Postmodernism and Law

The International Library of Essays in Law and Legal Theory
Series Editor: Tom D. Campbell

Schools

Natural Law, Vols I & II *John Finnis*
Justice *Thomas Morawetz*
Law and Economics, Vols I & II *Jules Coleman and Jeffrey Lange*
Critical Legal Studies *James Boyle*
Marxian Legal Theory *Csaba Varga*
Legal Reasoning, Vols I & II *Aulis Aarnio and D. Neil MacCormick*
Legal Positivism *Mario Jori*
American Legal Theory *Robert Samuel Summers*
Postmodernism and Law *Dennis Patterson*
Law and History *David Sugarman*
Law and Language *Fred Schauer*
Sociological Theories of Law *Kahei Rokumoto*
Rights *Carlos Nino*
Law and Psychology *Martin Lyon Levine*
Feminist Legal Theory, Vols I & II *Frances Olsen*
Law and Society *Roger Cotterrell*
Contemporary Criminological Theory *Francis T. Cullen and Velmer S. Burton Jr.*

Areas

Criminal Law *Thomas Morawetz*
Tort Law *Ernest J. Weinrib*
Contract Law, Vols I & II *Larry Alexander*
Anti-Discrimination Law *Christopher McCrudden*
Consumer Law *Iain Ramsay*
International Law *Martti Koskenniemi*
Property Law, Vols I & II *Elizabeth Mensch and Alan Freeman*
Constitutional Law *Mark V. Tushnet*
Procedure *D.J. Galligan*
Evidence and Proof *William Twining and Alex Stein*
Company Law *Sally Wheeler*
Privacy, Vols I & II *Raymond Wacks*
Lawyers' Ethics *David J. Luban*
Administrative Law *D.J. Galligan*
Child Law *Harry D. Krause*
Family Law, Vols I & II *Harry D. Krause*
Welfare Law *Peter Robson*
Medicine and the Law *Bernard M. Dickens*
Commercial Law *Ross Cranston*
Environmental Law *Michael C. Blumm*
Conflict of Laws *Richard Fentiman*
Law and Religion *Wojciech Sadurski*
Human Rights Law *Philip Alston*
European Community Law, Vols I & II *Francis Snyder*
Tax Law, Vols I & II *Patricia D. White*
Media Law *Eric Barendt*
Labour Law *David L. Gregory*
Alternative Dispute Resolution *Michael D.A. Freeman*

Legal Cultures

Comparative Legal Cultures *Csaba Varga*
Law and Anthropology *Peter Sack*
Hindu Law and Legal Theory *Ved Nanda*
Islamic Law and Legal Theory *Ian Edge*
Chinese Law and Legal Theory *Michael Palmer*
Socialist Law *W. Butler*
Common Law *Michael Arnheim*
Japanese Law and Legal Theory *Koichiro Fujikura*
Law and Development *Anthony Carty*
Jewish Law and Legal Theory *Martin P. Golding*
Legal Education *Martin Lyon Levine*
Civil Law *Ralf Rogowski*

Future Volumes
African Law and Legal Theory and Cumulative index.

Postmodernism and Law

Edited by

Dennis Patterson

Professor of Law, School of Law, Rutgers, The State University of New Jersey

NEW YORK UNIVERSITY PRESS
REFERENCE COLLECTION

Manufactured in Great Britain

First published in the U.S.A. in 1994 by
NEW YORK UNIVERSITY PRESS
Washington Square
New York NY 10003

Library of Congress Cataloging-in-Publication Data
Postmodernism and law / edited by Dennis Patterson.
p. cm. – (The International library of essays in law and legal theory. Schools : 14)
"New York University Press reference collection."
Includes bibliographical references and index.
ISBN 0-8147-6550-5
1. Law–Philosophy. 2. Postmodernism. I. Patterson, Dennis M. (Dennis Michael), 1955- . II. Series.
K235.P67 1994
340'.1–dc20 94-17303
CIP

Contents

Acknowledgements

The editor and publishers wish to thank the following for permission to use copyright material.

Cardozo Law Review for the essay: Richard Hyland (1990), 'Babel: A She'ur', *Cardozo Law Review*, **11**, pp. 1585–612.

Cornell University for the essay: Dennis Patterson (1992), 'Postmodernism/Feminism/Law', *Cornell Law Review*, **77**, pp. 254–317. © Copyright 1992 by Cornell University. All Rights Reserved.

McGill University for the essay: Alan Hunt (1990), 'The Big Fear: Law Confronts Postmodernism', *McGill Law Journal*, **35**, pp. 507–40.

Michigan Law Review Association for the essays: J.M. Balkin (1992), 'What is a Postmodern Constitutionalism?', *Michigan Law Review*, **90**, pp. 1966–90; Francis J. Mootz III (1992), 'Postmodern Constitutionalism as Materialism', *Michigan Law Review*, **91**, pp. 515–25.

Monash University for the essay: Peter Murphy (1991), 'Postmodern Perspectives and Justice', *Thesis Eleven*, **30**, pp. 117–32.

Texas Law Review for the essays: Pierre Schlag (1991), 'The Problem of the Subject', *Texas Law Review*, **69**, pp. 1627–743; Rosemary J. Coombe (1991), 'Objects of Property and Subjects of Politics: Intellectual Property Laws and Democratic Dialogue', *Texas Law Review*, **69**, pp. 1853–80. © Copyright 1991 by the Texas Law Review Association. Reprinted by permission.

University of Pennsylvania Law Review for the essay: Sanford Levinson and J.M. Balkin (1991), 'Law, Music and Other Performing Arts', *University of Pennsylvania Law Review*, **139**, pp. 1597–658.

University of Utah Press for the essay: Richard Rorty (1990), 'Feminism and Pragmatism', in Grethe B. Peterson (ed.), *The Tanner Lectures on Human Values*, **13**, Salt Lake City: University of Utah Press, pp. 1–35.

Yale Journal of Law & the Humanities for the essay: Robert Post (1992), 'Postmodern Temptations', *Yale Journal of Law & the Humanities*, **4**, pp. 391–8. © Copyright 1992 by Yale Journal of Law & the Humanities.

Every effort has been made to trace all the copyright holders, but if any have been inadvertently overlooked the publishers will be pleased to make the necessary arrangement at the first opportunity.

Series Preface

The International Library of Law and Legal Theory is designed to provide important research materials in an accessible form. Each volume contains essays of central theoretical importance in its subject area. The series as a whole makes available an extensive range of valuable material which will be of considerable interest to those involved in the research, teaching and study of law.

The series has been divided into three sections. The Schools section is intended to represent the main distinctive approaches and topics of special concern to groups of scholars. The Areas section takes in the main branches of law with an emphasis on essays which present analytical and theoretical insights of broad application. The section on Legal Cultures makes available the distinctive legal theories of different legal traditions and takes up topics of general comparative and developmental concern.

I have been delighted and impressed by the way in which the editors of the individual volumes have set about the difficult task of selecting, ordering and presenting essays from the immense quantity of academic legal writing published in journals throughout the world. Editors were asked to pick out those essays from law, philosophy and social science journals which they consider to be fundamental for the understanding of law, as seen from the perspective of a particular approach or sphere of legal interest. This is not an easy task and many difficult decisions have had to be made in order to ensure that a representative sample of the best journal essays available takes account of the scope of each topic or school.

I should like to express my thanks to all the volume editors for their willing participation and scholarly judgement. The interest and enthusiasm which the project has generated is well illustrated by the fact that an original projection of 12 volumes drawn up in 1989 has now become a list of some 60 volumes. I must also acknowledge the vision, persistence and constant cheerfulness of John Irwin and the marvellous work done by Mrs Margaret O'Reilly and Sonia Hubbard.

TOM D. CAMPBELL
Series Editor
The Faculty of Law
The Australian National University

Introduction

Part I Postmodernism and Justice

The word 'postmodernism' and its cognates have become a common feature of everyday thought and speech. Whether as an adjective or a noun, a term of art or one of opprobrium, 'postmodern' is finding its way into almost every facet of language. And yet, as the term becomes more familiar and its uses less novel, we seem to be no closer now to understanding its meanings than we were when the term first appeared in the contexts of architecture and aesthetics. The reasons for the continuing elusiveness of the meaning of postmodernism are numerous but not infinite. Many have a vested interest in certain understandings of postmodernism.[1] Others see postmodernism as a way to liberate themselves from modes of understanding they are eager to throw off; yet many are not quite able to articulate what it is they find attractive in postmodernism, save the possibility of redemption.

'Postmodernism and Law' is the theme for the present collection of essays. These were not collected from the point of view of a 'school' or movement, in the way one might put together a collection on positivism, natural law or some other school of thought. While there is no singular point of view or problematic for the present collection, the essays do exhibit certain common themes, problems and questions. It is my purpose in this Introduction to highlight certain of these and to say something of a substantive nature about postmodernism and law.

Part II Postmodernism and Culture

There are at least two levels at which one may approach postmodernism. While some interdependence exists between the two, there are sufficient differences to merit a division along the lines of culture and thought. In the realm of culture, postmodernism usually manifests itself at two levels of critique. Take the distinction between high and low culture. The postmodern critique of this aesthetic norm is violated by artists at the level of materials, subject matter and even mode of presentation.[2] The museum is declared a tomb or, worse, a relic.[3] Notions like the avant-garde and 'progress' in art are put in question, if not rejected out of hand. In architecture, where postmodernism gained an early foothold, we are told that all we have to look forward to is the endless recycling of past styles, for there is not now – nor will there ever be – anything new. All the tradition can do is repeat its past accomplishments in an endless cycle of recursive cynicism and irony.

There is nothing particularly postmodern about the desire to explain contemporary culture. Consider the neo-Marxist argument that fetishization of commodities is nothing more than late capitalism 'playing itself out'.[4] The explanation for *why* things are as they are can be, and almost always is, modernist in form. As some of the essays in the present volume illustrate, we may, indeed, be *in* postmodernity; but that does not preclude us from offering modernist explanations of how and why we got there. Again, making sense of culture – contemporary or otherwise – is not unique to postmodernism. What is unique, and worth pondering, is what it means to say that we live in a new epoch, that of 'postmodernity'.

The present volume makes a contribution to understanding postmodernism more at the level of thought than culture. What is of interest here is not so much the particulars of contemporary culture, legal or otherwise. Rather, from the perspective of thought, postmodernism concerns itself with a key component of the enterprise under scrutiny, that is law. The aspect of law to which our attention is drawn is justification. If it is anything, a postmodernist jurisprudence offers a new conception of legal justification. In this connection, it is important to remember that while our practices may not look vastly different from those of 50 years ago, what *has* changed are the grounds for those practices. As I shall now explain, postmodernist jurisprudence represents a break with the past in so far as it embodies a conception of justification which is at odds with the key assumptions of modernism.

Part III Postmodernism and the Subject

Before addressing the postmodernist conception of legal justification, we need to consider the particulars of the modernist perspective.[5] Epistemology and metaphysics are two categories basic to this perspective. Epistemology is the study of knowledge or, perhaps more perspicuously, what 'counts' as knowledge. The modern era in epistemology begins in the 17th century with Descartes. For the Cartesian, nothing can count as knowledge unless based on infallible cognitions (beliefs). The entire focus of epistemology is the identification of beliefs that depend not at all on other beliefs. Such beliefs are indubitable. From these indubitable beliefs (the foundations), deductive inference is possible.

The foundationalist approach to epistemology invites its opposite – scepticism. The most famous of the philosophical sceptics, the 18th-century empiricist David Hume, argued that all knowledge begins in experience (sense impressions). However, sensory experience cannot be a basis from which deductive inference is possible. In Hume's hands, epistemology is cut down to the analysis of the psychology of our experiences, to induction and probabilistic reasoning.

Metaphysics is often described as a semantic theory about the meaning of truth.[6] From the metaphysical perspective, 'truth' names a relation between word and world. An asserted proposition is 'true' if it corresponds to the way things are in the world. In short, language is conceived as representing states of affairs which it captures, mirrors or refers to. Thus, the task of metaphysics is to spell out how language reflects the way the world is.

Once conceived as representational, the role of language is essentially referential in nature. When a proposition refers correctly to a state of affairs (a fact), the proposition is true. Failure of reference engenders falsity. 'True' names this referring relation. But what of language that does not refer to states of affairs; say poetry, ethical and legal discourse? Language that is non-referential in nature is deemed expressive of the attitudes and feelings (sentiments) of the speaker. Some philosophers in the modernist tradition (e.g., the logical positivists) denigrated non-referential language as 'bad metaphysics'.

As is apparent from our discussion of epistemology and metaphysics, the individual is the central focus of modernism. It is the individual who has beliefs, asserts true and false propositions, and expresses opinions. Knowledge is something individuals possess, for it is the individual who has sensory impressions, draws inferences therefrom, and makes correct and incorrect judgements about facts. In sum, the modernist picture is composed of the following three elements: (1) epistemology–foundationalism v. scepticism; (2) language –representationalism or expressivism; and (3) individualism.

Part IV Postmodern Contexts

Central to the metaphysics of modernism is the idea of a 'truth-maker'. Recall that a central tenet of modernist metaphysics is the idea that the truth of propositions depends upon some feature of the physical, conceptual or normative realm which makes the proposition true. Owing to its referential capacity, the state of affairs to which the asserted proposition refers is the 'truth-maker'. From the modernist perspective, the nature of truth lies in the relationship between word and world. Thus, if metaphysics is a matter of a word–world relation, epistemology is naturally the enterprise concerned with revealing how we come to know the truth of the asserted proposition. Again, it is the individual who makes all the needed connections.

A central feature of postmodern thought is the elimination of the distinctions between epistemology and metaphysics, truth and belief, and meaning as reference and meaning as expression. The philosophical engine of modernism is the belief that there is a reality beyond our thoughts (and language) and that the truth and falsity of our beliefs is independent of our practices of justification and verification. In short, the hallmark of modernism is the separation of beliefs along the lines of truth and falsity, together with an account of truth and falsity in terms of a 'representational' metaphysics.

The modernism just sketched was the central organizing scheme until the middle of the present century. In the 1950s, the philosophical empiricist W.V.O. Quine questioned the distinction between knowledge and belief in a way that forever altered the modernist picture. In a famous passage in one of the most important essays in analytic philosophy, Quine said:

> The totality of our so-called knowledge or beliefs, from the most casual matters of geography and history to the profound laws of atomic physics or even of pure mathematics and logic, is a man-made fabric which impinges on experience only along the edges. Or, to change the figure, total science is like a field of force whose boundary conditions are experience. A conflict with experience at the periphery occasions readjustments in the interior of the field. Truth values have to be redistributed over some of our statements. Reevaluation of some statements entails reevaluation of others, because of their logical interconnections – the logical laws being in turn simply certain further statements of the system, certain further elements of the field. Having reevaluated one statement we must reevaluate some others, which may be statements logically connected with the first or may be the statements of logical connections themselves. But the total field is so underdetermined by its boundary conditions, experience, that there is much latitude of choice as to what statements to reevaluate in the light of any single contrary experience. No particular experiences are linked with any particular statements in the interior of the field, except indirectly, through considerations of equilibrium affecting the field as a whole.
>
> If this view is right, it is misleading to speak of the empirical content of an individual statement – especially if it is a statement at all remote from the experiential periphery of the field. Furthermore it becomes folly to seek a boundary between synthetic statements, which hold contingently on experience, and analytic statements, which hold come what may. Any statement can be held true come what may, if we make drastic enough adjustments elsewhere in the system.[7]

Of course, what Quine speaks of in this paragraph is 'holism', the view that the truth or falsity of any statement cannot be assessed in isolation from everything else we take to be true. We do not confront the world one statement at a time. Rather, we interact with the world in a medium which Quine identified as a web of beliefs. The truth value of any of those beliefs is settled, not by the world, but by how conflicts at the periphery are adjusted across the entire field (web) of knowledge. Within this paragraph lies the basic outline of the postmodern account of knowledge and experience.

When we say that a belief is 'true', what is it that we have said? For the modernist, 'true' means 'made true'; that 'making true' is a relation that 'obtains between non-beliefs and beliefs rather than between beliefs and other beliefs'.[8] Quine's point – a postmodernist one – is that no sense can be made of the idea of something making our beliefs true other than other beliefs.[9] In the spirit of Quine, Hilary Putnam develops Quinean holism with the observation that it makes no sense to speak of objects apart from a language of description:[10]

> The suggestion I am making, in short, is that *a statement is true of a situation just in case it would be correct to use the words of which the statement consists in that way in describing the situation*. ... [W]e can explain what 'correct to use the words of which the statement consists in that way' means by saying that it means nothing more nor less than a sufficiently well placed speaker who used the words in that way would be fully warranted in counting the statement as true of that situation.[11]

To appreciate just how radical a break Putnam's position represents, we need to return our attention to the role of truth in modernist thought. In modernist thought, truth (metaphysics) is the primordial notion. Truth names a relation between language and the world. The reason the expressive side of the linguistic axis is shaken off is that language as mere expression can never be factual. Because it can never be factual, no truths can be stated. Hence, the metaphysics of truth drives the theory of meaning.

Postmodernism abandons the metaphysics of truth and with it the distinction between truth as a metaphysical relation and meaning as reference. Instead of separating truth and meaning, each is married to the other. Richard Rorty makes this point in the following passage:

> [T]he thing to do is to marry truth and meaning to nothing but each other. The resulting marriage will be so intimate a relationship that a theory of truth will *be* a theory of meaning, and conversely. But that theory will be of no use to a representationalist epistemology, nor to any other sort of epistemology. It will be an explanation of what people *do*, rather than of a non-causal, representing, relation in which they stand to non-human entities.[12]

From the abandonment of the modernist programme of espistemology, of metaphysics and meaning comes not a rejection of philosophy, but a new focus. Instead of producing theories of truth and meaning, philosophy now takes as its task the perspicuous description of linguistic practices.[13] In law, this means describing legal practices of justification, what I have elsewhere referred to as 'forms of argument'.[14] Nothing – not the world, not morality, not economy – makes a proposition of law true. We use forms of legal argument (such as arguments from text, history, structure and doctrine) to justify our assertion of the truth of legal propositions. The forms of argument are the grammar of legal justification. They are the way in which a proposition of law is shown to be true.

In the space of this short Introduction, I am able to present only the barest outline of a postmodern jurisprudence. I hasten to add that the account just given is completely my own and is in no way endorsed by any of the authors whose work appears within these covers. In fact, some of these authors would, and do, disagree with the account of postmodern jurisprudence just offered. I have not chosen the contributions to this volume on the basis of agreement or disagreement with any particular conception of postmodernism. Rather, I have sought to bring to the reader's attention the full range of thinking on the topic of postmodernism and law. It is up to the reader to decide which arguments state the truth of the matter.

Notes

1 I have in mind the use of the term in literary criticism of the contemporary French variety.
2 An example here is the work of Robert Rauschenberg.
3 See Douglas Crimp (1983), 'On the Museum's Ruins' in Hal Foster (ed.) *The Anti-Aesthetic*, pp. 43–56.
4 See Frederic Jameson (1991), *Postmodernism, or, The Cultural Logic of Late Capitalism*, Durham, North Carolina: Duke University Press.
5 The discussion which follows is indebted to the work of Nancey Murphy. See Nancey Murphy (1990), 'Scientific Realism and Postmodern Philosophy', *British Journal for the Philosophy of Science*, **41**, p. 291.
6 A good discussion of the relationship between metaphysics and truth in the analytic tradition of philosophy is to be found in Hilary Putnam (1978), *Meaning and the Moral Sciences*, Boston and London: Routledge & Kegan Paul. For discussion of the point in the context of realism and anti-realism, see Michael Dummett (1978), *Truth and Other Enigmas*, Cambridge MA: Harvard University Press, pp. 145–7.
7 W.V.O. Quine (1953), 'Two Dogmas of Empiricism' in his *From a Logical Point of View*, Cambridge MA: Harvard University Press, 2nd edn. (1961), pp. 42–3.
8 Richard Rorty (1992), 'Putnam on Truth', *Philosophy and Phenomenological Research*, **52**, p. 415.
9 With this, Quine breaks decisively with modernist foundationalism, for he rejects the idea that there can be foundational beliefs.
10 Quine has recently made the same point in his (1993) article, 'In Praise of Observation Sentences', *Journal of Philosophy*, **90**, pp. 107, 113: 'Asking after the thing in itself, apart from human conceptualization, is like asking how long the Nile really is, apart from our parochial miles or kilometers'.
11 Hilary Putnam (1988), *Representation and Reality*, Cambridge, MA: MIT Press, p. 115.
12 Richard Rorty (1991), 'Representation, Social Practise, and Truth', in his *Objectivism, Relativism, and Truth* (Philosophical Papers, Vol. 1), New York, Cambridge: New York University Press, p. 154.
13 Of course, this is Wittgenstein's exhortation. See Ludwig Wittgenstein, *Philosophical Investigations* (G.E.M. Anscombe trans., 3d edn. 1958).
14 See Dennis Patterson (1993), 'Conscience and the Constitution', *Columbia Law Review*, **92**, p. 270 (reviewing Philip Bobbitt (1991), *Constitutional Interpretation*, Oxford, Cambridge MA: Blackwell).

Part I
Postmodernism and Justice

[1]

POSTMODERN PERSPECTIVES AND JUSTICE

Peter Murphy

Postmodernism is a reflection on — and in that respect is also parasitic upon — the modern condition. The modern condition arises from the fact that we, moderns, live in a differentiated society, and that society is divided into different, co-existent, spheres — the *communal, economic/bureaucratic, civic, cultural,* and *reconstructive* spheres. Standing apart, yet again, from each of these spheres is the *public* sphere, whose function is to reconcile and mediate between the other spheres, to internalize, dramatize, and moderate the conflicts between all of the differentiated spheres of modernity. Each of these spheres is constituted by its own, distinctive norms, ends, rules, procedures and processes, values, transformations, and equilibriums.[1] Each of the spheres, moreover, gives emphasis to one or other of these aspects. Community emphasizes norms; the economy, reciprocal ends and roles; bureaucracy, organizational goals and rules; the civic realm, procedures and processes; the cultural sphere, values; the reconstructive sphere, changes; and, finally, the public sphere, equilibrium and balance. Each of these spheres makes distinctive claims. Each backs-up its claims with its own vision of a good society. And each imparts its own sense of what counts as the fair or impartial, that is just, treatment of persons, so that each might hope to enjoy a good life. Correspondingly, there is not *a* justice in society. Rather, there is a co-existent (sometimes hostile, sometimes friendly) *multiplicity of justices.* There are, in other words, a number of *spheres of justice.* And, corresponding to each sphere is a system of discourse. Religion, science, philosophy, hermeneutics, and art articulate the differentiated spheres of the modern world. Each of these discourses — which we can also call logics or language games or paradigms or epistemes — in conjunction with the basic values they represent — generate rules, prescriptions, and laws, that is, the "oughts, shoulds, and musts" that guide actions *imperatively.* These systems of discourse are also *reflective.* That is, they have the capacity to appraise what they generate. They also have the ability to appraise the rules generated by other discourses. Art asks the question of its rules: are they "original" or do they promote "innovativeness"? Science asks the question

Thesis Eleven, Number 30

of its rules: are they "true" and do they promote "effectiveness"? Theology asks the question: are the rules "right" and do they promote "integration" or "community"? Hermeneutics asks: what "meaning" do the rules have — that is, what abstract "values", "patterns" or "contexts" can they be connected to so they can be "understood" — and do they, in turn, promote "understanding"? Philosophy asks the question: are the rules "reasonable" and do they promote "worthwhile activities"?

I.

Postmodernism assumes that different logics or paradigms, that is, different systems of discourse with their distinctive value axioms, can co-exist in the same social *space*. It is this, above all, that distinguishes postmodernism from enlightenment modernism.[2] The enlightenment modernist speaks of knowledge (in the singular) rather than discourses (in the plural). The Enlightenment view rests on temporal rather than spatial metaphors. That is to say, the Enlightenment view sees knowledge as a succession of paradigms through time. One system of knowledge succeeds another in a progressive, developmental sequence. This is the march of reason in history — from feudalism, to capitalism, to socialism or industrialism, or as Comte had it, from theology to metaphysics to positivism — with each developmental stage progressively more rational. For the postmodernist, history remains, but there is no march of reason in history. Measured against the benchmark of the Enlightenment's world history, that is, History with a capital H, postmodernism is also posthistory. But, of course, the romantics, a long time ago, up-ended the Enlightenment conception anyway, when they pronounced all cultures, past and present, equally close to God. History as we know it, with its display of a genuine curiosity about, and even affection for, the past derives from this romantic sensibility. And the pop historicism — that is, the quotations, eclecticism, and pastiche — of postmodernism, or for that matter, its questioning of closed or unified narratives, its emphasis on plural or heterogeneous histories and history-writing, and so on, adds little to this.[3]

What distinguishes postmodernism, of course, is not its sense of history. On the contrary, what it represents more than anything is a movement from temporal to spatial ways of understanding the relationship between different systems of knowledge in society. The conception of knowledge as an architectonic unity gives way to the idea of multiple discourses and perspectives. This is accompanied by a differentiation of the validity claims of distinctive knowledge systems. Postmodernism is identified, as a distinctive practice, by the spatial juxtaposition of fragments or units (rather than by their temporal succession). The postmodernist plays the role of a Benjaminite critic (in the manner of *The Origins of German Tragic Drama*) who constructs a *constellation* by juxtaposing what had been previously isolated. Meaning arises from the relative positions of the fragments in the constellation. The postmodernist works on what Crimp calls a "flatbed" surface that can receive a heterogeneous array of cultural images.[4] What the postmodernist does then is to create a kind of collage, a juxtaposition, simultaneously, of multiple and different representations, modes, values, images, and discourses. Postmodernism registers the fact that there is not just one single rationality in society, but that there are *plural rationalities*, and these rationalities are juxtaposed to each other, at the same time and in the same social space. There is no progress from one rationality to another. Postmodern thought then is polytheistic rather than monotheistic. It accepts Weber's proposition that there are a number of gods — paradigms or discourses or cultures — that claim our devotion in the postenlightenment world. Jean-François Lyotard, in fact, calls postmodern thought *pagan*.[5]

II.

One of the ways — although I do not think an especially illuminating way — that Lyotard distinguishes between the different paradigms or rationalities, or what he calls *language games*, that compete on the terrain of the modern world, is to distinguish between what he, following Anglo-American analytical philosophy, calls *prescriptive and descriptive* language games. This distinction actually is quite a misleading one. It ignores the fact that all language games are *both* descriptive and prescriptive in some crucial respect. All of them generate rules: all of them produce statements. Neither science, nor theology, nor philosophy, nor hermeneutics, nor art (to cite the principal language games that we are familiar with) are either exclusively prescriptive or exclusively descriptive. What is more, because all of these discourses are *reflective*, we can evaluate what is done in those games. We can judge both the *truth* of statements and the *justness* of the prescriptions we make.[6] But note, our evaluations are different as we pass from statement to imperative. This is because, as Lyotard observes, the prescriptive *use* of language is different from the theoretical use.[7] But different in what respect? Different, Lyotard suggests, because we have *criteria* to judge the truth of statements, but *no criteria to judge the justness of the prescriptions we make.* He puts it another way: *there is no knowledge in matters of ethics or politics, only opinions.*[8] Thus, we can only have knowledge of descriptive (or denotative) utterances because only in these cases do we have the criteria to evaluate them. Only theoretical, or scientific, discourse, apparently, can gain admittance to the house of knowledge.

What Lyotard suggests is that if we put forward a prescription — an ought, a must, a should, an obligation, a regulation, a law, etc. — we cannot tell, *with any certainty or conclusiveness*, whether it is just or not. Any reflections on the justness of prescriptions will be very allusive. *They will not have for us the status of knowledge.* Yet, we moderns live in settings which constantly demand that we reflect on the norms, rules, and imperatives of our world.

As Lyotard puts it, for moderns or postmoderns — as opposed to traditional societies—prescriptions *are never just received.*[9] They don't simply come to us from elsewhere. We, moderns, are more than addressees of prescriptions. We have to *decide between alternatives*, choose what is obligatory. This (almost paradoxical state of) having to decide (i.e. choose) what is obligatory (i.e. necessary or imperative) begins, Lyotard suggests, with some of the Greeks.[10] What does Greek mythology let us see, Lyotard asks? A society of gods that is constantly forced to redraw its codes. This is a theme one also finds, Lyotard indicates, amongst the sophists and rhetoricians of ancient Greece. Here are people for whom prescriptions *are subject to discussion*. Greek society is one of the seed-bed cultures for the modern world. In the modern world, as in the Greek enlightenment, norms are not given. We have to choose between alternatives. But, Lyotard argues, faced with this contingency, we cannot, in fact, judge which of the countervailing norms is just. All we can do is discuss. We have no criteria to judge between these alternative prescriptions. So there is always more talking to be done.[11] Is this what postmodernism is? A culture of interminable discourse? Certainly one side of Lyotard's thought drives in that direction. The only prescriptions or imperatives that we can judge as unjust are those that inhibit discussion. So that *what is just is being able to go on talking*. What is just *is to be able to continue the game of the just*. The only certain injustice that we know about, the only *absolute injustice* that the Lyotardian postmodernist recognizes, occurs when the possibility of continuing to play the game of the just (the prescriptive game, in other words) is excluded. So, according to this (criterion?), all politically-motivated terror, annihilation, massacre, and the imperatives, commands or duties to act in this manner are, by definition, unjust, because the people whom one massacres are no longer able to play the game of the just.[12]

But, beyond this, we are in *no* position to judge the justice of different prescriptive regimes. We can talk about them, but not judge them. The same reason remains. *We have no criteria*, according to Lyotard. There is no test for the just as there is for the true, he claims. One cannot compare what the rabbi says with a state of affairs.[13] That is to say, we can judge whether a statement is true or not according to whether it corresponds to the real state of affairs in the world. But what can we match prescriptions to? Lyotard objects to the Platonic conviction that there is a true being of society — an ultimate reality — and that society will be just if it is brought into conformity with this true being.[14] We, moderns, in judging prescriptions, have no model to guide us. We cannot, like Plato, produce a model that would be valid once and for all for the constitution of society.[15] We cannot test whether our prescriptions correspond to this model (this ultimate reality) like we might test or compare whether descriptive statements correspond to an actual state of affairs. For this reason Lyotard makes so much of the insistence that the prescriptive use of language is fundamentally different from the descriptive (or what Lyotard calls the theoretical) use of language. An "ought statement" *cannot be tested* for its validity. The postmodernist, unlike say the enlightenment modernist, is one who, in Lyotard's view, acknowledges this. Of course, there are those who now say that even descriptive statements cannot be judged or tested. Richard Rorty is preeminent amongst these.[16] Both Lyotard and Rorty converge in their *anti-realism.* Rorty simply takes it a step further than Lyotard. In Rorty's view, there is nothing outside of statements, outside of the language we use, *no reality,* that we can judge or evaluate statements by. All that we have are different vocabularies. Rorty insists on what he calls the *romantic thesis,* that what is important in human life is not what propositions we believe but what vocabularies we use. It is less important, he suggests, to find out whether a proposition is true than to find out whether a vocabulary is good. The logic of this is that postmodernism prides itself on what Rorty calls the autonomy and novelty of the language it uses, rather than on its truthfulness to experience or its discovery of pre-existing significance.

III.

Lyotard suggests that we are in the position of Aristotle's prudent individual who makes judgments about the just and the unjust without the least criterion. But is this so? I think not. It is *not* true that we have no criterion against which to judge prescriptions. This criterion may not be a Platonic ultimate reality. But to dismiss the Platonic option does not end the matter. For, in fact, we have the world of values, that is, a *value reality,* against which we judge prescriptions. This is not an ultimate, unchanging, reality. The world of values is part of our own world. It is not transcendent. It is made up of the historical movements and traditions, the legacies, the writings, the deeds of people who have endeavoured and struggled to realize in the world certain fundamental values or goods. These are the values of *belonging (community), participation (citizenship), inner worldly asceticism (work), understanding (humanistic scholarship), and autonomy (originality).* When we judge prescriptions in terms of these values, and the legacies, writings, and deeds which have grown up around them, we are not simply offering opinions, rather we are articulating knowledge. To stand Rorty on his head, we *can,* in other words, *discover the pre-existing significance* of the prescriptions we make.

It is questionable whether the anti-realism of Lyotard and Rorty is, of necessity, a postmodern position, at all. In fact, if we look at the work of Charles Jencks, a pioneer, and a much more convincing pioneer, of a postmodernism than Lyotard, we find no repudiation of realism but rather the argument that there is a distinctive postmodern realism: *the emphasis on the reality of a secondary reality* — the representation of a representation, the sign of a sign, etc.[17] I call this "secondary reality" a *value reality.* To be knowledgeable, rather than just opinionated, means to locate oneself in relation to various genres and categories of value. The quality of knowledge — its subtlety, its richness, its profundity, etc. — will depend on how well we *understand*, and are familiar with, the legacies, the literature, the traditions, and movements that make up the *value reality*. Unquestionably, the more we study, the more we find out. Consequently, whatever judgments we make (of the justness of prescriptions) will always be *provisional*. If we think of the complexity of the systems of knowledge that have grown up, over time, around the core values of Western societies, we must, with some humility, acknowledge the *inconclusiveness* of any of our attempts to judge. We can always learn more. We can always learn more about the literature, traditions, and movements of *belonging*, that is, those of *theology*. We can always learn more about the literature, movements and traditions of *civic participation*, and the great belief system of the city, *viz. philosophy*. The same applies, of course, to the values of *inner worldly asceticism and autonomy*. There is always something more we can add to our *understanding* of the traditions, movements, and literature of *science and art* as well. And, as our understanding grows, so also does the likelihood that we will revise judgments we have made in the past. But none of this means that we cannot make judgments. When we look to duties, rules, imperatives, regulations, and the actions they prescribe, we make judgments about their justice or worth by estimating whether they contribute to, or detract from, from fundamental goods or values.

Whether we judge well or not will of course partly depend on how *well informed* our judgment is. But the judging we do usually is of complex situations where we need not only knowledge but also *prudence*. We need to be prudent in judging, not because we lack criteria to judge, but because we need to take into account that in each case we are likely to judge there will be *more than one good at stake*. The real strength of postmodernism is that it recognizes that there are *plural rationalities*, that there is a *multiplicity of justices* in the modern world, and that *the claims of rival paradigms need to be taken into account whenever we judge and decide*. We cannot continue to play the game of enlightenment modernism of trying to exclude the claims and values of the other paradigms. Postmodernism is *inclusionary*. And this is all to the good. But, one of the consequences of this, is that it requires a *heightened prudence* on the part of anyone who makes judgments about the justice or worth of norms and rules. In the postmodern world we cannot rely just on one single criterion for judgment. We *judge according to multiple criteria*. We try and make decisions that in some way respect or acknowledge all of the logics of modernity.

But what of Lyotard's argument that if there were criteria that could ground judgments, there would have to be consensus on these criteria?[18] Interestingly, and ironically, the assumption made here is an enlightenment modernist one. The enlightenment modernist assumes that there is no point in making judgments based on criteria if those to whom we address our judgments do not share those criteria. The enlightenment modernist demands agreement on criteria. Of course, Lyotard knows that disagreement, rather than agreement, on criteria is the normal state of affairs in the modern world. So he concludes, therefore, that we have to *judge without criteria*. But what if we dispense with the notion that if we are to judge with criteria, then others must agree with our criteria? Let us begin with the way moderns actually behave. Moderns typically *judge in terms of one of five paradigms*. They render judgment from the perspective of religion, art, philosophy, hermeneutics, or science. This means, of course, that they often talk past each other. They invoke values, assumptions, and criteria which often those they address do not share. Or, if they do share the values, they rank them lower than some others. Of course, the converse also applies. So often they do speak in terms which are shared by their interlocutors. In such cases, they form communities of shared belief. But *either way*, it is not significant. It does not matter whether there is a consensus between interlocutors or not, so long as interlocutors *respect* the value systems of those they engage with; so long as they are prepared to accommodate them, to conciliate them, to adjust to them, and take them into account in their decision-making and action.

Postmodernism at its best makes us sensitive to the pluralism of belief systems. But this should not necessarily render us incapable of making judgments. This should not turn us all into indifferent relativists, or worse. But it may end up making our judgments less black and white, more subtle, more rich, *more attentive to and ready to take account of fundamental values different from those to which our primary allegiance is given*. We live in a world which is constituted not by one, but by several major traditions of discourse. We cannot without tyrannical and barbaric consequences eliminate those other traditions. We cannot without being arrogant dismiss those traditions.

IV.

Postmodernism comes down to this: *there are a multiplicity of language games in the modern world*. In Lyotard's version, postmodernism denies:

(i) that one language game should *dominate* any other language game;
(ii) that there is a metadiscourse, a grand narrative, that could unify or synthesize all the others.

Lyotard proposes (i) that the social universe is formed by a plurality of language games, without any one of them being able to claim that it can speak for all the others.[19] In this pluralized universe, persons leap from one language game to another.[20]

Lyotard also proposes (ii) that the different language games caught up in this polytheistic or pagan universe are incommunicable to each other. They cannot be synthesized into a unifying metadiscourse.[21]

To summarize: in Lyotard's conception, the postmodernist insists that there are many language games in the world, but that there is no common measure of them.[22]

With the first proposition I agree; with the second proposition, I disagree.

V.

The first proposition of the postmodernist accords, in significant measure, with the differentiated character of the modern world, with the fact that it is split up into distinctive spheres. These are the spheres of community, power, culture, citizenship, and reconstruction. Each of these spheres are organized in different ways. They have different norms and different values. Social actors spend their lives, in the modern world, shifting from one sphere to another. Corresponding to each of these spheres is a distinctive discourse and conception of justice.

The attitude of enlightenment modernism, as opposed to postmodernism, was to say: one sphere, one value, one conception of justice, etc., must triumph over all others. The attitude of postmodernism is to say: the different spheres and rival conceptions of justice must be accommodated to each other. The communitarian, the liberal or social democrat, the developmental liberal or humanist, the radical, and the romantic must find ways of living together in the same social space. They must find ways of reconciling or conciliating different conceptions of the law — the solidaristic-retributive or solidaristic-erotic, the contractual-civil, the administrative-regulatory, the developmental-formative, the constitutional-civic, and the reconstructive-transformative. They must find ways of accommodating the claims of rival conceptions of justice — the communitarian-protective, the compensatory-adjudicative, the social-allocative, the cultural-developmental, the civic-participatory, and contestatory-revisionist. Thus postmodernism calls for a *multiplication of justices.* No one "grand narrative" — whether it be Theology, Science, Philosophy, Hermeneutics, or Art — can claim our absolute allegiance. This also implies a change in our conception of political inquiry. We can no longer advocate a Political Science or a Political Philosophy, or a Humanistic, Theological or an Aesthetic Politics, and expect to expel all representatives of rival discourses from the house of knowledge. The political scientist, the culture critic, and the political philosopher, the political psychologists and the political sociologists, all must learn to give up imperialistic claims to dominate the field of knowledge. Postmodernism is, in some fundamental sense, postcolonial in its mentality.

In turn, politics as an activity is also transformed under the sign of postmodernism. Politics, conceived in postmodern terms, can no longer be *exclusively* of a civic or a pragmatic or a communitarian or a humanistic or a romantic kind. It cannot just be a participatory politics, or a power politics, or a politics of solidarity, or a developmental politics, or a politics of change.[23] In a sense, what politics is appropriate depends upon the sphere we are moving in and on the kind of activity we are engaged in. In Lyotard's terms, a postmodern politics is regulated by the idea of multiplicity. This politics would preserve pluralism.[24] *The pluralism of language games is its highest good.* A postmodern politics operates on the assumption that all known language games are to be maintained; none is to be privileged; none are to be dropped; and no game is to be played as the game of all other games.[25] This politics would act under a rule of divergence rather than convergence.[26] It would regulate itself by the idea of minority. *Each minority discourse would remain a minority discourse.* The radical, the romantic, the liberal or social democrat, the humanist, and the communitarian would all, always, remain in a minority. And a postmodern politics would ensure that minorities developed in such a way that *no minority could ever become a majority, and, on the contrary, that all majorities became minorities. No minority could prevail over any other.*[27]

VI.

It is not, however, only postmodernists who argue for such an emphatic pluralism. Indeed, postmodernism is only one part of a broader cultural turn away from hegemonic to pluralistic conceptions of justice, politics, ethics, and aesthetics. We see the resurrection of pluralism in a variety of quarters that cannot be identified as self-consciously postmodern. Hannah Arendt, long before Lyotard or Jencks, argued for comprehensiveness in judgment and the "representative" nature of political thought, while Agnes Heller, for the most part independently of postmodernism, has developed a pluralistic ethic of formidable dimensions.[28] We have also seen Michael Walzer argue for heterogeneous spheres of justices, and, more recently, Paul Hirst has set about reviving the tradition of English pluralism ... and so on.[29] I would not deny that there is a strong incipient connection, or elective affinity, between a postmodern standpoint and a pluralistic ethics or politics. As Jencks has noted, Hannah Arendt's work has been an important influence on certain postmodern architects,[30] while Agnes Heller, recently, has explicitly acknowledged the affinity between the language of postmodernism and her project of exploring the implications of the pluralized logics and heterogeneous value systems of the modern world.[31] Indeed, the term "postmodern" is not a bad term to describe these pluralistic thinkers so long as we accept a crucial qualification: *viz*, that they are "postmodernists" in the sense that Jencks employs the term, and *not* in the sense that Lyotard employs the term.[32]

There are really two kinds of postmodernists: Lyotardian and Jencksian. One of the crucial things that sets them apart is the question of *totality*. The

Lyotardian postmodernist repudiates the idea of totality: the Jencksian postmodernist does not. The question at stake here is the following: is it, necessarily, the case that there is no room for a "grand narrative", for a discourse that *synthesizes* all the other discourses? Is synthesis necessarily the same as domination? The answer to this is: no, it is not necessarily so. To put the question somewhat differently: is there a discourse that draws together all the other discourses or systems of knowledge without destroying them, without imposing a reign of tyranny over them? The answer to this question is: yes. There is one discourse in the modern world that is *unifying without dominating*. This is the discourse of rights or freedom, the "grand narrative" of emancipation. The story of freedom cannot dominate because, by itself, it is empty. It needs other stories — the stories of romance and of power, of belonging and excellence — to give it substance. The story of freedom (or rights) has *always* needed to be *supplemented*.[33] Moderns have always spoken of the freedom *to* associate, the freedom *of* trade, the freedom *in* aesthetic or life styles, the freedom *from* assault, and so on. Each of these freedoms, moreover, has been associated with different forms of life, different need structures, and different world views. Postmodernism, at its best, is a self-conscious admittance of this pluralism. But, at the same time, it can also represent a denial of the fact that this pluralism arises out of the modern idea of freedom, and that it *implicitly* extends, or rewrites, the "narrative" of freedom when it addresses the question of how it is possible to *eliminate domination* in the relations between the pluralistic cultures of modernity.

Why is it important that there should be a metadiscourse? Because, without it, there can be no real *inter*play of heterogeneous discourses, only their separation. *We need to distinguish between a master discourse and a metadiscourse*. A master discourse wants to impose itself on all the other discourses — it is progressive, they are reactionary; it is right, they are wrong. A metadiscourse, on the other hand, seeks to understand society as a *totality*.[34] By this I mean, it sets out to portray the contradictory nature of society and the complex interactions between the different spheres of society — their dramatic collisions and their dialogues, their tensions and reconciliations, their conflicts and accommodations. The Jencksian postmodernist accepts this as one of the key tasks of postmodernism. Postmodernism, Jencks, following Venturi, argues is concerned with complexity and contradiction, and precisely because it is concerned with complexity and contradiction, it in fact has a special obligation to the whole.[35] This is not the "harmonious whole" of canonic classicism, but rather the "difficult whole" of a pluralized and multi-dimensional world. Postmodernism, Jencks argues, is committed to synthesizing a "difficult whole" out of different fragments, references, and approaches. Its truth lies not in any part, but, as Venturi puts it, *in its totality or implications of totality*.[36] Lyotardian postmodernism, by contrast with this, is scandalized by the idea of totality.[37] Yet, in a totality, we see the fragments of modernity *in relation to each other*:

confronting, avoiding, colliding, remonstrating, debating, accommodating, outwitting, and judging each other. It is this — the drama of modernity and its mediations — that a Lyotardian postmodernism cannot convey. And, because it cannot do this, it cannot adequately portray or understand the *public sphere* in which the drama of modernity is not only played-out with its greatest intensity, but in which also the contestatory fragments of modernity have to communicate with each other and establish an equilibrium or balance. The Lyotardian postmodernist, of course, will reply that the idea of totality implies that history has a direction and that the contradictions of the modern world can be resolved.[38] This, the Lyotardian postmodernist says, is a myth — the tensions between the contradictory logics of modernity can never be dissolved. There is a half-truth in this. Modernity is the sum of its oppositions. Its tensions are enduring. But if this was absolutely true — if old conflicts were never replaced by new ones, but simply persisted without resolve then there could be no accommodation, no productive intercourse, and no dynamic equilibrium established between the logics of modernity. There would be no mediation, and no rich articulations, between the fragments. How, then, would the fragments of modernity relate to each other? With indifference, incomprehension, disdain, violence, or hatred, perhaps?

The Lyotardian postmodernist may honour divergence. But there is divergence and divergence. Whatever their differences, the pluralistic cultures of modernity *need* to "hang together". They need each other. And, in fact and in deed, these fragments *can* "hang together", *only* insofar as they participate in the idea of freedom. A metadiscourse is a reflection on the relations between the fragments of modernity *a reflection which, moreover,* judges these relations — relations which are sometimes domineering, sometimes tragic, sometimes mutually enriching. But to judge we must have a *criterion of judgment* — a criterion that will justify us not only in refusing colonizing relations between the plural cultures of modernity, but will also allow those cultures to speak to, to argue with, and to understand each other, however gropingly. This criterion is the idea of freedom. Freedom is the common measure of all the discourses of modernity.

VII.

Lyotard, of course, rejects the "grand narrative" of emancipation, suspecting it of harbouring the will to domination that postmodernism rejects. But this rejection is tainted by inconsistency, because Lyotard, in the end, finds that he cannot escape the demands for a unifying or totalizing discourse, a system of knowledge that somehow makes sense of all the other fragmented and rival systems of knowledge. What Lyotard does is to introduce a "grand narrative" through the back door. What he does, in effect, is to substitute the story of modern art for the story of freedom.

The first proposition of postmodernism says that we should accept the fact that we can play several language games.[39] There are the games of art, religion, philosophy, hermeneutics, and science. Postmodernism gets rid of the exclusionary view that one must do Science at the expense of Art, or Religion, or Philosophy, or Hermeneutics, or vice-versa. But, Lyotard then goes on to suggest, approvingly, that in between or within language games, postmodern actors will be motivated principally by *aesthetic* considerations. What Lyotard emphasizes is originality, innovativeness, and creativeness in moving between and within language games. For Lyotard, the interesting thing (what makes each of the games interesting in itself) is to play moves, and to play moves means *to set the imagination to work*.[40] What marks out the postmodern player is that he or she *develops* language games. Lyotard means development not in the (scientific) sense of cumulative progress, or in the humanist sense of forming and enriching individual capacities and comprehension, but in the romantic/aesthetic sense of introducing forms of language that are *unexpected* or *unheard of*.[41] He means development in the sense of original innovations and transformations. What counts, thus, for the Lyotardian postmodernist is *new* theology, new science, new philosophy, new hermeneutics, new art. Of course, Lyotard admits, for many of us, probably for most of us, when we play these games, we play them without inventiveness. That is, we do not make any "master strokes". But, to be pagan or postmodern, in Lyotard's sense, is to display the inventive restlessness typical of the modern romantic artist. It means to move from one game to another, and in each of these games to try and figure out new moves and, even better, to try and invent new games.[42]

We began with the problem of "what is a just prescription?". Each of the paradigms of knowledge, of course, answer this in different ways. Science judges prescriptions in terms of whether or how they contribute to the efficiency and effectiveness of social actors. Science gives rise to a power politics. Theology judges prescriptions in terms of how they contribute to social solidarity. Theology gives rise to a communitarian politics. Hermeneutics judges prescriptions in terms of how they contribute to the enlargement of human understanding. Hermeneutics gives rise to a humanistic politics. Philosophy judges prescriptions in terms of how they contribute to actors' participation in complex and demanding practices. Philosophy gives rise to a civic or participatory politics. Art (here I am speaking of the autonomous art that emerged with the appearance of romanticism towards the end of the 18th century) judges prescriptions in terms of the way in which they express, or promote, change. Art gives rise to a transformative politics.

Lyotardian postmodernism says that there are no criteria for judging prescriptions. There is no criterion of justice. Or is there? For it also says that one should be able to move between, and play different, language games without prohibition. One language game should not outlaw another game. Such attempts are unjust. Postmodernism, thus, represents the *justice of multiplicity*.

Postmodernism judges prescriptions in terms of how they contribute to cognitive diversity. Postmodernism gives rise to a pluralistic politics. But what about when the postmodernist enters one or other of the language games? On the terrain of science, philosophy, art, hermeneutics, or theology, can the postmodernist make any judgments about what is just or not? Lyotard says that we have *no criteria by which to judge*. But, in saying that, Lyotard returns us to Immanuel Kant's great summing-up, at the end of the 18th century, of the then newly emergent system of modern art that the romantics pioneered. In the *Critique of Pure Reason* and the *Critique of Practical Reason* Kant differentiated between science and morality. In his *Metaphysics of Morals* the idea of civility was, yet again, differentiated from both science and morality. While in his *Anthropology*, Kant began to pose the question of what others, later, would call understanding, that is, the notion of a pluralistic conception of thought (an enlarged mentality) as the ground of a humanistic or developmental-liberal culture. This, then, left Kant only to sum-up the logic of romanticism which he did with extraordinary insight in the *Critique of Judgement*. In the *Critique of Judgement*, Kant foreshadowed Lyotard's notion of judgment without rules or criteria. This is how the system of modern art judges. As Lyotard puts it, the ability to judge does not rest on criteria.[43] There is no external or established model to tell the artist what is a good or bad move to make in producing a work of art. The artist has to rely on his or her imagination. And this imagination is constitutive. It not only gives the artist the ability to judge without criteria (or rules); it is, in fact, the power to invent criteria (or rules). That is to say, a work of art is produced according to a set of rules; but its goodness is not judged in terms of the rules. Does this mean that it cannot be judged at all? Of course not. Modern art (romantic fine art) judges in terms of whether the rules, the artists' "style", is original or innovative. Is it then "judgment without criteria"? It is only if we accept both Kant and Lyotard's assumption that rules and criteria are the same thing. But, in point of fact, they are not. In fact, one always *judges* rules *according to criteria*. Originality is a criterion. One judges a work of art (i.e. modern art) according to the criterion of originality — just as one judges a moral rule according to the criterion of solidarity, or an organizational rule according to the criterion of efficiency, and so on. While Lyotard proclaims that the postmodernist "judges without criteria", he, in fact, readmits a singular criterion through the back door.

This singular criterion — originality — is the criterion of modern art. Lyotard's "postmodern" slogan of "judging without criteria" is simply a rewrite of *modern* aesthetics.[44] It leaves behind the dictatorial habits, of course, of the modernist *avant garde* which tended to insist on the dominance of *one* new style at a time. The Lyotardian postmodernist prefers, instead, to think in terms of the metaphors of *proliferation* rather than those of the Leninist or vanguard *party*. It is also true to say that the Lyotardian postmodernist leaves behind the functionalist aesthetic — rooted in the world view and logic of science — that influenced so much of 20th century modern art. Lyotardian postmodernism is definitely *post*-modern so long as one is happy to identify modernism and functionalism. But this is too simple, for modernity has *plural* logics, and one of those logics — the romantic-aesthetic/Fine Art logic — represents the separation of aesthetic value from industrial-technological-functional value. Certain modern art movements may have wanted to conflate the two; Lyotard may want to oppose the two.[45] But this still means that his "postmodernism", in the final analysis, borrows an enormous amount from the paradigm of modern art. So much indeed that one must question its claims to be genuinely polytheistic in its attitudes. Is there not, in fact, a covert monotheism hidden beneath its polytheistic surface? It certainly spends a lot of its time worshipping at the altar of modern art.

As Lyotard puts it, the postmodernist is an artist.[46] What we call an artist is *someone who proposes new rules* of a game. The point, Lyotard explains, is not to keep the game we play in existence, but rather, in each of the existing games, to *effect new moves*. One opens up the possibilities of *new efficacies* in the games with their present rules. In addition, one *changes* the rules. One plays a given game with *other* rules. Artists always establish rules that did not exist before. To be able to do this, or not to be impeded from doing this, is to enjoy the *justice of multiplicity*. To do this is to be postmodern. But is it?

Notes

1. For a further discussion of the differentiated spheres of modernity, looked at from the vantage-point of value-rationality, see P. Murphy, "Radicalism and the Spheres of Value", *Thesis Eleven* 25 (1990).
2. Amongst the best discussions of postmodernism are Charles Jencks's *Post-Modernism* (Rizzoli, 1987), the contributions to Hal Foster (ed.), *The Anti-Aesthetic: Essays on Postmodern Culture* (Bay Press, 1983); and the brilliant essay by David Roberts, "The Postmodernity of Art: Beyond Hegel and Adorno", *Thesis Eleven* 18/19 (1987).
3. On postmodern approaches to history, see, for example, Linda Hutcheon, *The Politics of Postmodernism* (Routledge, 1989), ch. 3.
4. Douglas Crimp, "On the Museum's Ruins" in Foster, op. cit.
5. Jean-François Lyotard and Jean-Loup Thebaud, *Just Gaming* (Manchester University Press, 1985).
6. For a more extensive discussion of this, see P. Murphy, "Meaning, Truth and Ethical Value", Part 1, *Praxis International* 5, 3 (1985) and "Meaning, Truth and Ethical Value", Part 2, *Praxis International* 7, 1 (1987).
7. *Just Gaming*, p. 24.
8. ibid., pp. 28, 73.
9. ibid., p. 17.
10. ibid.
11. ibid.

12. ibid., p. 66.
13. ibid.
14. ibid., p. 24.
15. ibid., p. 27.
16. Richard Rorty, "Nineteenth Century Idealism and Twentieth Century Textualism" in *Consequences of Pragmatism* (University of Minnesota Press, 1982). The argument is developed in *Contingency, Irony and Solidarity* (Cambridge University Press, 1989), ch. 1. I discuss Rorty's, and other comparable postmodern, views in the review of R. Rajchman and C. West (eds), *Post-Analytic Philosophy* in *Telos* 68 (1986).
17. Jencks, op. cit., p. 349.
18. *Just Gaming*, pp. 15–16.
19. ibid., p. 58.
20. ibid., p. 93.
21. ibid., p. 58.
22. ibid., pp. 50–51.
23. For a discussion of rival conceptions of politics in the modern world, see P. Murphy, "Socialism and Democracy", *Thesis Eleven* 26 (1990); "Between Romanticism and Republicanism: The Political Theory of Claude Lefort", *Thesis Eleven* 23 (1989); and "Pluralism and Politics" in John Burnheim (ed.), *Essays for Agnes Heller* (Reidel, forthcoming, 1991).
24. *Just Gaming*, pp. 94–96.
25. ibid., p. 60.
26. ibid., pp. 95–96.
27. ibid., p. 96.
28. See, for example, Hannah Arendt, "Truth and Politics" in *Between Past and Future* (Penguin, 1977); and the posthumously edited *Lectures on Kant's Political Philosophy* (University of Chicago Press, 1982). See also, Agnes Heller, *Radical Philosophy* (Basil Blackwell, 1984); "Rationality and Democracy" in *The Power of Shame* (Routledge and Kegan Paul, 1985); and *Beyond Justice* (Blackwell, 1987).
29. Michael Walzer, *Spheres of Justice* (Blackwell, 1985); and Paul Hirst (ed.), *The Pluralist Theory of the State* (Routledge, 1990).
30. Charles Jencks, *The Language of Post-Modern Architecture*, 5th edition (Academy Editions, 1987), p. 108.
31. See, for example, Agnes Heller and Ferenc Fehér, *The Postmodern Political Condition* (Polity, 1988).
32. For a very insightful analysis of the competing, and sometimes antithetical, definitions of postmodernism, see Blaine McBurney, "The Post-Modern Transvaluation of Modernist Values", *Thesis Eleven* 12 (1985). As McBurney observes: given that the definition of postmodernism is essentially contested, the question of "what is postmodernism?" can now be replaced in favour of the question "what *should* postmodernism be?".
33. I discuss this further in "Freedom and Happiness: The Pathos of Modernity in Agnes Heller", *Thesis Eleven* 16 (1987); and in "Pluralism and Politics" in John Burnheim

(ed.), *Essays for Agnes Heller*, op. cit.

34. The classic discussion of the idea of totality still remains that of Lukács. See, in particular, *The Historical Novel* (Merlin, 1962) and *Writer and Critic* (Merlin, 1978). While Lukács's discussion of the idea of totality is tainted by the strong residues of an enlightenment philosophy of history, it remains remarkably nuanced and free of dogmatism.
35. Jencks, *Post-Modernism*, op. cit., pp. 280–281. Robert Venturi, *Complexity and Contradiction in Architecture* (MOMA Publication, 1966).
36. This is central to Jencks's notion of a symbolic architecture. See his very interesting argument in chapter 10 of *Post-Modernism*.
37. *Just Gaming*, pp. 86–88.
38. See, for example, Hutcheon, op. cit., ch. 3.
39. *Just Gaming*, p. 60.
40. ibid., p. 60.
41. ibid., p. 60.
42. ibid., p. 61. See also *The Postmodern Condition* (Manchester University Press, 1984), ch. 14.
43. *Just Gaming*, p. 17.
44. Charles Jencks, in a more general way, has also commented on the modernist tenor of Lyotard's work. In *Post-modernism* (p. 12) Jencks writes: "The prefix 'post' has several contradictory overtones, one of which implies the incessant struggle against stereotypes and hence, by implication, the fetish of the new. The French philosopher JeanFrançois Lyotard has focused exclusively on this connotation ..." Jencks suggests that Lyotard is really a Late-Modernist rather than a Post-Modernist; that *The Post-Modern Condition* should, in fact, have been called "The Late-Modern Condition", and that Late-Modernism is just an exaggerated, purified and incessantly revolutionizing form of Modernism. Although there is a lot of truth in all this, Lyotard nonetheless does defend a genuine pluralism, and in that sense, actually steps beyond Modernism. In other respects though, Jencks is absolutely right to identify Lyotard as a Late-Modernist.
45. The flagship of modernist architecture — International Style — is a good example of the former.
46. *Just Gaming*, p. 62.

[2]

Feminism and Pragmatism

RICHARD RORTY

THE TANNER LECTURES ON HUMAN VALUES

Delivered at

University of Michigan
December 7, 1990

RICHARD RORTY is Professor of Humanities at the University of Virginia. He received his Ph.D. degree in Philosophy from Yale University in 1956 and, after service in the U.S. Army, taught at Wellesley and Princeton universities. Professor Rorty has been awarded grants from the American Council of Learned Societies and the John Simon Guggenheim Memorial Foundation and has held numerous fellowships and visiting professorships. He has received the following lectureships: Howison Lecturer, University of California, Berkeley; Northcliffe Lecturer, University College, London; Clark Lecturer, Trinity College, Cambridge; and Romanell Lecturer, Phi Beta Kappa. Many of his works are translated and internationally published, including *Philosophy and the Mirror of Nature* (1979) and *Contingency, Irony and Solidarity* (1989).

When two women ascended to the Supreme Court of Minnesota, Catherine MacKinnon asked, "Will they use the tools of law as women, for all women?" She continued as follows:

> I think that the real feminist issue is not whether biological males or biological females hold positions of power, although it is utterly essential that women be there. And I am not saying that viewpoints have genitals. My issue is what our identifications are, what our loyalties are, who our community is, to whom we are accountable. If it seems as if this is not very concrete, I think it is because we have no idea what women as women would have to say. I'm evoking for women a role that we have yet to make, in the name of a voice that, unsilenced, might say something that has never been heard.[1]

Urging judges to "use the tools of law as women, for all women" alarms universalist philosophers. These are the philosophers who think that moral theory should come up with principles which mention no group smaller that "persons" or "human beings" or "rational agents." Such philosophers would be happier if MacKinnon talked less about accountability to women *as* women and more about an ideal Minnesota, or an ideal America, one in which all human beings would be treated impartially. Universalists would prefer to think of feminism as Mary Wollstonecraft and Olympe de Gouges did, as a matter of rights which are already recognizable and describable, although not yet granted. This describability, they feel, makes MacKinnon's hope for a voice saying something never heard before unnecessary, overly dramatic, hyperbolic.

Universalist philosophers assume, with Kant, that all the logical space necessary for moral deliberation is now available — that

[1] McKinnon, *Feminism Unmodified: Discourses on Life and Law* (Cambridge: Harvard University Press, 1987), p. 77.

all important truths about right and wrong can not only be stated, but be made plausible, in language already to hand. I take MacKinnon to be siding with historicists like G. W. F. Hegel and John Dewey, and to be saying that moral progress depends upon expanding this space. She illustrates the need for such expansion when she notes that present sex-discrimination law assumes that women "have to meet either the male standard for males or the male standard for females. . . . For purposes of sex discrimination law, to be a women means either to be like a man or to be like a lady." [2] In my terms, MacKinnon is saying that unless women fit into the logical space prepared for them by current linguistic and other practices, the law does not know how to deal with them. MacKinnon cites the example of a judicial decision that permitted women to be excluded from employment as prison guards, because they are so susceptible to rape. The court, she continues, "took the viewpoint of the reasonable rapist on women's employment opportunities." [3] "The conditions that create women's rapeability as the definition of womanhood were not even seen as susceptible to change." [4]

McKinnon thinks that such assumptions of unchangeability will only be overcome once we can hear "what women as women would have to say." I take her point to be that assumptions become visible *as* assumptions only if we can make the contradictories of those assumptions sound plausible. So injustices may not be perceived as injustices, even by those who suffer them, until somebody invents a previously unplayed role. Only if somebody

[2] Ibid., p. 71. See also Carolyn Whitbeck's point that "the category, lesbian, both in the minds of its male inventors and as used in male-dominated culture is that of a physiological female who is in other respects a stereotypical male" ("Love, Knowledge and Transformation," in *Hypatia Reborn*, ed. Azizah Y. al-Hibri and Margaret A. Simons [Bloomington: Indiana University Press, 1990], p. 220). Compare Marilyn Frye's reference to "that other fine and enduring patriarchal institution, Sex Equality" (*The Politics of Reality* [Trumansburg, N.Y.: Crossing Press, 1983], p. 108).

[3] McKinnon. *Feminism Unmodified*, p. 38.

[4] Ibid., p. 73.

has a dream, and a voice to describe that dream, does what looked like nature begin to look like culture, what looked like fate begin to look like a moral abomination. For until then only the language of the oppressor is available, and most oppressors have had the wit to teach the oppressed a language in which the oppressed will sound crazy — *even to themselves* — if they describe themselves *as* oppressed.[5]

McKinnon's point that logical space may need to be expanded before justice can be envisaged, much less done, can be restated in terms of John Rawls's claim that moral theorizing is a matter of attaining reflective equilibrium between general principles and particular intuitions — particular reactions of revulsion, horror, satisfaction, or delight to real or imagined situations or actions. McKinnon sees moral and legal principles, particularly those phrased in terms of equal rights, as impotent to change those reactions.[6] So she sees feminists as needing to alter the data of moral theory rather than needing to formulate principles which fit preexistent data better. Feminists are trying to get people to feel indifference or satisfaction where they once recoiled, and revulsion and rage where they once felt indifference or resignation.

[5] Frye remarks that "for subordination to be permanent and cost effective, it is necessary to create conditions such that the subordinated group acquiesces to some extent in the subordination" (*Politics of Reality*, p. 33). Ideally, these will be conditions such that a member of the subordinate group who does not acquiesce will sound crazy. Later, Frye suggests that a person's sounding crazy is a good indicator that you are oppressing that person (p. 112). See also McKinnon, *Feminism Unmodified*, p. 105: "Especially when you are part of a subordinated group, your own definition of your injuries is powerfully shaped by your assessment of whether you could get anyone to do anything about it, including anything official." E.g., a non-crazy claim to have been raped is one acceptable to those (usually males) in a position to offer support or reprisal. Only where there is a socially accepted remedy can there have been a real (rather than crazily imagined) injury.

[6] When Olympe de Gouges appealed in the name of women to the Declaration of the Rights of Men and Citizens, even the most revolution-minded of her male contemporaries thought she was crazy. When Canadian feminists argued, in the 1920s, that the word *persons* in an act specifying the conditions for being a senator covered women as well as men, the Supreme Court of Canada decided that the word should not be so construed, because it never had been. (The Judicial Committee of the Privy Council, be it said, later ruled in the feminists' favor.)

One way to change instinctive emotional reactions is to provide new language which will facilitate new reactions. By "new language" I mean not just new words but also creative misuses of language — familiar words used in ways which initially sound crazy. Something traditionally regarded as a moral abomination can become an object of general satisfaction, or conversely, as a result of the increased popularity of an alternative description of what is happening. Such popularity extends logical space by making descriptions of situations which used to seem crazy seem sane. Once, for example, it would have sounded crazy to describe homosexual sodomy as a touching expression of devotion, or to describe a woman manipulating the elements of the Eucharist as a figuration of the relation of the Virgin to her Son. But such descriptions are now acquiring popularity. At most times, it sounds crazy to describe the degradation and extirpation of helpless minorities as a purification of the moral and spiritual life of Europe. But at certain periods and places — under the Inquisition, during the Wars of Religion, under the Nazis — it did not.

Universalistic moral philosophers think that the notion of "violation of human rights" provides sufficient conceptual resources to explain why some traditional occasions of revulsion really are moral abominations and others only appear to be. They think of moral progress as an increasing ability to see the reality behind the illusions created by superstition, prejudice, and unreflective custom. The typical universalist is a moral realist, someone who thinks that true moral judgments are *made* true by something out there in the world. Universalists typically take this truth maker to be the intrinsic features of human beings qua human. They think you can sort out the real from the illusory abominations by figuring out which those intrinsic features are, and that all that is required to figure this out is hard, clear, thought.

Historicists, by contrast, think that if *intrinsic* means "ahistorical, untouched by historical change," then the only intrinsic features of human beings are those they share with the brutes — for example, the ability to suffer and inflict pain. Every other feature is up for grabs. Historicists agree with the Wittgensteinian view Susan Hurley summarizes as "the existence of certain shared practices, any of which might not have existed, is all that our having determinate reasons . . . to do anything rests on."[7] So they think we are not yet in a position to know what human beings are, since we do not yet know what practices human beings may start sharing.[8] Universalists talk as if any rational agent, at any epoch, could somehow have envisaged all the possible morally relevant differences, all the possible moral identities, brought into existence by such shared practices. But for MacKinnon, as for Hegel and Dewey, we know, at most, only those possibilities which history has actualized so far. MacKinnon's central point, as I read her, is that "a woman" is not yet the name of a way of being human — not yet the name of a moral identity, but, at most, the name of a disability.[9]

Taking seriously the ideas of as yet unrealized possibilities and of as yet unrecognized moral abominations resulting from failure to envisage those possibilities requires one to take seriously the suggestion that we do not presently have the logical space necessary for adequate moral deliberation. Only if such suggestions are

[7] Hurley, *Natural Reasons* (Oxford: Oxford University Press, 1989), p. 32. Hurley is here offering the implications of Wittgenstein's views, rather than stating her own.

[8] In a recent article on Rawls, Susan Moller Okin points out that thinking in Rawls's original position is not a matter of thinking like a "disembodied nobody" but rather of thinking like lots of different people in turn — thinking from the point of view of "every 'concrete other' whom one might turn out to be" ("Reason and Feeling in Thinking about Justice," *Ethics* 99 [1989]: 248). Hurley (*Natural Reasons*, p. 381) makes the same point. The historicity of justice — a historicity which Rawls has acknowledged in his papers of the 1980s — amounts to the fact that history keeps producing new sorts of "concrete others" whom one might turn out to be.

[9] See the theme of "woman as partial man" in Carolyn Whitbeck, "Theories of Sex Difference," in *Women and Values*, ed. Marilyn Pearsall (Belmont, Calif.: Wadsworth, 1986), pp. 34–50. This theme is developed in fascinating detail in Thomas Laqueur, *Making Sex: Body and Gender from the Greeks to Freud* (Cambridge: Harvard University Press, 1990).

taken seriously can passages like the one I quoted from MacKinnon be read as prophecy rather than empty hyperbole. But this means revising our conception of moral progress. We have to stop talking about the need to go from distorted to undistorted perception of moral reality and instead talk about the need to modify our practices so as to take account of new descriptions of what has been going on.

Here is where pragmatist philosophy might be useful to feminist politics. For pragmatism redescribes both intellectual and moral progress by substituting metaphors of evolutionary development for metaphors of progressively less distorted perception. By dropping a representationalist account of knowledge, we pragmatists drop the appearance-reality distinction in favor of a distinction between beliefs which serve some purposes and beliefs which serve other purposes — for example, the purposes of one group and those of another group. We drop the notion of beliefs being made true by reality, as well as the distinction between intrinsic and accidental features of things. So we drop questions about (in Nelson Goodman's phrase) the Way the World Is. We thereby drop the ideas of the Nature of Humanity and of the Moral Law, considered as objects which inquiry is trying to represent accurately, or as objects which make true moral judgments true. So we have to give up the comforting belief that competing groups will aways be able to reason together on the basis of plausible and neutral premises.

From a pragmatist angle, neither Christianity nor the Enlightenment nor contemporary feminism are cases of cognitive clarity overcoming cognitive distortion. They are, instead, examples of evolutionary struggle — struggle which is Mendelian rather than Darwinian in character, in that it is guided by no immanent teleology. The history of human social practices is continuous with the history of biological evolution, the only difference being that what Richard Dawkins and Daniel Dennett call "memes" gradually take over the role of Mendel's genes. Memes are things like turns of speech, terms of aesthetic or moral praise, political slogans, proverbs, musical phrases, stereotypical icons, and the like. Memes compete with one another for the available cultural space as genes compete for the available lebensraum.[10] Different batches of both genes and memes are carried by different human social groups, and so the triumph of one such group amounts to the triumph of those genes or memes. But no gene or meme is closer to the purpose of evolution or to the nature of humanity than any other — for evolution has no purpose and humanity no nature. So the moral world does not divide into the intrinsically decent and the intrinsically abominable, but rather into the goods of different groups and different epochs. As Dewey put it, "The worse or evil is a rejected good. In deliberation and before choice no evil presents itself as evil. Until it is rejected, it is a competing good. After rejection, it figures not as a lesser good, but as the bad of that situation."[11] On a Deweyan view, the replacement of one

[10] Michael Gross and Mary Beth Averill, in their "Evolution and Patriarchal Myths" (in *Discovering Reality*, ed. Sandra Harding and Merrill B. Hintikka [Dordrecht: Reidel, 1983]), suggests that the term *struggle* is a specifically masculist way of describing evolution and ask, "Why not see nature as bounteous, rather than parsimonious, and admit that opportunity and cooperation are more likely to abet novelty, innovation and creation than are struggle and competition?" (p. 85). The question gives me pause, and I have no clear answer to it. All I have is the hunch that, with memes as with genes, tolerant pluralism will sooner or later, in the absence of interstellar travel, have to come to terms with shortage of space for self-expression. There is a more general point involved here, the one raised by Jo-Ann Pilardi's claim that Hegel, Sigmund Freud, and others "were burdened with a notion of identity which defines it as oppositional, one which was derived from the psychosocial development of male children" ("On the War Path and Beyond," in al-Hibri and Simons, *Hypatia Reborn*, p. 12). Just such a notion of identity is central to my claims in this lecture — and particularly to the claims about the possible benefits of feminist separatism I make later. So I am employing what many feminist writers would consider specifically male assumptions. All I can say in reply is that the notion of identity as oppositional seems to me hard to eliminate from such books as Frye's *Politics of Reality* — and especially from her discussion of feminist anger. Anger and opposition seem to me the root of most moral prophecy, and it is the prophetic aspect of feminism that I am emphasizing here.

[11] John Dewey, *Human Nature and Conduct*, in *The Middle Works of John Dewey*, vol. 14 (Carbondale: Southern Illinois University Press, 1983), p. 193. See also "Outlines of a Critical Theory of Ethics," in *The Early Works of John Dewey*, vol. 3 (Carbondale: Southern Illinois University Press, 1969), p. 379: "Goodness is not remoteness from badness. In one sense, goodness is based upon

species by another in a given ecological niche, or the enslavement of one human tribe or race by another, or of the human females by the human males, is not an intrinsic evil. The latter is a rejected good, rejected on the basis of the greater good which feminism is presently making imaginable. The claim that this good is greater is like the claim that mammals are preferable to reptiles, or Aryans to Jews; it is an ethnocentric claim made from the point of view of a given cluster of genes or memes. There is no larger entity which stands behind that cluster and makes its claim true (or makes some contradictory claim true).

Pragmatists like myself think that this Deweyan account of moral truth and moral progress comports better with the prophetic tone in contemporary feminism than do universalism and realism. Prophecy, as we see it, is all that nonviolent political movements can fall back on when argument fails. Argument for the rights of the oppressed *will* fail just insofar as the only language in which to state relevant premises is one in which the relevant emancipatory premises sound crazy. We pragmatists see universalism and realism as committed to the ideas of a reality-tracking faculty called "reason" and an unchanging moral reality to be tracked, and thus unable to make sense of the claim that a new voice is needed. So we commend ourselves to feminists on the ground that we can fit that claim into *our* view of moral progress with relative ease.

We see it as unfortunate that many feminists intermingle pragmatist and realist rhetoric. For example, MacKinnon at one point defines feminism as the belief "that women are human beings in truth but not in social reality." [12] The phrase "in truth" here can only mean "in a reality which is distinct from social reality," one which is as it is whether or not women ever succeed in saying what has never been heard. Such invocations of an ahistoricist realism

badness: that is, good action is always based upon action good once, but bad if persisted in under changing circumstances."

[12] MacKinnon, *Feminism Unmodified*, p. 126.

leave it unclear whether MacKinnon sees women as appealing from a bad social practice to something which transcends social practice, appealing from appearance to reality, or instead sees them as doing the same sort of thing as the early Christians, the early socialists, the Albigensians, and the Nazis did: trying to actualize hitherto undreamt-of possibilities by putting new linguistic and other practices into play, and erecting new social constructs.[13]

Some contemporary feminist philosophers are sympathetic to the latter alternative, because they explicitly reject universalism and realism. They do so because they see both as symptoms of what Jacques Derrida has called "phallogocentrism" — what MacKinnon calls "the epistemological stance . . . of which male dominance is the politics."[14] Other such philosophers, however, warn against accepting the criticisms of universalism and realism common to Friedrich Nietzsche, Martin Heidegger, and Derrida — against finding an ally in what is sometimes called "postmodernism." Sabina Lovibond, for example, cautions against throwing Enlightenment universalism and realism overboard. "How

[13] Suppose we define a moral abomination, with Jeffrey Stout, as something which goes against our sense of "the seams of our moral universe," one which crosses the lines between, as he puts it, "the categories of our cosmology and our social structure" (*Ethics after Babel* [Boston: Beacon Press, 1988], p. 159). Then the choice between a realist and a pragmatist rhetoric is the choice between saying that moral progress gradually aligns these seams with the *real* seams, and saying that it is a matter of simultaneously reweaving and enlarging a fabric which is not intended to be congruent with an antecedent reality. Giving an example of such a seam, Stout says, "The sharper the line between masculine and feminine roles and the greater the importance of that line in determining matters such as the division of labor and the rules of inheritance, the more likely it is that sodomy will be abominated" (p. 153). Later he says, "The question is not whether homosexuality is intrinsically abominable but rather what, all things considered, we should do with the relevant categories of our cosmology and social structure" (p. 158). As with the abominableness of homosexual sodomy, so, we pragmatists think, with the abominableness of the absence or presence of patriarchy. In all such cases, up to and including the abominableness of torturing people for the sheer pleasure of watching them writhe, pragmatists think that the question is not about intrinsic properties but about what we should do with the relevant categories — a question which boils down to what descriptions we should use of what is going on.

[14] MacKinnon, *Feminism Unmodified*, p. 50.

can any one ask me to say goodbye to 'emancipatory metanarratives,'" she asks, "when my own emancipation is still such a patchy, hit-or-miss affair?"[15] Lovibond's universalism comes out when she says, "It would be arbitrary to work for sexual equality unless one believed that human society was disfigured by inequality *as such*." Her realism comes out in her claim that feminism has a "background commitment . . . to the elimination of (self-interested) cognitive distortion."[16]

I share Lovibond's doubts about the apocalyptic tone and the rhetoric of unmasking, prevalent among people who believe that we are living in a "postmodern" period.[17] But, on all the crucial

[15] Sabina Lovibond, "Feminism and Postmodernism," *New Left Review*, Winter 1989, p. 12. For a somewhat more tempered account of the relation of postmodernism to feminism, see Kate Soper, "Feminism, Humanism, and Postmodernism," *Radical Philosophy* 55 (Summer 1990): 11–17. In their "Social Criticism without Philosophy: An Encounter between Feminism and Postmodernism," in *Universal Abandon?* ed. Andrew Ross (Minneapolis: University of Minnesota Press, 1988), Nancy Fraser and Linda Nicholson argue that "a robust postmodern-feminist paradigm of social criticism without philosophy is possible" (p. 100). I of course agree, but I am less sure about the need for, and utility of, "social-theoretical analysis of large-scale inequalities" (p. 90) than are Fraser and Nicholson. This is because I am less sure than Fraser about the possibility that "the basic institutional framework of [our] society could be unjust" (Fraser, "Solidarity or Singularity?" in *Reading Rorty*, ed. Alan Malachowski (Oxford: Blackwell, 1990), p. 318), and hence about "the utility of a theory that could specify links among apparently discrete social problems via the basic institutional structure (p. 319). I suspect my differences with Fraser are concrete and political rather than abstract and philosophical. She sees, and I do not see, attractive alternatives (more or less Marxist in shape) to such institutions as private ownership of the means of production and constitutional democracy, attractive alternatives to the traditional social-democratic project of constructing an egalitarian welfare state within the context of these two basic institutions. I am not sure whether our differences are due to Fraser's antifoundationalist theory hope (see n. 17 below) or to my own lack of imagination.

[16] Lovibond, "Feminism and Postmodernism," p. 28. See Lovibond's reference at p. 12 to "remaking society along rational, egalitarian lines." The idea that egalitarianism is more rational than elitism, rational in a sense which provides reasons for action *not* based on contingent shared practices, is central to the thinking of most liberals who are also moral realists.

[17] A rhetoric of "unmasking hegemony" presupposes the reality-appearance distinction which opponents of phallogocentrism claim to have set aside. Many self-consciously "postmodern" writers seem to me as trying to have it both ways — to view masks as going all the way down while still making invidious comparisons between other people's masks and the way things will look when all the masks have been stripped off. These postmodernists continue to indulge the bad habits char-

philosophical issues. I am on the side of Lovibond's postmodernist opponents.[18] I hope that feminists will continue to consider the possibility of dropping realism and universalism, dropping the notion that the subordination of women is *intrinsically* abominable, dropping the claim that there is something called "right" or "justice" or "humanity" which has always been on their side, making their claims true. I agree with those whom Lovibond paraphrases as saying "the Enlightenment rhetoric of 'emancipation,' 'autonomy' and the like is complicit in a fantasy of escape from the embodied condition." [19] In particular, it is complicit in the fantasy of escape from a historical situation into an ahistoricist empyrean — one in which moral theory can be pursued, like Euclidean geometry, within an unalterable, unextendable, logical space. Although practical politics will doubtless often require feminists to speak with the universalist vulgar, I think they might profit from thinking with the pragmatists.

One of the best things about contemporary feminism, it seems to me, is its ability to eschew such Enlightenment fantasies of escape. My favorite passages in MacKinnon are ones in which she says things like "we are not attempting to be objective about it,

acteristic of those Marxists who insist that morality is a matter of class interest, and then add that everybody has a moral obligation to identify with the interests of a particular class. Just as *ideology* came to mean little more than "other people's ideas," so *product of hegemonic discourse* has come to mean little more than "product of other people's way of talking." I agree with Stanley Fish that much of what goes under the heading of "postmodernism" exemplifies internally inconsistent "antifoundationalist theory hope." See Fish, *Doing What Comes Naturally: Change, Rhetoric and the Practice of Theory in Literary and Legal Studies* (Durham, N.C.: Duke University Press, 1989), pp. 346, 437–38.

[18] I am not fond of the term *postmodernism* and was a bit startled (as presumably was MacIntyre) to find Lovibond saying that Jean-François Lyotard, Alasdair MacIntyre, and I are "among the most forceful exponents of the arguments and values which constitute postmodernism within academic philosophy" (p. 5). Still, I recognize the similarities between our positions which lead Lovibond to group the three of us together. Some of these similarities are outlined by Fraser and Nicholson, "Social Criticism," pp. 85ff.

[19] Lovibond, "Feminism and Postmodernism," p. 12.

we're attempting to represent the point of view of women."[20] Feminists are much less inclined than Marxists were to fall back on a comfortable doctrine of immanent teleology. There is a lot of feminist writing which can be read as saying: we are *not* appealing from phallist appearance to nonphallist reality. We are *not* saying that the voice in which women will some day speak will be better at representing reality than present-day masculist discourse. We are not attempting the impossible task of developing a nonhegemonic discourse, one in which truth is no longer connected with power. We are not trying to do away with social constructs in order to find something that is not a social construct. We are just trying to help women out of the traps men have constructed for them, help them get the power they do not presently have, and help them create a moral identity as women.

I have argued in the past that Deweyan pragmatism, when linguistified along the lines suggested by Hilary Putnam and David Davidson, gives you all that is politically useful in the Nietzsche-Heidegger-Derrida-Foucault tradition. Pragmatism, I claim, offers all the dialectical advantages of postmodernism while avoiding the self-contradictory postmodernist rhetoric of unmasking. I admit that insofar as feminists adopt a Deweyan rhetoric of the sort I have just described, they commit themselves to a lot of apparent paradoxes and incur the usual charges of relativism, irrationalism, and power worship.[21] But these disadvantages are, I think, outweighed by the advantages. By describing themselves in Deweyan terms, feminists would free themselves from Lovibond's demand for a general theory of oppression — a way of seeing oppression on the basis of race, class, sexual preference, and gen-

[20] MacKinnon, *Feminism Unmodified*, p. 86; see also pp. 50, 54, for the "postmodernism" suggestion that the quest for objectivity is a specifically masculist one.

[21] We pragmatists are often told that we reduce moral disagreement to a mere struggle for power by denying the existence of reason, or human nature, conceived as something which provides a neutral court of appeal. We often rejoin that the need for such a court, the need for something ahistorical which will ratify one's claims, is itself a symptom of power worship — of the conviction that unless something large and powerful is on one's side, one shouldn't bother trying.

der as so many instances of a general failure to treat equals equally.[22] They would thereby avoid the embarrassments of the universalist claim that the term *human being* — or even the term *woman* — names an unchanging essence, an ahistorical natural kind with a permanent set of intrinsic features. Further, they would no longer need to raise what seem to me unanswerable questions about the accuracy of their representations of "woman's experience." They would instead see themselves as *creating* such an experience by creating a language, a tradition, and an identity.

In the remainder of this lecture I want to develop this distinction between expression and creation in more detail. But first I want to insert a cautionary remark about the relative insignificance of philosophical movements as compared with social-political movements. Yoking feminism with pragmatism is like yoking Christianity with Platonism, or socialism with dialectical materialism. In each case, something big and important, a vast social hope, is being yoked with something comparatively small and

[22] Developing this point would take too long. Were more time and space available, I should argue that trying to integrate feminism into a general theory of oppression — a frequent reaction to the charge that feminists are oblivious to racial and economic injustice — is like trying to integrate Galilean physics into a general theory of scientific error. The latter attempt is as familiar as it is fruitless. The conviction that there is an interesting general theory about human beings or their oppression seems to me like the conviction that there is an interesting general theory about truth and our failure to achieve it. For the same reasons that transcendental terms like *true* and *good* are not susceptible of definition, neither error nor oppression has a single neck which a single critical slash might sever. Maria Lugones is an example of a feminist theorist who sees a need for a general philosophical theory of oppression and liberation. She says, for example, that "the ontological or metaphysical possibility of liberation remains to be argued, explained, uncovered" ("Structure/Antistructure and Agency under Oppression," *Journal of Philosophy* 87 (October 1990): 502). I should prefer to stick to merely empirical possibilities of liberation. Although I entirely agree with Lugones about the need to "give up the unified self" (p. 503), I do not see this as a matter of ontology, but merely as a way of putting the familiar point that the same human being can contain different coherent sets of belief and desire — different roles, different personalities, etc. — correlated with the different groups to which he or she belongs or whose power he or she must acknowledge. A more important disagreement between us, perhaps, concerns the desirability of harmonizing one's various roles, self-images, etc., in a single unifying story about oneself. Such unification — the sort of thing which I described below as overcoming splits — seems to me desirable. Lugones, on the other hand, urges the desirability of "experiencing oneself in the limen" (p. 506).

unimportant, a set of answers to philosophical questions — questions which arise only for people who find philosophical topics intriguing rather than silly. Universalists — of both the bourgeois liberal and the Marxist sort — often claim that such questions are in fact urgent, for political movements *need* philosophical foundations. But we pragmatists cannot say this. We are not in the foundations business. *All* we can do is to offer feminists a few pieces of special-purpose ammunition — for example, some additional replies to charges that their aims are unnatural, their demands irrational, or their claims hyperbolic.

So much for an overview of my reasons for trying to bring feminism and pragmatism together. I want now to enlarge on my claim that a pragmatist feminist will see herself as helping to create women rather than attempting to describe them more accurately. I shall do so by taking up two objections which might be made to what I have been saying. The first is the familiar charge that pragmatism is inherently conservative, biased in favor of the status quo.[23] The second objection arises from the fact that if you

[23] For a good example of this charge, see Jonathan Culler, *Framing the Sign: Criticism and Its Institutions* (Oklahoma City: University of Oklahoma Press, 1988), p. 55: "the humanities must make their way between, on the one hand, a traditional, foundationalist conception of their task and, on the other, the so-called 'new pragmatism' to which some critics of foundationalism have retreated. If philosophy is not a foundationalist discipline, argues Richard Rorty, then it is simply engaged in a conversation; it tells stories, which succeed simply by their success. Since there is no standard or reference point outside the system of one's beliefs to appeal to, critical arguments and theoretical reflections can have no purchase on these beliefs or the practices informed by them. Ironically, then, the claim that philosophers and theoreticians tell stories, which originates as a critique of ideology . . . becomes a way of protecting a dominant ideology and its professionally successful practitioners from the scrutiny of argument, by deeming that critique can have no leverage against ordinary beliefs, and that theoretical arguments have no consequences. This pragmatism, whose complacency seems altogether appropriate to the Age of Reagan, subsists only by a theoretical argument of the kind it in principle opposes, as an ahistorical 'preformism': what one does must be based on one's beliefs, but since there are no foundations outside the system of one's beliefs, the only thing that could logically make one change a belief is something one already believes." Culler is right in saying that we pragmatists hold the latter view, but wrong in suggesting that we think that *logical* changes in belief are the only respectable ones. What I have called "creative misuses" of language are *causes* to change one's belief, even if not *reasons* to change them. See the discussion of Davidson on metaphor in various

say that women need to be created rather than simply freed, you seem to be saying that in some sense women do not now fully exist. But then there seems no basis for saying that men have done women wrong, since you cannot wrong the nonexistent.

Hilary Putnam, the most important contemporary philosopher to call himself a pragmatist, has said that "a statement is true of a situation just in case it would be correct to use the words of which the statement consists in that way in describing the situation." Putting the matter this way immediately suggests the question: correct by whose standards? Putnam's position that "truth and rational acceptability are interdependent notions" makes it hard to see how we might ever appeal from the oppressive conventions of our community to something nonconventional, and thus hard to see how we could ever engage in anything like "radical critique." [24] So it may seem that we pragmatists, in our frenzied

---

essays in my *Objectivity, Relativism, and Truth* (Cambridge: Cambridge University Press, 1991) for more on this cause-reason distinction, and for the claim that most moral and intellectual progress is achieved by non-"logical" changes in belief. Culler is one of the people I had in mind in n. 16 above — the people who want to hang onto the primacy of logic (and thus of "theoretical reflection" and "critique") while abandoning logocentrism. I do not think this can be done. Culler's charge can be found in many other authors, e.g., Joseph Singer, "Should Lawyers Care about Philosophy?" *Duke Law Journal* 1989, p. 1752: "Rorty . . . has marginalized the enterprise of philosophy, thereby depriving pragmatism of any critical bite." On my view, pragmatism bites other philosophies, but not social problems as such — and so is as useful to fascists like Mussolini and conservatives like Michael Oakeshott as it is to liberals like Dewey. Singer thinks that I have "identified reason with the status quo" and defined "truth as coextensive with the prevailing values in a society" (p. 1763). These claims are, I think, the result of the same inference as Culler draws in the passage quoted above. Both Singer and Culler want philosophy to be capable of setting goals, and not to be confined to the merely ancillary role I describe in n. 26 below.

[24] Putnam's *Representation and Reality* (Cambridge: MIT Press, 1988), pp. 114–15. See also Robert Brandom's formulation of "phenomenalism about truth" as the view that "being true is to be understood as being *properly* taken-true (believed)." Brandom says that what is of most interest about the classical pragmatist stories (C. S. Peirce, William James) is "the dual commitment to a normative account of claiming or believing [Alexander Bain's and Peirce's account of belief as a rule for action] that does not lean on a supposedly explanatory antecedent notion of truth, and the suggestion that truth can then be understood phenomenalistically, in terms of features of these independently characterized takings-true" (Brandom, "Pragmatism, Phenomenalism, Truth Talk," *Midwest Studies in Philoso-*

efforts to undercut epistemological skepticism by doing away with what Davidson calls "the scheme-content distinction," have also undercut political radicalism.

Pragmatists should reply to this charge by saying that they cannot make sense of an appeal from our community's practices to anything except the practice of a real or imagined alternative community. So when prophetic feminists say that it is not enough to make the practices of our community coherent, that the very *language* of our community must be subjected to radical critique, pragmatists add that such critique can only take the form of imagining a community whose linguistic and other practices are different from our own. Once one grants McKinnon's point that one can only get so far with an appeal to make present beliefs more coherent by treating women on a par with men, once one sees the need for something more than an appeal to rational acceptability by the standards of the existing community, then such an act of imagination is the only recourse.

This means that one will praise movements of liberation not for the accuracy of their diagnoses but for the imagination and courage of their proposals. The difference between pragmatism and positions such as Marxism, which retain the rhetoric of scientism and realism, can be thought of as the difference between radicalism and utopianism. Radicals think that there is a basic mistake being made, a mistake deep down at the roots. They think that deep thinking is required to get down to this deep level, and that only there, when all the superstructural appearances have been undercut, can things be seen as they really are. Utopians, however, do not think in terms of mistakes or of depth. They abandon the contrast between superficial appearance and deep reality in favor

---

phy 12 [1988]: 80). Brandom (as well as Davidson and I) would agree with Putnam that "truth does not transcend use" but I think all three of us might be puzzled by Putnam's further claim that "whether an epistemic situation is any good or not depends on whether many different statements are true" (*Representation and Reality*, p. 115). This seems to me like saying that whether a person is wealthy or not depends on how much money she has.

of the contrast between a painful present and a possibly less painful, dimly seen, future. Pragmatists cannot be radicals, in this sense, but they can be utopians. They do not see philosophy as providing instruments for radical surgery, or microscopes which make precise diagnosis possible.[25] Philosophy's function is rather to clear the road for prophets and poets, to make intellectual life a bit simpler and safer for those who have visions of new communities.[26]

So far I have taken MacKinnon as my example of a feminist with such a vision. But of course she is only one of many. Another is Marilyn Frye, who says, in her powerful book *The Politics of Reality*, that "there probably is really no distinction, in the end, between imagination and courage." For, she continues, it takes

[25] Joseph Singer, "Should Lawyers Care about Philosophy?" praises Elizabeth Spelman for "using the tools of philosophy to promote justice," and suggests that one such use is to show that "the categories and forms of discourse we use . . . have important consequences in channeling our attention in particular directions." Surely it is no disrespect to Spelman's achievement, nor to philosophy, to insist that it takes no special tools, no special philosophical expertise, to make and develop this latter point. The use of notions like "powerful methods" and "precise analytical instruments" in the rhetorics of analytic philosophy and of Marxism constitutes, to my mind, misleading advertising. An unfortunate result of such mystification is that whenever philosophy professors like Spelman or I do something useful, it is assumed that they were doing something distinctively philosophical, something philosophers are specially trained to do. If they then fail to go on to do something else which needs to be done, they will usually be charged with using an obsolete and inadequate set of philosophical tools.

[26] See John Dewey, "From Absolutism to Experimentalism," in *Later Works of John Dewey*, vol. 5 (Carbondale: Southern Illinois University Press, 1984), p. 160: "Meantime a chief task of those who call themselves philosophers is to help get rid of the useless lumber that blocks our highways of thought, and strive to make straight and open the paths that lead to the future." There is a lot of this road-clearing rhetoric in Dewey, rhetoric which is continuous with John Locke's description of himself as an underlaborer to those who seemed to him the prophetic spirits of his time—corpuscularian scientists like Newton and Boyle. Both metaphors suggest that the philosophers' job is to drag out-dated philosophy out of the way of those who are displaying unusual courage and imagination. Singer, "Should Lawyers Care about Philosophy?" says that "Dewey, unlike Rorty, saw the problems of philosophy as inseparable from the problems of collective life," and that "by separating philosophy from justice, Rorty's vision reinforces existing power relations" (p. 1759). It is true that Dewey often speaks as if social problems and philosophical problems were interlocked, but I should argue that all these passages can best be interpreted in the road-clearing sense I have just suggested. Dewey never, I think, saw pragmatism in the way in which Marxists saw dialectical materialism—as a philosophical key which unlocks the secrets of history or of society.

courage to overcome "a mortal dread of being outside the field of vision of the arrogant eye." This is the eye of a person who prides himself on spotting the rational unacceptability of what is being said — that is, its incoherence with the rest of the beliefs of those who currently control life chances and logical space. So feminists must, Frye goes on to say, "dare to rely on ourselves to make meaning and we have to imagine ourselves capable of . . . weaving the web of meaning which will hold us in some kind of intelligibility." [27] Such courage is indistinguishable from the imagination it takes to hear oneself as the spokesperson of a merely possible community, rather than as a lonely, and perhaps crazed, outcast from an actual one.

MacKinnon and many other feminists use *liberalism* as a name for an inability to have this sort of courage and imagination. "In the liberal mind," MacKinnon says, "the worse and more systematic one's mistreatment, the more it seems justified. Liberalism... never sees power as power, yet can see as significant only that which power does." [28] The phenomenon she is pointing to certainly exists, but *liberalism* seems to me the wrong name for it. So, of course, does *pragmatism*. I think the main reason — apart from some reflexes left over from early Marxist conditioning — why pejorative uses of the terms *liberal* and *pragmatist* are still common among political radicals is that if you say, with Putnam, that "truth does not transcend use," you may easily be taken as referring to actual, present use. Again, if you deny that truth is a matter of correspondence to reality, you may easily be taken as holding that a true belief is one that coheres with what most people currently believe. If you think that emancipatory moral or social thought requires penetrating to a presently unglimpsed reality beneath the current appearances, and find pragmatists telling you that there is no such reality, you may easily conclude that a pragmatist cannot help the cause of emancipation.

[27] Frye, *Politics of Reality*, p. 80.

[28] McKinnon, *Feminism Unmodified*, p. 221; cf. p. 137.

When, however, we remember that John Dewey — a paradigmatic liberal as well as a paradigmatic pragmatist — spent a great deal of time celebrating the sort of courage and imagination Frye describes, we may be willing to grant that the relation between pragmatism and emancipation is more complex. Dewey said remarkably little about the situation of women, but one of the few things he did say is worth quoting:

> Women have as yet made little contribution to philosophy, but when women who are not mere students of other persons' philosophy set out to write it, we cannot conceive that it will be the same in viewpoint or tenor as that composed from the standpoint of the different masculine experience of things. Institutions, customs of life, breed certain systematized predilections and aversions. The wise man reads historic philosophies to detect in them intellectual formulations of men's habitual purposes and cultivated wants, not to gain insight into the ultimate nature of things or information about the make-up of reality. As far as what is loosely called reality figures in philosophies, we may be sure that it signifies those selected aspects of the world which are chosen because they lend themselves to the support of men's judgment of the worth-while life, and hence are most highly prized. In philosophy, "reality" is a term of value or choice.[29]

Suppose we think, as feminists often do, of "men's habitual purposes and cultivated wants" as "the habitual purposes and cultivated wants of the males, the half of the species which long ago enslaved the other half." This permits us to read Dewey as saying: if you find yourself a slave, do not accept your masters' descriptions of the real; do not work within the boundaries of their moral universe; instead, try to invent a reality of your own by selecting aspects of the world which lend themselves to the support of *your* judgment of the worth-while life.[30]

[29] John Dewey, "Philosophy and Democracy," in *Middle Works* 11:145.

[30] To use an analogy suggested by Charlotte Perkins Gilman's poem "Similar Cases," it is as if one said to the creatures which were eventually to become the

Dewey's doctrine of the means-end continuum might have led him to add: do not expect to know what sort of life is worthwhile right off the bat. for that is one of the things you will constantly change your mind about in the process of selecting a reality. You can neither pick your goals on the basis of a clear and explicit claim about the nature of moral reality, nor derive such a claim from clear and explicit goals. There is no method or procedure to be followed except courageous and imaginative experimentation. Dewey would, I think, have been quick to see the point of Frye's description of her own writing as "a sort of flirtation with meaninglessness — dancing about a region of cognitive gaps and negative semantic spaces, kept aloft only by the rhythm and momentum of my own motion, trying to plumb abysses which are generally agreed not to exist."[31] For meaninglessness is exactly what you have to flirt with when you are in between social and, in particular, linguistic practices — unwilling to take part in an old one but not yet having succeeded in creating a new one.

The import of Dewey's pragmatism for movements such as feminism can be seen if we paraphrase Dewey as follows: do not charge a current social practice or a currently spoken language with being unfaithful to reality, with getting things wrong. Do not criticize it as a result of ideology or prejudice, where these are tacitly contrasted with your own employment of a truth-tracking faculty called "reason" or a neutral method called "disinterested observation." Do not even criticize it as "unjust" if "unjust" is supposed to mean more than "sometimes incoherent even on its own terms." Instead of appealing from the transitory current

---

mammals: "Do not try to imitate the ways in which those larger and more powerful fish cope with their environment. Rather, find ways of doing things which will help you find a new environment." ("Similar Cases" is perhaps most easily available at pp. 363–64 of Ann Lane, *To Herland and Beyond: The Life and Works of Charlotte Perkins Gilman* (New York: Pantheon, 1990). The point of the poem is that if it were true that, as feminists were often told, that "you can't change your nature" we should have had neither biological nor cultural evolution).

[31] Frye, *Politics of Reality*, p. 154.

appearances to the permanent reality, appeal to a still only dimly imagined future practice. Drop the appeal to neutral criteria, and the claim that something large like Nature or Reason or History or the Moral Law is on the side of the oppressed. Instead, just make invidious comparisons between the actual present and a possible, if inchoate, future.[32]

[32] As I suggested earlier, it is easy to reconcile Dewey's claim that, in philosophy, *real* is as evaluative a term as *good* with "postmodernist" views — for example, those found in Chris Weedon's book *Feminist Practice and Poststructuralist Theory* (Oxford: Blackwell, 1987). Pretty much the only difference between Weedon's criticism of the philosophical tradition and Dewey's is one which also separates contemporary pragmatists like Putnam and Davidson from Dewey — the use of *language* instead of Dewey's word *experience* as the name of what it is important for the oppressed to reshape. Weedon, like Putnam and Davidson and unlike Dewey, is what Wilfrid Sellars called a "psychological nominalist" — someone who believes that all awareness is a linguistic affair. She says, "Like Althusserian Marxism, feminist poststructuralism makes the primary assumption that it is language which enables us to think, speak and give meaning to the world around us. Meaning and consciousness do not exist outside language" (p. 32). The difference with Dewey has few consequences, however, since Dewey would have heartily agreed with Weedon that one should not view language "as a transparent tool for expressing facts" but as "the material in which particular, often conflicting versions of facts are constructed" (p. 131). The only real advantage to psychological nominalism for feminists, perhaps, is that it replaces hard-to-discuss (I am tempted to say "metaphysical") questions about whether women have an *experience* different from that of men, or Africans an experience different from that of Europeans, or about whether the experience of upper-class African women is more like that of lower-class European men than that of upper-class European women, with easier-to-discuss (more evidently empirical) questions about what *language* these various groups of people use to justify their actions, exhibit their deepest hopes and fears, etc. Answers to the latter questions are jumping-off places for practical suggestions about different languages which they might use, or might have used. I share MacKinnon's skepticism about the idea that "viewpoints have genitals" and Sandra Harding's skepticism about the utility of notions like "woman's morality," "woman's experience," and "woman's standpoint." See Harding, "The Curious Coincidence of Feminine and African Moralities: Challenges for Feminist Theory," in *Women and Moral Theory*, ed. Eva Kittay and Diana Meyers (Totowa, N.J.: Rowman and Littlefield, 1987), pp. 296–315. Although most of the doctrines (e.g., essentialism, Cartesian individualism, moral universalism) which Weedon attributes to "liberal humanism" are doctrines Dewey (a notorious liberal humanist) also targeted, Weedon does not seem able to eschew a longing for what Mary Hawkesworth calls "a successor science which can refute once and for all the distortions of androcentrism" (Hawkesworth, "Knowers, Knowing, Known: Feminist Theory and the Claims of Truth," in *Feminist Theory in Practice and Process*, ed. Micheline R. Malson, Jean F. O'Barr, Sarah Westphalwihl, and Mary Wye [Chicago: University of Chicago Press, 1989], p. 331). But once you put aside universalism, you should neither hope for knock-down refutations nor talk about "distortion." Hawkesworth goes on to criticize Harding for saying that "feminist analytical categories *should* be unstable at this

So much for the relations between pragmatism and political radicalism. I have been arguing that the two are compatible and mutually supporting. This is because pragmatism allows for the possibility of expanding logical space, and thereby for an appeal to courage and imagination rather than to putatively neutral criteria. What pragmatism loses when it gives up the claim to have right or reality on its side it gains in ability to acknowledge the presence of what Frye calls "abysses which are generally agreed not to exist." These are situations which give the universalist and the realist trouble — ones in which plenty of assent-commanding descriptions are available, but such that none of these descriptions do what is needed.

I turn now to the paradox I noted earlier: the suggestion that women are only now coming into existence, rather than having been deprived of the ability to express what was deep within them all the time. I take MacKinnon's evocation of a "role that women have yet to make" as a way of suggesting that women are only now beginning to put together a moral identity *as* women. To find one's moral identity in being an X means being able to do the following sort of thing: make your X-ness salient in your justification of important uncoerced choices, make your X-ness an important part of the story you tell yourself when you need to recover your self-confidence, make your relations with other X's central to your claim to be a responsible person. These are all things men have usually been able to do by reminding themselves that they are, come what may, *men*. They are things which men have made it hard for women to do by reminding themselves that they are women. As Frye puts it, men have assigned themselves the status of "full persons" — people who enjoy what she calls "unqualified

---

moment in history" (Harding, "The Instability of the Analytical Categories of Feminist Theory," in the same collection, at p. 19). But prophecy and unstable categories go together, and Harding's claim chimes with many of the passages I have been quoting from Frye. Harding's further claim that "we [feminists] should learn how to regard the instabilities themselves as valuable resources" is one that Dewey would have cheered.

participation in the radical 'superiority' of the species" — and withheld this status from women.[33] The result of men constantly, fervently, and publicly thanking God that they are *not* women has made it hard for women to thank God that they are. For a woman to say that she finds her moral identity in being a woman would have sounded, until relatively recently, as weird as for a slave to say that he or she finds his or her moral identity in being a slave.

Most feminists might agree that it was only with the beginnings of the feminist movement that it began to become possible for women to find their moral identities in being women.[34] But most feminists are probably still realist and universalist enough to insist that there is a difference between the claim that one cannot find one's moral identity in being an X and the claim that an X is not yet a full-fledged person, a person to whom injustice has been done by forbidding her to find her moral identity in her X-hood. For the great advantage of realism and universalism over pragmatism is that it permits one to say that women were everything they are now, and *therefore* were entitled to everything they are now trying to get — even when they did not know, and might even have explicitly denied, that they were entitled to it.

For us pragmatists, however, it is not so easy to say that. For we see personhood as a matter of degree, not as an all-or-nothing affair, something evenly distributed around the species. We see it as something that slaves typically have less of than their masters. This is not because there are such things as "natural slaves" but because of the masters' control over the language spoken by the slaves — their ability to make the slave think of his or her pain as fated and even somehow deserved, something to be borne rather than resisted. We cannot countenance the notion of a deep reality which reposes unrecognized beneath the superficial appearances.

33 Frye, *Politics of Reality*, pp. 48–49.

34 I am too ignorant about the history of feminism — about how long and how continuous the feminist tradition has been — to speculate about when things began to change.

So we have to take seriously the idea, made familiar by such writers as Charles Taylor, that interpretation goes all the way down: that what a human being is, for moral purposes, is largely a matter of how he or she describes himself or herself. We have to take seriously the idea that what you experience yourself to be is largely a function of what it makes sense to describe yourself as in the languages you are able to use. We have to say that the Deltas and Epsilons of Aldous Huxley's *Brave New World* and the proles of George Orwell's *1984* were persons only in the sense in which fertilized human ova or human infants are persons — in the sense, namely, that they are capable of being made into persons. So we pragmatists have to identify most of the wrongness of past male oppression with its suppression of past potentiality, rather than in its injustice to past actuality.

In order to say that women are only now in the process of achieving a moral identity as women, I do not need to deny that some women have, in every epoch, had doubts about, and offered alternatives to, the standard, androcentric, descriptions of women. All I need to deny is that women have been able to *forget* the latter descriptions — the ones which make them seem incapable of being full persons. I am denying that women in previous epochs have been able to avoid being torn, split, between the men's description of them and whatever alternative descriptions they have given to themselves. As an example of the sort of thing I have in mind — of the need to name, and thus to begin to bridge, what Frye calls "abysses generally agreed not to exist" — consider Adrienne Rich's description of her situation when young. She was, she says, "split between the girl who wrote poems, who defined herself as writing poems, and the girl who was to define herself by her relationships with men." [35] I want to interpret Rich's individual situation as an allegory of the more general situation in which women found themselves before feminism achieved lift-

[35] Rich, *On Lies, Secrets, and Silence: Selected Prose 1966–1978* (New York: Norton, 1979), p. 40.

off — of their inability to stop defining themselves in terms of their relationships with men. To envisage this inability, consider how Rich's situation differed from that of a young man in a similar situation.

Since Byron and Goethe men have thought of writing poems as one of the best ways to create an autonomous self, to avoid having to define oneself in the terms used by one's parents, teachers, employers, and rulers. Since 1820 or thereabouts, a young man has had the option of defining himself as a poet, of finding his moral identity in writing verse. But, Rich tells us, this is not easy for a young woman.

What is the difficulty? It is not that there is any dearth of true descriptions which Rich might have applied to herself. There were no well-formed — that is, generally intelligible — questions to which Rich could not have given true, well-formed answers. But nevertheless there was, she tells us, a split. The various true descriptions which she applied did not fit together into a whole. But, she is implicitly suggesting, a young male poet's descriptions would have fitted together easily. Rich was, in her youth, unable to attain the kind of coherence, the kind of integrity, which we think of as characteristic of full persons. For persons who are capable of the full glory of humanity are capable of seeing themselves steadily and whole. Rather than feel that splits are tearing them apart, they can see tensions between their alternative self-descriptions as, at worst, necessary elements in a harmonious variety-in-unity.

Rich's account of herself as split rings true, for, as she shows in her essay on Emily Dickinson and elsewhere, the language-games men have arranged that young women should play forces them to treat the men in their lives (or, the absence of men in their lives) as the independent variable and everything else — even their poems — as dependent variables. So insofar as Rich could not tie her poems in with her relationships with men, she had a problem. She was split. She could not be, so to speak, a full-time poet, because a language she could not forget did not let one be both a full-time poet and a full-time female. By contrast, since Byron, the language has let one be a full-time poet and a full-time hero (just as, since Socrates, it has been possible to be a full-time intellectual and a full-time hero).

What might solve Rich's problem? Well, perhaps nowadays it is a little easier for a young woman to define herself by and in her poems than when Rich was young — simply because she may have read books by Rich, Frye, and others. But only a little easier. What would make it *really* easy? Only, I would suggest, the sort of circumstances which made it easy for a young man in the generation after Byron to make his poetic activity the independent variable in the story he told himself about himself. In the previous generation there had been what now looks to us like a band of brothers — Hölderlin and Keats, Byron and Goethe, Shelley and Chamisso. Bliss was it in that dawn to be alive, and to be a young male with poetic gifts was to be able to describe oneself in heroic terms, terms which one could not have used earlier without sounding crazy. That band of brothers founded an invisible club, a very good club, one which is still giving new members a warm welcome.[36] So young male poets do not face abysses when they attempt self-definition. But, as Rich points out, Emily Dickinson was not allowed into that club.[37] So, to make things *really* easy

[36] The continued attractions of this club in our own cynical century are evidenced by the fact that, even as Bernard Shaw was having Candida make fun of Marchbanks, Joyce had Stephen Dedalus write that he would "forge in the smithy of my soul the uncreated conscience of my race." Joyce was not making fun of Stephen, and even Shaw admitted that Candida "does not know the secret in the poet's heart."

[37] "What might, in a male writer — a Thoreau, let us say, or a Christopher Smart or William Blake — seem a legitimate strangeness, a unique intention, has been in one of our two major poets [Dickinson] devalued into a kind of naivete, girlish ignorance, feminine lack of professionalism, just as the poet herself has been made into a sentimental object. ('Most of us are half in love with this dead girl,' confesses Archibald MacLeish. Dickinson was fifty-five when she died.)" (Rich, *On Lies, Secrets, and Silence*, p. 167).

for future Dickinsons and Riches, there would have to be a good, well-established club which they could join.

Here, I take it, is where feminist separatism comes in. Rich asks that

> we understand lesbian/feminism in the deepest, most radical sense: as that love for ourselves and other women, that commitment to the freedom of all of us, which transcends the category of "sexual preference" and the issue of civil rights, to become a politics of *asking women's questions*, demanding a world in which the integrity of all women — not a chosen few — shall be honored and validated in every aspect of culture.[38]

Someone who tries to fit what Rich is saying into a map drawn on a universalist and realist grid will have trouble locating any space separate from that covered by "the category of 'sexual preference' " or by "the issue of civil rights." For justice, on this universalist view, is a matter of our providing each other with equal advantages. Nothing, in this vision, *could* transcend civil rights and the realization of those rights by institutional change. So, for example, lesbian separatism is likely to be seen simply as an arrangement by which those with a certain sexual preference can escape stigma until such time as the laws have been extended to protect lesbians' rights and the mores have caught up with the laws.

Frye offers a contrasting view of the function of separatism when she writes,

> *Re* the new being and meaning which are being created now by lesbian-feminists, we *do* have semantic authority, and, collectively, can and do define with effect. I think it is only by maintaining our boundaries through controlling concrete access to us that we can enforce on those who are not-us our definitions of ourselves, hence force on them *the fact of our exis-*

[38] Ibid., p. 17.

> *tence* and thence open up the *possibility* of our having semantic authority with them.[39]

I take Frye's point to be, in part, that individuals — even individuals of great courage and imagination — cannot achieve semantic authority, *even semantic authority over themselves*, on their own. To get such authority you have to hear your own statements as part of a shared practice. Otherwise you yourself will never know whether they are more than ravings, never know whether you are a heroine or a maniac. People in search of such authority need to band together and form clubs, exclusive clubs. For if you want to work out a story about who you are — put together a moral identity — which decreases the importance of your relationships to one set of people and increases the importance of your relationships to another set, the physical absence of the first set of people may be just what you need. So feminist separatism may indeed, as Rich says, have little to do with sexual preference or with civil rights, and a lot to do with making things easier for women of the future to define themselves in terms not presently available. These would be terms which made it easy for "women as women" to have what Dewey calls "habitual purposes and cultivated wants" — purposes and wants which, as Rich says, only a chosen few women presently have.

To sum up: I am suggesting that we see the contemporary feminist movement as playing the same role in intellectual and moral progress as was played by, for example, Plato's academy, the early Christians meeting in the catacombs, the invisible Copernican colleges of the seventeenth century, groups of workingmen gathering to discuss Tom Paine's pamphlets, and lots of other clubs which were formed to try out new ways of speaking and to gather the moral strength to go out and change the world. For groups build their moral strength by achieving increasing semantic authority over their members, thereby increasing the ability of

[39] Frye, *Politics of Reality*, p. 106n.

those members to find their moral identities in their membership in such groups.

When a group forms itself in conscious opposition to those who control the life chances of its members, and succeeds in achieving semantic authority over its members, the result may be its ruthless suppression — the sort of thing that happened to the Albigensians, and which Margaret Atwood has imagined happening to the feminists. But it may also happen that, as the generations succeed one another, the masters, those in control, gradually find their conceptions of the possibilities open to human beings changing. For example, they may gradually begin to think of the options open to their own children as including membership in the group in question. The new language spoken by the separatist group may gradually get woven into the language taught in the schools.

Insofar as this sort of thing happens, eyes become less arrogant and the members of the group cease to be treated as wayward children, or as a bit crazy (the ways in which Emily Dickinson was treated). Instead, they gradually achieve what Frye calls "full personhood" in the eyes of everybody, having first achieved it only in the eyes of fellow members of their own club. They begin to be treated as full-fledged human beings, rather than being seen, like children or the insane, as degenerate cases — as beings entitled to love and protection, but not to participation in deliberation on serious matters. For to be a full-fledged person in a given society is a matter of double negation: it is *not* to think of oneself as belonging to a group which powerful people in that society thank God they do *not* belong to.

In our society, straight white males of my generation — even earnestly egalitarian straight white males — cannot easily stop themselves from feeling guilty relief that they were not born women or gay or black, any more than they can stop themselves from being glad that they were not born mentally retarded or schizophrenic. This is in part because of a calculation of the obvious socioeconomic disadvantages of being so born, but not entirely. It is also the sort of instinctive and ineffable horror which noble children used to feel at the thought of having been born to non-noble parents, even very rich non-noble parents.[40]

At some future point in the development of our society, guilty relief over not having been born a woman may not cross the minds of males, any more than the question "noble or base-born?" now crosses their minds.[41] That would be the point at which both males and females had *forgotten* the traditional androcentric language, just as we have all forgotten about the discussion between base and noble ancestry. But if this future comes to pass, we pragmatists think, it will not be because the females have been revealed to possess something—namely, full human dignity—which everybody, even they themselves, once mistakenly thought they lacked. It will be because the linguistic and other practices of the common culture have come to incorporate some of the practices characteristic of imaginative and courageous outcasts.

The new language which, with luck, will get woven into the language taught to children will not, however, be the language which the outcasts spoke in the old days, before the formation of separatist groups. For that was infected by the language of the masters. It will be, instead, a language gradually put together in separatist groups in the course of a long series of flirtations with meaninglessness. Had there been no stage of separation, there would have been no subsequent stage of assimilation. No prior antithesis, no new synthesis. No carefully nurtured pride in

[40] This is the sort of ineffable horror which creates a sense of moral abomination (at, e.g., intercaste marriage), and thus furnishes the intuitions which one tries to bring into reflective equilibrium with one's principles. To view moral abominableness as capable of being produced or erased by changing the language taught to the young is the first step toward a nonuniversalist conception of moral progress.

[41] To realize how far away such a future is, consider Eve Klossofky Sedgwick's point that we shall only do justice to gays when we become as indifferent to whether our children turn out gay or straight as we are to whether they become doctors or lawyers. Surely she is right, and yet how many parents at the present time can even imagine such indifference? For the reasons suggested by Stout, in *Ethics after Babel* I suspect that neither sexism nor homophobia can vanish while the other persists

membership in a group which might not have attained self-consciousness were it not for its oppression, no expansion of the range of possible moral identities, and so no evolution of the species. This is what Hegel called the cunning of reason, and what Dewey thought of as the irony of evolution.

Someone who takes the passage I quoted from Dewey seriously will not think of oppressed groups as learning to *recognize* their own full personhood and then gradually, by stripping away veils of prejudice, leading their oppressors to confront reality. For they will not see full personhood as an intrinsic attribute of the oppressed, any more than they see human beings having a central and inviolable core surrounded by culturally conditioned beliefs and desires — a core for which neither biology nor history can account. To be a pragmatist rather than a realist in one's description of the acquisition of full personhood requires thinking of its acquisition by blacks, gays, and women in the same terms as we think of its acquisition by Galilean scientists and romantic poets. We say that the latter groups invented new moral identities for themselves by getting semantic authority over themselves. As time went by, they succeeded in having the language they had developed become part of the language everybody spoke. Similarly, we have to think of gays, blacks, and women inventing themselves rather than discovering themselves, and thus of the larger society as coming to terms with something new.

This means taking Frye's phrase "new *being*" literally, and saying that there were very few female full persons around before feminism got started, in the same sense in which there were very few full-fledged Galilean scientists before the seventeenth century. It was of course *true* in earlier times that women should not have been oppressed, just as it was *true* before Newton said so that gravitational attraction accounted for the movements of the planets.[42] But, despite what Scripture says, truth will not neces-

[42] Pragmatists need not deny that true sentences are always true (as I have, unhappily, suggested in the past that they might — notably in my "Waren die

sarily prevail. "Truth" is not the name of a power which eventually wins through, it is just the nominalization of an approbative adjective. So just as a pragmatist in the philosophy of science cannot use the truth of Galileo's views as an explanation either of his success at prediction or of his gradually increasing fame, so a pragmatist in moral philosophy cannot use the rightness of the feminist cause as an explanation either of its attraction for contemporary women or of its possible future triumph.[43] For such explanations require the notion of a truth-tracking faculty, one which latches onto antecedently existing truth makers. Truth is ahistorical, but that is not because truths are made true by ahistorical entities.

Frye's term *new being* may seem even more unnecessarily hyperbolic than McKinnon's *new voice*, but we pragmatists can take it at face value and realists cannot. As I read Frye, the point is that before feminism began to gather women together into a kind of club, there were female eccentrics like Wollstonecraft and de Gouges, but these were not women who existed *as* women, in MacKinnon's sense of "as." They were eccentric because they failed to fit into roles which men had contrived for them to fill, and because there were as yet no other roles. For roles require a community — a web of social expectations and habits which define the role in question. The community may be small, but, like a club as opposed to a convocation, or a new species as opposed to a few

---

Gesetze Newtons schon vor Newton wahr?" *Jahrbuch des Wissenschaftskollegs zu Berlin* [1987]). Stout (*Ethics after Babel*, chap. 11) rightly rebukes me for these suggestions and says that pragmatists should agree with everybody else that "Slavery is absolutely wrong" has always been true — even in periods when this sentence would have sounded crazy to everybody concerned, even the slaves (who hoped that their fellow-tribespeople would return in force and enslave their present masters). All that pragmatists need is the claim that this sentence is not *made* true by something other than the beliefs which we would use to support it — and, in particular, not by something like the Nature of Human Beings.

[43] I have criticized realists' claims to explain predictive success by truth in part 1 of my *Objectivity, Relativism, and Truth* (Cambridge: Cambridge University Press, 1991). A related point — that the success of a true theory needs just as much historicosociological explanation as the success of a false one — is made by Barry Barnes and other members of the so-called Edinburgh school of sociology of science.

atypical mutant members of an old species, it only exists insofar as it is self-sustaining and self-reproducing.[44]

To sum up for the last time: prophetic feminists like MacKinnon and Frye foresee a new being not only for women but for society. They foresee a society in which the male-female distinction is no longer of much interest. Feminists who are also pragmatists will not see the formation of such a society as the removal of social constructs and the restoration of the way things were always meant to be. They will see it as the production of a better set of social constructs than the ones presently available, and thus as the creation of a new and better sort of human being.

[44] It may seem that the view I am offering is the one which Frye rejects under the name of "the institutional theory of personhood" — the theory that, as she puts it, " 'person' denotes a social and institutional role and . . . one may be allowed or forbidden to adopt that role" (*The Politics of Reality*, p. 49). She says that this view "must be attractive to the phallist, who would fancy the power to create persons." But I do not want to say that men have the power to make full persons out of women by an act of grace, in the way in which sovereigns have the power to make nobles out of commoners. On the contrary, I would insist that men could not do this if they tried, for they are as much caught as are women in the linguistic practices which make it hard for women to be full persons. The utopia I foresee, in which these practices are simply forgotten, is not one which could be attained by an act of condescension on the part of men, any more than an absolute monarch could produce an egalitarian utopia by simultaneously ennobling all her subjects.

Part II
Postmodernism and Culture

[3]

ESSAY/BOOK REVIEW

LAW, MUSIC, AND OTHER PERFORMING ARTS

SANFORD LEVINSON AND J. M. BALKIN†

> "[I]nterpretation" is a chameleon. When a performing musician "interprets" a work of music, is he expressing the composer's, or even the composition's, "meaning," or is he not rather expressing *himself* within the interstices of the score?
>
> —Richard Posner[1]

> Today the conductor, more than any one musical figure, shapes our musical life and thought. That may not be how things *should* be, but it is the way they are. In a future, fully automated age, it may be that the conductor, along with all performing musicians, will be obsolete. Musical creators are working toward that day, assembling electronic scores that, once put on tape, never vary. . . . But until that unfortunate day is here, let us be thankful that there still remain interpretive musicians to synthesize the product of the composer. For without the interplay between the minds of the creator and interpreter, music is not only stale, flat and unprofitable. It is meaningless. . . . Musical notation is an inexact art, no matter how composers sweat and strive to perfect it. Symbols and instructions on the printed page are subject to various interpretations, not to one interpretation.
>
> —Harold Schonberg[2]

> The legislature is like a composer. It cannot help itself: It must leave interpretation to others, principally to the courts.
>
> —Jerome Frank[3]

---

† Levinson is St. John Garwood Chair in Law, University of Texas School of Law. Balkin is Charles Tilford McCormick Professor of Law, University of Texas School of Law. The authors wish to thank Joseph Dodge, Doug Laycock, Dennis Patterson, Richard Posner, Robert Post, Tom Seung, Allan Stein, Carol Weisbrod, and Jay Westbrook for their comments on previous drafts, as well as the participants in faculty workshops at Rutgers-Camden School of Law and the University of Texas School of Law, where earlier versions of this essay were presented.

1 R. POSNER, THE PROBLEMS OF JURISPRUDENCE 271 (1990).

2 H. SCHONBERG, THE GREAT CONDUCTORS 23-24 (1967).

3 Frank, *Words and Music: Some Remarks on Statutory Interpretation*, 47 COLUM. L. REV. 1259, 1264 (1947).

I. Problems for the Performing Artist: Beethoven's F-Natural, Schubert's Repeats, and the Federal Land Policy and Management Act of 1976

The eminent pianist and writer Charles Rosen has noted that "[t]here is an irritating or piquant wrong note in the [score of the] first movement of Beethoven's first piano concerto, a high F-natural where the melody obviously calls for an F-sharp."[4] What accounts for an "obvious" error by this giant of classical music? The answer, says Rosen, lies in the developmental state of the piano when Beethoven composed the concerto: the piano keyboard stopped at F-natural, which therefore established the limit of what was physically possible for a performer to play. To be sure, Beethoven might have written "aspirationally" and composed what, though impossible under current conditions, could nonetheless be aspired to under some future imagined state. Thus Rosen writes of a piano sonata in which Beethoven "asks for a successive *crescendo* and *diminuendo* on a single sustained note," even though "the instrument that can realize this has not yet been invented."[5] But at least this suggests that Beethoven was capable of envisioning the possibility of radical transformation regarding piano design and wanted to signify an intention should those possibilities ever be realized. What, then, does the performer do with the F-natural, where Beethoven appears instead to have acquiesced to the limits of the instrument?

Though the piano that can simultaneously heighten and reduce the sound level of the same note apparently still awaits its development, the piano has indeed been transformed beyond the instrument known to Beethoven in Vienna. Indeed, the expansion of the keyboard happened only shortly after the composition of the first concerto; high F-sharps soon were available to both composers and performers, as exemplified by Beethoven's own use of this note in a number of subsequent compositions, including, interestingly enough, a cadenza meant to be performed as part of the first concerto.[6] He did not, however, return to the initial composition and physically change the notation of the earlier F-natural, in spite of an announced intention, in Rosen's words, "of revising his early

[4] Rosen, *The Shock of the Old* (Book Review), N.Y. REV. BOOKS, July 19, 1990, at 46, 48.

[5] *Id.* at 48.

[6] *See id.*

works in order to make use of the extended range."[7] What, then, is a performer to do when she comes to the measure in question? Should she feel bound by the "plain meaning" of the written score, which displays the F-natural, or ignore it and play what Rosen, a gifted pianist, calls the "obviously" preferable F-sharp?

What note should be played is only the first question. Just as important is another. Should we expect the performer, along with playing whatever note she thinks preferable, to offer a "theory" of musical performance that explicitly offers a justification for the note played? Such a theory, for example, would recognize the presence of such contending factors as the standard meaning of musical notation (to those trained in reading music), the composer's presumed intent, the likely sound heard by the initial audiences of the piece, the expectations of the modern audience, or purely aesthetic desirability–i.e. (or is it e.g.?) the production of beautiful and satisfying sequences of sound. Consider also our reactions if the performer gave as a response to our question, "Why did you play that note?" something like, "I just perform and play the note that feels right to me. If you want a theory of performance, go ask someone else. I can't imagine why you would expect one from me, or why you would feel that being given a theory would be of any use."[8]

If we expect the performer to be able to defend her choice to F-sharp or not to F-sharp, would we (however that "we" is defined) advise the performer to look not only at traditional musical materials, but also at what lawyers have done when deciding the meaning of legal notation? It should already be obvious that a lawyer (including, paradigmatically, an adjudicator) engaged in the performance of legal practice–for example, by being asked to construe a statute or a Constitution–can easily be presented with what appear to be equally "obvious" mistakes and be confronted by similar dilemmas of interpretation. Consider, for example, a provision of the Federal Land Policy and Management Act of 1976 that requires firms with unpatented mining claims on federal lands annually to reregister those claims "prior to December 31."[9] What is the status of a claim filed *on* December 31?[10] What do we

---

[7] *Id.*

[8] *Cf.* Fish, *Dennis Martinez and the Uses of Theory*, 96 YALE L.J. 1773 (1987) (asserting a lack of a relationship between theory and practice).

[9] Federal Land Policy and Management Act of 1976 § 314, 43 U.S.C. § 1744(a) (1988).

[10] *See* United States v. Locke, 471 U.S. 84 (1985). This case is discussed by Judge

expect from the legal performer faced with giving meaning to the ink on the page, and how, beyond the obvious difference in subject matter, would those expectations differ from those directed at the musical performer?

Before answering that question, we ask our readers to consider one more musical example, this time from the piano sonatas of Franz Schubert. The great pianist Alfred Brendel has indicated that he feels no duty to follow the repeat signs that appear at the end of the first sections (the so-called "expositions") of Schubert's last piano sonatas.[11] It has, apparently, been believed since at least the late nineteenth century that "these repeats were vestigial manifestations of an archaic mentality and therefore merely pro forma."[12] One reason offered for skipping the repeats is that most members of a modern audience have in fact heard, perhaps repeatedly, the pieces in question (and, of course, they can, by purchasing a record, repeatedly hear the piece, even if previously unknown to them, in the future); they therefore do not benefit from the repeats being played in the same way as did earlier audiences who only rarely could hear any given piece of music.

A second reason deals with contemporary concert practices. Most modern audiences expect three sonatas in the course of a concert, to be played within a two-hour period. Taking all of the repeats would require violating one of these expectations. People would either feel "cheated" by being presented with a meager program or imposed upon by the demand that they remain in the concert hall for two-and-a-half hours in order to get their full allotment of three sonatas.

Brendel's advice to skip the repeats has not met with universal enthusiasm. Neal Zaslaw, a professor of music at Cornell University, believes that "there is no evidence that the repeats . . . were not meant at face value," and he goes on to add that "[r]epeats are repeats, not question marks. They are there because the composers intended them."[13] To be sure, Professor Zaslaw is no fanatic. He

---

Posner in R. POSNER, *supra* note 1, at 267-69, in which he criticizes the majority of the Court for barring claims filed on December 31 because they are not "prior" to that date.

[11] *See* Brendel, *Schubert's Last Sonatas: An Exchange* (Book Review), N.Y. REV. BOOKS, Mar. 16, 1989, at 42, 42-43; see also Zaslaw, *Repeat Performance* (Book Review), N.Y. REV. BOOKS, Apr. 27, 1989, at 58-59 for a lengthy letter to the editor responding to Brendel's argument.

[12] Zaslaw, *supra* note 11, at 59.

[13] *Id.*

"see[s] nothing wrong with omitting them if time is short, the evening growing late, the performer or the audience seeming tired."[14] He laconically notes that even the greatest composers, "who made their livings by composing and performing frequently and to order, understood and accepted the realities of adapting the music to the occasion."[15] Still, he seems to suggest, one ought at least both have a good reason for ignoring the repeats and have the decency to admit that one is rejecting the composer's intentions on the matter. Again, one wonders, what is a performer to do, with what rationale, and might a conversation with one's counterparts in the law be at all helpful?

This essay is a review of *Authenticity and Early Music*,[16] a collection of essays that exemplify the heated debates now occurring over what is variously called the Early Music Movement or the Authentic Performance Movement. The movement itself has diverse features, including the rediscovery of forgotten music, especially that of the pre-Baroque period, and the careful reconstruction and renovation of period instruments.[17] But the more controversial aspect of the Early Music Movement is the claim of its followers that music should be played according to the "authentic" performance practices of the era in which it was composed.[18] The phrase "early music" has thus become somewhat of a misnomer. The study and application of performance practices of the Renaissance has paved the way in the past twenty years for authentic performances of the Baroque period–Vivaldi, Bach, and Handel, and then on to the music of the classical period–Beethoven, Haydn and Mozart. Nor have the devotees of authentic performance been content to rest with the close of the eighteenth century. For example, one of the most controversial early music conductors of Beethoven, Roger Norrington, has begun issuing "authentic" renditions of Berlioz, Mendelssohn, and Schumann symphonies. If Schumann's *Spring Symphony* is made authentic, can Brahms be far behind?

As Will Crutchfield explains in his essay, these developments have created considerable anxiety in "traditional musicians," an anxiety, Crutchfield argues, that is well justified:

---

[14] *Id.*

[15] *Id.*

[16] AUTHENTICITY AND EARLY MUSIC (N. Kenyon ed. 1988).

[17] *See* Kenyon, *Authenticity and Early Music: Some Issues and Questions*, in AUTHENTICITY AND EARLY MUSIC, *supra* note 16, at 1.

[18] *See id.* at 4-5.

> They know it will not stop with Beethoven any more than it stopped with Bach ten years ago. The movement not only hits them in the pocketbook, but questions the very basis of their art. It is as though we told a generation of scientists that their Ph.Ds were based on a now discredited body of theory–say Ptolemaic astronomy–and now, sorry, the degrees are no good. Worse: it is as though we had been told that Ptolemy was right after all.[19]

As Crutchfield suggests, great sums of money–in recording contracts and record sales–and great professional power and prestige are at stake in the debates over authentic performance. It is no accident that Raymond Leppard, one of the foremost interpreters of Baroque music in an earlier generation, looks askance at the claims made by disciples of authenticity, some of whose recordings inevitably compete with his own.[20] The monetary interest alone, a cynic might suggest, is enough to attract the attention of lawyers. Of course, that is not quite the reason we became interested in these matters. Our interest is in the theory of interpreting commands. We are legal academics writing primarily, we presume, for other legal academics, who are either legal performers in their own right or, with at least some regularity, critics (in the sense of evaluators) of the legal performances of others.

There are two obvious questions raised by our writing this review, even prior to the specific points we will be making below. The first concerns competence. Are we reviewing the book as "experts" who can claim some special training in the areas being discussed by the book's contributors and offer critical assessments of and contributions to the scholarly literature of musicology? The answer, in the case of one of us (Levinson), is unequivocally no; though he listens to music a great deal, his critical acumen is limited almost entirely to "knowing what he likes." The case for the other (Balkin) is a bit more complicated,[21] but he would also make no claims to being a member of the musicological scholarly community to which one ordinarily looks for "authoritative" pronouncements about the quality of scholarly work. But so what? Why would one believe that one must be an "expert" in an area in order to have

---

[19] Crutchfield, *Fashion, Conviction, and Performance Style in an Age of Revivals*, in AUTHENTICITY AND EARLY MUSIC, *supra* note 16, at 19, 20.

[20] *See* Kenyon, *supra* note 17, at 7-8.

[21] Balkin, unlike Levinson, studied composition and orchestration in his youth, and has published an article on Puccini's opera *Turandot*. *See* Balkin, *Turandot's Victory*, 2 YALE J. OF L. & HUM. 299 (1990).

interesting things to say about a given book? And this question, it should be noted, is as true for books about law (about which we *are* suitably certified experts) as for books about early music. One of us (Levinson) has written a book explicitly attacking the notion that conversation about constitutional law should be restricted to those who have been properly credentialed.[22] Thus, if we are so bold to review a book on early music, we should not be afraid to see books on law reviewed in *Early Music*, the leading journal in that field. On the contrary, we would welcome such reviews, at least if musicians think there are any useful comparisons to be made.

This last point leads to a second, equally obvious, question: Why should any lawyer care in the slightest about the debates occurring in the alien field of music (or musicologists about the debates played out in the legal academy)? Richard Posner, the author of one of the quotations opening this essay, devoted much of his book *Law and Literature: A Misunderstood Relation*[23] to attacking the premise that legal analysts really have anything to learn, at least professionally, from the interpretive dilemmas faced by their colleagues in departments of literature. "[T]here are," wrote Posner, "too many differences between works of literature and enactments of legislatures [or of constitutional conventions] to permit much fruitful analogizing of legislative to literary interpretation."[24] One of us (Levinson) had written that "[t]here are as many plausible readings of the United States Constitution as there are versions of *Hamlet*."[25] Though agreeing that *Hamlet* and the Constitution both present many genuine interpretive puzzles, Posner insists that they are "so different from each other that it is unlikely that a *Hamlet* scholar will have anything useful to say about the Constitution or a constitutional scholar anything useful to say about *Hamlet*."[26] Posner's allusion to musical performance in the

---

[22] *See* S. LEVINSON, CONSTITUTIONAL FAITH 49-50 (1988) (defending a "protestant" approach that minimalizes institutional authority and invites all citizens to participate as equals in constitutional dialogue).

[23] R. POSNER, LAW AND LITERATURE: A MISUNDERSTOOD RELATION (1988).

[24] *Id.* at 218.

[25] Levinson, *Law as Literature*, 60 TEX. L. REV. 373, 391 (1982). Interestingly, most readers have read this passage as asserting the infinite malleability of the Constitution rather than, say, the limited number of plausible versions of *Hamlet*. This probably says more about the layman's views about plausible artistic interpretation than it does about Levinson's views of the Constitution. *See infra* note 64. Here Posner attacks the utility of discussing *Hamlet* and the Constitution together rather than the view that either has a particular set of plausible meanings.

[26] R. POSNER, *supra* note 23, at 263.

opening quotation notwithstanding, it is unclear whether his skepticism about insights from literary scholars would dissipate if they were replaced by insights from musicologists.

We think that Posner is wrong in dismissing the potential benefits of communication between literary and legal analysts, but we also think that the question is not truly a theoretical one, as suggested by Posner's use of the word "unlikely" rather than, say, "inherently impossible." The ultimate test in regard to the interplay of law and literature, music, or any other field is the practical aid given the analyst, the felt sense of illumination provided by thinking about Beethoven's F-natural or *Hamlet* while wrestling with the possible meanings of a statute, regulation, or the Constitution of the United States.

Posner's dismissal of the potential interaction between legal analysts and disciplinary outsiders (or vice versa) begs a number of important questions. One is the assumption that there would have to be a transdisciplinary theory of interpretation-in-general that could be applied to all texts in order for different disciplines to have important things to say to each other. In fact, many modern students of hermeneutics have rejected the plausibility of a "science" of "interpretation in general."[27] As a tradition now identified with Wittgenstein and his successors insists, there are only "practices," each constituted by inchoate and unformalizable standards that establish one's statements or, indeed, pianistic performances, as "legitimately assertable"[28] by persons within the interpretive community[29] that constitutes the practice in question.

At the same time, an increasingly common practice in the contemporary academy is precisely to look outside the narrowest disciplinary boundaries for potential insight in solving the puzzles presented by one's own disciplinary materials. To adopt Claude Lévi-Strauss's famous notion, the essence of the post-modernist, post-structuralist interpreter is to be a *bricoleur,* who resourcefully and opportunistically borrows whatever tools might be available to solve particular problems at hand.[30] There are obvious similarities

---

[27] *Cf.* R. RORTY, PHILOSOPHY AND THE MIRROR OF NATURE 8-11 (1979) (arguing that standards of correct judgment differ among various disciplines and that neither philosophy nor any other master discipline can impose its own external standards on them).

[28] S. KRIPKE, WITTGENSTEIN ON RULES AND PRIVATE LANGUAGE 78 (1982).

[29] *See* S. FISH, IS THERE A TEXT IN THIS CLASS? 303-71 (1980).

[30] *See* C. LÉVI-STRAUSS, THE SAVAGE MIND 16-36 (1966); G. GARVEY, CONSTITUTIONAL *BRICOLAGE* 15 (1971).

between bricolage and contemporary pragmatism. The *bricoleur* is not a self-conscious theorist. What justifies using any given tool is its usefulness. There is no theoretically *a priori* way of deciding what tools are either "essential" or "absolutely inappropriate." Thus the pragmatist temperament, which is most likely to reject the notion of a transcendental science of interpretation, is also the most likely to look to other disciplines for analogies and comparisons that might be useful in the pragmatist's own work. Ironically, it is only after one gives up the dream of a single tool useful on every occasion that one begins to see the merits of the diverse tools available for construction, whether of buildings or of theories.

Indeed, Judge Posner, who has recently announced himself a pragmatist in his book, *The Problems of Jurisprudence*,[31] has hardly practiced what he preached in *Law and Literature: A Misunderstood Relationship*;[32] and his later writing suggests he may now be somewhat more latitudinarian. He has, for example, recently published a devastating review of Robert Bork's originalist jurisprudence under the title *Bork and Beethoven*.[33] Posner raises, but does not consider at any real length, some of the questions elaborated in the present review. He notes particularly, and valuably, that conservative intellectuals associated with the magazine *Commentary* seem both to embrace Bork's originalism—the view that "original intent" should control constitutional interpretation—and to be hostile to what on the surface seems to be a very similar view, identified with partisans of "authentic" performance—that a musical performer should try, as much as possible, to recreate the original sounds of a musical composition.[34] He is certainly correct in noticing that explanation of this apparent inconsistency requires some analysis of the cultural moment in which both make their respective appearances. Indeed, it is precisely the insight displayed by juxtaposing Bork and Beethoven (or, more accurately, Bork and *Commentary*'s music critic Samuel Lipman) that seems to disconfirm the rigid disciplinary separations advocated in *Law and Literature: A Misunderstood Relation*.

---

[31] R. POSNER, *supra* note 1.

[32] R. POSNER, *supra* note 23.

[33] Posner, *Bork and Beethoven* (Book Review), 42 STAN. L. REV. 1365 (1990) (reviewing R. BORK, THE TEMPTING OF AMERICA: THE POLITICAL SEDUCTION OF LAW (1990)).

[34] *See id.*

Given that we, too, consider ourselves pragmatists, we certainly have no desire to criticize Posner's argument by positing another equally aprioristic notion that reading literary theory or musicology will *necessarily* be helpful. Nor, certainly, do we wish to argue that law, literature, and music are identical enterprises operating under similar rules of practice. They are not. But to concede that law and music are importantly different does not necessarily imply that they do not also share enough similarities to make comparison useful (and, once more, we emphasize that pragmatic usefulness is the primary criterion we are employing).

Rudyard Kipling put the matter succinctly: "[W]hat should they know of England who only England know?"[35] Presumably one can paraphrase (though not parody) Kipling by asking "what should they know of Texas tort law who only Texas tort law know" (the justification, presumably, for teaching in our classes *de facto* comparative tort law rather than concentrating on the law of a single jurisdiction); "what should they know of tort law who only tort law know" (the justification, presumably, for asking our students to compare the notion of warranty as developed in contract law against developments in the products liability branch of tort law); or "what should they know of American tort law who only American tort law know" (the justification, presumably, for offering to our students courses on other societies' responses to the problems treated by American tort law). So the question ultimately becomes, "What should they know of law who only law know"? Obviously one can know a great deal about England without leaving its shores, and one can make the same claim about the other examples. But is Kipling really "refuted" by that recognition? Would we not, instead, say that few people cannot learn more about their own society by experiencing another? Is this not why most of us refer to travel as "broadening"? Surely this term implies more than simply amassing information about a different society. Rather, it suggests that a realization of how they do things in Tanzania will provide insights into how we behave here in the States. This has certainly been our own experience, and, we are confident, the experience of most of our readers.

Why does Posner, who is notably catholic in his own intellectual interests and well aware of the importance of looking outside

---

[35] Kipling, "The English Flag," *quoted in* OXFORD DICTIONARY OF QUOTATIONS 298 (3d ed. 1979).

traditional legal materials for insight into the law, reject the utility of a lawyer's reading literary theory? The primary reason seems to lie in Posner's insistence that law and literature are fundamentally different enterprises, with fundamentally different points. "A poet tries to create a work of art, a thing of beauty and pleasure."[36] This is, for Posner, presumably true of literary writers in general, even if their genre is the novel or short story rather than the poem. The legislature (or the constitutional convention), on the other hand, "is trying to give commands to its subordinates in our government system."[37] The notion of "command" is central to Posner's theory. "A command," he says, "is designed to set up a direct channel between the issuer's mind and the recipient's; it is a communication, to be decoded in accordance with the sender's intentions."[38] Nor is Posner alone in this view. Robin West, normally no great ally of Posnerian thought, concurs: "legal interpretation is the attempt to ascertain the meaning behind a command; literary interpretation is the attempt to ascertain the meaning behind an artistic expression."[39]

In their differentiation of law and literature, both Posner and West take the poem and the novel as the model of artistic expression. This is a fortunate example for both scholars, since the poem and the novel seem to have little to do with the phenomenon of command. Although Shelley might have claimed that poets were the unacknowledged legislators of mankind,[40] that designation is clearly metaphorical in a way that is not true of the senator or representative anguishing about a vote or the military commander ordering troops into action. Posner thus argues that "[l]aw is coercion rather than persuasion,"[41] and he offers the interpretation of military orders as a good analogue to statutory interpreta-

---

[36] R. POSNER, *supra* note 23, at 240.

[37] *Id.*

[38] *Id.*

[39] West, *Adjudication is not Interpretation: Some Reservations about the Law-as-Literature Movement*, 54 TENN. L. REV. 203, 277 (1987).

[40] *See* M. SHELLEY, A DEFENCE OF POETRY (1821), *quoted in* OXFORD DICTIONARY OF QUOTATIONS, *supra* note 35, at 505. See also Samuel Johnson's quite similar statement, "[The poet] must write as . . . the legislator of mankind, and consider himself as presiding over the thoughts and manners of future generations; as a being superior to time and place." S. JOHNSON, RASSELAS (1759), *quoted in* OXFORD DICTIONARY OF QUOTATIONS, *supra* note 35, at 282.

[41] R. POSNER, *supra* note 23, at 249. *See also* R. POSNER, *supra* note 1, at 296 (1990) ("Agreement on the meaning of legal texts may in many cases depend ultimately on force—law's ultimate backing.").

tion in general.[42] For her part, West asserts that "[l]aw is a product of power," and that legal interpretation is criticism of power.[43]

It is not the purpose of this review to question Posner's or West's reliance on law-as-command or law-as-emanation-of-power, although both of us believe that undue emphasis on this theory produces an impoverished account of law.[44] Indeed, for purposes of this review, we will gladly accept their view that law does indeed often command in a way that a poem or a novel does not. We will also acknowledge that there has been too much insistence that techniques of poetic interpretation could prove useful to the legal analyst, and that law-and-literature scholars have overemphasized the similarities between law and literature and underemphasized the differences. But note that what is interesting about the examples that lead off this review—Beethoven's F-natural and Schubert's repeats—is that they appear to be law-like commands. Consider in this context the comments of early music apostle Christopher Hogwood regarding the discovery of new material relevant to a composer's presumed intentions: "That's the wonderful thing, I think, about coming across new versions of pieces or new evidence. Suddenly that gives you this extra energy: 'Ah, a new set of instructions for embellishment . . . ah, wonderful!'"[45] If this is not a command theory of language, we do not know what would be.

Indeed, when one looks at any musical score, one is faced predominantly not with expression, but command. For what is a musical score but a series of *directions* concerning tempo, meter, pitch, rhythm, attack, and orchestration that are to be carried out over time by a group of performers? To be sure, the skilled musician can read a score like the ordinary person can read a novel, but this is not normally the way either enjoys music. Rather, one listens to the result of the commands brought to life by the performers so instructed. We can therefore imagine a continuum of artistic genres, some of which are more command oriented, like the musical score, and others which are less so, like the poem and

---

[42] *See* R. POSNER, *supra* note 1, at 272-73.

[43] West, *supra* note 39, at 277.

[44] At the same time, we believe that an account of law which focuses only on community-enhancing or permissive aspects is equally impoverished. *See, e.g.*, Levinson, *Conversing about Justice*, 100 YALE L. J. 1855 (1991).

[45] Taruskin, *The Pastness of the Present and the Presence of the Past*, in AUTHENTICITY AND EARLY MUSIC, *supra* note 16, at 150 (ellipsis in original) (quoting Christopher Hogwood).

the novel. The differences are, like those in all continua, a matter of degree. Even a poem may contain instructions (whether explicit or implicit) on how it is to be read—for example, through punctuation and accent marks. Far closer to the musical score is the play, which includes both the lines to be spoken by actors and the relevant stage directions. To be sure, plays can be read silently without performing them, and studied and appreciated like poems and novels. But most people would agree that the artistic expression in a play is not fully realized except through its performance on the stage. Dramatic genres thus undermine the distinction between interpretation of artistic expression and interpretation of command, for a play's artistic interpretation requires interpretation and observance of commands.

At first glance it might seem odd to speak of the lawyer or the judge as a "performer" of law. But in fact, the comparison, first noted by Jerome Frank, is quite apt.[46] As John Chipman Gray, one of the precursors of realism, pointed out at the turn of the century, the texts we call law are not law-in-action but only sources of law—they require the interpretation and application of lawyers, judges, and other legal officials to become law in the sense of a practice of social regulation.[47] Just as the music of the *Eroica* is not identical with its score, but needs a performer to realize it, so too the social practice of law is not fully identical with its written texts, but needs the activity of those entrusted with its performance to be realized.[48]

Another reason often given to doubt the relevance of artistic interpretation to legal interpretation is the differences in consequences that flow from the interpretive act. Legal interpretation affects people's lives and fortunes, whereas nothing of consequence flows from what literary interpreters do. A second, related claim is that unlike artistic interpretation, adjudication is distinctively an act of power.[49] Thus, Professor West argues that adjudication, although in form an interpretive act, is actually an "imperative act"—"an exercise of power in a way in which truly interpretive acts, such as literary interpretation, are not."[50]

---

[46] *See* Frank, *supra* note 3, at 1264.

[47] J. GRAY, THE NATURE AND SOURCES OF LAW 170 (2d ed. 1921).

[48] *See* Frank, *supra* note 3, at 1270-71. For a similar argument, see D. KORNSTEIN, THE MUSIC OF THE LAWS 108 (1982). The foreword to this book of essays, interestingly, was written by Robert Bork. *Id.* at 9-12.

[49] West, *supra* note 39, at 277.

[50] *Id.* at 207.

As to the first point, it seems clear that more rides on whether a young lieutenant obeys what she believes to be a mistaken order of her commander than if Alfred Brendel takes a repeat in a Schubert sonata. But that is true only because of the particular examples offered. In fact, much more may turn on certain directorial decisions in mounting productions of plays or operas than the adjudicated result of the average fender-bender. As noted above, the authentic performance movement is controversial not merely because of its hermeneutic claims, but because it threatens to throw a large number of traditional performers out of a job. If Maestro Norrington is correct, the New York Philharmonic would be best advised to keep its nose out of Schubert, Dvořák and the Romantics–the backbone of the modern symphony orchestra's repertory–to say nothing of Beethoven and Mozart. It had best stick to music it can play authentically–Shostakovich and perhaps Walter Piston. No doubt this will have a significant impact on its subscriptions. It will have an even greater effect on recording contracts, whose royalties often make up a sizeable chunk of a first-class orchestra's revenues. The authentic performance movement is controversial because it has thrown down the gauntlet–play Beethoven with extra woodwinds and an extremely astringent string tone or do not play him at all.

To be sure, Roger Norrington does not have the same power that the Supreme Court does. He cannot enjoin the New York Philharmonic from playing music "incorrectly," and those who disagree with him can offer competing readings of the music, unlike lower courts who are presumably bound by Supreme Court interpretations of federal law.[51] But even if Norrington has less power to enforce conformity with his views than an appellate court, it is a mistake to view him as having no power at all, especially to the extent that his devotees gain control and influence over institutions that shape our musical tastes and preferences.

One need only look at changes in the *Penguin Stereo Record Guide*[52]–a record collector's bible authored by contributors to *Gramophone Magazine*–to see what is at stake in the debates over authenticity in terms of economic power, status, and artistic prestige. In the second edition, published in 1975, the authors speak paternalistically but often approvingly of the very small

[51] We are indebted to Richard Posner for this point.

[52] E. Greenfield, R. Layton & I. March, The Penguin Stereo Record Guide (2d ed. 1975).

number of authentic performances of Baroque music then recorded; in their view, it's quite all right if you like that sort of thing.[53] But traditional performances constitute virtually all recommended albums of Baroque music. As the Eighties progressed, more and more authentic performances, first of Baroque, and then of Classical music appeared. In the 1984 successor volume, *The Complete Penguin Stereo Record and Cassette Guide*,[54] the authors express their approval of many individual "authentic" performances, tempered with occasional distress at the new fundamentalism that appears to inform them.[55] "Traditional," rather than "authentic," performances, however, constitute the lion's share of recommendations.[56] In the work's latest incarnation, *The Penguin Guide to Compact Discs*,[57] published this past year, the field of Baroque music has been largely ceded to authentic performers. It is assumed that most listeners will want such performances, although recommendations are still offered for those who insist on more traditional

---

[53] Discussing Nikolas Harnoncourt's and Gustav Leonhardt's cycle of Bach cantatas for Telefunken records, which at that time was virtually the only example of authentic performance committed to record, the authors note that the use of boys instead of female sopranos "will undoubtedly deter some collectors." *Id.* at 45. Although generally supportive of the project, the authors complain of "a certain want of rhythmic freedom" and too much "expressive caution" in the performances, so that "the grandeur of Bach's inspiration is at times lost to view." *Id.* The tendency to accent all main beats heavily, they note, is "a constant source of irritation throughout the series." *Id.* at 47.

[54] E. GREENFIELD, R. LAYTON & I. MARCH, THE COMPLETE PENGUIN STEREO AND CASSETTE RECORD GUIDE (1984).

[55] For example, in the middle of a highly positive review of Herman Bauman's recording of the Mozart Horn Concertos on a valveless horn, the authors note:

> We are not convinced that the playing of 'original instruments' always demonstrates their full expressive potential and in the case of the french horn it would seem perverse to use a valveless instrument, when a narrow bore modern horn . . . can sound the same, yet produce uniformity of timbre and stay in tune throughout its compass.

Id. at 682. Similarly, in the book's introduction, the authors argue:

> While it is undoubtedly valuable to have an educated opinion of what the music sounded like in the composer's own time, sometimes considerations of scholarship—however dedicated—seem to inhibit the spirit of the music-making. Advocates of the 'authentic' school often seem to regard any kind of expressive licence as reactionary . . . .

Id. at vii.

[56] *See, e.g., id.* at 21-24 (offering recommendations for Bach's *Brandenburg Concertos*); *id.* at 65-67 (Bach's *St. Matthew Passion*); *id.* at 1165-69 (Vivaldi's *Four Seasons*).

[57] E. GREENFIELD, R. LAYTON & I. MARCH, THE PENGUIN GUIDE TO COMPACT DISCS (1990) [hereinafter GUIDE TO DISCS].

versions.[58] With millions of classical music discs sold each year on the recommendations of *Gramophone* and similar magazines, it is clear that interpretive debates are hardly exclusively about matters of expression.[59]

As for Professor West's second point—that legal interpretation is an act of power, while artistic interpretation is not—we think this borders on the naive. One does not have to be a Nietzschean to recognize the struggles for power and prestige involved in debates over artistic interpretation. Indeed, the essays in *Authenticity and Early Music* speak of nothing so much as the battle for authority between early music acolytes and their traditional opponents.[60] Richard Taruskin complains loudly of the "authoritarian" appropriation of the word "authenticity" by early music advocates,[61] while

---

[58] *See, e.g., id.* at 22 (recommending Trevor Pinnock's performance of Bach's *Brandenburg Concertos* while suggesting alternatives "[f]or those who still cannot quite attune their ears to the style of string playing favoured by the authentic school").

[59] And, as Nicholas Kenyon reports in his introduction to *Authenticity and Early Music*, record companies have indeed found that authenticity sells:

> [I]t quickly became clear to the record companies that the legend 'Performed on Authentic Instruments' was regarded as some sort of seal of Good Musical Housekeeping, and the implication of much of their activity was that the use of such instruments guaranteed or at least went some considerable way to ensuring 'authentic' performance. Eventually we reached the absurd situation where the American company releasing the Academy of Ancient Music's recording of the Pachelbel Canon affixed a sticker to the disc proclaiming: 'Authentic Edition. The famous Kanon as Pachelbel heard it.' Those of us who had difficulty knowing what Pachelbel looked like, never mind what he heard like, had some problems with this.

Kenyon, *supra* note 17, at 6.

[60] *See, e.g.,* Taruskin, *supra* note 46, at 139 (noting that the classical music scene "has lately taken on the appearance of a 'battlefield,' . . . [and] we are fighting it out, in this book and elsewhere.") (quoting Crutchfield, *A Report From the Battlefield*, N.Y. Times, July 28, 1985, at 1.).

[61] Taruskin, supra note 45, at 138-39 ("One is hardly free to say, 'I prefer inauthenticity to authenticity,' or, 'I prefer inappropriateness to appropriateness,'—at least if one is interested in maintaining respectability with the crowd that swears by the *Harvard Dictionary* [*of Music*]."). Interestingly enough, Judge Posner has also criticized the "authoritarianism" of those who look to "tradition" for privileged insight into the law. *See* R. POSNER, *supra* note 1, at 448.

Will Crutchfield begins his essay by noting that the authentic performance movement "has come to resemble a juggernaut, a steamroller, a conquering army."[62]

Like Professor West, we also may have too easily accepted that the paradigm of interpretive debate was a solitary scholar lecturing on Keats' *Ode to a Nightingale* from a lectern. Yet it has become increasingly clear that many acts of interpretation are performative utterances which simultaneously constitute acts of power.[63] Rather than seeing the legal act of interpretation as exceptional in its complicity with power, we would suggest that it is quite the other way around. The legal act of interpretation, which clothes power through an act of cognition, is the normal, paradigmatic act of interpretation, while an imagined quiet "powerless" lecture on Keats is the exception.

Moreover, we think that West's and Posner's arguments about legal power confuse the effects of interpretive difficulties with their causes. It may well be true that because the meaning of the Constitution is debatable, people's lives will be affected by what interpreters do. Thus, significant consequences turn on the existence of interpretive difficulties. But this fact is not the *cause* of interpretive difficulty. The cause is the semiotic nature of the command—the fact that the Constitution contains commands encoded in signs requiring interpretation in the light of existing conditions. It is because both the text of the Constitution and the score of Beethoven's *Pastorale* Symphony are commands inscribed in signs that must be interpreted by performers that difficulties of interpretation arise. Once again, we do not deny that the consequences of the exercise of interpretive power should be in the mind of the interpreter as she interprets, and that they might serve as reasons for interpreting one way rather than another. But the interpreter's power does not create her interpretive difficulties—

---

[62] Crutchfield, *supra* note 19, at 19. Crutchfield reports that the opera director Frank Corsaro has even coined a phrase for the increasingly common experience of being frustrated in one's artistic attempts by the new musicological fundamentalism: he calls it being "gesellschafted." *Id.* at 20.

[63] *See* S. Fish, Doing What Comes Naturally: Change, Rhetoric and the Practice of Theory in Literary and Legal Studies 135-36, 306, 309 (1990).

rather it is the interpretive difficulties which give rise to her power over others.[64]

---

[64] In discussing the relationship of law to music with colleagues, we have also witnessed again and again the unquestioned assumption that, unlike legal interpretation, there are really no standards for judging artistic interpretation, and that, in contrast to legal interpretation and legal scholarship, there is really no good way to say that one performance or interpretation is better, richer, or more faithful than another. We suspect that lawyers and legal scholars who speak in this way have never attended a piano competition. Indeed, the entire system of education and training for musicians is premised on the assumption that some performances are better than others. The same assumption underlies record reviews, critical reviews of concerts, and a host of other institutions that are devoted largely to sorting, judging, and evaluating musical performance and musical talent. This is not to say that people do not disagree heatedly over these matters, or that views about interpretation do not change historically; we would only point out that the same is true of legal interpretation and of legal judgments of quality in scholarship or in judicial reasoning.

We think that the exaggerated emphasis on artistic subjectivity by lawyers and legal scholars forced to confront the analogies between law and music is a projection of what are thought to be undesirable characteristics of the self onto the Other. By opposing law to art in this manner, one is able to suppress the emotional and subjective elements of legal judgment by projecting them onto the opposite, art, while simultaneously downplaying the possibility of reasonableness and impartiality in artistic judgment. *See* Balkin, *The Domestication of Law and Literature*, 14 LAW & SOC. INQUIRY 787, 794 (1989); *cf.* Torres and Brewster, *Judges and Juries: Separate Moments in the Same Phenomenon*, 4 LAW & INEQUALITY 171, 181-85 (1986) (Ideological construction of juries as "emotional" allows judges to suppress recognition of their own biases and unreasonableness.).

As this essay went to press, we came across a fascinating case that yokes legal and artistic interpretation together, and thus actually requires a legal judgment about the plasticity of artistic standards. The Tams-Witmark Music Library, which licenses the rights to the Cole Porter musical "Anything Goes," has denied director Martin Teitel the right to stage the musical with a man in the lead role of Reno Sweeney (created on Broadway by Ethel Merman). *See* Shewey, *Anything Goes . . . Well Almost*, Village Voice, Apr. 23, 1991, at S2, col. 4. Previous productions on Fire Island and in Dallas were such a success that Teitel's unusual casting was reported in the trade press, at which point Tams-Witmark objected. (Teitel has met Tams-Witmark's action with a sex discrimination suit of his own.) *Id.* The standard Tams-Witmark licensing contract states that there will be "no additions, transpositions, or interpolations of any kind," although the musical is regularly performed in a modified, edited, and reconstituted fashion without complaint. *Id.* Thus in practice, at least, the question may boil down to whether the proposed innovations go too far. Shewey argues that "[i]t's patently clear that Tams-Witmark's objections stem from homophobia, especially dismaying considering Porter's own homosexuality." *Id.* Perhaps Teitel's alteration is no more a breach of the agreement than setting the musical in the present rather than in the 1930's. Nevertheless, in interpreting the contract, we would think it highly irresponsible for a court to find in the director's favor solely on the grounds that no one can tell whether or not a production is faithful to the musical's score and book. No matter how this particular case should be decided, there must be some point at which outraged theatergoers could demand their money back on the grounds that the play promised to them had not, in fact, been performed. We thus maintain once again that legal and musical interpretation are not as different as they first appear; for in musical, as well as in legal interpretation, not anything goes.

II. How to Perform Music Authentically—*A la Recherche du Temps Perdu*[65]

To take up Kipling's metaphor again, perhaps the best way to understand what other countries and cultures contribute to our understanding of England is to begin the journey itself. One quickly discovers that examples like Beethoven's F-natural or Schubert's repeats do not even begin to exhaust the many different kinds of controversies that may arise over performing the music of the (relatively distant) past. We begin, then, with the interpretation of commands in Beethoven's Symphony No. 6 in F, the *Pastorale*. Consider the following exegesis, given in a booklet accompanying the compact disc recording of Beethoven's Sixth Symphony by The Hanover Band, an English group fully committed to the task of performing music "in a form which [the composer] would recognise."[66] There is a certain irony in the Hanover Band's aspiration, given that Beethoven went deaf well before the composition of the *Pastorale* Symphony. It becomes a zen-like question (as in "what is the sound of one hand clapping?") to ask how one would have the slightest idea what Beethoven might "recognise" as the sound of a symphony that in fact he never heard or could hear fully, save in his own mind.

But of course the Hanover Band probably intended to produce the sonic effects experienced by Beethoven's non-hearing-impaired contemporaries. Even if one grants the plausibility of the Hanover Band's ambitions, their achievement is a daunting task, as illustrated by some of the issues discussed in the booklet. They include, but are not limited to, such aspects of musical performance as trying to recreate "the original orchestral sound" (which means in effect offering "an intimate, chamber music approach"), assigning to notes

---

[65] We allude here not only to the title of Proust's epic example of twentieth century modernism, but to the implications of the different English translations offered in its stead. The standard translation is *In Remembrance of Things Past*. Vladimir Nabokov, among others, has preferred the more "literal" *In Search of Lost Time*. *See* V. Nabokov, Lectures on Literature 208 (F. Bowers ed. 1980). The two titles have quite different implications. We believe that the debates over "authentic" musical performance turn on whether one can truly recover the past or whether one must realize that those times are irredeemably lost, and the concomitant necessity of recognizing that we live exclusively in our own time, separated and alien from the past.

[66] C. Brown, The Hanover Band (1988) (pamphlet accompanying compact disc version of *Beethoven's Symphony No. 6 'Pastoral'* (Nimbus Records 1988)).

the pitch assigned to them in the eighteenth century, mimicking "a late 18th-century feeling for tempo," and presenting "the dramatic address to rhythmic accent and dynamic colour which eyewitnesses [earwitnesses?] describe in Beethoven's own performances."[67] Also characteristic of "authentic" performance is the Hanover Band's emphasis on the use of "original" instruments, which can mean physical objects either originally produced at the time of composition and performance or built more recently in conformity to what is known about the instruments available at the relevant time. This means, among other things, that horns will have no valves, that pianos will produce sounds quite different from a modern Steinway, and that violins will use catgut instead of contemporary metallic strings.

The sonic effects produced by early music enthusiasts like Hogwood, Norrington, and the members of the Hanover Band are clearly different from what many listeners will be used to. For example, modern string players move their fingers slightly on sustained notes to produce a warmer tone, an effect called vibrato.[68] Early music players eschew vibrato, producing a string tone that has variously been described as sour, astringent, or vinegary.[69] Woodwinds and horns often sound out of tune, despite the best of intentions and the most skilled players. In the classical piano concerto, the pianoforte is replaced by the earlier fortepiano, which despite its name produces sounds that are more often piano than forte. Hogwood's tempi are usually much faster than even the fastest traditional performances and display a certain rigidity, while the Hanover Band apparently believe that authenticity requires more flexible changes in tempo than those often heard in traditional performances. Above all, authentic performance produces lighter and more transparent textures in Baroque and Classical music, with

---

[67] *Id.*

[68] THE NEW HARVARD DICTIONARY OF MUSIC 910 (D. Randel ed. 1986) [hereinafter THE NEW HARVARD DICTIONARY].

[69] One of the most amusing aspects of the reviews in *The Penguin Guide to Compact Discs* is their constant assurances to readers that the strings in their recommended authentic performances do not sound half as bad as one would expect. *See, e.g.*, GUIDE TO DISCS, *supra* note 57, at 299 ("Collectors fearful of the vinegary tone often produced by period violins will find their ears beguiled by sounds of great beauty."); *id.* at 29 ("Kuijken . . . shows that authentic performance need not be acidly over-abrasive."); *id.* at 23 (describing Pinnock's performances as "not too abrasive"); *id.* at 35 ("[T]hese accounts [of Bach solo violin music] are as little painful or scratchy as you are likely to get in the authentic field.").

a corresponding loss of weight and, some would say, grandeur.[70] The more expressive utterances–for example those in the slow movements of Mozart symphonies–tend to be downplayed,[71] and the general feeling is one of buoyancy and even lack of seriousness, or in Richard Taruskin's words, of music that "seems ready virtually to blow away."[72]

Do these innovations bring us closer to authentic performance, whatever that might mean? Let us begin with the insistence on using original instruments. Malcolm Bilson, an early music specialist who has recently recorded a cycle of Mozart's piano concerti using a fortepiano, has argued not only that Mozart's sonatas sound significantly different when played on a late-eighteenth century piano, but that a performance played on such a piano was importantly better, because more authentic, than one played on a modern Steinway. Charles Rosen disagreed, and he used Bilson's protest as an example of the ideological nature of the "authentic" performance movement in early music.[73] Professor Zaslaw, whom we have earlier seen in a debate over repeats with Alfred Brendel, tried to mediate between Rosen and Bilson. Zaslaw argued that the eighteenth-century Stein or Walter pianos used by Mozart and the twentieth-century Steinway or Bösendorfer pianos available to Rosen "are extraordinarily sophisticated instruments, each perfect in its own way. The two types are quite different, having been consciously designed to satisfy two very different aesthetics. Each can do things that the other, with all the good will, musicianship, and brilliant pianistic techniques in the world, cannot do."[74]

Rosen responded, however, that Zaslaw's attempted reconciliation still subscribed to the "erroneous and anachronistic assumption that the conception of an eighteenth-century work was identical with the sound we think the composer expected to hear."[75] He particularly took exception to Zaslaw's statement that both the Stein and

---

[70] *See, e.g., id.* at 447 (reviewing Trevor Pinnock's performance of Handel's *12 Concerti grossi*, Op. 6).

[71] *See, e.g., id.* at 682-83 (reviewing Hogwood's performances of the late Mozart symphonies).

[72] Taruskin, *The Pastness of the Present and the Presence of the Past*, in AUTHENTICITY AND EARLY MUSIC, *supra* note 16, at 188.

[73] *See* Rosen, N.Y. REV. BOOKS, Nov. 8, 1990, at 60 (replying to letter by Malcolm Bilson).

[74] Zaslaw, N.Y. REV. BOOKS, Feb. 14, 1991, at 50 (letter to the editor).

[75] Rosen, N.Y. REV. BOOKS, Feb. 14, 1991, at 50 (responding to Zaslaw's letter in the same issue).

Steinways are "each perfect in their own way," responding that "there are aspects of the music of Stravinsky, Bartok, Boulez, and Carter that can only be imperfectly realized on a Steinway. I see no reason to accept a claim of perfection on behalf of the Stein."[76] To the extent that anyone believes that a Stein is "perfect" for the performance of Mozart, Rosen argued, "that is only and tautologically because Mozart *is* to them what he sounds like on a Stein."[77] To believe that the Stein was "really so 'perfect' for Mozart" would presumably require that one believe as well that "the greater sustaining and singing power of the new pianos made soon after Mozart's death would be a falling-off from this absolute state."[78] Rosen freely concedes that "the 'improvements' in construction entailed a loss of certain tonal qualities as well as a gain of others. Zaslaw's position, however, implies that all the changes be seen as nothing but a loss and a degeneration from the ideal sound."[79] Zaslaw's assertion that Stein pianos were "'consciously (and successfully) designed to satisfy' an aesthetic" is dismissed as "a naive claim that ignores conflicting aesthetic ideals and all manner of mechanical problems that stand in the way of constructing pianos."[80] Rosen thus accuses Zaslaw (and Bilson) of being committed to a notion that there is one best way of presenting Mozart, and he writes a sentence that certainly should strike a familiar chord in anyone familiar with equally acrimonious disputes in the world of legal interpretation: "Multiple possibilities of realizing a musical text are a basic tradition of Western music . . . ."[81]

But deciding on what kinds of instruments to play is only the beginning. One must also decide on the numbers of instruments, which can obviously make a significant difference in terms of volume, tonal balance, and the like. Yet Harold Schonberg notes that "[o]ften Bach, like most other composers of the time, did not specify instrumentation, and he would use whatever was at hand."[82] What explains this? The answer is that, "[u]ntil Haydn and Mozart came along—and, indeed, for many years later outside of the big European cities—the orchestra was altogether a flexible

---

[76] *Id.*
[77] *Id.* (emphasis in original).
[78] *Id.*
[79] *Id.*
[80] *Id.*
[81] *Id.*
[82] H. SCHONBERG, *supra* note 2, at 29.

affair" in terms of the numbers of particular instruments represented and, of course, the quality of the particular players.[83] Thus a specific "composer's orchestration depended upon the groups involved," and, indeed, "[o]rchestration would be adapted to fit the needs of individual players."[84] There is no proof that previous composers expected that later generations would confine themselves to the same size orchestras they were forced to accept. Roger Norrington's attempt to achieve an authentically sized orchestra for his performance of Berlioz's *Symphonie Fantastique* based on 1830 Paris models is particularly troublesome in this respect; if there is one thing we know about Berlioz, it was that no orchestra was too large for his tastes.[85]

The Hanover Band is considerably smaller than most contemporary orchestras, with a far greater emphasis on the woodwinds. The reason, of course, is that this reflects the orchestras found in Vienna at the end of the eighteenth century. The members of the Band are directed not by a conductor standing on a podium, as is contemporary practice, but rather "either from the violin or from the keyboard as is in keeping with the period and according to the repertoire."[86] We are told, no doubt accurately, that "Beethoven directed many performances from the fortepiano added by propulsive internal direction given by the first violin."[87] What was good enough for Beethoven should, presumably, be good enough for Bernstein, at least if one's goal is fidelity to the former. It does not appear, though, that any early-music enthusiasts adopt the practice of early conductors who kept time by loudly beating a stick on the floor so as to be heard by the members of the orchestra.[88]

"The matter of pitch," we are told, "is crucial to a faithful reconstruction."[89] Today's "standard pitch" sets the A above

---

[83] *Id.* at 28.

[84] *Id.*

[85] *See id.* at 113-14 (describing Berlioz's ideal orchestra of 465 instruments and a 360 person chorus).

[86] C. BROWN, *supra* note 66.

[87] *Id.*

[88] *See* H. SCHONBERG, *supra* note 2, at 26, 28.

[89] C. BROWN, *supra* note 66. On pitch, see Fantel, *Equipment That Plays in the Key of Flexibility*, N.Y. Times, Aug. 26, 1990, at 26, col. 1. Fantel, who writes about "sound" for the *New York Times*, notes that "Beethoven's notion of C differs from ours," and goes on to observe not only that "[t]oday's performances, adhering to the modern convention of 'standard pitch,' take no account of this," but also the fact that compact disk players generally do not allow the listener to adjust the pitch of a recording. *Id.* The market has recognized this defect, though, and it is now possible to buy CD players that "are capable of tuning the music up or down by as much as

middle C at 440 cycles per second. The Hanover Band, after much research, adopts "an A sounding at 430 cycles per second."[90] Not surprisingly, such differences in pitch produce somewhat different sounds. It is worth mentioning in this context what is perhaps the *reductio ad absurdum* of this striving for historically-informed reproduction of sound. In Christopher Hogwood's recording of Beethoven's Third Symphony, the *Eroica*, he purports to recreate the initial performance of the music by "a very powerful company (consisting almost entirely of amateurs)."[91] Thus the performance features, among other things, the "uncomplicated, rhythmical" approach found in amateur performances even in the present.[92] If the first performance of the *Eroica* was mediocre, Hogwood seems to be arguing, well then, that is the price one pays for authenticity.

If the aural picture historically experienced by the work's first audience is the true test of authenticity, it is difficult to know whether Hogwood's suggestion is to be dismissed out of hand or fervently embraced. Indeed, one might go even further in the reconstruction of the exact sounds produced at the premieres of the Beethoven symphonies. Instruments used during the late eighteenth century were often out of tune, especially as the performance progressed, because of the limitations of the stings used at the time, for example. Presumably, then, it would violate the "rule of recognition," as adopted by the Hanover Band or by Hogwood, to play the music consistently in tune, as that is a distinctly "modern" expectation, based on subsequent developments in the technology of musical instruments.[93] Emphasis on recreating the actual

---

a whole note." *Id.* Fantel somewhat naively suggests, however, that the listening public might "leave the matter of pitch strictly in the hands of the performers." *Id.* The members of the Hanover Band would respond, though, that most performers cannot be trusted, that only *they* are presenting the *authentic* Beethoven experience.

[90] C. BROWN, *supra* note 66.

[91] Hogwood, *Hogwood's Beethoven*, THE GRAMOPHONE, Mar. 1986, at 1136, *quoted in* Taruskin, *supra* note 45, at 140.

[92] *See* Taruskin, *supra* note 45, at 141 (quoting Clive Brown, notes to Oiseau-Lyre 414338).

[93] This is by no means a fanciful concern. We normally expect top-flight modern symphony orchestras to play in tune, but our expectations about what "in tune" performance consists in depends upon several factors, including the invention of horns with valves and the universal adoption of the even tempered scale in the nineteenth century. To preserve acoustically pure intervals in one key necessitates that some intervals in other keys will deviate from acoustic perfection, and the more harmonically distant the key, the greater the disadvantage. *See* THE NEW HARVARD DICTIONARY, *supra* note 68, at 422, 837-38. Different methods of "tempering" or slight adjustment of the scale to compensate for this problem were devised and

conditions of performance, finally, leads one to ask whether recordings proclaiming such "authenticity" should not include coughs, wheezing, and other sounds that were undoubtedly heard in Viennese drawing rooms and concert halls during the playing of the music. At some point one crosses the line that separates scrupulousness from absurdity, but unfortunately one's confidence in the ability to locate that line has been seriously undermined by Hogwood's and the Hanover Band's pronunciamentos.

Of course, not everyone agrees with the Hanover Band's approach to correct interpretation. And indeed, the authors of *Authenticity and Early Music* are united primarily by their skepticism, if not outright hostility, to the ideology revealed in the Hanover Band booklet. For these writers, Proust's title[94] should undoubtedly be translated to emphasize the "lostness" of the past and, consequently, the inability to present a performance today that could meaningfully replicate earlier performances. All of them would agree with Robert P. Morgan's observation that "we cannot re-create the 'aura' of the original (to borrow Walter Benjamin's useful term), no matter how hard we try."[95] Difficulties concerning the maintenance or manufacture of "original" instruments or the "proper" pitch of C are only the beginning. Thus, writes Morgan, "[p]erhaps even more critical . . . than original performance inflections is the deeper context in which the works were originally experienced–their status as integral components of a larger cultural environment that has disappeared and is fundamentally irrecoverable."[96] Morgan offers as "only the most obvious" example that much "early music was not intended to be performed in concert."[97] To take another example, Bach composed his

employed during the 1600s and 1700s. The title of Bach's *Well-Tempered Clavier* refers to one such method, no longer used today. *See id.* at 838. Eventually, the equal temperament approach gained dominance, but this temperament is not necessarily the same one originally used when early music was first performed. *See id.* at 624, 838. Valveless horns of the type used in Beethoven's era play notes that do not precisely match an even tempered scale, *see id.* at 364, 380, and thus performers must use various devices (such as partially closing off the bell of the horn with the right hand) to approximate the correct pitch. *See id.* at 381. Some out of tune performance on original instruments is also due to the performer's inability to control various aspects of the instrument, for example the gradual loosening of the sounding strings on early stringed instruments or pianos.

[94] *See supra* note 65.

[95] Morgan, *Tradition, Anxiety, and the Current Musical Scene*, in AUTHENTICITY AND EARLY MUSIC, *supra* note 16, at 71.

[96] *Id.*

[97] *Id.* In the classical and Romantic periods, chamber and solo instrumental music

masses and his religious cantatas to be performed in church as part of the devotional exercises of committed Lutherans.[98]

Perhaps the best way of understanding the problem is by pondering a recent promotional advertisement offered by an Austin, Texas public radio station promising a performance of a Bach mass "just as Bach would have heard it." This advertisement was presumably directed to people eating dinner in their homes, to others working at their places of business, and to still others driving in their cars. The idea that if we wish to recapture the "authentic" experience of Bach or Beethoven all that is necessary is to pop a tape of Hogwood into our car stereo as we speed down interstate 35 seems increasingly preposterous the more that one thinks about it. Moreover, the very idea of *recorded* music that can be purchased as a commodity in stores (the *St. Matthew Passion*—on sale now for only $3.99!)—and can be played over and over again at our whim—is completely foreign to the phenomenology of musical performance in Bach's time, and indeed, of all musical culture until well into the twentieth century.[99]

As Morgan writes, "if we take the notion of context at all seriously, we are left with the painful realization that *any* concert performance of this music constitutes a basic perversion of its original intentions."[100] What he terms "[t]he authentic function of the music," an interesting term for him to adopt, "is lost to us and cannot be reconstituted. As soon as we place these works in a museum, we wrench them out of their own frame and utterly transform their original meaning."[101] Morgan concludes his essay by accusing the authenticity movement of "plac[ing] older music in a museum," which, he goes on to note, is an essentially "modern invention,"[102] created precisely at the moment in our culture when we recognized the ineluctable pastness of the past and thus felt the necessity to preserve what was no longer part of our living

---

would usually be performed in the home or at small social gatherings. *See* Rosen, *supra* note 4, 75, at 50; Holland, *Heard the One About the Madcap Trill?*, N.Y. Times, Apr. 7, 1991, at 25, col. 1 ("[A] lot of music we now listen to silently was written for noisy dinner parties.") (interview with Alfred Brendel).

[98] *See* Taruskin, *Facing Up, Finally, to Bach's Dark Vision*, N.Y. Times, Jan. 27, 1991, at 25, col. 1.

[99] *See* W. BENJAMIN, *The Work of Art in the Age of Mechanical Reproduction*, in ILLUMINATIONS 217-251 (H. Zohn trans. 1969).

[100] Morgan, *supra* note 95, at 71.

[101] *Id.*

[102] *Id.* at 81.

experience in an antiseptic environment suitable for distanced observation.

Morgan draws a contrast between placing early music in the equivalent of a museum and treating it as part of an ongoing tradition. Ironically enough, a *living* tradition involves participants who feel (and this word is used advisedly) comfortable engaging in their own interpretations, their own transformations of the materials that constitute their identity. What allows one, for example, to consider him or herself a "traditional" Jew is surely not some fantasy that one is doing exactly what was done 3000 years ago in ancient Israel, but rather a felt confidence that one is participating as the latest member of a recognizable way of life whose transhistorical identity has endured whatever the surface changes. Few traditions assume stasis as the operative condition of life.

As Will Crutchfield writes, "[o]ne of the unthought-of things the great composers assumed, wanted, and needed was the conviction and passion of great performers,"[103] who would offer their own emendations of the composer's score. Exemplifying Crutchfield's point is the distinguished theater and opera director Jonathan Miller, who writes of his hope "that by the first night a performance has emerged that has the possibilities of an enormous amount of spontaneous growth and amplification" generated by the performers themselves.[104] He mentions his delight, upon seeing a particular performance of *Rigoletto* that he had directed for the English National Opera, in discovering a host of "things that I had never seen before and never asked them to do." Indeed, "Whenever I have gone back to watch *Rigoletto* I have been delighted to find that it is a truly emergent production,"[105] a collaborative relationship among composer or playwright (who may, of course, be long dead), director, actors and singers, and audience.

For most of us, this notion of living tradition is most obvious in popular music. What makes Thelonious Monk's *Round Midnight* a true "classic" of jazz is most certainly *not* its ability to be endlessly re-presented in a single canonical note-for-note form, but rather its ability to serve as the basic setting for creations by other great musicians. Even if one exempts jazz from the discussion due to its deliberately improvisatory form, one can find much the same idea of a living tradition in performances of pop, soul, and rock music.

---

[103] Crutchfield, *supra* note 19, at 25.
[104] J. MILLER, SUBSEQUENT PERFORMANCES 117 (1986).
[105] *Id.* at 118.

One might also adopt, as Jonathan Miller does in his discussions of the interpretation of plays, Noam Chomsky's distinction between the deep and surface structures of grammar. In Miller's words, "there are an infinite series of sentences, all of whose *surface structures* are different but that can nevertheless express the same *deep structure*."[106] It is therefore altogether possible (and legitimate) that "an enormous variety of actual performances" can be faithful to the underlying deep structure of the particular piece that is being interpreted.[107]

Nevertheless, (and, we might add, alas), there are popular musicians who themselves are increasingly indicating disdain for those who ostensibly "'distort[popular music] in all kinds of insidious ways that are losing track of [the composer's] original authentic sound.'"[108] Morgan is quoting a "bright young star" of the New York cabaret scene, Michael Feinstein, who has produced an album which "attempts a re-creation of Gershwin's popular songs in their original form," using original orchestrations and texts.[109] Morgan fumes: "This from, of all things, a cabaret singer—a type *traditionally* committed to extremely personal, even blatantly idiosyncratic stylizations."[110] Feinstein's album is entitled, as might be expected, *Pure Gershwin*. The work of cultural anthropolo-

---

[106] *Id.*

[107] J. MILLER, *supra* note 104, at 118. Having introduced Chomsky into the discussion, we hasten to distance ourselves from any commitment to the general structuralist program that Chomsky is famous for (and that Miller is adopting). Post-structuralist critiques, after all, have argued forcefully against the notion of unique and identifiable deep structures that provide the kind of baseline that Miller strongly endorses to constrain interpretive license. One might respond to Miller's distinction by wondering whether continuous changes in surface over time might lead to what everyone would admit were really profound changes in structure. If the evolution of *Rigoletto* continued apace for ten years in his absence, Miller might well discover, upon his return, that the cumulation of so-called "surface alterations" had made his original artistic conception virtually unrecognizable. *Cf.* Balkin, *Constitutional Interpretation and the Problem of History* (Book Review), 63 N.Y.U. L. REV. 911 (1988) (discussing cumulative effects of commerce clause decisions). Similarly, the history of jazz music has demonstrated that the original notion of variations in melody, while preserving "deep" harmonic structure, eventually led to substituted harmonies in the be-bop era, the adoption of improvisation on modal scales in lieu of harmonic structure in the work of Miles Davis' first quintet, and finally to Ornette Coleman's "free jazz." M. GRIDLEY, JAZZ STYLES 40, 44, 51, 120-22, 177-78, 195-201 (1978). For a general discussion, see J. COLLIER, THE MAKING OF JAZZ: A COMPREHENSIVE HISTORY (1978).

[108] Morgan, *supra* note 95, at 78 (quoting Holden, *Cabaret's Bright Young Star*, N.Y. Times, June 29, 1986, § 6 (Magazine), at 33, col. 2).

[109] *Id.*

[110] *Id.*

gists may be particularly helpful in understanding what lies behind the use of the "pure" in such settings.[111] To label those whose interpretations differ from one's own "impure" is no small rhetorical feat. Indeed, it is structurally similar to describing one's opponents as "heretics."[112] Such language suggests the smell of the *auto-de-fe* rather than a willingness to acknowledge the legitimacy of competing perspectives. As Morgan observes with regard to Feinstein's ambitions, "[a]pparently it is no longer Mabel Mercer's or Bobby Short's Gershwin we want [or will even tolerate as an acceptable possibility], it is some sort of reincarnation of Gershwin himself."[113] To switch back to "classical" music, it is no longer Leonard Bernstein's or the New York Philharmonic's Beethoven we should want, but rather the Hanover Band's reincarnation. Such an approach, ironically enough, seems not only to embalm a tradition, but to be unfaithful to what is historically known about "original" performance practice, which allowed, indeed celebrated, improvisation.[114]

Richard Taruskin is perhaps the most polemical (and entertaining) of the opponents of the authentic performance school, which he rechristens "authenticistic."[115] His essay, "The Pastness of the Present and the Presence of the Past," casts scorn upon almost all of the claims suggested or implied by the proponents of "authenticity" in early music. Thus, as against the comment by one writer that "an ideal performance is one that perfectly realizes the composer's intentions,"[116] Taruskin responds that "[w]e cannot know intentions, for many reasons—or rather, we cannot know we know them."[117] In Taruskin's view, "'once the piece is finished, the composer regards it and relates to it either as a performer if he is one, or else simply as a listener.'"[118] As for fidelity to text, he

[111] *See, e.g.*, M. DOUGLAS, PURITY AND DANGER: AN ANALYSIS OF CONCEPTS OF POLLUTION AND TABOO (1978) (describing the cultural construction of "impurities" that must be suppressed).

[112] *See* R. BORK, *supra* note 33, at 4, 11 for just such a denunciation of opponents.

[113] Morgan, *supra* note 95, at 78.

[114] *See* Brett, *Text, Context, and the Early Music Editor*, in AUTHENTICITY IN EARLY MUSIC, *supra* note 16, at 106-07.

[115] Taruskin, *supra* note 45, at 148.

[116] *Id.* at 138 n.8 (quoting Grant, *On Historical Authenticity in the Performance of Old Music*, in ESSAYS ON MUSIC IN HONOR OF ARCHIBALD THOMPSON DAVISON 341 (1957)).

[117] *Id.* at 145.

[118] *Id.* at 147 (quoting Taruskin, *On Letting the Music Speak for Itself: Some Reflections on Musicology and Performance*, 1 J. MUSICOLOGY 340 (1982)).

quotes the composer George Perle's view that "[t]he greatest single source of bad performance . . . is literalism . . . 'It's what you expect nowadays.'"[119]

Taruskin also joins most of his fellow essayists in criticizing the historical tendentiousness of many of the "authentic performance" devotees. He argues that many early music performers are simply imposing their own aesthetic preferences under the guise of "authentic" performance practices. He gives the example of David Wulstan's performances of Renaissance choral music, which attempted to "'obtain as nearly as possible the sound of the great English Sixteenth Century Choirs.'"[120] After some experimentation with the traditional men-boy choirs, Wulstan switched from boy trebles to women, arguing that "'[b]ecause boys' voices now break early, they tend to find the high vocal parts . . . overtaxing: with proper training, however, girls' voices can produce exactly the right sound.'"[121] This seems a perfectly plausible accommodation until Taruskin points out that Wulstan (like everyone else alive today) had never heard the sound of a "great English Sixteenth Century Choir."[122] Authentic performance, Taruskin argues, is really the imposition of a post-Stravinskian modernist aesthetic to the music of the past. It is a creation of our own times, satisfying modern aesthetic preferences which are nevertheless justified and even sanctified by claims of historical accuracy.

Interestingly, Taruskin does not condemn *per se* the practice of making Mozart and Beethoven sound like Stravinsky; he objects, rather, to the claim that this modernization of sound is in fact authentic, and the related claim that this "authentic" practice is the only permissible way to perform early music. Taruskin at last reveals himself to be both a pluralist and a pragmatist in matters of musical performance. The test of an artistic interpretation for him, presumably, is whether it "works" aesthetically—whether it produces a pleasing and satisfying experience to the persons of our own era.[123]

We have purposely forborne from pointing to all of the obvious affinities between the arguments made (and attacked) by those interested in the performance of early music and those made by

---

[119] *Id.*

[120] *Id.* at 144 (quoting Chislett, notes to Seraphim LP 60256 (works of Tallis)).

[121] *Id.* (quoting Chislett, notes to Seraphim LP 60256 (works of Tallis)).

[122] *Id.*

[123] *See id.* at 204-07.

legal analysts concerned with how one should engage in legal performance. A statute or a constitution is, indeed, *not* a poem; it *is* designed to structure other people's behavior in certain important ways. But, then, so is the score of a symphony or the text of a play. And the word "structure" is purposely elusive, leaving open the possibility that the particular passions (and, dare we say, political commitments) of the gifted performer might have as much to do with the performance possibilities she chooses as some impossible fidelity to purportedly timeless and acontextual commands contained in the texts. *Authenticity and Early Music* should thus be of interest to anyone interested in problems of legal interpretation.

But that is only one of the reasons for suggesting that a law-and-music scholarship can complement the already flourishing genre of law-and-literature. Perhaps more important than recognition of the affinities of interpretive dilemmas generated by having to work with texts, as important as that recognition may be, is the insight provided into more general issues of cultural development.

III. Interpretation and Modernist Anxiety

It is our thesis that the early-music movement is best understood as attempting what the English historian Eric Hobsbawm calls the "invention of tradition."[124] Hobsbawm defines "'invented' traditions" as "responses to novel situations which take the form of reference to old situations, or which establish their own past by quasi-obligatory repetition."[125] Faced with "the constant change and innovation of the modern world," one engages in an "attempt to structure at least some parts of social life within it as unchanging and invariant."[126]

Hobsbawm contrasts this pseudo-traditionalism to participation in a living and developing tradition, and, interestingly, one example he gives is the English common law, which he argues is characterized by a remarkable combination of "flexibility in substance and formal adherence to precedent."[127] In Hobsbawm's view, the common law could never "afford to be invariant, because even in 'traditional' societies life is not so."[128] Variance means change,

---

[124] *See* Hobsbawm, *Introduction: Inventing Traditions,* in THE INVENTION OF TRADITION 1-14 (E. Hobsbawm & T. Ranger eds. 1983).

[125] *Id.* at 2.

[126] *Id.*

[127] *Id.*

[128] *Id.*

which means history and the realization of "break[s] in continuity."[129] Paradoxically, to the extent that one feels firmly rooted in a culture, such changes may be easily assimilated and treated, as we saw earlier, merely as surface manifestations of deeper unchanging continuities that legitimate the enterprise. Thus, it is crucial to note that Charles Rosen, after arguing that "[m]ultiple possibilities of realizing a musical text are a basic tradition of Western music," immediately follows with the clause, "a tradition which no longer apparently has any reality"[130] for "authentic" performance devotees. As "breaks" increasingly become defined as "ruptures" separating the past and the present, the stage is set for those who, dismayed by present practice, preach return to the purity of the past. Such revivalist movements, "common among intellectuals since the Romantics, can never develop or even preserve a living past (except conceivably by setting up human natural sanctuaries for isolated corners of archaic life), but must become 'invented tradition,'"[131] committed to stasis and condemning as impurity, heresy, and defilement what a truly living tradition might see simply as admirable "adaptability."[132]

Many of the essays in *Authenticity and Early Music* are not centrally concerned with "proper" standards of interpretation at all. They ask a much deeper question: What explains the development at this juncture of our culture of a movement organized around the notion of authenticity in musical performance? This question has implications reaching far beyond the particularity of music; it touches on central aspects of the experience of modernity in Western culture as a whole, including, most certainly, its legal aspects. Thus the study of music, on the surface so different from law, enables us to see things in our own discipline that were there all along but hidden by our very familiarity with it. By studying what the crisis of modernity has meant in music, we can better understand its impact on the law. To handle this crucial topic adequately would require a book of its own. This essay can do nothing more than sketch some points of comparison and suggest further questions for investigation.

There are many ways of describing the phenomenon of modernity and its relation to what has come to be called the

---

[129] *Id.* at 7.
[130] Rosen, *supra* note 75, at 50.
[131] Hobsbawn, *supra* note 124, at 8.
[132] *Id.*

postmodern condition. We might view modernity as the increasing recognition, especially since the Enlightenment, of the conflict between reason and tradition, including revealed religion, as modes of understanding the world.[133] We might understand it as the increasing victory of secular or worldly conceptions of life over the religious and transcendent.[134] We might view it as the increasing replacement of traditional modes of social organization by the bureaucratization and rationalization of society,[135] or as the eventual collapse of the concept of reason into a barren instrumentalism.[136]

We emphasize that modernity is a contested theoretical concept, which might be extended to much of Western culture since the Renaissance or restricted to the particular cultural issues of the late nineteenth and twentieth centuries, which is our particular focus.[137] Moreover, the features often ascribed to modernity are not always peculiar to the "modern" age, however it is defined. For example, the tension between reason and tradition characteristic of the modern age scarcely begins with the twentieth century, or even with the Enlightenment. One can find anti-traditionalism in the rationalism of Descartes and the skepticism of Hobbes, and still further back in debates in ancient Greek thought. Although we see the conflict between reason and tradition, and the concomitant sense of the disintegration and collapse of tradition as an integral part of what we call "modernity," we do not claim that it is unique to the modern era. Indeed, it is more likely that history is full of what might be called "modernist crises" in many different lands and

---

[133] *See* I. KANT, *What is Enlightenment?*, in FOUNDATIONS OF THE METAPHYSICS OF MORALS AND WHAT IS ENLIGHTENMENT? 85 (L. Beck trans. 1959); D. HARVEY, THE CONDITION OF POSTMODERNITY: AN ENQUIRY INTO THE ORIGINS OF CULTURAL CHANGE 12 (1989).

[134] *See* T. SEUNG, CULTURAL THEMATICS 246-59 (1976); G. HEGEL, PHILOSOPHY OF HISTORY 442 (1902).

[135] *See* 2 M. WEBER, ECONOMY AND SOCIETY, AN OUTLINE OF INTERPRETIVE SOCIOLOGY 1381-1462 (G.Roth & C. Wiltich eds. 1968); M. WEBER, THE PROTESTANT ETHIC AND THE SPIRIT OF CAPITALISM 182 (T. Parsons trans. 1958).

[136] This theme is probably most associated with the Frankfurt School of critical theory. *See* J. HABERMAS, LEGITIMATION CRISIS (1975); M. HORKHEIMER, ECLIPSE OF REASON (1947); M. HORKHEIMER & T. ADORNO, THE DIALECTIC OF ENLIGHTENMENT (1972).

[137] *Compare, e.g.*, T. SEUNG, *supra* note 134 (describing the creation of a modern "Faustian ethos" which separates the Middle Ages from the Renaissance) *with* M. BERMAN, ALL THAT IS SOLID MELTS INTO AIR: THE EXPERIENCE OF MODERNITY 16-17 (1982) (suggesting that the first phase of modernity begins in sixteenth century, but emphasizing modernity as a creature of the nineteenth and twentieth centuries).

times. To speak of modernity, thus, is to speak of one particular cultural moment in Western thought, when the conflict between reason and tradition not only becomes central, but is commingled with other elements that are more peculiarly of our age, such as mass industrialization, and the increasing rationalization and bureaucratization of society.

In this essay we focus on a single strand of the experience of modernity—our relation to the past and, in particular, to the cultural traditions that constitute it. From this perspective, the experience of modernity is the increasing sense of isolation and estrangement from the past and from tradition, spurred on by constantly accelerating changes in culture, economy, and technology.[138] Viewed solely as the collapse of tradition and separation from the past, "modernity" is surely nothing new. Each generation throughout history has probably spoken of the "good old days" that are long past.[139] One can find jeremiads bewailing the loss of past tradition to change and cosmopolitanism throughout human history, and to the this extent the present era has more in common with previous ones than theorists of modernity often admit.[140] What distinguishes our own particular "modern" period is an accelerating spiral of technology and bureaucracy unlike any other in human history; as a result, the sense of distance and fragmentation from the past appears to have become a central, pervasive, and seemingly permanent element of the experience of culture.[141]

---

[138] *See, e.g.*, L. SCAFF, FLEEING THE IRON CAGE: CULTURE, POLITICS, AND MODERNITY IN THE THOUGHT OF MAX WEBER 18 (1989) (describing progenitors of modernism as sharing a "consciousness of a dynamic and wrenching destabilization of transmitted cultural traditions"); C. SCHORSKE, FIN-DE-SIÈCLE VIENNA: POLITICS AND CULTURE xix (1980) (describing the modern sense of demise of tradition in "a whirl of infinite innovation"); M. BERMAN, *supra* note 137, at 15, 13 (describing the modern period as "a maelstrom of perpetual disintegration and renewal, of struggle and contradiction, of ambiguity and anguish[,]" which generates in people both "a will to change—to transform both themselves and their world—and . . . a terror of disorientation and disintegration, of life falling apart").

[139] *See* Luban, *Legal Traditionalism*, (forthcoming 43 STAN. L. REV. (1991)).

[140] *See id.*

[141] As Marshall Berman argues, nineteenth and twentieth century modernism is distinguished by a

> dynamic new landscape . . . . [of] steam engines, automatic factories, railroads, vast new industrial zones; of teeming cities that have grown overnight, often with dreadful consequences; of daily newspapers, telegraphs, telephones and other mass media, communicating on an ever wider scale; of increasingly strong national states and multinational aggregations of capital; of mass social movements fighting these modernizations from above with their own modes of modernization from below; of

Moreover, "modernity," as suggested by Hobsbawm's essay, is linked to the development of a specifically historical sensibility that focuses on the cultural segmentation of time rather than its continuity. An increased attention to the historicist elements of culture brings with it an understanding of the profound differences between the perceptions of times past (and irrevocably lost) and those of our own. It is just such an understanding that leads us to develop periodizations of time—e.g., "ancient times," the "middle ages," and the like—that serve not only to divide the calendar but also to mark significant changes of consciousness that separate the inhabitants of one culture from those of another. Some may applaud such changes as have occurred, as is true of those who see history as a progressive liberation from the cultural blinders dominating past epochs. Others may instead bewail these changes and see them instead as symptoms of decline from some presumably better state of things in the past.[142] But perhaps now more common is the rejection either of applause or of dejection, which are themselves recognized as the products of specific cultural moments, in favor of a somewhat more detached acceptance of the inevitability of change and our inability to place such changes as occur within any master narrative. Our awareness of the breaks between the past and our present situation is joined with a confidence (if that is the right word) that the future will bring equal ruptures that will lead to our own epoch being understood as merely one specific cultural moment. As one of the greatest living historians, David Brion Davis, reminds us, "in the future our own mixtures of insight and blindness will be interpreted from that then-present perspective from which one tries to understand the past. *We will then be perceived in ways that we cannot perceive ourselves.*"[143] It is precisely this awareness of perceptual gaps, of commitments to such fundamentally different paradigms of understanding that characterizes much of modernist sensibility.

> an ever-expanding world market embracing all, capable of the most spectacular growth, capable of appalling waste and devastation, capable of everything except solidity and stability.

M. BERMAN, *supra* note 137, at 18-19.

[142] *See, e.g.*, A. BLOOM, THE CLOSING OF THE AMERICAN MIND 85 (1987) ("Country, religion, family, ideas of civilization, all the sentimental and historical forces that stood between cosmic infinity and the individual, providing some notion of a place within the whole, have been rationalized and have lost their compelling force.").

[143] D. DAVIS, THE PROBLEM OF SLAVERY IN THE AGE OF REVOLUTION, 1770-1823, at 15 (1975) (emphasis added).

The literary scholar Paul Fussell, writing about the impact of World War I on Anglo-American culture, argues that "the most pervasive contribution of modern war to modernist culture is irony, widely perceived to be . . . the 'normative mentality' of modern art."[144] Just as Roland Barthes is said to have noted that one can unabashedly say "I will love you forever" only once in one's life, so does an awareness of historical situatedness cause us to stand at a suitable distance from our own most deeply held convictions. To put it mildly, questions about the meaning of authenticity, whether of one's beliefs or practices, go to the heart of modernist culture.[145]

As Will Crutchfield notes in his essay "Fashion, Conviction, and Performance Style," the word *authenticity* has many meanings. It may refer to fidelity to the composer's intentions, or to the composer's text.[146] Yet, Crutchfield insists, there is a more appropriate meaning of authenticity of performance: "This authenticity is what the standee at the opera means when he says he has heard 'the real thing,' 'the genuine article.'"[147] When a performance is authentic in the sense of genuineness, "we feel the music and musician are one . . . . The Irish theologian William Fitzgerald supplied . . . the right citation for this: 'That is called Authentic, which is sufficient unto itself, which commends, sustains, proves itself, and hath credit and authority from itself.'"[148]

The notion of authenticity as genuineness is deeply tied to the concept of tradition and one's relation to the past. The authentic performance is immersed in a tradition, so that the tradition springs from within it unself-consciously; it is the living embodiment of tradition, of the past. That is why it is sufficient to itself, and needs authority from no outside source. Hence another meaning of "authentic" is idiomatic, sincere, and unaffected. Nevertheless, this conception of authenticity leads to what we might call the "paradox of authenticity." The more one self-consciously tries to be authentic to a tradition, the less authentic one's practice becomes; conversely, true authenticity always emerges where one least expects it, and indeed, it emerges virtually without any effort on the part of the actors who are enmeshed in authentic practice.

---

[144] Fussell, *Introduction* to THE NORTON BOOK OF MODERN WAR 24 (1991).

[145] *See* L. TRILLING, SINCERITY AND AUTHENTICITY 97-98 (1972).

[146] Crutchfield, *supra* note 19, at 24.

[147] *Id.*

[148] *Id.* at 24-25.

At the risk of frivolity, we might offer a gustatory example drawn from our mutual experiences in the Southwestern United States. We refer, of course, to Tex-Mex cuisine. For those who have not been introduced to this contribution of the great state of Texas, Tex-Mex is an adaptation (some purists would say adulteration) of traditional Mexican dishes by both Chicanos and Anglos living in Texas. Tex-Mex cuisine has by now become quite popular around the United States. Indeed, from Seattle to New York City one can see signs advertising "Authentic Tex-Mex Cuisine." As one might suspect, those of us from Texas have only contempt for such assertions of authenticity, similar, we suspect, to the response of a French visitor to being taken to the "Paris Restaurant, featuring authentic French cuisine." Yet at the same time, there is something quite bizarre about the notion of *authentic* Tex-Mex food. This is, after all, a cuisine whose delicate flavors are produced by prodigious quantities of canned Ro-Tel tomatoes and great slabs of Kraft Velveeta. From the standpoint of "authentic" Mexican food, Tex-Mex is itself an abomination, a veritable monument to inauthenticity.

And yet, at the same time, there is no doubt that Texans can always spot an authentic Tex-Mex institution.[149] The streets of East Austin are full of them, and people are quite vocal about their favorites. Indeed, some people even prefer Tex-Mex to other types of Mexican food. The inauthentic has become the standard of authenticity. The alteration of old habits, the addition of new ingredients, the catch-as-catch-can recombination of elements has produced a new cuisine in its own right that can be authentically or inauthentically reproduced. And the moment that we realize that there can be "authentic" Tex-Mex cuisine—itself the product of a previous inauthenticity—at that moment the possibility of "inauthentic" Tex-Mex cuisine arises.

It is perhaps only a slight exaggeration to say that many of the problems of modernity and its relation to tradition are summed up in the sign that promises us "Authentic Tex-Mex Cuisine." Each tradition is the result of previous adulteration and abomination. Each tradition by becoming a tradition nevertheless asserts its own authenticity. The self-conscious search to regain and recapture that

---

[149] Of course this statement simply raises the issue of authenticity in the form of another question: Who, after all, counts as a "Texan?" For example, both Levinson and Balkin live in Texas but hail originally from North Carolina and Missouri, respectively.

authenticity nevertheless produces inauthentic performance. And the very unself-conscious activity involved in adulteration nevertheless produces ever new examples of the authentic, the authentic that is not yet recognized as such.

We can understand an important aspect of modernity through the concept of authenticity, by which we mean the idea of an organic connection to tradition. Modernity might be described as the experience of feeling self-conscious about one's relationship to the past and to tradition, isolated and alienated—in a word, inauthentic. The paradox of authenticity promises us that the modernist will both invariably fail at regaining this lost authenticity and invariably succeed in epitomizing an authentic experience—the authentic experience of separation from the past, which is the authentic experience of modernity.[150]

All of which brings us back to the early music movement. A question that fascinates several of the authors in *Authenticity and Early Music* is why the concept of authenticity has taken center stage, whether as hero or villain, in our own lifetimes. The idea of "authentic" performance practices would have seemed bizarre to earlier ages. A composer of early music, wrote the music historian Donald Grout, would be "astonish[ed] at our interest in such matters. Have we no living tradition of music, that we must be seeking to revive a dead one?"[151] Will Crutchfield notes:

> [I]f you were an Italian singer in 1888, you did not think of singing Rossini style for Rossini and Mozart style for Mozart and Verdi style for Verdi. You just *sang*. The way you sang—how you felt a crescendo, where you would instinctively accelerate, where you would feel the need to make an ornament, what a good pianissimo note sounded like to you—would have been in the style of the cultural situation of 1888, a style that developed in symbiosis with the middle and late operas of Verdi, along with the secondary composers such as Ponchielli who were active at the

---

[150] Because people usually desire what they feel they most lack, often the more self-conscious a person is, the more avidly she will seek authentic experience. Thus, it was no accident that the Romantic era was both an era of extreme self-consciousness and an age which stressed the importance of authenticity. *See* M. BERMAN, THE POLITICS OF AUTHENTICITY: RADICAL INDIVIDUALISM AND THE EMERGENCE OF MODERN SOCIETY 312-15 (1970) (emphasizing the importance of Montesquieu and Rousseau to the development of the romantic concern for authenticity, and showing the roots of the modern concern for authenticity in romantic self-consciousness).

[151] Taruskin, *supra* note 45, at 141 (quoting Grout, *On Historical Authenticity in the Performance of Old Music*, in ESSAYS ON MUSIC IN HONOR OF ARCHIBALD THOMPSON DAVISON 346 (1957)).

> time. . . . The concept did not yet exist of different style-complexes that could be stuck into the heads of performers like a floppy disc into a word processor depending on what program was desired that evening.[152]

There are several reasons for the previous lack of concern with authentic performance. During the nineteenth century there was still a continuous outpouring of what we *now* label "classical" music. Thus performers focused more on performing the new music of the 1800s, and less upon preserving a repertory of old classics, as is the case today. One played Mozart and Beethoven as one would play other music. There was no division of classical versus early romantic versus late romantic music. There was simply music, and it was performed according to the best stylistic practices of the day.[153] These stylistic practices colored the music of the past in terms of the tastes of the present. But this coloration was not noticed, because the cultural subject saw herself as at one with the past, not even conscious of following a tradition of performance.

To modern ears, the difference between Mozart and Mahler, or between Rossini and Puccini, is so great that it is difficult to comprehend this mindset. Perhaps the best analogy is to the popular music of today—rock and roll. When Bruce Springsteen plays a cover of "Twist and Shout" during a 1990's rock and roll concert, he simply plays the music as a rock and roll song. He does not engage in self-conscious inquiry into early 1960's performance practices. Nor does the audience find this at all unseemly. Nevertheless, rock and roll performance has changed greatly since the 1950s and 60s, due in part to developments in electronic instrument and recording technology, the increased importance of

---

[152] Crutchfield, *supra* note 19, at 22-23.

[153] In understanding this point, it is important to distinguish compositional from performance styles. The music of Liszt and Wagner, for example, shocked their nineteenth century contemporaries because of its harmonic audacity, and was often seen as a betrayal of sound compositional principles and traditions. But these qualms about new harmonic practices did not lead nineteenth century critics to think that earlier music should be *performed* differently than contemporary music. We emphasize, however, that the gradual breakdown of the tonal system of harmony by the beginning of the twentieth century, and the development of a musical avant-garde divorced from popular tastes, did eventually contribute to the modern experience of separation between performers and composers of "classical" music, as discussed *infra* text accompanying notes 155-57. We simply note here that these effects had not yet fully been felt in the nineteenth century.

the large stadium or arena as a venue for concerts, and even the development of the music video.[154]

Interestingly, no one *yet* thinks it very important to duplicate the earlier sound exactly. That is because, to paraphrase the song, it's still rock and roll to us. One can easily predict, however, that future Michael Feinsteins will make it their mission to present purportedly pure Buddy Holly or Little Richard songs and to denigrate as illegitimate and contemptible the versions played by performers like Springsteen and others whom we now benightedly identify as great rock-and-rollers in their own right.

There is an important connection between being unself-consciously within a cultural tradition that is still growing and developing, and a similar unself-consciousness about authenticity in performance. It is precisely because we don't think about authenticity very much when it comes to rock music that we can be quite sure that rock and roll is still a living tradition of popular culture, in a way that (for example) ragtime is not. As Will Crutchfield puts it:

> The great benefit of this close, narrow correspondence between contemporary composition and performing style—as we can still observe it in popular music, on historic recordings, in a very few elder statesmen among today's artists, and in specialists centering their work in the music of today—is that the performer can be so confident in the basic grammar and syntax of his stylistic language that true improvisation, true spontaneity of utterance, becomes possible within it. If the thriving triangular relationship between composers, performers, and the public had not broken down, historically informed performance would be neither likely nor desirable today.[155]

This triangular relationship between new music, audience, and performer began to deteriorate for what is now called "classical" music around the turn of the century. Although contemporary "classical" music continues to be written and performed, it has lost much of its audience, partly because of its deliberate embrace of atonality and partly because of its avant-gardist tendencies. A new generation of performers has sprung up who see their basic task not as the performance of contemporary music but the preservation of a classical repertory which extends roughly from the Baroque period to the beginning of the twentieth century. The classical performer becomes less and less the advocate of new music and more and

---

[154] *Watch, e.g.*, MTV.

[155] Crutchfield, *supra* note 19, at 23.

more the curator of museum pieces. But the very notion of the museum, which suggests preservation of the past, also suggests separation from it as well.[156] This distancing and alienation of the performer from the cultural tradition that spawned the music she regularly performs occurs in stages, and it appears differently in different subjects. The process is gradual; the performances of the 1950s seem more distanced than the performances of the 1920s, even if the former in turn seem terribly old-fashioned by today's standards.

The recognition of one's separation from a cultural tradition triggers two characteristic reactions. The first is to cling ever more tenaciously to the tradition as it is perceived to exist. The fear that the center will not hold, and that one must therefore reassert its centrality all the more urgently, creates a feeling of uncertainty and apprehension. This is the experience of modernist anxiety. The unease of modernism, where "all that is solid melts into air,"[157] produces the emotional search for resonance, tranquility, solidity, and stability.

And yet the problem of modernity is precisely the self-consciousness that we have become partly alienated from the past. For the past, once the process of alienation has begun, can never fully be recaptured. The further removed in time one is from tradition, the less one can regain the sense of organic unity with it. Because one cannot recapture the spirit of what has been lost, one attempts to recapture the letter—that is, the concrete historical manifestations of the tradition. The result in classical music is what Crutchfield calls the "museum model" of authenticity—"the precise reconstruction of sounds as near as possible to those heard by the composer."[158] This attempt is doomed to failure, if its goal is to recapture authenticity in the sense of organic connection to tradition. The mere imitation of a tradition does not really bring the tradition back to life. A crucial difference separates improvisation within the tradition and careful imitation of previous examples. The improvisor extends and alters the tradition by unself-consciously living

---

[156] For an illuminating discussion of the problem, see Donath, *The Gene Autry Western Heritage Museum: The Problem of an Authentic Western Mystique*, 43 AM. Q. 82 (Mar. 1991) (criticizing the Autry museum for displacing historical meaning in favor of an unreflective worship of the western mystique).

[157] M. BERMAN, *supra* note 137, at 15. The original phrase, of course, comes from Marx. *See* K. MARK & F. ENGELS, *Manifesto of the Communist Party*, in THE MARX-ENGELS READER 338 (1972).

[158] Crutchfield, *supra* note 19, at 25.

within it, while alteration is precisely what the imitator fears most. It is precisely this fear of alteration, Crutchfield argues, that the Early Music Movement must overcome if it is to avoid becoming a sterile and lifeless project:

> If we resurrect historical information on performing style simply to settle on 'correct' ways of playing, to promulgate and refine rules, to settle questions . . . if we seek nothing more than to write dozens more programs for the floppy discs we insert in students' brains—then it would be better if we had never started. If instead we seek an immersion in the disciplines of the past . . . because we aspire to the freedom and the power that can be gained through purposeful accomplishment—then historically informed performance may enable some of our performers to create anew for themselves the life-giving musical culture that swarmed around musicians in healthier times without their having to think about it. . . . The crucial challenge is to keep that aliveness in mind as the goal; though it can be approached only indirectly, it is more important than the correctness.[159]

The deliberate search for authenticity thus inevitably fails but, paradoxically, also inevitably succeeds. The experience of this search to regain authenticity is itself authentic to our time—it is the authentic experience of modernity. Thus, as Richard Taruskin suggests, the "authentic" performance movement is really the imposition of the aesthetic of modernism on the music of the past.[160] Despite the claims of its advocates, "authentic" performance of music does not present music as it really was, whatever that mysterious phrase might mean. Rather, "authentic" performance presents music how we really like it (or at least how contemporary musicians like it)—dressed in modernist garb to suit the tastes of our era, not Bach's or Mozart's.[161] The advocate of authenticity is quite right that her goal is to make Mozart sound fresh and new to our ears. But this goal has not been achieved by producing what Mozart really sounded like. Rather, it has been achieved by making him sound modern—with lighter textures, faster tempi, and austere and astringent string tone.[162] We have adapted Mozart to our age just as the romantics adapted him to theirs, only we have done it under the banner of "authenticity." However,

---

[159] *Id.* at 25-26.

[160] *See* Taruskin, *supra* note 45, at 152, 155, 167-69.

[161] *See id.* at 197-98, 203-04.

[162] *See id.* at 187-88, 190-91 (tracing stylistic changes in performances of Bach's Fifth Brandenburg Concerto).

the felt need to make performance "authentic," even when the result is really quite modern, is wholly authentic to the modern era.

The second characteristic reaction produced by modernity is the recognition that the past cannot be regained. It is to embrace, or at least to accept, the alienation of the spirit from its historical moorings. It is to comprehend our relation to the past as artificial and instrumental—to see the past as separate from us, but nevertheless something we can use for our own purposes. This reaction to modernity leads to the eclectic use of the past, to the juxtaposition of different elements of different traditions, in short, to pastiche. It is the type of modernist response that eventually leads towards what is now called post-modernism. When tradition becomes instrumental, we embrace it with a wink and a nod. Everyone, including the interpreter, knows that the performance is, in some sense, inauthentic, and that the interpreter is playing a role. But this does not raise concern, as long as it serves the purposes (aesthetic or otherwise) of the interpreter. By forsaking modernist anxiety, the interpreter moves closer and closer towards post-modern irony.[163]

The post-modern response to the crisis of modernity in art creates a artistic discourse that closes in upon itself and becomes increasingly self-referential. Postmodernism shares this feature with some earlier forms of artistic modernism. The subject of culture increasingly becomes culture itself. This tendency meshes with the postmodernist practice of pastiche, as previous cultural artifacts are juxtaposed and referred to in order to call up their various cultural associations in the mind. It meshes as well with the postmodernist attitude of irony and detachment—the previous work of art is referred to not to reassert what it means or conveys, but to comment on it or even undermine it. A good example of post-modern pastiche, irony, and self-reference is the recent film, *The Freshman,*[164] in which the actor Marlon Brando deliberately parodies his earlier role as the mafia chieftain Don Corleone in *The*

[163] Because of the similarities between postmodernism and modernism, there is considerable debate among philosophers and historians of culture over whether postmodernism is truly a different and separate stage of culture, or is instead merely a later stage of modernism. *See* D. HARVEY, *supra* note 133, at 113-18. This should hardly be surprising, as both concepts are heavily contested in theoretical discussion. In this essay, we view postmodernism as furthering some but not other features present in modernism—for example, modernist irony as opposed to modernist anxiety.

[164] *The Freshman* (Tristar Pictures 1990).

Godfather.[165] The creators of the film make the young hero a film student who attends classes on cinematic history and technique, so that lectures about and scenes from *The Godfather* can be liberally interspersed throughout the movie. The hero is taken under the wing of Marlon Brando's character, who reminds the student eerily of the Godfather in the film he is studying in class. In turn, Brando does not play a mafia don; rather, he plays Marlon Brando playing a mafia don. Brando's performance is a continual reminder to the audience that he is playing a role, that he knows he is playing a role and that he knows that the audience knows he knows he is playing a role, and so on indefinitely.[166]

Robert Morgan's essay identifies these two reactions to the modernist predicament—anxiety and detachment—with the different compositional approaches of Arnold Schoenberg and Igor Stravinsky.[167] Schoenberg, the founder of atonal composition, represents the earlier stage of modernist anxiety. Already fully self-conscious of the tradition of western classical music from Bach and Beethoven to the present day, Schoenberg feels the weight of

---

[165] *The Godfather* (Paramount Studios 1972).

[166] It is worth mentioning in this context the movie's remarkable final scene, which involves Bert Parks serenading a group of very rich gourmets who have gathered to feast on the meat of freshly killed endangered species. As the latest victim-to-be is paraded before them, Parks proudly sings "[t]here she goes, your komodo dragon." A few moments later, he is offering a spirited rendition of Bob Dylan's "I Ain't Gonna Work on Maggie's Farm No More." Parks' presence in the movie is left completely unexplained. What is the meaning of juxtaposing Parks—a longtime symbol of the Miss America Pageant (itself a symbol of American values of an earlier era)—with the selfish excesses and insatiable appetites of 1980's materialism represented by the slaying of the hapless reptile? Is the reference to the soon-to-be devoured dragon a sly accusation that the Miss America Pageant is nothing more than a ritualized "meat market"? What is meant by the juxtaposition of Parks with the music of Bob Dylan, a symbol of the rebellious 1960s, which began to put the values characterized by the Miss America Pageant into question? Is Parks' refusal "to work on Maggie's farm" a reference to his firing by ungrateful pageant directors who (it is rumored) felt that because he had so visibly aged, he no longer presented the right image? Is Parks, like Brando, a knowing participant in the ironies of the movie, or is he, as his performance suggests, blissfully unaware of the subtexts and subsubtexts of his performance? Finally, are the creators of the movie really making a statement through this pastiche of cultural icons, or are they simply having fun and perhaps even laughing at us for noticing the inexhaustible possibilities of cross reference? The mind boggles—and of course, that is precisely the way the postmodern artist would have it. To take the movie seriously is not to take what it says seriously. To be engaged with it is simultaneously to become detached from the cultural symbols that it invokes.

[167] *See* Morgan, *supra* note 95, at 60.

tradition heavily on his back.[168] He routinely describes his artistic goals in terms of progress—of moving forward with the project of the western musical tradition. Schoenberg sees himself as one who must carry on the traditions that burden him in the best way he knows how.[169] He thus views atonal composition as an inevitable development of western musical practices:

> Schoenberg . . . holds the traditional view, but in a form whose very extremity shows that it is reaching a critical, and perhaps even terminal stage. He understood his own development as a logical and necessary continuation of the dominant compositional tendencies that had (in his view) consistently shaped the mainstream of serious western music. This explains Schoenberg's discomfort at being considered a revolutionary—a composer in some way fundamentally separated from the past. In his own eyes, the course he followed offered the only possible realization of the musical implications inherent in the work of his greatest predecessors. Schoenberg believed his music to be progressive, certainly, but not in its basic aesthetic (or even technical) assumptions, fundamentally different from the music of the past.[170]

In contrast, Stravinsky shows much more of the ironic detachment of a later stage of modernism. Although he is not himself a postmodernist, he displays several modernist attitudes that in the hands of later artists will eventually blossom into what we now call the postmodern temperament. He picks and chooses different stylistic features from different eras, melding them in compositions by the force of his personality.[171] Unlike Schoenberg, Stravinsky sees himself as fully separated from the past, studying it not to continue it but to borrow from it piecemeal for his own purposes. The result is a compositional eclecticism characteristic of Stravinsky's style. As Morgan argues, Stravinsky's modernism presaged the compositional attitudes of the present day, in which "[c]omposers adopt and discard musical styles at will, not only from work to work but within single compositions."[172] In their search for musical styles to adopt for their own purposes, contemporary composers are considerably more eclectic even than Stravinsky, for "[t]hey do not limit themselves to the repertory of western concert music, but extend their grasp to music of other cultures, popular music, folk

---

[168] *See id.* at 60-61.
[169] *See id.* at 61-62.
[170] *Id.* at 60-61 (footnotes omitted).
[171] *See id.* at 65-66.
[172] *Id.* at 66.

music, jazz, etc., moving freely back and forth across cultural boundaries as well as temporal ones."[173]

Yet this eclecticism of the modern composer itself betrays a fact about the culture of the present—the felt absence of a cultural center, of a tradition of one's own. There is, Morgan says, "no well-defined sense of the musical present."[174] The loss of a cultural center, he argues, is simply the flip side of the Stravinskian attitude towards history. "Only when the current moment loses an essential character and personality of its own, and thus loses its ability to cast its own peculiar coloration on the past, is one able to look upon the past with such detachment and objectivity."[175] According to Morgan, one who recognizes, even embraces, such a notion of our situation, must also recognize that "the concept of culture, at least as previously understood, becomes extremely shaky."[176] More important, perhaps, is the recognition that "[o]ur sense of the musical present, and thereby of our own musical selves, is fatally threatened, dissolving into a patchwork of disconnected fragments snatched from here, there, and everywhere."[177] Few have better described the postmodernist sensibility.

It is interesting in this light to compare Stravinsky's compositional practices with his attitudes about musical performance. Stravinsky demanded strict adherence to the musical text.[178] Indeed, he pronounced that "[t]o interpret a piece [of music] is to realize its portrait, and what I demand is the realization of the piece itself and not of its portrait."[179] Elsewhere he invidiously contrasted, against loathsome "interpretation," what he termed objective "execution"—"the strict putting into effect of an explicit will that contains nothing beyond what it specifically commands."[180] As Taruskin argues, the essence of performance for

---

[173] *Id.*

[174] *Id.*

[175] *Id.* at 67.

[176] *Id.*

[177] *Id.*

[178] *See* Taruskin, *supra* note 45, at 181.

[179] I. STRAVINSKY, PROGRAM, STRAVINSKY FESTIVAL, LONDON SYMPHONY ORCHESTRA 41 (1979), *quoted in* Levinson, *On Interpretation: The Adultery Clause of the Ten Commandments*, 58 S. CAL. L. REV. 719, 724 (1985).

[180] I. STRAVINSKY, THE POETICS OF MUSIC 163 (A. Knodel and I. Dahl trans. 1956). Of course Stravinsky's demand for objectivity does not avoid interpretive difficulties, even of his own works. In the 1920's, desperate for money, Stravinsky arranged his orchestral compositions for player piano. On these pianola rolls, the dance at the end of his famous ballet *Rite of Spring* "is much faster than on any recordings, including his own 'final' versions of 1960 and 1961." *A Dance to the Death*, THE

Stravinsky was "scrupulous fidelity to the letter of the text, and an ascetic avoidance of unspecified nuance in the name of expression."[181] As we should already have come to expect, Stravinsky denounced those whose interpretations differed from his own not only as mistaken, but also, far more significantly, as perpetrators of "criminal assaults" and "betrayals."[182] In fact, Stravinsky's eclecticism and his demands for "objectivity" in performance are two sides of the same coin. It is precisely because one has become so detached from the past and thus from a living tradition encompassing earlier music that one must make reference to "objective" indicia—for example, the written text, the actual size of the musical forces at the first performance, and so on.

Indeed, not only are detachment and objectivity two sides of the same modernist coin, but, more surprisingly, so are the desires for authenticity and novelty.[183] Morgan points to the deep connection between the search for novelty in musical culture—whether it be new techniques of composition or the desire to make Bach and Mozart sound fresh and new to our ears—and the search for performance practices of the past. Both searches are a means of expressing dissatisfaction with the present.[184] One can escape the present either by catapulting to the future, or by attempting to recapture the past and make it one's own. The modernist always runs, even if she cannot hide.

If modernity has so thoroughly dominated musical culture in this century, it would be surprising if we did not see similar effects in legal culture as well. Obvious examples abound, the most obvious, ironically, being the insistence on the unique legitimacy of original intention as a guide to constitutional meaning.[185] With

---

ECONOMIST, Apr. 6, 1991, at 89. Ben Zander, the conductor of the semi-amateur Boston Philharmonic, has studied the piano rolls and concluded that they reflect Stravinsky's original intentions, but that Stravinsky compromised later because the first orchestras that tackled the piece simply could not perform his complex music at the speed he desired. *Id.* Is a conductor who performs the *Rite* at the faster speed engaging in objective "execution" or loathsome "interpretation"? Did Stravinsky, who performed and recorded the *Rite of Spring* in more than one way, engage in fraudulent "interpretations" of his own music?

[181] Taruskin, *supra* note 45, at 181.

[182] *Id.*

[183] *See* Morgan, *supra* note 95, at 75.

[184] *Id.* at 75-76.

[185] *See* R. BORK, *supra* note 33, at 6-8. We are grateful to Robert Post for pointing out that Thomas Hobbes (whose pessimism, skepticism about values, and statism have much in common with Judge Bork's philosophy) also developed a highly originalist theory of interpretation. *See* D. HERZOG, HAPPY SLAVES: A CRITIQUE OF CONSENT

modernity comes historicism—the understanding that the past has become alien to us and the desire to recapture what is slipping away. With detachment comes anxiety, and, as Hobsbawm suggests, the desperate attempt to deny the meaningfulness of history even as one denounces one's contemporaries for having deviated so far from purported models of the past.[186] Those who disagree are, as Stravinsky asserted, not merely mistaken, but criminal assailants on the uniquely legitimate way of performing constitutional analysis.

Our thesis is that we will find evidence of modernist anxiety and detachment, with a concomitant quest to regain "objective" indicia of performance and the invention of sacralized "traditions," in many different areas of culture, including, most certainly, both the general legal culture and its bastion of self-consciousness, the legal academy. By focusing on Robert Bork's jurisprudence of original intention as a quintessentially modernist response, we suggest an important difference between our perspective and that presented by David Luban in his interesting and important article, *Legal Modernism*.[187] Luban argues that the Critical Legal Studies movement represents the best analogy of modernist art to law.[188] The work of CLS scholars, in Luban's view, shares with modernist art a penchant for provocation, a feeling of homelessness in the world, and a tendency towards self-consciousness and self-commentary about its own production.[189] Although Luban takes as his model of inquiry modern art rather than musical performance, and although he assigns to the modern what some might now call postmodern, his discussion of the characteristic features of modernity is largely consistent with our own. For example, Luban's emphasis on "homelessness" as a recurring motif in modernist art[190] describes from another perspective the sense of separation

---

THEORY 145 (1989). Thus the turn to "originalism" is not unique to our current (twentieth century) brand of modernism; it also shows how twentieth century modernism has many antecedents. Moreover, Post's example is an excellent demonstration of how heavily contextual judgments of modernism are. Hobbes is certainly not "modern" in contrast to twentieth century thinkers, but in another sense he is a veritable architect of modernism in his demolition of Aristotelian traditionalism. *Cf.* Balkin, *Nested Oppositions* (Book Review), 99 YALE L.J. 1669, 1678-82 (1990) (depending on context, cultural concepts are always both exemplified by and in opposition to their concrete historical manifestations).

[186] *See supra* text accompanying notes 125-32.

[187] *See* Luban, *Legal Modernism*, 84 MICH. L. REV. 1656 (1986).

[188] *See id.* at 1656-59.

[189] *See id.* at 1657-59.

[190] *See id.* at 1660.

from tradition and from the past we have seen as characteristic of modernity.

There is much insight in Professor Luban's article. Nevertheless, we disagree with its thesis that legal modernism manifests itself most clearly in the work of CLS scholars or others on the left side of the political spectrum. It is worth noting that, as a historical matter, many leading cultural modernists were scarcely left-wing. As Daniel Bell has written, "[i]n discussing modernism, the categories of 'left' and 'right' make little sense. . . . Nietzsche, Yeats, Pound, and Wyndham Lewis were politically to the right."[191] Although Picasso's radical political sympathies were well known,[192] so were Ezra Pound's proclivities towards fascism.[193] Lionel Trilling has noted the irony of contemporary liberal intellectuals' embrace of modernists as heroes, noting that Proust, James Joyce and Andre Gide were "indifferent to, or even hostile to, the tradition of democratic liberalism as we know it," and "do not seem to confirm us in the social and political ideals which we [liberals] hold."[194]

Yet modern culture—and the response to modernity—comprises far more than those who are selectively identified as "modernists." A culture embraces *all* who live within it. Jerry Falwell is just as much a part of the contemporary American culture produced by the experience of modernity as is Cher, even though each is almost totally uncomprehending of the other (and even though each is in some way a reaction to the other). Modernity is an experience felt by all persons in a culture, even if in different degrees, and even if the reactions to it may be different in different quarters. Two billiard balls may move in opposite directions because of the same cause, a third billiard ball which has struck each object differently. Thus, to adopt Robert Morgan's example, Schoenberg's self-conscious attempt to follow tradition is just as modernist in its own

---

[191] D. BELL, THE CULTURAL CONTRADICTIONS OF CAPITALISM 51 (1976).

[192] *See* A. HUFFINGTON, PICASSO: CREATOR AND DESTROYER 282-311 (1988).

[193] On Pound, see J. DIGGINS, MUSSOLINI AND FASCISM: THE VIEW FROM AMERICA 246-47, 437-39 (1972). Even Wallace Stevens, the newly found darling of contemporary legal pragmatists, was not immune from the allure of facism. *See id.* at 245 (describing Stevens' support of Mussolini and his belief that fascism would merely be "'a transitional phase' of a state which hopefully would, like [Stevens'] poetry, wrest order from chaos and thereby lessen the 'disillusionment' and 'misery' in the modern world" (quoting W. STEVENS, LETTERS OF WALLACE STEVENS 289-90, 295 (H. Stevens ed. 1966))).

[194] L. TRILLING, THE LIBERAL IMAGINATION: ESSAYS ON LITERATURE AND SOCIETY 286 (1954).

way as Stravinsky's embrace of eclecticism. And Stravinsky's detachment led to both his instrumental use of the past for novelty's sake and his moralistic pursuit of the past via "objective" indicia of performance. In legal terms, modernity has brought us both Critical Legal Studies *and* Robert Bork.[195]

Luban's account of legal modernism, we think, overemphasizes the avant-gardist response to modernity at the expense of those trying to come to terms with tradition and the past either through an anxiously self-conscious adherence to tradition (Schoenberg) or through objectifying the past in concrete terms (Stravinsky). And here the modernist tendencies of the early music movement can provide a useful corrective. The fear that the past is slipping away and the redoubled search to regain tradition is not a *retreat* from modernism—it *is* one manifestation of the modernist experience, one version of modernist anxiety. The difference between the modernist and the premodernist is precisely that the modernist feels that there is something that has been lost. The conserving (but not necessarily conservative) response to modernism that is represented by Schoenberg is precisely the desire to cling to a receding tradition in order to relieve this sense of anxiety. While the modernist complains of anxiety, the premodernist asks "what anxiety?"[196]

For this reason, an inquiry into legal modernity must consider both the Schoenbergian as well as the Stravinskian attitudes towards tradition and the past.[197] It follows that we are likely to see the effects of legal modernity not only in the structural equivalent of the avant-garde in law, but in more mainstream reactions as well. If there are undoubted modernist themes in the work of CLS scholars, they are no less present in the work of the political right or the political center. Throughout the political spectrum one will find analogies both to Stravinsky's dual detachment and objectivity and Schoenbergian anxiety. No single view is uniquely "modernist"; all join in trying to make sense of our particular cultural moment, which features an ever-growing sense of disorder and fragmentation.[198]

---

[195] *See* Schlag, *Missing Pieces: A Cognitive Approach to Law*, 67 TEX. L. REV. 1195, 1216, 1228 (1989).

[196] And, we should add, the postmodernist also asks, "what anxiety?"

[197] This is not, of course, to say that Schoenberg and Stravinsky represent the only two possibilities. We agree with Morgan, however, that these two examples throw considerable light on the experience of modernity in music, as well as in culture generally.

[198] For a discussion emphasizing the presence of fragmentation in American law

IV. Legal Modernism and the Pursuit of "Authenticity"

What we have called legal modernity, like so much else in American law, can already be seen in the thought of Oliver Wendell Holmes, and in particular in his most iconoclastic work, *The Path of the Law*,[199] an essay which, almost 100 years after its presentation, still contains the power to startle.[200] Although *The Path of the Law* has many themes, one of its most striking is its author's attitude towards history and tradition. "[I]f we want to know why a rule of law has taken its particular shape, and more or less if we want to know why it exists at all," argues Holmes, "we go to tradition."[201] But one does not study history and historical doctrine for the purpose of veneration. Quite the opposite, for the understanding that a rule is historical "is the first step toward an enlightened scepticism, that is, towards a deliberate reconsideration of the worth of those rules."[202] In a truly remarkable metaphor, Holmes tells us that "[w]hen you get the dragon out of his cave on to the plain and in the daylight, you can count his teeth and claws and see just what is his strength."[203] Perhaps reflecting the origins of Holmes's own modernist thought in the maelstrom of the Civil War,[204] he makes clear that examining the "dragon" of historically-rooted rules "is only the first step. The next is either to kill him, or to tame him

---

and jurisprudence, see R. POSNER, *supra* note 1, at 203, 296. For a postmodern explanation of legal fragmentation and a delightful romp through the categories of modernism and postmodernism, see Schlag, *supra* note 195. While Schlag emphasizes the epistemological aspects of modernity and postmodernity, we emphasize their broader cultural manifestations.

199 O.W. HOLMES, *The Path of the Law*, in COLLECTED LEGAL PAPERS 167 (1920).

200 One is tempted to say that legal modernity begins with Holmes, but in fact the history of legal modernity is considerably more complicated. Moreover, Holmes's thought did not arise out of a vacuum. One of us (Levinson) has devoted considerable effort to showing the influence of a much earlier stream of thought—Emersonianism—on Holmes. S. Levinson, Skepticism, Democracy, and Judicial Restraint: An Essay on the Thought of Oliver Wendell Holmes and Felix Frankfurter, ch. 1 (Ph.D dissertation, Harvard University 1969). Thus, Holmes's thought combines both older and more foreword-looking elements, which is part of its endless fascination for historians and other scholars. In beginning our discussion of legal modernism with Holmes, we use Holmes as many others have—as less a progenitor than as a symbol of trends that have become central to American legal thought.

201 O.W. HOLMES, *supra* note 199, at 186.

202 *Id.* at 186-87.

203 *Id.* at 187.

204 *See* S. NOVICK, HONORABLE JUSTICE: THE LIFE OF OLIVER WENDELL HOLMES 43-52, 65-68, 71-73 (1989) (discussing profound impact of war on Holmes and describing the three times he was wounded in battle—at Ball's Bluff, Antietam, and Fredricksburg).

and make him a useful animal."[205] This stunning imagery precedes the well-known Holmesian injunction that "[i]t is revolting to have no better reason for a rule of law than that so it was laid down in the time of Henry IV."[206] And for Holmes "[i]t is still more revolting if the grounds upon which it was laid down have vanished long since, and the rule simply persists from blind imitation of the past."[207] The liberating cure is to reject "antiquarianism" and instead to become the student of economics and statistics. Thus, in a famous phrase, Holmes asks us to wash our traditional beliefs about law and legal traditions in "cynical acid."[208]

The modernism of Holmes is not the modernist anxiety of Schoenberg, who feels the past slipping away and must strive to regain it and follow its commands. It is rather the modernism of Stravinsky, for whom the past is an alien thing, to be used instrumentally in future compositions. The very comparison of history to a monster suggests that the past has already become strange to us, that we have already begun the process of detachment and separation. Another great modernist, James Joyce, speaking through the character of Stephen Daedelus, wrote of history as a nightmare from which he was trying to awake.[209] Whether Holmes would have gone quite that far, there can be no doubt that he had only disdain for those who put their faith in history and its "teachings" without reflection about the value and cogency of those purported lessons. The purpose of studying history is not to revere it, but to analyze it—to show it "in the daylight" and "count [its] teeth and claws."[210] And this analysis can only proceed, as Morgan points out, "when the current moment . . . loses its ability to cast its own peculiar colouration on the past [so that one] is able to look upon the past with such detachment and objectivity."[211] In *The Path of the Law*, the legacy of the past is now described as "dogma," itself a word richly redolent of Protestant reformers' critique of the encrusted traditions of the Church they sought to overthrow.[212]

---

205 O.W. HOLMES, *supra* note 199, at 187.

206 *Id.*

207 *Id.*

208 *Id.* at 174.

209 *See* J. JOYCE, THE PORTABLE JAMES JOYCE 674 (H. Levin ed. 1966) (excerpts from *Ulysses*).

210 O.W. HOLMES, *supra* note 199, at 187.

211 Morgan, *supra* note 95, at 67.

212 O.W. HOLMES, *supra* note 199, at 169.

The theme of detachment from the legal tradition is also clear in Holmes's call for a social scientific approach. If the legal tradition is a dragon, we are no longer its subjects. Rather, we are to become zoologists, whose purpose is to study and even dissect the creature. The "man of the future" is a social scientist because the goal of legal study has moved from exposition and interpretation of legal texts and doctrines to the study of law as a social phenomenon. "It is perfectly proper," as Holmes pointed out in his essay *Law in Science and Science in Law,* "to regard and study the law simply as a great anthropological document."[213] An anthropologist, unlike the native, observes the culture from a psychic distance rather than participating in its beliefs and performing its rituals unself-consciously.

Finally, Holmes's iconoclasm is consistent with another way of looking at the experience of modernism–as a perceived conflict between reason and tradition, a tension which manifests itself, for example, in the conflict between the search for truth through rational inquiry and the need for faith in the teachings of revealed religion.[214] Holmes makes quite clear that he reconciles this conflict in favor of what he perceives to be reason–in this case the instrumental reason of fitting means to ends–and against received dogmatic tradition. The future of the law is as the servant of reason, which for Holmes is nothing more than rational calculations designed to achieve most effectively what the community wants.[215] The inefficacious dogmas of the past, on the other hand, are to be eliminated as much as possible.

To be sure, the modernity we find in Holmes is not yet full–fledged. There is an undercurrent of optimism in these remarks that bears neither traces of anxiety about what is slipping away nor doubts about the efficacy of the scientific approach. One could well write an article on "Holmes's last paragraphs," the conclusions to his otherwise pessimistic and sometimes even savage remarks that suddenly transform the occasion into one of hope and (relative) optimism about one's place in the world. Thus *The Path of the Law* concludes by Holmes telling his audience that through the analysis

---

[213] O.W. HOLMES, *Law in Science and Science in Law,* in COLLECTED LEGAL PAPERS, *supra* note 199, at 210, 212.

[214] We emphasize here that this characteristic feature of modernity by no means originates with Holmes, or even with modernity itself. *See supra* notes 136-41 and accompanying text.

[215] *See* O.W. HOLMES, *supra* note 213, at 225.

1650 UNIVERSITY OF PENNSYLVANIA LAW REVIEW [Vol.139: 1597

of the "remoter and more general aspects of the law you not only become a great master in your calling, but connect your subject with the universe and catch an echo of the infinite, a glimpse of its unfathomable process, a hint of the universal law."[216] Whether a remnant of his grandfather's Calvinist sensibility or a continuing reflection of the influence of Ralph Waldo Emerson's transcendentalist faith in the ultimate resolution of all apparent tensions and contradictions,[217] there is little of the more contemporary sense of intellectual anxiety about the lack of even a "hint" of some unified perspective of the world. Nor is there any sense of irony about the situation that Holmes finds himself in; it does not occur to him that historicizing the work of previous judges calls into question whether his own work is simply another form of "dogma," to be treated as such by a later generation capable of placing *him* in a discrete historical setting and recognizing his own blindness and lack of insight.[218]

Nevertheless, the seeds of legal modernity are clear enough in *The Path of the Law.* It was therefore entirely fitting that Jerome Frank would see Holmes as a model in his appropriately titled book *Law and the Modern Mind.*[219] Frank's veneration of Holmes is characteristic of the further development of legal modernity we find in the work of the Realists. The Realists are commonly thought to have launched an attack on the autonomy of law and legal reasoning. But the autonomy of law is of at least two types. The first is the autonomy of law from politics or social beliefs. The second, and equally important sense of autonomy is the autonomy of law from other disciplines, which generates a faith that discrete "legal" methods of analysis will be sufficient to solve legal problems.[220] Because legal decisions might be better explained by the study of social forces than by the results of doctrinal argument, and because legal issues need the expertise of the economist or sociologist, "the

---

[216] *Id.* at 202. And those familiar with Holmes's famous dissent in *Lochner v. New York* are likely to overlook his argument that the test of legislative reasonableness is whether a statute would "infringe fundamental principles as they have been understood by the traditions of our people and our law." Lochner v. New York, 198 U.S. 45, 76 (1905) (Holmes, J., dissenting).

[217] For an extended comparison of Holmes and Emerson, see S. Levinson, *supra* note 200.

[218] Still less is Holmes's attitude post-modern in his desire to fashion a grand, all-encompassing theory of law.

[219] J. FRANK, LAW AND THE MODERN MIND (1930).

[220] *See* Balkin, *supra* note 64, at 795; Posner, *The Decline of Law as an Autonomous Discipline: 1962-1987,* 100 HARV. L. REV. 761, 762-66 (1987).

man of the future," as Holmes puts it, must be acquainted with social science.[221]

With the rise of legal realism, new forms of legal scholarship emerge. Previously, the goal of much legal scholarship had been to explicate or interpret existing law, to offer the best interpretation of legal materials through traditional forms of doctrinal argument. The rise of realism brings with it an additional goal—to suggest policy based reasons for development of legal doctrine in one direction rather than another, even if these policy based reasons are not suggested or implicated by the language of existing legal materials. The realist approach begins to separate the goals of scholarship from those of the bar, although eventually the practicing bar would assimilate the approach of "going beyond the cases," at least in part.[222]

A second and more significant development is the attempt to study law as a social artifact, as Holmes's "great anthropological document." The result is a scholarship where one studies the behavior of lawyers and judges, not to further or contribute to their interpretive enterprise, but rather to study the enterprise itself. The most extreme example of this approach is Herman Oliphant's suggestion that scholars might dispense with the study of doctrine altogether and investigate instead the effects that certain "stimuli" (i.e., facts) had on the "responses" (i.e., opinions) produced by judges.[223] Oliphant's behaviorist approach to legal scholarship, while not universally adopted by the realists, is nevertheless characteristic of a new sense of detachment from the practice of law. The legal scholar has, to a large degree, left the tribe and become an anthropologist. We normally think of realism as the study of "law in action" and thus a movement closer towards what the law "really is." Yet this very goal ironically produces a separation or estrangement between the student and the thing being studied. "Objectivity" requires that the member of the tribe no longer take at face value the natives' explanations for what they are doing. Dispassion requires distance. One cannot pour cynical acid on one's *own* skin.[224]

---

[221] O.W. HOLMES, *supra* note 199, at 187.

[222] *See* Rubin, *The Practice and Discourse of Legal Scholarship*, 86 MICH. L. REV. 1835 (1988).

[223] Oliphant, *A Return to Stare Decisis*, 14 A.B.A. L.J. 73 (1928).

[224] As Professor Schlegel reminds us, the realist study of law as a social artifact had at least two versions. One might engage in social scientific research with an eye to eventual suggestions for reform, a position that Schlegel associates with William

Modernity has had a lasting legacy on the forms of legal scholarship in at least three respects. The first is the self-consciously interdisciplinary character of legal scholarship. This essay is no exception. A second is the increasing amount of scholarship, especially in the elite journals, that is about other legal scholarship, rather than about primary legal materials like statutes and cases. Legal scholarship becomes an increasingly self-contained, self-referential discipline, which is "about itself" as much as it is about the legal world outside, either law on the books or law in action. As interdisciplinary movements like law and economics or law and literature spring up, they begin to focus not on their relationship to the work of lawyers and judges, but to their own internal coherence and justification. Legal interpretation is replaced by legal theory, which is replaced by meta-theory, which is replaced by meta-meta theory, and so on.

The third feature is the fragmentation of legal scholarship into new genres such as feminist scholarship, critical legal scholarship, or law and economics. As a result of this fragmentation, it is increasingly difficult for lawyers and legal academics to agree on what good legal scholarship is and how to evaluate it. To some extent, this was always true, as soon as legal scholarship specialized into different subject matters like pleading, property, trusts, and so on. Yet there was a feeling that good legal reasoning transcended doctrinal boundaries, and that the reasonably intelligent contracts professor could recognize it in the work of a colleague who wrote about equity or the law of agency and partnership. The creation of "genres" of scholarship, like law and economics or feminist jurisprudence, which cut across traditional legal departments and categories, undermines such confidence today. Both fields are highly specialized with separate canons; they have very different intellectual approaches and scholarly goals which may, in some instances, be mutually critical of each other. Giving a piece written in one genre to a person who specializes in another may produce consternation, and perhaps even outright rejection.

O. Douglas and Charles Clark. Or one might engage in the scientific study of legal institutions for its own sake, a position Schlegel finds most clearly in the work of Underhill Moore. *See* Schlegel, *American Legal Realism and Empirical Social Science: From the Yale Experience*, 28 BUFFALO L. REV. 459, 517-19, 539-45, 567-69, 578-85 (1979); Schlegel, *American Legal Realism and Empirical Social Science: The Singular Case of Underhill Moore*, 29 BUFFALO L. REV. 195, 293-95 (1980).

The idea of a common language and a common vocabulary among legal academics, and indeed, a common canon of legal materials, has increasingly become a fiction. There is now an identifiable group of scholars who have read *A Jury of Her Peers*[225] or *The Critical Legal Studies Movement*[226] and consider them canonical texts. Other scholars may not have heard of either of these works, much less consulted them. Still others, having heard of them, may view them as, at the least, "outside" the law or, indeed, dangerous to the enterprise of law. Robert Morgan's fear that today "we no longer have a [musical] culture of our own," and that such culture as we do have has become "a patchwork of disconnected fragments snatched from here, there, and everywhere,"[227] is easily translatable to legal culture. Faced with this Heraclitian whirl of flux and discontinuity in the legal academy, some may be tempted to form authentic performance-of-legal-scholarship movements with a concomitant attempt to delegitimize those they now perceive as contributing to the flux.

As these comments suggest, there is much work to be done in exploring what modernity means for American legal culture. But it also seems clear that the study of the effects of modernity on legal culture requires us to have a point of comparison in other aspects of culture with which our self-identity is not so bound up. The anthropological study of law, in Holmes's time as in our own, requires a form of distancing. One reason to study the effects of modernity in music is precisely because of its distance from law and from our own everyday experiences as lawyers and legal scholars. It is that very distance which allows us to see comparisons within our own discipline that might otherwise go unnoticed or underemphasized. For the student of legal modernity, then, a trip beyond our own cultural moorings may well be not only a helpful but even a necessary tool of research.

---

225 Glaspell, *A Jury of Her Peers*, in THE BEST SHORT STORIES OF 1917, 256-82 (E. O'Brien ed. 1918).

226 Unger, *The Critical Legal Studies Movement*, 96 HARV. L. REV. 563 (1983).

227 Morgan, *supra* note 95, at 67.

V. Conclusion: Law, Music, and Other Performing Arts

Felix Frankfurter described as "the single most important utterance in the literature of constitutional law"[228] John Marshall's admonition that "it is a *constitution* we are expounding."[229] Equally important is Marshall's insistence that the Constitution be interpreted so as to "endure for ages to come, and consequently, to be adapted to the various *crises* of human affairs."[230] It has always been feared, though, that too much "adaptation" would mean not the endurance, but rather the death of the Constitution. Yet how is one to tell the difference? Only half in jest do we announce that the subtext of this review is the question whether the performance of constitutional interpretation is better analogized to the Hanover Band's version of the *Pastoral Symphony* or to a jazz improvisation on Thelonious Monk's *Round Midnight*.[231] We do not mean to suggest that the choice must be exclusively between these two alternatives. Many other musical analogies might be suggested as well. We do mean to suggest that asking such questions–and wrestling over the answers–helps to illuminate the enterprise of constitutional analysis, including the particular problems posed by this enterprise for those who must confront the profound impact modernity has had on our political and legal culture.[232]

---

[228] F. Frankfurter, *John Marshall and the Judicial Function*, in Felix Frankfurter on the Supreme Court: Extrajudicial Essays on the Court and the Constitution 534 (P. Kurland ed. 1970).

[229] McCulloch v. Maryland, 17 U.S. (4 Wheat.) 316, 407 (1819).

[230] *Id.* at 415. Not the least of Marshall's rhetorically brilliant gestures is italicizing "crises" instead of "adapt" and "Constitution" instead of "we." *See* Schlag, *The Problem of the Subject*, 69 Tex. L. Rev. (forthcoming 1991).

[231] For a recent musing on the similarities between the Constitution and jazz, see Ely, *Another Such Victory: Constitutional Theory and Practice in a World Where Courts are No Different From Legislatures*, 77 Va. L. Rev. 833, 837 n.10 (1991) ("On the Constitution as a Lead Sheet.") (italics omitted).

[232] *Cf.* D. Kornstein, *supra* note 48, at 110 ("For all we know, one night this week Zubin Mehta . . . will stand at his podium and whisper to the New York Philharmonic: 'We must never forget that it is a *symphony* we are expounding.'").

Professor Ely suggests that "those who assert the possibility of differentiating valid from invalid constitutional interpretation on the basis of 'craft limits' of a sort they assert are recognized in the arts are likely to be badly disappointed when they get around to a close examination of the analogues." Ely, *supra* note 231, at 837 n.10. The reason is, apparently, that "every time there develops what appears to be a consensus among musicians (and their listeners), to the effect that a certain interval is unacceptable noise, someone who can't be dismissed on any principled basis as 'not a real musician' starts using it, and others often follow." *Id.* Of course, this does not demonstrate that the analogy is useless, only that it cannot serve to legitimate particular limits on the practice of constitutional interpretation by appeal to existing

It is often our proudest boast that we in the United States live within the embrace of a constitutional tradition whose origins we can locate and whose continuity we can celebrate even two centuries later. Yet, as we have seen, explaining what it means to adhere to a tradition, particularly in an age of modernist self-consciousness, is itself an extraordinarily difficult assignment. Although tradition seems to imply stasis as much as modernity implies change, in fact, as Roxana Waterston points out, "'tradition' really describes a process of handing down, and as such is just as dynamic and as historical as any other social process."[233] Yet the abstract ideals of fixed tradition and mutable modernity are simultaneously motivating factors in this dynamic of change. Thus "[t]radition, like history, is something that is continually being recreated and remodelled in the present, even as it is represented as fixed and unchangeable."[234]

"craft values." And that fact is itself quite interesting.

However, because Ely sees that the analogy to jazz is not much use in legitimating the sort of limits on constitutional interpretation he would like to exist, he conludes that it is not clear what we can learn from the analogy of jazz to constitutional law. *See id.* But for someone who is less interested than Ely in legitimating judicial review by distinguishing it from legislation, and is more interested in asking questions about how legitimation actually occurs, one learns a great deal from the analogy about how seemingly "objective" standards or craft values are constantly altering themselves. Thus, Ely sees his analogy as "not much use" precisely because it does not serve his particular project—because he does not want to conclude that the craft of judicial interpretation, like that of musical interpretation, is always altering itself historically. On the other hand, a person with a quite different project (understanding the phenomenon of constitutional interpretation and how elites justify it to themselves and to others) might find the analogy useful for precisely the reasons that Ely rejects it.

We think this example demonstrates something quite important about the pragmatic enterprise we are engaged in. First, for different projects (legitimation vs. anthropology) different tools may be more or less useful to the task, and thus different analogies will be more or less useful. Second, it does not follow from Ely's discussion that analogies between law and the arts are not possible, or that they will not stimulate thought, but rather that one's ability to use analogies to convince others with very different agendas will be limited because they will tend to reject analogies which move in directions they do not like, and the more unusual the analogy appears, the easier it will be for them to reject it out of hand. This should come as no surprise to anyone who has ever had a discussion with someone with a very different agenda. Thus while asserting that analogies can be helpful, the pragmatist always understands that analogies become more or less useful tools of discussion and persuasion depending upon the audience they are directed to.

[233] R. WATERSON, THE LIVING HOUSE: AN ANTHROPOLOGY OF ARCHITECTURE IN SOUTH-EAST ASIA 232 (1990).

[234] *Id. See also* Balkin, *Tradition, Betrayal, and the Politics of Deconstruction,* 11 CARDOZO L. REV. 1619 (1990) (discussing conceptual affinities between tradition and betrayal in constitutional law).

Perhaps the best illustration of the belief that we are participating in a living tradition is found in Justice John Marshall Harlan's well-known analysis of the meaning of "substantive due process" in *Poe v. Ullman*.[235] Harlan looked to the "balance [between the liberty of the individual and the demands of organized society] struck by this country, having regard to what history teaches are the traditions from which it developed as well as the traditions from which it broke. That tradition is a living thing."[236] Interestingly, Harlan's description of a "living" tradition explicitly involved both continuity with and alterations of previous tradition.[237] It is perhaps no coincidence that Robert Bork, the self-styled apostle of "original intent," describes Harlan's arguments as "entirely legislative" and denounces the opinion as simply a way station toward the "intellectual catastrophe" of *Griswold v. Connecticut*.[238]

We believe that in *Poe*, as elsewhere, Harlan showed himself to be a quintessential *performer* of constitutional law. Another major theme of this review is the importance of grasping the performative aspect of engagement with the law. This is obvious in the case of a judge, but it is present as well in the acts of a vigorous public critic of judges, such as Robert Bork.[239] Insofar as law is a performative art, insight can be gained from looking at performance practices (and theory) in other arts.

Thus, we believe that legal scholars have something to learn from Jonathan Miller's views on the challenges facing anyone called upon to direct a play, and in particular his attack on the notion "of the primary status of the text . . . as a literary work."[240] Those who hold such a view, he suggests, believe

> that in some peculiar way the play is at its very best when read quietly by the informed reader, who somehow manages to dramatize in his or her imagination a performance that is more congruent with the intentions of the author than *any* particular performance could ever be, and *all* performances then represent a lapse from this ideal state.[241]

---

[235] 367 U.S. 497 (1961).

[236] *Id.* at 542.

[237] *See* Balkin, *supra* note 234, at 1617-18.

[238] R. BORK, *supra* note 33, at 234.

[239] *See* S. LEVINSON, *supra* note 22, at 18-53; Balkin, *supra* note 107, at 937 n.116 (discussing role of non-judicial interpretations of the Constitution).

[240] J. MILLER, *supra* note 104, at 22.

[241] *Id.*

Though there may be an important sense in which "great plays can be said to exist without being theatrically performed,"[242] one would wonder "why a writer had chosen to cast his ideas in the form of a play at all"[243] inasmuch as the conventional meaning assigned the genre "play" includes performance.[244] "I cannot deny the fact that each time a play is staged the production is inevitably a limited version of the range of possible interpretations," but, nonetheless, "the destiny of a great play is to undergo a series of performances each of which is incomplete, and in some cases may prove misleading and perverse." Still, "[b]y submitting itself to the possibility of successive re-creation, . . . the play passes through the development that is its birthright."[245] Miller's analysis applies to music as well. Although it is surely possible to read a music score and to construct an "ideal" performance in one's mind, this is surely not the conventional practice of experiencing music. Enacted performance, for most of us, is inextricably linked with notes on a page.

Is this not also true of law, especially as conceptualized by those realists, influenced by Holmes, who emphasized "law in action"? Did they not ask us to focus on the *performances* of actual people—ordinary citizens, lawyers, police, public officials, and judges—rather than to concentrate on mere "law on the books," i.e., the text independent of its performance? To be sure, one can read the texts of the law as collected in statute books and the like, but in that guise they are only in a state of limbo. They await their performance by legal actors and actresses or, to shift the metaphor, by virtuosos of the law who can interpret melodic lines in the law in ways overlooked by previous players.

---

[242] *Id.* at 23.

[243] *Id.*

[244] Indeed, Miller points out, "[t]here is a tendency to forget that for a playwright like Shakespeare the written script was not intended for publication but as an aid to performance without any view to a distant posterity." *Id.* Miller would also presumably endorse recent suggestions by Shakespeare scholars that what we refer to today as the "texts" of the plays, deviation from which presumably is questionable, are themselves creations of a decidedly post-Shakespearean moment that overlooks the fact that his own actors felt altogether comfortable engaging in their own "contributions" to the manuscripts handed them. Thus Stephen Orgel notes that Shakespeare wrote his plays for performance rather than as publications to be read outside the theater. "Shakespeare habitually began with more than he needed," so that "his scripts offered the company a range of possibilities, and . . . the process of production was a collaborative one of selection as well as of realization and interpretation." *See* Brett, *supra* note 114, at 106 (quoting Orgel, *The Authentic Shakespeare*, 21 REPRESENTATIONS 1, 7 (Winter 1988)).

[245] J. MILLER, *supra* note 104, at 23.

It should now be clear why a review that began by considering how to perform Beethoven's first piano concerto should have gone on to address how those designated to engage in legal performance, like judges, interpret statutes or the Constitution. We believe that there is indeed a relation between law and music, derived in part from their common textuality and necessity for subsequent performance. And it should also by now be clear why studying this relationship of common textuality draws us more and more into the study of culture as a whole. For performance, whether legal or musical, is always situated in a culture and reflects the distinctive problematics of that culture. Thus, if ours is a modern culture, our interpretations, our subsequent performances of law and of music, must be understood in the light of the tangled and complicated experience of modernity and its gradual transformation into what is now called the postmodern. Although we have only begun to explore the complexities of the subject in this essay, we firmly believe that any deep understanding of legal thought in the twentieth century requires legal scholars to confront the meaning of modernity for law and legal culture. To the extent that the study of other aspects of culture, including music, must also confront questions of interpretation and subsequent performance under the shadow of modernity, we believe that comparative study can aid us in our more parochial task of understanding the law itself. We think we understand our own "England" better by having visited other shores, and we are confident that others can benefit from the same experience.

We are not suggesting that one best understands England by emigrating from it and establishing one's permanent life elsewhere; similarly, we doubt that one can best understand law by spending all of one's time on what follows the "and" in various "law and . . ." movements. But there are few people left who do not believe that at least some of one's time should be spent looking on what follows the "and," and the question is whether musical performance should become a suitable candidate for such study. We think that it should. We should have no trouble recognizing Richard Taruskin, Charles Rosen, Neal Zaslaw, and Christopher Hogwood as our own colleagues engaged in a common enterprise of trying to figure out how one meaningfully inhabits a practice of performance after innocence has been lost. They are all writing interesting, provocative, infuriating, and, most importantly, illuminating work that should interest any of us who daily wrestle with our own performance practices as lawyers, judges, or teachers of the law.

[4]

Book Reviews

Postmodern Temptations

Fredric Jameson, *Postmodernism, or, The Cultural Logic of Late Capitalism*. Durham: Duke University Press, 1991. Pp. xxii, 438. $34.95 (cloth), $19.95 (paper).

Robert Post

Pereat mundus, fiat philosophia, fiat philosophus, fiam![1]

Fredric Jameson has long been among our most sophisticated and influential cultural critics. Combining Marxism[2] and structuralism,[3] Jameson's persistent effort has been to locate and fix the social dimensions of structural cultural patterns.[4] In his most recent book, *Postmodernism, or, The Cultural Logic of Late Capitalism*, Jameson applies this perspective to the important phenomenon of postmodern-

1. Friedrich Nietzsche, On the Genealogy of Morals (Francis Golffing trans., 1956) 243.
2. Fredric Jameson, Marxism and Form: Twentieth-Century Dialectical Theories of Literature (1971); Fredric Jameson, Late Marxism: Adorno, or, the Persistence of the Dialectic (1990).
3. Fredric Jameson, The Prison-House of Language: A Critical Account of Structuralism and Russian Formalism (1972).
4. Fredric Jameson, The Political Unconscious: Narrative as a Socially Symbolic Act (1981).

ism.[5] The book ought to be required reading for the many legal academics who have greeted the advent of postmodernism with unrestrained enthusiasm. Jameson, through close attention to the actual cultural manifestations of postmodernism, tells a far darker tale.

Postmodernism, Jameson tells us, expresses "an inverted millenarianism in which premonitions of the future, catastrophic or redemptive, have been replaced by senses of the end of this or that."[6] The postmodern condition defines itself through its interrogation of the great movements of the past, especially of modernism. It is thus a particular way of organizing experience and most specifically of structuring time. In the postmodern moment the great upward march of history seems suddenly to have culminated and ceased. As Jameson explains, "[i]t is safest to grasp the concept of the postmodern as an attempt to think the present historically in an age that has forgotten how to think historically in the first place."[7]

This loss of history, and its resulting "structure of feeling,"[8] is the theme of Jameson's *Postmodernism*. His earlier influential essays on this subject compose the beginning of the book, which then goes on comprehensively and vigorously to explore the postmodern condition in contemporary architecture, video, painting, sculpture, photography, fiction, and cultural theory. Jameson's analyses of Paul de Man and Walter Benn Michaels, his readings of Robert Gober's "Untitled Installation" and the Frank Gehry House in Santa Monica, his assessments of the video work AlienNATION and Claude Simon's *Les Corps conducteurs*, to mention only a few, are deeply intelligent and, given the intrinsic difficulty of the terrain, surprisingly illuminating.

Taken together, these encounters sustain a convincing portrait of the generic characteristics of postmodern sensibility. These characteristics may be conceptualized as concentric circles of deprivation. There is, first, the loss of time as a dimension of social meaning and the substitution of synchronic for diachronic forms of explanation. The dominant metaphors of postmodernism are spatial rather than temporal. They evoke systemic interrelationships, a "logic of difference or differentiation"[9] instead of narrative continuity. Jameson brilliantly illustrates the point through his analysis of contemporary videowork, which continually defeats the instinctive effort to attain interpretive clarity by confronting the viewer with "a constant stream, or 'total flow,' of multiple materials, each of which can be seen as something like a shorthand signal

5. FREDRIC JAMESON, POSTMODERNISM, OR, THE CULTURAL LOGIC OF LATE CAPITALISM (1991) (hereinafter POSTMODERNISM).

6. *Id.* at 1.

7. *Id.* at ix.

8. *Id.* at xiv.

9. *Id.* at 342.

for a distinct type of narrative or a specific narrative process."[10] The viewer is thus forced to search for "synchronic" interconnections among a "ceaseless" barrage of images.

Synchronic analysis, however, requires that experience be abstracted and flattened so as to fit into whatever system (or "discourse" or "code" or "structure") is deemed relevant. The result is a second loss, that of "depth," which is everywhere "replaced by surface, or by multiple surfaces."[11] Exemplary is the replacement of

> the older language of the 'work'—the work of art, the masterwork . . . by the rather different language of the 'text,' of texts and textuality—a language from which the achievement of organic or monumental form is strategically excluded. Everything can now be a text in that sense (daily life, the body, political representations), while objects that were formerly 'works' can now be reread as immense ensembles or systems of texts of various kinds, superimposed on each other by the way of the various intertextualities, successions of fragments.[12]

Even the past is deprived of its specifically historical character and transformed into that unidimensional collection of "visual mirages, stereotypes, or texts"[13] which has become the signature of postmodern architecture and contemporary nostalgia films.

This textualization of the world is made possible by yet a third loss, that of nature. Jameson writes that postmodernism corresponds to "the effacement of Nature,"[14] which occurs because we have so dominated and reconstructed our human environment that the only reliable referents for reality have become those of our own culture. Jameson compares Van Gogh's "A Pair of Boots" to Andy Warhol's "Diamond Dust Shoes," and demonstrates how the tension between humanity and nature that sustains the former has entirely disappeared from the latter. He keenly observes the extent to which postmodern painting generally "reinvents the 'referent' in the form of . . . collective cultural fantasies."[15] While this etiolation of nature may sometimes be experienced as emancipatory, as for example in postmodern legal feminism, its ultimate effect is to undermine resistance to the proliferating codes and discourses that have so successfully colonized our world. As a result, "the pure and random play of signifiers that we call postmodernism"[16] proceeds unimpeded, for "reality" itself has been transmuted into a cultural construction.

10. *Id.* at 86.
11. *Id.* at 12.
12. *Id.* at 77.
13. *Id.* at 46.
14. *Id.* at 366.
15. *Id.* at 179.
16. *Id.* at 96.

Faced with such staggering deprivations, postmoderns can make a virtue of necessity and celebrate "the randomly heterogeneous and fragmentary and the aleatory"[17] through such familiar techniques as irony and pastiche. But when, lacking this confidence and tired of whistling in the dark, they attempt seriously to make sense of these "heaps of fragments,"[18] they betray a distinctive sensibility that Jameson aptly labels "schizophrenic nominalism."[19] The sensibility is nominalist because it radically distrusts abstraction and intellectualization; it is schizophrenic because it is consequently unable to locate any stable or useful meaning in the world.

Schizophrenic nominalism is most evident in the writings of postmodern academics. Jameson illustrates the point by reference to Paul de Man's implacable commitment to exposing "the *artificial* emergence of metaphoric abstraction and of the conceptual universal from the real of particularity and heterogeneity."[20] Such a perspective, when generalized, creates the present condition of postmodern theory, where "the mission of theoretical discourse . . . becomes a kind of search-and-destroy operation in which linguistic misconceptions are remorselessly identified and stigmatized, in the hopes that a theoretical discourse negative and critical enough will not itself become the target of such linguistic mystification in its turn."[21] Jameson dryly notes that the "hope is, of course, vain," so that postmodern intellectual life has truly become "a *bellum omnium contra omnes*."[22]

Like so many of the specific cultural perceptions in *Postmodernism*, the observation rings true. Jameson's great virtue lies in his capacious and relentless ability to identify and weave together symptoms of the postmodern. What emerges is a striking and instantly recognizable depiction of postmodern sensibility, a depiction that ought to provide a reasonably secure frame of reference for future analysis. This is no small feat, enabled in part by the intensity of Jameson's Marxism, which provides him with a useful critical distance from postmodernism.

This distance functions in two dimensions. Marxism inhabits a millenarian temporality, oriented toward a future of progressive political achievement and fulfillment. Jameson is therefore unsympathetic to postmodernism's repudiation of time; he views it with considerable suspicion as "the sequel, continuation, and fulfillment of the old fifties 'end of ideology' episode."[23] Marxism also focuses on the relationship between objective social conditions and ideological cultural formations. From the

17. *Id.* at 25.
18. *Id.*
19. *Id.* at 360.
20. *Id.* at 236 (emphasis added).
21. *Id.* at 392-93.
22. *Id.* at 393.
23. *Id.* at 263.

outset, therefore, Jameson is hostile to postmodernism's evisceration of nature and its tendency toward schizophrenic nominalism. His distrust is conveyed in the continual reversion of his prose toward tropes of history, depth, and reality. Jameson's ambition is truly to explain the emergence of the phenomenon of postmodernism itself.

While Jameson's diagnosis of postmodernism is sharp and penetrating, the premises of his own Marxism are left vague and unexamined. So, for example, Jameson's concern to retain Marxism's traditional emphasis on the continued possibility of Utopian (socialist) redemption are the weakest aspects of his book. His reiterated references to socialism seem primarily theological. His evidence of Utopian possibility goes no further than to adduce momentary oppositions to "the dominant poster-and-decorative culture,"[24] residual resistances to the discursive colonization of the world in the name of an alien and unknowable nature. Jameson thus concludes that "Utopian thought and even Utopian critique" are recognizable chiefly in their demonstration of "the *impossibility* of imagining Utopia."[25] Precisely by revealing the inescapable extent of the "systemic restrictions and repressions" that bind us, Utopian thought gestures toward "the desperate attempt to imagine something else."[26] Utopia, so starkly diminished, seems scarcely worth the candle.

Jameson is most successful in illuminating the historical predicates of postmodernism when he explores the social tensions that inform particular texts. His exegesis of Kafka's *The Trial*, for example, reveals the impact of the uneven pace of modernization within the Hapsburg empire; the interpretation is both exciting and memorable. But Jameson's style of theoretical Marxism will not let him remain content with such concrete observations, and prompts him instead to assay historical hypotheses of far broader sweep. He thus proposes that "the stages of realism, modernism, and postmodernism" correspond to the three forms of capitalism identified by Ernst Mandel as market capitalism, monopoly (or imperialist) capitalism, and multinational (or late) capitalism.[27]

The formula is manifestly important to Jameson, for he often repeats it. Quite apart from its manic simplification, however, the formula is almost entirely vacuous. Late capitalism is never analytically or empirically defined in any useful way, and it functions throughout the book merely as a placeholder for whatever various social conditions Jameson deems relevant for understanding postmodernism. It serves little other purpose than to mark Jameson's account as politically progressive.

In fact Jameson's appeal to an undifferentiated and totalizing concept like "late capitalism" hinders his effort to perform a Marxist analysis, for

24. *Id.* at 171.
25. *Id.* at 208.
26. *Id.* at 208.
27. *Id.* at 35-36.

it obscures what would otherwise be obvious, that postmodernism affects only certain segments of contemporary life. There is, for example, no postmodern physics, although there are postmodern accounts of physics. There is no postmodern medicine, although there are postmodern histories of medicine. There is no postmodern law, although there are postmodern commentaries on law. These comparisons suggest that postmodernism is not the result of anything so global as "the world space of multinational capital,"[28] but is rather connected to discrete and local positions within that space.

Physics, medicine, and law are all successful social practices. The philosopher Alasdair MacIntyre has convincingly demonstrated how such practices depend upon "standards of excellence and obedience to rules," so that engaging in a practice involves internalizing "the authority of those standards."[29] Jameson establishes, however, that the schizophrenic nominalism of postmodernism fundamentally repudiates the authority necessary to define and apply such standards. From a sociological perspective, therefore, postmodernism entails not so much an attack on coherence, as a full-scale assault on the authority required to make coherence meaningful.

We can thus expect a social practice to remain untouched by postmodernism if its participants retain a healthy respect for the authority of the relevant standards of the practice. Physics, medicine, and law will remain impervious to postmodernism so long as practicing physicists generally agree on the standards for the evaluation of theoretical logic and experimental design, so long as practicing doctors generally agree on the principles for assessing the success of therapeutic interventions, and so long as the institutional policing mechanisms of law retain general legitimacy among practicing lawyers and judges.[30] Academic accounts of these practices, however, display their postmodernism most precisely in their generic repudiation of the authority for these various standards. It is in this way that such accounts situate themselves as "academic" and outside of these practices.

An explanation of the social origins of postmodernism thus requires a sensitive topography of the patterns of contemporary authority. We need to understand, for example, why practices retain their vitality and legitimacy, which is no doubt related to their ability to accomplish social functions that are perceived to be important. Conversely, we need to inquire into the conditions under which social authority dissipates and ceases to order human action. In this regard Jameson usefully identifies

28. *Id.* at 54.

29. Alasdair MacIntyre, After Virtue 177 (1981).

30. MacIntyre is clear that acceptance of the standards of a practice does not mean that the standards are "themselves immune from criticism," *id.*, but rather that such criticism must occur from within a more general context of agreement. For a general discussion of how this can occur, *see* Michael Walzer, Interpretation and Social Criticism (1987).

the sensibility of the consumer in a mass market as a particular locus for postmodernism. Jameson shrewdly notes that postmodernism evokes a condition of "consumerism." It theorizes commodification from the point of view of a consumer shut out by a product "even from a sympathetic participation, by imagination, in its production. [The product] comes before us, no questions asked, as something we could not begin to imagine doing for ourselves."[31]

The essence of consumerism lies in the apotheosis of preference, and for this reason consumerism rejects independent standards and authority; it thus cannot function as a practice. From the angle of our preferences, products appear designed for our appropriation; they have no independent integrity apart from that appearance. The world of the consumer, therefore, lacks history, depth, and nature. One can easily discern the roots of schizophrenic nominalism in the sovereign prerogative that sustains our power to choose among competing products.

It would be a mistake, of course, to identify late capitalism merely with consumerism. Capitalism engenders not merely consumers, but also those who, through the application of instrumental reason, create and distribute the products and services that are consumed. David Lodge's recent novel, *Nice Work*, neatly makes this point by chronicling the improbable relationship between a postmodern literary academic and the managing director of a manufacturing plant; the two inhabit starkly different ideological worlds.[32] It would even be a mistake to identify consumerism with the generic act of consumption itself, for one can imagine forms of consumption, like connoisseurship, which are quite different. The question, therefore, is why postmodernism seeks culturally to privilege the particular kind of consumption that it does.

The answer to that question is no doubt complex and nuanced. It is not enough to adduce, as does Jameson, the extent and dominion of the market. One would want to know why the consumer's perspective on the market attains general cultural hegemony, which perhaps might entail an investigation of such issues as the nature of modern work, the division of labor, and the prevalence and structure of social practices. Such investigations would likely be local in scope. So, for example, an explanation of the recent explosion of academic postmodernism, and in particular its transformation of "works" into "texts," ought to begin with the collapse of the practice of aesthetic judgment and the consequent transfiguration of literary academics into consumers of the written word. Similarly, the attempt to explain the tendency of recent art to explore a condition of consumerism ought to begin with a detailed examination of the particular circumstances of contemporary artistic authority and production.

31. POSTMODERNISM, *supra* note 5, at 317.
32. DAVID LODGE, NICE WORK (1989).

One ought to keep in mind, moreover, the distinction between thematizing a particular structure of experience and exemplifying (or enacting) that structure. To the extent that academics and artists continue to engage in serious intellectual and aesthetic practices, practices that solicit and submit to standards of excellence and evaluation, their work cannot in an important sense be said to exemplify a condition of consumerism, but must rather be characterized as "about" that condition. We must distinguish, in other words, between postmodernism as an organization of experience and postmodernism as a particular set of thematic concerns.

I would like to think that Jameson would welcome such concrete inquiries, although their modest empirical and sociological specificity is a far cry from the sweeping historical drama of "late capitalism." What worries me, however, is Jameson's easy evasion of all serious engagement with the grubby particularities and difficulties of such social explanations. Throughout *Postmodernism* grand causal historical hypotheses effortlessly proliferate, as though society could be remade with the turn of a phrase. It seems to me deeply ironic that in the almost magical puissance assumed in this casual obliteration of the old fashioned principles of evidence and proof, Jameson re-enacts the postmodern denial of nature he elsewhere so penetratingly exposes.

Lured by the promise of Utopian redemption, intoxicated by the exercise of theoretical mastery, Jameson's uncontrollable speculation loses hold of the most subtle insight of its Marxist heritage—that reality, although perhaps unknowable in its noumenal essence, can nevertheless be engaged and respected through forms of human praxis. The very principles of evidence and proof abandoned by Jameson constitute for us a form of praxis by which history ceases to be merely our own cultural construction, and is instead made visible as stretching behind and beyond us in all its depth and integrity.

Of course it has become part of the recognizable international style of the new cultural criticism to radically subordinate history and sociology to "theory" in this fashion. The distinctive contribution of *Postmodernism*, however, is to expose the disturbing and self-defeating implications of that subordination, which, by depriving us of the presence of an independent world, drives us into the sovereign but stationary logic of consumerism. That this logic should ensnare even *Postmodernism*'s author, among the most astute of cultural critics, vividly illustrates the intense temptation of the postmodern structure of experience.

[5]

BABEL: A *SHE'UR*

for Sharka

*Richard Hyland**

Unserem Packmeister sind nun doch noch Bedenken gekommen.

The letter bearing the sentence surfaces again, long afterward, as we leaf through an old correspondence file. She slowly reads the sentence aloud, savoring the surprisingly literary quality of the prose from a German shipping firm, then asks whether it is possible to translate the sentence into English. I stare at it for a moment, and suddenly the little memory floods over me. One of the reasons translation is so time-consuming is that it causes the mind to wander . . . .

We were moving again. We had spent days dragging empty boxes from the market, packing them with books and padding them with crumpled pages from the sports section. Finally, we loaded them into a rented VW van and drove them to the freight forwarder. A worker pointed to a place for the boxes—on a wooden pallet in the middle of a gaping warehouse. The random-size boxes, however, piled high and tilting slightly, did not look stable. Yet the warehouser was confident: the pile would not topple. A month later, back in the U.S., we received the letter telling us that our belongings had been shipped, that everything was in order, except that the boxes of books had had to be adjusted on the pallet and strapped down with wide metal bands . . . .

Unserem Packmeister sind . . . To our packing master are . . . It is not yet the close of business. I call a moving company and ask for the term used to designate the member of the moving team who is in charge of packing. *The packer*, I am told. Is there no name for a specially skilled packer who, because of years of dedicated service and accumulated expertise, is consulted about particularly difficult questions? *You mean a supervisor*? Is there then no word like *packing master* or *master packer*? *Hey, what's this all about*? I manage to extricate myself, offer thanks, and hang up. I then report the results of the conversation. We fall silent. Why, she asks, does the German language have the concept while English does not? And who is the subject of the *our*? To whom in the end does the master packer belong?

nun doch noch . . . now yet again . . . Adverbs, expletives, and

* Professor of Law, University of Miami Law School.

other German particles are packed with meanings as randomly as our boxes were packed with books. Some of the meanings can be approximated in English, but others can be translated only by a gesture—a shrug, a frown, a slap on the knee. The particles mean so much separately that they are able to mean almost anything when strung together.

Bedenken gekommen . . . thoughts-about come . . . Not just thoughts but apprehensions—doubts of some kind. The real question is where do the misgivings come from: What is the point of this odd sentence structure according to which the master packer, the human actor, serves only as the place at which thoughts come to rest?

Of course, the words can be interpreted to make at least some sense in English. *Nun* may well be the key. It seems to invoke a sigh of relief—*now, coming to a conclusion after long reflection*. *Doch* can be taken with *noch* to signify a contrast, to insist that the new conclusion is firm, despite the initial contrary opinion. And perhaps it would be best in English to camouflage somewhat the surprising implication from the sentence structure, namely that thoughts possess their own means of locomotion.

In the end, second thoughts did in fact occur to our master packer. If this is a translation, then I am a translator. And I suppose Gadamer would explain not only that I have thereby interpreted the original but also that my horizon and language have become fused with those of the text. Yet I do not experience the fusion. I experience my translation as a sad and sorry compromise, and one that, far from fusing anything, instead reveals the great distance separating the very different sentences involved in the drama. There is the original. There are the several possible word-for-word renderings. There is my own approximation, together with the numerous alternatives that I have rejected. And there are the various sentences that *I* might have written in American English in such a letter—if the thought had occurred to me and if, in such a situation, I had found it useful to write it down. *Our supervisor had second thoughts about the way your boxes were loaded on the pallet*, I might have written. Or, more likely, I would have been more direct. *We decided that it was necessary, before shipment, to secure your boxes to the pallet*. The fact is, however, that I probably would not have found it necessary to mention the thought at all.

The experience of translating produces in me not the pleasure of merger and comfort but rather the acute distress of things torn apart and a vain and frantic desire to hold them together. In the end, the text entreats *me* to be a master packer. And so I pack my translation, somewhat arbitrarily, with as much meaning as possible. But the translation is, after all, only a sentence, and I am only a packer. Much has found its way into the translation, but as rereading it continually reminds me, much more has been left out—enough, surely, for many other sentences. In contrast to the master packer, I do not feel that I have completed my job, that my horizon is at one with another's.

The notion of translation implies that there is some relationship between languages. The fact that there is difficulty indicates at least that there is no one-to-one correspondence between words in one language and those in another. Since the law is formulated in language, the difficulty of translation suggests a similar lack of continuity from one legal system to another. It might then be asked how exactly to characterize the relationship between one language and another, or between two different legal systems. At least in the West, the discussion about such questions traditionally implicates a Biblical text (Gen. 11: 1-9) that tells the story of the tower of Babel. The object of this essay is to explore the lesson of this story for the appreciation of diversity, particularly the diversity of legal systems.

Of God

There is no way around it: reflection about the meaning of Babel requires recourse to the notion of God. One of the difficulties in thinking about Divinity is that the prevailing tradition offers little margin for error. According to Revelations (3:12), the names of God are literally inscribed in the faithful. As Fray Luis de Léon (*De los nombres de Cristo*) remarked, those names are the essence that God communicates to the fortunate—brief ciphers wherein God miraculously encapsulates all that human understanding can and may perceive of Godhood. Since, in this tradition, all names of God partake of Divinity, the stakes in theological discussion are high: any assertion may not only be challenged as incorrect, but also branded as blasphemy. Even English, despite its extravagantly rich resources, lacks the necessary vocabulary for a completely open discussion about the nature of God.

Hebrew offers a convenient distinction—one which might easily be incorporated into English—that serves to relax the tension in theological discussion. Hebrew distinguishes between those names used exclusively when addressing the Holy One and others that may be employed in both discussion and everyday conversation.

Though there is some dispute about whether Hebrew contains a single word for *God*, it does contain numerous names *of* God. There is a twelve-letter name, and there is also a forty-two letter name, both long since forgotten. There is the word that was spoken to Moses when he inquired of the name he was to tell to the Children of Israel. In fact, it is said that the Torah contains nothing other than the names of God. Seven of these names are distinguished by the fact that, once written, they may not be erased. The first of these, the ineffable Tetragrammaton, may no longer be pronounced—a prohibition that leads to some confusion, since the true pronunciation has been forgotten. Even in the days of the priests, it was spoken aloud only in the Temple, most notably by the High Priest, after ritual purification on the holiest of days, in a whisper muffled by song. The six remaining names are used today when directly addressing the Holy One and may not be uttered outside of prayer or blessing. When, even in study, reference is made to these names, their pronunciation is altered, slightly but perceptibly, in order to avoid sacrilege.

In discussion or conversation about God, use is made of other names—oblique references, really. One such name is *HaShem*, which means simply *The Name*. It refers not directly to God, but rather to the Holy Name. Names such as this create space between the signifier and the signified and are therefore sufficiently removed from the name of God that their inadvertent misuse must not necessarily be considered irreverent. That is why they are needed here.

Even once a name has been agreed upon, the preliminaries are not over. A form must be found in which to discuss such matters. Theological discussion almost necessarily assumes that there is a fundamental ordering to the universe and thus does not proceed as though it involved a typical question from the law or politics. The Talmudic tradition offers a form for this sort of disputation. It is called the *she'ur*. The word *she'ur* may well be derived from a Hebrew verb signifying *to measure* or *estimate*. On one level, it indicates the measured or circumscribed time available between religious services for such discussions. Yet the idea of measurement reveals something of the substantive goal as well, the desire to open the nature of Divine order to human understanding—to demonstrate that, at least to some extent, humanity can grasp something about infinity. The *she'ur* begins by revealing a puzzle—usually an apparent inconsistency between two texts of the Written or Oral Laws. Since it is assumed that both texts were transcribed from Divine dictation, and since it is further assumed that Divine texts do not contain inconsistencies, the problem is to resolve the dissonance and restore meaning to the Holy Text. At the same time, precisely because the topic is the infinite and the Divine, no *she'ur* claims to be absolutely right, and none need fear being absolutely wrong. It is clear from the outset that every suggestion will enrich the discussion and equally clear that none will ever close it.

Though the *she'ur* was developed as a form for discussing the *Chumash* (the Five Books or Torah) and the Talmudic texts, its usefulness is not limited to that context. It may be understood more broadly to offer form to a discussion about the relationship between harmony and diversity—to the investigation of the affinities between empirically existing activities once it is assumed that there is order in the cosmos. The question here, for example, involves the relationship between homogeneity and diversity with respect to the human languages—and with respect to the various systems of law. The name *HaShem* is meant to serve here as a convenient reference to the idea of reason in diversity. The *she'ur* is employed as a mode for its elaboration.

Of History

The story of the tower built at Babel is based on the assumption that humanity once shared a single language. It was the language of Noah's family, for only Noah and his wife, together with their three sons and their wives, survived the Flood. According to the *Chumash*, all nations are descended from this family. After the death of Noah, as humankind journeyed from Ararat, the mountain of the East where the ark of Noah had come to rest, it came upon the plain of Shinar. As the group looked out onto the plain, everything about the place must have reminded them of death, for the bodies of those who had died in the Flood had washed down onto Shinar. Perhaps it was the very proximity of the plain to death, together with humanity's desire to conquer mortality, that convinced the group to settle there and to build a city and a tower. Because of the events that soon transpired, the city became known as Babel, which may be derived from *Bab-ilu* (*Gate of God* in Assyrian, perhaps signifying the portals through which the nations were to go out), and, at least by popular etymology, is related to *balal*, the Hebrew for *to mix up* or *confuse*. The tower to be built there was designed to reach to Heaven. After construction of the tower was well along, *HaShem* came down to examine it. Upon seeing the tower, the Holy One destroyed it, confounded the speech of the various nations so that they could no longer understand one another, and scattered them over the face of the earth.

Tradition has had much to say about the tower. It is said to have contained two sets of stairs. The eastern stairs were used by workers carrying bricks to the top, while the stairs to the west were used by those who returned for new bricks. The tower was tremendously tall, so much so that its top appeared to touch the sky. When the tower was destroyed, the bottom third of it sank into the ground, the top third was consumed by fire, and only the middle third remained. Yet what remained of the tower was so immense that one might have walked for three days without leaving its shadow. (Some of the traditional stories about the tower are collected in *The Torah Anthology* [*MeAm Lo'ez*].)

From Rashi to Derrida (Des Tours de Babel, in *Difference in Translation* (Graham ed. 1985)), the scholars have unanimously interpreted the confusion of language as a well-deserved punishment, one particularly designed to prevent the completion of the tower. The diversity of language and the inevitability of mutual misunderstanding have been considered elements of a curse brought on by Divine annoyance at human pride, particularly at the vanity implicit in the conception of the tower—the belief that human beings might reach Heaven, and therefore immortality, without the journey through death.

Despite its persistence, there is something peculiarly unsatisfying about this interpretation of the story. The tower, of course, could never have reached Heaven. The Holy One had no reason for concern. Moreover, pride of accomplishment and the desire to postpone or transcend death are constant elements of the human condition and certainly not its least attractive ones. Furthermore, though *HaShem* is capable of rage (metaphorically understood), the Rambam demonstrated that not every human failing is capable of inducing Divine anger: an examination of the incidents of wrath in both the Torah and the prophetic writings reveals that only one very particular sin provokes the Holy One, and that is idolatry. And finally, the confusion of language involves much more than the simple creation of a barrier to communication. If all that *HaShem* had desired was to obstruct human discourse, that could have been achieved by hindering the human ear or by slowing the tongue. In other words, the building of the tower seems to provide little enough reason for punishment at all, let alone for a punishment of this particular type. The difficulty then becomes to discover a connection between the confusion of language and the building of the tower than can be reconciled with the all-encompassing wisdom of the Holy One.

Once the problem is posed in this manner, the story of Babel is so evocative that numerous resolutions suggest themselves. My own favorite interprets the story as a fable of post modernism. The first step in conceiving of the story in this way is to reexamine its status as history. In my view, none of the stories recounted at the beginning of the *Chumash* need be interpreted as history, at least not history as we are used to conceiving of it. Though the sages do not deny the historicity of these stories, a few of their sentences seem to point to the possibility of a nonhistorical reading. Woe unto them, remarked Rabbi Shimon bar Yochai in the *Zohar*, who see in the Torah merely worldly stories and history. To Rabbi Yaakov Culi, the few stories retold in the Torah are really mysteries, enshrouded in words that make them appear like history. For the nonhistorical reading, it is irrelevant whether the incidents described in those stories actually took place, whether a tower was actually built or human language actually confused as described in the Torah. Rather the stories present analysis in the *form* of history. To decipher this curious form, the story of Babel must be read in context.

The *Chumash* presents a code of laws—613 commandments, 248 mandating some positive act, the remaining 365 enumerating the prohibitions—interspersed with what appears to be an historical narrative. The culmination of the narrative is the recounting of the single Divine revelation in human history, the appearance of the Holy One and the giving of the Law at Sinai. What precedes the giving of the Law is an account of the formation and education of the people chosen to receive it, which begins with the story of Abraham our Father. Before beginning the story of Abraham and his descendants, the *Chumash* focuses on three events—the stories of Eden, the Flood, and Babel.

The three stories may be read as the preface to a legal text, a reminder of the three preconditions that are necessary for a functioning legal system. These stories describe not the past but the present, each designating a necessary element of the whole. Each story illustrates one of the prerequisites by means of an *as though* analysis, what Hans Vaihinger (*The Philosophy of "As If"*) might have called a heuristic fiction. The very possibility of the law is rooted in these three aspects of the human condition, yet they seem so natural that they are virtually imperceptible until they have been problematized—scandalized really—by ascribing to them fictional origins: it is *as though* humanity had been Divinely created and then suffered a Fall, *as though* it had received a covenant from the Lord after a terrible destruction, *as though* an original common language had been fragmented. The challenge is to redeem the wisdom sealed in the metaphors.

In Eden, our first ancestors tasted of the forbidden fruit, and thereby gained the ability to distinguish between good and evil. The story of the Fall recognizes in human nature an attraction to evil as well as an understanding of good, together with the ability to distinguish between the two, and the insight that they are often intertwined. The story describes one aspect of the human condition that serves as a prerequisite for a functioning legal system, a feature so essential that it is difficult to conceive of a legal system without it. If human beings did not both recognize the good and yet, at the same time, desire evil, the notion of a legal prohibition backed by coercion would be incoherent. There is also something more to the story. The teller of the tale must have marveled at the human ability to appreciate the distinction between right and wrong. It may have seemed that the knowledge of good and evil results not from reasoned inquiry but rather from a quality innate in human nature. And yet human beings are clearly not predetermined to do good. The knowledge of good seems to be Divinely inspired, as though the human race initially had been Divinely created and subsequently had fallen from the perfect identification with Divine will that constituted grace.

Unfortunately, the knowledge of good and evil, unguided by morality, did not prove sufficient to overcome temptation. Beginning with Cain and Abel, what resulted was such human iniquity that the Holy One decided to drown the world. After the Flood, *HaShem* covenanted with Noah that the world would never again be destroyed by calamity. By making the promise, the Lord demonstrated to Noah the nature of obligation and thereby initiated him and his family into the concept of duty. The sense of duty or morality is the second prerequisite of a legal system, for there can be law only if humanity struggles to comply with the demands of duty. The daily, heroic, and largely successful human struggle to overcome desire makes it seem as though humankind is attempting to fulfill promises made in exchange for the Lord's own covenant.

An understanding that right differs from wrong and a moral commitment to the good are still not sufficient for the establishment of a legal system, at least according to the author of the *Chumash*. The final requirement is an understanding of the necessity of particularity. The Divine Text expressed the requirement by portraying the fragmentation of a single original language. This account raises two difficulties. The first is to make sense of the claim that the various natural languages have a common origin. The second is to understand why the notion of particularity is a necessary prerequisite for a code of laws.

Of Language

As our ancestors were resolving to build the city and the tower of

Babel, it is written that they also decided to make for themselves a name, in order to avoid being scattered over the face of the earth. Confronted by the splendid yet frightening multifariousness of existence, they wished to prevent their dispersion by gathering together, by reducing everything to a unique name, to a single understanding. They sought transcendence beyond the realm of diversity in a unique foundational principle. The idea of the single name influenced the conception of the tower. Finding no stones, we are told, they made bricks and burnt them thoroughly. The tower's foundation was thus a human construction. Yet the tower builders believed that, if they were to construct a tower, even on such foundations, on a plain encountered by chance, they would be able to dominate Creation and, from the top of the tower, enter into Eternity.

The story of the tower of Babel suggests how easily the human mind can be seduced by reductionism. The story expresses the frantic yet persistent hope that it is possible to escape uncertainty by glorifying the theory of the moment: if only the tower is tall enough, our ancestors thought, it can reach to Heaven. The story reminds us that human intuition seeks truth in unity, in monocausal explanation, rather than in multiplicity. If humanity were possessed of but a single language, it would inevitably believe that there is but a single valid understanding. In the end, Babel reveals the limitation of the human imagination, its difficulty in conceiving of infinite possibility.

This is an important limitation, because the ability to conceive of possibility is the difference between Divine and human understanding. The Holy One understands the world as it is, both in its existence and in its potential. That is what Heidegger called original being (*das ursprüngliche Sein*). Humankind, on the other hand, tends to focus on the given and the finite and to reduce it to a single explanation. However great its comprehension, no human mind can ever discover more than an extremely limited number of the possible alternatives.

Hashem destroyed the tower and scrambled language not to punish those who had sought to reach Heaven, but rather to open the human mind to the appreciation of possibility. For this purpose it was necessary to establish at least some of those possibilities empirically and to permit them to flourish independently. The confusion of language, by making it difficult for one nation to communicate with the next, permitted each group to develop relatively autonomously the possibilities inherent in the language it received.

The development of a particular language over time is a cultural tradition. There is of course never homogeneity within a tradition. For one, languages are often composed of numerous competing dialects. Moreover, each cultural tradition is the expression of a debate—at times only an unvoiced tension—between the rulers and the ruled, between sexes and races and religions, majorities and minorities of all kinds. There is also constant Babel or confusion even within the same language. And, of course, history matters too. To begin with, the tradition is constantly reorganizing itself, emphasizing today what it yesterday rejected. Moreover, at some point, cultural developments that occurred much earlier may prove difficult to interpret, so that, like Middle English, they are no longer fully able to contribute to the contemporary discussion. Yet despite the internal conflict and confusion, each tradition shares a common understanding. In fact, what distinguishes one tradition from another are the terms in which the various conflicts are fought out.

From the standpoint of Babel, in other words, language is not transparent. If the various languages were merely neutral instrumentalities for the communication of thought, it would be impossible to explain their extraordinary multiplicity and diversity. The tradition is that seventy nations received languages at Babel. These languages ultimately differentiated themselves into what may have been as many as ten thousand languages, of which possibly five thousand survive today. The reason for the diversity is that each language is constituted by, expresses, and reproduces a particular intelligibility. In Heidegger's phrase, language is *die redende Gliederung*, speaking articulation. Since each language represents only one of the many possible understandings, the existence of thousands of languages confirms the possibility of at least so many lived articulations of meaning. In fact, the number of possibilities may well be endless. The mission confided by the Holy One to human hands is to discover, explore, and develop these endless possibilities. It is *as though* an original common language had once been fragmented.

Of Translation

The Babelian understanding of language irrevocably alters the notion and goal of translation. Translation as traditionally understood—the phrase-by-phrase rendering of a message from one language into another while *retaining the sense* (Samuel Johnson)—proves to be impossible. The problem is not that languages are totally incommensurable with each other. It is not that it is inherently impossible to express in one language the meaning of a word or phrase from another. Language determines not, as Benjamin Lee Whorf seems to have believed, what it is *possible* to see and understand, but rather what *easily* can be grasped and what, in contrast, requires more effort. If languages were impregnable fortresses, nothing could be learned from a foreign culture.

The principal problem is rather that languages communicate simultaneously on various levels. On one level, language is a tool by which human beings attempt to come to terms with their world, either by attempting to describe or represent the world that they perceive to be external to them or by seeking to express their inner awareness and conflicts. The question about whether language is adequate to the task, an issue about which Richard Rorty has expressed doubts, does not bar human beings from the attempt. Even on this level, no message can be comprehensively translated from one language into another without constant resort to asterisks and extensive explanatory notes.

This is not a problem that affects only a few well-known untranslatables, such as *Aufhebung* or the pair *langue/parole*. Even the English word *bread* does not have the same meaning as the French word *pain*. Though there are dozens of differences, the easiest to explain are found on the side of the signified. Not only are the breads referred to by the two words significantly different in form, texture, and taste, but also bread in America is usually bought pre-packaged, pre-sliced, and even pre-frozen and is rarely eaten with the main course, while French bread is bought fresh in bakeries shortly before it is to be consumed at the main meal. On the side of the signifier, the differences are just as stark. Though the two words share many connotations, such as the notion of *daily bread* (*pain quotidien*), colloquial English has developed the metaphor to produce the idea of the *breadwinner* and even equates *bread* with *money*, while French tends to use *pain* in metaphors related to the shape of the loaf, such as *pain de viande* (meat loaf) and *pain à cacheter* (sealing wax), and colloquial French even arrives somehow at having *pain* mean a slap in the face. Moreover, the literary associations of the two words are completely diverse. *Pain* rhymes with *sain* (healthy), *pin* (pine tree), and *vin* (wine), while *bread* rhymes with *dead*, *head*, and *said*. Upon hearing the word *bread*, it is unlikely that anyone but those with a childhood in English will recall the verse *"A loaf of bread," the Walrus said*, and suddenly feel the tug from the far side of the looking glass.

Language as a tool—the use human beings make of words—is not all there is to language. Languages, too, communicate. They speak through those who are attempting to use them in their own communication. As John Sallis notes, language is not primarily an articulation of meaning that we perform, but rather one that is always already performed for us, one we have already assumed inadvertently by virtue of our life in language. (Language and reversal, in *Martin Heidegger: in Europe and America* (Ballard & Scott eds. 1973)). The particular intelligibility that a language conveys may be at cross purposes with the intent of the individual speaker. If, as we are used to saying, language is a game, it is not a game that we play with language, but rather one that language plays with us. This is one of the senses in which one might say, with Heidegger, that it is actually language that speaks (*Denn eigentlich spricht die Sprache*).

The consequences for translation are considerable. The problem is not simply that the meaning of a particular word or phrase in one language cannot find an exact equivalent in another. The problem is rather that there is nothing identical across languages. Languages are simply not equivalents as media for communication. The different understandings implicit in the natural languages render every one of their words, phrases, and sentences untranslatable—unless the translation in accompanied by an absurdly compendious and extraordinarily subtle textual apparatus.

Thus, if there is a relationship at all among languages—and only then would translation even be conceivable—it arises only in terms of the whole that, together, the various languages may have constituted. If the Holy Name is in fact the organizing principle of the universe, and if all of the world's languages are fragments of the original language spoken at Babel, then each language represents a piece of a much larger jigsaw puzzle. No piece can reveal its meaning alone, but each may acquire coherency when examined together with some of the other pieces. One problem, of course, is that, by now, we have lost half the pieces, even assuming that we ever once had them all. As a result, whatever the whole may once have signified will remain forever concealed from us.

The absence of a direct relationship among languages provides reason for skepticism about Gadamer's confidence in translation. For Gadamer, translation is simply a particular kind of understanding. All understanding is interpretation, the fusion of the reader's language and horizon with the language and horizon of a text. Since translation involves a similar fusion, it too would be merely interpretation. It would represent both an extreme form of and a model for understanding. Gadamer's confidence would be warranted if the task were merely to understand what human beings do with words. But his method is unable to account for what is communicated by the language itself. Another and very different strategy is needed in order to reproduce in one language the understanding constituted by another. As Walter Benjamin was probably the first to note, translation could solve this problem only by importing from one language into another an entire fragment of the foreign culture, and not merely the thing meant. In this sense, successful translation not only enriches the target language but also reminds us of its limitations.

Of Law and Legal Education

The story of Babel is particularly important as the preface to a legal text. It emphasizes the particularity of any single code of laws. No code promulgated in a post-Babelian language—even if conceived in Divine inspiration—can be universal. Every law is a particular law. It is part of a particular language, embedded in a particular cultural tradition, and designed for a particular people. The laws codified in the *Chumash*—the 613 *mitzvos*, including the Ten Commandments—apply directly only to the people in whose language the code is written.

Like languages, legal systems express particular understandings. And as with languages, the particular understandings are constituted in conflict and debate, are what the debaters share. Thus, no matter how successful, no particular legal system can make a direct claim to universality—none can overcome the particularity of the language in which it is formulated. Each legal system articulates the meaning of law and justice in a particular way. Wisdom in the law is not located within any particular understanding, but results rather from grasping all of these articulations at once.

The understandings incorporated in the numerous particular systems of law and justice may be accessed in several ways, but it may be easiest to begin at what might be called the beginning: not a beginning buried in the past but rather the beginning all new jurists experience as they are initiated into their craft—the various and extraordinarily diverse systems of legal education. Intuition suggests that legal education will differ greatly between traditions that are geographically dispersed and culturally disparate. But even a common cultural heritage does not prevent difference. For this reason, in order to suggest the range of methods in legal education, it is especially important to consider legal education in countries whose traditions seem to be closely related. Those established in West Germany, France, and the United States will be examined here. Though the skills taught in the three systems may seem to overlap somewhat, there is something very different about the manner in which they are articulated. The focus here is on those differences. In order to avoid a much more extensive discussion, I ignore other related processes in the law, such as the manner in which cases are decided and the methods of legal scholarship.

The principal object of German legal education is to develop the skill of the *Fallösung* or case resolution, a particular method for finding a legal solution to a hypothetical fact situation. It is the skill required for success at the German state examination, which is given at the conclusion of law school and which alone determines a student's final grade and rank in class. The technique of the *Fallösung* is considered so important that upper-level German law students often abandon university instruction entirely for the year or two prior to their state exam and follow courses taught by one of the many private tutors, the *Repetitoren*, who relentlessly drill and develop the skills required.

Substantively, German legal education tends to center in the private law, especially the law of contracts, particularly of sales contracts. The focus there is on questions of remedy, specifically on the relationship between the remedies and defenses available under general contract law and those provided by sales law. The complex set of rules provided in the German Civil Code and in the relevant case law to govern these matters involves elaborate cross-references, repeated resort to the interaction of principle, exception, and exception to exception, and reliance on elusively subtle distinctions. For those to whom intricate elegance is a virtue, this structure must be counted, with the verb forms in classical Greek, among the sublime creations of the human imagination. Needless to say, this part of German law is *Professorenrecht*, a matter for specialists. The complexity of the field is what recommends it as a test for the student's mastery of legal technique.

Success in resolving the German hypothetical requires a thorough knowledge of the remedial scheme and a comprehensive and systematic examination of the relevance of the various remedial provisions to the facts at hand. If the claimant in the hypothetical has several potential opponents, the claims against each must be discussed separately. If the claimant has more than one type of claim (*Anspruch*) against a particular party, the claims must be examined in the appropriate order. Much of German academic discussion focuses on questions of organization, and there are competing views on these questions. In general, primary claims are to be reviewed before secondary claims (specific relief before damages, replevin or ejectment before contract claims) and the claimant's primary objective before a secondary one. For each type of claim, there may be more than one potentially relevant basis for the claim (*Anspruchsgrundlage*)—the specific provision in the code or a well-established principle from the case law that offers the particular remedy to the claimant. Each substantive discussion begins with a statement of the relevant *Anspruchsgrundlage*, and all of the conceivably relevant bases for the claim must be examined in order—special before general norms, contractual before extra-contractual provisions, property-based provisions before restitution. For each particular provision, there is also an established order for the review of the legal requirements (*Tatbestandsmerkmale*). In tort, for example, though there is debate about the appropriate scheme, and any one of two or three alternatives is acceptable, the discussion traditionally begins with the nature of the harm, and then proceeds through the type of right that was violated, the tortious act, causation between the tortious act and the violation of the right, causation between the violation of the right and the harm, breach of duty (*Rechtswidrigkeit*), and fault (*Verschulden*). (The technique of the *Fallösung* is described in Uwe Diederichsen, *Die BGB-Klausur* 80-88 (6th ed. 1984), and in Dieter Medicus, *Bürgerliches Recht* 1-14 (14th ed. 1989).)

In short, greater emphasis is placed on the framework for the analysis than on the result. What is essential for success in the state examination is that the student subsume the facts correctly under the elaborated system of remedies. Of course, policy arguments may be raised in the answer, but only if they are incorporated into the appropriate phase of the discussion. In any case, nothing is to be mentioned that is not directly relevant to the question at hand. At the same time, no logically necessary step may be omitted. A serious error in construction may lead to failure even if the theories and policies are adequately examined. Most importantly, no step may be taken and no argument advanced unless it finds authority in a code provision or a well-established case-law principle. Though there may be slightly more flexibility and openness to innovation outside of the private law, adherence to preconceived outlines is cherished throughout German legal education.

Exclusive focus on the logic of the *Anspruchsgrundlage* encourages the German student to develop extraordinary rigor and orderliness and to pay close attention to subtle distinctions between the various remedial provisions. This emphasis, however, is not without its limitations. It tends to avoid explicit and wide-ranging discussion of policy alternatives and leaves the skill of advocacy largely undeveloped. Moreover, by concentrating on the accepted view and the firmly established remedial provisions, and by emphasizing the virtues of predictability and certainty, the *Fallösung* acquires a somewhat conservative cast.

German legal education, as it analyzes and orders the remedial scheme, enunciates a moral and political understanding of the nature of justice and of freedom under law. It asserts that a people is free when it deliberates in a parliamentary manner and when the commands of the legislature are rigorously executed by the judiciary. The implication is that progress in the law should be left to the political process and fine-tuning to the highest courts. The role of the individual judge is not to provide a remedy merely because it may seem just to do so but rather to respect the will of the people as promulgated in legislative enactments. The common lawyer may experience the German method as somewhat inflexible in reaching a legal conclusion and inattentive to the constellation of possibilities offered by the law. Yet, at the same time, the vision implicit in German legal education expresses not only a belief or yearning that is widely shared both inside and outside of Germany, but also a thought that may represent an element of every complex legal system.

French legal education focuses on a different skill and embodies a distinct understanding of the nature of law. To begin with, the French law professor avoids the hypothetical as a teaching tool: French law students are virtually never asked to consider a complicated fact pattern, identify the issues, and resolve the dispute. Instead, the focus is on a particular kind of synthesis. French students are taught to develop an overview of a legal topic or of a court decision and to convey that overview not only convincingly but also in a specific form.

The keystone of the French synthetic method is the *plan*, the organizational structure for the *exposé* or presentation. French jurists have developed the *plan* into an art form, one they elaborate according to strict rules. One rule is the maxim of elegance: the topic headings of the *plan*, when taken together, must envelop the entire subject matter, and each element of the whole must in fact be subsumed under one of the topic headings. Second, the *exposé*, between its brief introduction and its even briefer conclusion, generally contains exactly two parts, each divided into exactly two subparts. (A *plan* may include three principal parts—in its classical form, virtually never more than that—only if it is impossible to subsume one of the three under one of the other two.) The role of the introduction is to present and justify the *plan*. It begins from a commonplace that a legally educated reader would surely accept and then presents the subject matter in such a manner that the structural divisions of the *plan* seem convincing, even obvious. Each of the two principal parts of the *exposé* must be of approximately equal length. Each of two corresponding subparts must also be of similar proportion. Parallel topic headings must be symmetrical in syntactic form. In sum, the successful *exposé* gains clarity and persuasiveness by following the canons of balance and harmony. (The technique of the *plan* is described in Jean-Pierre Gridel, *La dissertation et le cas pratique en droit privé* 21-45 (2d ed. 1986).) This rule of two parts and two subparts is followed rigorously by students in both oral presentations and written examinations, and with some variation, by doctoral candidates writing dissertations, by the authors of law-review articles, and even by specialists when drafting comprehensive treatises.

The binary structure of the *exposé* may seem somewhat arbitrary and rigid, but, as with the rhyme scheme of a sonnet or the number of syllables in a *haiku*, the appearance is deceptive. The *plan* is essential to the French understanding of the nature of law. The insight underlying the French conception of the *plan* is that legal topics are best presented from the point of view of a fundamental tension or contradiction. Until a basic tension is discovered and the subject examined from that standpoint, any understanding is unsatisfying: the details will seem to have outflanked the author and the subject matter still to lie beyond the grasp. It is important to note that the French understanding does not represent a camouflaged metaphysical assertion about a supposed dialectical structure implicit in the law. There is nothing absolute or objective about the *plan* as the French conceive it. For any one subject, there could be as many *plans* as—or even more *plans* than—there are jurists.

The French conception of the *plan* is intoxicating to the point of addiction. No one who has successfully apprenticed in the French system deems a presentation successful, whether written or oral, unless it has been harmoniously organized into two parts, each with two subparts. From this perspective, any other organization of a legal discussion suggests only that the author has not yet fully mastered the material. The *plan* renders it uncommonly easy to see and retain the structure of the law and is capable of displaying the relationship among even the most far-flung topics. In the end, a persuasive *plan* is about as satisfying as intellectual things can be.

The single-minded French concentration on synthesis necessarily neglects much of what is otherwise interesting in the law. For example, French legal education fails to develop in its students a sensitivity to the facts or an understanding of the art of advocacy. It also produces an overly harmonious and unified vision of the law. It places the law student outside the law, at the point of synthesis, and removes all but the most accomplished jurists from active participation in legal change.

The vision implicit in French legal education is that the law is the organizing force in a society wrought with tension and contradiction. To organize contradiction, of course, does not mean to deny it. The law's task is to recognize the tension, to perceive how every legal question is divided against itself, to evaluate the contradictory views and present them in a balanced manner, and to offer, if only temporarily, an elegant and satisfying reconciliation of opposites. Law, in this perspective, both guarantees the realm of freedom and creates social unity and cohesiveness. It squares the circle, imposes order upon chaos. It is the center that holds against centrifugal force.

American legal education offers yet a different understanding. As are many other systems, it is principally the study of decided cases. But cases are not studied in America as they are studied elsewhere. In many other systems in which cases are read, the case serves almost exclusively to demonstrate to the law student how to apply the law to the facts, how to evaluate the comportment of individual parties by recourse to the norms available in the legal order. The object is to understand which party acted appropriately and which did not. In America, the study of cases may often fulfill a similar function, but the power of the case method lies elsewhere.

For one, cases are not generally taught alone. They are taught in pairs, triplets, or even entire series. The coupled cases may seem at first glance to provide differing solutions to the same set of facts. The task is then to reconcile the cases, to distinguish their facts in a convincing manner so that it becomes clear why each deserves the result the common law judge accorded to it. The challenge is to discover the perspective from which seemingly identical cases appear to be opposites.

In addition, the facts in reported cases are frequently used in American legal education as a challenge. The aspiration in many classrooms is for students to use the case to reconstruct the legal system. Legal norms are then not used to decide which of the two opposing parties acted properly. The answer to *that* question—this is one lesson from legal realism—is not an exclusively legal matter. Instead, American law teaching often uses a particular case as an occasion to evaluate the appropriateness of the legal rules. The object of such class discussion is to determine how the legal order should be structured so that it would resolve the case before the court in a satisfactory manner. The student learns to stand up in class and argue that, despite statute, regulation, and precedent, a rule is not what it ought to be. The goal is not merely for students to learn to spot the difficult issues, but also for them to learn that the difficulties must be resolved in a socially and politically responsible manner. For this reason, the case law method is neither rigorous nor formal. It is an impressionistic attempt to integrate statutory provisions, case law, policy considerations, jurisprudential theories, and notions of fairness and justice. What counts is what works, what convinces the socially and politically concerned listener.

The beauty—and the limitation—of American legal education is that it does so much with the rather limited resource of the appellate court opinion. Probably more than any other system of legal education, it encourages and develops the skill at drawing fine distinctions between the facts of similar cases and turning those distinctions into convincing legal arguments. It also teaches students not only to spot issues—to create them, really—but, at least to some extent, to advocate and achieve change. The case method can expand a student's imagination and creative potential in a way that may best be described as psychedelic. Of course, by concentrating on these skills very much to the exclusion of others, American law students often fail to achieve technical proficiency at manipulating code provisions and rarely gain a comprehensive overview of the relationship between the diverse fields of the law.

American law schools aspire to reorganize the past and prepare the future. The understanding of the law implicit in such a system is that the judge, the lawyer, and the individual litigant each has a role to play not only in vindicating, but in fact in creating individual rights. It is a vision of decentralized decision making, of a state in which every individual has direct access to a rule maker. It is the conception of the courtroom as a forum for democracy.

Of Legal Education and Cultural Projects

The diversity of meaning articulated in the various languages and systems of legal education suggests that every cultural tradition is distinct. Each pursues a particular goal, which it might be useful here to call a *cultural project*. The project is present in the language that is spoken, in the method of legal education, in the manner in which bread is baked—in short, in every aspect of life in a particular tradition.

Everyone who has lived abroad is aware of this. Yet, because it smacks of stereotyping, it seems slightly immoral to recognize it. One of the reasons stereotyping is such a serious sin is that the admission of global distinction may suggest grounds for prejudice and discrimination. For this reason, comparativists of all kinds usually attempt to demonstrate that, contrary to appearances, everything is really the same everywhere. Whatever the reason, little attention has been paid to the particularities of cultural projects. But the lesson of Babel is difficult to grasp until an effort is made to understand the peculiarities—and the potential contributions—of each of the various cultural traditions. What follows is a preliminary and subjective speculation about how language is related to the law in the three cultural traditions whose methods of legal education were examined above.

One particular feature of the German language is the manner in which abstraction is generated. It is part of the genius of the language that abstraction never loses touch with the concrete. In German, abstractions are living metaphors. They almost universally consist of two or more easily recognizable elementary words that have been yoked together. The basic, concrete meanings are generally active and present. The word *aufheben* is a good example. It consists of a prepositional prefix (*auf = up*) and a basic verb (*heben = to lift*). Its primary meaning is simply *to lift* or *to pick up* (to pick up a pencil from the floor) and the word is used in daily conversation in that sense. When used more abstractly, as is also common, the verb gains two virtually contradictory meanings. It can mean *to preserve* (to put something away in order to save it) as well as *to cancel* or *to set aside* (to abrogate or repeal a statutory restriction). Hegel employed the word philosophically to incorporate all of these meanings at once. To him it signified the process of transcending a stage of development by preserving it at a higher level.

The poetic and philosophical quality of the German language derives to a considerable extent from this constant resonance of the concrete in the abstract. For example, Hegel and Heidegger repeatedly interrogated the individual elements of composite words to discern their contribution to the resulting abstract concept. Both used the hyphen as the surgical tool for their investigation. Hegel, for example, on the last page of the *Phenomenology*, discovered in *Er-Innerung* (remembrance/internalization) not only an indication of Spirit's reimmersion into itself, but also the suggestion that history is the result of Spirit's own internal development. Heidegger transposed the technique mythopoeically to classical Greek, interpreting *Existenz* (existence) from the perspective of *Ek-sistenz* (to cause to stand and be exposed to), and *aletheia* (truth) as *a-letheia* (recovered from forgetfulness). Thus, one of the German language's central preoccupations is to assure that the individual element has been carefully and meaningfully integrated into the whole. Even basic words, when properly arranged with other words, gain metaphysical significance. The implication is that the individual not only gains meaning through, but to a large extent is identified with, its role in the complex whole.

Of course, this is not to say that this feature is unique to the German language. English, for example, occasionally employs the technique as well (*overcome, headhunter*), though English characteristically distinguishes between abstractions, which have Latin roots, and words for the concrete, which are derived from Anglo-Saxon. (Of course, *trans-late* too is a composite, both to those who know Latin and to English speakers who are aware of other *trans-* words (*transgress*) and other *-late* words (*elated*), but the elements are much less apparent than they are in the corresponding German compounds.) Moreover, the generation of abstraction is only one of the German language's central linguistic features. Another peculiarity, for example, is the delay of the verb until the end of the sentence, which requires a discipline in speaker and listener and an ability to anticipate and postpone gratification. Only after these and other elements have been illuminated can the nature of the German project become entirely clear.

This preoccupation with the role of the part in the whole, though only one of its elements, is constitutive of the German cultural project as well. The individual, though of course respected in its own right, is largely identified by its particular role in the community. It is a trait of Germanic languages, shared to some extent by English, that common proper names suggest the identification of the individual with its social role—*Schmidt* (smith), *Müller* (miller), *Wagner* (wainwright), *Krämer* (shopkeeper), *Bauer* (peasant farmer). The intensity of the German concern with these issues is what makes it so difficult to translate a sentence such as *Unserem Packmeister sind . . . Bedenken gekommen*. The suggestion of expertise implicit in the notion of the *Packmeister* or master packer emphasizes the importance of the development of a socially relevant skill to the identity of the individual. Moreover, by referring to the *Packmeister* as *unser* (our), the shipping firm both confirmed that the packer was in its employ and suggested that the master packer is a cultural resource, the polity's master packer, a person specially skilled in the craft and therefore deserving of job security and social insurance, a craftsperson of whom the entire nation might be proud. Furthermore, as the sentence suggests, master packers themselves are, in the end, only conduits for the tradition. The second thoughts arose from the practice of the craft over centuries, and merely came to rest in the person of the master packer. And, of course, the master packers' awareness of their role in the tradition redefines in turn how they conceive of themselves.

At the same time, there can be little doubt that the thoroughness with which the German project is organized generates a highly energized tension with individual rights and a heightened concern for the individual. That concern—which is also implicit in the Hegelian and Heideggerian hyphen—helps explain the focus in German philosophy on the status and nature of human freedom.

The German focus on the role of the part in the whole, though only one of its contradictory moments, is of great consequence to German legal education. The focus suggests the importance to the individual of a reliable social division of labor, both because of the security it affords and the opportunity it provides for the cultivation of craft and the mastery of technique. German legal education is simply a further expression of the same understanding. One of the hallmarks of a stable division of labor is a careful delimitation of the various social roles. The legislature makes the laws, while the lawyer and judge assure technical proficiency in their application. It seems, therefore, that central features of German legal education run parallel to the fundaments of the German language.

One of the exquisite qualities of spoken and written French lies in the distinction and alternation between the indicative and subjunctive moods of its verbs. Verbs in the indicative mood often end with syllables pronounced as open (despite the orthography), while those of the subjunctive are usually and emphatically closed (*vient/vienne*). The French subjunctive appears chiefly in subordinate clauses, generally after principal verbs expressing personal feeling, such as desire, joy, and sadness. Thus, as a simple proposition, *she is coming* (*elle vient*) is in the indicative, but is placed in French in the subjunctive following statements such as *I wish that . . .* (*je veux qu'elle vienne*). The subjunctive may also appear in relative clauses that indirectly express similar emotions, and even in principal clauses, namely in a few fixed idioms expressing a great personal commitment or excitement that coincides with a socially recognized injunction (*Vive la France! Sauve qui peut!* Run for your life!). Much of the concern in teaching French and the joy in learning it revolves around the mastery of the forms and distinctions involved in the use of the subjunctive. The poetic quality of the French language also derives in part from the interplay between the two moods. (*Vienne la nuit sonne l'heure/Les jours s'en vont je demeure*).

The French indicative describes the objective, the verifiable, the repeatable. The subjunctive invokes the subjective, the personal, the desired. To delimit the appropriate sphere for the pursuit of individual desire within the structure of social cohesion is the central concern. The opposition between the two moods legitimates a role for individual exuberance within the framework of social convention. From this perspective, the French project attempts to maintain sufficient room for the expression of individuality while maintaining a cohesive centralized order. Once again, legal education seems to be structured like the language, for this of course is also the object of the *plan*. The *plan* both recognizes the tension that may result from the assertion of individual interest and demonstrates the necessity of the law as the structure for social organization.

Of course, the alternation between indicative and subjunctive is not unique to French—in fact it is shared with the other Romance languages. Moreover, French has other characteristic features, such as the double negative (*ne . . . pas*, *ne . . .rien*), that must be explored before the French project can be thoroughly understood.

It would be useful to include here a short discussion of American English and of the American cultural project. A sense of the particularity of American English, however, is largely barred to me. One of the most direct lessons of the story of Babel, as Paul de Man has noted, is that the most alienated and uncomprehending relationship one can have with a language is usually the one native speakers have with their own. However, those I have consulted who speak English as a foreign language usually tend to note the same peculiarities. Spelling does not coincide with pronunciation (tough/though/through, read/read). Prepositions are employed in an apparently idiosyncratic manner (the alarm went *off*, to study *under*). Word formation often ignores etymology (hamburger/cheeseburger) (sandwich/fishwich). There are some rules that few master (the distinction between *that* and *which*, the proper use of the comma), other rules that tend to be honored chiefly in their breach (the prohibitions against the split infinitive and against ending a phrase with a preposition), elaborate rules that are seldom used (much about the various past tenses), and vast stretches with no enunciated rule and nothing to assist the foreigner who has not yet acquired a sense of the underlying enterprise. The stated rules seem to be of little importance, while the effective rules seem to be unstatable. In fact, idiomatic expressions are so prevalent that it is possible to master all the rules and still not speak the language fluently. The consensus is that it is a language of infinite imagination but little discipline, a restless language in constant innovation. ("We got the repeat," San Francisco 49ers running back

Roger Craig announced to the press after his team won the Super Bowl for the second year in a row. "now we want the *three*-peat.")

Needless to say, there is much in common here with American legal education, especially its impromptu and unsystematic character, the joy with which principles and theories are created, employed, and forgotten. The pragmatic American mode of politics, the role of individual initiative, and all the rest seem intimately bound up in all of this. But it can only be seen clearly by someone who takes it up from the perspective of another tradition. (Indeed, what I suggest above about the particular understanding implicit in American legal education is not my own insight but comes rather from Michel Pêcheux, who mentioned the idea in conversation shortly before his death.).

One lesson is that each system of legal education, like the language in which it is formulated, constitutes a part of a larger cultural project and represents a particular articulation of meaning. The even more far-reaching lesson from the story of Babel is that diversity deserves to be recognized, preserved, cultivated, and developed. The political and theoretical implications of this lesson are perhaps best observed from the point of view of postmodernity.

First, the story of Babel seems to confirm much of what postmodernity has to say about the implication of madness in understanding. The idea is that understanding is fundamentally constituted by the desire to escape from chaos. (The idea is discussed by William Corlett in *Community without Unity* (1989).) In the hope of domesticating chaos, understanding constructs polar oppositions and forces every element of existence to adhere to one or the other of two poles—male and female, white and black, right and left, sick and healthy, individual and collectivity. Understanding thus not only bears the trace of fear in its constitution, but is itself a kind of derangement.

This, in fact, is what the story of Babel is all about. The confusion of language resulted directly from the seemingly unavoidable tendency to think in terms of polar opposition. Certainly each of the cultural projects examined here, including their systems of legal education and their languages, attempt to conquer chaos in this manner. German legal education emphasizes the obedience of the judge to the will of the legislature in a way that reflects the concerns of the German cultural project about the importance of integrating the individual into the collectivity. French legal education emphasizes that the opposition between individual desire and legal order is to be expounded by binary opposition, and thereby mirrors the oppositions found in its language between subjunctive and indicative, subjective and objective, individual and collective. American legal education emphasizes the conflicting demands of judicial creativity and precedent—another version of the tension between individual and collectivity, which parallels the opposition in American English between idiomatic expressions and traditional rules.

Each cultural project and each system of legal education seems to attempt to escape from chaos by constructing its own set of polar oppositions, oppositions that can be ordered on many axes, including the relationship between individual and collectivity. The deconstructionists are justly worried about the power of these oppositions and are correct in suggesting that we try to defuse them. In this sense, *HaShem* was the original deconstructionist, for that was also *HaShem*'s concern. What *HaShem* noticed upon descending to Babel was that humankind recoiled in fright from the unknown, and that it was quick to try to protect itself by articulating meaning in terms of oppositions—Heaven and earth, life and death, unity and dispersion, naming and chaos. *HaShem* thereupon confused language and sent humankind out into the unknown that it most feared. By creating a multitude of languages, *HaShem* hoped to melt the dichotomies into diversity and to assist humanity in overcoming its reduction of meaning.

In sum, the understanding present in any one language or cultural project is plagued with the structure of opposition that deconstruction has taught us to notice and reject. Each of these understandings is therefore not only particular and limited, but in fact suffused with fear and madness, or rather constitutes one kind of madness in order to escape from another. That is why translation can be not only frustrating but literally maddening: it tends to lead the translator beyond the habitual bulwarks against insanity. Hölderlin's translations of Sophocles were some of the last lines he composed before he plunged into almost forty years of crazed silence.

A second concern of postmodernism is the problem of the unitary origin. As I understand it, one of the goals of postmodern politics is to demonstrate the importance of differential plurality and to create a society that takes advantage of the potential synergism of all types of difference. In this perspective, the postmodern philosophies of difference attempt to demonstrate that differences cannot be confined within an original unity or totality in which they might, in the end, be reconciled. Difference, we are told, is *anoriginal*. (The term is from Andrew Benjamin, who summarizes the argument in *Translation and the Nature of Philosophy* (1989).) The danger that postmodernity thereby seeks to avoid is the single totalizing structure that may be imposed upon, and thereby destroy, diversity.

Yet not all stories of origins have this problem. Accounts of origins are problematic only when they imply that it would be beneficial to reduce diversity to unity or to return to an original golden age. An example is the extraordinarily conservative and nostalgically romantic myth of return that inhabits Marx's thought and that seems to have led Heidegger to Nazism. But there is not the least suggestion in the story of Babel that humanity would be better off returning to the Noachian condition. Moreover, as the story makes clear, there was never any meaningful unity at the origin. The original language must have teemed with an incredible multitude of patterns and ideas. Otherwise its confusion could never have produced ten thousand human languages. What led to calamity was rather the human insistence on reducing that incredible wealth to one set of simple oppositions. Furthermore, it is clear that there is no way, starting from the natural languages that survive today, to piece together the original language. Language is and will remain for us always already disarticulated into difference. Any unity that might once have existed can never be resynthesized. Since the remaining languages can never be reduced to a single meaning, all that results from piecing them together is the understanding of how each represents the kind of intentionality that Walter Benjamin referred to as pure language (*die reine Sprache*). Thus, the story of Babel is not so much the story of an origin as the indication of a trace.

One last theoretical issue raised by the story of Babel concerns the status of diversity. This is a problem that is never really resolved in the garden variety philosophies of difference. These theories attempt to demonstrate the plausibility of a way of thinking that conceives of difference as primary. But the mere existence—or even the primacy—of difference cannot alone convince us that difference is good. Instead of a normative argument demonstrating the value of diversity, the philosophies of difference offer only a clutter of difference, what might better be called *indifference*. Though these philosophies may be read to imply that we should respect those who hold views that differ from our own, there is nothing in them to encourage us to devote our energy to examining with care articulations of meaning that we initially find unconvincing or strange. Theirs is a position at which one might arrive just as easily by indolence as by conviction.

It is in this sense that the story of Babel demonstrates how much more there is to diversity than the philosophers of difference have perceived. For the message of the story is not simply that difference is an unavoidable fact of life. It is rather that diversity expands the limits of intelligibility. The reason is as follows. Language does not simply take the world as it is, but rather constitutes intelligibility as it communicates. There is no intelligibility outside of language. This thought, which Heidegger took from Stefan George—No thing can be where the word is wanting (*Kein ding sei wo das wort gebricht*)—suggests that every language, and every tradition, is entitled to profound respect. However limited and deranged, the understandings in the surviving natural languages are the sum total of intelligibility. If each language constitutes a different fragment, then each is a treasure. We are the shepherds and not the masters of language.

The potential wealth of diversity is at least threefold. First, since the articulations of meaning present in the particular languages and traditions are each limited, each will find much that is evidently and practically useful in the other cultural projects. And this is true whether or not there was ever a single original language of which the surviving languages may be fragments. Second, the interplay between diverse traditions offers one of the few opportunities for the creation of truly new ideas, ideas that arise outside the scope of any one tradition's particular experience. Finally, diversity is a prerequisite to serious self-reflection. Without the existence of diverse traditions, it would become literally impossible to assess the peculiar characteristics of any particular understanding. Human beings who know only one language have little alternative but to consider the articulation of meaning within that language to be absolute. There is little they can do to step outside that understanding in order to relativize it. The articulation of meaning in their language will permeate everything they think or write and render it difficult to avoid totalizing reductionism. Should they become aware that other and different perspectives exist, they are of course capable of tolerance. But wisdom is not simply tolerance, never merely a recognition *of* diversity, no matter how generous and humanitarian. Wisdom rather is a vision *from* diversity, an understanding constituted in fragmentation. The multiplicity of languages is its irreducible condition. It is a blessing and not a curse.

Of Blessings

Blessings are opportunities. They are no less so because their realization requires effort and often suffering. The study of a foreign language and the initiation into a foreign culture can be intriguing and delightful, but they also involve mindless memorization, incessant repetition, and a painful reorientation of thought. When pursued seriously, they may result in a throbbing loneliness, the constant companion of foreigners who isolate themselves from their compatriots long enough to master the essentials of a foreign language. And apprenticeship in a foreign legal system can be even more disorienting and disturbing than learning the foreign language in the first place.

No one who succeeds at the enterprise does so without a good reason. Some have had their lives shattered in their homelands, been scattered into exile, and have been subjected involuntarily to the destructive force of diversity. They are thankful for the hospitality their hosts show them, but equally frustrated by the incomprehension they encounter. They survive the experience chiefly by clinging to the possibility of return. For others, diversity is a constant reminder of incompleteness, of the wound left in the soul by the dismemberment that occurred at Babel. Their awareness of the impoverished character of any single articulation of understanding requires them to reach out to embrace foreign cultures. But even for them, diversity is no more than a scar over a wound that can never heal.

There is no perspective from which the disastrous consequences of the confusion of language can be denied. But a blessing is not distinguished from a curse by the intensity of pain thereby avoided or by the quality of comfort it affords. What makes of Babel a blessing is that it offers, though at terrible cost, the otherwise unavailable challenge of possibility.

(I am deeply indebted to Susan Bender, Rabbi David Bleich, David Carlson, Mary Coombs, Michael Fischl, Christoph Grigoleit, Pat Gudridge, Arthur Jacobson, Dennis Patterson, Robert Rosen, Simon Schneebalg, Nicolo Trocker, Elisabeth Weber, and Steven Winter. And thanks to Nora de la Garza for helping me find the books.)

Part III
Postmodernism and the Subject

[6]

Papers

The Problem of the Subject

Pierre Schlag*

* Professor of Law, The University of Colorado. This Article was presented at the University of Toronto legal theory workshop. I am grateful to the participants for their helpful comments. In addition, I wish to thank Jamie Boyle, Tom Grey, Debbie Maranville, Bob Nagel, Jeremy Paul, Jack Schlegel, Steven Smith, Mark Tushnet, and Steven Winter for their comments.

This Article is part of a larger enterprise—an attempt to understand the character and status of contemporary normative legal thought. For other installments, see Schlag, *Normativity and the Politics of Form*, 139 U. PA. L. REV. 801 (1991); Schlag, *Normative and Nowhere to Go*, 43 STAN. L. REV. 167 (1990); Schlag, *"Le Hors de Texte, C'est Moi": The Politics of Form and the Domestication of Deconstruction*, 11 CARDOZO L. REV. 1631 (1990).

Texas Law Review Vol. 69:1627, 1991

"Subjectivity was not waiting for philosophers . . . . They constructed, created it, and in more than one way. And what they have done must perhaps be undone."

—Maurice Merleau-Ponty[1]

Sometimes it seems as if there is only one story in American legal thought and only one problem. The story is the story of formalism and the problem is the problem of the subject. The story of formalism is that it never deals with the problem of the subject. The problem of the subject is that it's never been part of the story.

* * *

Until now.

Now, the problem of the subject is fast becoming part of the story. But in the beginning it was not so. For instance, in the celebrated case of *McCulloch v. Maryland*,[2] Chief Justice Marshall wrote, "[W]e must never forget that it is *a constitution* we are expounding."[3] In that sentence, Marshall emphasized the terms "*a constitution*" as the locus of significance. By contrast, the "we" who do the expounding, the "we" who must "never forget" were relegated to relative unimportance.

Marshall's objectivist emphasis on the constitution and his corresponding forgetting of the subject, the "we," is neither odd nor surprising to us. On the contrary, this forgetting of the subject is an echo of the foundational rhetoric of *Marbury v. Madison*[4] itself. Indeed, it was precisely the "we" who do the expounding that Chief Justice Marshall made a point of forgetting (over and over again) as he crafted his magnificent, captivating, perfectly circular arguments in *Marbury*.[5]

In his systematic and foundational forgetting, Marshall established an extremely important precedent for American legal thought. This for-

1. M. MERLEAU-PONTY, *Everywhere and Nowhere*, in SIGNS 153 (1964).
2. 17 U.S. (4 Wheat.) 316 (1819).
3. *Id.* at 407 (emphasis in original).
4. 5 U.S. (1 Cranch) 137 (1803).
5. For discussion of the circularity of Marshall's arguments, see Van Alstyne, *A Critical Guide to* Marbury v. Madison, 1969 DUKE L.J. 1.

getting of the "we" who do the "expounding," this bracketing of the "I"—in short, this eclipse of the problem of the subject—became a vital, pervasive, constitutive characteristic of American legal thought. Indeed, American legal thought has been conceptually, rhetorically, and socially constituted to avoid confronting the question of who or what thinks or produces law.

In a nutshell, then, this is the problem of the subject. Notice that it has already become at least two problems. One problem is that we are missing any convincing accounts of who or what it is that thinks or produces law. Another problem is that apparently we and our legal rhetoric have been constituted to avoid inquiry into this question of who or what produces law.[6] Hence, rather than sharing a rich matrix of intellectual or cultural understandings that would help us inquire into the character of the subject, we share a rich matrix of intellectual and cultural understandings that enables us to avoid inquiry into the character of the subject (over and over again).[7]

6. If the problem of the subject already manifests a dual structure, by the end of this Article the problem will have become thoroughly pluralized. Here's one way of stating the problem: Just who or what is it that thinks about or produces law? Here's another way: What must be true or potentially true about the character of the agents that construct law, in order for law to be a legitimate or viable enterprise? Here's yet another way to pose the question: What conception of subject-object relations is implicit in the rhetorical and social forces that are constructing us?

Now, in one sense, these questions are somewhat startling. They are startling, I think, because the problem of the subject has been kept off the stage of legal thought for a very long time. We are simply not accustomed to asking these kinds of questions, much less answering them.

7. Nonetheless, some of us have begun to explore, in different idioms, the various ways in which the legal and social formation of subjects contributes to the production of law and legal thought. *See* Boyle, *Is Subjectivity Possible? The Postmodern Subject in Legal Theory*, 62 U. COLO. L. REV. 489 (1991); Coombe, *Room for Manoeuver: Toward a Theory of Practice in Critical Legal Studies*, 14 LAW & SOC. INQUIRY 69 (1989); Coombe, *"Same as It Ever Was": Rethinking the Politics of Legal Interpretation*, 34 MCGILL L.J. 603 (1989); Cornell, *Institutionalization of Meaning, Recollective Imagination and the Potential for Transformative Legal Interpretation*, 136 U. PA. L. REV. 1135 (1988); Minow, *Identities*, 3 YALE J.L. & HUMANITIES 97 (1991); Schlag, *Fish v. Zapp: The Case of the Relatively Autonomous Self*, 76 GEO. L.J. 37 (1987) [hereinafter *Fish v. Zapp*]; Schlag, *Missing Pieces: A Cognitive Approach to Law*, 67 TEXAS L. REV. 1195 (1989) [hereinafter *Missing Pieces*]; Schlag, *"Le Hors de Texte, C'est Moi": The Politics of Form and the Domestication of Deconstruction*, 11 CARDOZO L. REV. 1631 (1990) [hereinafter *"Le Hors de Texte"*]; Schlag, *Normative and Nowhere to Go*, 43 STAN. L. REV. 167 (1990); Schlag, *Normativity and the Politics of Form*, 139 U. PA. L. REV. 801 (1991) [hereinafter *Politics of Form*]; Winter, Bull Durham *and the Uses of Theory*, 42 STAN. L. REV. 639 (1990) [hereinafter *Bull Durham*]; Winter, *Indeterminacy and Incommensurability in Constitutional Law*, 78 CALIF. L. REV. 1441 (1990) [hereinafter *Indeterminacy*]; Winter, *Contingency and Community in Normative Practice*, 139 U. PA. L. REV. 963 (1991) [hereinafter *Contingency and Community*].

My sense is that much of these recent efforts to inquire into the problem of the subject are at once influenced by and a reaction to earlier treatments of the legal subject in critical legal thought. This earlier work includes D. KENNEDY, LEGAL EDUCATION AND THE REPRODUCTION OF HIERARCHY: A POLEMIC AGAINST THE SYSTEM (1984); R. UNGER, PASSION: AN ESSAY ON PERSONALITY (1984); Heller, *Structuralism and Critique*, 36 STAN. L. REV. 127 (1984); Kennedy, *The Structure of Blackstone's Commentaries*, 28 BUFFALO L. REV. 205 (1979) [hereinafter *Blackstone's Commentaries*]; Kennedy, *The Political Significance of the Structure of the Law School Curriculum*,

Texas Law Review Vol. 69:1627, 1991

So far I've stated the problem in epistemic terms: "we are missing convincing accounts of . . .". But the problem could be posed in political terms: how can the agencies of social action or social transformation be activated? It could be posed in cultural terms: what is the current state of our capacities for constructing or reproducing our social world? These are very sweeping ways of asking about the problem of the subject. And it is doubtful that many legal thinkers would want to approach the problem on such a sweeping scale.

Nonetheless, in more concrete, local ways, the problem of the subject is fast emerging on the scene of contemporary American legal thought as the locus of inquiry for a variety of jurisprudential approaches. In this Article, my aim is to try to reveal the various ways in which the problem of the subject arises within several important contemporary modes of legal thought including rule-of-law, critical legal studies (cls), neopragmatism, and cultural conservatism. Because these various modes of legal thought are differently situated and advance different intellectual agendas, the problem of the subject arises in different ways for each of them.

It is important to attend carefully to these differences, but it is also important not to overdo it. In our postmodern context, so marked by the celebration of difference and the exaltation of pluralism, it is unlikely that differences in the appearance of the problem of the subject will be missed. It may well be the recognition of sameness that has become the more difficult enterprise. Moreover, because so many of us, as legal thinkers, are engaged in disagreements whose very sense and meaningfulness depend upon distinguishing rule-of-law from cls from neopragmatism from cultural conservatism from . . .,[8] it may be very difficult for us to appreciate the ways in which all these ostensibly opposed jurisprudential modes nonetheless share and reproduce a certain sameness.

And yet they do. As will be seen, there is *a recurring sameness to the ways in which the problem of the subject arises within each of these modes of contemporary legal thought.* That is because, in their very rhet-

14 SETON HALL L. REV. 1 (1983); Peller, *The Metaphysics of American Law*, 73 CALIF. L. REV. 1151 (1985).

Much of the recent work is also (consciously or not) influenced by and a reaction to the work of Stanley Fish who rarely mentions the subject or the self by name, yet in a sense speaks of little else. S. FISH, DOING WHAT COMES NATURALLY: CHANGE, RHETORIC, AND THE PRACTICE OF THEORY IN LITERARY AND LEGAL STUDIES (1989) [hereinafter DOING WHAT COMES NATURALLY]. *See* Lippucci, *Surprised by Fish*, 63 U. COLO. L. REV. (forthcoming 1991); Schlag, *Fish v. Zapp*, *supra*.

8. . . . all the other modes of thought that comprise the contemporary jurisprudential field. For a helpful articulation of the various kinds of legal thought that currently comprise the jurisprudential landscape, see Radin & Michelman, *Pragmatist and Poststructuralist Critical Legal Practice*, 139 U. PA. L. REV. 1019 (1991).

The Problem of the Subject

oric, all of these modes of contemporary legal thought establish, depend upon, and eclipse a quintessentially liberal individual subject—what I have elsewhere called the relatively autonomous self or the relatively autonomous subject.[9] As this subject emerges from its eclipsed condition, we will see that it emerges as a problem for each of these modes of contemporary legal thought.

The enterprise here is to reveal and articulate the problem of the subject as a problem for rule of law, cls, neopragmatism, and cultural conservatism. It is to reveal this problem in all its vitality and import for each of the modes of legal thought discussed—to reveal it as a problem for each of them.[10] The effort here is to retrieve a whole set of critical inquiries from their presently concealed condition so that we might begin to think about them.

Now, of course, since "problems" are generally viewed negatively in our (legal) culture, what follows could easily be understood as a kind of "critique" in the nontechnical sense of "criticism" or "argument against" the various modes of legal thought. To the extent possible, I would like to caution against such a reading. The conclusion to be drawn here should not be that these modes of thought are wrong, flawed, bad, incorrect, mistaken, intellectually weak, or anything of the sort.[11] Rather, I hope that the conclusion will be that each of these modes of thought has a serious problem, a recursive problem, and that it is in some senses the same problem—the problem of the subject.

This Article is thus organized around some recognizable descriptions of the various modes of contemporary legal thought—rule of law, cls, neopragmatism, and cultural conservatism. In each section, I describe these modes of thought and trace the ways in which the problem of the subject becomes a problem for them. As you might guess, this effort is not just a completely disinterested, purely altruistic attempt on my part to give various schools of thought something to think about. I have an agenda—and I will explain that agenda in the last section, when

9. Schlag, *Fish v. Zapp*, *supra* note 7, at 42-50; Schlag, *"Le Hors de Texte," supra* note 7, at 1667-73.

Steven Winter has helpfully elaborated some of the intellectual and political implications of the recursive reinscription of this (pervasive) liberal subject. Winter, *Indeterminacy*, *supra* note 7, at 1444-46. And now, in his contribution to this symposium, Jack Balkin joins us as well in recognizing the importance of the social construction of this relatively autonomous subject. Balkin, *The Promise of Legal Semiotics*, 69 TEXAS L. REV. 1831 (1991); *See also* Balkin, *Ideology as Constraint* (Book Review), 43 STAN. L. REV. 1133 (1991) (reviewing A. ALTMAN, CRITICAL LEGAL STUDIES: A LIBERAL CRITIQUE (1990)).

10. My sense is that the problem of the subject extends well beyond the particular modes of contemporary legal thought discussed in this Article.

11. It is not that such conclusions would themselves be "wrong" or the like. Rather, it is that such conclusions would be askew to the enterprise pursued here.

Texas Law Review Vol. 69:1627, 1991

the problem of the subject returns (explicitly) to trouble my own enterprise.

But before we turn to each of these modes of thought, we must return to the primal scene—Langdellian jurisprudence.

I. A Brief Survey of the Langdellian Jurisdiction

The very first article written by Christopher Columbus Langdell in Issue 1 of the Harvard Law Review begins with this sentence:

> Equity jurisdiction is a branch of the law of remedies; and as it affects, or is affected by, nearly the whole of that law, *it is impossible to obtain an intelligent view of it as whole without first taking a brief view* of the law of remedies as a whole. Moreover, as all remedies are founded upon rights, and have for their objects the enforcement and protection of rights, *it is impossible to obtain an intelligent view* of remedies as a whole, without first considering the rights upon which they are founded.[12]

The same article concludes with these sentences:

> *So it seems* that any wrongful extinguishment by the obligee of an obligation which is itself the subject of an equitable obligation, though it is a breach of the equitable obligation is also a tort to the equitable obligee. *So it seems* that the alienation by its owner of any right which is the subject of an equitable obligation, in disregard of such obligation is a tort to the equitable obligee.[13]

Now, between what the Introduction proclaims as necessary for "*obtaining an intelligent view*" of the matter and what the Conclusion presents as a series of declarative *So it seems*'s, there is never once any explicit articulation, much less discussion, of who it is that will be obtaining the intelligent view or by what mode of thought or reflection he will be enabled to do it.

In Langdell's universe, things happen, thoughts get thought, and the passive voice gets used a lot: "For example, a debtor becomes personally bound to his creditor for the payment of the debt . . . ."[14] It is as if Langdell had not only read, but decided to simulate the early Stanley Fish: Langdell's work reads like law's immaculate conception. When it is law that is produced, the "I" is kept out of sight (and out of mind). Langdell's law poses as the discourse without an individual subject.[15]

And even when Langdell is confronted with those dicey transitions

12. Langdell, *A Brief Survey of Equity Jurisdiction*, 1 HARV. L. REV. 55 (1887) (emphasis added).

13. *Id.* at 72 (emphasis added).

14. *Id.* at 68.

15. Before there were "interpretive communities" there was "Equity." (Puns retracted).

The Problem of the Subject

where it seems as if the individual subject (Langdell himself) will have to make an appearance, if only in the indicative mode to decide where the text should go next, the individual subject is still kept hidden. Consider, for instance, this close call: "Having thus treated with sufficient fulness of equitable rights, *it remains to speak* briefly of the violation of such rights."[16] Here, with a finesse Stanley Fish could admire, Langdell manages at once to invoke and yet deny the presence of the "I." The individual subject (if there is one) is off center stage—out of sight.

For Langdell this eclipse, this exclusion of the individual subject is perfectly natural. The main event featured on center stage has little to do with the individual subject. On the contrary, occupying the center stage of Langdellian jurisprudence there is the intrinsic, essential order of law—the order of law that is busy being discovered by true science.

> We have also constantly inculcated the idea the library is the proper workshop of professors and students alike; that it is to us all that the laboratories of the university are to the chemists and physicists, the museum of natural history to the zoologists, the botanical garden to the botanists.[17]

All of this is very tidy. But where's the subject?

This is an interesting question—rendered even more so when one considers that Langdell was probably not a precocious antihumanist seeking to decenter the individual subject. We know Langdell. We've worked with Langdell. He's no Stanley Fish. On the contrary, Christopher understood perfectly well that he was an individual subject.[18] And he could use the "I" indicatively and ontologically as well as the rest of us. Indeed, the preface to *The First Edition of A Selection of Cases on the Law of Contracts*[19] is peppered with Christopher's use of the first person singular. Hence Chris begins the preface, "*I* cannot better explain the design of this volume . . . ."[20] Later he tells us, "*I* was called upon to consider directly the subject of teaching . . . ."[21] And so on. Indeed, whenever Chris addresses a matter of pedagogy in his preface, the "I" is all over the place. And yet, quite mysteriously, as soon as the law makes its appearance in the preface, the "I" vanishes.[22] Chris disappears. Dean Langdell is removed. Even you, the reader, begin to experience a certain

16. *Id.* at 71 (emphasis added).
17. *Harvard Celebration Speeches*, 3 LAW Q. REV. 118, 124 (1887).
18. Not that I want to suggest, mind you, that Stanley Fish doesn't understand this.
19. C. LANGDELL, A SELECTION OF CASES ON THE LAW OF CONTRACTS (1871).
20. *Id.* at v.
21. *Id.*
22. *Id.* at vi.

ego loss. Could it be God?[23] Is it love? No, it's law—law and science: "Law, considered as a science, consists of certain principles or doctrines . . . ."[24]

A. *Look Ma No Subject: The Transcendental Object Does It All*

How is it that law comes to occupy center stage in this way—relegating all individual subjects to the periphery of consciousness? What subject-object relations underwrite this grand and sober drama? One way to begin an understanding of the subject-object relations instanced in Langdell's discourse is to take seriously his nineteenth century science metaphors. Tom Grey does:

> The heart of the theory was the view that law is a science. Langdell believed that through scientific methods, lawyers could derive correct legal judgments from a few fundamental principles and concepts, which it was the task of the scholar-scientist like himself to discover.[25]

This image of the scientist "discovering" principles and concepts can easily be understood as the self-effacement of the individual subject in the presence of a transcendental order of the object—the order of law.[26] According to this representation, law itself comes to occupy the space of the object, leaving the subject to efface himself so that he might "discover" the objective order of law.[27]

Now, much of Langdell's writing is consistent with such a view. We have already witnessed that when he speaks of law, in contrast to pedagogy or something else, Langdell eclipses the individual subject. The "I" is almost invariably relegated to some implicit space off the rhetorical center stage. Langdell does not write, "*I think* the law is . . . ." Rather, his individual subject formation is much more hesitant, much more modest. "So it seems" he writes, leaving the reader to imagine and at the same time discount the individual subject to whom the "So it seems" might seem.

This depersonalization and deprivileging of the individual subject is an accomplishment of the formal style. Within the formal style of law (or diplomacy or etiquette) the space of the individual subject is narrowly

23. Well, sort of, actually. *See* K. BURKE, A GRAMMAR OF MOTIVES 355 (1945) ("For a God term designates the ultimate motivation, or substance, of a Constitutional frame.").

24. C. LANGDELL, *supra* note 19, at vi.

25. Grey, *Langdell's Orthodoxy*, 45 U. PITT. L. REV. 1, 5 (1983).

26. Hence, not only is law a science, as Langdell proclaims, but "all the available materials of that science are contained in printed books." *Harvard Celebration Speeches*, *supra* note 17, at 124.

27. One of the best philosophical expressions of this kind of objectivist aesthetic in contemporary legal thought is found in Moore, *The Interpretive Turn in Modern Theory: A Turn for the Worse?*, 41 STAN. L. REV. 871, 881-87 (1989).

circumscribed precisely because any active contribution of the individual subject could only interfere with (not help maintain) the objective order of meaning. In formal diplomatic negotiations or formal marriage ceremonies, for instance, the opportunities for contributions by the individual subject are severely restricted precisely because at the end of the events there can only be one set of meanings; the event's meanings are already choreographed, already scripted, already pre-ordained. The only thing required of the individual subjects is that they play their parts—in the most self-effacing manner possible. Now, it is in exactly the same sense that the formal tone of the Langdellian discourse enables Langdellian law to continue to provide the self-same, invariant, stabilized meanings—meanings that are *contained in* and can thus be discovered *in* a transcendental order of the object.[28]

To understand Langdellian formalism as a rhetoric of a transcendental order of the object before which the individual subject is effaced and marginalized coincides with some of the salient features we typically associate with legal formalism. If the meaning of the law is located in an object-form (*i.e.*, the doctrines and principles) whose operative meaning requires almost[29] no contribution from any individual subject, then law itself is stable, self-identical, foundationally secure and bounded; it is, in other words, just like an object. Moreover, the severe restriction of the rhetorical space of the subject removes a potential threat to the stability, self-identity, foundational security, and closure of Langdellian formalism. First, because the role of the subject is so weakened, no subject can easily develop or organize itself in sufficient strength to create a strong subject-object conflict. On the contrary, the overwhelming rhetorical domination of the subject by the object at the level of structure translates into the same domination at the level of event, at the level of everyday. The occasions for live subject-object confrontation have thus been delimited. In a second sense, they have also been marginalized. Within Langdellian formalism, the possible remonstrances of a questioning or rebellious subject have already been confined to the margins—very far

28. In Lakoff-Johnson terms, the use of the expression "contained in" is an instance of what they call the container metaphor. Here the use of the metaphor yields its prototypical effect: objectification. We have the objectification of Law (the container) as well as the doctrines and principles (its contents). G. LAKOFF & M. JOHNSON, METAPHORS WE LIVE BY 29-30 (1980) (describing the container metaphor and its implications); Winter, *Bull Durham*, *supra* note 7, at 673-74, 679-82 (showing how Stanley Fish relies upon the container metaphor to make his arguments against "theory"); Winter, *Transcendental Nonsense, Metaphoric Reasoning, and the Cognitive Stakes for Law*, 137 U. PA. L. REV. 1105, 1146-52 (1989) (showing the links between the container metaphor and objectivist epistemology).

29. As we will see, this a very problematic "almost." *See infra* text accompanying notes 112-15.

Texas Law Review Vol. 69:1627, 1991

from the action on center stage. Hence should any deviant individual subject (say, a Felix Cohen or a Duncan Kennedy) attempt to assert himself against this sort of formalism, the rhetorical spaces and paths that might potentially enable and legitimate such self-assertion have already been relocated to the periphery, if not altogether banished. The performative significance of self-assertion by a deviant individual subject is thus already structured to signify that this subject is outside the discourse of formalism and hence outside the discourse of law—beyond the pale.

Any strong self-assertion against the transcendental order of the object is always and already beyond consideration. And certainly for Langdellian formalism, this is exactly as it should be. Indeed, once meaning has been located in the transcendental order of the object, the individual subject emerges only as a potential threat. In more contemporary descriptions, for instance, the individual subject often features as the misguided "activist" judge who derails the law by imposing his "own personal values."[30] Hence, both the rhetoric and the substantive jurisprudential commitments of Langdellian formalism converge to suppress the space of the individual subject. And this suppression in turn coincides with the well-known formalist celebration of aesthetic values that suppress the individual subject:[31] *universality*, *neutrality*, and *objectivity*.[32]

Now, to the extent that Langdellian formalism can be understood as shaped by a transcendental object strategy,[33] can this strategy be secure? For us, it hardly seems possible to secure meaning solely by reference to a transcendental objective order of meaning *unless* we start quite problematically to "subjectify" the object—to project the categories of the subject onto the transcendental order of the object.[34] For us, even if

30. *See, e.g.*, Kress, *Legal Indeterminacy*, 77 CALIF. L. REV. 283, 285 (1989) (observing that the debate about judicial activism rests upon the "presupposition that a judicial decision is . . . open to question, if not downright immoral, if it reflects nonlegal factors such as the judge's personal preferences or political ideology").

31. Beale describes the essential characteristics of law as *generality* (law as a body of general principles, not a collection of special commands), *universality* (law as all extending over all human action), *continuity* (law as temporally uninterrupted), *justice* (conformity to ethical standards of the people), *predictability* (knowledge in advance of decision), *regularity* (restriction of judicial discretion), and *systematicity* (capable of extension by means of principle). 1 J. BEALE, TREATISE ON THE CONFLICT OF LAWS 45-48 (2d ed. 1935).

32. "Objectivity implies that the interpretation can be judged by something other than one's own notion of correctness. It imparts a notion of impersonality." Fiss, *Objectivity and Interpretation*, 34 STAN. L. REV. 739, 744 (1982).

33. I make no claims here that Langdellian formalism *is* in fact grounded in a transcendental object strategy—only that it can be understood this way and that such an understanding coincides with many of the salient features we typically associate with Langdellian formalism.

34. But this argument, by introducing the contributions of various subjects, creates more

The Problem of the Subject

Langdellian formalism reduces the subject to a subordinate, trivial role, the performance of that trivial role remains essential to the "reading" of the object order of law. But was this a problem for the Langdellian formalists? Clearly, they did not deal with this problem as stated in this form. But some of the Langdellian formalists did confront a strikingly similar (if not the same) problem—namely, if law has an objective order, how is it that it can change? What is the agent that leads legal thought to change? Some formalists like Beale argued that professional, judicial, and scholarly opinion enabled "progressive" changes in the law. As Beale put it:

> It is assumed by most authorities that if the judges did not make, but discovered the law, then in the absence of legislation the law must remain what it has always been, and therefore by a process of backward projection, it is argued that unless the courts changed the law the law must have been the same in 1200 that it is today.[35]

Having stated the problem, Beale then made a precocious deconstructive move:

> This line of reasoning, which has seemed convincing to many persons, is quite obviously a mere begging of the question. It is certain that the common law changes; not merely the common law of a particular jurisdiction, but the common-law system in general. This must be true, or the science of law, differing from all other sciences, would be unprogressive. The law of today must of course be better than that of seven centuries ago, more in accordance with the general principles of justice, more in accordance with the needs of the present age, more humane, more flexible, and more complex.[36]

And now the subject appears:

> There are many sources of this change of law, of which, it is true the decisions of the courts are one and in many ways the most important. The law of a given time must be taken to be the body of principles which is accepted by the legal profession, whatever that profession may be; and it will be agreed that the judges have a preponderating share in fixing the opinion of the profession. They are, however, not the sole element in forming this opinion. Legal thinkers who are not judges have at all times played a considerable

problems than it resolves—at least in terms of safeguarding a transcendent order of object law from destabilization.

35. 1 J. Beale, *supra* note 31, at 39.

36. *Id.* at 39. Compare:

> [N]either interpretive communities nor the minds of community members are stable and fixed, but are, rather, moving projects—engines of change—whose work is at the same time assimilative and self-transforming. The conclusion, therefore, is that change is not a problem; and, indeed, to the extent that there is a problem, it would seem to be one of explaining how anything ever remains the same . . . .

S. Fish, Doing What Comes Naturally, *supra* note 7, at 152.

Texas Law Review Vol. 69:1627, 1991

part.[37]

Hence, by explaining change in the common law in terms of changes in the opinions of the legal profession—and in turn explaining these changes by reference to the influence of judges and legal thinkers—Beale refers the entire question of change in the law to the activity of the subject.

Of course, this throws into question the very transcendence of the transcendental objective order of law. If one concedes, as Beale in effect does, that the subject is necessary to read this order, what guarantees that this subject will read the order of the object correctly? It is not clear that this emerged as a serious problem for Langdell, but it has lingered in American legal thought up until the present day, appearing and reappearing under slightly different guises. Indeed, the problem of constraining the subject is reproduced as a series of conventional problematics of

delimiting judicial review
constraining interpretation
confining judicial activism
preventing judicial tyranny
securing objective meaning in adjudication
curtailing judicial discretion
and so on up until the present day.

We can already see something quite ironic about this constant reproduction of the concern with restraining the subject of law: this concern voiced by legal thinkers is almost invariably directed outward towards other subjects and (virtually) never *inward* to the legal thinker. The problem of restraining the subject, then, is almost invariably cast as the problem of restraining someone else (*i.e.*, the judge) not one's self (*i.e.*, not the Langdellian thinker). This irony skims the entire surface of Langdellian formalism. But to appreciate this point, we must back up.

Thus far, the intimation has been that Langdellian discourse is ruthless in its effacement of the individual subject. And in the senses suggested, I think this remains true. But in another sense, this effacement might well be understood as a ruse of discourse. It is quite possible that so long as the Langdellian "I" identifies with or collapses into the role of the legal scientist discovering the law, then such *a duly authorized and well disciplined* "I" is not required to self-efface at all. Instead, this sort of "I"—here you can picture a member of the old boys club—might very

37. 1 J. BEALE, *supra* note 31, at 39-40. It would not be until much later that Beale's notion of a "body of principles which is accepted by the legal profession" would be elaborated by Owen Fiss in his description of the character of "the interpretive community" of legal professionals and their "disciplining rules." *See infra* text accompanying notes 138-48.

well be authorized to project his own self-image onto the order of the object, only to then discover his own self-image as objective truth—all in the name of science.[38] The thing that makes this ruse of discourse a plausible feature of Langdellian formalism is that while the formalists were discursively quite self-effacing, their substantive self-image as scholars was nonetheless quite self-important. Indeed, in his own eyes, the Langdellian legal thinker was an extremely important player in the discovery, articulation, and arrangement of the law. Beale, for instance, was unabashedly self-aggrandizing:

> The teachers of law today have an increasing influence, and one which is comparable in degree with the part played by the judges, in the development of the law; and their power to mould professional opinion is likely to increase in the future more rapidly than that of the judges. The expressed opinions of writers on the law also is powerful in the moulding of professional opinion . . . .[39]

Now, of course, this description seems somewhat at odds with the self-effacing discursive practices of the Langdellian legal thinker described above.[40] Rather than depicting a retiring individual subject awed and humbled in the presence of The Law, Beale seems instead to be describing a kind of imperial legal scholar[41] who rules by representing his own creations as objectified thought-structures.

If we begin to understand Langdellian formalism in this way—as a ruse of discourse—then what previously seemed to be a process of individual self-effacement before The Law becomes, through an unseen and undisclosed moment of self-objectification, a kind of fetishism of the order of the object. Object-forms such as rules, doctrines, and principles

38. Interestingly, the structure of this ruse of discourse describes the structure of the argument that cls and feminist thinkers will make much later to the effect that objectivity, neutrality and universality in law are a mask, a vehicle for the reproduction and maintenance of the partial, subjective world views of white males. As Martha Minow and Elizabeth Spelman note, "[W]e emphasize context in order to expose how apparently neutral and universal rules in effect burden or exclude anyone who does not share the characteristics of privileged, white, Christian, able-bodied, heterosexual, adult men for whom those rules were actually written." Minow & Spelman, *In Context*, 63 S. Cal. L. Rev. 1597, 1601 (1990).

39. 1 J. Beale, *supra* note 31, at 40.

40. Langdell too had his moments of non-self-effacement. Here's one statement where Langdell seems to be just brimming with self or at least self-assurance:

> [T]he number of fundamental legal doctrines is much less than is commonly supposed; the many different guises in which the same doctrine is constantly making its appearance, and the great extent to which legal treatises are a repetition of each other, being the cause of much misapprehension.

C. Langdell, *supra* note 19, at ix.

41. This phrase was coined by Richard Delgado. The kind of intellectual practice that Richard Delgado describes (and criticizes) as imperial legal scholarship is enabled by the rhetoric of Langdellian formalism—and its simultaneous effacement of the individual subject together with the enthronement of the legal scholar as the oracle of The Law. *See* Delgado, *The Imperial Scholar: Reflections on a Review of Civil Rights Literature*, 132 U. Pa. L. Rev. 561, 573 (1984).

are worshipped in the manner of a fetish precisely because the Langdellian thinker never apprehends the moment of self-objectification. Thus, when the rules, doctrines, and principles discovered by the Langdellian thinker emerge already cast in his own image, they seem right and true and good—almost magically so.

If we are to understand Langdellian formalism as a ruse of discourse, its eclipse of the subject operates to cut off not subjectivity, but rather the recognition of the subject's role in creating and maintaining Langdellian law. In Langdellian formalism, the result is a fetishism of rules, doctrines, and principles. This fetishism of rules, doctrines, and principles continues virtually unmodified in rule-of-law thought.[42] In other later forms of legal thought, the same process leads to the fetishism of other artifacts—such as theory, methodology, extra-legal disciplines, extra-legal luminaries, and so on.[43]

For us, to understand these points is to recognize some obvious tensions in the Langdellian world view. For the Langdellian legal thinker, this tension was probably not as acute as we might take it to be—precisely because in Langdellian formalism the contributions of the individual self to self-objectification are not visible. If the Langdellian thinker sees himself as entitled to play an important role, it is because he considers himself a legal scientist—one who knows how to read the law with appropriate deference and respect and without reading too much into it.

The sublimation of the subject into the order of the object and the resulting fetishism is a move that is replayed endlessly in American legal thought. This self-effacement of the subject to the order of the object is precisely what enables legal thinkers to keep believing in their objectified thought-structures as off the shelf, stand-alone, self-sufficient, self-sustaining systems, completely independent of the activity of subjects. This sublimation of the subject is precisely the kind of process targeted by the reification critique of liberal legal thought offered by cls.[44] Ironically, however, the same sort of sublimation process is at work in critical legal thought itself,[45] as well as in neopragmatism[46] and, less surprisingly, in rule-of-law thought[47] and cultural conservatism.[48] Each of these ap-

42. *See infra* text accompanying notes 155-63 (discussing the judiciary's fetish with tests, prongs, and standards).

43. *See infra* text accompanying notes 281-93 (discussing critical legal thought); *infra* text accompanying notes 342-71 (discussing neopragmatism); and *infra* text accompanying notes 376-400 (discussing cultural conservatism).

44. *See infra* notes 197-293.

45. *See infra* text accompanying notes 281-93.

46. *See infra* text accompanying notes 342-71.

47. *See infra* text accompanying notes 146-77.

48. *See infra* text accompanying notes 376-400.

proaches to legal thought leads, in its own way, to its own kind of fetishism.

Now, of course, even if Langdellian formalism is understood as a kind of transcendental object strategy, we can hardly expect it to have broken down specifically along these lines. And yet, the sort of breakdown in transcendental object strategies described above is classic: first, the subject becomes aware that he is on the scene. Second, the subject notices that he is not just a spectator, but is actively contributing to the construction of what was supposed to be a self-sufficient transcendental order of the object.[49] Finally, the subject comes to understand that the order of the object is his own creation.

How are such startling recognitions achieved? Consider what Felix Cohen had to say about a question asked by the New York Court of Appeals—namely, "Where is a corporation?"

> Will future historians deal more charitably with such legal questions as "Where is a corporation?" Nobody has ever seen a corporation. What right have we to believe in corporations if we don't believe in angels. To be sure some of us have seen corporate funds, corporate transactions (just as some of us have seen angelic deeds, angelic countenances, etc.) But this does not give us the right to hypostatize, to "thingify" the corporation, and to assume that it travels about from State to State as mortal men travel.[50]

What Cohen's hypostatization critique does here is revealing in two ways. First, he is showing that the specific presumptions about the character of corporations (such as existence and location in geographical space) are bizarre. At the same time, he is also showing that the hypostatization of the corporation, as well as the corporation itself, are constructions of a subject—in this case the New York Court of Appeals. The problem of the subject arises here precisely because the description offered by reference to the transcendental order of the object is no longer experienced as plausible, as canonically self-evident. Once this is appreciated, everything is then referred back to a subject—a subject whose active beliefs contribute to the creation and maintenance of what was supposed to have been, but clearly is no longer, the transcendental order of the object. Cohen makes the point perfectly clear: "Legal concepts . . . are supernatural entities which do not have a verifiable existence *except to the eyes of faith*."[51]

49. For one recent attempt to produce such a recognition, consider Laurence Tribe's essay on the implications for law of the Heisenberg Uncertainty Principle. Tribe, *The Curvature of Constitutional Space: What Lawyers Can Learn from Modern Physics*, 103 HARV. L. REV. 1 (1989).

50. Cohen, *Transcendental Nonsense and the Functional Approach*, 35 COLUM. L. REV. 809, 811 (1935).

51. *Id.* at 821 (emphasis added).

Texas Law Review Vol. 69:1627, 1991

This recognition that various transcendental orders of the object are constructions of a subject—this demystification of fetishism—will be replayed over and over again in American legal thought as the layers of transcendental objectivism are successively peeled away.[52] For example, first we recognize that the framers' intent is a construction of the subject—and only one way to interpret the Constitution.[53] Then, we come to understand that the Constitution is itself a particular construction created by the subject of the text.[54] Then we come to understand that the text is itself a creation of an interpreting subject.[55] Then we come to understand that the supposition that the subject is doing the interpreting is itself a construction of [—].[56]

B. *Doing Flips With Langdell*

There is, of course, a limit (though not a static or a stable one) as to how far we can go on like this before, like Wittgenstein, we are reduced to wanting to utter silence.[57] In law, our oft-repeated displacement of transcendental objectivism through the recognition that its construction is the action of a subject is usually arrested at some point well before the potential of the deconstructive moves is exhausted.[58] What is striking is that not only defenders of the faith, but also critics of the faith, will seek to arrest the displacement of transcendental objectivism.

The defenders of an orthodox faith[59] will typically resist the very

52. . . . and re-inscribed elsewhere, sub-textually.

53. *See* Dworkin, *The Forum of Principle*, 56 N.Y.U. L. REV. 469, 476-82 (1981).

54. *See* Grey, *supra* note 25, at 1 (questioning "whether the constitutional text should be the sole source of law for purposes of judicial review, or whether judges should supplement the text with an unwritten constitution that is implicit in precedent, practice, and conventional morality").

55. *See generally* S. FISH, IS THERE A TEXT IN THIS CLASS? THE AUTHORITY OF INTERPRETIVE COMMUNITIES (1982) (discussing in various essays how readers, in essence, create what they read).

56. Indeed, many of the critical breakthroughs in American legal thought have come through ever more pronounced, ever more self-decentering recognitions that what previously seemed to be an obvious characteristic of the transcendental order of the object was instead a contribution of the subject. For instance, some of the key moves of the critical works of Felix Cohen, Ronald Coase, and Duncan Kennedy can be understood to fit this pattern. Cohen, *supra* note 50; Coase, *The Problem of Social Cost*, 3 J. LAW & ECON. 1 (1960); Kennedy, *Blackstone's Commentaries*, *supra* note 7.

57. L. WITTGENSTEIN, TRACTATUS LOGICO-PHILOSOPHICUS 151 (1961) ("What we cannot speak about we must pass over in silence."). Or, like Derrida, we are led to write "*sous rature*" in order to better approximate what we are made to want to mean. J. DERRIDA, OF GRAMMATOLOGY 60 (1976).

58. Cls thinkers have noted that legal realists aborted the deconstructive potential of their critiques. *See, e.g.*, Peller, *supra* note 7, at 1219-59 (pointing out various inadequacies in realists' deconstructive moves). I am generalizing the point here and including cls within the group of critics who fail to exhaust the deconstructive potential of their critiques. This is not necessarily meant as criticism. Indeed, I rather doubt that it is possible to do anything else. It is a question of more or less.

59. The expressions "defender" or "critic" of an "orthodox faith" are meant to denote not any

The Problem of the Subject

move that refers the purported objectivity back to a constituting subjectivity. If for the moment we can characterize Langdell, Bork, Fiss, and Dworkin as defenders of an orthodox faith, we can see that each, *at different conceptual points*, refuses to accept critical moves that would refer the order of the object back to the actions of a constituting subject. At some point, each of them holds out for a privileged description of the legal or doctrinal scene—one that will stand independently of the actions of subjects. Now, it is not surprising that those who occupy the role of defenders of an orthodox faith (whatever that orthodox faith may be) would at some point refuse the "referring-back" of the transcendental order of the object to some constituting subject. That is predictable.

What is less predictable and more interesting is that those who occupy the role of critics of an orthodox faith (whatever that orthodox faith may be) do the same thing. They, too, refuse to follow their critique of objectivism to its limits. For instance, the legal realists arrest their critique of formalist objectivism at precisely the point where they as legal subjects can begin to do what they consider to be *real* law: real functionalist law informed by real social science. In fact, it is striking how often critics of an orthodox faith advance their claims as crypto-objectivist pleas for recognizing "what is *really* going on."

This is a telling phrase: it reveals that the very move which allows the critics to refer a transcendental order of the object back to a constituting subject is actually a re-inscription of the order of the object at a different level. We can see this effect at work most clearly in the legal realist's stabilization of the new realm of the object as the realm of social science explanation and functionalist prescription.

This re-inscription of a transcendental order of the object is not the only, or even the most interesting, effect produced by the "referring-back to a subject" critique. After all, if this were the only kind of effect, we could count on increasingly serious—that is to say, increasingly radical—referring-back critiques to reveal any residual objectivism and to displace any remaining fetishism. But there is another kind of interesting and ironic effect produced by the "referring-back" critique: the arrest of this critique always leaves a *stabilized, untroubled, unexamined* subject in place. Critical legal thinkers thus arrest their critique of objectivism, often at precisely the point where they as legal subjects are enabled to recognize that "we must take responsibility for the judgments we make, rather than pretending that those judgments can be made for us by ap-

particular position or stance or closed category of stances within a conventional representation of the field of jurisprudence, but rather two modes of doing legal thinking, or reasoning, or arguing.

plying a determinate and comprehensive theory of justice."[60] What is really striking about this is that, despite the increasing radicalism of the "referring-back to a subject" critiques, including legal realism and critical legal studies, the subject has been left almost entirely untroubled, unquestioned. We thus face the startling possibility that the configuration of the legal subject today is much the same as it was at the zenith of Langdellian formalism.

How did we get here? In a sense, perfectly naturally. Our conception of Langdellian formalism as a kind of transcendental order of the object is, in its outlines, utterly conventional. Not only is it conventional to understand Langdellian formalism as a kind of excessive objectivism, but, more importantly, it is conventional for American legal thinkers to understand and to criticize any undesirable orthodoxy as shaped by an untenable objectivism—even to the point of getting their own critiques demonstrably wrong. For instance, even as astute a critic as Felix Cohen, in his famous criticism of *Tauza v. Susquehana Coal Co.*,[61] mistakenly criticized as "thingification"[62] a formalist instance of the personification, or animism, of the corporation.[63] If fetishism is the perennial risk run by the defenders of the faith, then a fetishistic critique of fetishism is the perennial risk run by the critics of the faith. Indeed, in American legal thought, undesirable orthodoxies (whatever they may be) are typically apprehended, conceptualized, and criticized as thingification, hypostatization, reification, formalization, conceptualization, and so on. In other words, they are typically[64] attacked either for being objectivist or for enacting the wrong sort of objectivism.[65] This is the American (juristic) way.

To some extent, I might be understood as following precisely that same path. Until now. Now, with this recognition another option presents itself. It presents itself as soon as we recognize that for any enterprise as complex and sophisticated as a jurisprudence, objectivism and subjectivism are the same moment organized in two different ways. This means that we don't have to follow the conventional American ju-

60. Singer, *Property and Coercion in Federal Indian Law: The Conflict Between Critical and Complacent Pragmatism*, 63 S. CAL. L. REV. 1821, 1830 (1990). For an elaboration of this elision of the problem of the subject in critical legal thought, see *infra* text accompanying notes 201-13.

61. 220 N.Y. 259, 115 N.E. 915 (1917).

62. *See* Cohen, *supra* note 50, at 815.

63. Steve Winter makes the point that Cohen, in comparing the corporation to a traveler, does not so much thingify as personify the corporation. Winter, *supra* note 28, at 1164.

64. But not invariably.

65. For example, the feminist jurisprudence movement has faulted objectivist legal thought for contributing to "distortion of reality." By this reasoning, objectivist attempts to fashion law using the rationale of "abstract universality" are no more than efforts to transform sexism into a legal code. Scales, *The Emergence of Feminist Jurisprudence: An Essay*, 95 YALE L.J. 1373, 1377 (1986).

ristic way and understand Langdellian formalism as shaped by a transcendent order of the object. Instead, we could try to understand Langdellian formalism as shaped by the presupposition of a certain kind of subject, by a kind of transcendental subject strategy. With these recognitions, we have just been invited to do a flip. We have just been invited to understand Langdellian formalism as shaped by, and composed of, not just a rhetoric of transcendental objectivism, but a rhetoric of transcendental subjectivism.

To try to understand Langdellian formalism as a kind of transcendental subjectivism may help us in several ways. First, to the extent that such an understanding proves to be convincing and yet contrary to the received stories of Langdellian formalism, we will have a graphic demonstration of our own erroneous objectivist propensities—the conventional tendency to "look for" and "find" law "in" the conceptual space of object-forms. Second, in carrying out this sort of understanding, we may come to understand how it is that transcendental subjects are insulated from recognition and challenge. Finally, we may gain some understanding of how to reveal the constituting subjects and their effects.

Much of Langdellian formalism can be understood as shaped by, and composed of, a transcendental subject strategy.[66] With this rhetorical strategy, once again one of the poles of the subject-object relation is severely marginalized. Formalism and its virtues are secured because the transcendental subject can be counted upon to repeat its same old recursive operative moves. Objectivity is secured by virtue of the stabilization and universalization of the gaze of the observer, the Langdellian legal scientist. This strategy stabilizes legal meaning and moral value by enshrining law as a paramount subject that legal interpreters are bound to honor and observe. That is, they must honor and observe the identity and teleology of this law as subject. This vision of law as subject secures legal meaning by effectively subordinating the acts and errancies of individual legal actors.[67] To the extent one understands the law as possessed of spiritual force, of will, the law can remain on track despite the deviations of errant legal actors. Legal meaning and moral value are secured because there is a force greater than all of us whose very purpose is to maintain that legal meaning and moral value.

Deviance is also kept to a minimum because any nonconforming

66. In Kant, "transcendental" means that which makes experience possible. A. KOJEVE, INTRODUCTION TO THE READING OF HEGEL 123 (1969). Here the transcendental subject would be that subject that renders the experience of law possible. But to be clear, I am not attempting here to follow Kant's conception of the transcendental subject.

67. *See* Fiss, *supra* note 32, at 747.

object can already be identified as extralegal.[68] As for the transcendental subject, its formal and formative faculties cannot be dethroned because the objective order of things—the things in themselves—are never knowable as such. On the contrary, they are always and already mediated by categories and concepts of the subject.

C. Langdell's Immaculate Conception: The Transcendental Subject

Recall that the occasion for conceiving Langdellian formalism as grounded in a transcendental order of the object was the almost invariable effacement of the individual subject (*e.g.*, "Chris Langdell") whenever he spoke of law. This feature, together with Langdell's propensity to objectify law as rules, doctrines, and principles, led us to conceive this system as grounded in a transcendental order of the object.

Rather than understanding the effacement of the "I" in the face of an awesome transcendental order of the object, however, we can now see it as the subordination of the individual subject to the law as a transcendental subject. And there is something to this notion because, in Langdell's discourse, law, like a subject, actually does things. At times, law is fully animated. In Langdellian thought Law, or rather Equity, does some amazing stuff—and, what's more, does it *all by itself*: "Equity will, however, annex to such a contract an obligation directly to B."[69] And as you can see, apparently equity will often do its stuff without the mediation of social actors—neither courts,[70] nor parties. In fact, Langdell tells

68. This is why those who argue on behalf of any established orthodoxy almost always demand not simply a critique (a depiction of the shortcomings of the transcendental approach), but the affirmative demonstration of a suitable substitute. This is a very safe and effective argument to make because, in so far as the scene (the social, the political, the intellectual scene) is already a construction of the transcendental subject, there are no objects, no affirmative pieces of evidence, that the critic can rely upon to make out his positive case. All of this is déjà vu:

> Having established the breakdown of the common law methods the task of the functionalists is not over. They must submit and establish a reform program and prove that it will function better than the traditional methods in vogue in our day and place . . . . In this period of transition and change, the proponents of the New Deal in the law must submit to the critical examination of their evidence, must bear the affirmative of the issues, and must establish the "experiential capacity" of the experts offered by functionalism before their testimony is given full credence and the formulas are translated into action.

Kennedy, *Functional Nonsense and the Transcendental Approach*, 5 FORDHAM L. REV. 272, 283 (1936) (citation omitted).

69. Langdell, *supra* note 12, at 71.

70. Indeed, in the Langdellian universe, courts are rarely mentioned explicitly. Equity, for instance, often traverses the linguistic space of the institutional mediation of the court without a moment's (or a sign's) notice. Equity is always doing this, annexing that, or creating those obligations and so on all by itself. This subordination of courts to the Law or to Equity is not an accident of style, but a key aspect of the ambition of Langdellian jurisprudence to scientific rigor.

After all, as mere mortals, judges are likely to err. Thus, when courts are explicitly mentioned, it is often to rebuke them for having departed from the Law:

> This doctrine had its origin in efforts of courts of equity to prevent the harsh and unjust discriminations which the law formerly made between creditors of persons deceased, whose

you so: "Many equitable obligations are created . . . *by equity alone* . . . . For instance, *it is by force of equity alone* that an equitable obligation follows the property . . . ."[71] In Langdell's discourse, the doctrines not only mean, they *do* things to each other—frequently in a visible way. Doctrines doing things to other doctrines is hardly a unique characteristic of Langdellian discourse. What is unique to Langdellian discourse is the uncharacteristic visibility and frequency of this doing and its apparent doctrinal self-actualization. Indeed, in Langdellian discourse the doctrines seem to negate, convert, modify, and limit each other without the apparent assistance of any social actor—not even the author.

Actually, if we pay attention to what Langdell says about law, we should not be surprised that his doctrines are animated. Langdell tells us that

> [e]ach of these doctrines has *arrived* at its present state by slow degrees; in other words, it is a *growth, extending* in many cases through centuries. This growth is to be *traced* in the main through a series of cases in which it is *embodied*.[72]

Note the metaphorical image of the law and its doctrines and principles. They *arrive*. They are a *growth*. They are *extending*. Their growth can be *traced*. They are *embodied*.[73] The law here is rendered in animistic terms. It is personified.[74] It is, in short, a subject—a transcendental subject that moves all by itself. Soon it will even go so far as to make an appearance. Watch. "[T]he many different guises in which the same doctrine *is constantly making its appearance* . . . [is] the cause of much misapprehension."[75] If Langdell's "I" disappears when law makes its appearance in Langdell's text, it is because law itself is operating as the subject. There is an important ratio operative here: the more the law becomes established as a subject, the more the "I" must be effaced. This is why whenever the law makes an appearance on the scene in Langdell's discourse, the "I" is relegated to an implicit space off-stage or to a passive subordinate position. This "I" can only say of the law, as Langdell

> claims were in equity and justice equal; and it seems that the doctrine as a general one, cannot be sustained upon any principle.

Id. at 70.

71. *Id.* at 67 (emphasis added). There are limits to how far I'm willing to follow Langdell.

72. C. LANGDELL, *supra* note 19, at viii (emphasis added).

73. I'm sorry, but this still seems reptilian to me. For my first thoughts on reptilian jurisprudence, see Schlag, *Cannibal Moves: An Essay on the Metamorphoses of the Legal Distinction*, 40 STAN. L. REV. 929 (1988).

74. This personification is one of the possible constructions of law enabled by what Steve Winter calls our idealized cognitive model of law. For the complete idealized cognitive model of law, see Winter, *supra* note 28, at 1207-24.

75. C. LANGDELL, *supra* note 19, at viii-ix (emphasis added).

says in his own inaugural Harvard article, "So it seems . . .".[76]

This ratio between the transcendental subject and the individual "I" is very important. As we will see, the same ratio is re-enacted in Stanley Fish's discourse where the totalizing power of "interpretive communities" institutes the complete conformity of the individual subject—so much so that in Stanley Fish's discourse, there is not even any room for self-consciousness.[77] To some extent, we will even see the same ratio operative in the discourse of critical legal studies, which sees the false necessity attributed to rights and to law itself as inversely related to the liberation of the existentialist individual subject.[78]

Now, one might think that the undoing of this transcendental subject strategy is precisely a function of an unfortunate encounter between the transcendental subject (say, law) and the individual subject (say, Chris Langdell) within the confines of the same sentence or the same text. One might think, then, that the problem of the subject for transcendental-subject formalism would arise precisely from an unfortunate dialectical encounter between the transcendental subject and a potentially or actually nonconforming, noncomplying individual subject.

76. Langdell, *supra* note 12, at 72. This point about the retreat of the "I" in the face of the transcendental subject tracks with Gary Peller's observations concerning the structure of what he describes as liberal knowledge:

> Liberal knowledge, whether based on the transcendental object or the transcendental subject, presumes that an act of cognition can occur separate from the object of cognition and separate from the social forces which it studies. The contemplative stance of liberal knowledge suggests that "truth" is reached by an effacement before a transcendental source and an ultimate nondifferentiated unity [*i.e.*, like "Law"], rather than by a historical, open-ended, and creative process unlimited by any transcendental laws.

Peller, *supra* note 7, at 1269.

77. *See* S. FISH, DOING WHAT COMES NATURALLY, *supra* note 7, at 394-95.

78. *See infra* text accompanying notes 203-13. Most critical legal thinkers decried this false necessity as the attribution of objectivity to law, rights, and legal reasoning. *See, e.g.*, Boyle, *The Politics of Reason: Critical Legal Theory and Local Social Thought*, 133 U. PA. L. REV. 685, 689 (1986) ("Critical legal theory has reacted against a set of claims about the naturalness, the neutrality, the objectivity, and the apolitical quality of various discourses."). I attribute the tendency of cls thinkers to frame mystification claims in terms of false projections of objectivity to a combination of the critique of reification influenced by Lukács and the critique of bad faith developed by Sartre in *Being and Nothingness*. For the classic explanations of these ideas, see G. LUKÁCS, HISTORY AND CLASS CONSCIOUSNESS 83-222 (R. Livingstone trans. 1971); J.-P. SARTRE, BEING AND NOTHINGNESS 47-70 (H. Barnes trans. 1956).

Critical legal thinkers have missed two things because of their fixation on the critique of the objectivity of law. First, they have missed the extent to which animistic forms of thought that create transcendental subjects such as "the framers" or "the constitution" or "the court" have an ideologically disabling and pacifying effect on individual actors. For one provocative exception, see Gabel, *Founding Father Knows Best: A Response to Tushnet*, 1 TIKKUN, Fall 1986, at 41.

Second, with their fascination with objectivity, many critical legal thinkers have missed the ideological implications of legal thought that are to be found not in reification per se or in the practice of animism per se, but rather in the play of relations between animism and reification in legal culture and the distribution of animism-reification relations in legal culture. For a notable exception showing sensitivity to the contingency, multiplicity, and play of subject-object relations, see Kennedy, *Spring Break*, 63 TEXAS L. REV. 1377 (1985).

The Problem of the Subject

One can imagine, for instance, Chris Langdell waking up one day, forgetting to use the imperial declarative mode, and writing not, "The law is . . ." but instead, "*I think* the law is . . .". By writing that sentence, Chris might have recognized that he (the "I"), far from passively receiving the commands of law, was actively engaged in *thinking* (*i.e.*, constructing) the law.[79] Now, if that had happened, we might have had a precocious dialectical encounter between the transcendental subject and a nonconforming individual subject. We might have had the beginnings of an inquiry into the problem of the subject. Langdell might have asked, "Is law the subject or is it the 'I' or are they both subjects, and, if so, what is their relation to each other?"

But note how improbable it is that Langdell would have formulated such a question. It's improbable in all sorts of ways, but the one of interest here goes well beyond who and when Langdell was. The reason it is improbable that Langdell would have formulated such a question—even if he had tripped up one day and written (as he probably did), "*I think* the law states . . ."[80]—is that the recuperative capacities of the transcendental subject strategy are absolutely awesome.

Dialectical encounters between the transcendental subject and the individual subject are not so easily produced. To produce such an encounter requires bringing to consciousness some sort of rhetorical, ontological, or epistemic dislocation, discrepancy, or contradiction between the individual subject and the transcendental subject. But one can't simply assume into existence such a diremption between the individual and the transcendental subject. On the contrary, most successful transcendental subject formalisms are already well defended against the attempt to inscribe or recognize such diremptions. In our time, this recuperative defense is perhaps best expressed and demonstrated by the work of Stanley Fish, who shows (repeatedly) that there is no self, no individual subject, apart from the transcendental subject (*i.e.*, the interpretive

79. And if he had, he would no doubt quickly have proceeded to cite most (if not all) of the following: P. Berger & T. Luckmann, The Social Construction of Reality (1966); P. Bourdieu, The Logic of Practice (R. Nice trans. 1990); S. Fish, Doing What Comes Naturally, *supra* note 7; M. Foucault, The Archaeology of Knowledge (1972); C. Geertz, The Interpretation of Cultures (1973); C. Geertz, Local Knowledge (1983); N. Goodman, Ways of Worldmaking (1978); D. Herzog, Without Foundations: Justification in Political Theory (1985); R. Rorty, Philosophy and the Mirror of Nature (1979).

80. Here, for instance, he comes very close to saying just that:

> It seemed to me, therefore, to be possible to take such a branch of the law as Contracts, for example, and without exceeding comparatively moderate limits, to select, classify, and arrange all the cases which had contributed in any important degree to the growth, development, or establishment of any of its essential doctrines.

C. Langdell, *supra* note 19, at ix.

communities) that has constructed this individual subject.[81] In other words, the transcendental subject strategy does not so much deny the existence of an individual subject as it fashions and refashions this individual subject in its own image.[82]

So when Steve Winter argues against Stanley Fish that self-consciousness is not only possible but helpful in understanding law and our selves,[83] Stanley Fish could nonetheless rightfully respond that there is no self-consciousness possible except within the sort of interpretive communities that enable the self-consciousness move to be made and to be represented as such.[84] This is to say (to simulate the prose of Stanley Fish) that self-consciousness is never possible because there is never any self apart from its interpretive community to be self-conscious about. Now, none of this is to say that Steve Winter is wrong. On the contrary, Steve Winter is right. This is just to show how this recuperative awesome re-envelopment, this capacious nesting move really works. First, one identifies within someone else's discourse those aspects that confirm one's own discourse. Then one highlights these aspects—bringing them to the foreground. And then one re-envelops[85] the other's discourse within one's own. It's very democratic,[86] very postmodern, very easy, and almost always very unconscious.

Now it is in precisely this way—by means of the recuperative awe-

81. Stanley Fish, for example, notes:

> [B]eing situated not only means that one cannot achieve a distance on one's beliefs, but that one's beliefs do not relax their hold because one "knows" that they are local and not universal. This in turn means that even someone . . . like me . . . who is firmly convinced of the circumstantiality of his convictions will nevertheless experience those convictions as universally, not locally, true.

S. Fish, Doing What Comes Naturally, *supra* note 7, at 467.

82. Proponents of self-consciousness often seem to be very confident that they are talking about something that is self-evident. But this sense that self-consciousness is easily distinguishable from consciousness of scene is attributable to the conventionally-embedded hypostatization of the self and its separation from scene. In other words, our conventional cultural linguistic forms for reporting instances of self-consciousness are far less opaque and much more precise than an adequate report of the experience itself would produce.

Consider that when you actually start thinking about what you are thinking about, it's not at all self-evident that what you are thinking about is the self: "Oh, this is the way I think about things. No—on further reflection, if I really push self-consciousness, it becomes clear that it's not really me who is thinking of things that way. It's also the way my culture, my discourse, and my computer lead me(?) to think about things."

83. Winter, *Bull Durham*, *supra* note 7, at 681-91.

84. This is close to what Stanley Fish actually does say: Self-consciousness for Fish "is impossible because there is no action or motion of the self that exists apart from the prevailing realm of purposes and therefore no way of achieving distance from that realm." S. Fish, Doing What Comes Naturally, *supra* note 7, at 464.

85. (analytically, grammatically, semantically, syntactically, etymologically, metaphorically, performatively, constatively, etc.).

86. Not only can everyone do it—but more than one person can actually win (at least theoretically).

some re-envelopment, the capacious nesting move—that the transcendental-subject strategy sustains and defends itself against the disruptive questioning of an errant individual subject. And the truth as well as the significance of the point becomes obvious as one takes note that God himself (the all-time champion transcendental subject) was, according to transcendentally authoritative reports, capable of recuperating and recasting in his own image as severe a risk of deviance as Job. Indeed, the story of Job is the ultimate in the demonstration of the power of the all-time transcendental subject to re-appropriate even the most serious diremptions between the individual and the transcendental subject.

Displacing an operative transcendental subject is thus very hard work. How then are operative transcendental subjects displaced? Certainly the exploitation of diremptions between the individual and the transcendental subject are helpful. But there is more. Again, Langdell furnishes an excellent example.

Soon after Langdell tells us in his celebrated preface that doctrines are constantly making their "appearance" in "many different guises" thus causing "much misapprehension," he proposes a solution: "If these doctrines could be so classified and arranged that each should be found in its proper place, and nowhere else, they would cease to be formidable from their number."[87] This taxonomic solution entails the objectification of law, the transcendental subject. In some less secular religions, such an act would be understood as crudely reductive, de-spiritualizing, and thus sacrilegious.[88] But Langdell goes ahead and does it: as Langdell says, "Law, considered as a science, consists of certain principles and doctrines."[89] In this sentence, law has already been reduced to identifiable, discrete (though still living) entities.[90] It is this objectification and partitioning of the transcendental subject into *identifiable*, *discrete*, and *causally related* sub-parts that allow Langdellian formalism to be what it is.[91]

In Langdell's brief article on equity jurisdiction, the partitioning action starts early—on the very first page:

87. C. LANGDELL, *supra* note 19, at ix.

88. No graven images. *See, e.g.*, *Deuteronomy* 5:8.

89. C. LANGDELL, *supra* note 19, at viii.

90. This representation of law in terms of entities may seem unexceptionable to the reader, but it is quite significant both in the kind of vision law enabled as well as the kind of vision law excluded. To understand law as consisting of propositional entities creates entirely different opportunities and problems than understanding law as a *process* as in Holmes, *The Path of the Law*, 10 HARV. L. REV. 457 (1897), a *field of forces* as in Cohen, *Field Theory and Judicial Logic*, 59 YALE L.J. 238 (1950), and so on. For a lucid demonstration of this point, see Winter, *supra* note 28, at 1105.

91. G. LAKOFF & M. JOHNSON, *supra* note 28, at 25-32. The metaphorical representation of [——] "as an entity allows us to refer to it, quantify it, identify a particular aspect of it, see it as a cause. . . . Ontological metaphors like this are necessary for even attempting to deal rationally with our experiences." *Id.* at 26.

Texas Law Review Vol. 69:1627, 1991

> Rights are either absolute or relative. Absolute rights are such as do not imply any correlative duties. Relative rights are such as do imply correlative duties . . . . Relative rights, as well as their correlative duties, are called obligations; *i.e.*, we have but one word for both the right and its correlative duty. The creation of every obligation, *therefore*, is the creation of both a right and a duty . . . .[92]

What is interesting in Langdell's objectification of the transcendental subject is that no glaring internal conflict appears to arise from his simultaneous treatment of law as a transcendental subject and as an objectified taxonomy. And the reason this is so is that, within the Langdellian universe, the transcendental subject is itself in charge of its own self-objectification. Rules, doctrines, and principles are identified and described in object-form, but it is almost always the law (the rules, doctrines, and principles) that determines, in the manner of a transcendental subject, the identity and meaning of *other* doctrines. Rules, doctrines, and principles act upon each other, giving each other the significance they have. This, of course, is precisely the awesome recuperative-envelopment-nesting strategy described above: the transcendental subject effects its own transformation into an objectified form.

There is a certain elegance to understanding Langdellian formalism as shaped by a transcendental subject strategy. This understanding seems to secure everything we want in Langdellian formalism.[93] In fact, this is such a secure representation of Langdellian formalism that exactly how this transcendental ordering breaks down becomes a real question.

To answer this question we must return to what seemed to be the perfectly choreographed doctrinal movements of Langdellian formalism; a world in which doctrines themselves operated on each other with only the slightest assistance from the individual subject. Watch the doctrinal dance at work. Langdell writes:

> With respect to the modes in which they are created, equitable obligations differ widely from legal obligations. Most legal obligations are created by means of contracts . . . . But a purely equitable obligation cannot be made in that way. . . .
>
> [E]quity cannot annex an obligation to a promise or a covenant to which the law refuses to annex any obligation. In a word, there is properly no such thing as an equitable promise or covenant, and no such thing as an equitable contract. The reason, *therefore*, why a contract cannot result in creating a purely equitable obligation is,

92. Langdell, *supra* note 12, at 55.

93. And as compared to a transcendental object strategy, a transcendental subject strategy is more complete. The main aporia in this account lies precisely in tracing the ways in which the transcendental subject objectifies itself. Just how does this occur? How is it that law comes to be crystallized into this particular matrix of rules, doctrine, and principles? How do these object-entities come to be?

> that a contract always results in creating a legal obligation.[94]

To summarize then—going backward from the conclusion:[95] Contracts cannot create purely equitable considerations because contracts can only create legal obligations. And why is that? Because purely equitable obligations cannot be created in the same manner as legal obligations. And why is that? Well, because purely equitable obligations cannot be created by contract, whereas legal obligations can. Aaaaaah.[96] Got it? Well, even if you don't, the important thing to note is that Langdell's definitions and doctrines *act* upon each other to give each other content and meaning. It is generally thought improper to say that doctrines "impact" upon other doctrines, but in the Langdellian world they really do.

The transcendental subject is in charge of everything, including itself—its own identity, its own meaning, its own doctrinal elaboration. Now, in one sense, this is a very stable system. It is very stable because it is perfectly circular. That, of course, is also why it falls apart. Felix Cohen tells the story as follows:

> Legal arguments couched in these terms are necessarily circular, since these terms are themselves creations of law, and such arguments add precisely as much to our knowledge as Moliere's physician's discovery that opium puts men to sleep because it contains a dormitive principle.[97]

Now it's possible, particularly to the extent we are under the influence of American, Anglo-Saxon academic philosophy or any other form of rationalist practice, to understand Cohen's argument about circularity here as a logical objection. But there is a far richer understanding of Cohen's argument. The problem is not circularity per se, but the very *shallowness* of the circularity Cohen reveals. The Langdellian formalism fails, not because it has committed a logical error, but because it ceases to tell us very much of what we want to know. It's as if the Langdellian transcendental subject had been revealed to be not merely a sham, not just a fraud, but something much more serious: an intellectual lightweight. The problem with transcendental subject formalism is that it stops speaking to us. In Felix Cohen's thought, the transcendental subject stopped speaking to him when the system was revealed to be a rather *shallow*, self-referential system. Indeed, it is at that point that the system itself becomes identifiable as a transcendental subject—*i.e.*, one that no longer speaks, but whose own internal structure can now be dissected in a postmortem.

94. Langdell, *supra* note 12, at 64-65 (emphasis added) (citation omitted).
95. Actually, it could go either way.
96. Didn't you always suspect it was something like that?
97. Cohen, *supra* note 50, at 820.

At this point we can begin to understand (just as Felix Cohen did) the *shallow*, self-referential character of the particular transcendental subject formalism that we are operating under. Phenomenologically, this breakdown of the transcendental subject can be experienced in various ways. It can be experienced with contempt and impatience, as in the case of Felix Cohen.[98] It can also be experienced in more insecure terms as a fear of nihilism.[99] For the participants, the breakdown of a transcendental subject formalism is thus experienced as a loss of meaning and significance. Or it can be experienced as a kind of boredom—the sense that the old moves are being replayed without producing anything new.[100]

Now, it is in precisely the same ways—with the same losses of meaning and the same affective experiences—that the problem of the subject arises in the contemporary modes of legal thought that we are about to consider. This is no accident. The various modes of contemporary legal thought can all be understood as variations on the transcendental subject strategy, the transcendental object strategy, or the disintegration of these strategies.[101]

I would like to move beyond the Langdellian scene.[102] But first there's a lingering question that may have to be answered: *Which is it?* Is Langdellian formalism a kind of transcendental subject strategy or a kind of transcendental object strategy? While this question arises predictably enough, it is not a terribly interesting or helpful one.[103] You will

98. *See* Cohen, *supra* note 90, at 242 (arguing that "so far the logicians, having concentrated their vision on the logical heavens where words continue at rest and mean the same thing forever, have not fully explored the imperfect efforts of human beings to communicate with each other").

99. *See* Fiss, *supra* note 32, at 746; (explaining that "literary critics are so unconstrained that no claim of objectivity can be made for any of their interpretations . . . ."); Carrington, *Of Law and the River*, 34 J. LEG. EDUC. 222, 227 (1984) ("[P]rofessionalism and intellectual courage of lawyers . . . cannot abide . . . the embrace of nihilism and its lessons that who decides is everything and principle nothing but cosmetic.").

100. Schlag, *Normative and Nowhere to Go*, *supra* note 7, at 173-80 (noting that normative legal thought, even in its reaction to postmodernism, functions as a well-internalized routine).

101. Indeed, the coming to consciousness of the problem of the subject within the various modes of legal thought can be seen as an increasingly sophisticated awareness of the extent to which they already depend upon the presence of a satisfactory account of the transcendental subject *and* an increasingly sophisticated awareness of the extent to which such dependence, while unavoidable, is itself always and already insufficient.

102. Wouldn't we all?

103. If Langdell and his formalist confreres had been philosophically inclined, perhaps they might have experienced a need to answer this question. As it is, they didn't. Suppose the question is asked of us. How would we answer it?

It is extremely unlikely that we can understand Langdellian formalism as resting on a transcendental subject. For one thing, the intellectual tradition that underwrites this position was and is foreign to American culture. For another, Langdell's very insistence on the science metaphors, on the "empirical" observation of case law, on the rejection of natural law (a natural jurisprudential embodiment for the transcendental subject) make it difficult for us to understand Langdellian formalism as grounded in a transcendental subject.

For us to try to understand Langdellian formalism as grounded in a transcendental order of the

The Problem of the Subject

notice that the asking of *this* question (rather than others) repeats what we have just revealed as the embedded objectivist orientation of American legal thought. In asking *this* question—"So which it?"—attention is directed again towards the *object* part of our inquiry—namely, on determining the identity of Langdellian formalism. Correspondingly, with the asking of *this* question, we are drawn away from the *subject* part of the inquiry—namely, away from questioning *our* use of transcendental subject and transcendental object strategies to make sense of Langdellian formalism.

If I stress this ironic point, it is to give just one more example of the way we are primed to focus on whatever occupies the conventional space of objectivity and to simultaneously elide the problem of the subject. Indeed, this brief survey of the subject-object relations of Langdellian formalism has helped reveal the ways in which our own objectivist tendencies lead us to eclipse the "space" of the subject. Our intellectual conventions in legal thought repeatedly direct our attention toward that which is already represented or easily representable as an object-form. It is "there," in the object-form, that we unconsciously expect to find legal

object is also difficult. The imperial pose of the Langdellian scholar looms too large for us to accept at face value his discursive self-image as some sort of self-effaced individual subject timidly observing the objects of law at work. But this transcendental object understanding is disabled precisely because it doesn't make sense for us. We cannot start with the object (of law) and move from there to the subject (us). In fact, we cannot even start with the object, period. What can we do—take the object's point of view? That's a projection of the categories of the subject onto the object.

Perhaps, then, we can understand Langdellian formalism as a kind of philosophically inelegant jurisprudence resting at times on a transcendental subject and at other times on a transcendental object. Or we have a transcendental subject objectified or a transcendental object subjectified.

Now, we could do any of these things. But I do not think answering the question "So which is it?" in the way that question is posed is particularly helpful. Rather, I think the reason we are having difficulties finding suitable answers to the question as posed is that the question itself presupposes that the transcendental subject and the transcendental object are *substantive positions* that underwrite Langdellian formalism in the same manner in which academic philosophy usually understands its constructions to underwrite other practices.

Looking at things in such a way—that is, in the manner of academic philosophy—is of limited help. If, after the manner of academic philosophy, the transcendental subject and the transcendental object are understood to be two competing positions, two competing ideas of subject-object relations, then we will indeed have difficulty understanding how it is that Langdellian formalism could have combined both and still sustained itself as a viable *formalism*. But if the transcendental subject and the transcendental object moves are considered instead to be rhetorical strategies, then the apparent contradiction dissipates, not just as a rhetorical matter, but as a philosophical one. If these are rhetorics of argument, strategies of representation, then what before seemed, in the rationalist representation of academic philosophy, to be an unacceptable contradiction, falls away. The contradiction falls away because the transcendental object and the transcendental subject become rhetorical moves—moves that the participants may or may not be conscious of.

Now, there's much to be said for this understanding of the matter. For one thing, it helps makes sense of what seem to be both objectivist and subjectivist tendencies in Langdellian transcendentalism. For another, it actually conforms to the lines of attack used by realists such as Felix Cohen against the Langdellian formalists. Cohen advanced both a hypostatization critique aimed at objectivism and a circularity critique aimed at the subjectivist or animistic character of Langdellian thought.

meaning and legal significance, as well as legal problems—the stuff of legal meaning and the stuff of critique.

What we have revealed thus far, however, are possibilities for a new and different kind of jurisprudential intellectual inquiry—an inquiry into the kind of subject pre-supposed by the various schools of legal thought. Interestingly, this new possibility for inquiry also enables a different kind of jurisprudential "critique"—one which would seek to criticize a school of thought, not in terms of the truth, adequacy, or normative appeal of its representations of or in the objective realm, but rather in terms of the kind of subject that the school of thought presupposes or celebrates.

But in this Article, it is not critique that matters. Instead, given that the transcendental object and the transcendental subject strategies of Langdellian formalism have broken down, the question is, "What happens next?"

Meanwhile—onward to disintegration.

D. *Learning to Do Without: When the Transcendentals Are Out to Lunch*

Sometimes these object-forms and subject-forms seem to float around in no apparent order or pattern. This is a moment of *disintegration*. Sometimes the subject-forms and object-forms seem to coalesce in some grander pattern with operant or generative regularities. Here we can speak of *reconstruction*. When a previous reconstruction breaks down and legal thinkers seek to escape the chaos of disintegration and at the same time avoid the demonstrable falsity of reconstruction, they use the strategy of *collapse*: an arrangement of subject- and object-forms that eschews strong specifications of the subject-object relation. These three moments are not necessarily mutually exclusive. Each can, in various ways, be subsumed within the others spatially (*e.g.*, partitions in a field), temporally (*e.g.*, cycles), and in various nesting relationships (*e.g.*, a collapse strategy that contains moments of reconstruction).

1. Disintegration.—We see, for instance, the law as object-form evidenced in frequent ontological assertions that there exist such *things* as "*the* framers' intent" or "*the* plain meaning of a statute" or "*the* positive law" or even "*the* constitution."[104] Likewise, the law as object-form remains the principal image that informs such crucial legal operations as legal analysis (*i.e.*, breaking the whole into its parts), legal synthesis (*i.e.*, putting the parts together into a whole), and so on. The law as object-

104. *See, e.g.*, Grey, *supra* note 25, at 13-17 (discussing the constitution as an "instrument").

form is prevalent among such legal thinkers—even those who try to reject it on theoretical or philosophical grounds.

The prevalence of the object-form of law is supported by the metaphorical and syntactical structure of language; they combine to produce what has been called the conventional metaphor: *ideas are objects.*[105] In turn, this metaphor subconsciously structures the manner in which we deal with ideas. To the extent that we subconsciously treat ideas as objects, we perform the same kind of operations on these ideas that we typically perform on objects. Thus, we end up treating ideas as if they were substantial, stable, unified and divisible. For instance, the conventional notion that the text has "a plain meaning" is underwritten by the projection of object-like characteristics on communicative activity: its reduction to a text, the text's further reduction to a series of object-like features including substantiality, stability, unity, and so on. In the ALI Restatements and in Gilbert's, this objectification finds further mimetic expression in the large block letters used to announce important doctrines—the big block letters suggesting solidity and permanence.[106]

The ease with which we can recognize law as object-forms is largely attributable to our own prereflective constitution as legal thinkers. Our own prereflective constitution situates us (you and me) as individual subjects who are reading or authoring objective statements of law. Because we already implicitly understand ourselves to be occupying the space of the subject, this prereflective constitution makes it more difficult for us to apprehend the moments when the law is cast as a subject-form rather than as an object-form.

Yet the law as subject-form is very much a part of our legal discourse. The law as subject-form is reflected, for instance, in the hopeful and optimistic view that law adapts and grows, that it confers meaning and value on our practices. As Justice Brandeis said, "Government is

105. The law-as-object vision is principally a cognitive or linguistic phenomenon—not principally a philosophical or an interpretive one. Indeed, recent work in cognitive science has identified the ways in which our cognitive and linguistic structures tend to produce the prototypical treatment of ideas as objects. To mention but one example, there is a persistent tendency to think of meaning as something that is *in* the text, somehow "contained" in words. This tendency, known as the "conduit metaphor," tends to transform meaning into a thing contained by the text-container. The net effect is to endow the meaning-as-object with all the usual qualities of object such as substantiality, stability, etc. Reddy, *The Conduit Metaphor—A Case of Frame Conflict in Our Language About Language*, in METAPHOR AND THOUGHT 284 (A. Ortony ed. 1979). *See also* Schlag, *"Le Hors de Texte," supra* note 7, at 1634 (noting that "traditional legal discourse has already framed its own form as . . . a container for 'substantive' thought"); Winter, *Death is the Mother of Metaphor*, 105 HARV. L. REV. (forthcoming 1991).

106. *See, e.g.*, RESTATEMENT (SECOND) OF TORTS § 17 (1959) (featuring headings with large, block lettering); J. CHOPER & M. EISENBERG, CORPORATIONS (Gilbert 1983) § 65 (featuring a similar format).

the potent, the omnipresent teacher."[107] For instance, the notion that law must "keep up with the times" or the view that in time "law works itself pure," both originate in the law-as-subject vision. The widespread and largely unexamined assumption that there is and must be some connection between what law is and what it ought to be (*e.g.*, just, right, or good) is typically sustained by the ascription of subject-like characteristics to the law, such as will, direction, and motivation. Indeed, much like any other subject, the law arrives on the scene of contemporary legal thought already normatively charged and already inherently meaningful.

On the cognitive and linguistic plane, the law-as-subject strategy is at once signalled and constituted by the deployment of the "meat-and-bones" imagery of the animated organism. As Felix Frankfurter said, for example, "law isn't something that exists as a closed system within itself, but draws its juices from life."[108] Frankfurter further noted that the "common law is not a brooding omnipresence in the sky, but the articulate voice of some sovereign . . . ."[109] In the law-as-subject vision, the law is often presented as a traveler on a journey.[110] The law speaks with many voices.[111] Etc., etc., etc.

Much of the legal discourse left after the collapse of Langdellianism is steeped in both the subject-form and the object-form. The objectification of law is underwritten largely by metaphysical metaphors, while the subjectification of law is underwritten largely by metabiological metaphors. Sometimes these object-forms and subject-forms are simply floating around in no apparent pattern, unnoticed and unremarkable. To describe law in this way is to describe law in a moment of disintegration.

2. *Reconstruction.*—At some times, the subject-forms and object-forms of law appear to crystallize into different arrangements that are actually patterned. For the sake of nomenclature, we can speak of this as a moment of reconstruction. An example of this reconstruction strategy is found in the great and grand recursive dispute over whether ours is "a machine that will work of itself" or "a living constitution." As Morton Horwitz put it:

> [T]he issue is sometimes described by historians as an argument between an eighteenth century Newtonian Constitution and a nineteenth century Darwinian Constitution. The Newtonian view of

107. Olmstead v. United States, 277 U.S. 438, 485 (1928).

108. H. PHILLIPS, FELIX FRANKFURTER REMINISCES 168 (1960).

109. Southern Pac. R.R. v. Jensen, 244 U. S. 205, 222 (1916) (Holmes, J., dissenting).

110. *See* Holmes, *supra* note 90.

111. *See* Yudof, *'Tea at the Palaz of Hoon': The Human Voice in Legal Rights*, 66 TEXAS L. REV. 589 (1988).

> the universe was of a perfect machine set in motion by a deist God at the beginning of time. Everything subsequent was determined by the operation of physical laws, present at the beginning and themselves never changing. The Newtonian Constitution corresponded to these physical laws, and like them was meant to last for all time. The Newtonian world view of the framers certainly encouraged this sort of imagery. By contrast, the Darwinian ideal of the nineteenth century, the idea of evolution, supposed the unfolding of gradual but inevitable change in the Constitution. As society changed, the Constitution would also change, adapting to the environment in which it functioned.[112]

This description of the Newtonian and Darwinian constitution reconstructs the floating subject-form and object-form metaphors into patterned arrangements. In contemporary legal thought, we can see instances of this sort of reconstruction in the opposition of liberal pluralist theories of constitutional decision making (object-form dominance) to republican dialogic theories of constitutional decision making (subject-form dominance).[113] We can also see this reconstruction at work in the cls attempts to describe and organize legal thought along a "structuralist strand" (object-form dominance) and a "phenomenological subjectivist strand" (subject-form dominance).[114] More broadly we can see this pattern of reconstruction at work in the conflicting positions of "law-and-economics and its satellites on the one hand [object-form dominance] and what might loosely be called 'cultural legal studies' on the other [subject-form dominance]."[115]

Reconstruction never quite manages to entirely restabilize subject-object relations. The reconstruction always seems to depend on some subject-object relation that is transverse or askew to the attempted reconstruction. This is easiest to see in the simple visions of the Darwinian and Newtonian constitutions above. The objectivist Newtonian representation implicitly relies on a suppressed subject. The subjectivist Darwinian representation of the Constitution as an organic form relies on a suppressed object. Indeed, the objectivist Newtonian vision is "set in motion" by an unspecified "God," whereas change in the subjectivist Darwinian vision is constrained and limited by an unspecified changing "society" or social "environment." The problem of the subject arises when "God" stops speaking and when it is recognized that some subject

112. Horwitz, *The Meaning of the Bork Nomination in American Constitutional History*, 50 U. PITT. L. REV. 655, 657 (1989).

113. *See, e.g.*, Michelman, *Law's Republic*, 97 YALE L.J. 1493, 1503 (1988) (contrasting the roles that the individual plays under the republican dialogic model and the liberal pluralist model).

114. *See infra* text accompanying notes 272-73.

115. Grey, *Hear the Other Side: Wallace Stevens and Pragmatist Legal Theory*, 63 S. CAL. L. REV. 1569, 1571 (1990).

Texas Law Review Vol. 69:1627, 1991

is required to specify that previously unspecified social "environment." What we have at this point is the *disintegration* of the transcendentals.

3. Collapse.—Collapse is the attempt to escape both disintegration and reconstruction through the collapse of subject-object relations. In order to maintain reconstruction, legal thought must deny the extent to which the subject-form and the object-form depend on each other. When legal thought can no longer sustain this denial, it either falls back into disintegration or emerges in a collapse strategy.

In the collapse strategy, legal meaning is located neither in the subject nor in the object, but in some *unspecified* synthesis, circumvention, mediation, or transcendence of the subject-object relation.[116] The appeal of this strategy for both naive and sophisticated legal thought lies in its frank admission that legal meaning is simply too complex to cabin within any specific articulation of the subject-object relation.

Although the collapse strategy is obviously open to the charge of mysticism, its importance in shaping legal thought should not be underestimated. The collapse strategy is often exemplified in those approaches that (in essence) equate law with wisdom, sound judgment, practical reason, craft, or convention.[117] All such concepts of collapse must remain unspecified if they are to serve the collapse strategy. Any approach that claims to have overcome the subject-object dichotomy will resort frequently to at least one such unspecified term. Indeed, to the extent that the content or structure of any these collapse concepts are specified, they risk lapsing back into some sort of reconstruction or disintegration. So the critical concepts of collapse must remain virtually empty. Typically, the concepts of collapse are at once extremely abstract (as opposed to specific) and extremely earthy (as opposed to technical). The concepts of collapse often operate as theoretical unmentionables—those wonderful spaces and gaps that cannot be specified but can be named and in the naming apparently serve to resolve all the difficulties that the theory may have had.[118] Here, the concepts of collapse mysteriously serve to secure legal meaning and moral value. It is in the spaces described as wisdom, sound judgment, practical reason, craft, or that professional *je ne sais quoi* that legal meaning and moral value are secured.

116. In his foreword to this symposium, Steve Winter also uses the term "collapse" to describe a particular state of subject-object relations. Our uses of the term, "collapse," are not the same. *See* Winter, *Foreword: On Building Houses*, 69 TEXAS L. REV. 1595, 1610 (1991).

117. For a quick summary and citations to the literature, see Sherry, *The Ninth Amendment: Righting an Unwritten Constitution*, 64 CHI.-KENT L. REV. 1001, 1012-13 (1988).

118. For an example of a theoretical unmentionable, see *infra* text accompanying note 148 (suggesting that Owen Fiss's "disciplining rules" function as a theoretical unmentionable).

The Problem of the Subject

The concepts of collapse work to secure legal meaning because they authorize whatever combination of subject-form and object-form that happens to be in place. That, of course, is also the undoing of the collapse strategy. At some point, the need to secure legal meaning or moral value against some perversion requires that the concepts of collapse be given explicit content or structure. And at that point we are back to some form of reconstruction.

Most of contemporary legal thought exists in this state of collapse. This means that it has no overarching structure specifying the subject-object relation. More specifically, the overarching structure is itself a theoretical unmentionable. Within collapsed legal thought, subject and object relations remain unregulated—except to the extent that any strong specification is disallowed. This means that virtually any sort of relation (except consciously specified relations) can occur within collapsed legal thought, including:

Rapid shifts between subjectification and objectification,
interpenetration of subject by object (or vice versa),
collapsed conceptualizations,
and so on.

Any sort of relations (except consciously specified relations) are authorized in collapsed legal thought, but this does not imply that collapsed legal thought is transparently disorderly or aesthetically unpleasing. On the contrary, it can be (and often is) extremely graceful in negotiating its own shifts, penetrations, and collapse—so much so that it is difficult for the participants to even perceive that there has been anything like collapse.[119]

Most sophisticated legal thought strives very hard to present itself as collapsed: that is, as refusing to specify any strong subject-object relation. The current prevalence of the collapse strategy is expressed in the work of Ronald Dworkin and confirmed by the popularity of his theories.[120] Moreover, much sophisticated legal thought goes to great lengths to present itself as antifoundational, nonfoundational, situational, situated, contextualist, pragmatic, antiformalist, anticonceptualist, and interpretive. Sophisticated legal thought will generally attempt to privilege hermeneutics over epistemology and, in turn, to privilege epistemology

119. *See* Kennedy, *A Rotation In Contemporary Legal Scholarship*, in CRITICAL LEGAL THOUGHT: AN AMERICAN-GERMAN DEBATE 353 (D. Trubek & C. Joerges eds. 1989).

120. I have previously tried to show how Dworkin's theories work as an elegant and sophisticated rhetorical structure that gains content and meaning through the projection and displacement of the legal reader's beliefs onto the Dworkinian text and the Herculean judge. *See* Schlag, *"Le Hors de Texte," supra* note 7, at 1660-64; Schlag, *Politics of Form*, *supra* note 7, at 875.

Texas Law Review Vol. 69:1627, 1991

over ontology.[121] This methodological distancing from ontology serves to defuse, delay, and to some extent trivialize the reckoning with the subject-object relation. Indeed, given sufficient methodological sophistication, the interpretive and the epistemological turn can succeed in postponing any articulation of a strong specification of the subject-object relation.

The problem with collapse, however, is that it cannot locate or secure meaning or value—neither theoretically nor practically. Collapse strategies thus seldom serve the instrumental, political, or normative goals of legal thinkers. Even as legal thinkers practice the collapse strategy, they are engaged in some sort of reconstruction. Indeed, in order to stabilize meaning and value, collapse strategies typically attempt a covert deployment of reconstruction.[122]

II. Rules of Law (a Whole Lot of Them)

"The genius of the common law does not lend itself to codification . . . ."[123]

—Joseph H. Beale

Initially, the rule-of-law approach is best understood as a kind of collapse strategy: an abandonment of the attempt to situate legal meaning entirely in the object or entirely in the subject. Both of these transcendental moves are eschewed, and any specification of subject-object relations is studiously avoided.

But how is it possible to effect a collapse? How is it possible to avoid specifying subject-object relations and still present an intellectually compelling vision of law? The rule-of-law approach accomplishes this task with the rubric of *craft*—a professional way of doing things that cannot be reduced to any formula, algorithm, or theory.[124] The notion of craft is at once the image and the rhetorical mechanism that enables rule-

121. *See* Moore, *supra* note 27, at 902.

122. *See, e.g.*, *infra* text accompanying notes 145-53 (describing how rule-of-law thinkers use the strategies of collapse and reconstruction simultaneously).

123.

> The increasing mass of decisions, however, in America has called for some palliative, and in 1923 the American Law Institute was founded for the purpose of restating the effect of the law as it was found to be at the time of restatement.

1 J. Beale, *supra* note 31, at 43.

124. It is, however, difficult to identify the core jurisprudential commitments of this school of thought because these core commitments are rarely expressed in theoretical form. This is no accident: rule-of-law thinkers are typically suspicious of theory, and, thus, few have tried to articulate the theoretical structure of their own practices. Typically, this is not the sort of project that would interest rule-of-law thinkers. For them, the theoretical enterprise is almost always geared toward reducing law to some sort of algorithm, model, or paradigm, and they think that law cannot be

of-law thinkers to avoid dealing specifically and explicitly with the problem of the subject and its analogues.

The craft notion allows rule-of-law thinkers to maintain a desired ambiguity in answering the question of whether law is principally, or even usually, theory or practice, universal or contextual, immanent or transcendent, and so on. Precisely because the rule-of-law approach represents law as a craft—as a way of doing things—the approach is simultaneously easy to recognize in gestalt terms but difficult to identify in terms of its constitutive jurisprudential commitments.

We will start with the gestalt. Rule-of-law thinkers tend to think of law as doctrines, principles, and policies properly understood—that is to say, understood in the manner of competent members of the legal profession.[125] Within the legal community, these concepts have integrity, identity, and a certain constancy, all of which enable sound and roughly predictable decision making. Typically, these doctrines, principles, and policies are represented in object-form—with identity, constancy, and boundedness, along with a location and presence within the field of other related doctrines, principles, and policies. For rule-of-law thinkers, the doctrines, principles, and policies thus have an object-like character. They are there to be read and can be read with the accepted procedures, methods, and norms of legal thinkers.

For rule-of-law thinkers, law "works." What's more, it works fairly well. Rule-of-law thinkers hold that the legal institutions of the United States, the prevailing mode of legal reasoning, the legal decisions actually rendered are all, by and large, pretty good. For these kinds of legal thinkers, jurisprudential problems such as illegitimacy, indeterminacy, or incoherence are largely illusory. They attribute these jurisprudential problems to misguided attempts to impose from the outside—from the economics department, the philosophy department, or the *Quartier Latin*—a series of intellectual constructs and criteria that are foreign to law properly understood. The foreign imports are seen as inappropriate in either of two ways. They may be seen as inappropriate because they conflict with some important, explicit aspect of law properly understood or because they are crudely reductivist, meaning they fail to take into account all of law properly understood.

These responses are very convincing to the rule-of-law thinker. They are convincing precisely because the rule-of-law thinker always and

reduced to such one-dimensional representations. Rather, law is not capable of sound or accurate representation in theoretical form because it is much more like a craft.

125. *See* 1 J. BEALE, *supra* note 31, at 40-41; *see also supra* text accompanying note 37 (quoting same).

already understands himself as immersed *within* the rule of law and thus as competent to identify the character and composition of law properly understood. Jurisprudentially, this authority to make determinations about what is and what is not law properly understood is established and defended by the metaphor of inside and outside. The rule-of-law thinker asserts that there is an internal perspective to law that is distinct from the external perspective to law. The internal perspective is asserted to be that of the judge, with whom the rule-of-law thinker identifies implicitly. The external perspective is that of other social observers, such as sociologists and moral philosophers. The effectuation and maintenance of this distinction between the internal and external perspective creates a domain—the internal perspective on the rule of law—that is autonomous from the rest of social life and that is implicitly the rightful dominion of the rule-of-law thinker and his projected alter ego, the judge. The space of the external perspective serves as a rhetorical dumping ground for misguided, irrelevant, and threatening lines of inquiry about the rule of law.[126] Although he would never use this expression, the rule-of-law thinker understands himself to be a "privileged reader" of the law.

The interesting thing about rule-of-law thinkers is that while their most appealing self-image depends heavily on the notion that law is a craft, their scholarly and pedagogical interest has been centered almost exclusively on the articulation, improvement, and perfection of legal doctrine.[127] From law as craft to law as mastery-of-doctrine there is, of course, a certain reductive operation.[128] Yet rule-of-law thinkers are unlikely to experience this reductive operation as reductive at all. On the contrary—for rule-of-law thinkers there is an implicit and unquestioned equation of the craft of law with the mastery of doctrine and doctrinal argument. What this reductive equation avoids is the problem of the subject: what kind of subject—more precisely, what kind of person—is presupposed, is necessary to practice law as a craft? What kinds of moral virtues, talents, and faculties are required in order to make the law-as-craft vision not only plausible but actual in contemporary American culture? These are questions that typically do not arise for the rule-of-law thinkers.[129]

126. For an elaboration of how the internal-external distinction is used to construct, stabilize, and insulate The Law, see Schlag, *Politics of Form*, *supra* note 7, at 916-26.

127. There is a sense in which, although the rule-of-law thinkers have moved far beyond Langdell and the formalists, nonetheless the actual role they play in their scholarship and teaching has remained essentially the same. *See infra* text accompanying notes 412-15.

128. *Cf.* Winter, *Without Privilege*, 139 U. PA. L. REV. 1063, 1065 (1991) (noting pragmatists Margaret Jane Radin and Frank Michelman's characterization of the practice of normative legal thought as "a unitary, static, or invariable 'thing,' [rather than] a dynamic pattern of performance").

129. In a related context Anthony Kronman has pointed out that the question of why one

The Problem of the Subject

And yet, these are crucial questions for the rule-of-law vision. They are crucial because the rule-of-law thinker imagines that legal meaning is produced and secured by a well-trained professional who possesses the moral virtues and epistemic capacities necessary to read doctrines, principles, and policies in a manner that secures and preserves their true (or best) meaning. The capacity of the rule-of-law vision to avoid lapsing back into one or the other of the transcendental strategies of the legal formalist (*i.e.*, reconstruction) or disaggregating into an unappealing pile of fragmented doctrines and principles (*i.e.*, disintegration) depends precisely upon the continued presence on the legal scene of such a competent individual subject.

Sometimes the rule-of-law thinker answers this problem by suggesting that it is a nonproblem, that common sense or good judgment are sufficient to safeguard the rule-of-law enterprise and to assure that each doctrine, principle, or policy is used "correctly." But there is something tendentious in such an approach. To say that good judgment allows the rule-of-law thinker to "know" which doctrine applies when is a bit too self-congratulatory. Is good judgment here something more than a nice name for arresting certain potentially problematic lines of inquiry? And if so, is "good judgment" all that different from "lack of imagination" or "intellectual mediocrity?"[130]

In one sense the rule-of-law thinker might try to put an end to these questions by answering, "No." To put it in less charged terms: it may in some sense be correct to say that the rule of law "works" because the legally trained have acquired through years of arduous training serious perceptual and intellectual deficits and limitations. I would say that the rule of law "works" precisely to the extent that its practitioners have lost the ability to perceive and apprehend how law doesn't "work." Now, there is a sense in which this is undoubtedly true. But still, this quasi-

should care about being or becoming a lawyer has been largely ignored. Kronman, *Living in the Law*, 54 U. CHI. L. REV. 835, 837 (1987).

By contrast, Kronman recognizes that "[t]o practice law well requires not only a formal knowledge of the law (a knowledge of what the legal realists termed the 'paper' rules or rules 'on the books') but certain qualities of mind and temperament as well. Most lawyers recognize this . . . ." *Id.* at 841 (footnote omitted).

130. My point here is not that distinctions cannot be drawn. Rather, my point is to show that the isolation of virtues from vices is not as easily achieved (theoretically or practically) as we are often led to believe. Consider the following list and ask yourself what enables practical or theoretical distinctions between

common sense	and	slavish conventionalism
good judgment	and	intellectual mediocrity
sympathy	and	prejudice
detachment	and	lack of empathy
intelligence	and	shrewdness

Texas Law Review Vol. 69:1627, 1991

Kantian move is not terribly satisfactory. A quasi-Kantian attempt to ground the rule-of-law vision on the intellectual limitations of its practitioners is problematic precisely to the extent that the legitimacy of the rule-of-law vision depends upon the pursuit of truth, justice, and reason.[131]

Recently, the intellectual heat on identifying a competent individual subject for the rule-of-law vision has been turned up. Intellectual currents—notably critical legal thought and moral and economic theory—have created great intellectual pressure to answer precisely this question. The moral and economic theorist's insistence on coherence and elegance in legal thought[132] and the critical insistence that rule-of-law thinking is recursively contradictory raise the stakes for rule-of-law thinkers in locating and reproducing a legal subject who can meet the theorist's intellectual requirements and rebuff the cls critique. What is needed here is an account of the subject that can make the view of law as a craft at once plausible and appealing. More than that: What is needed is a reconstitution of the kind of subject who could give the lie to the malaise so well described by David Kennedy:

> Doctrinal argument seems increasingly complex and ever less able to determine outcomes. The normative moorings of the most basic doctrinal discourse by lawyers, scholars and judges seem infirm .... The more diverse the sphere of an argument's application, the thinner it seems to become until its manipulability becomes more apparent than its persuasive clout. The result has been ever more polarized arguments, ever more sophisticated doctrinal diversity, and ever more narrowly applicable holdings.[133]

What matters in David Kennedy's description is not whether doctrinal argument is or is not determinate or how much. Framed in that way, the question presupposes that what matters is the state of the law conceived in objectified terms. But that's precisely what is not in issue. What is in issue, and what is so well captured by David Kennedy's account, is that doctrinal argument is experienced as infirm, indeterminate, and manipulable. What is in issue is precisely the condition of the subject, that a large number of legal thinkers of David Kennedy's generation and

131. I don't discount the possibility of resurrecting some vision of the rule of law by appeal to a notion of institutionally inculcated intellectual and perceptual deficits. In some sense, the inculcation of intellectual and perceptual deficits is precisely what the first year of law school (with its rule-of-law orientation) accomplishes. But my sense is that to ground the rule-of-law vision in some sort of description of the socially instituted limitations of the legal thinker is likely to be normatively and aesthetically offensive to the academic practitioners of the rule-of-law vision.

132. *See, e.g.*, Posner, *Utilitarianism, Economics and Legal Theory*, 8 J. LEGAL STUD. 103, 110 (1979).

133. Kennedy, *Critical Theory, Structuralism and Contemporary Legal Scholarship*, 21 NEW ENG. L. REV. 209, 211-12 (1986).

The Problem of the Subject

younger often (not always) experience doctrinal argument as infirm, indeterminate, and manipulable.

The problem here is the problem of the subject. Doctrinal legal argument simply increasingly fails to speak. And this state of affairs is not going to be repaired by complex arguments that Wittgenstein or William James can help underwrite the practice of doctrinal argument. Suppose they do. So what? Even if the Wittgensteinian or pragmatic arguments are correct, the connection still needs to be made between what those philosophical arguments tell us is true and the social condition or cognitive practices of the subject. Absent an extreme philosophical idealism (which would treat law as philosophy's colony), there is no reason to suppose that these kinds of philosophical arguments have any practical or desired effect on the practices or condition of the subject. Philosophical accounts drawn from Wittgenstein or William James can help fend off certain kinds of arguments launched against the rule-of-law vision.[134] But these philosophical accounts fail to reconstitute the legal subject as epistemically and normatively competent to realize the rule-of-law vision. It is not enough—not socially, rhetorically, or intellectually—simply to reaffirm that law is a craft and then invoke the support of Wittgenstein or William James. Law may very well be a craft or a language game, but that does not tell us *what kind* of craft or language game it is—or whether its self-representations are adequate or not. And the reason these arguments fail in this way (not in all ways) is that they don't address this question of the subject's competence. On the contrary, these accounts implicitly assume—they have to assume—an epistemically and normatively competent subject. In other words, these sorts of philosophical accounts assume, and thus assume away, precisely what is in question: the problem of the subject.

Now, in one sense, the rule-of-law vision has largely ignored this problem. For much of its history, the rule-of-law vision has simply presupposed the existence of such a competent subject. In its scholarship, for instance, the rule-of-law vision has quite systematically and unconsciously assumed the perspective of a normatively and epistemically competent agent and, in turn, reduced the agent to a certain idealized image of the appellate judge. Indeed, most rule-of-law scholarship is addressed to this idealized image of the appellate judge—an image that depicts appellate judges as important legal decision makers who operate more or

134. *See* Williams, *Critical Legal Studies: The Death of Transcendence and the Rise of the New Langdells*, 62 N.Y.U. L. Rev. 429, 451-57, 492 (1987) (explaining that to Wittgenstein "concepts need not be secured against every possible contingency, nor need rules be developed to deal with all the situations that people can imagine").

Texas Law Review Vol. 69:1627, 1991

less autonomously within a field of legal doctrine, but who are receptive to rational legal argument and committed to accepting the better argument.[135] The idealized appellate judge is one who does a "close reading" of the cases, venerates legal precedent, and rarely departs from the traditional pathways of conventional legal interpretation or reasoning. In this way, by presupposing the effective presence of such a competent agent, rule-of-law thinking has elided the problem of the subject.

Yet there is another crucial sense in which the rule-of-law vision has always been concerned with at least one version of the problem of the subject. Rule-of-law thinkers have been persistently concerned that, insofar as law as craft depends upon the individual subject, his or her actions and thoughts need to be constrained in some way. Typically, the problem of the subject first presents itself to the rule-of-law vision as the risk that some errant individual subject, some person occupying the critical role of judge, might fail to read the doctrine "correctly" and thus might "impose his personal values" on the rest of us.[136] This way of thinking about the problem of the subject is so deeply ingrained in rule-of-law thinkers that they are often incapable of or unwilling to think about the subject in any other way. Instead, they often subsume or reformulate other very different concerns about the problem of the subject within this problematic strategy of constraining the deviant autonomous individual subject.

Consider, for instance, Owen Fiss's reply to what he perceives as a threat of nihilism posed by critical legal thinkers and deconstructionists. He experiences and conceptualizes this threat, not so much as a loss of meaning, but as a loss of objectivity—a loss of constraint in legal interpretation.[137] Indeed, it is remarkable how passionately Fiss fears the loss of objective constraints on interpretation, how much he dreads the errancy of a deviant individual subject: "The nihilist would argue that for any text . . . there are any number of possible meanings, that interpretation consists of choosing one of those meanings, and that in this selection process the judge will inevitably express his own values. All law is masked power."[138]

For Fiss, then, the nihilist threat is personified in the radical individ-

135. Schlag, *Politics of Form*, *supra* note 7, at 848-52, 925; *see also supra* text accompanying notes 412-22 (describing the continued dominance of Langdellian formalism in defining the aesthetics of law, the jurisprudential field, and the role of the legal thinker).

136. *See, e.g.*, Fiss, *supra* note 32, at 751 (arguing that in a judicial decision, "[w]hat is being interpreted is a text, and the morality embodied in that text, not what individual people believe to be the good or right").

137. *See id.* at 742.

138. *Id.* at 741.

ual subjectivist—the one who, upon discovering that meaning is not located in the object, concludes that "anything goes." This representation of the nihilist threat as radical individual subjectivism is central to Fiss's text. And it is against this threat that Fiss sets out to reconstruct the site of legal meaning and moral value.[139]

Fiss begins his reconstruction with a frank admission of what it cannot accomplish. This retreat serves to moderate our expectations; a theoretical attempt to secure legal meaning and moral value cannot yield a wholly deterministic account of interpretation. This would be neither possible nor desirable. The only possible or desirable objectivity is a "bounded one." Between the mechanistic determinism of the naive objectivist and the "anything goes" of the radical individual subjectivist, Fiss tries to reconstruct the middle ground of a "bounded objectivity."[140]

Identifying himself as a "conventionalist," Fiss nevertheless makes an *ontological* claim for the existence of both disciplining rules and the interpretive community. For Fiss, disciplining rules constrain the interpreter and serve as the standards by which to determine the validity of judicial interpretation. The authoritative character of these rules is secured by an interpretive community that considers the rules authoritative and that is itself constituted by these rules.

Examples of well-known disciplining rules are those insisting that one consult the framers' intent, observe precedent, and justify decisions on universalizeable grounds.[141] These disciplining rules constrain interpretation. But they do not do so in the naive manner of the transcendental order of the object. They constrain inasmuch as they constitute the conditions for a community of intersubjective meaning—"the interpretive community."[142] Accordingly, it is possible within that community to disagree about the meaning of the disciplining rules. In turn, the interpretive community imbues these disciplining rules with legitimacy. Further, unlike the naive transcendental subject vision, Fiss's conception of the interpretive community is not a totalizing one. It remains possible

139. Fiss notes that he offers his disciplining rules to combat the excessive freedom Sanford Levinson bestows upon individual interpreters. Fiss, *Conventionalism*, 58 S. CAL. L. REV. 177, 186-87 (1985). Fiss also acknowledges that there is another version of nihilism. This version, rather than holding that texts can mean anything (*i.e.*, anything goes) holds instead that texts mean nothing at all. Fiss, *supra* note 32, at 763; *see also supra* text accompanying note 154 (explaining how Fiss's main defense is framed in objectivist terms).

140. Fiss, *supra* note 32, at 745-46. Fiss further elaborates on the extreme positions and firmly places himself in the middle in Fiss, *supra* note 139, at 178-83.

141. Fiss, *supra* note 32, at 754.

142. *See id.* at 745 ("Rules are not rules unless they are authoritative, and that authority can only be conferred by a community. Accordingly, the disciplining rules that govern an interpretive activity must be seen as defining or demarcating an interpretive community consisting of those who recognize the rules as authoritative.").

Texas Law Review Vol. 69:1627, 1991

for individual interpreters to play an important personal role in the meaning-giving process.[143] The result is that "[w]e can find in this conceptualization a recognition of both the subjective and the objective."[144] Or as he says elsewhere, "I conceive the interpretive process as a dynamic interaction between the text and the reader."[145]

It is clear, then, that Fiss wants very much to reconcile the subject and the object in the medium of interpretation. But, at the same time, he wants very much to make legal interpretation constraining. The first desire leads him to the strategy of *collapse*, that is, the refusal to specify strong subject-object relations. The second desire—to constrain interpretation—leads him to a displacement and a *reconstruction*, one which resituates the transcendental object in the disciplining rules and supplants the transcendental subject with the interpretive community.

In the collapse mode, the disciplining rules and the interpretive community—the object and the subject—stand in a reciprocally constitutive and constraining relation.[146] Without more, of course, this leaves the relation of subject and object rather unspecified.[147] Indeed, both disciplining rules and the interpretive community are concepts that appear to have substance and meaning, but in fact have very little. For instance, consider what Fiss says about disciplining rules:

> 1. They receive their authority from the interpretive community.
> 2. They also constitute and define the interpretive community.
> 3. They are norms.
> 4. They can be internalized.
> 5. They can also be objects of conscious self-reflection.
> 6. They must be interpreted.
> 7. They are the standards by which the correctness of interpretation is to be judged.
> 8. They constrain legal interpretation.[148]

In defining disciplining rules in items one through eight above, Fiss at first appears to provide an answer to the problem of stabilizing legal meaning. And the answer he gives ("disciplining rules") looks like an answer. But if instead of looking at the answer, one looks closely at the

143. *Id.* at 750.

144. *Id.*

145. Fiss, *supra* note 139, at 184.

146. The constraining effect stems precisely from the fact that the interpretive community is "constituted by, and confers authority upon, the disciplining rules." *Id.*

147. It is also difficult to understand in what way their relation mutually constrains given that all Fiss can say is that it is mutually constituting. Indeed, the account provided by Fiss does not specify things much beyond the suggestion that interpretation stems from the interaction of the text, the author, the reader, and their respective communities.

148. *See id.* at 184-94.

list above, the answer loses the character of an answer and becomes instead a shorthand reference to a series of problems. Indeed, how could a text-analogue like a disciplining rule satisfy all eight characteristics above all at once? How can disciplining rules receive their legitimacy from the interpretative community, yet constrain legal interpretation? How is it that disciplining rules can be at once norms that are susceptible to internalization and yet are also objects of conscious self-reflection? What, apart from Fiss's own affirmation that these rules constrain, would make us think that they do in fact constrain?

What we have in the concept of disciplining rules is a paradigm example of the theoretical unmentionable—a concept that appears to provide a positive solution to a problem, but that is in fact nothing more than the name for a whole series of unresolved difficulties, aporias, and contradictions.[149]

To the extent that Fiss succeeds in making a compelling case that disciplining rules constrain, it is because he objectifies these disciplining rules or, better yet, because he allows the reader to do the objectifying for him.[150] In other words, the potential constraining effect of the disciplining rules (if any) stems from the fact that, despite the apparent prevalence of his collapse strategy, Fiss objectifies the rules. One very important moment of objectification lies in Fiss's assertion that the disciplining rules are contained in the delimited and ascertainable text of law[151]—a text that can apparently be distinguished from the moral or social text.[152] This assertion serves to locate the possible set of materials from which the disciplining rules might be drawn and to exclude other sources. Second, the disciplining rules apparently take a flat, static and ostensibly self-coinciding form—just like objects. The objectified form of the disciplining rules is evident in their interrelations. Fiss says very little about the relations among the various disciplining rules—but what he

149. *See supra* text accompanying note 118.

150. Indeed, this vision of rules as constraining objects is part of the conventional metaphorics of our conceptual system. *See* Winter, *supra* note 28, at 1216-17 ("It is LAW personified that lays down the rules (from the Latin *regula*, meaning straightedge, and *regere* meaning to lead straight). . . . This understanding . . . views LAW as a constraint on motion, much as a path constrains travel. . . . Thus, it is the objectified constraint of the path that is the object referred to in the phrase 'to break the law.' ").

151. Fiss, *supra* note 32, at 740.

152. *See id.* at 750. By situating the disciplining rules within the legal text, as opposed to the moral or social text, Fiss has located these rules within an objectified form. In one sense, he clearly needs to do this to constrain interpretation and to prevent the creation of law from materials that are not themselves legal. On the other hand, this move in effect situates the disciplining rules in an objectified field—a field of delimited legal materials. Fiss's rules constrain precisely to the extent that he objectifies them. And yet, as he correctly notes, objectification is precisely the sort of naive strategy that does not work. *Id.* at 762-63.

does say suggests a relation that is at once objectified and, not surprisingly, constraining. Says Fiss:

> The image I have in mind is that of a judge moving toward judgment along *a spiral of norms that increasingly constrain*. At any point in the spiral there might be a disagreement over the meaning of a rule . . . . To resolve this dispute, the disciplining rules must be interpreted and the process of interpreting those rules must itself be constrained by other norms further along or higher up the spiral.[153]

This spiral—or, really, hierarchical arrangement—of disciplining rules is, of course, an extremely orderly and stable depiction of the relation among the various disciplining rules. Each rule has its place in the hierarchy.

In sum, the strategy deployed by Fiss goes as follows: First, as in any collapse strategy, he recognizes the futility of reconstruction. He notes, for instance, that law is both subject and object. But no sooner does he acknowledge the futility of reconstruction than he displaces objectivity from the text of ordinary law to the realm of disciplining rules and projects the subjectivity of the rule-of-law thinker onto the interpretive community. Next, by noting that disciplining rules and the interpretive community are reciprocally constituting, he effectuates a *collapse*. One might speak of a dialectical collapse here: dialectical in the sense that the subject and object have become mutually dependent and collapse in the sense that the relation of both remains relatively vacant and unspecified. For Fiss, however, one unfortunate implication of the collapse is that the disciplining rules and the interpretive community are one and the same and, therefore, will not be available to sufficiently constrain each other—that is, themselves. Accordingly, Fiss remedies this lapse of constraint by objectifying the disciplining rules and authorizing the reader to engage in similar acts of objectification. Fiss is remarkably effective in simultaneously authoring and authorizing such objectifications. He rehearses some examples of disciplining rules that the reader is bound to recognize and thereby inscribes the form as well as the structure of the disciplining rules: they are clear, they are static, and they cohere. They certainly are not contradictory.

All this provides an elegant theoretical structure in which the rule-of-law thinker can project his or her own set of beliefs about law. If Fiss's account is believable because of the logic of projection, then the account hardly secures what Fiss most wants secured: constraint of the deviant subject. On the contrary, whatever constraint the individual

153. Fiss, *supra* note 139, at 185 (emphasis added).

The Problem of the Subject

legal subject experiences turns out to be his own projections of constraint. All of this, of course, throws the plausibility of the rule-of-law project—and the existence of constraint—back onto the character and composition of the legal subject.

But this is an issue that Fiss never fully confronts: for Fiss, the *initial* enablement, competence, and capacity of the individual legal subject is never really in question. On the contrary, in the routine framing of the problem of the subject as one of constraining *deviant* individual subjects, Fiss and the rule-of-law thinkers implicitly presuppose and establish the presence of a *normal* individual legal subject who is always already O.K.. They presuppose and establish an individual legal subject who is always and already competent to discharge the rule-of-law mission.

What is eclipsed in this process is a much more serious and possibly much more interesting problem of the subject: how is the legal subject rendered epistemically and normatively competent in the first place? In a telling passage at the end of *Objectivity and Interpretation*, Fiss reveals simultaneously the avoidance and the recognition of *this* problem of the subject:

> My defense of adjudication as objective interpretation, however, assumes that the Constitution has some meaning—more specifically, that the text embodies the fundamental public values of our society. I have confronted the nihilism that claims the Constitution means everything . . . . My defense does not work if it is said that the Constitution has no meaning, for there is no theory of legitimacy that would allow judges to interpret texts that themselves mean nothing.[154]

With this passage, Fiss reveals that his essay—or his "defense" as he tellingly puts it—has missed the problem of the subject. The difficulty with this defensive conceptualization is that it assumes there is something *in* the Constitution to defend in the first place. But that is to frame the question in object-form terms. And that's not the question; that's not the problem. The problem is one of the subject: is there anyone who is normatively and epistemically competent to make the Constitution mean *in a way that Fiss might approve*? Fiss presumes that legal knowledge, legal capacities, and legal aptitudes will be transmitted from generation to generation without difficulty. The problem of the subject for a rule-of-law thinker like Fiss is that the sort of subject who would be capable of interpreting the Constitution to mean something *in a way Fiss might approve* is fast disappearing from the legal scene.

154. Fiss, *supra* note 32, at 762-63.

The reasons for this disappearance are quite simple. First of all, the professional forms of argumentation and interpretation—those used by the courts—are fast becoming lifeless forms. The current judicial style

> emphasizes formalized doctrine expressed in elaborately layered sets of "tests" or "prongs" or "requirements" or "standards" or "hurdles." The judicial opinions in which these "analytical devices" appear tend to be characterized by tireless, detailed debates among the Justices.[155]

Lawyers and judges go through the motions, but the rule of law is no longer an animated vision. It rarely elicits respect or admiration.

> Think for example of the piles of books and journal articles that litter your office: With what expectations and what feelings do you turn to them? If you are at all like me, you do so with a feeling of guilty dread and with an expectation of frustration. We live in a world of specialized texts and discourses, which all too often seem marked by a kind of thinness, a want of life and force and meaning.[156]

The gods are leaving the rule-of-law temple. The most thoughtful and reflective young scholars and students understand that doctrinal argument is to be used in the same way that one uses a complaint to get a lawsuit started or a postage stamp to get a letter mailed. Postage stamps, complaints, doctrinal legal argument—all have performative value. None is to be sneered at. Each has its use in appropriate circumstances. It is even appropriate to admire the intellectual or cultural achievement required to bring each into being. But do they inspire *intellectual* respect, *moral* attention, or *aesthetic* admiration? Doubtful. Postage stamps are useful to get letters mailed. Doctrine is helpful to get a doctrinal judge to bring certain relations of coercion into play.[157] Period.

> We need note only that to the extent the writing of the judicial branch, or of the lawyer giving advice on what the law is, is the outcome of bureaucratic processes, to that extent it is in danger of losing its claim upon us and failing to leave us with a sense of obligation and willing obedience after we read and hear it . . . .[158]

For the rule-of-law thinker, this is a horrifying picture. And for the rule-of-law thinker, it is very tempting to argue that this picture must not come to pass, that belief in the rule of law and its virtues should be main-

155. Nagel, *The Formulaic Constitution*, 84 MICH. L. REV. 165, 165 (1985) (citation omitted).

156. White, *Intellectual Integration*, 82 NW. U.L. REV. 1, 5-6 (1987). "How often, for example, do you simply skim-read what is before you, and how often do you feel that nothing is lost?" *Id.* at 6.

157. *Cf.* Cover, *Violence and the Word*, 95 YALE L.J. 1601, 1617-18 (1986) (discussing how doctrine renders judges capable of overcoming any inhibitions against bringing coercive mechanisms of society to bear).

158. Vining, *Law and Enchantment: The Place of Belief*, 86 MICH. L. REV. 577, 594 (1987).

tained. But this response misses the point again—and in a very stereotyped way.[159] The question is not whether the rule-of-law vision *should* be maintained. The question for the rule-of-law thinker is much more acute and much more interesting: where is the subject who will reconstruct the rule-of-law vision?[160]

This is an acute question—rendered all the more so when one recognizes that the older generation of rule-of-law thinkers have no readily apparent successors. What remains of the lawyer's craft, of doctrinal argument tempered by public values is something that rule-of-law thinkers would probably not want to recognize as their own. As Judge Posner says, "Many students regard a law school as an obstacle course . . . . They come in believing the law is something you look up in a book somewhere. All they want to know is which book. They discover it's Gilbert's and Emmanuel's."[161] And this cannot surprise, for, as Judge Posner observes, the opinions of judges and the writings of legislators are "essentially mediocre texts."[162] As for indigenous practices of legal scholars, they entail the application of "analytical tools of no great power or beauty."[163]

For rule-of-law thinkers, then, the problem of the subject comes to be experienced as the disappearance of the subject. Few if any subjects are left on the scene—either in the courts or in the academy—who are epistemically capable of appreciating, for instance, the fascinating puzzles presented in the Hart & Sacks legal process materials.[164] Doctrinal sophistication is fast becoming a superfluous faculty—one that has lost meaning as the kind of subjects who have maintained it as a practice recede ever more rapidly into history.

Precisely because the problem of the subject presents itself to rule-of-law thinkers in such stark terms—as the death of the subject—it is difficult for rule-of-law thinkers to take cognizance of the problem. Af-

159. *See* Schlag, *Normative and Nowhere to Go*, *supra* note 7, at 178 (noting that a normative legal thinker will typically ask a challenger to engage in norm-selection with the question, "What should we do?"); Schlag, *Politics of Form*, *supra* note 7, at 805-06 (noting that when you're utterly lost it is not helpful to ask, "Where should we go?").

160. Or even more acutely (and even more interestingly): By what process might conditions be created to enable the reconstruction of a competent subject? *Cf.* Winter, *Contingency and Community*, *supra* note 7, at 989-91 (noting that the various rules constituting the "self" are created through interaction with the community).

161. Statement of Richard Posner at AALS Conference, Jan. 5, 1991, *reprinted in* Myers, *At Conference, Posner Lambasts Academics for Weak Scholarship*, NAT'L L.J., Jan. 21, 1991, at 4, col. 3.

162. *Id.* at 4, col. 4.

163. *Id.*

164. H. Hart & A. Sacks, The Legal Process: Basic Problems in the Making and Application of Law (tent. ed. 1958) (unpublished manuscript).

ter all, from their perspective, it is extremely unpleasant. Among rule-of-law thinkers, denial is thus a predictable and, *for them*, perhaps even healthy response.[165]

And yet, some rule-of-law thinkers have attempted to confront the problem. Owen Fiss is one of them. In an essay entitled *The Death of the Law?*,[166] Fiss courageously confronts the question. Characterizing both law and economics and critical legal thought as ascendant intellectual movements that reject "law as an embodiment of a public morality"[167] he writes:

> We will never be able to respond fully to the negativism of critical legal studies or the crude instrumentalism of law and economics until a regenerative process takes hold, until the broad social processes that fed and nourished those movements are reversed. The analytic arguments wholly internal to the law can take us only so far. There must be something more—a belief in public values and the willingness to act on them.[168]

And then Fiss asks the question that the rule-of-law thinkers need to ask: "Where will that belief come from?"[169] That is the critical question—or at least a way of posing it: who is the subject, and what is the social process that will regenerate a belief in the rule-of-law vision?

But then having asked the question—the *right* question—Fiss retreats to old and familiar ground: "In speaking of . . . morality . . . *I am sustained* by a historical vision—by remembering the 1960's, and the role that the law played in the struggle for racial equality."[170] This invocation of the sixties is disappointing—it seems to be a nostalgic avoidance of the problem of the subject. Then, in an unexpected and promising turn, Fiss engages again: "But for a generation born after *Brown*, after Ole Miss, [etc.] *this vision does not work*."[171] Right, exactly so, one wants to say, looking forward to Fiss's renewed attempt to engage the problem of the subject. But then—no go: Fiss proceeds to look for the regeneration of the subject in modern-day analogues of the civil rights movement. He finds feminism, expresses some doubts about the analogy and then in despair concludes, "Beyond that, it is difficult to know how a belief in

165. *See* Altman, *Beyond Candor*, 89 MICH. L. REV. 296 (1990) (arguing that jurisprudential denial and repression is not all bad); Schlag, *Contradiction and Denial* (Book Review), 87 MICH. L. REV. 1216, 1220 (1989) (reviewing M. KELMAN, A GUIDE TO CRITICAL LEGAL STUDIES (1987)) (noting that denial has the advantage of being easier, if less interesting, than acknowledgement).

166. Fiss, *The Death of the Law?*, 72 CORNELL L. REV. 1 (1986).

167. *Id.* at 15.

168. *Id.*

169. *Id.*

170. *Id.* at 14-15 (emphasis added).

171. *Id.* at 15 (emphasis added).

The Problem of the Subject

public values might be regenerated."[172]

Now, this sort of on-again, off-again attempt to deal with the problem of the subject is emblematic of the difficulties facing rule-of-law thinkers. Fiss is ultimately not able to engage the problem of the subject—because he wants to do so on his own terms, and his terms do not let him imagine any source of regeneration for the subject other than rather rigid, rather literal social analogies to the civil rights movement of the 1960s. This rigidification of the rhetorical and jurisprudential framework over time is one consequence of the lack of engagement with the problem of the subject. As history proceeds, intellectual frameworks reveal more readily, more visibly their moments of inflexibility as they show themselves increasingly incapable of mapping onto the social or political scene and incapable of adapting.

Fiss does not engage the problem of the subject because the problem is always and already framed for him within the project of entrenching and preserving his vision of law—the one informed by the civil rights movement of the 1960s—for later generations. In part there is something admirable about this highly political enterprise, especially if the relevant frame of comparison is the uninspired, uninspiring jurisprudence of the Burger and the Rehnquist Courts. But, at the same time, there is something not at all admirable about Fiss's attempt to entrench the jurisprudence of the 1960s Warren court. Fiss is attempting to force us to relive *the past* . . . and not just the past, but *his* past . . . and not just his past, but his past as *The Law*. What is particularly problematic about this is that this authoritarian strategy is inconsistent with and, in effect, neutralizes the more democratic, empowering Warren Court vision that Fiss champions. In a repetition of the sublimation of the subject that we saw at work in the Langdellian formalism,[173] rule-of-law thinkers typically situate themselves at the center of the discipline as if they were oracles whose own projections, whose own subjectivity were somehow beyond question. Again, this pattern is an entailment of the presupposition that the subject need not be questioned . . . because the subject is always already O.K. . . . because the subject is always already *us*.

This failure to engage the problem of the subject is tragic for the rule-of-law thinkers (as well as for others). For rule-of-law thinkers, it is tragic because they have thus far failed to understand that the cultural reproduction of an intellectual or moral vision is not so much a matter of handing down stone tablets (doctrinal or otherwise) as it is a matter of

172. *Id.*
173. *See supra* text accompanying note 37.

engaging the next generation. And this means engaging the kind of subject they are. In an older, somewhat objectivist and thus somewhat inadequate idiom, it means engaging the next generation *on its own turf.* This is ironic in some sense because the warning signs that the stone tablet strategy, the "restatement" approach would not work were there early. In 1970, just before Owen Fiss joined the Yale faculty, one Yale law student (later to become quite famous in legal academic circles) wrote:

> I have a strong feeling that when a professor speaks about "intellectual response" in a classroom at the Law School, what he really means is an enthusiastic, eager, involved response to the particular question he has identified for the class as "interesting." Few teachers anywhere show an enormous amount of interest in exactly what it is that makes their students enthusiastic and excited until *it becomes apparent to them that for some reason or another they have lost the capacity to evoke that response.*[174]

So the problem of the subject for rule-of-law thinkers is cast in very stark terms. The question is very much one of succession: who (if anyone) will follow in their footsteps?

Owen Fiss, at times, indicates an awareness of this problem. And yet, tellingly, the solutions he offers are either extremely grim or strikingly implausible. First, extremely grim—*The Death of the Law?*:

> [I]f the two jurisprudential movements of which I have spoken are victorious, . . . there will be people who wear black robes and decide cases, but it will be a very different kind of law. . . . In neither case will it be capable of sustaining or generating a public morality. It will be law without inspiration. This will mean the death of the law, as we have known it throughout history, and as we have come to admire it.[175]

Second, strikingly implausible—*The Law Regained*:[176]

> Sensitive to the difference between law and politics and determined to uncover the liberating potential of the law, Catherine MacKinnon and the legal practice she has developed now stand as an inspiration to an entire generation of law students. She has shown them what they can do with the law, not simply as power, but as an especially disciplined kind of power.[177]

Fiss's statements concerning Catharine McKinnon, as well as his entire effort to assimilate feminist jurisprudence into his vision of the 1960s civil rights movement, seems a strained and unsatisfactory attempt to

174. Kennedy, *How the Law School Fails: A Polemic*, 1 YALE REV. L. & SOC. ACTION 71, 79 (1970) (emphasis added).

175. Fiss, *supra* note 166, at 15-16.

176. Fiss, *The Law Regained*, 74 CORNELL L. REV. 245 (1989).

177. *Id.* at 253.

produce (if only rhetorically) a jurisprudential heir—one that just isn't there.

Now, it is important not to overstate the point. Even if the rule-of-law thinkers continue to fail to address the problem of the subject, orthodox doctrinal legal thought will no doubt continue to occupy the vast majority of hours in the classroom and most of the pages of the law reviews. But it will become an increasingly uninspiring, hackneyed, and mediocre form of thought—one which fails to engage the problems or the generations of the day, a way of talking that has to be used because the powers that be have lost the imaginative capacity to talk any other way. It'll be just a bunch of rules of law.

III. Critical Legal Sartre

"But he did not like structuralism."

—Simone de Beauvoir (on Jean-Paul Sartre)[178]

Instead of beginning with the stereotypical scholarly frameworks for examining cls (indeterminacy, contradiction, incoherence, or the "law is politics" slogan), consider the social situation of young, left, liberal legal thinkers circa 1975. This is a group of young scholars whose defining political and cultural experiences are significantly influenced by the civil rights movement, the Vietnam war, and the counterculture. This is a generation pervasively alienated from mainstream American culture—more likely to find resonant meaning and guidance in *Being and Nothingness* than in *Huckleberry Finn*.[179] This is a generation that, as a result of government policy—lies during the Vietnam war—has acquired a permanent distrust of authority, authority structures, and authority figures, or any word w/6 of authority.[180] This is a generation that has gained an acute, highly developed, pervasively internalized understanding that reasoned argument (particularly the best and brightest reasoned argument) can never be taken just on its own terms but must always be read for the violence,[181] the death, and the power that the argument simultaneously

178. S. de Beauvoir, Adieux: A Farewell to Sartre 33 (1984).

179. This is, of course, a premature anticipation of a critique to arrive many years later in which Paul Carrington will remonstrate with the crits for not loving the river enough and for trying to replace Mark Twain with a nihilistic worm at the heart of being. *See* Carrington, *supra* note 99, at 222, 227.

180. Of course, if the Vietnam war was a demonstration of this point, Watergate was its protracted confirmation.

181. "It should not be so difficult to admit that a substantial part of the pleasure of being aggressive in class consists of being able to demolish students. And that another substantial part consists of being able to impose on them, by 'main force' of reason, a concept or conclusion they might not have reached alone." Kennedy, *supra* note 174, at 74 (commenting as a law student at Yale Law School).

Texas Law Review Vol. 69:1627, 1991

effects, engenders, and disguises.[182] This is a generation that has lived through virulent reversals of the Oedipal myth: Daddy kills his young—literally and figuratively.

So here it is 1975, and this generation is entering the ranks of teaching in law schools. Here they are going to lectures at the AALS. Here they are listening to talks at various faculty colloquia throughout the country. Here they are arguing in the hallways adjoining the faculty offices. Here they are eating their lunches from paper bags in the faculty lounges of American law schools everywhere. Here they are—and what do they hear? What do they encounter?

What they encounter, over and over again, is the deeply doctrinal,[183] judge-identified, un-self-conscious,[184] self-satisfied,[185] stiff, and pompous[186] rule-of-law rhetoric. Now for them this rule-of-law stuff is déjà vu with a vengeance.[187] If you are a young liberal thinker circa

182. This critical approach to interpretation is as good an explanation as any for the well-known virulence of the critical legal thinkers' reaction to the jurisprudence of Ronald Dworkin. When Ronald Dworkin announces that interpretation consists of "making the material the best it can be" it is as if he had just declared himself to be the William Westmoreland of Jurisprudence. *See* R. DWORKIN, LAW'S EMPIRE 413 (1986) (noting, after an extended discussion of "what law is," that the definition holds true "for the people we want to be and the community we aim to have").

For critical legal thinkers, "making the material the best it can be"—the principle of charity in interpretation—is precisely the sort of interpretive approach that led Americans to believe the lies of their government and to overlook the violent realities implicit in such expressions as "Vietnamization," "pacification," "no longer operative," "post-traumatic stress syndrome," and all the other double-talk that emerged during the Vietnam war.

Note that this double talk reemerged during the war with Iraq. We did not *bomb* targets, we "*visited*" them. If necessary, we "*revisited*" them. The targets were not *destroyed*; they were "*acquired*." We had lots of military "*assets*" from which, of course, we got "*dividends*." All of these euphemistic expressions served to avoid the evocation of the violence, carnage, death that war is. Professor William Lutz notes that "you start getting two to three times removed from the reality that you're supposed to be talking about." *Morning Edition* (NPR radio broadcast, Jan. 28, 1991) (transcript on file at *Texas Law Review*).

183.

> What is needed is a feeling that for once a piece of doctrine will be challenged from a *new* direction rather than confronted for the thousandth time with some well known countervailing principle . . . . After a certain amount of this, the impression grows that the law is without what could properly be called theoretical or philosophical problems. There are only "conflicting principles", factors to be "balanced", and problems to be "left" to this, that or the other institution . . . .

Kennedy, *supra* note 174, at 84 (emphasis in original).

184. "At a bare minimum it seems to me that the faculty as a group is guilty of an astounding lack of awareness of what they are doing." *Id.* at 73.

185. "It is hard for the student not to wince at the air of magisterial self-satisfaction with which professors tend to approach questions they know little about." *Id.* at 72.

186. "One of the first and most lasting impressions that many students have of the Law School is that the teachers are either astoundingly intellectually self-confident or just plain *smug*." *Id.* at 71 (emphasis in original).

187. This is Kissinger jurisprudence. It's early McNamara doctrine. It's all the same.
From (Southeast Asian) domino theories to (constitutional) slippery slopes;
from reason of state to institutional competence;
from military latinate abstractions to Weschlerian conceptions of neutrality;
from fetishism of the free world to fetishism of the rule of law;

1975, you experience this jurisprudential rhetoric not at all as an exercise of reasoned argument (which it represents itself to be), but as a kind of rhetorical police action—the intellectual or discursive equivalent of police lines. Not only are there things that you cannot do or say—lines you cannot cross—but you are not even permitted to talk about the fact that there are lines you cannot cross or inquire into the whys or wherefores. Indeed, you have just landed in a rhetorical zone whose recursive argument pathways (such as neutrality, objectivity, universality, and a curiously intense fascination with authority-based arguments) immediately rule out or disable your kind of argument as extralegal and overly political, not to mention bad and probably nontenurable. What you experience as a rhetorical assault on your self[188] does not stop here. Not only are you prevented from making the kinds of arguments and articulating the kinds of visions of law you want, but you are being groomed (like it or not) to become the next Dean Rusk of Property, the next Dr. Kissinger of Contracts, the next William Westmoreland of Torts. In a word, you are being asked to become the one thing you are quite sure you don't want to become: "Dad."

Now, if you were a young scholar and you stepped into this sort of psycho-socio-political setting—one where virtually all the rhetorical action is tightly patterned to preserve the prestige, status, and conceptual matrices of the old school—wouldn't you be just a little bit tempted to do a structuralist number on them? Wouldn't you show some interest in concepts like "indeterminacy" and "antifoundationalism"? Wouldn't you show at least mild interest in something that announces itself as "deconstruction"?

Of course you would. And if you did, you would likely help construct what is now known as critical legal studies. In this sense, then, critical legal thought is like the thought of all other jurisprudential schools: its formative intellectual structure is a working out of its reaction to the recursive projection of its own primal, generation-specific encounters with The Law as it is represented by the elders in the faculty lounge . . . or in the first year classroom.[189]

> from the objectivity of (technocratic) expertise to the objectivity of (technocratic) doctrine;
> from Vietnamization to cost internalization.

Note that these equivalencies will form part of the experiential source field for the cls slogan "Law is Politics."

188. "A great many students . . . feel the socratic [sic] method . . . is an assault. The observation that students often respond physically and emotionally to questioning as though they were in the presence of a profound danger is simply *true*." Kennedy, *supra* note 174, at 72-73 (emphasis in original) (citation omitted).

189. . . . or in the legal theory workshop, or in . . . . You get the metonymic point.

Texas Law Review Vol. 69:1627, 1991

Here, then, is how the cls reaction might have been played out.[190] After years of bumping up against rule-of-law rhetoric, you might try to understand how the rhetoric is structured in a way that keeps you from making your arguments. This inquiry would present itself as at once intellectually fascinating (how does this work?) and politically significant (I can try to scuttle or use this structure once I understand how it produces its effects).[191]

In collecting these patterns of argument, you notice that they are all arranged in a systemically contradictory order.[192] And as you collect and document all this, you are stripping doctrinal argument of its power. You are no longer within the game that finds these doctrinal moves compelling or even interesting. On the contrary, you have gained a distance and achieved a perspective from which these moves begin to seem rather silly and unconvincing.[193] No longer a pawn in somebody else's chess game, you can now see the entire board: you are now a player.[194]

And at this point, of course, you have a new insight: the rule-of-law doctrinal arguments are indeterminate. They are indeterminate in oh so

190. Here I'm offering a speculative *motivational* account of the rise of the critical legal strategies—all the better to prepare you to accept my description of the subject-object permutations instanced in critical legal writings. For an excellent account of the early days of cls, one that rises beyond the merely speculative to the authoritatively anecdotal, see Schlegel, *Notes Toward an Intimate, Opinionated, and Affectionate History of the Conference of Critical Legal Studies*, 36 STAN. L. REV. 391 (1984). For a more "political" account, see Tushnet, *CLS: A Political History*, 100 YALE L.J. 1515 (1991).

191. For two different views of the instrumental, intellectual, and political character of structuralist analysis of legal argument, see Balkin, *The Hohfeldian Approach to Law and Semiotics*, 44 MIAMI L. REV. 1119, 1137-40 (1990); and Paul, *The Politics of Legal Semiotics*, 69 TEXAS L. REV. 1779, 1795-99 (1991).

192. For descriptions of the dominant recursive contradictions in early critical legal thought, see R. UNGER, KNOWLEDGE & POLITICS 76-81 (1975) (subjectivity of value versus objectivity of reason); Kennedy, *Form and Substance in Private Law Adjudication*, 89 HARV. L. REV. 1685, 1687-1713 (1976) (rules v. standards); *id.* at 1713-37 (altruism v. individualism); Kennedy, *Blackstone's Commentaries*, *supra* note 7, at 211-13 ("the fundamental contradiction").

193. Consider, for example, Boyle's admonition to torts students:

> My description should show you that these argumentative techniques are, by themselves, incapable of explaining the cases or the "rules," because for each argument or technique there is a counterargument. Without some political choice as to which side one is going to favor, *the arguments are just like pairs of cliches, e.g., many hands make light work vs. too many cooks spoil the broth; a stitch in time saves nine vs. cross your bridges when you come to them*.
>
> Like cliches they appear convincing because the judge only uses one of them at a time . . . but you have to learn that there is always another opposite one . . . . Until you learn to do this, *you will be fooled by the shell game of judicial rhetoric, which appears to deduce solutions from "legal reasoning," when in fact those decisions rest on political, moral or economic decisions*.

Boyle, *The Anatomy of a Torts Class*, 34 AM. U.L. REV. 1003, 1051 (1985) (emphasis omitted and added).

194. If you are socially constructed as a pawn, you have reason to fear the knight. But if you learn chess, you can stop being a pawn—you can actually become a player. The pawn, of course, is caught up within the moves on the board. The player, in contrast, enjoys a meta-view. And it is precisely that meta-perspective that constitutes part of the appeal of structuralism in legal thought.

The Problem of the Subject

many ways, but mostly because they are systemically contradictory—that is, it is only if one supplements these arguments with an extralegal infusion of moral, political, social, or economic context that one or the other side of the doctrinal argument can be made to prevail.[195] Once one starts to question that context, the doctrinal arguments begin to lose their power. The next insight is that there is no way to freeze the baselines. Freezing baselines is a kind of naive foundationalism—one that is not only wrongheaded, but impossible in any event.[196]

195. *See* Boyle, *supra* note 193, at 1052. The aesthetics of the description of the source or character of indeterminacy varies among the various critical legal writers—perhaps an unwitting testimony to the difficulty of freezing shared baselines (even among friends).

Here is a non-exhaustive list:

1. *The normative indeterminacy claim (Version #1)*:

Liberal legal thought is committed to systematically contradictory norms or justifying principles. Each prong of the contradiction will in any given case justify the opposite result. Thus, "[w]hile settled *practice* is not unattainable, the CLS claim is that settled *justificatory schemes* are in fact unattainable. Efforts at norm legitimation are radically indeterminate not because the source of authority *cannot* speak clearly (though, rather incidentally, she often cannot) but because if pressed, she would not want to." M. KELMAN, *supra* note 165, at 13 (emphasis in original).

2. *The normative indeterminacy claim (Version #2)*:

In order to render legal reasoning determinate and consistent with decisions actually reached, one would have to introduce political, aesthetic, and empirical assumptions that could not be (or that no one would want to see) justified on a normative basis. Since no one really wants to acknowledge these political, aesthetic and empirical assumptions as normatively legitimate, the system of legal reasoning remains on the whole normatively indeterminate. *See* Singer, *The Reliance Interest in Property*, 40 STAN. L. REV. 611, 625 n.40 (1988) (arguing that in terms of fostering desired political change within the system of law, it is more helpful to see the law as conflictual and indeterminate rather than coherent and outside of political controversy).

3. *The early-Sartre phenomenological ("I'm taking the perspective of the individual agent") indeterminacy claim*:

All legal decisions facing legal decision makers such as judges are indeterminate in that the legal decision maker remains at each instance free to choose (and responsible for choosing) the manner in which (the scope, the reach, the meaning, the structure, the closure or lack thereof) the law binds him or her. *See* Kennedy, *Freedom and Constraint in Adjudication: A Critical Phenomenology*, 36 J. LEG. EDUC. 518 (1986).

4. *The political value choice insufficiency indeterminacy claim*:

Liberal legal thought is indeterminate because it cannot yield outcomes absent further specification of (unredeemed and controverted) political or aesthetic or rhetorical choices about how to characterize what is at issue and what is the context. Boyle, *supra* note 193, at 1052.

5. *The circular indeterminacy claim*:

The authority of all conceivable legal requirements (*e.g.*, facts, precedent, intentions of parties to the agreement, and policy considerations) ultimately rest upon each other in a circular manner and are thus always subject to destabilization in any given case. Frug, *Argument as Character*, 40 STAN. L. REV. 869, 870-71 (1988).

6. *The undeterminacy indeterminacy claim*:

The medium range regularities observed in the interpretation and application of legal rules in given contexts are not "*necessary* consequences of the adoption of a given regime of rules." Gordon, *Critical Legal Histories*, 36 STAN. L. REV. 57, 125 (1984) (emphasis in original).

196. The myth of the subject-object metaphor is the projection of some place either in the subject or the structure of things, that is outside social inscription. But there is no point beyond social inscription, no law separate from politics, no knowledge separate from power, no reason separate from imagination, no things underneath mere words, and no free subjects separate from social language. The myth of presence is the treachery of

As you look back at what this structuralist account reveals, what you see is contradiction, indeterminacy, and foundationalist attempts to cut off serious legal inquiry. At this point, given the unbelievably upbeat and cheery tone of doctrinal legal argument, it is a cinch for you to recognize that doctrinal thought is a species of legitimation.

Now, as we can tell from the foregoing, there are close connections between the social experiences of cls thinkers and their intellectual claims. Indeed, one can find in Duncan Kennedy's student essay, *How the Law School Fails: A Polemic*,[197] the expression of the experiential basis for virtually every major claim that not only Duncan Kennedy but cls was to make during the period from 1975 to 1984: the decline of liberal legal thought and the corresponding turn to structuralism, indeterminacy, and contradiction.[198] Indeed, these points are corroborated by the text-footnote interaction in this very Article.[199]

This close connection between the social experiences and the intellectual claims of cls thinkers hardly distinguishes cls from any other jurisprudential school. What does distinguish cls from other schools, however, is that these connections or relations have themselves become a focus of inquiry for critical legal thought. James Boyle, for instance, conceptualized this interaction in terms of a tension between the structuralist and the subjectivist strands of critical thought:

> On the philosophical level, the subjectivist strand stresses the importance of the individual's subjective experience. It develops its picture of the social world through phenomenological descriptions of that experience. . . . Conversely, the structuralist strand focuses, unsurprisingly, on structures. . . . [T]he structuralist strand . . . tries to expose the constraining quality of the structures of everyday life, which are embedded in legal decisions, standard arguments, or in the unproblematic assumptions on which a discussion is based.[200]

One of the interesting and valuable aspects of Boyle's account is that he articulates what appears to be an obvious tension between the subjectivist and the structuralist strand.

Boyle summarizes the tensions as follows: "Each strand, in other words, both contradicts and relies on the other. Each contains the dan-

> self-denial as we filter our perception and communication about social life through the official metaphors of validity.

Peller, *supra* note 7, at 1290.

197. Kennedy, *supra* note 174.

198. *Id.* at 79, 80-81.

199. *See, e.g.*, *supra* notes 183-88 and accompanying text (and accompanying interaction).

200. Boyle, *supra* note 78, at 741-43 (citation omitted).

gerous supplement . . . of its opposite."[201] This description appears symmetrical: it seemingly refuses to accord any privilege to either the structuralist or the subjectivist strand. In contrast to Boyle, Duncan Kennedy denies any incompatibility between the two strands.[202] But like Boyle, Kennedy accords symmetrical status to both the subjectivist strand (traced to Sartre's *Being and Nothingness*) and the structuralist strand (traced to Levi Strauss's *The Savage Mind*).[203]

This apparent symmetry is misleading; it covers up a problematic and relentlessly recursive subject-object hierarchy in critical legal thought. We can see this hierarchy at work and the asymmetry revealed once Jamie Boyle begins to describe the political and intellectual aims of both the subjectivist and the structuralist strands: "The subjectivist strand is informed by 'the idea of personal liberation.' By 'personal liberation' I mean the vision of an individual who expresses and affirms her personhood by bursting free of the *constraints* imposed by the *reified structures of social life*."[204] As for the structuralist strand, it has the same aim:

> By uncovering "what is really going on," the structuralist strand in critical legal studies tries to expose the *constraining quality* of the *structures of everyday life*, which are embedded in legal decisions. standard arguments, or in the unproblematic assumptions on which a discussion is based. And this philosophical description of structure is only meaningful insofar as it manages to evoke the actual *experience of constraint*—the profane feeling of limitation by the illusion of necessity.[205]

With this account of the aims of critical legal thought, the symmetry disappears in favor of an asymmetrical convergence on a single goal to be attained by a single means. The single means is the intellectual and political empowerment of the individual subject. The single goal is the liberation of the individual subject from the constraint of oppressive reified structures. Or as Jamie Boyle puts it: "Critical legal thought offers accounts of *structures* of thought with the aim of liberating *subjective* potential."[206]

Here cls establishes a very sharp subject-object hierarchy. The recurrent picture informing critical legal thought is that legal thinkers are already politically and morally competent subjects who are systemati-

201. *Id.* at 744 (footnotes omitted).

202. Kennedy, *A Cultural Pluralist Case for Affirmative Action in Legal Academia*, 1990 DUKE L.J. 705, 746.

203. *Id.* at 746 & n.80.

204. Boyle, *supra* note 78, at 742 (emphasis added).

205. *Id.* at 743 (emphasis added).

206. *Id.* at 745 (emphasis in original).

cally mystified and constrained by an oppressive object-order of legal structures and thingified social roles.[207] The critical image here is of the competent subject encased like a prisoner within the cage of objectivity[208]—a cage that is ironically of his own making. This leads to a politics aimed at setting the prisoner-subject free. This image and the politics it engenders are recursive throughout critical thought:[209]

> By criticizing those justificatory structures we "*open up space* to think and act in the world."[210]

> The thing that makes political phenomenology so attractive is its insistence that the subjective, immediate moment contains within itself vast possibilities, which are no sooner experienced than they are *covered over* by the *cloying film projected by a "thingified" set of social roles*.[211]

> This is not simply a description of the workings of legal discourse; it is a polemic against the experience of *structural constraint everywhere* in social life.[212]

> If you really take seriously the notion that freedom is *just* interstitial, doesn't have an essence, it's just things you can do in spite of the structured character of the situation, that's freedom—then it's always there; there are always millions of things you can do in spite of the structured character of the situation.[213]

Now, this prototypical cls image of the individual subject encased by reified legal structures and thingified social roles turns out to be the recursive playing out of Jean-Paul Sartre's phenomenology of consciousness. In turn, Sartre's phenomenology is the recursive playing out of a few excruciatingly rationalist moves[214] made early in *Being and Nothingness*. In the introduction to *Being and Nothingness*, Sartre wrote, "*consciousness is a being such that in its being, its being is in question in so far as this being implies a being other than itself*."[215] This inevitable noncoincidence of consciousness with itself, this "decompression of being"[216]

207. *See* Gabel, *Reification in Legal Reasoning*, 3 RES. LAW & SOC. 25, 26-29 (1980).

208. I am borrowing this image of the prisoner-subject from Balkin, *Ideology as Constraint*, *supra* note 9, at 1040-41.

209. *See* Boyle, *supra* note 78, at 766 ("What does all of this tell us? No matter which trace one looks at, the tension between subjectivism and structuralism seems to occupy center stage.").

210. *Id.* at 739 (emphasis added) (quoting Gary Peller).

211. *See id.* at 762 (emphasis added).

212. *Id.* at 765 (emphasis added).

213. Gabel & Kennedy, *Roll Over Beethoven*, 36 STAN. L. REV. 1, 53-54 (1984) (emphasis in original) (comments of Duncan Kennedy).

214. "Rationalist" as I describe this mode of thought in Schlag, *Missing Pieces*, *supra* note 7, at 1210-13.

215. J.-P. SARTRE, *supra* note 78, at 24 (emphasis in original).

216. *Id.* at 121.

is what, for Sartre, defines the being of the for-itself (roughly, the subject). Total self-coincidence, on the other hand, is the being of the in-itself (roughly, the object). As Sartre puts it, "[t]he in-itself is full of itself."[217] It is a "perfect equivalence of content to container."[218] Hence, for Sartre, the being of the for-itself (the subject) is radically and irretrievably separate and distinct from the being of the in-itself (the object).

This radical separation of the for-itself and in-itself, subject and object, ego and world is established early in Sartre's work by the privileging of an epistemological—some have said Cartesian[219]—phenomenology. Sartre starts his phenomenology with what consciousness can *know*; more precisely, he starts with what a highly intellectualized consciousness can know.[220]

The argument is extraordinarily rationalist in tenor. It goes like this: in order to be conscious of something—say, a table—it is necessary to be conscious of being conscious of the table. This follows because if one were not conscious of being conscious of the table, then we would have "a consciousness ignorant of itself, an unconscious—which is absurd."[221] How, then, is consciousness to be secured? If we keep thinking of consciousness as knowing consciousness then we are faced with two unattractive possibilities. Either we declare some arbitrary end to the series of reflexive knowings (*i.e.*, a knowing consciousness that (absurdly) is not conscious that it knows) or we run into an infinite regress. To avoid these two unattractive possibilities, we must do as Sartre says: "If we wish to avoid an infinite regress, there must be an immediate, noncognitive [*i.e.*, nonknowing, nonpositional] relation of the self to itself. . . . In other words, every positional consciousness of an object is at the same time a non-positional consciousness of itself."[222] Now, of course, as a result of this last move, consciousness becomes precisely that which escapes knowledge, as Sartre is quick to point out: "We . . . have apprehended a being which *is not* subject to knowledge."[223] Later Duncan Kennedy will echo the point: we have here a being that "is ineffable, unjudgeable, ungraspable with the apparatus of thought."[224] Sar-

217. *Id.* at 120.

218. *Id.* at 120-21.

219. *See* K. WHITESIDE, MERLEAU-PONTY AND THE FOUNDATION OF AN EXISTENTIAL POLITICS 71 (1988).

220. Sartre denies this. J.-P. SARTRE, *supra* note 78, at 17-18 ("Henceforth, we have escaped idealism. For the latter, being is measured by knowledge . . . . There is only *known* being; it is a question of thought itself. . . . We, on the other hand, have apprehended a being which is not subject to knowledge and which founds knowledge . . . ." (emphasis in original)).

221. *Id.* at 11.

222. *Id.* at 12-13.

223. *Id.* at 18 (emphasis added).

224. Kennedy, *supra* note 202, at 745.

tre's next move is to universalize this ineffable, nonpositional, noncognitive being of self-consciousness: "This self-consciousness we ought to consider not as a new consciousness, but as *the only mode of existence which is possible for a consciousness of something*."[225]

And from this beginning, everything (all of Sartre's philosophy) follows:

> If the standard of all certainty is uncovered in the Cartesian inner dialogue that strips existing things to their essence, then it follows logically that nothing else can possibly exist with the same degree of truth as my own ego. With nothing else do I have such intimate contact. Because the analysis starts from the cogito, because thought is made the measure of truth, everything external to the ego, including other persons, is first assimilated to the status of an object.[226]

Hence, despite Sartre's constant self-conscious efforts to avoid lapsing into idealism, to avoid according primacy to thought over being, his own beginnings betray his best ambitions. The kind of consciousness that Sartre starts out to secure is a *knowing consciousness*—one that he posits as knowing something like one knows a table (in the manner of a distinct object). That kind of knowing consciousness,[227] which already presumes a sharp separation of subject and object, is not universal.[228] And when it passes for a universal mode of being, as it does in Sartre's work, it falsely represents not only its own character, but the world and its situation in the world.

Failing to recognize the partiality of his own starting point, Sartre proceeds to project it right and left, even in areas of social life where it may not belong. The radical distancing of subject and object, ego and world, consciousness and role is re-enacted even in Sartre's famous example of the restaurant waiter playing at being a waiter:

> Let us consider this waiter in the cafe. His movement is quick and

225. J.-P. SARTRE, *supra* note 78, at 14 (emphasis in original).

226. K. WHITESIDE, *supra* note 219, at 78-79.

227. I would call it rationalist consciousness. *See* Schlag, *Missing Pieces*, *supra* note 7, at 1210-11.

228.

> The separation of subject and object is both real and illusory. True, because in the cognitive realm it serves to express the real separation, the dichotomy of the human condition, a coercive development. False, because the resulting separation must not be hypostatized, not magically transformed into an invariant . . . . The separation is no sooner established directly, without mediation, than it becomes ideology, which is indeed its normal form. The mind will then usurp the place of something absolutely independent—which it is not; its claim of independence heralds the claim of dominance. Once radically parted from the object, the subject reduces it to its own measure; the subject swallows the object, forgetting how much it is an object itself.

Adorno, *Subject and Object*, in THE ESSENTIAL FRANKFURT SCHOOL READER 497, 498-99 (A. Arato & E. Gebhardt eds. 1987).

> forward, a little too precise, a little too rapid. He comes toward the patrons with a step a little too quick. He bends forward a little too eagerly; his voice, his eyes express an interest a little too solicitous for the order of the customer. Finally there he returns, trying to imitate in his walk the inflexible stiffness of some kind of automaton while carrying his tray with the recklessness of a tight-rope-walker by putting it in a perpetually unstable, perpetually broken equilibrium which he perpetually re-establishes by a light movement of the arm and hand. All his behavior seems to us a game .... He is playing, he is amusing himself. But what is he playing? We need not watch long before we can explain it: he is playing at *being* a waiter in a cafe.[229]

Now, this passage presents itself as a phenomenological description of "being a waiter in a cafe." But it is not that at all. On the contrary, this is a phenomenological description of being an intellectual in a cafe—waiting for one's food, observing the waiters, and entertaining one's intellectual friends with philosophical reflections on the being of a waiter.[230] This is not the phenomenology of waiting tables. This is the phenomenology of intellectual observation while waiting for one's food.

And if we think about it, the conclusion that the waiter is playing at being a waiter doesn't have all that much to do with the waiter that Sartre is describing. I don't mean to say that the waiter could not have a moment of self-reflection and think of himself as playing at being a waiter. But if he thought about this in the manner of Sartre (and particularly if he were seriously self-reflective) he would say: "*Ah, Mais oui, en effet*—just a moment ago, I was playing at being a waiter. But now that I think about *ces choses* in this way, I am playing at being a Sartrean existentialist intellectual—that is, one who observes others from a great (virtually unbridgeable) distance in a manner already required, already legislated by an epistemic description of consciousness that radically sep-

229. J.-P. SARTRE, *supra* note 78, at 101-02. Compare Peter Gabel's description of his interaction with a bank teller: "her words are somehow 'processed'; her gestures, ever so slightly delayed, have been 'subject to review.' In other words she is playing the role of being a bank teller, while acting as if her performance is real." Gabel, *The Phenomenology of Rights-Consciousness and the Pact of the Withdrawn Selves*, 62 TEXAS L. REV. 1563, 1568 (1984).

230. And just to show this is not mere idle speculation, consider Simone de Beauvoir's reminiscence:

> On one of their weekends in Paris, they met Sartre's fellow *normalien* and friend Raymond Aron for drinks, in what has since come to be considered an encounter of epic, if not mythic, proportions. Aron was home on holiday from the year he was spending at the French institute in Berlin, where he had a scholarship to study philosophy and write a thesis. ... [W]hile they were actually imbibing the drink Aron said the liquor reflected Husserl's remark that a phenomenologist could create philosophy from anything in life. From then on, Sartre regarded that casual comment as the moment when he began to formulate his own Existential system.

D. BAIR, SIMONE DE BEAUVOIR: A BIOGRAPHY 187 (1990).

arates the subject from its object and precludes fusion."[231]

In this reflexive (admittedly ironic) reversal of Sartre's description of playing at being a waiter, we are provided with yet another example of how Sartre's thought covertly privileges the epistemic phenomenology of the intellectual knower and projects this phenomenology onto others. Sartre's observation of the waiter is already an anticipation of another crucial aspect of Sartrean thought: "the gaze" as constitutive of the relation between the self and the other. In *Being and Nothingness*, Sartre describes a jealous lover peeping through a key-hole. The lover is a subject reducing those who are seen to an object. But when the jealous lover feels observed by a third party, he is instantly degraded to the status of an object—his possibilities alienated, in the control of another.[232] "Thus being-seen constitutes me as a defenseless being for a freedom which is not my freedom."[233] This dominance of the subject-object relation governing the self-other relation enables Sartre to describe the relation between self and other as alternating moments of sadism (mastery) and masochism (self-denial).[234]

It is this universalization of the non-coincidence of the for-itself and the in-itself, this radical separation between the being of the for-itself and the being of the in-itself, between subject and object, between self and other, and between consciousness and social roles that enables Sartre as well as critical legal thinkers to imagine and conceptualize the problem of the subject as its imprisonment in reified legal structures and thingified social roles.[235]

As Sartre himself put it, "There are indeed many precautions to *imprison* a man *in* what he is, as if we lived in perpetual fear that he might escape from it, that he might break away and suddenly elude his condition."[236] Many precautions indeed. And here we encounter some irony. One of the ironic aspects of critical legal thought is that it too has become a kind of prison, a kind of critical legal orthodoxy, a sort of recur-

231.

> [T]he very being of self-consciousness is such that in its being, its being is in question; this means that it is pure interiority. . . . Its being is defined by this: that it *is* this being in the mode of being what it is not and of not being what it is. Its being, therefore, is the radical exclusion of all objectivity. . . . In short the *for-itself* as for-itself can not be known by the Other. The object which I apprehend under the name of the Other appears to me in a radically *other* form. The Other is not a *for-itself* as he appears to me . . . .

J.-P. SARTRE, *supra* note 78, at 326-27 (emphasis in original).

232. *See id.* at 348-58.

233. *Id.* at 358.

234. *See id.* at 474-534.

235. *See* H. MARCUSE, STUDIES IN CRITICAL PHILOSOPHY 166-68 (1972) (tracing the connections between Sartre's subject-object relations and the self-other relation in terms of conflict, competition, alienation, and reification).

236. J.-P. SARTRE, *supra* note 78, at 102 (emphasis added).

sive re-enactment of the Sartrean rehearsal of the subject and object, the for-itself and in-itself, consciousness and role incommensurabilities. The intellectual attempts of critical legal studies to dislodge the objective reified structures of thought in order to allow the Sartrean-existentialist subject to awaken to his or her freedom and responsibility have themselves crystallized into a frozen thought structure, into "a pod." Indeed, this point is presaged in James Boyle's observation that "[s]ubjectivism and structuralism seem to be *necessary*, almost definitional components of any kind of legitimation theory or consciousness analysis, *perhaps of any theory* about ideology and the social world."[237]

Now, of course, this possibility is itself envisioned by Sartre's phenomenology:

> If bad faith is possible, it is because it is an immediate, permanent threat to every project of the human being; it is because consciousness conceals in its being a permanent risk of bad faith. The origin of this risk is the fact that the nature of consciousness simultaneously is to be what it is not and not to be what it is.[238]

So the reification of critical legal thought can be understood within the Sartrean problematic of the radical discontinuity between the for-itself and the in-itself. To some extent, Duncan Kennedy himself provides such a Sartrean account of the reification of critical thought in *Roll Over Beethoven*.[239]

In that article, Duncan Kennedy expresses concern over the reification of certain of his own critical contributions—namely, "the fundamental contradiction" and the altruism-individualism split. Kennedy's concern is that these notions have become "absolutely classic examples of 'philosophical' abstractions,"[240] which are then manipulated and applied as if they contained some sort of overarching truth about the character of legal reality. Kennedy recants these critical artifacts and then states that they nonetheless did contain "a truth."[241] What then follows in the interchange between Peter Gabel and Duncan Kennedy is an acute Sartrean attempt simultaneously to state this truth and yet escape the objectifying implications of having stated it. The Sartrean anxiety is at fever pitch. It is, as the notorious Hindu learning on turtles suggests,[242]

237. Boyle, *supra* note 78, at 767 (emphasis added).
238. J.-P. SARTRE, *supra* note 78, at 116.
239. *See* Gabel & Kennedy, *supra* note 213, at 17.
240. *Id.* at 15-16.
241. *Id.* at 16-17.
242. *See* Crampton, *Demystifying Legal Scholarship*, 75 GEO. L.J. 1, 1 n.4 (1986) ("Like the old woman in the story who described the world as resting on a rock, and then explained that rock to be supported by another rock, and finally when pushed with questions said it was rocks all the way down.").

Texas Law Review Vol. 69:1627, 1991

Sartre all the way down. Watch.

Kennedy announces the truth identified by the fundamental contradiction as Sartre's idea that "[n]othingness is the worm at the heart of being,"[243] adding, "I'm willing to embroider that on the flag."[244] Not skipping a beat, Peter Gabel aptly responds: "Is that a universal? That you're willing to be pinned down to?"[245] This is exactly the right question. And Duncan Kennedy's response confirms that it *is* the right question—because immediately Duncan Kennedy walks away from the flag, its embroidery, and the worm at the heart of being: "Yes. As long as it's clear that the concept of a 'worm' is like 'making the kettle boil.' The idea that nothingness is the worm at the heart of being is no more defensible, but because it's an image, a metaphor, almost a joke . . . ."[246] Now here, on the constative level, Duncan Kennedy seems to be taking some distance from Sartre's proclamation that nothingness is the worm at the heart of being. It's a joke, he says. And yet, on a performative level, Kennedy's trivialization, his virtual retraction, of Sartre's slogan is precisely the re-enactment of the distance, the non-coincidence that the Sartrean subject, the for-itself, must always and already take from objectified thought-structures—from the in-itself.[247]

So, what appears to be Kennedy's conflicted stance towards the articulation of knowledge (*i.e.*, "I'm saying it,—but now I take it back") is an ironic playing out of, a repetition of his *pregiven* commitment to the Sartrean metaphysic. The problem is that there's a self-defeating aspect to Sartre. Indeed, so long as Duncan Kennedy keeps on faithfully playing the part of Sartre, he will never be able to take back enough. It is not just the fundamental contradiction that has to be recanted. It's not just the altruism-individualism split. What has to be recanted is *the very structure* (a telling phrase) of critical legal thought as divided along the lines of a thoroughly objectified structuralist moment and a subjective, Sartrean phenomenological moment. In other words, so long as it adheres to the Sartrean metaphysic, critical legal thought must (and likely will) recant whatever *knowledge* it produces. And this *must* happen because the Sartrean subject (absent bad faith) can never find itself to coin-

243. Gabel & Kennedy, *supra* note 213, at 17.

244. *Id.*

245. *Id.*

246. *Id.*

247. As noted elsewhere, "constative utterances simply describe or report states of affairs, and performative utterances are actions directed at other ends. The classic performative utterance is 'I promise'—by saying the words, the speaker engages in the act of promising." Schlag, *Missing Pieces*, *supra* note 7, at 1205 n.53 (discussing terms borrowed from J. AUSTIN, HOW TO DO THINGS WITH WORDS 3-15 (J. Uromson ed. 1965)).

cide with the in-itself.[248] Ironically then, in the ultimate reflexivity the Sartrean-existentialist subject (including the critical legal thinker) must rebel at the very confinement, the very structural jurisdiction that Jean-Paul Sartre has reserved for that subject. It is precisely that rebellion that I have been trying to provoke in the last two paragraphs: Sartre is the worm at the heart of critical legal studies.

Sartre's metaphysic is the one that prevents critical legal thought from ever fully coinciding with itself. It is Sartre's metaphysic that introduces, locates, and shapes the recursive dislocation at the heart of critical legal thought—the recursive rejection of the logic of identity at the heart of cls.[249]

It is important not to understate the significance of the Sartrean worm at the heart of cls. Indeed, despite the significant influence of poststructuralist thinkers like Derrida and Foucault on recent critical legal thought, virtually all of this poststructuralist thought has been received by cls within the formative aesthetic of the Sartrean metaphysic—the ontological non-coincidence of the for-itself and the in-itself. Indeed, Jack Balkin's recent writings confirm the point:

> I am sure that I am not the first person to note the curious relationship between deconstruction and an earlier French import—existentialism . . . . If we see life itself as the general text, the textual freedom of the deconstructionist becomes quite similar to the pragmatic (action-oriented) freedom of the existentialist.[250]

248. The point was put in more expressly political terms by Merleau-Ponty who saw Sartre's radical subjectivism as tending towards violence: "When negativity descends into the world and takes possession of it by force [then all] that opposes it appears as negation and can be put pell-mell in the same bag." M. Merleau-Ponty, The Adventures of the Dialectic 163 (1973); *see also* K. Whiteside, *supra* note 219, at 243-45.

249. In part this explains why cls has been so difficult to understand even for sophisticated critics like John Stick and Larry Solum. Working from within an Anglo-Saxon philosophical tradition that is unreflectively steeped in the logic of identity, most critics of cls (and some cls proponents as well) have been unable to understand the deliberately unstable, the designedly dislocated and dislocating character of a critical legal thought that is steeped in a continental tradition that follows Hegel. *See infra* text accompanying notes 252-54. Instead, the strategy of cls critics like Solum and Stick has been to try to pin cls claims down (in an objectified manner) to a series of stabilized propositions and then to harvest the resulting incoherence. *See generally* Stick, *Can Nihilism Be Pragmatic*, 100 Harv. L. Rev. 332, 389-401 (1986); Solum, *On the Indeterminacy Crisis: Critiquing Critical Dogma*, 54 U. Chi. L. Rev. 462, 462-70 (1987). Sophisticated critical legal thinkers typically feel unmoved and unscathed by such critiques precisely because they do not see their thought as implicated in the objectified thought representations of critics like Stick and Solum. Sophisticated critical legal thinkers—those who have done the most to escape the routine aesthetic of Anglo-Saxon analytical philosophy—understand critics like Stick and Solum to be projecting their own philosophical aesthetics onto the text of critical legal thought. *See* Schlag, *supra* note 165. In fairness to Stick and Solum and for the sake of accuracy, the unappealing nesting of Hegelian-inspired critical thought within the Anglo-Saxon analytical form is something that (some?) (many?) critical legal thinkers unfortunately accomplished all by themselves.

250. Balkin, *Tradition, Betrayal, and the Politics of Deconstruction*, 11 Cardozo L. Rev. 1613, 1629-30 (1990).

Now, from the perspective of analytical Anglo-Saxon philosophy, there does seem to be a "curious relationship" here. In fact, from that perspective, we can even refine and deepen this curious relationship by moving back from freedom to being.[251] Indeed, we can trace this curious relationship back to what must seem like the even more curious correspondence between Sartre's "nothingness" that lies at the heart of being and Derrida's "differance."[252] To analytical Anglo-Saxon thinkers, it must seem as if there is great significance in the fact that both Sartre and Derrida accord dislocation and non-self-coincidence such key roles in their own thought. But, of course, within the continental tradition so heavily influenced by Hegel, the presence of such dislocations is simply an entirely expected entailment of any approach that rejects the logic of identity—which is to say, basically *any* approach.[253] Within the continental tradition, therefore, the presence of a dislocating dislocation at the heart of Sartre and Derrida is about as significant and as interesting as the fact that both are speakers of French.[254]

For analytical thinkers who implicitly accept the logic of identity, it is much easier to see Sartrean and Derridean thought as curiously similar. And it is thus easy for analytical Anglo-Saxon thinkers to conflate Derrida with Sartre. While it is easy for critical legal thinkers to conceive of Sartrean existentialism and Derridean deconstruction as natural complements, we should not fall into that trap here. If Sartre and Derrida seem like such natural complements in critical legal thought, it is because critical legal thinkers have received (and deformed) Derridean deconstruction through the Sartrean formative metaphysic and its frozen subject-object ontology. In critical legal thought, deconstruction is typi-

251. For Sartre, human freedom is grounded in the non-self-coincidence of the for-itself with itself. *See* H. MARCUSE, *supra* note 235, at 165 ("Human freedom [as] conceived [by Sartre] is not one quality of man among others, nor something which man possesses or lacks . . . , but is the human being itself and as such.").

252. In Sartre, *nothingness* is the source of the subject's non-self-coincidence and freedom. J.-P. SARTRE, *supra* note 78, at 239. In Derrida, *differance* is the problematic and highly problematized name given to the free play of the text. *See* J. DERRIDA, *Differance*, in MARGINS OF PHILOSOPHY 1, 11-22 (A. Bass trans. 1982).

253. *See* C. TAYLOR, HEGEL 76-94 (1975).

> Hegel holds that the ordinary viewpoint of identity has to be abandoned in philosophy in favour of a way of thinking which can be called dialectical in that it presents us with something which cannot be grasped in a single proposition or series of propositions, which does not violate the principle of non-contradiction: (p.p̄). The minimum cluster which can really do justice to reality is three propositions, that A is A, that A is also Ā; and that A show itself to be after all A.

Id. at 80.

254. Or as Jacques Derrida responded himself (in a stage whisper): "Sure, sure. Same university. Same city. Same Planet." Remark made at the Cardozo Law School Conference on Deconstruction and the Possibility of Justice (Oct. 2, 1989).

The Problem of the Subject

cally (not always) depicted and used as an "analytical tool"[255] by a purportedly free individual subject. What is in Derrida the free play of signifiers becomes in Sartre the free play of the individual deconstructionist who makes the text mean what he "wants it to mean."[256] It is in this way that deconstruction gets stuffed in the stabilized, reified, acritical, and relatively uninteresting space of the *analytical tool*. The reification of deconstruction in critical legal thought is almost palpable: "Described in its simplest form, the deconstructionist project involves the identification of hierarchical oppositions, followed by *a temporary reversal* of the hierarchy."[257] What do these deconstructive operations get us? A helpful *thought experiment*: "The point is not to establish a new conceptual bedrock, but rather to *investigate* what happens when the given, 'common sense' arrangement is reversed. Derrida believes that we derive *new insights* when the privileging in a text is turned on its head."[258]

Now, of course, this is not Derrida, and it is not deconstruction. Deconstruction is not *an analytical tool* or a "method." On the contrary, as Derrida says, "We here note a point/lack of method."[259] And Derrida is not into *temporary reversals* of hierarchies—but rather "an overturning of the classical opposition and a general displacement of the system."[260] And deconstruction is not a *thought experiment* designed to provide new *insights*. Rather, deconstruction seeks to *intervene* in the field of oppositions that it criticizes, which is also a field of nondiscursive forces."[261]

How then has it been possible for critical legal thinkers to claim to practice Derridean deconstruction while manifestly following an altogether different approach? The answer is Sartre. Indeed, consider the following account of deconstruction by Jack Balkin and watch for the Sartre:

> I believe that in each case, one deconstructs because one has a particular ax to grind, whether it be a philosophical, ideological, moral, or political ax. [Even t]he deconstructor of the self is still *picking* her targets . . . . And this *choice (for we can find no other word to describe it)* is still the grinding of a particular ax . . . .[262]

255. Balkin, *Deconstructive Practice and Legal Theory*, 96 YALE L.J. 743, 786 (1987).
256. Balkin, *supra* note 250, at 1630.
257. Balkin, *supra* note 255, at 746 (emphasis added).
258. *Id.* at 746-47 (emphasis added).
259. J. DERRIDA, DISSEMINATION 271 (1981).
260. J. DERRIDA, *Signature Event Context*, in MARGINS OF PHILOSOPHY, *supra* note 252, at 329.
261. *Id.* at 329 (emphasis in original).
262. Balkin, *supra* note 250, at 1627-29 (emphasis added).

Texas Law Review Vol. 69:1627, 1991

Now, this description assumes—right down to its very choice of an agent (*i.e.*, in Balkin's sentence it is the deconstructor, not the deconstruction, that is pre-scripted as the agent doing the choosing)—precisely the sort of radically free autonomous subject that is at the heart of Sartre. This is the enclosure, the nesting of Derrida within the Sartrean metaphysic. Indeed, compare the grand role Balkin accords to the individual subject in the deployment of deconstruction with what Derrida says in the following and experience the dissonance:

> [Deconstruction is an] incision precisely [because] *it can be made only* according to lines of force and forces or rupture that are localizeable in the discourse to be deconstructed.[263] The topical and technical determination of the most necessary sites and operators—beginnings holds, levers, etc.—in a given situation depends upon an historical analysis. The analysis is made in the general movement of the field *and is never exhausted by the conscious calculation of a "subject."*[264]

Of course, the kind of subject presupposed in Balkin's account is much more consistent with Sartre than with Derrida; it is much more consistent with the subject usually presumed within legal academic thought than with the troubling of the subject usually effected by deconstruction.

It is not hard to understand how critical legal thinkers might have come, through the Sartrean metaphysic, to subscribe to Derridean deconstruction without actually practicing it. The consequences for critical legal thought, however, are quite serious. It is precisely this Sartrean metaphysic (so congenial to orthodox descriptions of the subject-object scene) that is pervasively inscribed throughout critical legal thought, and it is precisely this Sartrean metaphysic that has contributed to the self-immobilization of critical legal thought.

Now, that doesn't make Sartre all bad. Indeed, one of the important and critical contributions of cls has been to demonstrate the extent to which our socially constructed knowledge can lead to pacification and to our own personal-political immobilization.[265] After having pushed Sartre to his limits, however, we can consider precisely what kind of subject is presupposed in critical legal thought. As Jean-Paul himself said, "There are indeed many precautions to imprison a man in what he is."[266]

263. This is why Balkin is correct when he notes that deconstruction does not "seize upon every word in the text as the source of a deconstructive reverie." *Id.* at 1627. But it is only the pervasively inscribed binary, either-or form of thinking, together with the usual logocentric privileging of the normatively competent individual subject, that leads Balkin to imagine that, therefore, individual subjects must be the ones who are choosing what and how to deconstruct.

264. J. DERRIDA, POSITIONS 82 (1981) (emphasis added).

265. *See, e.g.*, Gabel, *supra* note 207, at 28-29.

266. J.-P. SARTRE, *supra* note 78, at 102.

The Problem of the Subject

And no doubt one such precaution is the configuration of the space defining him as a subject. I suggest, then, that we pause to consider the extent to which this precaution applies to critical legal thinkers. One good reason for doing so is that the development in cls of the subjectivist Sartrean strand and the structuralist strand have produced a political and intellectual image of subject-object relations that appears—shockingly enough—to be utterly conventional. Indeed, the subject at the heart of critical legal thought, the Sartrean subject, is a stunningly liberal subject.[267]

The apparent radicalism of critical legal thought does not stem from a new conceptualization of the subject, but rather from a reversal of the valences in the same old rule-of-law depiction of subject-object relations.[268] Whereas the rule-of-law thinkers radically separate and distinguish subject and object, seeking to restrain and constrain the legal subject by means of "objective law," critical legal thinkers adopt the mirror image and strive to accomplish exactly the reverse.[269] For critical legal thinkers, as for Sartre, the perpetual problem is that the subject is always constrained by "reified structures" and "thingified social roles" and that everything turns into "pods."

The only change in this picture of subject-object relations is the reversal of the traditional valences. Critical legal thought celebrates precisely what the rule of law fears: the emancipation of the individual subject. In turn, this cls reversal authorizes a whole series of aesthetically analogous reversals on the political plane—the reversal of the orthodox preference for rules over standards[270] and the reversal of the orthodox preference for freedom of contract as opposed to paternal-

267. If Sartre is the worm at the heart of critical legal studies, then the liberal subject is the worm at the heart of Sartre:

> [Sartre] attempts to found existential understanding on Cartesian categories. Being-in-itself updates Descartes' conception of a dense material world that is absolutely other to the consciousness. Being-for-itself revives Descartes' pure thinking substance that freely surveys the world. Sartre deliberately sets himself the task of standing between a deterministic positivism and an unconstrained idealism. But he is unable to define that position theoretically because the Cartesian spirit virtually possesses his philosophy.

K. Whiteside, *supra* note 219 at 71.

268. *Cf.* Genovese, *Critical Legal Studies as Radical Politics and World View* (Book Review), 3 Yale J.L. & Humanities 131, 149 (1991) (reviewing M. Kelman, *supra* note 165) ("Kelman, like Unger, Kennedy, and others, begins with the conflicted concerns of the individual and ends with his liberation . . . . In this respect they follow proudly in the tradition of the great bourgeois theorists from Hobbes to Locke and Blackstone and Burke, and beyond.").

269. This sense that critical legal theory can be understood as a recursive inversion of liberal legalist valuations is also suggested in Boyle, *supra* note 7, at 506 ("Are there uses of subjectivity rather than objectivity in order to privilege, to armor, to give authority to particular statements, particular theories, particular visions of society? I think the answer is clearly 'yes' . . . .").

270. *See* M. Kelman, *supra* note 165, at 16 ("One should expect that those on the political left like the cls writers would contribute most heavily to the pro-standards position.").

Texas Law Review Vol. 69:1627, 1991

ism.[271] What we find, then, in orthodox critical legal thought is a kind of upside-down version of liberal legalism: the valences change, but the aesthetic structure remains the same.

One consequence of this critical reversal is that all the critical hopes—political, aesthetic and intellectual—are staked on the (liberal) individual subject who, once freed from the reifications of thought and role, is to emerge as a competent intellectual and normative agent. Terrific pressure is thus placed on the individual subject, both in theory and in practice, to develop all the right normative moves and to do the right thing. As Mark Kelman puts it: "We think in prepackaged categories, clusters, reified systems. We forget the degree to which we invent the social world. We come to think that rules make us act impersonally; we often forget that we must continually choose to act impersonally."[272] This, of course, is not so much a radical vision as it is a repetition of the quintessentially liberal-legalist aggrandizement of the individual subject as a self-determining agent who fashions his or her world by choosing to realize *this* moral vision as opposed to *that* one.

Now, in a sense this is precisely the sort of understanding of the subject and of politics that we should have expected. It is precisely what one should expect from the Sartrean existentialist metaphysic, which ceaselessly saddles the individual subject with an inexhaustible responsibility to bridge the chasm of the subject and the object on the basis of ungrounded value choices. It is also what should be expected if one understands the history and the social situation of critical legal thinkers. The cls adoption of Sartrean existentialist phenomenology (the subjectivist strand) and structuralism (the structuralist strand) is a mimetic replay of precisely the relation of the personal social situation of critical thinkers circa 1975 to the intellectual claims that they advanced.

Indeed, if you reconsider the beginning paragraphs of this section, it becomes evident that the structure of critical legal thought is a projection of the social situation of critical legal thinkers onto the intellectual plane. Sartre's existentialist subject very easily describes the critical legal thinker circa 1975 sitting in the faculty lounge, experiencing rule-of-law rhetoric as an objectified thought-structure that is at once alien and hostile.

From there, it is fairly easy to get to the basic structure of orthodox cls thought. In orthodox cls thought, the spaces occupied by the legal

271. *See* Kennedy, *Distributive and Paternalist Motives in Contract and Tort Law, With Special Reference to Compulsory Terms and Unequal Bargaining Power*, 41 MD. L. REV. 563, 624-49 (1982) (suggesting that compulsory terms motivated by paternalism are both pervasive and desirable).
272. M. KELMAN, *supra* note 165, at 294.

subject are almost always explored from a phenomenological perspective (and never from a structuralist perspective). One result, then, is that these spaces are in effect immunized, removed as they are from the purview of structuralist interpretation. A second result is that the subject is almost always conceived as a projection of the critical thinker himself.

On the other side of the ledger, the objective moment in law (*i.e.*, doctrines and policy arguments) is almost always approached from a structuralist perspective (never a phenomenological one).[273] One result is that doctrine, policy, and other objectified sites of the law are almost always represented as alien and object-like, never quite resonant with the subject. A second result is that the reappropriation of doctrine and policy by the subject is not possible except in a very distanced instrumental sense. Yet a third result is that phenomenological accounts of law remain mediated by a subject who already experiences himself as free, as the original creator of his own meanings.

What we get, then, in orthodox critical legal thought is a kind of structuralism that remains confined to the most object-like moments in law: a structuralism of appellate doctrine. On the phenomenological side, what we get is a sense of the tremendous freedom of the critical subject, who cannot be constrained or confined by the objective moments of law because these objective moments are never *him*. The unbearable lightness of being a subject is a consequence of never recognizing one's self in the meaningless solidity of dead doctrine.

Notice the black holes created on both the structural and phenomenological sides of the ledger by this highly structured critical practice. Structuralism never proceeds beyond the object-forms already privileged by traditional legal thought. Hence, the deep structure turns out to be located in an utterly conventional, superficial place—in appellate doctrine. This is why structuralist interpretation has been so successful pedagogically and at the same time so visibly threatening to traditional legal thinkers. Now, in a sense this represents a victory for cls. But it is also a bit of a defeat: this sort of work does nothing to displace the conventional spaces, the conventional conceptual and social aesthetics established by traditional legal thought. To give a concrete example, even after cls structuralist interpretation, appellate doctrine remains the place where law school says the law is to be found.

Now, on the phenomenological side of the ledger, there is another

273. More accurately, the phenomenology of doctrine, policy, and other objectified sites of law is, for the orthodox critical legal thinker, almost always experienced in structuralist terms. The orthodox critical legal thinker's experience of doctrine, policy, etc. is already mediated by the structuralist framework.

black hole. Since we are always dealing with the phenomenology of a subject who is free to create his own meaning, critical phenomenology never proceeds beyond the phenomenology of freedom to "real" experiences of constraint.[274] Constraint always and already has to be experienced (at least in theory) as an illusion—always and already susceptible to structuralist dismantlement.

Ironically, what I have been trying to suggest is that this structured practice of critical legal thought is itself disabling. It is not that there is anything wrong with doing a structuralist number on doctrine or moral theory. Nor is phenomenological inquiry misguided. What is wrong is that this division among the structuralist (appellate doctrine in itself) strand and the phenomenological subjectivist (value choices) strand has become, consciously or not, the master rule, the totalizing framework. Not only is this totalizing, structured practice intellectually limiting, it is politically disabling and oppressive.

The Sartrean metaphysic constantly calls for individual subjects to recognize their responsibilities and to choose. The message is this: Avoid bad faith—choose! But, in a Foucaultian sense, this construction of the subject entails a prevailing unfreedom. Each and every social, legal, and political event is immediately represented as an event calling for a value-based choice. You are free to choose between this and that. But, of course, you are not free. You are not free because you are constantly required to reenact the motions of the prescripted, already organized configuration of the individual being as chooser. You have to, you already are constructed and channeled as a choosing being.[275] Not only is this social construction of the self extraordinarily oppressive—but it often turns out to be absurd as well. Much of its absurdity can be seen in the normative visions that routinely issue from the legal academy urging us to adopt this utopian program or that one—as if somehow our choices (I like decentralized socialism, you like conservative pastoral politics, she likes liberal cultural pluralism) had any direct, self-identical effect on the

274. Duncan Kennedy gets pretty close in Kennedy, *supra* note 195, at 526.

275.

> What I am afraid of about humanism is that it presents a certain form of our ethics as a universal model for any kind of freedom. . . . [N]ow this idea of man has become normative, self-evident, and is supposed to be universal. Humanism may not be universal but may be quite relative to a certain situation. What we call humanism has been used by Marxists, liberals, Nazis, Catholics. . . . I think there are more secrets, more possible freedoms, and more inventions in our future than we can imagine in humanism as it is dogmatically represented on every side of the political rainbow: the Left, the Center, the Right.

Truth, Power, Self: An Interview with Michel Foucault (Oct. 25, 1982), in TECHNOLOGIES OF THE SELF: A SEMINAR WITH MICHEL FOUCAULT 9, 15 (L. Martin, H. Gutman & P. Hutton eds. 1988) (sentence order rearranged).

construction of our social or political scene. The critical insistence on making political value choices is utterly captive to a conventional and nostalgic description of the political field—a description and definition of the field that is guaranteed to yield political disablement and disempowerment.[276] To tell people that they are already empowered to make political value choices is, in effect, to bolster the dominant culture's representation that we are free-choosing beings and to strengthen the forces that lead to our own repeated, compelled affirmation of (meaningless) choices.[277] By presupposing the authenticity of the Sartrean subject, critical legal thought has greatly underestimated the extent to which this "free" subject, in its very "freedom to choose," is already constructed to compulsively act out choosing behavior—regardless of whether the social, political, or rhetorical scene warrants or even enables a choice to be made at all.

In legal thought, the sterility of this approach is manifest in articles that exhort us to engage in choosing behavior while refraining from telling us what to choose. For instance, a while back John Stick argued that cls-ers and liberals ought to drop epistemic warfare and start arguing about what really counts: politics (conceived, of course, as political value choice).[278] But nothing happened and, of course, that's not surprising. All dressed up and nowhere to go. What are legal thinkers supposed to say? Three cheers for democratic socialism? I (really) like Ike? The Rawlsian difference principle really does require the Rule in Shelley's Case? There is a big and very widespread category mistake at work here: the presupposition that arguing about political values is somehow synonymous with engaging in politics.[279] Talking and arguing about political values is not necessarily (or even usually) political, anymore than talking about football is political.[280] To engage in politics is to engage with

276. *See* Schlag, *Politics of Form*, *supra* note 7, at 805-07.

277. I like:

Desert Rose corn chips (regular flavor, lightly salted, if the date of expiration has more than 10 weeks to go and the bag is not crumpled),
Japanese cars built after December 1988,
Non-tyrannical, watered-down, deontological moral theory,
Decentralized, pluralistic socialism—but only in combination with strong legal protection for the traditional liberal freedoms,
Small to medium size firms with an emphasis on corporate litigation,
Four out of six large Eastern seaboard cities but only if the commute is less than 35 minutes,
Ike.

278. *See* Stick, *supra* note 249, at 389-401.

279. *See* Schlag, *Politics of Form*, *supra* note 7, at 906-09; Winter, *Indeterminacy*, *supra* note 7, at 1473-85.

280. Now talking about football *is* in some senses political—because it typically excludes certain types of people from the conversation (women) and because it establishes and reaffirms certain bonds of solidarity and trust among other kinds of people (male sports fans). Talking about football is also

power. Arguing about political values may or may not engage with power. It depends. But there is no reason to presuppose that academic political value talk has any desired political effect whatsoever. Whether such talk has any desired political effect depends on how the aesthetics of power have enabled and constituted this political value talk and on the context within which this political value talk is issued and heard (assuming it is heard at all).

Now, it seems that critical legal thought has not considered these kinds of problems because cls thinkers have not inquired into the problem of the subject.[281] In turn, that is because critical legal thought already presupposes—indeed, is enabled by—the tacit construction of the space and the configuration of the subject. The space and configuration of the subject have been presupposed in two ways. First, á la Sartre, the individual subject "is ineffable, unjudgeable, ungraspable with the apparatus of thought,"[282] that is, he is that nothingness, that worm at the heart of being. In a second sense, however, the subject of cls thought is also understood as the people who got together in Madison, Wisconsin in 1977—complete with their rich, counterculture, new-left, oppositionalist social identities. Both of these tacit understandings of the subject converge to eclipse the problem of the subject. Sartre's metaphysic makes the subject irretrievable in such a way that there is simply no point in pursuing the problem: there is no motivation to look for the subject, because there is literally nothing to find. But even aside from that point, there is no motivation to even *start* thinking about the problem of the subject, because the primal experience is that the subject is O.K. and all the problems are situated on the outside—in the external objectified thought structures that *constrain* the critical legal thinker (and all other legal thinkers).

Of course, now the problem of the subject does arise. And it arises for critical thought in several virulent forms. First, we are coming to understand that orthodox critical legal thought is structured in terms that turn out to be antithetical[283] to the Sartrean subject.[284] The very

political because it occupies conversational space and recursively rehearses certain highly stereotyped aesthetics of social life: the corporate form, the primacy of competition, the zero-sum nature of social life, the spatialization of conflict, the importance of strategy and capital asset management, the artificiality of socio-economic and racial class, and so on. Now, if talking *about* political value choices is political, it is political in the same kind of ways.

281. *See* Boyle, *supra* note 7, at 489 (noting that cls "has concentrated too much on critiques of objectivity, wrongly assuming that 'subjectivity' was an unproblematic term").

282. Kennedy, *supra* note 202, at 745.

283. Antithetical, that is, to the extent that the subject does not actualize the permanent possibility of bad faith.

284. Hence it is really no surprise that Jean-Paul Sartre

did not like structuralism. He gave his reasons: "The specialists in linguistics try to treat

identification of legal thought as consisting of two unbridgeable and incommensurable subjectivist and structuralist moments turns out to be an intolerable burden for the Sartrean critical legal thinker to bear. What is unbearable is *the freezing of this division* as accepted or operative truth.

Second, cls thought is constantly driven by this subjectivist-structuralist division to reject whatever positive knowledge it produces.[285] This is why the highest political-intellectual program of cls is conceived as an "intersubjective zap"—a sort of ecstatic jurisprudential moment in which the false consciousness of thingified social roles dissipates, and the subject becomes one with the group.[286] But this intersubjective zap never lasts; the sort of subject required to achieve "it"—that wonderful Sartrean moment in which one recognizes one's total freedom—is of necessity unsupported and unsupportable by any objective social structure. Understood in Sartrean terms, the for-itself, despite its best intentions, is always and already transforming itself into the in-itself.[287] Cls thinking leaves us oscillating within the Sartrean metaphysic—alternating between ecstatic moments of triumph and abject moments of utter failure. Never a dull moment, but never an enduring one either.

Third, the problem of the subject arises for critical legal thought because the realization of a radically free subjectivity always seems to elicit an equal and opposite radical objectivism. In other words, a certain symmetrical supplementarity is at work here. The more the subject is conceived, constituted, or called forth as a *radical* subjectivity, the more the object will also have to be conceived, constituted, or called forth as a *radical* objectivity. This symmetrical supplementarity has already been acted out in several ways. First, of course, it has already been acted out in Sartre's *Being and Nothingness*.[288] Second, it has been acted out in the critical interventions of cls thought.[289] Indeed, the theoretical alternative that many critical legal thinkers conceive as most plausible, most serious, and most worthy of critical attention is precisely the most objectivist ju-

> language *from without*, and the structuralists, who base themselves on linguistics, also deal with a whole *from outside*; for them it is a matter of carrying concepts to their utmost limit. But I cannot do that because I set myself not on a scientific but a philosophic plane, and that is why *I do not need to exteriorize* what is entire."

S. DE BEAUVOIR, *supra* note 178, at 33 (emphasis added).

285. *See supra* text accompanying note 248.

286. This is close to Sartre's notion of "groupe en fusion." J.-P. SARTRE, CRITIQUE DE LA RAISON DIALECTIQUE (PRÉCÉDÉ DE QUESTIONS DE MÉTHODE) (TOME 1) 627 (1960).

287. Critical legal thinkers have a direct experiential confirmation of this point as they see their thought systematically reified and thus neutralized by unfriendly as well as friendly commentators. *See* Gabel & Kennedy, *supra* note 213, at 7 (suggesting that some critical thinkers have turned the fundamental contradiction into a "pod").

288. *See supra* text accompanying notes 214-35.

289. *See supra* text accompanying notes 272-87.

risprudence on the legal landscape—namely, law and economics.[290] Moreover, on a more local level, the most routine dismissal in the academy (with or without accompanying personnel action[291]) is accomplished through the tendentious objectivist claim that cls thought is not "law." In these ways, then, we can see that radical individual subjectivism tends to call forth a radical objectivism in response.

These instantiations of symmetrical supplementarity remain relatively unimportant compared to what announces itself as a much more significant political problem for cls: the resurgence of the order of the object in the form of the bureaucratic structuring of thought and life. Cls is not the only movement to insist upon the radical freedom of the individual subject. On the contrary, that theme is pervasive throughout American culture. And the problem is that this insistence on the radical freedom of the individual subject is accompanied and effectuated by the increasing pervasiveness and dominance of technology-centered, market-bureaucratic instrumentalist practices. Thus, the problem for critical legal thought is this: Critical legal thought insists on the radical freedom of the subject—but it does so at precisely the same time that the technology-centered, market-bureaucratic practices are insisting on the same thing. It thus becomes highly questionable whether the critical insistence on the radical freedom of the individual subject has any political or intellectual significance other than to help constitute a subject who is already missing the critical capacity to understand or resist the techno-instrumentalism of our private-public, market-bureaucratic practices.

Now, perhaps the Sartrean existentialist subject is competent to deal with issues like:

socialism v. capitalism
liberation v. colonialism
communalism v. individualism
or any other conventional, value-based description of the political field.[292]

The problem for critical thought, however, is that the Sartrean subject and its value-based description of the political field provide no critical or epistemic or ethical competencies to deal with the sort of politics implicit in the techno-instrumentalism of our private-public, market-bureaucratic practices. Indeed, inasmuch as the Sartrean existentialist subject and its

290. *See* M. KELMAN, *supra* note 165, at 114 (noting that "the Law and Economics movement . . . is the best worked-out, most consummated liberal legal ideology of the sort that CLS has tried both to understand and to critique").

291. or inaction

292. At the very least, one can say that the Sartrean subject is theorized and constituted as a subject who can take cognizance of these types of issues and respond cogently. This value-based description of the political field is one in which the Sartrean subject can fit.

morality are already captive to and collaborative with these practices, they are politically regressive phenomena.[293]

This brings us to the fourth and, indeed, the most serious form of the problem of the subject for cls: the subject, having been already specified as non-self-coinciding, as "ineffable" and "ungraspable" through thought, becomes that blank space in which dominating ideologies do their work free from critical inquiry. The subject presupposed by critical legal thought is precisely the sort of subject that is (in the current structuralist-subjectivist configuration of critical legal thought) impervious to critical inquiry and to thematization. For critical legal thinkers to confront the problem of the subject thus requires a reconsideration or, more accurately, a displacement of the Sartrean metaphysic that has defined and confined the enterprise of critical legal thought thus far. That, of course, is precisely the sort of reconsideration or displacement that I have been trying (ever so gently) to prompt here.

IV. Neopragmatism: Within the Context of No Context

> Wonder was the grace of the country. Any action could be justified by that: the wonder it was rooted in. Period followed period, and finally the wonder was *that things could be built so big*. Bridges, skyscrapers, *fortunes*, all having a life first in the marketplace, still drew on the force of wonder. But then a moment's quiet. What was it now that was built so big? Only the marketplace itself. Could there be wonder in that? The size of the con?[294]

A. Freedom From Theory-Guilt Now!

The remarkable advent of pragmatism in the past five years is no accident. Pragmatism is featured as an initially plausible candidate for the answer to several different but related jurisprudential embarrassments. After rule-of-law thinking stalls in a series of interpretive contretemps, pragmatism arrives to explain how the interpretive enterprise can be stabilized. After a devaluation of normal doctrinal science by fancy theorists, pragmatism arrives to lend legitimacy to standard doctrinal

293. For a profoundly alienated and apocalyptic vision of an order of the object working itself through without regard for and not subordinate to the control of individual subjects, see J. BAUDRILLARD, LA TRANSPARENCE DU MAL—ESSAI SUR LES PHÉNOMÉNES EXTRÊMES (1990). As description, Baudrillard's essay tends towards the anti-humanist extremes. Nonetheless, taken in fragments it aptly describes the sort of anti-humanist social circumstances we may have stumbled into. It is a reminder of the extent to which our social constructions work and work and continue to work regardless of us, without regard for us, through us. Baudrillard's work is helpful because it is a new marker extending the intellectual field—one that makes Weber's iron cage look like a picnic.

294. G. TROW, WITHIN THE CONTEXT OF NO CONTEXT 3 (1981) (emphasis in original).

work.[295] After grand theory fails to provide constraints on adjudication,[296] pragmatism arrives to provide a new theory of decision making.[297] After the normative aspects of critical legal thought risk devolving into irrationalist particularism, pragmatism arrives at once as the inspiration, the structure, and the legitimation of contextualism.[298]

There is thus a great deal in pragmatism to like—apparently from a great many directions. Part of the appeal of pragmatism is no doubt captured in Tom Grey's slogan: "Pragmatism is freedom from theory-guilt."[299] Pragmatism provides an intellectually respectable justification for one's inability or refusal to provide a theoretically cogent account of what one is doing.[300] Pragmatism is the indigenous American substitute for the Wittgenstein cite.[301] It is the indigenous intellectual tradition for

295. *See* Farber, *The Case Against Brilliance*, 70 MINN. L. REV. 917, 929 (1986) ("Perhaps the current bias in favor of brilliant, 'paradigm shifting' work should be abandoned. The more pedestrian 'normal science' may be the worthier endeavor."); Farber, *Legal Pragmatism and the Constitution*, 72 MINN. L. REV. 1331, 1334 (1988) ("A growing number of scholars share my discontent with foundationalism.").

296. *See* M. TUSHNET, RED, WHITE AND BLUE 1-4 (1989) (positing grand theory as an attempt to constrain judicial decision making); Minow & Spelman, *supra* note 38, at 1601 (noting the failure of abstract universal principles to resolve problems).

297. Sherry, *The Ninth Amendment: Righting an Unwritten Constitution*, 64 CHI. KENT L. REV. 1001, 1013 (1989) ("In light of the failure of the 'grand theories' to produce a useful and noncontroversial theory of constitutional constraints, many constitutional scholars have recently turned instead to anti-formalist, anti-theoretical approaches.").

298. It would be too much to suggest that critical legal thinkers have adopted pragmatism as their own approach. Hutchinson, *The Three R's: Reading/Rorty/Radically* (Book Review), 103 HARV. L. REV. 555, 572 (1989) (criticizing Rorty's pragmatism as vaguely quiescent). Yet, clearly, pragmatist approaches hold some appeal for critical legal thinkers. *See, e.g.*, Singer, *The Player and the Cards: Nihilism and Legal Theory*, 94 YALE L.J. 1, 25-26 (1984).

299. Grey, *supra* note 115, at 1569.

300. "The pragmatist thus possesses a general antidote to statements of the form 'We cannot proceed with X until we have an adequate theory of Y,' where X is a socially constituted practice and Y is an academic subject or theoretical topic." *Id.* at 1569. Now, of course, this "antidote" quality is not a distinguishing characteristic of pragmatism. The Hegelian, the Marxist, the French Existentialist, the poststructuralist, or anyone with any sort of sophisticated (*i.e.*, nonrationalist) understanding of the relations of theory and practice has a "general antidote" too.

By comparison with all these other approaches, the distinguishing mark of pragmatism is that it can provide the "general antidote" while least disturbing the already existing intellectual and social constitution of the American legal intellectual. That is why pragmatism can seem appealing (in varying degrees) to such widely different intellectual personages as Tom Grey, Richard Posner, Margaret Jane Radin, Dan Farber, Martha Minnow, Frank Michelman, and Suzanna Sherry. *See generally Symposium on the Renaissance of Pragmatism in American Legal Thought*, 63 S. CAL. L. REV. 1569 (1990).

301. The Wittgenstein cite goes like this:

> "So you are saying that human agreement decides what is true and what is false?"—It is what human beings *say* that is true and false; and they agree in the *language* they use. That is not agreement in opinions but in form of life.

L. WITTGENSTEIN, PHILOSOPHICAL INVESTIGATIONS ¶ 241, at 88E (G. Anscombe trans. 2d ed. 1958). The Wittgenstein cite is used in three prototypical ways in legal thought. First, it is a way of arresting an infinite regress in the search for rational foundations. Second (and relatedly) it is a way of indicating that the way in which a particular theoretical or regulative inquiry or question has been framed is miscast—misconstruing not only what is to be sought, but the searching that is to seek it.

defusing (miscast) theoretical inquiries and for disassembling overly formalized, overly ambitious forms of thought. It is the traditional American way in which being—apparently any being—revolts against the imperialism of thought.

This all sounds very good—but it raises a certain identity crisis problem for pragmatism. What is it? One thing's for sure: pragmatism is not a theory—at least, not as the term "theory" is commonly understood among legal thinkers. Pragmatism cannot be the sort of intellectual artifact that occupies the customarily reified space of theory.

Of course, having pointed this out, we needn't be so miserly, so rationalist, in our conception of the space accorded to "theory." We can redefine our terms:

> Theories understood in the pragmatist ("pensive") way are not Euclidean axioms or Kantian categorical imperatives, but graffiti, practical guidelines to be noticed by the alertly street-wise when context makes them applicable. It is a lively and attractive, if not particularly inspiring, picture of the way the pragmatist makes use of theory.[302]

Now, here the question of what kind of theory pragmatism may be is ultimately referred back to the identity of the user: the pragmatist who "makes use of theory."[303] This reference of theoretical questions back to the pragmatist is a critical recursive move in pragmatic legal thought. The move can be understood in terms of two related moments.

First, pragmatism strives to decompress the space legitimately to be accorded to theory—that is, the theories of others, as well as the theories of pragmatists. This is pragmatism's negating moment. As Posner says, "Pragmatism remains a powerful antidote to formalism."[304] It "clears the underbrush; it does not plant the forest."[305] Radin agrees: pragmatism (along with feminism) shares "a commitment against abstract idealism, transcendence, foundationalism, and atemporal universality; and in favor of immanence, historicity, concreteness, situatedness, contextuality, embeddedness, narrativity of meaning."[306] More bluntly, Rorty says, "I think it is true that by now pragmatism is banal in its application to

Third, the Wittgenstein cite is a performative move (and not always a polite one) designed to communicate something like, "Oh be quiet, and stop bothering me with *your* problems."

For a playful, that is to say, deadly serious, deconstruction of this Wittgenstein Maneuver, see Schlag, *supra* note 73, at 938-42 (1988).

302. Grey, *supra* note 115, at 1593.

303. *Id.*

304. Posner, *What Has Pragmatism to Offer Law?*, 63 S. CAL. L. REV. 1653, 1663 (1990).

305. *Id.* at 1670. Richard Posner even goes further, endorsing T.S. Eliot's conclusion: "[T]he great weakness of Pragmatism is that it ends by being of no use to anybody." *Id.* at 1653 (citing T.S. ELIOT, *Francis Herbert Bradley*, in SELECTED PROSE OF T.S. ELIOT 204 (F. Kermode ed. 1975)).

306. Radin, *The Pragmatist and the Feminist*, 63 S. CAL. L. REV. 1699, 1707 (1990).

Texas Law Review Vol. 69:1627, 1991

law."[307]

In the second moment, all remaining questions are then referred back to the identity or character of the pragmatist. As Posner says, pragmatism "signals an attitude, an orientation, at times a change in direction."[308] And as Tom Grey says, "To become a pragmatist is to undergo a paradigm-switch, a change in attitude or outlook as much as a change in belief."[309] And since, in the pragmatic world view, it is intuition, experience, context, and perspectivism that count, it can hardly surprise anyone that the precise identity and location of the one having the intuition, experience, and perspective should matter greatly.[310] It is thus understandable that a pragmatist like Margaret Jane Radin, for instance, eschews writing about pragmatism, preferring instead to write about the pragmatist—what she thinks, what she does.[311] Likewise, it is also aesthetically fitting that in confronting some difficult problems posed about the status of pragmatic perspectivism, Tom Grey eschews a theoretical resolution and instead traces in detail the way in which "Stevens's poetic practice shows a way for perspectivists to move on."[312]

B. Being a Pragmatist Is Hard to Do

All of this, of course, places great intellectual and social pressure on the character and the identity of the pragmatist. In a sense, we have a replay of the problem of the subject faced by the rule-of-law thinkers. But here we must ask, who is the pragmatist? Who is this personage, this individual subject so critical to the pragmatic enterprise? Not surprisingly, the pragmatist is the one who understands, who recognizes what it means to be a thinking, acting individual subject. To understand what it means to be an individual subject means to understand that the individual and his thoughts are socially constructed. His thinking is "always embodied in *practices*—habits and patterns of perceiving and conceiv-

307. Rorty, *The Banality of Pragmatism and the Poetry of Justice*, 63 S. CAL. L. REV. 1811, 1811 (1990).

308. Posner, *supra* note 304, at 1670.

309. Grey, *supra* note 115, at 1570; *see also* Kronman, *Alexander Bickel's Philosophy of Prudence*, 94 YALE L.J. 1567, 1569, 1573 (1985) (emphasizing the importance of "attitude" or "temperamental disposition" in his own "prudentialist" version of pragmatism).

310. Tushnet, *Character as Argument* (Book Review), 14 LAW & SOC. INQUIRY 539, 547-48 (1989) (reviewing H. KALVEN, A WORTHY TRADITION: FREEDOM OF SPEECH IN AMERICA (1988)) (criticizing Kalven's "theory" of the First Amendment as entirely dependent on Kalven's character).

311. Radin, *supra* note 306, at 1699 (reflecting even in her article's title the importance of the pragmatist agent).

312. Grey, *supra* note 115, at 1577.

The Problem of the Subject

ing"[313]—most of which are collectively produced through the culture.[314] At the same time—and in apparent tension—the pragmatic view "grants no special authority to unconscious habit and slowly evolved custom; self-conscious reflection and innovative reason are equally central . . . ."[315] The pragmatist recognizes the subject as reflective, deliberative, even contemplative—capable through his thought of guiding action—so much so that beliefs are to be "judged by their efficacy in leading the agent through experience successfully."[316]

Now, as between the image of the subject as socially constructed and the image of the subject as in charge of his own thought and action, there is a certain tension. The pragmatist deals with this tension by invoking the image of mediation. The pragmatist subject is conceived as the site for mediation. This conceptualization of the subject is not surprising given that "James offered pragmatism as a '*mediating* way of thinking.' "[317] Indeed, the term "mediating" and its location in the thinking of the pragmatist subject recurs frequently throughout the neopragmatic literature, not just to mediate the specific tension of the contextualist and the instrumentalist strands of pragmatism, but to identify the site for the mediation of a whole series of recursive binary conflicts:

reason	feeling[318]
mind	body[319]
nature	nurture[320]
connection	separation[321]
means	ends[322]
public (man)	private (woman)[323]
optimism	pluralism[324]

313. Grey, *Holmes and Legal Pragmatism*, 41 STAN. L. REV. 787, 798 (1989) (emphasis in original).

314. *Id.*

315. *Id.* at 801.

316. *Id.* at 803.

317. Radin, *supra* note 306, at 1715 (emphasis added) (quoting W. JAMES, PRAGMATISM 26 (1975)).

318. Radin, *supra* note 306, at 1707.

319. *Id.*

320. *Id.* at 1708.

321. *Id.*

322. *Id.*

323. *Id.*

324.

> Pragmatism is a way of understanding our simultaneous commitments to optimism *and* pluralism, to concrete empiricism *and* principles, to an incomplete and dynamic universe *and* to the possibility of perfection that our ideals impel us unceasingly to hope for and work for.

Radin, *supra* note 306, at 1715 (emphasis in original).

Texas Law Review Vol. 69:1627, 1991

concrete empiricism	principles[325]
an incomplete dynamic universe	the possibility of perfection[326]
all previous truths	certain new experiences[327]
tough-minded philosophical realism	tender-minded idealism[328]
philosophical positions that stress the determining force of material, physical, or biological reality	philosophical positions that stress the shaping power of the imaginative capacity for cultural development[329]

Pragmatists almost always seem to be dealing with bipolar tensions and almost always seem to respond by mediating them.[330] For pragmatism, then, it is the pragmatist subject who must already be competent to mediate these and other tensions. Not surprisingly, given its mediating function, the space of the pragmatist subject is left relatively unstructured and unspecified.

This minimalist aesthetic representation of the pragmatist's subject need not produce uncertainty or unpredictability or anything of the sort. If pragmatists take or are led to take a strong conventionalist turn—and the conventions already in place happen to be monistic and univocal (rather than pluralistic and dissonant)—then some degree of stability can be achieved. But it is quite clear that many pragmatists seem disinclined to adopt this tack. Many pragmatists disclaim any such conservative or "complacent" agenda.[331] On the contrary, the kind of mediating that the pragmatist subject is supposed to accomplish is left generously unclear, virtually free flowing:

> A corollary of pragmatism, derived from the tenets that thought is always both situated and instrumental, is a kind of perspectivism. Because new beliefs emerge out of a complex of already existing beliefs that can never be made fully conscious and explicit, all use-

325. *Id.*

326. *Id.*

327. Radin, *supra* note 306, at 1709 n.26 ("[O]ur theory must mediate between all previous truths *and* certain new experiences." (emphasis added) (quoting W. JAMES, *supra* note 317, at 104)).

328. Grey, *supra* note 115, at 1571 (suggesting that a Wallace Stevens poem "captures pragmatism's double focus—its mediation of 'tough minded' philosophical realism . . . and 'tender-minded' idealism").

329. *Id.* at 1572 ("These are the chief American legal theorists who have followed the pragmatist middle way, the *mediation* between philosophical positions that stress the determining force of material, physical, or biological reality, *and* those that stress the shaping power of the imaginative human capacity for cultural development." (emphasis added)).

330. I think that the pragmatist makes a valuable contribution in bringing to our attention the conventionally embedded dualisms of our (legal) culture. I am, however, rather doubtful that pragmatic mediating or oscillating moves in any significant way beyond these embedded dualisms. For a critique and an alternative to the latent binary tendency of pragmatism, see Winter, *supra* note 105.

331. *See, e.g.*, Radin, *supra* note 306, at 1711 (arguing that the feminist perspective of domination prevents the complacency seen in some pragmatists).

> ful beliefs may not ultimately prove commensurable with each other. Furthermore, because inquiry is at root an instrument to guide action (including the action of further inquiry), its products are subject to revision as the ends sought in action change. This double relativity of situation and purpose implies a tentative attitude toward all beliefs, including especially those "theoretical" and "fundamental" ones to which we are most likely to attribute permanent and universal validity. The pragmatist recognizes that the best account of a phenomenon (such as law) from one angle, for one purpose, at one time, might not serve as well from another perspective, rooted in another temporal context, and aimed at different goals.[332]

To read this description of the pragmatic approach can yield a sense of jurisprudential vertigo: the passage reads like the description of reflective equilibrium[333] in the context of all contexts. Among the socially situated, instrumentalist, and perspectivist themes of pragmatism, there is always the possibility of changing the *social situation* one finds oneself in, the *goals* one seeks to pursue, or the *perspective* that one is using to understand one's social situation or goals.[334] Tom Grey highlights this phenomenon with the thought of Wallace Stevens: "Stevens moves from *idealism* to *realism*, then dialectically to an integrating *perspectivism*, then to a renewed dialogic oscillation between *idealism* and *realism*, with the partners reconceived as *perspectives*."[335] Interestingly, even Grey's sensitive rendition slips into essentialism and thus understates the vertiginous potential of pragmatism. Indeed, rather than conceiving *idealism*, *realism*, and *perspectivism* as distinct moments, we can begin to understand the extent to which any act of thought might be understood as a [—][336] *nesting* of idealism within realism within perspectivism (or any other combination). In other words, within the pragmatic vision, we can become structuralists and recognize that utterances, language, and

332. Grey, *supra* note 313, at 804-05.

333. *See generally* J. RAWLS, A THEORY OF JUSTICE 48-51 (1971) (arguing that our sense of justice comes from matching prereflective intuitions with proposed reconceptions until we achieve a kind of balance, called "reflective equilibrium").

334. As Tom Grey points out, a pragmatist will not go round and round forever trying to understand these instabilities, because inquiry is itself a kind of action (or inaction) and might thus interfere with the pursuit of goals, or even the understanding of one's social situation. Grey, *supra* note 313, at 797-99.

This is an important point for the pragmatists (and non-pragmatists) to recognize, but it really doesn't provide much in the way of stabilizing pragmatic inquiry. As the micro-economists would put it: the absolute value of transaction costs are neither here nor there. You need to know something about the value of what is at stake to understand whether the transaction costs are worth incurring. *See* A. SCHMID, PROPERTY, POWER, AND PUBLIC CHOICE: AN INQUIRY INTO LAW AND ECONOMICS 104 (2d ed. 1981).

335. Grey, *supra* note 115, at 1583 (emphasis added).

336. Fill in the blank:

thought are structured like Russian dolls.[337] We can even become poststructuralists and understand that utterance, language, and thought are like Russian dolls, in which the boundaries between each doll can fuse, disappear, or be relocated depending upon changes in the frame of reference that are not [—][338] within our control.[339]

In short, it would seem that the pragmatic approach can, in effect, slide into anything—including the adoption of what might otherwise appear to be highly nonpragmatic, essentialist a priori approaches. It could, for instance, become a pragmatic imperative to adopt a nonpragmatic approach so as to carry out very pragmatic, instrumental goals. Nonpragmatism can also become the pragmatic program in so far as the self of the pragmatist is shaped by a highly formalist, essentialist culture of thought. Notice that *in a sense* everyone (even the essentialist, the bad a priori thinker) can always already make a pretty good claim[340] to being a pragmatist.[341] What is more, everyone can always already make a pretty good claim that any ostensible violation of the pragmatic approach, such as "bad" essentialist a priori thinking, is already instrumentally justified. What is more, on pragmatic grounds the retort is always ready. It's the standard reflexive perspectivist response: "So you say I am essentialist, an a priori thinker? By reference to what view of

(case specific?)	contextualism
(stereotypical?)	structuralism
(recursive & recombinant?)	poststructuralism
(abstractly stable?)	essentialism
and so on.	

337. Jack Balkin and Duncan Kennedy "use the term 'nesting' to describe this sequential ordering of legal questions in which the second issue raises concerns seemingly put to rest by resolution of the first issue." Paul, *supra* note 191, at 1795 (footnote omitted). The import of Kennedy's and Balkin's conception lies in identifying the extent to which moral and policy questions, presumably resolved at one level of decision making (*i.e.*, substantive doctrinal rule) may resurface as a live dispute at another level of legal decision making (*i.e.*, evidentiary standard). *Id.* at 1795 n.36. This is akin to the *linear* infinite regress.

My use of the term "nesting" is more general and is designed to include far less orderly recursive patterns. It is designed to identify the presence of a logic of containment or envelopment or reappropriation. None of my Russian dolls have to look alike; they don't have to belong to the same set; they don't even have to get along very well. In fact, very often, they don't. *See* Schlag, *Missing Pieces*, *supra* note 7, at 1222-28 (demonstrating how rationalism reappropriates and refashions modernist and postmodern thought in its own rationalist image thereby defusing both).

338.
(often?)
(necessarily?)
(usually?)
(always?)
and so on.

339. *See generally* Schlag, *supra* note 73.

340. (This is a technical term.)

341. *See* Smith, *The Pursuit of Pragmatism*, 100 YALE L.J. 409, 435-37 (1990) ("In short, the pragmatist suggests that . . . [w]e should talk things over, and we should look at problems in context. All of this seems eminently sensible. Who does—who *could*—disagree?" (emphasis in original)).

The Problem of the Subject

reality, pray tell? Uh, huh, yes. And where's your tap into the heart of being, guy?"

Now, I don't think that Grey or Radin or any other sophisticated pragmatist would disagree with any of this. They could, of course, reply with a standard pragmatist move: All of these vertiginous gyrations and uncertainties are possible—but only in a (bad?) *theoretical* sense. The *pragmatic* possibilities of pragmatism—as distinguished from the *theoretical* possibilities of pragmatism are, for Radin and Grey, far narrower. But how so? Again, I think we are referred to the pragmatist subject who is at once situated and guided by instrumental concerns. It is *this* situatedness and *this* instrumentalism of the subject that keeps the lid on what would otherwise be the wild Nietzschean poststructuralist perspectivism. But how?

If Grey or Radin thinks that pragmatism means something, it is because pragmatism refers questions to the character and temperament of the pragmatist subject.[342] Tom Grey, for instance, keeps on talking about "what it feels like" to be a pragmatist.[343] Now, one has to have some sympathy for the enterprise that Grey and Radin are pursuing: in some sense they are trying to describe pragmatism phenomenologically—that is, in terms of what it feels like to be a pragmatist. The usual objectivist matrix of jurisprudential discourse makes this exercise in description by Grey and Radin very difficult. Part of their point, presumably, is that being a pragmatist does not reduce to any one position in the usual aesthetic matrix of jurisprudential discourse. That is why, for instance, Grey adopts the unusual jurisprudential strategy of trying to describe pragmatism by tracing the philosophical implications of Wallace Stevens's poetry.[344] This is definitely not the usual taxonomic (*i.e.*, which box do you fit in?) approach to jurisprudence.

The rejection of the box approach to jurisprudence (which Radin correctly identifies as tendentiously leading towards essentialism)[345] is precisely what leads both Radin and Grey to experience some difficulty expressing their thinking when the boxy dualistic matrices resurface in their own work. Whenever the dreaded dualities return, Radin and Grey use opaque verbs like "mediate" or "oscillate" to describe how

342. In contrasting the pragmatist to the poststructuralist, Radin and Michelman insist on temperament as a key difference. Radin & Michelman, *supra* note 8, at 1043-44; *see also* Smith, *supra* note 341, at 437-40 (noting the importance of "temperament" to neopragmatism).

343. Grey, *supra* note 115, at 1570.

344. *Id.* at 1583.

345. *See* Radin & Michelman, *supra* note 8 at 1049-51 (cautioning that some feminists have adopted an "essentializing" stance that entrenches the current, injurious cultural understanding of women's limited nature).

Texas Law Review Vol. 69:1627, 1991

pragmatists deal with binary representations. This opacity, this deflection, is perfectly understandable in as much as both Grey and Radin want to avoid representing the pragmatist subject in terms of these dualities. They seek to arrest the infinite regress and to avoid jurisprudential vertigo. They do this by invoking a pragmatist subject—one who mediates. But this move, of course, refers all the problems to the identity of the pragmatist subject. The question still remains, who is this pragmatist subject?

The short answer is that the pragmatist subject is them (Radin, Grey, etc.). "Today the legal pragmatist stands—to oversimplify as one must for summary purposes—between law-and-economics and its satellites on the one hand, and what might loosely be called 'cultural legal studies' on the other."[346] Now, of course, this description of the legal pragmatist coincides almost perfectly with a description of both Radin's and Grey's jurisprudential stances, as they see them.

The longer answer requires a new question: how is it that the pragmatist subject came to be them (Radin and Grey) as opposed to someone else, say Duncan Kennedy or Frank Easterbrook? Radin and Grey would likely answer that Duncan Kennedy and Frank Easterbrook (whatever their virtues) simply do not have the temperament, the attitude, or the quality of mind of pragmatists. Kennedy and Easterbrook are not pragmatists because they do not "take our present descriptions with humility and openness."[347] Within the conventional understanding of "humility and openness" in the legal community, this judgment will likely seem right to many people. But notice what is going on here: our ability to identify a quality of mind, a temperament, the pragmatist subject himself, turns out to depend upon a thoroughly conventionalist representation of the field of contemporary jurisprudence.

"Precisely so," Radin and Grey might say, "that is exactly what pragmatism prescribes. We are all creatures of the conventions we learn."[348] But such a response is belied by their drive to describe the pragmatist subject in a transcontextual manner—a manner that will cut across contexts.[349] In changing the context by discussing Wallace Ste-

346. Grey, *supra* note 115, at 1571.

347. Radin, *supra* note 306, at 1726. If Duncan Kennedy is not a pragmatist for Grey or Radin, it is because he does these structuralist things that look to them very *a priori*, essentialist and somewhat formalistic. Roughly the same is true of Frank Easterbrook. Now, no doubt such a judgment will ring true to many legal academics. But what vision of jurisprudence is being presupposed here? I'm sure if we asked Easterbrook or Kennedy if they were being a priori, essentialist or somewhat formalistic, each would say something like—"no, not at all, no more than I need to be: I've got it just right, thank you."

348. *See supra* text accompanying note 346.

349. This is understandable: they are both theorists. And both, to some extent, understand the

vens's poetry and thought, Grey hopes to provide an understanding of "what it feels like" to be a pragmatist. But this is a transcontextual project. It is clear that the motivation for a discussion of the life, thought, and poetry of Wallace Stevens is driven by Grey's desire to escape from the clichés of conventional jurisprudential "reality" through a metaphor: Wallace Stevens as metaphor, a metaphor for how *to be*. But this transcontextual attempt to capture the identity of the pragmatist subject cannot work. We would fly off once again, in the context of all contexts, with the unbearable-lightness-of-being-a-subject blues again.[350] There is simply no describing the character, temperament, or sensibility of the pragmatist subject *outside* the representation of the field within which that subject's character, temperament, and sensibility is constituted—both as concept and as determinable content.[351] That is why, to understand what pragmatism means for law, Grey had to come down to jurisprudential earth and tell us in a highly conventionalist representation of the legal field: "Today the legal pragmatist stands—to oversimplify as one must for summary purposes—between law-and-economics and its satellites on the one hand, and what might loosely be called 'cultural legal studies' on the other."[352]

But what is Grey *doing* with this answer? He is doing what pragmatists are almost always driven to do: he is "mediating" or "oscillating" between two poles. Usually, this standard pragmatic answer in the face of conflicting dualisms has at least the appearance of plausibility. But here, the standard pragmatic "mediating" answer is particularly inappropriate. It is particularly inappropriate precisely because the question here is *who* or *what* is it that is doing the mediating? One answer, of course, is the conventionally oscillating self. This is a bit déjà vu, a bit too close to Sartre for comfort.

And yet it may be right. The mediation, the oscillation of the pragmatist subject are in several senses quite conventional. First, the pragmatist is always mediating, always oscillating between a highly conventional set of dualities: subject-object, imagination-reality—in short, the usual binary suspects. Pragmatism can hardly be faulted for recognizing the patterned binary character of intellectual and social culture in the West.

extent to which the theory-game as it is currently practiced and structured within the legal academy resists their attempt to re-present pragmatism. Believe me; I empathize. *See* Schlag, *Politics of Form*, *supra* note 7, at 889-95.

350. "Am I being a bit too referential here?" No, not at all: this is the context of all contexts.

351. This sort of problem is pointed out by Martha Minow and Elizabeth Spelman. *See* Minow & Spelman, *supra* note 38, at 1639 ("[O]ur discussion of a conception of judging founded in the particulars of a circumstance and in the situated sensibilities of the judge risks sounding abstract in the absence of a specific context.").

352. Grey, *supra* note 115, at 1571.

Texas Law Review Vol. 69:1627, 1991

What is striking about legal pragmatism, however, is that its understanding of the situation, role, and effect of these dualities is stunningly conventional. Legal pragmatism (unlike, for instance, some kinds of poststructuralist, rhetorical, or cognitive approaches) locates these dualities in the spaces of mind, thought, and theory. Hence, neopragmatists may claim to "oscillate" or "mediate" between idealism and materialism, thought and practice, mind and body, but the oscillation, the mediation itself always and already takes place within a conventional discourse field that is already configured or formatted in the image of idealism, thought, and mind.[353] Pragmatists are thus limited to a highly conventional form of "oscillation" or "mediation." In consequence, while pragmatists *may claim to oscillate* between theory and practice, *the oscillation they do* remains quite conventionally confined to theory's idea of theory as well as to theory's idea of practice. Theory, idealism, and mind are the conventionally inscribed formats and there is nothing in the pragmatic repertoire to suggest that neopragmatists have recognized that they are operating within this format. Indeed, as pragmatists, how could they achieve such a recognition? What's more, even if they did, there is no indication that they have the moves to escape from or to reconfigure this conventional format.

The practical implication is that neopragmatists do not yet understand that these dualities *have a material, bodily, practical dimension.*[354] That is why pragmatists can talk in overly audacious ways of a "*refusal* to think the world divisible by categorical oppositions,"[355] or of having "*rejected* the dichotomies of reason and feeling."[356] Within the conventional conceptual structure of orthodox legal thinking, such *refusals* or *rejections* are generally considered meaningful. But they are considered meaningful within conventional legal thought precisely because conventional legal thought has already been conventionally formatted in the image of idealism, mind, and theory. Neopragmatism thus remains a protest against philosophical idealism, rationalism, and transcendentalism that ironically remains confined to the realms, the matrices already carved in the self-images of philosophical idealism, rationalism, and transcendentalism.[357]

353. The computer metaphor here is deliberate—as deliberate as deliberate can be.

354. For elaboration, see Schlag, *Politics of Form*, *supra* note 7, at 897-99.

355. Michelman, *Private Personal but not Split: Radin Versus Rorty*, 63 S. CAL. L. REV. 1783, 1783 (1990) (emphasis added).

356. Radin, *supra* note 306, at 1707 (emphasis added).

357. *See* Schlag, *supra* note 73, at 955-57 & n.95; Schlag, *Missing Pieces*, *supra* note 7, at 1223-24. For a similar point in connection with the already neutralized practice of cls-deconstruction, see Schlag, *"Le Hors de Texte," supra* note 7, at 1660.

The Problem of the Subject

Neopragmatism is, in short, a *stance*—a stance that would like to be a *practice*. But that is the standard-issue idealist dream. When Tom Grey writes that "the legal pragmatist *stands* . . . between law-and-economics and . . . 'cultural legal studies,' "[358] the critical term is "stands." Notice that once the legal pragmatist *stands* on this conventional jurisprudential spectrum, he is somewhere between the two extremes. His position has become localized (within a highly conventional depiction of the jurisprudential universe as arranged along a spectrum). The pragmatist is no longer open or critical. Instead, he is located at a precise point with a precise position between the extremes of the jurisprudential spectrum.

How did he get here? This is not his critical pragmatism. This is not his humble openness. He's got a stance: the pragmatist *stands* between the two poles. He is no longer embedded in a traditional field of jurisprudence. Still less is this field embedded in him. No, on the contrary: the legal pragmatist *stands*—thus separating himself from the grounds of his own social constructedness. And in standing, he has acquired the necessary distance from convention so that he may "consult" history and "treat" law as "policy coupled with tradition."[359] Here the legal pragmatist stands outside his social construction as a kind of epistemic free agent who decides what to make (hermeneutically, intellectually, and politically) of his own social constructedness. This understanding of the self—its agency and its situation—is, of course, utterly conventional—an instance of what I have elsewhere described as the "relatively autonomous self."[360]

Interestingly, this moment of critical lucidity in which the pragmatist subject takes distance from its own social constructedness is precisely the moment that pragmatists seize upon to counsel a critical, open, revisionary attitude. Michelman and Radin warn, for instance, that "[o]nly by constant attentiveness to the commonplace can pragmatist critical practice keep faith with its postmodernist commitments to suspect facile consensus and pursue epistemic openness."[361] But warning is not enough; it does not get at the problem. The problem is with the way the pragmatist subject is already socially constituted to understand the warning. "Be more self-conscious" doesn't tell you anything more than that you should be self-conscious in accordance with the usual *conventionally*

358. Grey, *supra* note 115, at 1571.

359. Grey, *supra* note 313, at 807 (quoting O.W. HOLMES, THE COMMON LAW 5 (Mittowe ed. 1963)).

360. Schlag, *"Le Hors de Texte," supra* note 7, at 1667-68.

361. Radin & Michelman, *supra* note 8, at 1048 (footnote omitted).

Texas Law Review Vol. 69:1627, 1991

(limited) forms of self-reflection that constitute you as a self-conscious creature.[362] The convention-transcending moment in pragmatism—the perspectivist moment—is extremely weak. It is an invitation, an urging, "to take our present descriptions with humility and openness."[363] But again, given a conventionally constructed pragmatist subject, this invitation can mean no more than "be as humble and as open as convention allows and has constructed you to be."

Radin, Grey, and the other neopragmatists are stuck within a conventional representation of the scene in which they are operating. Indeed, (on their own pragmatic grounds) how could they not be? They talk about "dissolution of traditional dichotomies."[364] But in the context of a rhetoric that systematically reinscribes these traditional dichotomies in the very construction of discourse, action, *and the subject*, what critical move does pragmatism provide that would enable the pragmatists to practice what they preach? None. All the moves refer back to the pragmatist subject—his temperament, her sensibility, their character—and thus to the conventions that have constituted this subject. How then, by what moves are the pragmatists to move beyond (as they think they must) the conventional context they are in? If the subject is already colonized by undesirable conventions, how does pragmatism propose to "rescue" this subject?

Now, for pragmatists, the problem raised here is unlikely to seem acute—at least, not yet. The problem does not seem acute for pragmatists precisely because they arrive on the scene of pragmatic jurisprudence as already-constituted individual subjects with pregiven political agendas in a pregiven political division of the field in which they "stand."[365] One of the things that is attractive for some legal thinkers is that, even in its perspectivist moment, pragmatism does very little to initiate an interrogation of the pragmatist subject or its political agenda. If it did, we would be back to jurisprudential vertigo.

But we're not. Instead, we see neopragmatists providing the most

362. *See generally* S. FISH, *Critical Self-Consciousness, or Can We Know What We're Doing?*, in DOING WHAT COMES NATURALLY, *supra* note 7, at 436. I am not urging this point as a criticism of the practice of self-consciousness. I agree with Winter on this point. *See supra* text accompanying notes 83-84. But practicing self-consciousness (or showing how self-consciousness is practiced) and saying that one should be self-conscious are quite different events. And it is only the usual (legal academic) supposition that thought controls practice that allows us to (erroneously) see one as referring unproblematically to the other.

363. Radin, *supra* note 306, at 1726.

364. *Id.* at 1707.

365. Indeed, as will be suggested below, pragmatism is likely to seem most appealing to legal thinkers who already have relatively well-defined, deeply sedimented social-political-intellectual identities within the conventional jurisprudential description of the field (*i.e.*, precisely persons like Michelman, Grey, Radin, Posner, and Fish). It's in large part a generational thing.

strikingly *conventional* description of their own scene and doing so uncannily at precisely the moment when they are also insisting upon the need for critical perspectivism and the recognition of indeterminacy. Listen to, for instance, Ruth Putnam's opening remarks for her talk at the pragmatism conference at U.S.C.:

> We pragmatists believe that inquiry begins in an indeterminate situation. I take it that the inquiry to which this conference is devoted begins as follows: We find ourselves in a situation in which society has disappointed the hopes and legitimate expectations of the poor and the powerless (women and minorities, children, and those who are ill) in spite of legislation and Supreme Court decisions that promised to meet those hopes and expectations.[366]

Now, this is a very conventional, even if contestable, view of "the situation." This is exactly what you would expect a liberal academic to say at a conference on pragmatism. But of course, although this is one situation—one context—that these academics find themselves in, it is important not to overlook the others. For example, here is another way describing "the situation" at the U.S.C. conference—one that pragmatists seem to routinely overlook as if it had no effect on what they are saying or doing:

> I take it that the inquiry to which this conference is devoted begins as follows: We find ourselves in a situation in which social and rhetorical forces have constructed an assembly of highly respected legal scholars meeting with other highly respected scholars to exchange papers on pragmatism. The audience is largely composed of law students (most of whom will become lawyers) and legal academics who will mostly remain legal academics. At this conference, any number of things will go on: idle chatter, micro-politics, career advancement, career retardation, play, sex, love, hate, put downs, revenge, eating, drinking, drives to the beach—punctuated at times by refreshing displays of wit and insight against a background of relentless standard rhetorical moves.[367] Now, within

366. Putnam, *Justice in Context*, 63 S. CAL. L. REV. 1797, 1797 (1990).

367. I'm a bit ambivalent about these standard rhetorical moves. On the one hand, they are part of the fabric of our thought marking out its borders, the structure of its interior region, the pathways that lead nowhere, and the pathways that might lead somewhere. It seems miserly to object to these rhetorical moves—akin to objecting to the weather. "I wish we didn't even have any weather today."

On the other hand, these standard rhetorical moves are to legal thought as public opinion polls are to politics. The standard performative contradiction move, for instance, becomes a standard problematic objection organizing the development of the discourse precisely because everybody repeats it and everybody seems to think it's a real problem. Now consider the public opinion poll. It provides useful information—and objecting to such polls is, again, very much like objecting to the weather. On the other hand, note that public opinion polls implicitly and subconsciously (because it's not thought about) establish and regulate the content and form of important political issues. The political import of public opinion polls is not in the information they provide, but in the organization of the questions they ask. The same sort of thing is true of standard rhetorical moves. The impor-

> this sur-pragmatic description of context and the social actors, the question is how does our own social construction, our own rhetoric enable or disable us from helping the poor or the powerless (women and minorities, children and those who are ill)?

Now this strikes me as a *serious* way of asking the question: *who* are you talking to? What can they *do*? And what (if anything) is or could be *done* here? But pragmatists would not ever raise these questions seriously. They would not raise them precisely because to pose this question in this way requires an upsetting of the conventions of legal thought. Because pragmatists understand themselves as constituted by convention and because pragmatism furnishes little in the way of critical moves to upset or displace convention, they cannot pose this question in this way.

If pragmatism "means," it is because the pragmatist subject makes it "mean." And if the pragmatist subject makes pragmatism mean something, it is because he or she arrives on the scene already conventionally constituted with a series of pregiven political aims. It is pragmatism's conventional depiction of the field of action, of thought, and of plausible political aims that leads the pragmatist subject to make pragmatism mean something.

It is the security of a conventional depiction of the field, of the subject, and of plausible political aims, that make pragmatism seem attractive to certain kinds of legal thinkers. And it has to be acknowledged that, given a certain conventional picture of law and jurisprudence, pragmatism can seem very attractive. Pragmatism is attractive if the judge is a Holmes or Cardozo or Brandeis; if law is a self-conscious, self-critical enterprise; if culture is produced by thoughtful or artistic or wise artisans of meaning; if social institutions echo the needs of the self. But . . . .

This is not our context. This is simply one of our contexts—the standard legal academic romanticization of the scene of legal thought. It is our convention to pretend that judges have the wit, the intelligence and the craft of an Oliver Wendell Holmes. But once the romance stops, we see the judge for what he or she usually is: a harried bureaucrat of limited intellectual and perceptual faculties. This is a man or a woman whose mind has been addled by Restatements and C.F.R., and (what now amounts to the aesthetic equivalent) the constitutional opinions of the Supreme Court. It is our convention to pretend that law is a self-conscious, self-critical enterprise, but in fact its meaning is largely instrumental and performative; that is, governed by its ability to deliver the

tance of the standard performative contradiction move lies not in whether one has a solution to it or not, but rather in regulating the kinds of theories and ideas that can even be thought and published and heard from in the first place.

The Problem of the Subject

goods—goods whose identities are largely decided upon elsewhere. It is our convention to pretend that culture is produced by artisans of meaning, but culture is now shaped by the techno-bureaucratic service strategies of the mall, the HMO, the school, the prison, and the day-care. It is our convention to pretend that social institutions are or should be subject to the needs of individual selves, but the dominant configuration (and thus the potential) of the individual self are themselves the product of institutional mechanisms and devices that appear, in large part, to work of their own accord.

Who or what is the subject in such a world? Currently, every human contact between selves who are declared, *ab initio*,[368] to be self-directing and already free is mediated and constructed by techno-bureaucratic strategies. There is no human participation in the creation of culture or relations with others that is not already an instance of the regimen of techno-bureaucratic strategies: Sesame Street, MTV, Federal Express, malls, HMO's, word processing, endless ratings, endless polls, endless interest groups, endless reflexive commentary on commentary, endless processing of services, endless differentiation of culture, and endless celebration of difference, all ironically leading to a regime of pervasive sameness:[369] the radical de-differentiation of life and meaning,[370] the context of no context, the crash.

So the problem of the subject for the pragmatist also arises in very stark terms. The pragmatist subject, understood in pragmatic terms, is the shopper at the universal mall making meaning with the commodified signs of our traditions and culture while the social aesthetics of techno-bureaucratic strategies are making him think he means something.[371] Everything else is just nostalgia.

V. Cultural Conservatism Twenty Minutes into the Future

"Yet if the only form of tradition, of handing down, consisted in following the ways of the immediate generation before us in a blind or timid adherence to it successes, "tradition" should positively be discour-

368.
In first grade,
In the declaration of independence
And on t.v.

369. Note the exquisite post-modern differentiation of that quintessential modernist emblem: Coke is it. Only now, Coke is Classic Coke, to be distinguished from New Coke. I haven't done the homework, but I strongly suspect that each of these sub-brands already has strong sub-brand consumer allegiance.

370. Or in short, mud. *See* Lash, *Discourse or Figure? Postmodernism as a "Regime of Signification?,"* 5 CULTURE, THEORY & SOCIETY 311, 333 (1988).

371. This is definitely not the subject initially contemplated by pragmatists.

aged. . . .Tradition is a matter of much wider significance. It cannot be inherited, and if you want it you must obtain it by great labour."

—T.S. Eliot[372]

The classic problem of the subject for conservatives poses itself as a question of time.[373] Conservatism implies a slowing down of time. It is a call to retain for the future by action in the present what the past has provided. But no one lives in the past except through the mediation of the present. The perennial problem for the conservative is thus whether the present allows any sort of action that might preserve a cherished past. In our terms, the question is whether there is any subject capable of sustaining this cherished past—capable of sustaining it in a way that does not transform it into a mere image of itself, a mere simulation.

Anthony Kronman's recent article illustrates the point well.[374] Taking a neo-Burkean approach, Kronman distinguishes "a world of culture" from "a world of thought." The world of culture is accumulative and susceptible to ruin if not maintained.[375] The world of thought, by contrast, "differs from the world of culture in two decisive ways, in its unchanging sameness and its invulnerability to ruin."[376] The two worlds are thus defined as rigorously separate. Indeed, "whenever a person begins to think he leaves the cultural world behind, and enters a different realm in which progress and loss do not exist."[377]

Given that the world of culture needs to be protected from ruin and that the world of thought is rigorously separated from the world of culture, it is no surprise to discover that "the activity of thinking encourages an indifference to the world of culture as a whole and to its accumulation of decaying artifacts."[378] It follows, then, that the world of thought is a threat to the world of culture—a corrosive influence.[379]

372. T.S. Eliot, *Tradition and the Individual Talent*, in The Sacred Wood: Essays on Poetry and Criticism 48-49 (1950).

373. *See* Cornell, *Time, Deconstruction, and the Challenge to Legal Positivism: The Call for Judicial Responsibility*, 2 Yale J. L. & Humanities 267 (1990).

374. Kronman, *Precedent and Tradition*, 99 Yale L.J. 1029 (1990).

375. *Id.* at 1058.

376. *Id.* at 1061.

377. *Id.* at 1063.

378. *Id.*

379. Compare Steven Winter's more generalized objection to historicism:

> A common thread runs through each of these distinctions: some things are dependable, others not; some things are solid, others ephemeral. Mostly, of course, reality, the rules, and the past are (relatively) solid and reliable. On the other hand, values are contingent; the spirit or purpose of the inherited rules are unknowable; and contemporary people are unreliable. If any of this sounds vaguely familiar, it is because it replicates the subject/object dichotomy. The object—that is, reality, the rule, the past—is good. The subject—that is, current values, the intention behind the rules, present-day humans—is subjective and bad.

The Problem of the Subject

Kronman, in his own way, wants us to recognize the importance of our embeddedness in culture, in history, in the past. In an equally if not more important sense, he also wants us to recognize that culture, history, and the past are embedded in us. Kronman's argument can easily be understood as a cultural conservative's caution against the corrosive rationalism of the contemporary world of thought.[380] Kronman seems to *want* to say that "the distinctiveness of our humanity is tied to our participation in the world of culture"[381] and that "[t]he world of culture makes us who we are."[382] But he never quite manages to say just that: the quotes above have been taken out of context. They have been removed from their original rationalist[383] envelope. What Kronman *does* say is this:

> We must, if we are to be human beings at all *adopt* toward the past the custodial attitude Burke recommends. . . . We must respect the past because the world of culture *that we inherit from it* makes us who we are . . . .[384]

The world of culture is thus something we *inherit*—something like a legacy—and towards which we must *adopt* a custodial attitude. It seems, then, that our connection to this world of culture is mediated by a realm allowing us to choose what attitude to adopt toward this legacy of the past. And what is this realm that allows us to *choose* our stance toward the world of culture? Well, what could it be other than the world of thought?

In fact, this is precisely the conclusion that Kronman is somewhat uncomfortably driven to advance: "The past," he says, "cannot enforce its claim against us if *we choose* to disrespect it."[385] But what would allow us to choose to disrespect this past, if not the world of thought? That is to say, despite Kronman's best intentions, the world of culture is nested in, is enveloped in, is mediated by the rationalist world of thought. And indeed, Kronman's article is a performative confirmation of this very point. His article is a sustained rationalist argument in favor of our thinking of ourselves as "cultural beings, as opposed to animals or thinkers."[386] And that creates a serious problem for him. Indeed, while

Winter, *Indeterminacy*, *supra* note 7, at 1511.

380. For other arguments against the corrosive character of rationalism, see Nagel, *Rationalism in Constitutional Law*, 4 CONST. COMM. 9, 15-22 (1987); Nagel, *supra* note 155, at 182.

381. Kronman, *supra* note 374, at 1066.

382. *Id.*

383. "Rationalist" in the sense explored in Schlag, *Missing Pieces*, *supra* note 7, at 1197 n.7 (using "rationalism" to "refer generally to a cognitive perspective that privileges ego-centered reason as its foundation").

384. Kronman, *supra* note 374, at 1066 (emphasis added).

385. *Id.* at 1067 (emphasis added).

386. *Id.* at 1066.

Texas Law Review Vol. 69:1627, 1991

Kronman would like to say that it is "the world of culture" that "makes us who we are," his text ends up saying something quite different—namely, that it is our thinking about the world of culture that makes us who we are.

Once again, we see that this kind of argument presupposes a subject. This subject's identity is neither secured nor exhausted by culture—the very thing that is, according to Kronman, supposed to make her what she is. We have at the heart of Kronman's thought a free agent whose identity cannot be pinned down by the world of culture, but whose thought is absolutely necessary to Kronman's project of conserving that world of culture.

We have already seen that thought must come to the rescue of culture. We have already seen how problematic this position is for Kronman's argument. It remains now to consider the character of the subject that is to do this thinking. Kronman acknowledges that "[t]hinking always begins within the context of a particular cultural milieu."[387] Even though the questions—and therefore the structure of thought—may be determined by the culture a person inhabits, it is nonetheless "a *person* [who] *chooses* to think about [them]."[388] It is precisely that moment of unconstructed, undetermined, unspecified *choosing* that allows the subject to "leave" the world of culture for what Kronman calls the activity of thought—an activity that "is *wholly disconnected* from [that] world."[389] In fact, the two realms are so separate that you have to "leave" one in order to "enter" the other.[390]

The realms of culture and of thought are thus conceived on the spatial metaphor of two contiguous, bounded, nonoverlapping realms.[391] They are, in this sense, objectified spaces, like rooms in a mansion through which the individual subject can pass. Indeed, this metaphor of a mansion is apt, because Kronman recursively describes culture in the image of a building.[392]

387. *Id.* at 1059.

388. *Id.* (emphasis added).

389. *Id.* at 1058 (emphasis added).

390. *See id.* at 1058-59. *See also supra* text accompanying notes 376-77.

391. They are not unrelated—but their relations are relations of exteriority. One realm provides the *context* for the other. One realm may *depend* upon the other. One realm may even *determine* the other. *Id.* at 1059.

392. "[A] separate world of culture thus depends on . . . a constant effort *at upkeep and repair* . . . . This is easy enough to see in the case *of physical structures like buildings* . . . ." *Id.* at 1053 (emphasis added). "To the extent that he views himself . . . as adding to or refining the achievements of his predecessors in that tradition, *contributing so to speak a few bricks of his own to the construction of some common edifice* . . . ." *Id.* at 1057-58 (emphasis added). "To begin with, the world of thought, unlike the world of culture, does not need *to be kept up as a building* or a legal system does." *Id.* at 1060 (emphasis added).

The Problem of the Subject

Now, if the role of the subject is to maintain culture in the way that one maintains a building,[393] then what we have here is a vision of the subject as concierge.[394] Implicit in this vision is not only the duty of upkeep and repair, of devoting "considerable resources" to preserve the world of culture, but also of passing it on from generation to generation for the benefit of the occupants.[395]

No doubt for conservatives there is an appeal to the notion of subject as concierge—to the idea that the present generation serves basically to transmit the productions of the past as faithfully as possible. The appeal of this vision is that the past is merely forwarded without transformation, without perversion, without deformation. And yet in this conservative vision the past has already made a problematic contribution to the present—namely, in its the notion that the past can be contained in object-form and transmitted by a subject who does nothing more than play the role of concierge. And ironically, this contribution of the present is itself corrosive of culture. One has only to think here of the effect of the Restatements, with their big, block, object-like Roman letters, on the practice of common-law lawyering to recognize that culture is not transmittable in object-form.[396]

If one understands culture as a building (as opposed to, for instance, designs for a building, or the knowledge for constructing buildings, or the understanding of how buildings affect the patterns of social life), one is likely to think of culture as substance (forgetting form) and as outcome (forgetting process). One is likely, in other words, to devote all of one's efforts to preserving cultural artifacts, while neglecting the process of cultural signification within which the artifact might have meaning.[397] Certainly, that is precisely the sort of tendency that Kronman exhibits—a concern for artifacts and a lack of attention to the process that invests them with meaning. As Kronman himself puts it: "In all these cases, a ceaseless effort at preservation is required if the *artifact* in question is to retain its meaning within the system of signs that constitutes the world of culture: if, that is to say, it is to survive as a *cultural artifact* at all."[398]

393. *See* Winter, *supra* note 116, at 1600 (discussing the conventional metaphor that *theories are buildings*).

394. The Harvard Law School equivalent is the subject as custodian. *See* R. DWORKIN, *supra* note 182, at 239 (portraying the legal subject as the legendary and mythic cleaner of Aegean stables—a.k.a. Hercules).

395. Kronman, *supra* note 374, at 1054.

396. Unless, of course, it is a kind of dead culture.

397. Or as David Luban suggests, missing from Kronman's account is the recognition that cultural construction itself requires action—a creative moment, a break with tradition. Luban, *Legal Traditionalism*, 43 STAN. L. REV. 1035, 1041 (1991) ("[T]he artifacts of human culture require constant tending.").

398. Kronman, *supra* note 374, at 1053 (emphasis added).

We see here the irony that is the conservative ambition: preservation of the past depends upon the contributions of the present. And when the social aesthetics of the present are not kind to the past, the past is preserved in a museum, as dead culture.[399] The problem for conservatism is that whenever the conservative impulse arises, whenever it becomes focused on a specific desire, it is always already too late. The culture is already ready for the museum. It is, in a word, already dead.[400]

The problem of the subject for conservatism is that it conceives of the subject as a concierge. This is a very restrained and highly regulated job description. After all, the concierge as the keeper of artifacts is a kind of bailee, subject to a stringent standard of care. Cultural conservatism needs to presuppose this sort of subject. The arch-enemy of cultural conservatism is the artist, who with unforgivable arrogance believes that he or she might actually create something, something life-giving. The last thing conservatism wants is to acknowledge that the subject might be an artist. Art implies change, and that is what the cultural conservative fears most. So the pregiven role of the subject among cultural conservatives is that of concierge. But making past culture continue to live is simply not part of the present job description of a concierge.

The underlying problem with conservatism is that it always wants to stay the same, and it never can. From its own perspective, conservatism is always already twenty minutes into the future—and, thus, without a clue as to what subject it might entrust with its mission.

VI. Recursive Recursions

The problem of the subject arises for various approaches in different ways. For rule-of-law thinkers, it arises as a recognition that the problem has been misstated. Rule of law is traditionally fixated on restraining and constraining deviant individual subjects.[401] Yet the most significant problem for rule-of-law thinking is not that some deviant subject may get out of control—but rather that there is no longer a subject on the scene who is normatively and epistemically competent to practice

399. *See supra* text accompanying note 372.

400.

> To adopt the self-conscious attitude of traditionalism requires historical distance from the traditional—a sense of loss, indeed a sense that one has become cut off from the past. Thus, traditionalism waxes as tradition itself wanes; like Hegel's owl of Minerva, traditionalism always arrives on the scene too late. It is the political counterpart of what individuals experience as nostalgia for lost innocence.

Luban, *supra* note 397, at 1057.

401. That is, the judicial equivalents of Felix Cohen or Duncan Kennedy.

and realize the rule-of-law vision in the first place. The mistake of rule of law was in presupposing the continued presence of a competent subject in the first place.

Ironically, critical legal thought borrows much from the rule-of-law aesthetic and tends to repeat the same mistake. Replicating the Sartrean metaphysic, critical legal thought presupposes that the subject is O.K. and needs only to be liberated from objectified thought-structures to become politically and intellectually free. But again, this is not all that is needed. The Sartrean individual subject may be equipped to take stands on colonial wars, racism, or other "grand" political issues, but he is strikingly ill-equipped to deal with the political framework defined by techno-bureaucracies. What's more, as a political matter, rather than liberating the existentialist subject, critical legal thought tends to reinforce the dominant cultural aesthetic that constructs individuals as free-choosing beings who are compulsively driven to choose and to require others to choose. "What should we do?", "What do you think should be done?", "What would you put in its place?", etc.—in a virulently recursive sort of way.

For neopragmatism, the problem of the subject announces itself as the recognition that all of its answers ultimately refer back to the pragmatist subject—and this subject has yet to be understood in a cogent pragmatic manner. For neopragmatism, then, the subject is a creature of context. But neopragmatism keeps treating the subject as the context of all contexts. Currently, this subject finds itself in the context of all contexts—shopping at the cultural-intellectual mall without a clue as to what its place might be in the free play of signifiers. Neopragmatism thus encounters the problem of the subject in the recognition that pragmatism doesn't have much to offer the subject—that the work to be done is perhaps in *becoming* a subject in the first place.

Starting too late turns out to be the problem of the subject for cultural conservatism. For conservatism, as for all the other approaches, the problem of the subject announces itself as a recognition that the available subjects are not adequate to the tasks required. Cultural conservatism needs a subject to conserve the past. Unfortunately, the past has not been very forthcoming in producing such a subject. What cultural conservatism faces, then, is a present rudely taken out of context: "the extraordinarily unappetizing prospect"[402] that "we are all we have."[403]

402. Leff, *Unspeakable Ethics, Unnatural Law*, 1979 Duke L.J. 1229, 1249.
403. *Id.*

Texas Law Review Vol. 69:1627, 1991

Clearly, the problem of the subject is conceptualized and arises for these various approaches in many differing ways. One difference has to do with the ways in which the various approaches represent themselves as advancing a vision of the *full* or *empty* subject. Indeed, as Merleau-Ponty suggested, "There are at bottom only two ideas of subjectivity—that of empty, unfettered, and universal subjectivity, and that of full subjectivity sucked down into the world—and it is the same idea . . . ."[404]

For instance, both rule-of-law and critical legal thought privilege a representation of the individual subject as empty.[405] For rule of law, the individual subject is empty and thus cannot have any positive contribution to make to the field of law. The individual subject is to submit to or efface himself before it; he is thus outside the jurisdiction of the rule of law. He is off-scene, out of jurisprudential sight. To the extent he appears on the scene at all, it would be as an interloper, a trespasser. Critical legal thought also privileges the empty subject. But now this emptiness is given a positive valuation: the subject is empty, ineffable, and thus cannot be reduced to its legal context. Thus, the individual subject is a source of intellectual and political promise rather than a threat. Both neopragmatism and cultural conservatism also place the subject beyond inquiry, but they do so by privileging an individual subject that is so full of convention that he has neither the motive nor the distance necessary to engage in anything but the most conventional sort of self-understanding.[406] There is no access to the subject because the subject is already saturated by convention.

Ironically, in American legal thought the full subject understands his fullness as having been chosen freely, autonomously, through a series of well-considered, conscious choices. Also ironically, the empty subject is a completely conventional cultural construction. I have tried to capture this phenomenal construction of the self under the rubric: "the relatively autonomous" self—a not altogether inappropriate name considering that the expression "relative autonomy" is traceable to Sartre[407] and that Sartre's conception of the self is traceable to a conventional liberal conceptualization of the subject.[408]

Now, neither the full nor the empty subject is a particularly stable entity. On the contrary, the empty subject needs to be stabilized and

404. M. MERLEAU-PONTY, *supra* note 1, at 154.

405. This, of course, does not mean that rule-of-law and critical legal thought *invariably* represent the individual subject as empty. *See infra* text accompanying notes 407-08.

406. This, of course, does not mean that neopragmatism and cultural conservatism invariably represent the individual subject as full. *See infra* text accompanying notes 407-08.

407. J.-P. SARTRE, SEARCH FOR A METHOD 68-70 (1963).

408. *See supra* text accompanying notes 267-71.

filled up. The full subject, by contrast, needs to account for its own subjective experience. Thus, in both areas which arguably privilege the empty subject—rule of law and critical legal thought—we see a tendency to seek out a full subject. Conversely, in cultural conservatism and legal neopragmatism, both of which privilege the full subject, we see a sort of longing for transcendence manifested in a tendency to achieve the state of the empty subject.

For all the differences I have insisted upon in describing how the problem of the subject arises for these various modes of contemporary legal thought, there is ironically a certain sameness nonetheless. In each case, we find that the problem of the subject arises in the unwelcome recognition that the approach already presupposes the existence of a particular subject—and that this subject is nowhere to be found. This can, of course, be a disturbing recognition. Each approach goes to great lengths to avoid this recognition. Each approach, when it is engaging with intellectual challenges, rhetorically reinscribes its own subject-object aesthetic in a way that systematically elides the recognition that the very kind of subject it presupposes is missing.[409] The subject can be missing in different ways. It can be missing in the sense that it is undertheorized, incompetent or simply no longer viable. These recognitions are routinely elided in one of two ways—in the presupposition of an empty subject or in the presupposition of a full subject. Hence, the subject can be depicted as empty, such that there really is nothing to say about the subject. Or, the subject can be depicted as "us" and "we" (as full subjects, extensions of a rich interpretive community), and *we*, of course, are always O.K..

Even the most critical strategies of American legal thought succeed in re-inscribing and re-instating the subject as beyond inquiry. The two basic critical moves in American legal thought are to dissolve a purported objectivity back to the actions of a constituting subject or to show that the transcendental subject is really a fraud, a masquerade, an intellectual lightweight. In either instance, however, the critical move is arrested at precisely the point where the new presupposed subject can begin to do its work. Thus, the legal realists arrest their deconstructive critique at the point where Langdellian conceptualism is destroyed and law can be reconstructed by a subject competent in functional, purposive think-

409. For a brief illustration of this process, see Schlag, *Normative and Nowhere to Go*, *supra* note 7, at 173-80 (showing how normative legal thought routinely defuses postmodernist challenges by reformulating them within its own normative aesthetic). For a discussion of the workings and implications of this process, see generally Schlag, *Politics of Form*, *supra* note 7 (describing how normative legal thought reproduces itself and its aesthetic political effects).

ing and social science. Similarly, critical legal thinkers arrest their deconstructive critique at precisely the point where the newly freed existentialist individual subject emerges as a "choosing being" who takes responsibility for her choices. Legal neopragmatists arrest their critique of rationalist metaphysics at precisely the point where all theoretical questions are thrown back on the mediated mediating mediator, the pragmatist subject. In all three instances, despite the critical ambitions of these movements, we have an arrested critique which leaves unexplored and untroubled the space occupied by a presupposed competent individual subject.

Now, all of this prompts several questions. First, what is the character of this unexplored space of the subject?[410] Second, how is it that legal thought seems systematically to avoid not only exploring but even noticing this space of subjectivity? Third, what are the implications of this kind of subjectivity? Fourth, how might we move beyond this type of arrested political and intellectual practice?

A. *The Liberal Subject*

First, if we are to understand how the subject is constituted, we must understand how the space he inhabits is constituted. Absent a lapse into a naive philosophical idealism, we cannot simply take what various jurisprudential approaches say about their own contributions at face value. The question, then, is not what these approaches say substantively about the subject. The question is what relations does their rhetoric establish between author and reader. What kind of author and reader are imagined and instituted by these various approaches?

Once we ask the questions in this way, it becomes evident that all of these approaches presuppose and construct the subject as a conscious, sovereign individual subject—the conventional liberal subject. In his most educated moments, this liberal subject understands that he is socially and rhetorically constructed, but nonetheless retains his autonomy to decide just how constructed or autonomous he really is. This divided individual subject[411] is precisely the kind of subject rhetorically presupposed by virtually all contemporary American legal thought. The supposition is that the individual subject is essentially—a word deliberately chosen—autonomous, coherent, self-directing, integrated, rational, and originary. This means that what might seem on the level of "substantive

410. If I speak here of the subject in the crypto-objectivist metaphor of "space," it is because that is the way contemporary legal thought (with its objectivist tendencies) first represents the problem of the subject to itself.

411. *See supra* note 360 and accompanying text.

propositional content" to be a dominant conventionalist or constructivist moment in legal neopragmatism and cultural conservatism is as a matter of rhetoric, practice, and form, subordinated to the actions, rule, and rhetoric of the sovereign individual subject. This also means that the apparent total erasure of the individual subject in cls and rule-of-law thinking is an ineffectual erasure—one that leaves the conscious sovereign individual subject untroubled, unquestioned, and in charge.

This sovereign individual subject—this relatively autonomous self is a kind of default subject—one that is routinely re-enacted and reproduced in legal thought. Because the relatively autonomous subject is in its very configuration unstable, it enables a series of other kinds of subjects or selves to be represented in substantive propositional legal thought. In other words, the very instability of the relatively autonomous self enables its own rhetorical reproduction even as it accommodates different and potentially destabilizing representations of the subject. Only rarely, then, will we find legal thought itself attempting to establish a radically different kind of subject in its very form, practice, or rhetoric.

B. The Langdellian Paradigm

How is it that legal thought has managed to create this space of the subject that seems to systematically survive any critique untroubled and unexplored? Each approach objectifies the world in order to make it safe for its own favorite individual subject. The subject-object relations are frozen at some highly abstract level, and this frozen relation is then replayed recursively throughout the jurisprudential approach.[412] In effect, this frozen subject-object relation eclipses the problem of the subject; it puts the problem of the subject beyond consideration. How does

412. Rule of law, for instance, attempts to locate legal meaning in the doctrines, rules, and policies and concerns itself with the subject only as something that needs to be constrained and restrained. Rule of law is thus fixated on perfecting "law" in a so-called objective realm demarcated by appellate doctrine, rules, and other reified thought-spaces.

Critical legal thought concerns itself with liberating the individual subject from reified thought structures and thingified social roles. Ironically, this subject-object picture is itself a captive of rule-of-law thought and, although the valences get reversed, the subject-object aesthetic and separation remain the same.

Legal neopragmatism, unlike rule of law and cls, is not primarily informed by a spatial representation of subject-object relations. On the contrary, legal pragmatism is informed by a dominant temporal metaphorics. Indeed, the stock move of legal pragmatism is to dissolve and refer all theoretical questions back to a prior moment of agency: the character of the pragmatist subject, the one who "mediates"—or more accurately the already mediated mediating mediator.

Cultural conservatism is a sort of intense reification of the pragmatic recognition of the constitutive character of convention. Like legal neopragmatism, cultural conservatism refers identity and meaning back to an agency. Here the agency turns out to be the past itself. Hence, cultural conservatism attempts to restrain the space of the subject as much as possible.

this happen? More to the point: how is it that this happens over and over again?

We must remember how we got here. Langdell said early on:

> I have tried to do my part towards making the teaching and the study of law in that school worthy of a university . . . .
>
> To accomplish these objects, so far as they depended upon the law school, it was indispensable to establish at least two things—that law is a science, and that all the available materials of that science are contained in printed books.[413]

We must remember that the enterprise that we as legal thinkers have been engaged in from the very start has been to construct and reconstruct law in the image of a discipline worthy of the university—in other words, to legitimate and institutionalize our work and our selves.[414] In a sense, then, from the very beginning we have tried to construct and to create the study of "law" as something that would be independent of the particular individuals who would study that law.

One of the attractive features of the Langdellian orthodoxy for legal thinkers is the extraordinarily flattering role that it carved out for them. Inasmuch as the Langdellian orthodoxy required the conceptual subordination of case decisions to the harmonious arrangement of legal principles, the legal thinker (as the discoverer of the principles of law) enjoyed a privileged intellectual position relative to that of the judge (the author of case decisions). In contrast to the modern dominance of court positivism,[415] the Langdellian thinker reserved for himself the right to pronounce whether or not some judicial decision in an actual case was or was not law. Whether or not a decision was law would depend (within the Langdellian universe) on its conformity to the principles of law.[416]

413. *Harvard Celebration Speeches*, *supra* note 17, at 123-24.

414.

> I think Langdell's world was attractive to legal academics because it gave them a piece of the academic division of labor that no one else claimed, and gave them a distinctive method, the hallmark of any modern science, from which they could build a professional identity much as had other academic disciplines like history or economics around the turn of the century. From this perspective, the choice to renounce Langdell's legacy is an implausible one, for in so doing the legal academic would renounce his or her own professional identity.

Schlegel, *Langdell's Legacy or, The Case of the Empty Envelope*, 36 STAN. L. REV. 1517, 1533 (1984).

415. *See* Powell, *Constitutional Law as Though the Constitution Mattered* (Book Review), 1986 DUKE L.J. 915, 915 (reviewing W. MURPHY, J. FLEMMING & W. HARRIS, AMERICAN CONSTITUTIONAL INTERPRETATION (1986)) ("[T]hat perception of the meaning of constitutional law leads to what might be called 'Court-positivism'—the almost automatic assumption that the Constitution is indeed 'what the judges say it is.' " (citations and footnotes omitted)); *see also supra* note 70 (discussing the Langdellian subordination of case law to principles).

416. Schlegel, *American Legal Theory and American Legal Education: A Snake Swallowing Its Tail* in CRITICAL LEGAL THOUGHT: AN AMERICAN-GERMAN DEBATE, *supra* note 119, at 52.

The Problem of the Subject

The custodian of these principles and their harmony was, of course, none other than the legal thinker—whose task it was to continually arrange legal decisions and legal rules in accordance with the architecture of Langdellian principles.

Most legal thinkers will represent legal thought as having come a long way from the days of Langdell. No doubt, the substantive propositional content of legal thought has changed greatly since Langdell. The institutional role of the legal thinker, however, has remained much the same.

Indeed, much of the epistemic structure of contemporary legal thought was already in place in Langdellian times. The classical orthodoxy developed by Langdell, Beale, and the other legal formalists established the identity of the legal thinker, his role, his audience, their relation, the proper modes of communication, the relation of theory to practice, and basic notions of historical and political agency.[417] While it would be crude to claim that the Langdellian paradigm has remained unchanged to the present, there is not much risk—at least among legal academics—of falling into that type of error. On the contrary, given widespread contemporary hostility to the Langdellian approach, legal academics have, if anything, been too quick in disclaiming or denying the continued hold of the Langdellian orthodoxy.[418] Indeed, it is striking as we look at the role of the Langdellian legal thinker how much that role is our role. The explicit (and widely known) tenets of the Langdellian orthodoxy—for instance, the view of legal study as a science or the depiction of law as autonomous—had very specific (and relatively unnoticed) *formative* implications for:

the relation between the academy and the courts
the identity of the audience
the identity of the author
the relation between the author and the audience
the role of the text in legal culture
the relation between theory and practice.

1. The Relation Between the Academy and the Courts.—One effect of placing the legal academic in this position was to make the legal academic the judge of judges. The legal academic was superior to the judge (at least potentially) in the sense that if the judge's decision did not accord with the Langdellian architecture, it simply was not law and could thus be treated as some sort of pathological departure. In some sense

417. *See* Winter, *Indeterminacy*, *supra* note 7, at 1455-56.

418. Grey, *supra* note 25, at 57 (noting that "[a]part from the balancing idiom, legal discourse largely retains its orthodox form").

Texas Law Review Vol. 69:1627, 1991

then, the ultimate pronouncer of the law was not the judge, but the legal thinker himself.

But if the Langdellian academic enjoyed an epistemic privilege over the courts, he was also their *ally*. The Langdellian academic was an ally in several senses. As the primary custodian of the principles of law, the Langdellian academic furnished ultimate guidance on what counted as law and what did not. The Langdellians discharged this duty by producing copious and cleanly integrated treatises that organized the law in a manner that was fiercely hierarchical and thoroughly coherent.[419] These treatises, of course, were aimed at realizing in case law the Langdellian view of law as coherent, gapless, and hierarchically arranged. Inasmuch as cases were the raw materials for the science of law, it was part of that science to show that the case law did have the coherent, hierarchical, gapless order that the Langdellians claimed it had. Thus, it was necessary to the Langdellians that the Langdellian architecture be realized not just in the treatises, but in the case law as well. While the Langdellian thinker may have enjoyed an epistemic privilege relative to the courts, the acquiescence of the courts in the Langdellian pronouncements was still quite necessary.

Accordingly, within the Langdellian paradigm the relations between the academy and the judiciary were exceedingly cordial. The Langdellian thinker addressed his thoughts to the courts to inform them as to what was and what was not the law. In turn, the courts and the bar were expected to listen and to heed the pronouncements of the legal thinker whose taxonomic efforts lent coherence, order, and legitimacy to the law. Legal thinkers wrote for judges, and judges were supposed to listen.

2. *The Identity of the Audience.*—One implication of writing for judges, of course, is that judges (as the audience) were accorded the typical respect that an author—at least an author bent on persuasion—reserves for his anticipated audience. Persuasive rhetoric typically entails respecting the self-image of the reader and, at the very least, avoiding statements that will injure that self-image. For the Langdellian thinker, this meant that the self-image of the judge as an intelligent, well-meaning, autonomous, and even wise individual had to be respected. And this image had to be respected not only as a matter of substance, but as a matter of form. For the Langdellian, of course, this was hardly a difficult problem. Given that law was an autonomous discipline, it was natural for the Langdellian thinkers to treat judges as conscious sover-

419. *See, e.g.*, 1-3 J. BEALE, *supra* note 31; C. LANGDELL, *supra* note 19.

eign individual subjects—individuals beyond the reach of the insulting knowledges of social science, psychology, economics, and their (quasi-) determinist structures. Indeed, little could have been further from the Langdellian mind than to treat judges as an object of study—either generally or more particularly, as a class of bureaucratic decision makers whose rhetorical and cognitive patterns are prompted by the relatively intense socialization processes of law schools and law firms. The very fact that Langdellian thinkers wrote for judges thus established as a matter of form the tacit image of judges as self-directing, autonomous, rational individuals. The judge, of course, was not the only figure to receive this beneficent treatment. To some extent, this image of the autonomous, self-directing individual was extended as a matter of form to all persons engaged in the enterprise of law. Indeed, one of the consequences of treating law as an autonomous discipline is that, at least for purposes of doing law, the participants in the discipline are also treated as autonomous individuals—including, of course, the Langdellian thinker himself.

3. The Identity of the Author.—The Langdellian thinker was a "scientist" in the nineteenth-century sense that his discovery of the principles of law from the data (the cases) was grounded in a secure sublimation into a transcendental order of the object or the subject. The Langdellian scientist discovered principles already extant in the law.[420] Accordingly, no reason ever arose to question the identity of the professional self of the legal scientist. It was beyond question—normatively, socially, psychologically, and so on.

4. The Relation Between the Author and the Audience.—Within the Langdellian orthodoxy, the author and his audience are complicitous in confirming their own epistemic privilege. The author's implicit assumption that he is addressing self-directing, autonomous individuals in a rational manner, of course, implicitly extends that status to his readers. Interestingly, in the very act of addressing such a community, in the very act of claiming to be a part of this community, the author performatively confirms his own status as an autonomous, self-directing individual. Ironically, it is the readers who constitute the author in this way. Inasmuch as the readers already view themselves as autonomous, self-directing, and rational, they rhetorically compel the author to write in precisely that voice. In a formal and formative sense, the Langdellian orthodoxy tacitly imagines and thereby constitutes a community of self-

420. *See supra* notes 24, 413 and accompanying text.

directing, autonomous, rational individuals bound by the common enterprise of law.

This symbiotic fantasy is largely stable and self-perpetuating. In order to escape the fantasy, the author would have to do one of two self-destructive things. He would have to question (and thus injure) the self-image of his readers as autonomous, self-directing individuals. Or he would have to question (and thus injure) his own self-image as an autonomous, self-directing, and rational individual. Either tactic is likely to prompt some sort of regulatory rhetorical response: a thought-police action. As will be seen later, the stability and appeal of this symbiotic fantasy makes it extremely difficult to discard as a structural or formal matter even though, of course, most modern thinkers would agree that the fantasy is substantively ludicrous.

5. *The Role of the Text in Legal Thought.*—Viewing law as an autonomous discipline with its own rational order, the Langdellian orthodoxy views the text of legal thought as the medium for clarifying the order and for redressing isolated deviances. Thus, the Langdellian treatise and Langdellian thought equivocate between what moderns might call descriptive and prescriptive scholarship. In Langdellian orthodoxy, the two are not firmly separated. Law has a certain order quite independent of what particular courts may do. The description of that order, however, carries the implicit suggestion that courts ought to bring their decisions in line with that order. In turn, any prescription offered to courts on an unsettled problem purports to be description. In this manner, the legal text conflates description and prescription.

It is easy to see how such a conflation might occur within the Langdellian framework. Because law is an autonomous discipline, the hierarchical and coherent *arrangement* of the principles, rules, and decisions is to be accomplished immanently through the use of *legal* argument—the very sort of argument to be used by judges and lawyers. Thus, legal argument is itself part of law. To engage in Langdellian legal arguments is at once to describe and prescribe a particular doctrine. Thus, the text within the Langdellian scheme is at once descriptive and prescriptive—rarely distinguishing between the two.[421]

As a matter of form, the great Langdellian treatises and articles were clearly designed to guide judges in decision making. Langdellian thought was principally addressed to the judges and to the bar with

421. It is precisely this conflation of the is and the ought in the very definition of law that was criticized by Felix Cohen. Cohen, *supra* note 50, at 838 (criticizing Blackstone's definition of law for conflating what the sovereign commands with what is right and wrong).

whom the Langdellian scholars identified.[422] Relative to modern thought, there is thus an apparent lack of critical distance between Langdellian thought and judicial or lawyerly argument. Consistent with the view that they were engaged in the scientific discovery of the principles embedded in the case law, the Langdellian scholars had virtually no self-conscious apprehension of the constitutive role of their own jurisprudential commitments. Indeed, the Langdellians were gifted with an amazing capacity for lack of self-awareness. Consistent with the view that law is an autonomous discipline, Langdellian thought shows no awareness of the psychological or social dimension of legal communication. On the contrary, the Langdellian text aims to be transparent to autonomous, self-directing, rational individuals. Hence, the Langdellian text is relentlessly rationalist. Consistent with the Langdellian constitution of the author and the reader as self-directing, autonomous selves, Langdellian texts seek to persuade by giving rationalist reasons *for belief*.

6. The Relation of Theory and Practice.—The Langdellian claim that legal study was a science, legal scholars were scientists, and law was autonomous led to an extremely simple and idealist conception of the relation of theory to practice. The rigorously hierarchical and gapless character of the Langdellian ordering of law reveals much about the Langdellian view of the relation of theory to practice. This relation seems to be virtually unidirectional: theory governs practice in an unproblematic way. Higher level principles control the rules which, in turn, control the case decisions. Within the Langdellian universe, there is not the slightest sense that theory might be embedded in practice, that theory might be epiphenomenal, that theory is itself a practice or anything of that nature. Rather, for the Langdellian, the conceptual structure of law rules legal practice in a straightforward manner. Isolated case anomalies or deviations are simply the result of a lack of intelligence or legal acumen.

Now, it seems to me that, as a matter of substantive propositional content, our contemporary visions of law have arguably changed significantly from this Langdellian paradigm. In terms of the actual practice, rhetoric, and form of contemporary legal thought, however, there has been very little change. What is interesting to note is that, even as change has occurred at the level of substantive propositional content, the

422. *See* Barnhizer, *Prophets, Priests, and Power Blockers: Three Fundamental Roles of Judges and Legal Scholars in America*, 50 U. PITT. L. REV. 127, 132 (1988) (noting that the Langdellian approach formed lasting and close links with the American judiciary).

Langdellian formal relations nonetheless continue in a slightly different guise.

In fact, perhaps the *only* change from this Langdellian paradigm is that many of us no longer think the courts are listening to much of anything we say or write and that many of us seem to be well on the way to abandoning communication with judges altogether.[423] But even as these changes are occurring, the arguments of legal thinkers about what law is or should be continue to be mediated and channeled by a highly traditional and romanticized image of the kind of reasoning used by the appellate judge. This is evidenced, for instance, in the *Hercules phenomenon*, which aptly symbolizes the apparent legal academic belief that the appellate judge is somehow the central site for the creation and maintenance of the law and its meaning.[424]

Now, I think it is precisely because the reigning configuration of legal thought is embedded in regions and processes that are obscured from the critical reaches of that same legal thought that this rhetoric has been so resilient. The rhetoric has been structured as a kind of forgetting of the forgetting, a repression of the repression. The rhetoric has been inscribed in the legal subject—and that is what has been put off-scene, out of reach, beyond inquiry. In the same way, the problem of the subject has been obscured in virtue of the legal thinkers' construction as a conscious sovereign individual subject, who does not even recognize that the subject is a problem.

C. *The Subject as Problem*

But the subject is a problem. We have already seen how the subject becomes a problem for various kinds of contemporary legal thought and their projects. The problem arises as each school recognizes that its own intellectual architecture, its own normative ambitions rest upon the presupposition of a subject—a subject whose epistemic, ontological, and normative status is now very much in question.

Now this is not simply an intellectual problem; it has political implications. The political implications are easy to describe. The constitution of legal thinkers and others as conscious sovereign individual subjects produces a politics that works perfectly—assuming that we do indeed

423. *See* Winter, *Indeterminacy*, *supra* note 7, at 1452-53.

424. For my discussion of the Hercules phenomenon, see Schlag, *"Le Hors de Texte," supra* note 7, at 1663-66; Schlag, *Politics of Form*, *supra* note 7, at 845-52. Owen Fiss exemplifies the Hercules phenomenon succinctly when he says, "My conception of adjudication starts from the top—the office of the judge—and works down . . . . I start with the conception of power embodied in the judge." Fiss, *The Supreme Court, 1978 Term—Foreword: The Forms of Justice*, 93 HARV. L. REV. 1, 41 (1979).

The Problem of the Subject

have conscious sovereign individual subjects situated to control the levers of the social machinery.[425]

Once articulated, however, that vision fast becomes implausible. In the legal academy, this vision of social life is maintained by an elite of legal thinkers who systematically confirm themselves in this vision by relentlessly rehearsing its aesthetic. They seem to be either incapable or unwilling to recognize that this conventional aesthetic of social life is fast becoming unbelievable.

Now, the resistance of legal academics to a reconsideration of the conventional aesthetic of the liberal subject is easy to understand. If the liberal subject disappears from the scene, a number of very troublesome questions immediately surface: who (or what) is controlling the levers running the social machinery?[426] And if there's no one operating the levers, then what has been the effect of all that good, admirable, serious, normative legal thought?[427]

As legal thinkers, we like to think we are doing good, normative legal work—advancing noble causes and the like—but if the liberal subject is no longer operating the levers, our work product can take on a different character. We may simply be rehearsing and reproducing the instrumentalist logic of bureaucratic practices.[428] Indeed, the main significance of noble normative work is in the rehearsal of a false aesthetic of social life—one which falsely represents

instrumentalist strategies as within the control of individual subjects
the unfolding of bureaucratic logic as the choices of individuals
the discursive mechanisms of coercion as normative dialogue.

Now, there is nothing wrong with instrumental control in and of

425.

> This picture is deeply attractive to moderns, both flattering and inspiring. It shows us as capable of achieving a kind of disengagement from our world by objectifying it. We objectify our situation to the extent that we can overcome a sense of it as what determines for us our paradigm purposes and ends, and can come to see it and function in it as a neutral environment within which we can effect purposes which we determine out of ourselves . . . .

1 C. TAYLOR, HUMAN AGENCY AND LANGUAGE: PHILOSOPHICAL PAPERS 4 (1985).

426. Of course, if the liberal subject is disappearing from the scene, we will also have to reconsider the related objectivist metaphor of "the social machinery".

427. *See* Schlag, *Politics of Form*, *supra* note 7, at 899 (characterizing normative legal thought as a "blockage" which prevents "inquiry into the process, form, and practice" of legal thought); Schlag, *Normative and Nowhere to Go*, *supra* note 7, at 173-81 (describing normative legal thought as the bureaucratic routine of the legal academy).

428. *See* Schlag, *Politics of Form*, *supra* note 7, at 832 (noting that normative legal thought enables legal thinkers to incorrectly assume they are themselves immune from "the bureaucratic power games"); Schlag, *Normative and Nowhere to Go*, *supra* note 7, at 188-91 (noting that teaching normative legal thought may be merely training students to become well-versed in the rhetoric of bureaucratic logic as opposed to humanistic principles).

Texas Law Review Vol. 69:1627, 1991

itself. Indeed, instrumental control is often valued—it bears names like efficiency, effectiveness, and wisdom. But the supposition that instrumental control is desirable presupposes that there is an epistemically and normatively competent subject at the levers. And that is precisely what is being thrown in question: if the subject is constituted by its discourses and its context, who or what is in charge?[429]

Viewed in this light, we can understand normative legal thought not as a noble attempt to criticize and reform the structures and practices of bureaucratic domination, but rather as a kind of discourse that has already been unconsciously captivated by those very same structures and practices. The pathways, the issues, the problems of normative legal thought are already constituted by bureaucratic domination. That is why normative legal thought can seem at once normatively ineffectual and unappealing. Rather than contributing to our understanding or to the realization of the good or the right, all this normative argument simply perpetuates a false aesthetic of social life—one that prevents "us"[430] from even recognizing the sort of bureaucratic practices that constitute and channel our thought and action.

The plausibility of this sort of systemic misrepresentation is evident as one considers that the governing criteria of knowledge in legal thought—of what counts as good argument—are invariably represented in terms of reason, yet are closely linked to a conception of power as instrumental control. Among the regulative criteria for sound legal thought, the following recur frequently:

1. representational accuracy[431]
2. consensual acceptability[432]
3. coherence[433]
4. elegance[434]
5. sweep[435]
6. determinacy[436]
7. realizability.[437]

429. This, of course, is a preliminary (not satisfactory) way of asking the question—one which is still shaped by a certain subject-object aesthetic that is itself being put in question.

430. This is a very problematic "us."

431. The theory must not rely on assumptions or advance propositions that do not correspond to its referents.

432. The theory must not rely on assumptions or advance claims that are or entail offensive, absurd, or unbelievable implications for the relevant audience.

433. The theory must avoid internal contradiction and performative contradiction.

434. The theory must rely on as few explanatory or justificatory variables as possible.

435. The theory must be as encompassing as possible and must explain or justify all aspects that are within its legitimate scope.

436. The theory must restrict as much as possible the number of relevant and plausible conflicting interpretations it can sustain.

437. The theory must be capable of guiding its own realization in practice.

The Problem of the Subject

These aesthetic criteria, which are usually represented as related to the form and content of truth are used to assess the value of theory.[438] These are the regulative discursive criteria that authorize the stock of arguments and objections of much of contemporary legal thought. Yet, these regulative aesthetic criteria are also linked to *instrumental control.*

We can formulate the point in (at least) two interesting ways. *Ex post*: satisfaction of these regulative criteria facilitate deployment—they facilitate activation of the theories that are produced by the existing practices and institutions of instrumental control. *Ex ante*: these regulative criteria channel and shape the kinds of normative, explanatory, and prescriptive theories that will be produced—disabling and devaluing those intellectual efforts that do not comply with the strategies, structures, and practices of instrumental control.

Each of the modes of thought we have considered is (to varying degrees) enabled and delimited by an unconscious construction of what the legal thinker is supposed to do. Implicit in each vision is an understanding that the legal thinker will develop some approach that will allow reason to be used as control. Virtually all legal thinkers are involved in this enterprise, which is why the recursive theme for each generation of American legal thinkers is some (typically formalistic) variant of a struggle between formalism and anti-formalism:

formalism vs. realism
universalism vs. contextualism
rules vs. standards
and so on.

If we understand social aesthetics in this way, then it is easy to recognize that most of the intellectual-political disagreements among the various schools of thought we have discussed are—at least as far as their own substantive propositional content is concerned—epiphenomenal. All these disagreements are grounded upon and made meaningful by a shared misunderstanding of the aesthetics of contemporary social life—a shared misunderstanding that is inscribed in generations of legal thinkers whose stature and dialogic engagement are themselves supported and sustained by this shared misunderstanding.

D. *The Subject Reconsidered*

Now, if this is right, then the problem of the subject takes on an important significance. Recognizing and addressing the problem of the subject is not simply a question of resolving a particular kind of error in

438. Schlag, *The Brilliant, the Curious, and the Wrong*, 39 STAN. L. REV. 917, 921-22 (1987).

our jurisprudence, our theories, our institutional practices. Rather, addressing the problem begins with the recognition that the sort of subject formation we have been constructed to be is one that systematically reproduces a false aesthetic of social life.

I have tried to show how this subject formation is unconsciously reproduced and maintained by ostensibly very different, even radical and critical modes of contemporary legal thought. These modes of legal thought are nested within a Langdellian form and rhetoric which shapes the kinds of subjects who practice these modes of thought. The result is that regardless of their (good) intentions, these subjects unconsciously replicate the Langdellian paradigm and its subject formation. This is the process that I call *the politics of form*.

What is perhaps most powerful about the politics of form is that it is not and cannot be recognized within our conventional representations of the political or the jurisprudential field.[439] On the contrary, the politics of form *is* the process that shapes us and our aesthetic conceptualization of the political and jurisprudential field. And in shaping us and our aesthetic conceptualizations, the politics of form shapes us to systematically elide the kinds of subject formations we have been constructed to be and the politics of form that has constructed us to become those subject formations.

If the problem of the subject and the politics of form are currently of concern (and possible to articulate) it is because the Langdellian subject formation—that is, the subject formation of the contemporary legal thinker—is intellectually *exhausted*. Indeed, that is in part why so "[m]any of the critiques developed over the past twenty years or so seem to have reached, if not dead ends, then at least a measure of exhaustion."[440] Indeed, there is an important sense in which, for all the differences among the various modes of legal thought discussed here, they all exhibit a prevailing and repetitive sameness.[441] This is the sameness of the Langdellian paradigm—the sameness produced through a subject constructed to rehearse the same social aesthetic, the same form of intel-

439. In this sense, Radin and Michelman's suggestion that the arguments of *Normativity and the Politics of Form*, *supra* note 7, do not conform very well with Radin and Michelman's conventional representation of the jurisprudential field is, in a sense, absolutely right. The politics of form is an account of the politics that shape our very conceptualization of the political (including, the jurisprudential) field in the first place. *Compare* Radin & Michelman, *supra* note 8, *with* Schlag, *Stances*, 139 U. PA. L. REV. 1059 (1991).

440. Levinson, *Strolling Down the Path of the Law (and toward Critical Legal Studies?): The Jurisprudence of Richard Posner*, 91 COLUM. L. REV. 1221, 1252 (1991).

441. This is a sameness that becomes cognizable once the enablements and disabilities of the Langdellian paradigm and its subject formation have been left behind. For those who remain Langdellian subject formations, it is the differences between the various approaches of legal thought, not their sameness, that remain of paramount significance.

lectual action, the same rhetorical relations regardless of the substantive propositional content at stake.

What concerns me about this Langdellian subject formation is that despite its exhaustion, it nonetheless remains dominant in the legal academy. Not only does the dominance of this subject formation prevent the development and recognition of other subject formations, but it effectively colonizes and homogenizes otherwise interesting and potentially edifying intellectual approaches.[442] Perhaps most significant is that this Langdellian subject formation is deeply implicated in the reproduction of images of law, society, culture, and politics and their relations that are now *seriously* out of date and positively detrimental to the intellectual and social construction of our world. For instance, the aesthetic that enables the formation and currency of political categories such as "conservative," "liberal," and "radical" is fast being eviscerated. What we have now is simulated conservatism, simulated liberalism, and simulated radicalism.[443] One can bemoan this state of affairs, but, of course, the risk is that this will be simulated bemoaning.

VII. Conclusion

Sometimes it seems that there is only one story in American legal thought and only one problem. The story is the story of formalism and the problem is the problem of the subject. The story of formalism is that it never deals with the problem of the subject. The problem of the subject is that it's never been part of the story.

* * *

Until now.

442. *See, e.g.*, Schlag, *"Le Hors de Texte," supra* note 7.
443. *See generally* J. BAUDRILLARD, SIMULATIONS (1983).

[7]

Objects of Property and Subjects of Politics: Intellectual Property Laws and Democratic Dialogue

Rosemary J. Coombe*

"[T]he self becomes itself only through a transaction of signs with other selves—and does so, moreover, without succumbing to the mindless mechanism of the behaviorists."

—Walker Percy[1]

"*[C]onsciousness itself can arise and become a viable fact only in the material embodiment of signs*. . . . [U]nderstanding is a response to a sign with signs. . . .

. . . .

. . . The individual consciousness is nurtured on signs; it derives its growth from them; it reflects their logic and laws."

—Valentin Voloshinov[2]

"[My] purpose . . . is to make explicit the systems of operational combination . . . which also compose a 'culture,' and to bring to light the models of action characteristic of users whose status as the dominated element in society . . . is concealed by the euphemistic term 'consumers.' Everyday life invents itself by *poaching* in countless ways on the property of others."[3]

* Assistant Professor, Faculty of Law, University of Toronto. B.A. 1981, University of Western Ontario; LL.B. 1984, University of Western Ontario; J.S.M. 1988, Stanford University; J.S.D. 1991, Stanford University. The author was the 1990-91 Karl Loewenstein Fellow in Jurisprudence and Political Thought at Amherst College. She would like to thank the Trustees of Amherst College and her colleagues Austin Sarat and Tom Dumm in the Department of Political Science. Conversations with Michael Blazer, Barbara Yngvessen, and Pierre Schlag helped to clarify my arguments. Paul Stoller helped me to give the Article a form that more fully reflects the spirit of the enterprise and the ethnographic sensibility with which I approach this topic; I thank him for the inspiration. The research assistance of Amanda Pask is greatly appreciated.

1. W. Percy, *A Semiotic Primer of the Self*, in Lost in the Cosmos: The Last Self-Help Book 88 n.* (1984).

2. V.N. Voloshinov, Marxism and the Philosophy of Language 11-13 (L. Matejka & I.R. Titunik trans. 1973).

3. M. de Certeau, The Practice of Everyday Life xi-xii (S. Rendall trans. 1984) (emphasis in original).

Texas Law Review Vol. 69:1853, 1991

"Marginality today is no longer limited to minority groups, but is rather massive and pervasive; this cultural activity of the non-producers of culture, an activity that is unsigned . . . remains the only one possible for all those who nevertheless buy and pay for the showy products through which a productivist economy articulates itself. Marginality is becoming universal. A marginal group has now become a silent majority."

—Michel de Certeau[4]

"[T]he ruling class strives to impart a supraclass, eternal character to the ideological sign, to extinguish or drive inward the struggle between social value judgments which occurs in it, to make the sign uniaccentual."

—Valentin Voloshinov[5]

I. Introduction

Who authorizes Thumper? I want to express the nature of my stunned disbelief when I noticed that, in a recent law review article, Pierre Schlag *cited authority* for the proverb, "If you can't say anything nice, don't say anything at all."[6] Perhaps he had his tongue in cheek. Or it may be that the editors made him do it. Either way, there are readers who no doubt feel that it is entirely appropriate to find authorization for taking the words out of Thumper's mouth. This, despite the fact that a lot of us cried when Bambi's mother died in that fire, that for many of us it's the closest thing we have to a shared cultural memory of childhood,[7] and that we may well share a socialization in which our own mothers were grateful to be able to echo Thumper's words of wisdom. In other words, notwithstanding his role in our collective cultural heritage, Thumper must be authorized. Who authorizes Thumper? Those who own the intellectual property rights in him, of course, and Schlag appropriately cites Walt Disney studios and the date of their copyright in *Bambi* as the relevant authority with which to credit Thumper's proverbial wisdom. It is the political dimension of this relationship between legal ownership and cultural authority that I wish to address, as I try to

4. *Id.* at xvii.

5. V.N. VOLOSHINOV, *supra* note 2, at 23.

6. Schlag, *Normative and Nowhere to Go*, 43 STAN. L. REV. 167, 175 & n.23 (1990).

7. Well, of course there's Santa. Santa has long been with us as a European saint named Nicholas. What few people realize, however, is that until 1931, the old saint was a thin, dark man dressed in drab green or brown. His reincarnation as a plump, twinkling, jolly, white-bearded old chap in a red suit originated in a Coca-Cola advertising campaign (if pressed, I'll provide N. Cornell, *Collecting Christmas*, SKY, Dec. 1990, at 67, 72 as authority for this. I found this magazine in the seat pocket of an airplane). Fortunately for North American children and commercial culture, the Coca-Cola Company did not claim trademark rights in the figure. Had they done so, Santa, like Thumper, might also require authorization in this context.

develop what Schlag, in the same article, both implies and denies—the possibility of a normative postmodern vision.[8]

To make this argument, I must first reiterate philosophical arguments made elsewhere about the inadequacies of the understanding of subjectivity and objectivity as dichotomous that prevails in dominant perspectives on legal reasoning and the relation between law and social life. I will attempt to move beyond critique, however, and consider the relation between law, culture, and (the commodity) form. Moreover, I will put these arguments in their proper historical context and suggest that for a postmodern subject[9] occupying the cultural space of postmodernism[10] in contemporary consumer societies, political action must involve a critical engagement with commodified cultural forms.[11] I make this point by way of an elaboration of the concept of dialogism as it was developed by the late philosopher and literary theorist Mikhail Bakhtin, who argued that dialogic practice was constitutive of our humanity.[12] In the current climate, however, intellectual property laws stifle dialogic practices—preventing us from using the most powerful, prevalent, and accessible cultural forms to express identity, community, and difference.

I want to make it clear at the outset that this Article will speak simultaneously from several dissonant cognitive frameworks[13] and that its polymorphous perversity[14] is intentional, to the extent that my historically-situated and culturally-mediated gender-, age-, and class-specific intent is at all relevant to the rationalist[15] within you. As the following discussion of subjectivity and objectivity will make apparent, I reject the

8. *See* Schlag, *supra* note 6, at 175 n.22.

9. As Pierre Schlag puts it: "Postmodernism questions the integrity, the coherence, and the actual identity of the humanist individual self . . . . For postmodernism, this humanist individual subject is a construction of texts, discourses, and institutions." Schlag, *supra* note 6, at 173.

10. I distinguish postmodernism as a cultural context from postmodernity—the related historical condition of late capitalism. *See* R. Coombe, Publicity Rights and Political Aspirations: Mass Culture, Gender Identity and Democracy (1991) (unpublished manuscript on file at the *Texas Law Review*).

11. I explore the cultural nature of postmodern politics more fully elsewhere. *See* R. Coombe, The Celebrity Image and Cultural Identity: Publicity Rights and the Subaltern Politics of Gender (1991) (unpublished manuscript on file at the *Texas Law Review*).

12. *See infra* notes 138-148, 152-154.

13. I have borrowed the term "dissonant cognitive framework" from Schlag who argues that although the dissonance among incomprehensible cognitive frameworks characterizes legal thought, legal argument, and legal texts, to characterize incommensurability as dissonance itself implies a rational belief in a unified ego. *See* Schlag, *Missing Pieces: A Cognitive Approach to Law*, 67 TEXAS L. REV. 1195, 1228-36 (1989).

14. Schlag says that nearly all legal texts are polymorphously perverse. *Id.* at 1209.

15. Schlag defines the rationalist world view as one that constantly asks for the redemption and justification of all descriptive and normative claims and that privileges the individual rationalist self and its ability to make normative recommendations about the law's ideal structure through ego-centered reason. *See id.* at 1208, 1210-12.

rationalist privileging of the autonomous self and its claims to know an objective social world. Like the modernist, I seek to de-center the subject and its claims to ontological and epistemological primacy,[16] but I reject the modernist insistence that a single underlying structure may be privileged as *the* objective reality underlying the cultural epiphenomena of everyday life and consciousness.[17] I am postmodernist in my refusal to believe that we can find solace in any of the totalizing visions that modernism offers us[18] and in my suggestion that the social world is constituted only in and through representational relations of difference that are constantly shifting in our all-too-human efforts to give meaning to its terms.

As a postmodernist, I believe that form has implications for the issues that we address[19] and that conventional forms of discourse limit and shape the realities we recognize.[20] Like Schlag, I believe that "the typical supposition within the legal community that intellectual endeavor can and must converge in 'points' or 'solutions' or 'ideas'—or 'conclusions'—has a real tendency to kill thought,"[21] but I am not sufficiently rationalist to believe that it is possible to convey an "is" without imparting an "ought." This argument will be made by way of anecdote and appropriative dialogue, using irony, irreverence, and polemic—fashions in form that mirror the modus operandi of the social practices with which I am concerned. I will also cease to cite endless references in incessant footnotes,[22] as if an abundance of small typeface enabled us to "speak in the name of the real."[23] First, however, I will permit Pierre Schlag to give

16. *See id.* at 1214 ("Modernism thus demands a de-centering of ego-centered reason. It demands that individual ego renounce its claims to the status of the *fundamental* epistemological, ontological, or methodological unit." (emphasis in original)).

17. *See id.* at 1213, 1216. For a longer discussion of the modern and the distinction between modern and postmodern forms of explanation, see Coombe, *Encountering the Postmodern: New Directions in Cultural Anthropology*, 28 CANADIAN REV. OF SOC. AND ANTHROPOLOGY 188 (1991).

18. Schlag suggests that modernism at least offers solace with its totalities (*e.g.*, class relations, the unconscious) that postmodernism rejects. *See* Schlag, *supra* note 13, at 1218.

19. *Id.* at 1217-20. Postmodernists breach rules of discourse because they believe that form has implications and conventional forms of discourse may be inadequate to express alternative visions. The postmodernist voice is irreverent and typically bent on irony. *See, e.g.*, Schlag, *supra* note 6, at 167-77 (comparing normative legal thought to the Top 40 radio charts).

20. Normative legal thought is in part a routine—our routine. It is the highly repetitive, cognitively entrenched, institutionally sanctioned, and politically enforced routine of the legal academy—a routine that silently produces our thoughts and keeps our work channelled within the same old cognitive and rhetorical matrices. *See id.* at 179.

21. Schlag, *supra* note 13, at 1243.

22. Well, at least I'll try.

23. I have appropriated this phrase from Paul Stoller, who borrowed it from Ivan Brady, who appropriated it from Michel de Certeau, who discusses reading and writing as textual poaching in THE PRACTICE OF EVERYDAY LIFE. For the original sources of these borrowings, see (in turn) Stoller, *Speaking in the Name of the Real*, 29 CAHIERS D'ÉTUDES AFRICAINES 113 (1989); Brady, *Introduction to Speaking in the Name of the Real: Freeman and Mead in Samoa*, 85 AM. ANTHRO-

Intellectual Property Laws and Democratic Dialogue

me authority to speak:

> [T]he blunting of . . . postmodernism means that it is eighteenth century conceptions—conceptions of responsibility, of agency, of harm, of language and meaning itself—that continue to rule the decisions of a late twentieth century technological society. Such a state of affairs is at once an intellectual embarrassment and a form of violence.[24]

II. Transcending the Subject-Object Dichotomy: The Cultural Construction of Self and World

The idea of an objective world that can be known with certainty by a subject whose capacity for knowledge is independent of that world has been repeatedly undermined in recent legal scholarship.[25] Arguing that

POLOGIST 908 (1983); and M. DE CERTEAU, *History: Ethics, Science and Fiction*, in SOCIAL SCIENCE AS MORAL INQUIRY (N. Haan, R. Bellah, P. Rabinow & W. Sullivan eds. 1983).

24. Schlag, *supra* note 13, at 1248.

25. *See, e.g.*, Brainerd, *The Groundless Assault: A Wittgensteinian Look at Language, Structuralism, and Critical Legal Theory*, 34 AM. U.L. REV. 1231, 1232 (1985) (stating that "[m]uch of critical legal theory has involved attempts to either reject or prove the possibility of an independent subject"); Coombe, *Context, Tradition, and Convention: The Politics of Constructing Legal Cultures*, 13 ASS'N FOR POL. AND LEGAL ANTHROPOLOGY NEWSL., Oct. 1990, at 15 (suggesting that the legal academy's objectification of legal culture results from a false belief in culture and consciousness as "singular, internally consistent system[s] of meanings"); Coombe, *Room for Manoeuver: Toward a Theory of Practice in Critical Legal Studies*, 14 LAW & SOC. INQUIRY 69, 70, 121 (1989) (arguing that critical legal theorists should stop characterizing structure and subjectivity as "two poles of an ineluctable dichotomy" as a critical first step towards freeing CLS from its relative "theoretical inadequacy") [hereinafter *Room for Manoeuver*]; Coombe, *"Same As It Ever Was": Rethinking the Politics of Legal Interpretation*, 34 MCGILL L.J. 603 (1989) (describing the theory of legal hermeneutics, its history, its relation to other social sciences, and its empirical and theoretical limitations) [hereinafter *"Same As It Ever Was"*]; D. Cornell, *Institutionalization of Meaning, Recollective Imagination and the Potential for Transformative Legal Interpretation*, 136 U. PA. L. REV. 1135 (1988) (critiquing the arguments of Dworkin, Hegel, and Pierce, and concluding that although there can be no final culmination of the interpretive process, the conversion principle of dialogue can justify a break with precedent); D. Cornell, *Toward a Modern/Postmodern Reconstruction of Ethics*, 133 U. PA. L. REV. 291, 299 (1985) (arguing that "[t]he insistence on the intersubjective dynamic inherent in the construction of humanity—our shared spirit—permits us to expand the concept of rationality to encompass ethical questions and also to provide a vision of our prospects rooted in our actual life situation") [hereinafter *Reconstruction of Ethics*]; Peller, *The Metaphysics of American Law*, 73 CALIF. L. REV. 1151 (1985) (investigating law as a system of representation and the incorporation of legal realism into mainstream legal discourse); Schlag, *supra* note 13, at 1198 (noting that "it has become a characteristic gesture of contemporary legal scholarship to scorn Cartesian rationalism"); Schlag, *supra* note 6 (criticizing normative legal thought as self-indulgent and obstructive of a real understanding of political and moral situations); Schlag, *Fish v. Zapp: The Case of the Relatively Autonomous Self*, 76 GEO. L.J. 37 (1987) (exploring the rhetorical structure and appeal of Stanley Fish's arguments about interpretive communities) [hereinafter *Fish v. Zapp*]; Winter, Bull Durham *and the Uses of Theory*, 42 STAN. L. REV. 639 (1990) (proposing to reconceptualize the law in light of modern knowledge of the human mind with the goal of describing law in a cognitively meaningful manner) [hereinafter *Bull Durham*]; Winter, *Transcendental Nonsense, Metaphoric Reasoning, and the Cognitive Stakes for Law*, 137 U. PA. L. REV. 1105 (1989) (arguing that philosophical analysts of the law frequently shift from one cognitive framework to another in more or less systematic ways) [hereinafter *Transcendental Nonsense*]. This is by no means an exhaustive list of legal theorists who have addressed these issues.

Texas Law Review Vol. 69:1853, 1991

the objective world is the cultural construction of social subjects and that subjectivity itself is a product of language and cultural practice, this literature draws upon American pragmatism, cognitive theory, cultural anthropology, and continental philosophy to support its claims. I have recently argued that the replacement of positivism and empiricism with interpretive or hermeneutic models of social life in the social sciences has profound implications for legal theory, specifically for the way it conceptualizes the world in which law has meaning, effect, and consequence.[26] Human beings may never speak in the name of the real,[27] or grasp the world objectively, because the realities we recognize are shaped by the cultural contexts that enable our very cognizance of the world itself. As Stanley Fish argues, what we see in the world is not a product of the world, but a product of our cultural categories, which provide the very possibilities for perception.[28] What we experience as social reality is a constellation of cultural structures that we ourselves construct and transform in ongoing practice.[29]

Steven Winter uses the pragmatism of Richard Rorty and, to a lesser extent, cognitive linguistic anthropology to define and critique the objectivist assumptions that characterize traditional legal theory.[30] Objectivism, Winter notes, treats the world as

> filled with determinate, mind-independent objects with inherent characteristics unrelated to human interactions[,] understands categorization either as about natural sets of objects in the world or, when it recognizes categorization as humanly constructed, as about objects with ascertainable properties or criteria that establish their commonality[, and] treats reasoning as about propositions and principles that are capable of "mirroring" those objects and accurately describing their properties and relations.[31]

This set of assumptions is rejected by subjectivists and cultural relativists who argue that legal categories bear no accurate correspondence with a knowable reality[32] and that language, rather than describing an

26. Coombe, *"Same As It Ever Was," supra* note 25, at 605-10.

27. Another way to explain this would be to say that reality cannot authorize us to speak in its name.

28. *See* S. FISH, DOING WHAT COMES NATURALLY: CHANGE, RHETORIC, AND THE PRACTICE OF THEORY IN LITERARY AND LEGAL STUDIES 82-85 (1989); S. FISH, IS THERE A TEXT IN THIS CLASS? THE AUTHORITY OF INTERPRETIVE COMMUNITIES 167-73 (1980).

29. For a longer discussion of this process, see Coombe, *Room for Manoeuver, supra* note 25, at 88-99 (using cultural anthropology to develop and elaborate upon Robert Gordon's observations concerning the pervasiveness of social structures in Gordon, *New Developments in Legal Theory*, in THE POLITICS OF LAW: A PROGRESSIVE CRITIQUE 281, 286-89 (D. Kairys ed. 1982) [hereinafter POLITICS OF LAW]).

30. *See* Winter, *Transcendental Nonsense, supra* note 25, at 1108.

31. *Id.*

32. *Id.* at 1110-11.

Intellectual Property Laws and Democratic Dialogue

objective state of things in the world, is constitutive of the world itself.[33] Winter agrees that there are no objective descriptions of reality separate from our conceptual schemes for apprehending it[34] and that the world is a product of our imaginative processes of interacting as embodied, social creatures.[35] Although I have grave doubts about Winter's belief in the constraints and direction given to meaning by virtue of the experience of human embodiment,[36] I think we share a belief in the constitutive role of culture—socially established structures of meaning or relations among construable symbols or signs—in constructing the realities we recognize and our sense of self, community, and possibility.[37] The imaginative making of meaning is the quintessential human act, and culture is both this practice and its product.[38]

Drucilla Cornell evokes Hegelian philosophy to make a similar critique of objectivity and the conventional understanding of subjectivity with which it is associated.[39] Like myself and Winter, she seeks resources which will enable her to transcend liberalism's dichotomies. She attempts to reject the notion of a transcendental ego existing prior to its engagement in a social and historical context without either abandoning creative human agency or seeing the subject as imprisoned by determining structures.[40] Instead, the self is understood to be constituted through

33. *Id.* at 1119-20. *See generally* Coombe, *"Same As It Ever Was," supra* note 25, at 610-13.

34. Winter, *Transcendental Nonsense, supra* note 25, at 1131; *see also* Winter, *Bull Durham, supra* note 25, at 683 (noting that an antifoundationalist insight teaches that one's view of the world always depends on one's conceptual scheme and is therefore not objective); Winter, *The Cognitive Dimension of the* Agon *Between Legal Power and Narrative Meaning*, 87 MICH. L. REV. 2225, 2228 (1989) (reiterating that meaning is located in the process of interaction between the world and the human) [hereinafter *The Cognitive Dimension*].

35. Winter, *Transcendental Nonsense, supra* note 25, at 1132.

36. *See id.* at 1130-34. Winter seems to believe that because reason is grounded in social and embodied experience it is not arbitrary, that our shared experience of embodiment provides us with a common basis for the cultural structures we differentially elaborate. (In this sense, he is a modernist.) I fear that Winter overstates this effect. Possibly, the legal meanings that afford the greatest controversy are too abstracted from the body to be considered limited by it. Moreover, feminist, poststructuralist, and anthropological theorists suggest that the experience of embodiment is *not* a natural ground on which culture is built or a universal experience that is given cultural specificity through language, but rather a culturally and historically contingent experience. I have described the culturally sentient body elsewhere. *See* R. Coombe & P. Stoller, Consuming Power(s): Knowledge and Embodiment in West African Societies (1991) (unpublished manuscript); *see also* P. Stoller, The Sorcerer and his Body, Paper presented to the Department of Anthropology, University of Illinois-Champaign, Urbana (Apr. 11, 1991) (on file at the *Texas Law Review*).

37. *See* Winter, *The Cognitive Dimension, supra* note 34, at 2245 ("[O]ur very ability to construct a world is already constrained by the cultural structures in which we are enmeshed.").

38. Winter, *Foreword: On Building Houses*, 69 TEXAS L. REV. 1595, 1607 (1991). *See generally* Winter, *The Cognitive Dimension, supra* note 34, at 2230 (asserting that understanding narrative is essential to understanding the cognitive process).

39. *See* D. Cornell, *Reconstruction of Ethics, supra* note 25, at 292-99.

40. *See id.* at 297; *see also* Coombe, *Room for Manoeuver, supra* note 25, at 72-88 (drawing upon feminist and sociological literature to explore the possibilities for reconstructing subjectivity without denying agency).

communicative activity. Individuality and consciousness are embedded in and realized through language and shared cultural symbols.[41]

> [T]o understand ourselves as subjects constituted to be speaking subjects, is to understand ourselves as members of a dialogic community that is not a mere dead weight confronting the individual but rather is both the product and the medium of communicative relations. We transform speech even as we come to ourselves within it.[42]

The de-centering of the subject does not spell its demise, but "renders subjectivity thoroughly communicative."[43] Subjectivity, then, is fundamentally dialogic: "what is most characteristic of our humanity is that we are dialogical or conversational beings in whom language is a reality."[44] For Cornell, the concept of dialogue should serve as a powerful regulative ideal with which to orient our practical and political lives:

> If the quintessence of what we are is to be dialogical—and if this is not just the privilege of the few—then whatever the limitations of this ideal, it nevertheless can and should give practical orientation to our lives.[45]

Legal theory, however, tends to render its reconstitution of subjectivity and objectivity in utopian and optimistic gestures, as if legal tendencies to reify and dichotomize subjectivity and objectivity could be reversed with only a modicum of intellectual good faith and political good will. In the Dionysian social worlds Cornell and Winter describe, dialogue is always already our state of being and consciousness. If judges and decision makers were simply to recognize this state of affairs as the human condition, better laws and better decisions would further realize this immanent potential. Legal theorists generally evade consideration of the social processes at work in everyday life to fix meaning and stifle dialogue. They fail to examine the differential power that social agents have to make their meanings mean something and the material factors that constrain signification and its circulation in the late twentieth-century. Legal theory perhaps defines itself *as* theory by its loathing to address specific processes of hegemonic struggle or the political economies of communication in a late capitalist era.

It *is* important to celebrate the human capacity to engage in imagi-

41. D. Cornell, *Reconstruction of Ethics*, *supra* note 25, at 297-98.

42. *Id.* at 362 (footnote omitted); *see also* Coombe, *Room for Manoeuver*, *supra* note 25, at 88-99 (discussing the simultaneously constitutive and transformative, and constraining and enabling qualities of cultural structures).

43. D. Cornell, *Reconstruction of Ethics*, *supra* note 25, at 364 n.361 (quoting M. Taylor, Erring 142 (1984)).

44. *Id.* at 365 (quoting R. Bernstein, Beyond Objectivism and Relativism 162 (1983)).

45. *Id.*

native meaning making, but it is now necessary to go beyond abstract assertions about the nature of subjectivity and objectivity to examine concrete practices of self and world creation. To do so, it is imperative that we acknowledge the politics of meaning making and the conflictual nature of struggles to fix and transform meanings in a world where access to the means and the mediums of communication is limited. It is necessary to consider, concretely, what the optimal "material and cultural conditions for participation" in dialogue might be.[46] As a modest contribution to an ethics and politics based on the dialogical principle,[47] I will indicate how intellectual property laws may function to deprive us of possibilities for dialogic interaction with the cultural reality or lifeworld known as postmodernism.[48]

III. Making Meaning in Postmodernity

> In postwar America, media images have dominated our visual language and landscape, infiltrating our conscious thoughts and unconscious desires.[49]

> In a century that has seen the intrusion of saturation advertising, glossy magazines, movie spectaculars, and television, our collective sense of reality owes as much to the media as it does to the direct observation of events and natural phenomena.[50]

> A friend tells me about a cross-country plane ride between Los Angeles and Chicago with her eighteen-month-old son, Jimmy. There is a little Korean girl two rows ahead of them. She's about four and speaks no English. She sees Jimmy and before she waves or smiles, she tries to determine what kind of creature she's dealing with. Bobbing up and down in her seat, she cries, "Ninja, Ninja, Ninja Turtles!" and waits, expectantly. My friend restricts her son's television viewing and tries to protect him from the influence of mass culture. Little Jimmy can't respond, and the girl turns away, disappointed (All dialogue guaranteed overheard[51]).

> The women of Smith College experienced a fair degree of internal social turmoil in the fall of 1990 as the college dealt with demands for increased commitment to issues of multiculturalism and greater

46. *Id.* at 368.
47. *See id.*
48. For a definition of postmodernism, see *infra* text accompanying notes 54-57. Readers interested in an extended discussion and bibliography should refer to R. Coombe, *supra* note 10; Coombe, *supra* note 17.
49. M. HEIFERMAN & L. PHILIPS, IMAGE WORLD: ART AND MEDIA CULTURE 13 (1989).
50. *Id.* at 57.
51. This slogan sometimes accompanies STAN MACK'S REAL LIFE FUNNIES, a cartoon that appears in THE VILLAGE VOICE. It may well be copyrighted.

sensitivity to minority experience. In a show of community and solidarity, a number of women made, wore, and sold T-shirts parodying the internationally known Bennetton logo. "United Colors of Smith" were proudly proclaimed.[52]

The white kids had the counter-culture, rock stars and mysticism. The blacks had a slogan which said they were beautiful, and a party demanding power. Middle America had what it always had: Middle America. The hawks had Vietnam, and the doves the Peace Movement. The students had campus politics, and the New Left had Cuba and the Third World. And women had a voice. I had rejection from all of them. I also had Judy Garland.[53]

Social theorists identify the term "postmodern" both with an historical era of capitalist development[54] and with the particular forms of cultural practice that are characteristic to that era.[55] To simplify things, I will refer to the historical period as the condition of postmodernity, to the era's cultural qualities as postmodernism, and to the practices situated in these contexts as postmodern or postmodernist.[56] Postmodernity is distinguished by a dramatic restructuring of capitalism in the postwar period, a reconstruction of labor and capital markets, the displacement of production relations to non-metropolitan regions, the consolidation of mass communications in corporate conglomerates, and the pervasive penetration of electronic media and information technologies. Such processes have coalesced in the Western world societies oriented toward consumption. Consumption is managed by the mass media's capacity to convey imagery and information across vast areas to ensure a production

52. I think this story is in the public domain.

53. R. DYER, HEAVENLY BODIES: FILM STARS IN SOCIETY 141 (1986) (quoting Drag Queen, a character in the Grieg & Griffiths play, *As Time Goes By* (1981)).

54. *See* D. HARVEY, THE CONDITION OF POSTMODERNITY: AN ENQUIRY INTO THE ORIGINS OF CULTURAL CHANGE 107 (1989) (suggesting that postmodernism's insecurity derives from capitalism's destabilizing nature).

55. *See* L. HUTCHEON, THE POLITICS OF POSTMODERNISM 1 (1989) (noting that "postmodernism here is not so much what Jameson sees as a systemic form of capitalism as the name given to cultural practices which acknowledge their inevitable implication in capitalism without relinquishing the power or will to intervene critically in it"); Ross, *Introduction*, in UNIVERSAL ABANDON?: THE POLITICS OF POSTMODERNISM viii (A. Ross ed. 1988) ("[P]ostmodernist culture is a real medium in which we all live to some extent, no matter how unevenly its effects are lived and felt across the jagged spectrum of color, sex, class, religion, and nationality."). For a general discussion of postmodern cultural practices, see S. CONNOR, POSTMODERNIST CULTURE: AN INTRODUCTION TO THEORIES OF THE CONTEMPORARY (1989).

Frederic Jameson notes the difficulty in trying "to systematize a usage or to impose any conventional coherent thumbnail meaning [on the term postmodernism], for the concept is not merely contested, it is also internally conflicted and contradictory. . . . [F]or good or ill, we cannot *not* use it." F. JAMESON, POSTMODERNISM, OR THE CULTURAL LOGIC OF LATE CAPITALISM xxii (1991). Jameson uses the term in both senses in dealing with "both levels in question, infrastructure and superstructures—the economic system and the cultural 'structure of feeling.'" *Id.* at xx.

56. For further elaboration of the distinction, see Featherstone, *In Pursuit of the Postmodern: An Introduction*, in 5 THEORY, CULTURE AND SOCIETY 195 (1988).

of demand. Goods are increasingly sold by harnessing symbols, and the proliferation of mass media imagery means that we increasingly occupy a "cultural" world of signs and signifiers that have no traditional meanings within social communities or organic traditions.[57]

A proliferation of signification without social meaning,[58] these signs seem to come at us as from nowhere—across radio waves, fibers, unseen cables, and invisible microwaves and lasers. They spring up in our living rooms, flow from our telephones, bombard our paths, and fill our horizons wherever we walk. These images do, however, come from somewhere, and increasingly they come from fewer and fewer places. As the power of media widens, the power base is consolidating as corporations consolidate holdings in print and electronic media:

> In 1981 twenty corporations controlled most of the business of the country's 11,000 magazines, but only five years later that number had shrunk to six corporations.
>
> Today, despite 25,000 media outlets in the United States, twenty-nine corporations control most of the business in daily newspapers, magazines, television, books, and motion pictures.
>
> . . . [B]y the year 2000 all United States media may be in the hands of six conglomerates.[59]

Postmodernists suggest that we address the "textual *thickness* and the visual *density* of everyday life"[60] in societies saturated with commodified forms of cultural representation. Such images so pervasively permeate all dimensions of our quotidian lives that they are constitutive of the "cultures" in which most people in Western societies now live. Any consideration of contemporary life must take into account both the production and the consumption of media-disseminated cultural forms.

Elsewhere, I have argued that the consumption of commodified representational forms is productive activity in which people engage in meaning-making to adapt signs, texts, and images to their own agendas.[61]

57. Every day, according to the Association of American Advertising Agencies, the average person is exposed to 1,600 advertisements. M. Heiferman & L. Philips, *supra* note 49, at 18.

58. See D. Kellner, Jean Baudrillard: From Marxism to Postmodernism and Beyond (1989) for an extended discussion of Baudrillard's musings on this topic.

59. B. Bagdikian, The Media Monopoly 4 (2d ed. 1987). *See generally* H. Schiller, Culture, Inc.: The Corporate Takeover of Public Expression (1989).

60. McRobbie, *Postmodernism and Popular Culture*, in Postmodernism: ICA Documents 165 (L. Appignanesi ed. 1989) (emphasis in original).

61. *See* R. Coombe, *supra* note 10; Coombe, *Postmodernity and the Rumor: Recoding the Commodity/Sign in Late Capitalism*, in Culture, Power, Place: Explorations in Critical Anthropology (R. Rouse, J. Ferguson, & A. Gupta eds. forthcoming 1992). An abbreviated version of the latter appears as *Postmodernity and the Rumor: Late Capitalism and the Fetishism of the Commodity/Sign*, in Jean Baudrillard: The Disappearance of Art and Politics (W. Chaloupka & W. Stearns eds. 1991).

These practices of appropriation or "recoding"[62] cultural forms are the essence of popular culture[63] and are understood by theorists of postmodernism to be central to the political practices of those in subordinate social groups and those marginal to the centers of cultural production.[64] It is now evident that mass media imagery and commodified cultural texts provide the most important cultural resources for the articulation of identity and community in Western societies, as traditional ethnic, class, and cultural indicia fade, and minority groups must organize along alternative lines.[65]

If, as human selves in human communities, we are constituted by and constitute ourselves with shared cultural symbols, then it is important that legal theorists consider the nature of the cultural symbols "we" "share" in consumer societies and the recognition the law affords them.

IV. Fixing the Signifier/Owning the Sign

> [Within the science fiction fan community,] . . . there are distinct groups of fans that organize around the production, circulation, and consumption of fan magazines (fanzines). . . . [A]lmost exclusively female and predominantly heterosexual, [this movement] involves middle class women who . . . employ images, themes, and characters from a canonized set of mass culture texts [generally television series episodes] to . . . create new female communities [and] alternative gender identities . . . . In 'Slash' fiction, women write erotic stories and draw illustrations depicting a love relationship between [the male characters] . . . . [F]anzine writers ha[ve] depicted Luke Skywalker and Han Solo in an erotic relationship . . . . [F]andom has had an uneasy relationship with Lucasfilm . . . .[66]

62. *See generally* H. FOSTER, RECODINGS: ART, SPECTACLE, CULTURAL POLITICS (1985); H. FOSTER, THE ANTI-AESTHETIC: ESSAYS ON POSTMODERN CULTURE (1983).

63. *See generally* D. HEBDIGE, CUT'N'MIX: CULTURE, IDENTITY, AND CARIBBEAN MUSIC (1987); L. HUTCHEON, *supra* note 55, at 28; P. WILLIS, COMMON CULTURE (1990); McRobbie, *supra* note 60.

64. *See* D. HEBDIGE, *supra* note 63, at 8 ("Naming can be in and of itself an act of invocation, conferring power and/or grace . . . . [T]he names carry power in themselves."); L. HUTCHEON, *supra* note 55, at 8 ("[T]he postmodern appears to coincide with a general cultural awareness of the existence and power of systems of representation which do not reflect society so much as grant meaning and value within a particular society."); McRobbie, *supra* note 60, at 8-9 (discussing Shiite terrorists' use of Western media as a political platform and observing that "the media continues, relentlessly, to hijack events and offer in their place a series of theatrical spectacles whose points or relevance are only tangentially on what is going on, and whose formal cues came from other, frequently televisual, forms of representation").

65. Many inner city gangs mark their identities, communities, and turf with the logos of particular brands of athletic shoes. *See* Wilkerson, *Challenging Nike, Rights Group Takes a Risky Stand*, N.Y. Times, Aug. 25, 1990, § 1, at 10, col. 4.

66. R. Coombe, *supra* note 10, at 62-69 (citations and footnotes omitted).

Intellectual Property Laws and Democratic Dialogue

> Walking down the street in Toronto one day, pedestrians were surprised to see the following message flashing on an electronic billboard at the corner of Yonge and Wellesley: "Lesbians Fly Air Canada," it repeatedly flashed. The next day the message was gone. A gay rights group had broadcast the statement to remind people of the similarities between lesbians and all other Canadians by evoking the archetypal "normal" Canadian experience. The communication stopped when Air Canada threatened to apply for an injunction to stop the group from using its name.[67]

> From Harlem to Watts and nearly every urban enclave of black youths in between, black variations of the popular cartoon gradeschooler, Bart Simpson, have been the most enduring T-shirt images of the summer. . . . "There is a suppressed rage in the cartoon that black people are picking up on," [said Russell Adams, chairman of the Afro-American Studies Department at Howard University]. . . . Ultimately, the reasons for the popularity of the black Bart character may be as elusive as determining where the great masses of T-shirts come from . . . . [N]one of the Black Bart T-shirts are licensed by [20th Century] Fox. . . .[68]

> Only a few months ago, the T-shirt of choice in certain neighbourhoods was an image of Malcolm X next to the words, "It's a Black thing. You wouldn't understand." Now a chocolate-coloured Simpson has taken Malcolm's place, declaring, "I'm Black Bart. You wouldn't understand."[69]

> The only street phenomenon similar to this, in recent memory, was the bootleg, Afro-Americanized Mickey and Minnie Mouse T-Shirts of a few years ago. . . . But that was peanuts compared with the unmitigated appropriation of Bart Simpson. . . . "You have to have mixed feelings when you're getting ripped off," [artist Matt] Groening says. "I don't like these smokestack factories belching out bootleg Simpsons T-Shirts. It's a huge business. 20th Century Fox takes this matter extremely seriously. There have been busts all over the country."[70]

> A twelve year old boy was sued for producing Black Bart T-Shirts.[71]

If both objective social worlds and subjective desires, identities, and understandings are constructed with cultural resources, then legal atti-

67. Conversation with Professor Mariana Valverde, Professor of Sociology at York University, Toronto (May, 1989).

68. Marriott, *I'm Bart, I'm Black And What About It?*, N.Y. Times, Sept. 19, 1990, at C8, col. 5.

69. Klawans, *American Notes*, Times Lit. Supp., July 20, 1990, at 774, col. 1.

70. Mills, *Bootleg Black Bart Simpson, the Hip-Hop T-Shirt Star*, Wash. Post, June 28, 1990, at D13, col. 1.

71. This is only a rumor, but I think it is a telling one.

Texas Law Review Vol. 69:1853, 1991

tudes toward cultural forms may have profound implications. Laws creating and enforcing intellectual property rights permit, maintain, and perpetuate the commodification of cultural texts and images by securing their market value. For example, trademark laws create proprietary rights in the signs manufacturers use to market their goods[72] and publicity rights enable celebrities (and often their estates) to control the reproduction and circulation of the star's name, image, and other publicly recognizable features.[73] Copyright laws restrict the social flow of texts, photographs, music, and most other symbolic works. All of these forms retain their cultural qualities, however, and in a world where mass media tends to monopolize the dissemination of signifying forms, the cultural resources available to us (and within us) are increasingly the properties of others.

The political implications of cultural commodification (and the legal regimes supporting it) are largely unexplored. When the ramifications for the political ideal of democratic dialogic practice are addressed, it is generally in terms of the *material* limitations of access to dialogue caused by concentrations of capital and mass media monopolies.[74] What I'm suggesting here is that intellectual property laws may deprive us of the optimal *cultural* conditions for dialogic practice. By objectifying and reifying cultural forms—freezing the connotations of signs and symbols and fencing off fields of cultural meaning with "no trespassing" signs—intellectual property laws may enable certain forms of political practice and constrain others.

Arguably, fewer and fewer defenses are available in intellectual property infringement actions;[75] free speech defenses are inconsistently

72. E. VANDENBURGH, TRADEMARK LAW AND PROCEDURE 3 (1968).

73. *See* Felcher & Rubin, *The Descendability of the Right of Publicity: Is There Commercial Life After Death?*, 89 YALE L.J. 1125 (1980).

74. *See generally* L. TRIBE, CONSTITUTIONAL CHOICES 192-98 (1985); Fiss, *Why The State?*, 100 HARV. L. REV. 781, 787-90 (1987); Fiss, *Free Speech and Social Structure*, 71 IOWA L. REV. 1405, 1408-13 (1986); Kairys, *Freedom of Speech*, in POLITICS OF LAW, *supra* note 29, at 166; Moon, *Lifestyle Advertising and Classical Freedom of Speech Doctrine*, 36 MCGILL L.J. 76, 101 (1990); Moon, *The Scope of Freedom of Expression*, 23 OSGOODE HALL L.J. 331, 335-40 (1985).

75. A growing body of legal literature points to this decline in available defenses, along with (1) the massive expansion of the cultural forms now considered.to be private property, and (2) the use of intellectual property laws to impede the flow of imagery and information in the service of interested agendas. In a recent article, David Lange notes that copyright lends itself (recurringly) to efforts aimed at the direct suppression of speech; it validates some speech at the expense of other speech, frequently imperils the creative process, and often conflicts with our commitments to freedom of expression. *See* D. Lange, At Play in the Fields of the Word: Copyright and the Construction of Authorship in the Post-Literate Millennium, Paper presented at the Society for Critical Exchange Conference, Intellectual Property and the Construction of Authorship, Case Western Reserve University (Apr. 19-21, 1991) (on file at the *Texas Law Review*).

This is especially true in Canada, where copyright has become a virtually absolute property right increasingly used as a means of private censorship. *See* Vaver, *Intellectual Property Today: Of*

interpreted and often dismissed without due consideration.[76] More troubling, however, is the likelihood that freedom of expression arguments will not even be asserted. In most cases, the dispute will never be

Myths and Paradoxes, 69 CAN. B. REV. 98, 110-11 (1990). The prevailing attitude toward the scope of copyright protection was summed up in a report issued by Canada's Sub-Committee on the Revision of Copyright, which included the remarkable statement that "ownership is ownership is ownership. The copyright owner owns the intellectual work in the same sense as a landowner owns land." REPORT OF THE SUB-COMMITTEE ON THE REVISION OF COPYRIGHT, STANDING COMMITTEE ON COMMUNICATIONS AND CULTURE, A CHARTER OF RIGHTS FOR CREATORS 9 (1985).

The increasing judicial restriction of the type of activities that might be considered fair use of copyright material in the United States indicates that the scope of copyright protection is expanding throughout North America. *See* L. PATTERSON & S. LINDBERG, THE NATURE OF COPYRIGHT: A LAW OF USER'S RIGHTS (1991). Diane Conley has demonstrated that there is an increasing judicial presumption against fair use, a conclusory and dismissive attitude toward first amendment claims, a tendency to use copyright to protect the personal interests of the author (in a fashion that bears no relation to the incentive structure the copyright is constitutionally designed to provide), and a general discounting of the public interest. *See* D. Conley, Author, User, Scholar, Thief: Fair Use and Unpublished Works, Paper presented at the Society for Critical Exchange Conference on Intellectual Property and the Construction of Authorship, Case Western Reserve University (Apr. 19-21, 1991) (on file at the *Texas Law Review*). For other critical discussions of the judicial tendency to limit and confine the application of fair use, see Leval, *Toward a Fair Use Standard*, 103 HARV. L. REV. 1105 (1990); Abrams, *First Amendment and Copyright: The Seventeenth Donald C. Brace Memorial Lecture*, 35 J. COPYRIGHT SOC'Y 1, 4-12 (1987); Leval, *Fair Use or Foul? The Nineteenth Donald C. Brace Memorial Lecture*, 36 J. COPYRIGHT SOC'Y 167-81 (1989); and, for an economic perspective, see Fisher, *Reconstructing the Fair Use Doctrine*, 101 HARV. L. REV. 1659, 1698-1744 (1988). The unwillingness of the judiciary to consider the creative, productive, and culturally transformative nature in which copyrighted works may be used (and to insist upon a bright line distinction between "authors" and "users" that privileges and over-estimates the creativity of the former) is also discussed in Jaszi, *Theorizing Copyright Doctrine: Some Uses of "Authorship,"* 1991 DUKE L.J. (forthcoming), and Litman, *The Public Domain*, 39 EMORY L.J. 965 (1990). The increasing expansion of private copyright interests, the diminished arena of cultural forms that constitute the public domain, and the concomitant threat to the public interest in progress in the arts and sciences is explored in Yen, *Restoring the Natural Law: Copyright as Labor and Possession*, 51 OHIO ST. L. J. 517 (1990).

Jessica Litman argues that copyright law is inhospitable to actual processes of authorship precisely because it maintains untenable distinctions between (romantic) authors and (suspect) users and misunderstands the nature of creative authorship:

> All authorship is fertilized by the work of prior authors, and the echoes of old work in new work extend beyond ideas and concepts to a wealth of expressive details. Indeed, authorship *is* the transformation and recombination of expression into new molds, the recasting and revision of details into different shapes. What others have expressed, and the ways they have expressed it, are the essential building blocks of any creative medium.

J. Litman, Copyright as Myth, Paper presented at the Society for Critical Exchange Conference, Intellectual Property and the Construction of Authorship, Case Western Reserve University (Apr. 19-21, 1991) (on file at the *Texas Law Review*).

David Lange argues that both publicity rights and trademark protections are also expanding to the detriment of those engaged in creative authorship and at a significant cost to the public in *Recognizing the Public Domain*, in 44(4) LAW AND CONTEMPORARY PROBLEMS 147 (1981). A longer argument about the cultural losses occasioned by the expansion of publicity rights may be found in R. Coombe, *supra* note 10.

76. *See, e.g.*, Walt Disney Productions v. Air Pirates, 581 F.2d 751, 758 (9th Cir. 1978) (noting that the First Amendment claim of the defendants "can be dismissed without a lengthy discussion"), *cert. denied*, 439 U.S. 1132 (1979); McGraw-Hill, Inc. v. Worth Publishers, Inc., 335 F. Supp. 415, 422 (S.D.N.Y. 1971) (finding that the proffered First Amendment claims "fly in the face of established law"); *see also* Note, *Copyright, Free Speech and the Visual Arts*, 93 YALE L.J. 1565 (1989). But, for a more optimistic reading of judicial tendencies, see Note, *Trademark Parodies and Free Speech: An Expansion of Parodists' First Amendment Rights in* L.L. Bean, Inc. v. Drake Publishers, Inc., 73 IOWA L. REV. 961 (1988).

Texas Law Review Vol. 69:1853, 1991

tried on its merits. Faced with the threat of legal action, most local parodists, political activists, and satirical bootleggers will cease their activities.[77] They are also likely to be visited with ex parte injunctions and possibly even temporary restraining orders, in which their goods and records are seized without notice.[78] In any case, they are unlikely to have the resources and wherewithal to engage in protracted constitutional litigation.[79]

Examples of cases which *are* litigated are not difficult to find, as the subject is an amusing one for both intellectual property and constitutional scholars. The type of practice I am concerned with is most readily apparent in trademark law, but examples may also be found in the publicity rights and copyright fields. Regardless, in an era when characters, phrases, logos, and even names and faces from movies, novels, and television are the subject of merchandising rights and tie-in contracts, the distinction becomes rather negligible. Humphrey Bogart's estate, for example, might hold publicity rights and use "Sam Spade" to market hats, while his film producers license "Casablanca" to bar and hotel chains while collecting royalties for commercial usages of copyrighted dialogue.[80] In any case, these figures and moments from our cultural history become private properties that we parody, proliferate, or politicize at our peril.

Let me give a few examples drawn from the trademark field. In 1977 an environmental rights group distributed materials critical of the practices of the electric utility industry.[81] These materials contained a caricature of the Reddy Kilowatt trademark, a stylized cartoon stick man.[82] Confronted with the possibility of an injunction, the Environmental Action Foundation argued that it was exercising its right of free

77. *See* Dorsen, *Satiric Appropriation and the Law of Libel, Trademark and Copyright: Remedies Without Wrongs*, 65 B.U.L. REV. 1923, 1924-28 (1986) (noting that the risk of litigation can stifle creativity); Note, *The Parody Defense to Copyright Infringement: Productive Use After Betamax*, 97 HARV. L. REV. 1395, 1412 (1984) (finding that copyright law restricts parody).

78. Matt Groening's allusion to Twentieth Century Fox's "busts," *supra* note 70, no doubt refers to officials carrying out the authority given them under an Anton Piller order. Such operations are often ominously Kafkaesque as armies of officials across wide regions simultaneously surround and enter premises, seizing merchandise and business records as evidence for a forthcoming trial—a trial that is unlikely to take place once the alleged infringer has lost his inventory.

79. *Cf.* Note, *Copyright, Free Speech and the Visual Arts*, *supra* note 76, at 1568 & n.18 (noting that when threatened with litigation over his use of an appropriated photograph, Andy Warhol easily squashed the suit with a settlement consisting of artwork).

80. *See* Lugosi v. Universal Pictures, 603 P.2d 425, 160 Cal. Rptr. 323 (1979). Bela Lugosi's heirs sued a movie company for using Lugosi's likeness in promoting new Dracula movies. Although the company owned the copyright to the film, the court found that during his lifetime Lugosi could have created a "right of value" in his name or likeness. *Id.* at 428.

81. Reddy Communications, Inc. v. Environmental Action Found., Inc., 199 U.S.P.Q (BNA) 630, 631-32 (D.D.C. 1977).

82. *Id.* at 632.

Intellectual Property Laws and Democratic Dialogue

expression.[83] The defense was rejected by analogy to cases affirming the right of private property owners to exclude picketers.[84] In other words, you can't use someone else's property to express yourself. I will momentarily leave aside the question of whether trademark rights give you "ownership" of a sign or symbol in any and all contexts ("authorities" say they don't,[85] but then it is judges who authorize their use). This question certainly didn't concern the Manitoba Court of Appeals when it allowed the Safeway grocery chain to enjoin picketing workers from using the stylized "S" from the company's name in its strike literature.[86] Deciding that the insignia was known to the public, the court determined it was an asset connected with the company's goodwill and that the company therefore had proprietary rights in it. The court stated: "[T]here is no right under the guise of free speech to take or use what does not belong to [you]."[87] It was, of course, precisely because the insignia was publicly associated with the company that the union wished to use it; the union sought to inform the public that the sign was associated with unfair labor practices, as well as the more cheerful associations the store management projected. They were attempting to invest the symbol with another, alternative set of meanings.

The ability to fix the signifier, because you "own" the sign, has expanded dramatically with the increasing adoption and judicial enforcement of state antidilution statutes.[88] Traditional trademark theory

83. *Id.* A preliminary injunction was denied, *id.* at 636, and a permanent injunction was also denied. 477 F. Supp. 936, 948 (D.D.C. 1979).

84. *Reddy Communications, Inc.*, 199 U.S.P.Q. (BNA) at 633-34 & n.11. The Court concluded that the plaintiff's "property" had not "assume[d] . . . the functional attributes of public property devoted to public use," *id.* at 633 (quoting Century Hardware Co. v. NLRB, 407 U.S. 539, 547 (1972)), thus the enforcement of plaintiff's private rights was not considered state action. *See id.* at 633-34. In other words, because the private action was not inherently governmental, it was not subject to constitutional limitation. For a critique of this reasoning, see Denicola, *Trademarks as Speech: Constitutional Implications of the Emerging Rationales for the Protection of Trade Symbols*, 1982 WIS. L. REV. 158, 190-91 & n.146.

85. *See* 2 J. MCCARTHY, TRADEMARKS AND UNFAIR COMPETITION § 24:1, at 160-63 (1984 & 1990 Supp.) (noting that trademark law limits use of the mark only where consumer confusion is likely).

86. Canada Safeway Ltd. v. Manitoba Food and Chemical Workers, Local 832, 73 C.P.R. (2d) 234 (1983).

87. *Id.* at 237.

88. State antidilution statutes are a relatively recent phenomenon. Massachusetts adopted the first antidilution statute in 1947. Shire, *Dilution Versus Deception—Are State Antidilution Laws an Appropriate Alternative to the Law of Infringement?*, 77 TRADEMARK REP. 273, 278 (1987). Today, at least 24 states have antidilution statutes. See *infra* note 94 for a list of state antidilution statutes. See Note, *Trademark Parody: A Fair Use and First Amendment Analysis*, 72 VA. L. REV. 1079, 1088-92 (1986), and 2 J. MCCARTHY, *supra* note 85, § 24:13 (D), at 159-60, for examinations of increasing judicial acceptance of dilution statutes.

Canada does not, as yet, have any judicially developed dilution doctrine and given judicial interpretations of the its Trademarks Act, CAN. REV. STAT. ch. T-10, § 22(1) (1985), is unlikely to develop antidilution protections unless there are statutory amendments. However, the tendency of

protected rights in the sign only insofar as it was necessary to protect consumers from deception and confusion.[89] Increasingly, however, holders of trademark rights are enabled to prevent "misappropriation" even when there is no competition between the goods and the trademark use is unlikely to cause public confusion. The "dilution rationale" was first suggested by Frank Schechter in 1927 as additional justification for the protection of a mark used in association with noncompeting goods:

> The real injury in all such cases . . . is the gradual whittling away or dispersion of the identity and hold upon the public mind of the mark or name by its use upon non-competing goods. The more distinctive or unique the mark, the deeper is its impress upon the public consciousness, and the greater its need for protection against vitiation or disassociation from the particular product in connection with which it has been used.[90]

Justice Frankfurter put it this way:

> The protection of trade-marks is the law's recognition of the psychological function of symbols. If it is true that we live by symbols, it is no less true that we purchase goods by them. . . . The owner of a mark exploits this human propensity by making every effort to impregnate the atmosphere of the market with the drawing power of a congenial symbol. Whatever the means employed, the aim is the same—to convey through the mark, in the minds of potential customers, the desirability of the commodity upon which it appears. . . . If another poaches upon the commercial magnetism

those with distinctive trademarks to register them as copyrights augers in the same direction. Unlike the United States, Canada has no fair use defense for copyright infringement and only an anachronistic fair dealing defense to permit limited copying for the purposes of news reporting and scholarly review. *See* Copyright Act, CAN. REV. STAT. ch. C-30, § 27(2)(a) (1985).

89. *See, e.g.*, Waterman Co. v. Gordon, 72 F.2d 272, 273 (2d Cir. 1934) (enjoining defendant from selling razor blades under the name "Waterman," because the blades "might naturally be supposed to come from" plaintiff, who owned the trademark "Waterman's" registered for use on fountain pens and other writing instruments); Yale Electric Corp. v. Robertson, 26 F.2d 972, 974 (2d Cir. 1928) (affirming dismissal of plaintiff's suit to compel registration of its trademark, the word "Yale" inside an ellipse and octagon, on the ground that consumers were likely to confuse it with products made by Yale & Towne Manufacturing Company and marked "Yale"); Aunt Jemima Mills Co. v. Rigney & Co., 247 F. 407, 410, 412 (2d Cir. 1917) (enjoining defendant from marketing syrup under the name "Aunt Jemima," because consumers would believe it to be manufactured by plaintiff, who sold flour under the same name). As Denicola described the traditional approach:

> At a rhetorical level there is a certain convenience in speaking of a trademark "owner"; as the symbol of the goodwill enjoyed by an enterprise, the mark is indeed a valuable commercial asset capable of exploitation and assignment. Yet as a description of the legal consequences attaching to the adoption of a particular symbol as an indication of origin, the property conception is largely inadequate. Traditional trademark doctrine does not establish the general right to exclude others implied by the property designation. Protection is normally limited to instances in which there is a threatened appropriation or injury to goodwill arising through customer confusion. The danger in utilizing a property conception of trademark [is that it has a tendency to preclude] rational consideration of competing social, economic, and occasionally, constitutional interests.

Denicola, *supra* note 84, at 165 (footnotes omitted).

90. Schechter, *The Rational Basis of Trademark Protection*, 40 HARV. L. REV. 813, 825 (1927).

of the symbol he has created, the owner can obtain legal redress.[91]

According to Schechter, the chief value of the trademark lies in its capacity to convey positive meanings.[92] The use of a similar mark vitiates the original's unique or distinctive ability to convey meaning, thus diluting its strength in the consumer imagination.[93] Although the doctrine was not incorporated into federal trademark legislation, many states have enacted "anti-dilution" statutes[94] that provide that "likelihood of injury to business reputation or of dilution of the distinctive quality of a mark . . . shall be a ground for injunctive relief notwithstanding the absence of competition between the parties or the absence of confusion as to the source of goods or services."[95]

Although these statutes initially encountered judicial recalcitrance,[96] courts increasingly accepted the dilution doctrine in the 1970s and 1980s.[97] The dimensions of dilution now extend to include protection against the "blurring"[98] of a positive image caused by "dissonant"[99] usage, against "erosion"[100] of the "magic"[101] of the status of the mark,

91. Mishawaka Rubber & Woolen Mfg. Co. v. S.S. Kresge Co., 316 U.S. 203, 205 (1942).

92. *See* Schechter, *supra* note 90, at 818 ("The true functions of the trademark are, then, to identify the product as satisfactory and thereby to stimulate further purchases by the consuming public.").

93. *See id.* at 830 (arguing that a trademark symbol "would soon lose its arresting uniqueness and hence its selling power if it could be used on pianos, shaving cream, and fountain pens").

94. *See* ALA. CODE § 8-12-17 (Supp. 1984); ARK. STAT. ANN. § 4-71-113 (1987); CAL. BUS. & PROF. CODE § 14330 (West Supp. 1989); CONN. GEN. STAT. ANN. § 35-11i(c) (West 1987); DEL. CODE ANN. tit. 6, § 3313 (Supp. 1990); FLA. STAT. ANN. § 495.151 (West 1988); GA. CODE ANN. § 10-1-451(b) (1989); IDAHO CODE § 48-512 (1977); ILL. ANN. STAT. ch. 140, para. 22 (Smith-Hurd 1986); IOWA CODE ANN. § 548.11(2) (West 1987); LA. REV. STAT. ANN. § 55:223.1 (West 1987); MASS. GEN. LAWS ANN. ch. 110B, § 12 (West 1990); ME. REV. STAT. ANN. tit. 10, § 1530 (1980); MO. REV. STAT. § 417.061 (1986); MONT. CODE ANN. § 30-13-334 (1989); NEB. REV. STAT. § 87-112 (1987); N.H. REV. STAT. ANN. § 350-A:12 (1984); N.M. STAT. ANN. § 57-3-10 (1987); N.Y. GEN. BUS. LAW § 368-d (McKinney 1984); OR. REV. STAT § 647.107 (1989); 54 PA. CONS. STAT. ANN. § 1124 (Purdon Supp. 1990); R.I. GEN. LAWS § 6-2-12 (1985); TENN. CODE ANN. § 47-25-512 (1988); TEX. BUS. & COM. CODE ANN. § 16.29 (Vernon Supp. 1991).

95. MODEL STATE TRADEMARK BILL § 12 (1964), *reprinted in* 2 J. MCCARTHY, *supra* note 85, § 22.4, at 26-27.

96. *See* 2 J. MCCARTHY, *supra* note 85, § 24.13(B), at 156-59; Pattishall, *The Dilution Rationale for Trademark—Trade Identity Protection, Its Progress and Prospects*, 71 NW. U.L. REV. 618, 621-24 (1976).

97. *See* Note, *supra* note 88, at 1088-92; 2 J. MCCARTHY, *supra* note 85, § 24:13 (D), at 159-60.

98. *See, e.g.*, Mead Data Central, Inc. v. Toyota Motor Sales, U.S.A., Inc., 875 F.2d 1026, 1030 (2d Cir. 1989) (defining "dilution as either the blurring of a mark's product identification or the tarnishment of the affirmative associations a mark has come to convey").

99. *See, e.g.*, Exxon Corp. v. Exxene Corp., 696 F.2d 544, 550 (7th Cir. 1983) (explaining that similar names may cause dissonance in the minds of consumers: "It is the same kind of dissonance that would be produced by selling cat food under the name 'Romanoff,' or baby carriages under the name 'Aston Martin.' ").

100. *See, e.g.*, Jordache Enterprises, Inc. v. Hogg Wyld, Ltd., 625 F. Supp. 48, 52 (D.N.M. 1985) (stating that there is a risk of "erosion of the public's identification" of a trademark, diminishing its distinctiveness, uniqueness, effectiveness, and prestige (quoting Tiffany & Co. v. Boston Club, Inc., 231 F. Supp. 836, 844 (D. Mass. 1964))).

101. *See, e.g.*, Augusta National, Inc. v. Northwestern Mutual Life Ins. Co., 193 U.S.P.Q.

against "tarnishing"[102] the luster of a trade name, to prevent use of the mark in an "unwholesome or unsavory"[103] context, and to prevent the creation of an "unsavory mental association"[104] with the original mark.[105]

"Many of our culture's best known and most powerful symbols are trademarks."[106] Moreover, the "owners" of trademarks are the most powerful and wealthy members of North American society. Their production operations and management activities may be increasingly invisible to us, but their signifiers permeate our senses and surround us with sights, sounds, and smells.[107] Why should the most prominent indicia or symbols of corporate power be enabled to impart an exclusively favorable impression? Why should these symbolic forms be enabled to maintain a pristine innocence, abstracted from the history and the practices of the corporate bodies that produce them? Commodity fetishism, anyone?

The Coca-Cola Company, which polices its marks assiduously, is often (one could almost say routinely) successful in preventing unauthorized uses of its globally recognized bottles and logos. In 1972 it sued to enjoin entrepreneurs from marketing "ENJOY COCAINE" posters using the famous script employed by the multinational in its "ENJOY COCA-COLA" advertisements.[108] The court found that impermissible damage to Coca-Cola's reputation would be caused by this unwholesome association with an illegal drug.[109] The injunction was granted;[110] the judge commented that people seeing the posters might "refuse to deal with a company which would seek commercial advantage by treating a dangerous drug in such jocular fashion."[111] The court conveniently overlooked the company's historically established, more-than-symbolic

(BNA) 210, 214 (S.D. Ga. 1976) ("[T]here is reasonable certainty that the value of [Augusta National's Masters] mark will be eroded; a little now, more later, until the 'magic' of the Masters will be mortally dissipated if not completely dispelled.").

102. *See, e.g.*, *Mead Data Central*, 875 F.2d at 1031 (stating that dilution has been defined as "the tarnishment of the affirmative associations a mark has come to convey").

103. *See, e.g.*, Mutual of Omaha Ins. Co. v. Novak, 648 F. Supp. 905, 912, 231 U.S.P.Q. (BNA) 963, 967 (D. Neb. 1986) ("Trademark disparagement can be found where the defendant has used the same or a confusingly similar mark in a way that creates an undesirable, unwholesome or unsavory mental association with the plaintiff's mark.").

104. *Id.*

105. *See* 2 J. McCarthy, *supra* note 85, § 24:13, at 155-61.

106. Note, *supra* note 88, at 1079 (footnote omitted). I couldn't have said it better myself.

107. The United States Patent and Trademark Office determined on Sept. 19, 1990 that a distinctive smell could be registered as a trademark, thereby opening up a whole new realm of the senses to commodification. In re Clarke, 17 U.S.P.Q.2d (BNA) 1238, 1239-40 (1990) (holding fragrance added to applicant's yarn functions as a trademark for the yarn).

108. Coca-Cola Co. v. Gemini Rising, Inc., 346 F. Supp. 1183, 1193 (E.D.N.Y. 1972).

109. *Id.* at 1191.

110. *Id.* at 1193.

111. *Id.* at 1191.

associations with the drug at issue.[112]

Similarly, General Electric was granted an injunction against the use of GENITAL ELECTRIC on T-shirts and briefs, in a decision which manipulated the confusion rationale to deal with the threat of tarnishment to the company's image.[113] But what if one were to superimpose the company's advertising slogan, "GE, we bring good things to life," over a drawing of the missiles they produce or on a photograph of carnage in Iraq (presuming that it were established that GE played some role in manufacturing the thousands of bombs that inadvertently killed thousands of Iraqi civilians)? Would we be permitted to counter their media message with other mediations? Could we answer their assertion, even if we did have access to the same media channels and the same level of resources? Concepts as vague as tarnishment and loss of distinctiveness have the capacity to escalate into a general power to prohibit all reproductions of a mark and "grow into a powerful vehicle for the suppression of unwelcome speech."[114]

The legal doctrine of dilution provides a potent means for corporate actors to manage their public personas. Perhaps the full implications of these laws have yet to be realized.[115] In jurisdictions that enforce dilution laws, it might not be safe to comment upon the sexual objectification of women in a mattress company's ads by way of a feminist film suggesting a rape on a mattress identified with its trademark. Nor could you be sure of your freedom to comment upon multinational capital if you depicted a Nestle billboard in the midst of Third World squalor and malnutrition. By controlling the sign, trademark holders are able to control its connotations and potentially curtail many forms of social commentary. The stronger or more famous the mark, the greater the legal protection that is afforded it against noncompeting and nonconfusing

112. *See* E. KAHN, THE BIG DRINK: AN UNOFFICIAL HISTORY OF COCA-COLA 54-55, 101-03 (1960) (describing the invention of Coca-Cola as a therapeutic syrup containing cola nuts, caffeine, and a derivative of coca leaves including, before 1906, trace amounts of cocaine); *see also* Schatzman, Sabbadini & Forti, *Coca and Cocaine: A Bibliography*, 8 J. PSYCHEDELIC DRUGS 95, 97 (1976) (noting that 19th-century advertisements of Coca-Cola proclaimed it a "remarkable therapeutic agent," a "sovereign remedy," and a cure for headaches, neuralgia, hysteria, melancholy, biliousness, spring fever, and insomnia).

113. General Elec. Co. v Alumpa Coal Co., 205 U.S.P.Q. (BNA) 1036, 1037 (D. Mass. 1979) (finding that confusion was likely without ever addressing the possible damage to GE's reputation). The "expansive confusion analysis" is discussed in Note, *supra* note 88, at 1094-96, and Denicola, *supra* note 84, at 186.

114. Denicola, *supra* note 84, at 190.

115. It is difficult to know. No one is keeping a record of threatening phone calls and letters received by local parodists, political groups, and other "consumers" of corporate symbols, which are subjectively experienced "realities" that are never documented by those who quantify objective "reality" for the official record. In other words, the political effects of the exercise of these legal rights may well be (and may remain) invisible to us.

uses.[116] This means that the more powerful the corporate actor in our commercial culture, the more successfully it may immunize itself against oppositional (or ironic or simply mocking) cultural strategies that "recode"[117] those signifiers that most evocatively embody its presence in postmodernity.

The most egregious and perhaps the most well-known recent example involved the prohibition of the use of the word OLYMPIC by a gay rights advocacy group. In 1981, San Francisco Arts & Athletics, Inc. (SFAA), a nonprofit corporation, began to promote an international "Gay Olympic Games" to enhance the image of the gay community.[118] T-shirts, buttons, and bumper stickers were sold to finance the games.[119] The United States Olympic Committee attempted to prohibit any use of the term OLYMPIC in connection with these games.[120] Congress had granted the Committee exclusive rights to use the word under the Amateur Sports Act of 1978.[121]

The district court granted a preliminary injunction prohibiting the SFAA's use of the term, and the Ninth Circuit affirmed.[122] Eventually, the district court awarded a permanent injunction and compelled the nonprofit organization to pay the Committee's attorneys' fees.[123] Fi-

116. 2 J. McCarthy, *supra* note 85, § 24:6(F), at 136-37.

117. See the discussion of "recoding" as a cultural and political tactic, *supra* notes 61-65 and accompanying text.

118. According to the SFAA's president, the Gay Olympic Games were intended

> (1) To provide a healthy recreational alternative to a suppressed minority.
> (2) To educate the public at large towards a more reasonable characterization of gay men and women.
> (3) To attempt, through athletics, to bring about a positive and gradual assimilation of gay men and women, as well as gays and non-gays, and to diminish the ageist, sexist and racist divisiveness existing in all communities regardless of sexual orientation.

San Francisco Arts & Athletics, Inc. v. United States Olympic Comm., 483 U.S. 522, 535 n.13 (1987).

119. *Id.* at 525.

120. *Id.* at 525-28.

121. In particular, section 110 of the Act, set forth in 36 U.S.C. § 380 (1988), provides:

> (a) Without the consent of the [USOC], any person who uses for the purposes of trade, to induce the sale of any goods or services, or to promote any theatrical exhibition, athletic performance, or competition—
>
> . . . .
>
> (4) the words "Olympic", "Olympiad" . . . or any combination . . . thereof tending to cause confusion, to cause mistake, to deceive, or to falsely suggest a connection with the [USOC] or any Olympic activity . . .
> shall be subject to suit in a civil action by the [USOC] for the remedies provided in [the Lanham Act]. . . .
>
> . . . .
>
> (c) The [USOC] shall have exclusive right to use . . . the words "Olympic", "Olympiad" . . . subject to [lawful uses of these words established prior to 1950].

Amateur Sports Act of 1978, § 110, 36 U.S.C. § 380 (1988).

122. International Olympic Comm. v. San Francisco Arts & Athletics, 219 U.S.P.Q. (BNA) 982, 987-88 (N.D. Cal. 1982), *aff'd*, 707 F.2d 517 (9th Cir. 1983) (mem.).

123. *See* International Olympic Comm. v. San Francisco Arts & Athletics, 781 F.2d 733, 738

nally, in 1987 the Supreme Court upheld the Committee's exclusive rights to control the OLYMPIC signifier and determined, in effect, that the Committee had complete discretion to prohibit any use of the term that it found offensive.[124] The "property" rights of the Committee had priority over the expressive interests of an historically silenced minority.[125]

The term OLYMPIC has a long history of positive associations with human excellence and achievement. It is, therefore, a "key symbol,"[126] with which those in disadvantaged groups will associate to seek public recognition.[127] Indeed, the Committee had authorized youth groups and associations for the handicapped to hold OLYMPIC games. Homosexuals were not deemed worthy of the same privilege. As the judge writing the dissenting opinion for the Ninth Circuit remarked, "[I]t seems that the USOC is using its control over the term Olympic to promote the very image of homosexuals that the SFAA seeks to combat: handicapped, juniors, police, Explorers, even dogs are allowed to carry the Olympic

(9th Cir. 1986) (affirming permanent injunction but vacating and remanding for further proceedings on the award of the plaintiff's attorneys' fees), *reh'g denied and opinion amended*, 789 F.2d 1319, 1320 (9th Cir. 1986), *aff'd sub nom.* San Francisco Arts and Athletics, Inc. v. United States Olympic Comm., 483 U.S. 522, 548 (1987).

124. Moreover, it was determined that there were no defenses available to anyone who used the term without authorization. *San Francisco Arts & Athletics, Inc.*, 483 U.S. at 530-32. For longer discussions of the reasoning in the case, see Kravitz, *Trademarks, Speech, and the* Gay Olympics *Case*, 69 B.U.L. REV. 131, 160-84 (1989) (arguing that the Supreme Court's rationale in *San Francisco Arts & Athletics* distorted the analysis of what constitutes commercial speech to the detriment of SFAA's first amendment rights); Note, *A Sad Time for the Gay Olympics*, 56 U. CIN. L. REV. 1487 (1988).

125. Similarly, a suit has been filed against The Pink Panther Patrol, a group formed to deter gay bashing in Manhattan's West Village. The company that owns the rights to the Pink Panther movies claims that the group's use of the name with an emblem consisting of a paw print inside a pink triangle "diminish[es] the identity and reputation" of their trademark. The group considers this is a necessarily homophobic argument. Hays, *Gay Patrol and MGM in a Battle over Name*, N.Y. Times, May 27, 1991, § 1, at 21, col. 2.

126. For a discussion of the cultural significance of "key symbols," see Ortner, *On Key Symbols*, 75 AM. ANTHROPOLOGIST 1338, 1342-44 (1973) (suggesting that key symbols have both a summarizing function that catalyzes thought and action and an elaborating function that organizes conceptual experience or social action). Ortner updates her approach to key symbols in Ortner, *Theory in Anthropology Since the Sixties*, 26 COMP. STUD. SOC. & HIST. 126, 144-60 (1984) (suggesting that the trend in anthropology during the 1980s would be toward a more practice-oriented approach, focusing on either: (1) practice, praxis, action, and so on (*i.e.*, the things people do with cultural symbols, particularly with intentional or unintentional political implications); or (2) the agent, actor, self, subject, and so on (*i.e.*, the culturally constructed motivations of those who engage in such activities)).

127. Elsewhere I have discussed minority interests in "official signifiers" (or marks held by public authorities) and the political implications of bestowing unlimited discretion to control signs upon bodies who are not accountable for its use. *See* R. Coombe, Official Signifers: The Control of Signs and the [De]Construction of Difference, Paper presented to the American Society of Criminology (Nov. 7, 1990) and to the American Anthropological Association (Nov. 28, 1990) (on file at the *Texas Law Review*).

torch, but homosexuals are not."[128] In the dissent to the Supreme Court majority opinion, Justice Brennan (joined by Justice Marshall) noted that there were over 200 organizations listed in the Los Angeles and New York phone directories alone whose names began with the word OLYMPIC.[129] Indeed, the Committee's counsel (nominated by Ronald Reagan in 1987 for the position of district court judge) was a member of an exclusive all-male social club with a history of discrimination against minorities.[130] The name of this elite institution? You guessed it—The Olympic Club.[131] No legal injunction was launched on that front.

The ability to restrict and control meaning because you "own" the sign may be most readily apparent in the trademark field, but it is more widespread. Other writers have suggested that copyright law has developed without due regard for the public interest, raising the specter of likely recovery for "copying" of any kind, without consideration of the social interests in promoting expressive activity or protecting the public domain.[132] Publicity rights arguably enable celebrities, their assignees, and their estates to control the meaning of the celebrity image in a fashion that deprives us of access to our collective cultural heritage and the ability to reflect upon the historical significance of the celebrity aura.[133] Further, celebrity images provide the cultural resources which those in marginalized groups use to construct alternative gender identities. For example, in the pre-Stonewall era gay men used the image of Judy Garland to identify themselves to each other and to comment upon the relation between nature and artifice in the presentation of the gendered

128. International Olympic Comm. v. San Francisco Arts & Athletics, 789 F.2d 1319, 1323 (9th Cir. 1986) (Kozinski, J., dissenting).

129. *San Francisco Arts & Athletics, Inc.*, 483 U.S. at 568 n.32.

130. *See* Shenon, *Battle Looming over a Nominee for U.S. Court*, N.Y. Times, Jan. 14, 1988, at A14, col. 6 (characterizing it as a "private club that bars membership to women and has been criticized for having no minority members in recent years"); *see also* McLaughlin, *The Walker Nomination: A Bork-style Battle in San Francisco*, The San Francisco Bay Guardian, January 20, 1988, at 7 (noting Walker's membership in the "elitist" club, "which openly discriminates against gays, women and minorities").

131. *Id.*

132. *See, e.g.*, Kulzick & Hogue, *Chilled Bird: Freedom of Expression in the Eighties*, 14 LOY. L.A.L. REV. 57, 77-78 (1980) (lamenting that "[i]n the long run . . . both the writer and the viewing public will suffer from the inevitable chilling effect wrought by overbroad construction of the copyright monopoly"); Note, *Copyright Infringement and the First Amendment*, 79 COLUM. L. REV. 320, 320-21 (1979) (asserting that because "copyright protection results in a partial monopoly over expression, . . . it conflicts with the first amendment interest in free speech"); Vaver, *supra* note 75 (arguing that, upon examination, the social utilitarian justification of copyright law—that it protects authors, encourages creativity, and encourages dissemination—"dissolves into mythology"); *see also supra* note 75.

133. See the discussion of Elvis Presley and Madonna in R. Coombe, *supra* note 10, at 14-21. David Lange makes a similar argument. *See* Lange, *supra* note 75, at 165 (noting that the First Amendment is an inadequate tool for controlling the development of intellectual property rights).

self.[134] Similarly, James Dean provides lesbians with an icon which may embody a challenge to dominant understandings of the causal connections between biology, anatomy, desire, and sexual practice.[135] Thousands of women use Star Trek characters to rewrite the masculine, re-imagine the male body, and engender utopian "alternative universes."[136] Again, those who attempt to give novel and alternative meanings to popular and powerful signifiers come up against the law and the politics of the commodity form. Gene Roddenberry may have conceived the philosophy of IDIC (Infinite Diversity in Infinite Combination), but there is no guarantee that Paramount Pictures will respect its principles.[137]

V. Dialogism

The concept of dialogue, dialogism, and the dialogical principles of human life were central to the philosophical anthropology of Mikhail Bakhtin, who has been described as "the most important Soviet thinker in the human sciences and the greatest theoretician of literature in the twentieth century."[138] With Pavel Medvedev and Valentin Voloshinov, Bakhtin developed a body of philosophy about the constitutive role of language in human life and the cultural life of democracy, which he saw as quintessentially dialogical.[139]

I will borrow Bakhtin's authority here because he transcends and rejects the dichotomy of subjectivity and objectivity by understanding culture as the ongoing activity of transformative meaning-making.[140] Further, he does so without denying either the materiality of signs or the political importance of struggles to fix their meanings.[141] Bakhtin made extensive attacks both on the transcendental ego and on objectivist understandings of self, language, and the world. For Bakhtin, the self was a

134. R. Coombe, *supra* note 10, at 56-57.

135. *Id.* at 59.

136. *Id.* at 72-80.

137. *Cf. id.* at 76-77 (suggesting that fanwriters may "respect the legal prohibition against selling their writings, videotapes and artworks for profit," but still not be deterred by the possibility that many of their activities might be enjoined on copyright, trademark, or publicity grounds).

138. T. Todorov, Mikhail Bakhtin. The Dialogical Principle ix (W. Godzich trans. 1984). Most of Bakhtin's work is still untranslated, and it is necessary to refer to secondary sources to get a sense of the full range of his thought.

139. Hirschkop, *Introduction: Bakhtin and Cultural Theory*, in Bahktin and Cultural Theory 1-2 (K. Hirschkop & D. Shepherd eds. 1989).

140. *See* M. Holquist, Dialogism: Bakhtin and His World 41 (1990) (describing Bakhtin's theory that "[e]xistence is . . . a vast web of interconnections each and all of which are linked as participants in an event whose totality is so immense that no single one of us can ever know it. That event manifests itself in the form of a constant, ceaseless creation and exchange of meaning.").

141. *See id.* at 49 (noting that in dialogism "meaning comes about only through the medium of signs. . . . [And] a thing exists only in so far as it has meaning.").

Texas Law Review Vol. 69:1853, 1991

dialogic relation[142] with other selves that is never complete, but is always dominated by a "drive to meaning" in which meaning is understood as something always in the process of creation, never completed, for the world itself "is a vast congeries of contested meanings."[143]

The self authors itself with and through the social signs with which meaning is made:

> Meaning comes about in both the individual psyche and in shared social experience through the medium of the sign, for in both spheres understanding comes about *as a response to a sign with signs*. . . . "And nowhere is there a break in the chain, nowhere does the chain plunge into inner being, nonmaterial in nature and unembodied in signs."[144]

Bakhtin sees the relation between an individual and society not as a binary opposition, but as a continuum because the contents of the psyche and a culture are the same: signifying forms that simultaneously demand and elude closure as fixed signs with certain meanings. As one commentator has noted, "the nature of the linguistic sign is synergistic, a constant struggle and co-operation between the necessity to be static and repeatable, and the opposed but no less imperative necessity of the same material to be open to constantly new and changing circumstances . . . ."[145]

As human beings we live an existence of sheer semioticity, "surrounded by forms that in themselves seek the condition of mere being-there, the sheer givenness of brute nature,"[146] but at the same time we are compelled to invest these forms with new life and meaning so that we may understand them. Understanding is responding, answering. "Human being is the *production* of meaning . . . ."[147] We are fated to the condition of dialogue, "not only with other human beings, but also with the natural and cultural configurations we lump together as 'the world.' The world addresses us and we are alive and human to the degree that we are answerable, i.e. to the degree that we can respond to addressivity."[148]

142. *Id.* at 19; *see also* M. BAKHTIN, PROBLEMS OF DOSTOEVSKY'S POETICS 311-12 (1984) (C. Emerson trans. 1984) (arguing that "I achieve self-consciousness, I become myself only by revealing myself to another, through another and with another's help. The most important acts, constitutive of self-consciousness, are determined by their relation to another consciousness . . . .").

143. M. HOLQUIST, *supra* note 140, at 23-24; *see also* T. TODOROV, *supra* note 138, at 95.

144. M. HOLQUIST, *supra* note 140, at 49 (quoting V.N. VOLOSHINOV, *supra* note 2, at 11) (emphasis in original); *see* T. TODOROV, *supra* note 138, at 30. There is a vociferous debate about whether the works allegedly authored by Voloshinov were in fact written by Bakhtin. *See* M. HOLQUIST, *supra* note 140, at 8. I think Bakhtin would be amused.

145. M. HOLQUIST, *supra* note 140, at 175.

146. *Id.* at 66.

147. *Id.* at 158 (emphasis in original).

148. *Id.* at 29-30.

Intellectual Property Laws and Democratic Dialogue

If what is quintessentially human is the capacity to make meaning,[149] challenge meaning, and transform meaning,[150] then we strip ourselves of our humanity through over-zealous application and continuous expansion of intellectual property protections. Dialogue involves reciprocity in communication—the ability to respond to a sign with signs.[151] What meaning does dialogue have when we are bombarded with messages to which we cannot respond, signs and images whose significations cannot be challenged, and connotations we cannot contest?

The sign, according to Bakhtin and Voloshinov, is always an arena of social struggle, because it embodies the dialectical history of two contending social tendencies—the monologic and the dialogic.[152] Bakhtin often links monologic tendencies with the "official" in cultures, which must always contend with dialogic or "carnivalesque" tendencies. This is a sociopolitical opposition, with those in power attempting to give a brute facticity and singular meaning to the sign and to extinguish the "struggle between social value judgements which occurs in it, to make the sign uniaccentual."[153] Such centralizing forces must always contend with dialogism—ubiquitous, centrifugal forces that find expression in practices like those of satire, parody, irony, quotation, collage, stylization, and polemic.[154] These are practices like those "recodings" of commodified signs explored earlier,[155] practices that involve a generation of new meanings through metaphor and generative recontextualizations of the sign.

The struggles that take place on the terrain of the sign to define its symbolic boundaries are historically specific contentions in which those

149. "To be human is to seek coherence, constantly to engage in an 'effort after meaning.'" Winter, *The Cognitive Dimension*, *supra* note 34, at 2230 (quoting Bruner, *Foreword* to D. SPENCE, THE FREUDIAN METAPHOR: TOWARD PARADIGM CHANGE IN PSYCHOANALYSIS at xii (1987)).

150. We constantly use our imaginative capacities "to recast what we find and reconstruct our context by reconceptualization" and our "power of imagination to create new meanings not already shaped by what we believe." Winter, *Bull Durham*, *supra* note 25, at 674-76. "Freedom consists not in an unrestricted capacity to define meaning, but in an ability to modulate meanings." *Id.* at 684 (quoting K. WHITESIDE, MERLEAU-PONTY AND THE FOUNDATION OF AN EXISTENTIAL POLITICS 68-69 (1988)).

151. *See* V.N. VOLOSHINOV, *supra* note 2, at 11.

152. *See* Pechey, *On the Borders of Bakhtin: Dialogisation, Decolonisation*, in BAKHTIN AND CULTURAL THEORY, *supra* note 139, at 43-52.

153. V.N. VOLOSHINOV, *supra* note 2, at 23.

154. *See* M. BAKHTIN, *Discourse in the Novel*, in THE DIALOGIC IMAGINATION 259, 298-99 (M. Holquist ed. 1981) ("The prose writer does not purge words of intentions and tones that are alien to him, he does not destroy the seeds of social heteroglossia embedded in words . . . . [T]he writer of prose does not meld completely with any of these words, but rather accents each of them in a particular way—humorously, ironically, parodically and so forth . . . .").

155. *See supra* notes 61-65 and accompanying text. For specific examples of practices that recode commodified signs to produce alternative meanings, see text accompanying notes 51-53, 66-71, 81, 86.

with divergent social interests strive to establish legitimate meanings for the sign or to delegitimate the meanings established by others.[156] The sign is dynamic; it maintains the capacity for development, vitality, and social life to the extent that it is open to reconfiguration. In postmodernism, I fear, we see fewer and fewer signs of life, but more and more monologic monuments—commercial tombstones marking the demise of the carnivalesque in the condition of postmodernity.

Legal theorists who emphasize the cultural construction of self and world—the central importance of shared cultural symbols in defining us and the realities we recognize—need to consider the legal constitutions of symbols and the extent to which "we" can be said to "share" them. I fear that most legal theorists concerned with dialogue objectify, rarefy, and idealize "culture"—abstracting "it" from the material and political practices in which meaning is made.[157] Culture is not embedded in abstract concepts that we internalize, but in the materiality of signs and texts over which we struggle and the imprint of those struggles in our consciousness.[158]

This ongoing negotiation and struggle over meaning is the essence of dialogic practice. Many interpretations of intellectual property laws quash dialogue by affirming the power of corporate actors to monologically control meaning by evoking the concept of property. If both subjective and objective realities are constituted culturally—through signifying forms to which we give meaning—then we must critically consider the relationship between law, culture, and the politics of commodifying cultural forms.

156. I should at this point make it clear that I believe that we are always in a world where some meanings are being fixed, while others are changing. A world of free-floating signifiers in which *no* meanings were fixed would be an impossible one in which to live, as would a world where signification had reached a state of closure. Social actors have many different kinds of power to fix and to challenge meaning; intellectual property law is only one kind of power in a larger field. We are all always engaged in meaning-making. What I am arguing for here is a democratization of access to this practice such that all peoples have equal capacities to engage in it and economically powerful actors are not given even further resources and capacities to dominate cultural arenas than they already possess.

157. For example, Winter says that his conception of "culture" does not reify it into some monolithic, determinate "thing," but he never explores any social negotiations of meaning nor any conflictual practices or struggles to define meaning. Instead, he relegates the politics of meaning to a single phrase in a single footnote when he tersely notes that "people in power get to impose their metaphors." Winter, *Transcendental Nonsense*, *supra* note 25, at 1135 n.101 (quoting G. Lakoff & M. Johnson, Metaphors We Live By 157 (1980)). For a longer discussion of the tendency of legal theorists to avoid issues of power when discussing "culture," see Coombe, *"Same As It Ever Was,"* *supra* note 25, at 630-52.

158. But if legal theorists concerned with "culture" have a tendency towards idealism, those concerned with free speech tend towards an undue materialism in their consideration of dialogism. I discuss the left critique of the public-private dichotomy in liberal freedom of speech doctrine in R. Coombe, *supra* note 10, where I argue that critics on the left fail to consider the cultural dimensions of postmodernity in their critiques of commercial expression.

Part IV
Postmodern Contexts

[8]

POSTMODERNISM/FEMINISM/LAW

Dennis Patterson†

TABLE OF CONTENTS

---

† Professor of Law, Rutgers University School of Law-Camden; B.A., 1976; M.A., 1978; J.D., 1980; Ph.D. (Philosophy), 1980, State University of New York at Buffalo. I wish to thank Anita Allen, Dianne Avery, Jack Balkin, Jay Feinman, David Frankford, Richard Hyland, Tom Morawetz, Nancey Murphy, Robert Post, Jeanne Schroeder, Allan Stein, John Stick, Jim Tully, Mary White, Robin West, Joan Williams, and the audience and participants in a panel on Feminism and Institutions, held at the May, 1990 meeting of the International Association for Philosophy and Literature in Montreal, Canada, for their discussions of the ideas in, and text of, this Article. Special thanks to Anne Goldstein for the seminar and many other forms of support, to my students at Rutgers in the seminar on Postmodernism and Feminism for their ardor, and to Marion Townend, Anne Dalesandro, and David Batista of the Rutgers University Law Library for outstanding assistance in locating research materials.

Das heute baue sich auf das gestern auf, so wie sich das gestern auf das vorgestern aufgebaut hat.

Adolf Loos**

INTRODUCTION

Can feminism survive the postmodern critique of reason? Or are the emancipatory aspirations of feminists tied to the continuing viability of modernist forms of discourse? Recent feminist writing[1] indicates that this question is central to the future of feminism as an emancipatory enterprise: in short, feminism is unthinkable without philosophy.[2] Feminists seem to have two choices: stick with modernism or give up feminism. Are these the only choices available?

Some feminists fear that unless their arguments are clothed in the discourse of modernism[3]—objectivity, truth, and reason—feminist aspirations to break free of patriarchal shackles will be frustrated.[4] These feminists believe that only by transcending our

** ADOLF LOOS, *Meine Bauschule*, in 1 SÄMTLICHE SCHRIFTEN 323 (1962) ("Let today build itself on yesterday, just as yesterday built itself on that which came before it.").

1 *See* Sabina Lovibond, *Feminism and Postmodernism*, 178 NEW LEFT REV. 22 (1989); Nancy Fraser & Linda J. Nicholson, *Social Criticism Without Philosophy: An Encounter between Feminism and Postmodernism*, *in* FEMINISM/POSTMODERNISM 19-38 (Linda J. Nicholson ed., 1990).

2 "Philosophy" refers to the enterprise that seeks, through the power of reason, right representation, moral knowledge, truth, and other modernist artifacts. For a discussion of the end of philosophy, and what will succeed it, see AFTER PHILOSOPHY: END OR TRANSFORMATION? (Kenneth Baynes et al. eds., 1987).

3 Modernity's staunchest defender, Jürgen Habermas, describes the project of modernity in the following terms:

> [T]he project of modernity formulated in the 18th century by the philosophers of the Enlightenment consisted in their efforts to develop objective science, universal morality and law, and autonomous art according to their inner logic. At the same time, this project intended to release the cognitive potentials of each of these domains from their esoteric forms. The Enlightenment philosophers wanted to utilize this accumulation of specialized culture for the enrichment of everyday life—that is to say, for the rational organization of everyday social life.

Jürgen Habermas, *Modernity—An Incomplete Project*, *in* THE ANTI-AESTHETIC 9 (Hal Foster ed., 1983). For Habermas's critique of the critics of modernity, see JÜRGEN HABERMAS, THE PHILOSOPHICAL DISCOURSE OF MODERNITY (Frederick Lawrence trans., 1987) (leveling a broad attack on recent Continental thought, in particular the work of Jacques Derrida, Michel Foucault, and George Bataille). For a discussion of Habermas's self-conception of his place in the German modernist tradition of philosophy, see Dennis M. Patterson, *Hegel and Postmodernity*, 10 CARDOZO L. REV. 1665 (1989).

4 *See, e.g.*, Ruth Colker, *Feminism, Sexuality, and Self: A Preliminary Inquiry Into the Politics of Authenticity*, 68 B.U. L. REV. 217, 220 (1988) (book review).

> Our journey toward authenticity, however, requires more than discovering our inner selves. We also need to work to create a world in which we can freely *experience* our authentic selves. Society has strongly influenced our gender, as well as our larger personhood. We need to struggle against limiting forces in our lives to move toward authenticity, which, in terms of our feminist work, means struggling against the forces of patri-

current perspective—be it linguistic, social, or political—can women be emancipated.[5] In short, their contention is that women can only be liberated by getting their voice to a place it is not,[6] or by speaking a language that is not yet their own.[7]

This Article argues that the choice between feminism[8] and postmodernism[9] is a false one. The claim that these purported in-

---

> archy. Our glimpses of our authentic selves can provide us with the strength and direction necessary to struggle against the brokenness and subordination in our lives. Without a sense of our authentic selves, we would have no basis for selecting priorities in our feminist struggles.

Id. *But see* Jeanne Schroeder, *Abduction from the Seraglio: Peirce's Logic of Imagination and Feminist Methodologies*, 70 TEX. L. REV. 109 (1991) (arguing for the reconstruction of feminist jurisprudence by rethinking questions of scientific knowledge and hypothesis formation).

5 *See* Katharine T. Bartlett, *Feminist Legal Methods*, 103 HARV. L. REV. 829, 867 (1990).

> A point—perhaps *the* point—of legal methods is to reach answers that are legally defensible or in some sense "right." Methods themselves imply a stance toward rightness. If being right means having discovered some final, objective truth based in a fixed physical or moral reality, for example, verification is possible and leaves no room for further perspectives or for doubt. On the other hand, if being right means that one has expressed one's personal tastes or interests which have no greater claim to validity than those of anyone else, being right is a rhetorical device used to assert one's own point of view, and verification is both impossible and pointless.

Id.

6 *See, e.g.*, Carrie Menkel-Meadow, *Portia in a Different Voice: Speculations on a Women's Lawyering Process*, 1 BERKELEY WOMEN'S L.J. 39 (1985); Suzanna Sherry, *Civic Virtue and the Feminine Voice in Constitutional Adjudication*, 72 VA. L. REV. 543 (1986).

7 *See* CATHARINE A. MACKINNON, FEMINISM UNMODIFIED 32-45 (1987).

8 In light of the many projects, aspirations, and theories that can be denominated "feminist," it makes little sense to advance a definition of feminism. Like all notions, "feminism" has a grammar for its usage; this grammar, however, is contested. Hence, it seems silly to draw lines when no one is entirely reasonable. Better simply to notice and appreciate the multiplicity of meanings inherent in the term.

9 It is difficult to describe postmodernism in a sentence or two, for postmodernism "belongs to a network of 'post' concepts and thinking—post-industrial society, post-structuralism, post-empiricism, post-rationalism. . . ." ALBRECHT WELLMER, ZUR DIALEKTIK VON MODERNE UND POSTMODERNE 48 (1985). In discussing postmodernism, it is helpful to observe two dichotomies: modern-postmodern and modernity-postmodernity. The modern-postmodern dichotomy identifies philosophical positions. For example, if you believe that musical ideas have a nature that is expressed in the written score, and that composers work within musical traditions to give expression to musical ideas, then you are a modernist. If you believe that past musical traditions "exist" for the purposes of the composer, and that the tradition of understanding and developing musical ideas places no restrictions on what the composer can or ought to do, your attitude is postmodern. The connections between music, modernity, and postmodernism are spelled out in Sanford Levinson & J.M. Balkin, *Law, Music, and Other Performing Arts*, 139 U. PA. L. REV. 1597 (1991) (providing a modernist, psycho-social explanation by resorting to the mechanism or causal process of (legal) cultural anxiety in the movement from modernity to postmodernity). *See generally* Robert P. Morgan, *Tradition, Anxiety and the Current Musical Scene*, *in* AUTHENTICITY AND EARLY MUSIC 57-83 (Nicholas Kenyon ed., 1988). Modernity and postmodernity are, of course, epochal notions. The epoch of Modernity is that period in human history which begins with the Enlightenment and

commensurables represent the only choices available to feminism is itself the product of a distorted conception of the relationship between reason and critique. Properly understood, postmodernism

---

continues to the present. It is marked by an increasing control of nature, the separation of the subject from tradition, and the growth of reason as the arbiter of human conflict. Postmodernity is that epoch in which the defining features of Modernity are no longer a part of the terrain of human existence. Postmodernity is exemplified in culture by the presence of "pastiche"—the juxtaposition of unrelated elements in various cultural forms. For a discussion of this phenomenon in the culture of television, see E. ANN KAPLAN, ROCKING AROUND THE CLOCK: MUSIC TELEVISION, POSTMODERNISM, & CONSUMER CULTURE (1987).

Whether or not we are in postmodernity is, of course, very much open to question. This Article is concerned with the first of the dichotomies set forth above. Its focus is limited to the question of whether ideas have a life apart from the practices in which they are embodied. From the perspective of philosophy, the modernist answer is affirmative and the postmodernist answer negative. Thus, the postmodernist denies that ideas are autonomous: rather, they "exist," "have a life," or are "viable" only to the extent they are embodied in practices.

In addition to these qualifications, one must be careful in identifying particular thinkers as "postmodern." One name often tied to postmodernism is that of Jean-François Lyotard, who associates postmodernism with the death of "the metanarrative." *See* JEAN-FRANÇOIS LYOTARD, THE POSTMODERN CONDITION: A REPORT ON KNOWLEDGE xxiv (Geoff Bennington & Brian Massumi trans., 1984) ("I define *postmodern* as incredulity toward metanarratives."). Lyotard's argument is nothing less than a wholesale rejection of the picture of knowledge and justification that has supported much of the discourse of the human and natural sciences for the last three hundred years. Precisely what does Lyotard reject? In a word, legitimation. "Legitimation is the process by which a legislator is authorized to promulgate . . . a law as a norm." *Id.* at 8. Thus, the question "is this law valid?" has no point, for the "knowledge" required to answer the question is a knowledge that can never exist. In postmodernity, legitimation of first-order discourses (e.g., law and science) by resort to second-order discourses of reason (e.g., philosophy) is replaced with a picture of knowledge as a move within a game, specifically a "language-game."

> It is useful to make the following three observations about language-games. The first is that their rules do not carry within themselves their own legitimation, but are the object of a contract, explicit or not, between players (which is not to say that the players invent the rules). The second is that if there are no rules, there is no game, that even an infinitesimal modification of one rule alters the nature of the game, that a "move" or utterance that does not satisfy the rules does not belong to the game they define. The third remark is suggested by what has just been said: every utterance should be thought of as a "move" in a game.

Id. at 10 (citation omitted). Lyotard's principal focus in attacking the traditional conception of knowledge as rational scrutiny of claims to truth and validity is philosophy. What Lyotard seeks is the complete displacement (not replacement) of philosophy with knowledge of the pragmatics of interaction. He wants philosophy "forced to relinquish its legitimation duties." *Id.* at 41. Legitimation gives way to the agonistic play of the participants as they struggle with one another for control of the game.

Feminism aspires to a metanarrative about gender or patriarchy. For example, "different voice" feminism claims that women speak and think differently than do men, and that male forms of discourse and modes of understanding suppress their "voice." If Lyotard is right that the era of the totalizing and legitimating metanarrative is at an end, then feminism, at least in its totalizing forms, is impossible. Thus, postmodernism poses a threat to any form of feminist critique that issues from a perspective assuming or presupposing a position outside the (dominant) discourse of (gendered) law.

poses no threat to feminism.[10] In fact, all that postmodernism threatens is a conception of reason (the modernist[11] conception) which may have reached the end of its useful life.[12]

After reviewing the broad contours of contemporary feminist jurisprudence, Part I provides a description of modernism and postmodernism. The move from modernity to postmodernity is not depicted as the replacement of one mode of thought with another; rather, postmodernism is viewed as the unwillingness to be captivated by certain questions that animate modernist habits of thought. Part II turns to contemporary feminist jurisprudence. Having made the argument that the status of postmodernism is central to recent debates in feminist jurisprudence, the focus is shifted to the work of three feminists in support of this claim. The work of each feminist represents a different perspective on the question of postmodernism. For one, feminism is not possible without the modernist project. The second is skeptical of modernism but cannot escape modernist forms of argumentation. The third openly embraces postmodernism and uses her stance to criticize the shortcomings of radical feminists making their arguments from within modernist rhetorical forms.

Part III considers what a feminist jurisprudence would look like from the postmodernist perspective. Having moved beyond the modernist conception of knowledge, the emphasis shifts to the themes of practice, critique, and localism. This focus leads to a description of feminist jurisprudence as a form of narrative, viewing it as an enterprise devoted to reconstructing juridical conventions by rereading them in ways that can be described as "postmodern."

---

10 The epigram with which this Article begins signals the sense in which postmodernism and the manifold claims made for it should be understood.

11 I identify modernism with the spirit of the Enlightenment. "In the most general sense of progressive thought, the Enlightenment has always aimed at liberating men from fear and establishing their sovereignty." MAX HORKHEIMER & THEODOR W. ADORNO, DIALECTIC OF ENLIGHTENMENT 3 (John Cumming trans., 1972). Despite the broad tenor of Horkheimer and Adorno's language, the conception or aspect of modernism that is here identified by the term is quite specific (thus, extrapolation from this narrow focus is hazardous). The broadest way to frame the modernism with which I shall be concerned is this: freedom and rationality are ineluctably connected in some fashion. This idea, which stems from Kantian ethical philosophy, is given various expressions from the eighteenth century to the present. The most basic element in this view is that the relationship between ethics and reason is one of disclosure: the latter discloses the former. It is with this specific claim that I shall take issue.

12 It is important to remember that the point of modernist thought, particularly political thought, was to emancipate *humanitas* from a non-secular mode of existence that itself had become obsolete. As the contradictions of modernism mount, modernism too may give way to a form of thought, the parameters of which have yet to be defined.

I
Feminism, Modernity, and Postmodernity

A. The State of Contemporary Feminist Jurisprudence

Are women different from men? This seemingly simple question is immediately rendered problematic by further questions. Given that there are differences, whence come the differences? How can we know the truth of those differences? These questions in turn give rise to others addressed in feminist jurisprudence. Is sex identical to gender? Do women have a different psychic constitution than men?; one that impels them toward care[13] and compassion[14] rather than argument, contest, and even violence? And where do our images of women come from? Is gender something with which we come into the world, or is it produced in our language or culture?[15] These are important questions, and in attempting to answer them, all manner of contemporary feminist theory has become wedded to the "difference" issue.[16]

Another question presents itself—call it the question of critique. Underlying the difference question is a host of critique-based questions regarding epistemology, patriarchy, subordination, and power. For example, in her critique of rape law, Catharine MacKinnon accepts that men and women are different.[17] What MacKinnon rejects is the elevation into law of the male view of sex. Rape law has nothing to do with protecting women: to accomplish that goal, the law would have to look at sex, and rape, from "women's point of view."[18] This it refuses to do because the discourse of law is gendered, and its gender is male. Hence, critique, discourse, and liberation are inextricably woven together.

The project of providing a philosophical account of the differences between men and women has evolved into the "difference" question. If men and women are different, then what are the differences, and how should we take account of them? At this point, the

---

13 *See* NEL NODDINGS, CARING (1984).

14 *See* Ruth Colker, *Feminism, Theology, and Abortion: Toward Love, Compassion and Wisdom*, 77 CAL. L. REV. 1011 (1989). For a discussion of the nineteenth century opposition between reason and feeling, see IRIS M. YOUNG, *Impartiality and the Civic Public: Some Implications of Feminist Critiques of Moral and Political Theory*, *in* THROWING LIKE A GIRL AND OTHER ESSAYS IN FEMINIST PHILOSOPHY AND SOCIAL THEORY 92-113 (1990).

15 On this question, see ELIZABETH WILSON, ADORNED IN DREAMS: FASHION AND MODERNITY 117-33 (1985) (analyzing the role of fashion in the production of gender identity).

16 For an innovative effort to think through the implications of "difference" in the context of questions of social justice, see IRIS M. YOUNG, JUSTICE AND THE POLITICS OF DIFFERENCE (1990).

17 *See* MACKINNON, *supra* note 7, at 40.

18 Catharine A. MacKinnon, *Feminism, Marxism, Method, and the State: Toward Feminist Jurisprudence*, 8 SIGNS 635, 644 (1983).

difference question and the question of critique converge, and the internal debate in feminism heats up. First comes essentialism. Women *are* different, and their differences *are* universal: they include the mothering impulse,[19] biological differences,[20] and the capacity to nurture.[21] Because of these differences, women should be treated differently than men. *Is* implies (or could be made to imply) *ought*.

Long feminism's torment, essentialism has fallen on hard times.[22] As two feminist philosophers recently stated: "[V]estiges of essentialism have continued to plague feminist scholarship, even despite the decline of grand theorizing. In many cases . . . this represents the continuing subterranean influence of those very mainstream modes of thought and inquiry with which feminists have wished to break."[23] If, however, essentialism is abandoned, what will take its place?[24] One answer is this: a view of "woman" not as the instantiation of a universal category, but as the product of legal discourse.[25] Why not do away with the whole idea of the category "woman" altogether? Perhaps feminists would do better "to tolerate and interpret ambivalence, ambiguity, and multiplicity as well as

19 *See* NANCY CHODOROW, THE REPRODUCTION OF MOTHERING: PSYCHOANALYSIS AND THE SOCIOLOGY OF GENDER (1978).

20 *See* SHULAMITH FIRESTONE, THE DIALECTIC OF SEX: THE CASE FOR FEMINIST REVOLUTION (1970).

21 *See* CAROL GILLIGAN, IN A DIFFERENT VOICE (1982).

22 *See* Helen Vendler, *Feminism and Literature*, N.Y. REV., May 31, 1990, at 19, 22.

> Feminism's unacknowledged problem, visible from its inception, has been its ascription of special virtue to women. In its most sentimental form, feminism assumes that men, as a class, are base and women are moral; in its angry version, that men are oppressors and women are the oppressed. This is to ignore what some cooler feminist minds have suspected, that the possession of power, rather than whether one is a woman or a man, is what determines the act of oppression.

Id.

23 Fraser & Nicholson, *supra* note 1, at 33.

24 This question arises with great frequency with respect to projects that conceptualize feminism along poststructuralist lines. *See, e.g.*, Teresa de Lauretis, *The Essence of the Triangle or, Taking the Risk of Essentialism Seriously: Feminist Theory in Italy, the U.S., and Britain*, 1 DIFFERENCES 3, 9 (1989) ("I would insist that the notion of experience in relation both to social-material practices and to the formation and processes of subjectivity is a feminist concept, not a poststructuralist one . . . .").

25 One feminist summarizes the problem this way:

> If there is to be feminism at all, as a movement unique to women, we must rely on a feminine voice and a feminine "reality" that can be identified as such and correlated with the lives of actual women. Yet all accounts of the Feminine seem to reset the trap of rigid gender identities, deny the real differences among women (white women have certainly been reminded of this danger by women of color), and reflect the history of oppression and discrimination rather than an ideal to which we ought to aspire.

Drucilla Cornell, *The Doubly-Prized World: Myth, Allegory and the Feminine*, 75 CORNELL L. REV. 644, 644-45 (1990).

to expose the roots of our needs for imposing order and structure no matter how arbitrary and oppressive these needs may be."[26] But what would this change do to "feminism"? How can feminism be "something more than a reformist movement"[27] if it gives up the project of "calling the parish boundaries into question"?[28] In short, how can there *be* feminism without a systematic critique of gender relations?[29]

Faced with these questions, contemporary feminist jurisprudence has developed a variety of projects, all of which are aimed at the development of the tools necessary to critique the gendered discourse of law. Much of this literature is devoted to the development of feminist methods for use in the critique of doctrine,[30] judging,[31] and practical reasoning.[32] In the course of this development, a good deal of attention has been focused on what feminist jurisprudence should "look like."[33] To answer this question, one must first ask what *any* jurisprudence should look like. This raises further questions about method, knowledge, and critique.[34] It is also to raise the question of postmodernism.[35]

---

26 Jane Flax, *Thinking Fragments*, *in* FEMINISM/POSTMODERNISM, *supra* note 1, at 56.

27 Lovibond, *supra* note 1, at 22.

28 *Id.*

29 I owe this formulation of the question to Jack Balkin.

30 *See* SUSAN ESTRICH, REAL RAPE (1987).

31 *See* Judith Resnik, *On The Bias: Feminist Reconsiderations Of The Aspirations For Our Judges*, 61 S. CAL. L. REV. 1877 (1988).

32 *See* Bartlett, *supra* note 5, at 854-62. Professor Bartlett embraces method both as a substantive tool (it will get us closer to the "truth" of things) and as a legitimating device.

> Method matters also because without an understanding of feminist methods, feminist claims in the law will not be perceived as legitimate or "correct." I suspect that many who dismiss feminism as trivial or inconsequential misunderstand it. Feminists have tended to focus on defending their various substantive positions or political agendas, even among themselves. Greater attention to issues of method may help to anchor these defenses, to explain why feminist agendas often appear so radical (or not radical enough), and even to establish some common ground among feminists.
>
> As feminists articulate their methods, they can become more aware of the nature of what they do, and thus do it better. Thinking about method is empowering. When I require myself to explain what I do, I am likely to discover how to improve what I earlier may have taken for granted. In the process, I am likely to become more committed to what it is that I have improved.

Id. at 831.

33 *See, e.g.*, Martha Minow, *Beyond Universality*, 1989 U. CHI. LEGAL F. 115 (suggesting that the validity of feminism need not be connected to its distinctiveness).

34 It is also to raise the question of whether the notion of "ideology," so central to Marxist and Neo-Marxist critiques of political economy, is still viable. For a recent defense of critique's continuing viability in the realm of culturally produced objects, see JOHN B. THOMPSON, IDEOLOGY AND MODERN CULTURE 320-27 (1990).

35 *See supra* text accompanying note 2. *See generally* CHARLES JENCKS, WHAT IS POST-MODERNISM? (1986).

Just as feminists began to develop sophisticated theories of law, creating a jurisprudence of their own, postmodernism raised the question of whether a systematic jurisprudence was possible. This question arose naturally from feminist explorations in the realm of postmodernity, where issues of gender, sex, and identity are endlessly debated.[36] These debates are important—even critical—for feminist jurisprudence. A jurisprudence is no better than the general philosophical positions it assumes.[37] Thus, there can be no jurisprudence if there are no answers to questions of truth, justification, critique, knowledge, and normativity. By challenging the modernist stance on these topics, postmodernism necessarily calls into question the modes, manners, and methods of jurisprudence.

The connection between postmodernism and feminist jurisprudence, then, is determined by whether and to what extent feminist jurisprudence can tie its future to the future of modernist assumptions about truth, reason, and normativity. With respect to postmodernism, the stakes for feminist jurisprudence are clear: if modernism is considered to be at an end, has feminism reached its terminus as well? This is the question with which this Article is concerned. Before considering this question, we must take a closer look at modernism and postmodernism.

B. Mapping Modernity

Modernism is the form of thought identified with the spirit of the Enlightenment,[38] whose familiar story is captured by Jeffrey Stout's felicitous phrase "the flight from authority."[39] Spurred on by the power of science and its control over nature, philosophy replaced the medieval emphasis on custom, ritual, authority, and cos-

---

36 For a recent collection of papers on the social aspects of gender construction, see THE SOCIAL CONSTRUCTION OF GENDER (Judith Lorber & Susan A. Farrell eds., 1991).

37 *See* CAROL SMART, FEMINISM AND THE POWER OF LAW 69 (1989) ("The concept of jurisprudence presumes an identifiable unity of law, hence basic principles of justice, rights, or equity are presumed to underpin all aspects of law.").

38 As previously mentioned, the focus of this Article is on a small aspect of the vast picture of modernism. *See supra* note 11 and accompanying text.

39 *See* JEFFREY STOUT, THE FLIGHT FROM AUTHORITY: RELIGION, MORALITY, AND THE QUEST FOR AUTONOMY 2-3 (1981).

> [M]odern thought was born in a crisis of authority, took shape in flight from authority, and aspired from the start to autonomy from all traditional influence whatsoever; . . . the quest for autonomy was also an attempt to deny the historical reality of having been influenced by tradition; and . . . this quest therefore could not but fail.

Id.

mology with a self-conscious preoccupation with legitimacy,[40] progress, civility, rationality, and human emancipation.[41]

Modernism is exemplified by three axes which, together, provide a three-dimensional perspective.[42]

> 1. Epistemological Foundationalism: the view that knowledge can only be justified to the extent it rests on indubitable foundations;
> 2. Theory of Language: language has one of two functions—it represents ideas or states of affairs, or it expresses the attitudes of the speaker;
> 3. Individual and Community: "society" is best understood as an aggregation of "social atoms."[43]

These three components of the modernist picture should not be viewed as simply parts of a whole. Each represents not merely an idea or element in a picture, but an axis which, considered with the others, enables one to see a broad range of theories as all of a piece.

As the label suggests, epistemological foundationalism is an epistemological axis, with foundationalism[44] at one end and skepticism[45] at the other. Perhaps the most representative rationalist

---

40 *See* HANS BLUMENBERG, THE LEGITIMACY OF THE MODERN AGE (Robert M. Wallace trans., 1983) (defending the idea of progress as a secular notion).

41 If any single theme runs through the whole of modernity it is the idea of autonomy. In politics, the subject is free to decide her own conception of the good; in art, the work of art must be allowed to "speak for itself." Literature has the same hopes for itself, as does law. When the tradition starts to slip away, and the autonomy of the text is thereby threatened, the anxiety may be expressed in terms of fetishization. For a discussion of this phenomenon in music, see Howard M. Brown, *Pedantry or Liberation? A Sketch of the Historical Performance Movement*, *in* AUTHENTICITY AND EARLY MUSIC, *supra* note 9, at 27-56.

42 *See* Nancey Murphy & James W. McClendon, Jr., *Distinguishing Modern and Postmodern Theologies*, 5 MODERN THEOLOGY 199 (1989) (describing modernity by reference to three axes). *See also* Nancey Murphy, *Scientific Realism and Postmodern Philosophy*, 41 BRIT. J. PHIL. SCI. 291 (1990) (describing postmodern philosophy of science). One could reasonably take issue with many aspects of this representation of modernism. The story of modernism is far more complex than this simple representation of its genealogy can depict. These difficulties notwithstanding, this representation is heuristically defensible in that important aspects of modernism are identified and isolated for study. In short, used with appropriate caution, this picture of modernist thought is useful.

43 Murphy, *supra* note 42, at 292.

44 *See* D.W. HAMLYN, THE THEORY OF KNOWLEDGE 10 (1970).

> There is a tendency to think of the corpus of knowledge as a building that is rising upward and that those who increase the stock of knowledge are building additional stories on to the existing fabric. If the foundations are not secure the whole building will eventually come crashing to the ground.

Id.

45 *See id.* at 7-8 ("Philosophical skepticism . . . raises fundamental doubts about the possibility of knowing anything at all."). For a broad essay on skepticism in the tradition of analytic philosophy, see John Skorupski, *The Intelligibility of Skepticism*, *in* THE ANALYTIC TRADITION 1-29 (David Bell & Neil Cooper eds., 1990).

foundationalist[46] is René Descartes.[47] In essence, Descartes saw the problem of knowledge as a problem about certainty. Separating belief from illusion required a method, and in response to that need, Descartes invented the "method of doubt."[48] This process of validating a belief required that the belief be submitted to an inner (mental) tribunal wherein it was interrogated. An idea that survived this process of questioning earned the label "clear and distinct": that which could not be doubted—the indubitable—was valid and, thus, "knowledge."[49] Descartes' emphasis on method and validation led, not surprisingly, to the valorization of mathematics, science, and geometry, for it was in these areas that he found that which was most certain: axiom, system, and deduction.[50]

The other foundationalist approach to knowledge is empiricism. This theory replaces the rationalist emphasis on the formal relations between ideas with an appeal to our ordinary, commonsense understanding of experience.[51] When we see an object, we have a retinal impression of a thing that exists in space and time; to put it more colloquially, we have an experience of another body. Providing an explanation for such an experience (that is, demonstrating how it is possible and what having that experience involves)

---

46 For the rationalist, the flux of experience cannot be understood without resort to ideas, for it is through ideas that experience is organized and knowledge achieved. But which ideas are correct and which illusory? Rationalists of all stripes take this question seriously; however, the way in which they take it seriously cannot go unnoticed. The rationalist has no need to consult other people in answering the question "How do I know my beliefs are true?" With introspection, such an individual can gain knowledge of the world through the methodological discernment of ideas. True beliefs are those that accord with clear and distinct ideas. In short, "one could define rationalism as the view that knowledge about the world is the development of what, in some sense, we already know in the form of clear, distinct, and mutually consistent ideas present to our consciousness." ROBERT ACKERMANN, DATA, INSTRUMENTS AND THEORY 7 (1985).

47 For an interesting essay on Descartes' account of subjectivity and the relationship of his thought to modernity, see DALIA JUDOVITZ, SUBJECTIVITY AND REPRESENTATION IN DESCARTES: THE ORIGINS OF MODERNITY (1988).

48 For an excellent discussion of the place of Descartes' method of doubt in modernist arguments over validity and belief, see ROBERT B. PIPPIN, MODERNISM AS A PHILOSOPHICAL PROBLEM 23-25 (1991).

49 *See* ROY BOYNE, FOUCAULT AND DERRIDA: THE OTHER SIDE OF REASON 42 (1990).

> For Descartes, when the understanding perceives something clearly and distinctly, we can be sure that it perceives truly, because God, who is not a deceiver, gave us the powers that we have, and it is inconceivable that where we perceive something clearly God intended that we should be deceived. It follows from this that corporeal things "possess all the properties which I clearly and distinctly understand."

Id. (citation omitted).

50 *See* René Descartes, *Discourse on Method*, *in* ESSENTIAL WORKS OF DESCARTES 12 (Lowell Bair trans., 1961).

51 *See* HAMLYN, *supra* note 44, at 34.

without referring to anything "in" the mind is the gravamen of empiricism.[52] Empiricism is foundationalist in that, for the empiricist,

> verification and justification, telling whether something is true and backing up one's claims about what is true, must rely eventually upon the evidence of one's senses; not in the first instance, maybe, but at the end of the day. What else could we appeal to, to tell us whether something is true, than the evidence of our senses? This is a good sound empiricist question. So the evidence of our senses is what we start from when we need to construct a justification for our beliefs, on this approach.[53]

Skepticism[54] is not necessarily tied to either the rationalist or the empiricist strand of foundationalism. It is therefore a mistake to characterize the skeptic as one who denies the rationalist or the empiricist account of knowledge. The skeptic does not deny that what is described *as* knowledge is *in fact* knowledge. Rather, the skeptic denies that we ever *have* knowledge. For example, David Hume believed that, although we had to assume its existence, we could not *prove* the existence of the external world.[55] All we have on which to base our knowledge of causation is a constant conjunction of sense impressions. These impressions—raw input from the outside world—are the only available bases for knowledge.[56]

---

52 *See* DAVID HUME, ENQUIRIES CONCERNING HUMAN UNDERSTANDING AND THE PRINCIPLES OF MORALS 49-50 (L.A. Selby-Bigge ed., 1975) (noting that ideas in the mind are generated by sense impressions).

53 JONATHAN DANCY, AN INTRODUCTION TO CONTEMPORARY EPISTEMOLOGY 86 (1985).

54 The great critic of skepticism is, of course, Immanuel Kant. Kant takes seriously the skeptical claim that we can never "know" the truth of any proposition, advancing a "critical philosophy" of transcendental idealism. *See* IMMANUEL KANT, CRITIQUE OF PURE REASON (Norman Kemp Smith ed. & trans., 1929); IMMANUEL KANT, CRITIQUE OF PRACTICAL REASON (Lewis W. Beck trans., 1956); IMMANUEL KANT, CRITIQUE OF JUDGMENT (Werner S. Pluhar trans., 1987). A recent treatment of Kant's theory of knowledge is found in HUBERT SCHWYZER, THE UNITY OF UNDERSTANDING (1990). For a brilliant analysis of the aporias of judgment, and of Kant's solution to them, see HOWARD CAYGILL, THE ART OF JUDGEMENT (1989). For a breathtakingly quick run through the whole of Kantian critical philosophy, see GILLES DELEUZE, KANT'S CRITICAL PHILOSOPHY (Hugh Tomlinson & Barbara Habberjam trans., 1984).

55 *See* DAVID HUME, A TREATISE OF HUMAN NATURE 187 (L.A. Selby-Bigge ed., 1888) (We may well ask, "*What causes induce us to believe in the existence of body*? but 'tis in vain to ask, *Whether there be body or not*? That is a point, which we must take for granted in all our reasonings.").

56 Modern philosophy had wrestled with the relationship between epistemology and vision long before the Vienna Positivists turned their attention to the matter. *See* 2 ARTHUR SCHOPENHAUER, THE WORLD AS WILL AND REPRESENTATION (E.F.J. Payne trans., 1958) (criticizing Kant's aesthetics and epistemology for inattention to the physiology of apperception). For a discussion of vision as a theme in modernity, see JONATHAN CRARY, TECHNIQUES OF THE OBSERVER: ON VISION AND MODERNITY IN THE NINETEENTH CENTURY (1990). In our own century, the idea that knowledge is built up from simple elements in sensory experience was taken to new heights by the Vienna Circle. Led by the philosopher Rudolf Carnap, the Circle advanced a wide-ranging program for the consti-

In sum, knowledge on the modernist view is foundational, whether derived from rationalism or empiricism. For modernists, the only question is whether you believe in foundations or are dubious of the foundational enterprise. "Taking epistemology seriously" does not require a commitment to one end of the axis or the other: rather it merely requires that one be captivated by the questions that animate the poles of the axes.

The two poles of the language axis represent the two functions of language. Language either refers to objects in the world or is expressive of the attitudes, preferences, or emotions of the speaker. One pole, representationalism, is closely linked with epistemological foundationalism. If language is a medium for referring to objects in the world, then knowledge of what something is can be gleaned from that object's representation in language. The point of studying language is to study the ways in which words refer to things.

In their heyday, modernist philosophers advanced representational theories of language that viewed words as place holders or stand-ins for things.[57] In the twentieth century, the pre-1929 work of Ludwig Wittgenstein is the paradigmatic expression of such theories, establishing the program of "logical atomism," which empha-

---

tution of knowledge in fields as diverse as philosophy, sociology, architecture, and language studies. Underlying the subject-matter divisions of the Circle's broad program was a simple yet powerful approach to knowledge, one with philosophical, cultural and political dimensions. Peter Galison describes the details of the program in two seemingly disparate arenas: science and architecture. He notes that the Vienna Positivists' program

> sought to instantiate a modernism emphasizing what I will call "transparent construction," a manifest building up from simple elements to all higher forms that would, by virtue of the systematic constructional program itself, guarantee the exclusion of the decorative, mystical, or metaphysical. There was a political dimension to this form of construction: by basing it on simple, accessible units, they hoped to banish incorporation of nationalist or historical features.
>
> From simple observation reports ("protocol statements") and logical connectives (such as "if/then," "or," "and"), the logical positivists sought to ground a "scientific," antiphilosophical philosophy that would set all reliable knowledge on strong foundations and isolate it from the unreliable. Since all valid inferences would be built out of these basic statements, the sciences would be unified by their shared starting points. For their part, the Bauhäusler hoped to use scientific principles to combine primitive color relations and basic geometrical forms to eliminate the decorative and create a new antiaesthetic aesthetic that would prize functionality. So close had the two groups come in their shared vision of modernism that, when the Bauhaus reconvened as the New Bauhaus in Chicago after fleeing the Nazis, the New Bauhaus imported the Vienna Circle's logical positivism as a fundamental component of its basic design program.

Peter Galison, *Aufbau/Bauhaus: Logical Positivism and Architectural Modernism*, 16 CRITICAL INQUIRY 709, 710-11 (1990).

57 *See* RICHARD RORTY, PHILOSOPHY AND THE MIRROR OF NATURE 257-312 (1979).

sizes the reduction of sentence elements to their constituent parts in the world.[58] In describing Wittgenstein's theory, David Pears explains the method this way:

> We evidently do succeed in using this language to describe the world, but how is this done? [Wittgenstein's] answer is that we succeed only because there is a fixed grid of possible combinations of objects to which the structure of our language conforms. The grid must exist and connections must be made with it if language is going to work. But it clearly does work and so the metaphysical conclusions follow.[59]

Viewing language as the instantiation of some structure or grid is a way of answering the question, "How does language represent the world?" A related, and for law more important, question is, "How can one see a variety of situations as being the same thing?" This question focuses on the role language plays in connecting a variety of factual contexts which, despite their differences, can be said to be the same.[60]

If language is not a means of referring, then what else can it be? If one accepts the representationalist claim that language does refer to things in the world, then what becomes of ethical discourse? The Vienna Circle recommended that ethics, together with the whole of continental philosophy, be dismissed as "bad poetry."[61] On this view, the only alternative is to develop an account of language as a mode of expression. Thus, moral judgments are not "true," and do

---

58 LUDWIG WITTGENSTEIN, TRACTATUS LOGICO-PHILOSOPHICUS (D.F. Pears & B.F. McGuinness trans., 1974).

59 1 DAVID PEARS, THE FALSE PRISON: A STUDY OF THE DEVELOPMENT OF WITTGENSTEIN'S PHILOSOPHY 6 (1987).

60 For example, an offer can be accepted orally, in writing, by telegram, by smoke signal, and so on. What makes these different ways of acting "the same thing," that is, "acceptance"? Some modern philosophies of language unpack the idea that different contexts are "the same thing" by isolating those elements that are shared. There exists, it is argued, an "essence" that can be captured by language, mirrored in thought, and which reflects the external world. The following passage explicates this view:

> The meaning of words like "death," therefore, is not to be found in some set of conventions; meaning is neither a set of standard examples, nor a set of properties conventionally assigned to a symbol. The meaning of a word like "death" is only to be found in the best scientific theory we can muster about the true nature of that kind of event. By assuming that there are such true natures of natural kinds of things, the theory of meaning presupposed by our usage is aptly termed a *realist* theory of meaning.

Michael S. Moore, *A Natural Law Theory of Interpretation*, 58 S. CAL. L. REV. 279, 300 (1985). For a similar view, consciously adopting a semantics of "natural kinds," see David O. Brink, *Legal Theory, Legal Interpretation, and Judicial Review*, 17 PHIL. & PUB. AFF. 105, 111-12 (1988). For a critique of Brink's position, see Dennis M. Patterson, *Realist Semantics and Legal Theory*, 2 CANADIAN J.L. & JURISPRUDENCE 175 (1989).

61 For an entertaining summary of the tenets of the Vienna Circle and its program of logical positivism, see DONALD PALMER, LOOKING AT PHILOSOPHY: THE UNBEARABLE HEAVINESS OF PHILOSOPHY MADE LIGHTER 330-38 (1988).

not "represent" the world; rather, they are "expressions of preference, expressions of attitude or feeling, insofar as they are moral or evaluative in character."[62]

Finally, we address the third modernist axis, whose poles are individualism and collectivism. To the individualist, society is composed simply of "social atoms,"[63] each endowed with needs and desires the existence and identity of which are known (internally) to each.[64] Political economy is best understood from the perspective of individual motivation.[65] The individualist eschews all talk of public values, group norms, or "structures." Methodological individualism is the explanatory model for understanding.

The collectivist counters that the *class* to which a person belongs is far more foundational than the individual. Class is one of many constitutive social facts that shape the individual, making her what she is. At its most radical, collectivism maintains that the individual is not in control of her own fate, but is produced by forces beyond her control. Agents are individually capable of making free and rational decisions with respect to their preferences only to the extent they are able to become aware of and break free from the structures that shape their choices.[66]

Together, these three axes yield the following picture of modern thought.[67]

---

62 ALASDAIR MACINTYRE, AFTER VIRTUE 11 (1981).

63 *See generally* ELIZABETH H. WOLGAST, THE GRAMMAR OF JUSTICE 1-27 (1987) (discussing the ontological and conceptual foundations of liberalism, and specifically, the theory of individuality as social atomism).

64 There are two "spaces" that together compose the individual. The realm of right, which is created by reason, is divided into two spheres, the public and the private. The public sphere is one of right. In this realm, private action is restricted to the extent it impacts on the right of others to act similarly. The private sphere is the realm of individual choice in actions which, from the perspective of the individual, are good. This account of the relationship between reason, agency, and normativity was first established by Immanuel Kant. *See* IMMANUEL KANT, GROUNDWORK OF THE METAPHYSIC OF MORALS (H.J. Paton trans., 1964). For a discussion of this perspective in the light of the postmodern critique of agent-centered reason, see JOHN MCGOWAN, POSTMODERNISM AND ITS CRITICS 31-43 (1991).

65 *See* ADAM SMITH, THE WEALTH OF NATIONS 119 (1970).

> It is not from the benevolence of the butcher, the brewer or the baker that we expect our dinner, but from their regard to their own self interest. We address ourselves not to their humanity but to their self-love, and never talk to them of our own necessities but of their advantages.

Id.

66 For an application of argument to contract theory, see Jay M. Feinman, *The Significance of Contract Theory*, 58 U. CIN. L. REV. 1283 (1990).

67 This diagram is taken from Murphy & McClendon, *supra* note 42, at 199. As mentioned above, our focus with respect to modernism is on the question "In what does knowledge consist?" This Article advances the position that knowledge is the demonstrable ability to move within a linguistic practice. This view represents both a substantive position on knowledge and an alternative to views of knowledge labeled as

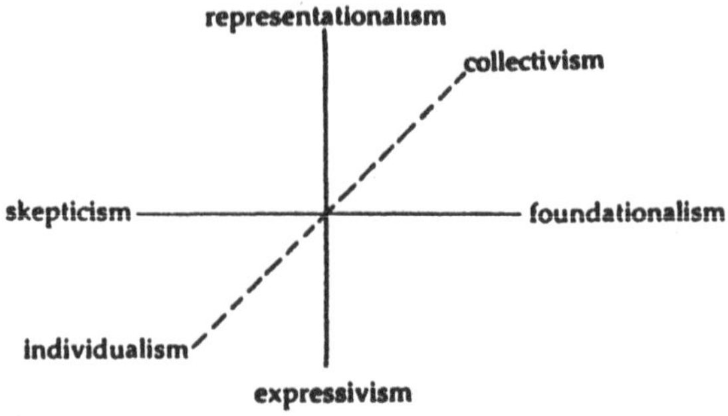

FIGURE 1

C. Postmodern Thought

Postmodern thought may be defined as "any mode of thought that departs from the three modern axes described above without reverting to premodern categories."[68] It must be emphasized that postmodernism does not involve the reconstitution of any or all of these axes. Postmodern projects depart from these axes, seeking to rethink the problems from a perspective that is nonuniversalist or "local" in character, holistic, and discursive.[69] As we shall see, the movement from the modernist picture of knowledge to the postmodern view of the world took place through a gradual shift in perspective. Not surprisingly, the shift began on modernist terms.

The story of science from the seventeenth to the twentieth century is best told as the rise of experimentation as the central focus of philosophical debates over the ground of knowledge.[70] This em-

---

modernist or postmodernist. One can be skeptical of claims that we are in postmodernity without forsaking a position in the modern-postmodern debate about knowledge.

68 Murphy & McClendon, *supra* note 42, at 199. These premodern categories are authority (specifically, religious authority) and cosmology—an understanding of the world that explains the existence of the universe by postulating the existence of a deity. *See* ANTHONY FLEW, A DICTIONARY OF PHILOSOPHY 77-79 (2d ed. 1979). For a broader version of the story of modernism, see STEPHEN TOULMIN, COSMOPOLIS: THE HIDDEN AGENDA OF MODERNITY (1990); MARSHALL BERMAN, ALL THAT'S SOLID MELTS INTO AIR: THE EXPERIENCE OF MODERNITY (1988). For a recent work concentrating on the cultural aspects of postmodernism, see FREDERIC JAMESON, POSTMODERNISM, OR, THE CULTURAL LOGIC OF LATE CAPITALISM (1991). An excellent bibliography on postmodernism is found in AFTER THE FUTURE: POSTMODERN TIMES AND PLACES 333-50 (Gary Shapiro ed., 1990).

69 I will argue in Part III that this position is best described as "narrational."

70 This is only a recent realization, first brought to light in ACKERMANN, *supra* note 46. *See also* PETER GALISON, HOW EXPERIMENTS END (1987) (reviewing experiments on gyromagnetic effects and the production of scientific knowledge). The usual story of the progress of scientific knowledge goes like this:

> It has become usual in recent history of science to rehearse the shortcomings of standard textbook presentations of scientific progress: observations not in accord with previous conceptions of the world accumulate until they force a new set of theoretical views on the scientific community.

phasis is due to the empiricist basis of positivism, the most influential theory of scientific knowledge.[71] During the 1950s and 1960s, the positivist picture of knowledge received close scrutiny and was found wanting. The first chink in the positivist armor resulted from a blow that came from within positivism's own ranks, dealt by the philosopher and logician W.V.O. Quine.[72] In Quine's view, the idea of knowledge as a process of building from the simple to the complex, as well as the concomitant notion that knowledge is a matter of resonance between word (concept) and world, had to be scrapped. In their place, Quine substituted holism. This theory maintains that the truth of any one statement or proposition is a function not of its relationship to the world, but of the degree to which it "hangs together" with everything else we take to be true.[73]

> The totality of our so-called knowledge or beliefs, from the most casual matters of geography and history to the profoundest laws of atomic physics or even of pure mathematics and logic, is a man-made fabric which impinges on experience only along the edges. Or, to change the figure, total science is like a field of force whose boundary conditions are experience. A conflict with experience at the periphery occasions readjustments in the interior of the field. Truth values have to be redistributed over some of our statements. Reëvaluation of some statements entails reëvaluation of others, because of their logical interconnections—the logical laws being in turn simply certain further statements of the system, certain further elements of the field. Having reëvaluated one statement we must reëvaluate some others, which may be statements logically connected with the first or may be the statements of logi-

---

> Even now it is not hard to find physics textbooks that recount the origins of special relativity in terms of the inexorable march of optical ether-drift experiments. According to these potted versions of history, Einstein "simply" generalized the clear observational fact that motion with respect to the ether could not be observed. In this way the strength of physical argumentation is rhetorically linked to its connection with observation (or experiment) and the historical sequence is described in such a way as to enhance the role of experience and denigrate the corresponding theoretical analysis.

Peter Galison, *History, Philosophy, and the Central Metaphor*, 2 SCI. CONTEXT 197, 198-99 (1988).

71 *See* DAVID OLDROYD, THE ARCH OF KNOWLEDGE 168-262 (1986) (tracing the origins of the positivist model of knowledge).

72 *See* WILLARD V.O. QUINE, *Two Dogmas of Empiricism*, *in* FROM A LOGICAL POINT OF VIEW 20-46 (1953) (arguing against the idea of a "basic" unit of knowledge and urging instead a view of knowledge as embedded in "the whole of science."). *See also* Galison, *supra* note 70, at 203 ("Quine strongly opposed the total separation of observation from other forms of knowledge; for him, all were up for evaluation."); Murphy, *supra* note 42, at 294 ("Quine not only replaced the foundationalist theory of knowledge with a holist account, but also provided a new picture or metaphor—that of a web or network of beliefs—to replace the 'layer-cake' model."). For a very quick tour through Quine's thought, see Hilary Putnam, *Misling*, LONDON REV. OF BOOKS, April 21, 1988, at 11-13.

73 QUINE, *supra* note 72, at 42-43.

cal connections themselves. But the total field is so underdetermined by its boundary conditions, experience, that there is much latitude of choice as to what statements to reëvaluate in the light of any single contrary experience. No particular experiences are linked with any particular statements in the interior of the field, except indirectly through considerations of equilibrium affecting the field as a whole.

If this view is right, it is misleading to speak of the empirical content of an individual statement—especially if it is a statement at all remote from the experiential periphery of the field. Furthermore it becomes folly to seek a boundary between synthetic statements, which hold contingently on experience, and analytic statements, which hold come what may. Any statement can be held true come what may, if we make drastic enough adjustments elsewhere in the system.[74]

Quine's picture of knowledge of the external world changed the way people thought about the construction of knowledge. His breakthrough was to see knowledge not as a matter of foundations—building up from bedrock—but as a function of one's ability to move about within a holistic web, be it a web of theory or of intersubjective practice. It is in this shift from simplicity, reductionism, and foundations to holism, network, and totality that Quine's epistemology earns the description "postmodern."[75] Quine's embrace of holism, together with his pragmatism on questions of truth,[76] invites comparison with the referential theory of language, the second of the three aspects of modernism displaced in postmodernity.

Language is the central preoccupation of contemporary philosophy.[77] But how does language work? Are we lost in the labyrinth of language, as Nietzsche thought,[78] or is language simply a medium through which the world is represented (or, to put the emphasis where it should be, *re*presented)? Does language have the power to represent nature as it is in itself, *sub specie aeternitatis*? That is, in language do words represent states of affairs in the world in such a way that the truth of any proposition may be discerned by comparing the proposition with the state of affairs it depicts?

---

74 *Id.*

75 *See* Murphy, *supra* note 42, at 294 ("As candidate for the title of postmodern epistemologist I nominate Willard V.O. Quine.").

76 For a discussion of this aspect of Quine's thought, see CHRISTOPHER HOOKWAY, QUINE: LANGUAGE, EXPERIENCE AND REALITY 50-58 (1988).

77 *See* RICHARD RORTY, CONSEQUENCES OF PRAGMATISM xiii-xlvii (1982) (providing a wide-ranging account of the function of language in philosophical discourse).

78 *See* Friedrich Nietzsche, *On Truth and Lies in a Nonmoral Sense*, *in* PHILOSOPHY AND TRUTH: SELECTIONS FROM NIETZSCHE'S NOTEBOOKS OF THE EARLY 1870'S 79-100 (Daniel Breazeale ed. & trans., 1979).

Postmodern approaches to language[79] do not present arguments *against* the modern, representationalist view.[80] Rather, postmodernist conceptions of the word-world relation see the modernist picture of propositional, representational truth[81] as unintelligible—as a project that never gets off the ground.[82] The focus of

---

79 For a discussion of the relationship between language and representation in modernism and postmodernism, see SCOTT LASH, SOCIOLOGY OF POSTMODERNISM 12 (1990) ("Modernism . . . had clearly differentiated and autonomized the roles of signifier, signified, and referent. Post-modernization on the contrary *problematizes* these distinctions, and especially the status and relationship of signifier and referent, or put another way, representation and reality.").

80 Rather, the postmodern emphasis is on the question of what can be *done* with language. *See* 2 RICHARD RORTY, PHILOSOPHICAL PAPERS (ESSAYS ON HEIDEGGER AND OTHERS) 58 (1991).

> [Donald] Davidson's account of human linguistic behavior takes for granted, as the later Wittgenstein also did, that there are no linguistic entities which are intrinsically relationless—none which, like the "simple names" of the Tractatus, are by nature relata. But Davidson's holism is more explicit and thoroughgoing than Wittgenstein's, and so its antiphilosophical consequences are more apparent. Whereas in the *Philosophical Investigations* Wittgenstein still toys with the idea of a distinction between the empirical and the grammatical, between nonphilosophical and philosophical inquiry, Davidson generalizes and extends Quine's refusal to countenance either a distinction between necessary and contingent truth or a distinction between philosophy and science. Davidson insists that we not think either of language in general or a particular language (say, English or German) as something which has distinct edges, something which forms a bounded whole and can thus become a distinct object of study or of philosophical theorizing.

Id. Rorty's claim that "Davidson's holism is more explicit and thoroughgoing than Wittgenstein's" is a red herring. Davidson's account of understanding is, in the vocabulary here in use, thoroughly modernist and empiricist—a far cry from the holist and pragmatist reading Rorty advances. The central reason Rorty's characterization of Davidson's position cannot be sustained is that, for Davidson, understanding is a matter of an empirical theory. *See* Donald Davidson, *A Nice Derangement of Epitaphs*, *in* TRUTH AND INTERPRETATION: PERSPECTIVES ON THE PHILOSOPHY OF DONALD DAVIDSON 433-446 (Ernest LePore ed., 1986).

> [C]laims about what would constitute a satisfactory theory are not . . . claims about the propositional knowledge of an interpreter, nor are they claims about the details of the inner workings of some part of the brain. They are rather claims about what must be said to give a satisfactory description of the competence of the interpreter. We cannot describe what an interpreter can do except by appeal to a recursive theory of a certain sort.

Id. at 438. Thus, understanding another person is a matter of having a theory about the sounds that emanate from her mouth. These sounds are interpreted by reference to a grid which is recursively mapped onto the audible output of the interlocutor. This, Rorty, claims, is pragmatism! For a Wittgensteinian critique of the pretensions and shortfalls of Davidson's account of understanding, see STEPHEN MULHALL, ON BEING IN THE WORLD: WITTGENSTEIN AND HEIDEGGER ON SEEING ASPECTS 91-122 (1990).

81 For a discussion of modernity, representation, and reason, see Adam B. Seligman, *Towards a Reinterpretation of Modernity in an Age of Postmodernity*, *in* THEORIES OF POSTMODERNITY 117-35 (Bryan S. Turner ed., 1990).

82 *See* JOSEPH ROUSE, KNOWLEDGE AND POWER 154 (1987).

> [The Realist] takes as already determined both the way the world is and our understanding of how our interpretations take it to be. The realist of

the dispute is the modernist theory of correspondence, specifically, the Sentence-Truth-World relation. To put it in a nutshell, the postmodern alternative replaces the modernist picture of Sentence-Truth-World with an account of understanding that emphasizes practice, warranted assertability, and pragmatism.[83]

In synthesizing the work of Dewey, Wittgenstein, Heidegger, and Davidson, Richard Rorty has rethought American Pragmatism.[84] His work, which ranges across areas as divergent as philosophy of mind and political theory, repeatedly returns to the argument

---

> course recognizes that we do not know in *advance* how the world is. But once we have some definite interpretations of the world, we can use them as the basis for our actions, which in turn test the adequacy of our interpretations. If our actions fail to achieve their aims, something must be wrong with the interpretations they were based on. If our actions succeed, this success of course does not entail that their underlying interpretations do accord with the reality they interpret. But if a wide variety of actions in differing circumstances generally succeed, the best explanation for their success is that those interpretations at least approximately accord with the way those objects really are. But where do we acquire our understanding of what our various interpretations do say about the world and of what would count as success in our actions? The realist needs to give some account of understanding such that we can understand how our interpretations take the world to be independent of how the world actually is. Otherwise the alleged independence of object and interpretation can never get off the ground. Sentences and practices do not have ready-made meanings, nor do they acquire meaning by convention. (How could the parties involved understand what they were agreeing to?) They acquire meaning only in their performance or use.

Id.

83 The following summary of the cumulative effect of Quine, the later Wittgenstein, and like-minded philosophers speaks to this point.

> When it comes to deciding between theories constructed within different conceptual schemes it is possible in Quine's view to have a situation of under-determination—that is, of there being no factually objective way to decide between them. Because ontology is relative to conceptual schemes there is no decisive fact of the matter. But Quine did wish to emphasize the importance of empirical enquiry to our understanding of the world. Empirical enquiry takes place at the boundaries of holistic networks or structures of theory—where they meet the world—and those boundaries gradually change, so altering the conceptual structure, but not in any sudden or pervasive way.
>
> A corollary of this position was a radically different conception of epistemology: seeing it not as the reconstruction of first principles of all knowledge, being transcendent of particular discourses, but rather as *psychology*, being the study of particular acts or behavioural patterns of knowing.
>
> This fundamental questioning of the nature of epistemology, associated also with the later work of Wittgenstein and to some extent with the later work of [Rudolf] Carnap, had a profound but unfortunate effect. In Quine's words, it "loosed a wave . . . of epistemological nihilism", reflected partly, as he says, in a tendency "to belittle the role of evidence and to accentuate cultural relativism."

Christopher Lloyd, Explanation in Social History 73 (1986) (citation omitted).

84 By "American Pragmatism" I refer to the thought of, among others, John Dewey, Charles S. Peirce, and William James.

that the modernist approach to truth is simply not worth the effort to keep it afloat. Rorty summarizes his position this way:

> For the pragmatist, the notion of "truth" as something "objective" is just a confusion between
>
> (I) Most of the world is as it is whatever we think about it (that is, our beliefs have very limited causal efficacy)
>
> and
>
> (II) There is something out there in addition to the world called "the truth about the world" (what [William] James sarcastically called "this tertium quid intermediate between the facts *per se*, on the one hand, and all knowledge of them, actual or potential, on the other").
>
> The pragmatist wholeheartedly assents to (I)—not as an article of metaphysical faith but simply as a belief that we have never had any reason to doubt—and cannot make sense of (II). When the realist tries to explain (II) with
>
> (III) The truth about the world consists in a relation of "correspondence" between certain sentences (many of which, no doubt, have yet to be formulated) and the world itself
>
> the pragmatist can only fall back on saying, once again, that many centuries of attempts to explain what "correspondence" is have failed . . . .[85]

Risking repetition, it must be emphasized that the modernist picture of successful communication is not being *replaced* with another explanatory picture. The postmodern approach to language eschews advancing explanations in favor of describing localized linguistic practices. Wittgenstein's later approach to language[86] is revolutionary[87] because his attack on modernist philosophical methods breaks down the distinction between explanation and the phenomenon being explained. All understanding occurs *in language*.[88] Lan-

---

85 RORTY, *supra* note 77, at xxvi.

86 I have detailed the parameters of Wittgenstein's linguistic philosophy and its importance for law in Dennis M. Patterson, *Wittgenstein and the Code: A Theory of Good Faith Performance and Enforcement Under Article Nine*, 137 U. PA. L. REV. 335, 352-73 (1988); Dennis M. Patterson, *Good Faith, Lender Liability and Discretionary Acceleration: Of Llewellyn, Wittgenstein, and the Uniform Commercial Code*, 68 TEX. L. REV. 169 (1989).

87 For a discussion of Wittgensteinian language philosophy in the context of modernism and postmodernism, see WELLMER, *supra* note 9, at 78 ("Wittgenstein's skeptical question is: 'How can I know what I am talking about? How can I know what I mean?' Language philosophy's critique destroys the subject as author and as the final judge of his meaning and intentions.").

88 This view disclaims the notion that "understanding" can occur in any private sense. Owing to its character as a public medium, language—and, thus, meaning—can never be relegated to the private realm. For a discussion of this point in the context of the philosophy of consciousness, see ERNST TUGENDHAT, SELF-CONSCIOUSNESS AND SELF-DETERMINATION 77-97 (Paul Stern trans., 1986) (discussing Wittgenstein on private language and its relationship to self-consciousness).

guage is the universal medium within which we think, act, and understand. The idea that language "corresponds" to something outside itself can never be fleshed out, because all talk about language itself remains *use of language*. No part of language can be torn from the whole and valorized as a meta-language, super-language, or "language about language." Wittgenstein addressed this matter in his first recorded thoughts about the language-world relation:

> But is *language* the *only* language?
> Why should there not be a mode of expression through which I can talk *about* language in such a way that it can appear to me in co-ordination with something else?
>
> Suppose that music were such a mode of expression: then it is at any rate characteristic of *science* that *no* musical themes can occur in it.
>
> I myself only write *sentences* down here. And why?
> *How* is language unique?[89]

So what does all of this mean for truth? If the modernist conception of truth is abandoned, are we not left with abject relativism?[90] Is not every claim to truth, every description of a state of

---

89 Ludwig Wittgenstein, Notebooks 1914-1916 52e (G.H. von Wright ed., G.E.M. Anscombe ed. & trans., 1969).

90 For a recent discussion of this theme, see Robert J. Lipkin, *Skepticism and the New Fuzziness*, 75 Cornell L. Rev. 811 (1990) (purporting to go "beyond fuzziness" in ethics and endorsing "moderate [healthy?] skepticism in normative discourse"). For a more partisan discussion of the relationship between epistemology, realism, and relativism in the light of recent debates in interpretive theory see Michael S. Moore, *The Interpretive Turn in Modern Theory: A Turn for the Worse?*, 41 Stan. L. Rev. 871 (1989). The "realist" ontology and epistemology Moore advocates is based on a model of science whose heyday was the nineteenth and early twentieth centuries. Its last gasp was uttered by Carl Hempel in the formation of the hypothetico-deductive model of truth. *See* Carl G. Hempel, Aspects of Scientific Explanation and Other Essays in the Philosophy of Science (1965). The empiricist proclivities of Hempelian method impel those blinded by its promise of objectivity and right representation to ignore the role of scientific practices and communities in the production of scientific knowledge. Of course, after Kuhn, few in the philosophy of science are as enthusiastic about realism in science as Moore is about realism in law or ethics. *See* Thomas Kuhn, The Structure of Scientific Revolutions (2d ed. 1970). For a recent, intelligent, and quite lively discussion of the current state of the philosophy of science, see Larry Laudan, Science and Relativism (1990) (narrating an imaginary dialogue between representatives of key positions in twentieth century philosophy and science, including those of Kuhn and Hempel).

In normative discourse, the realist view that Moore advocates assumes the following critical posture when describing positions that, in this Article, would be described as postmodernist:

> Telling us we must choose and that some choices will *seem* better than others, without giving any reasons why we should choose one way or the other or why the "seeming-better" should be taken to *be* better, does not engage us [read "does not engage me, (Moore)"]. Such suggestions are empty in the way that noncognitivist and existential ethics are always empty. For what it is worth, here in the realm of the noncognitivist, Rorty's world does not seem better to me. It seems a barren place in which all arguments are made only by pulling oneself out of deep existen-

affairs, as good or acceptable as any other? This is what the purveyors of "truth" would have us believe. The fact that we cannot demonstrate how language "cuts reality at the joints"[91] does not mean that we cannot come up with better or worse ways of carrying on our practices. This, at least, is the claim to be sustained.[92]

We saw earlier that in the modernist picture of knowledge, the individual controls her own fate. This picture presupposes "that any individual (given the basic sensory and intellectual equipment) is as competent as any other to form justified beliefs and speak the language."[93] To attain knowledge, the individual need not have contact with another self. Even when isolated from a community, an individual is capable of separating true from false beliefs. As Descartes demonstrated, all that is required is the right method, since truth and method are inextricably linked.

Postmodernism, on the contrary, challenges the primacy of the individual.[94] The postmodern conception of individuality casts the individual not as the subject in control of discourse, but as an arti-

---

> tial nausea, itself possible only by bad-faith forgetfulness that all arguments are rhetorical substitutes for the bullets one either does not possess or is unwilling to use.

Moore, *supra* at 904.

Moore's critique of Rorty utterly fails to come to terms with the philosophical problems that lead to the characterization of truth Rorty advances. Moore wants to marry truth to something that is mind-independent (for Moore, essences), and then create an epistemology that explains things, objects, properties, or relations and their representation in language. This is a failed project, as such diverse philosophers as Quine, Davidson, Wittgenstein, Sellars, Heidegger, and Putnam have shown. (Query: Are they all then existentialists?) What Moore refuses to see is that "[t]rying to make meaning accessible [on realist terms] has made truth inaccessible." Donald Davidson, *A Coherence Theory of Truth and Knowledge*, *in* TRUTH AND INTERPRETATION, *supra* note 80, at 313. By tying meaning to "the given" ("moral essences" for example) and truth to justification (here, an unexplicated notion of "best theory"), Moore embraces skepticism. What is the solution?

> [T]he thing to do is to marry truth and meaning to nothing and nobody but each other. The resulting marriage will be so intimate a relationship that a theory will *be* a theory of meaning, and conversely. But that theory will be of no use to a representationalist epistemology, nor to any other sort of epistemology. It will be an explanation of what people *do*, rather than of a non-causal, representing, relation in which they stand to non-human entities.

Richard Rorty, *Representation, Social Practice, and Truth*, 54 PHIL. STUD. 215, 219 (1988).

91 RICHARD RORTY, *Texts and Lumps*, *in* 1 OBJECTIVITY, RELATIVISM AND TRUTH: PHILOSOPHICAL PAPERS 80 (1991).

92 This claim is defended in Part III. *See infra* notes 231-91 and accompanying text.

93 Murphy, *supra* note 42, at 295.

94 *See generally* MANFRED FRANK, WHAT IS NEOSTRUCTURALISM? 362-454, *passim* (Sabine Wilke & Richard Gray trans., 1989) (reviewing the major theories and arguments of postmodernism); PAUL SMITH, DISCERNING THE SUBJECT (1988) (focusing on "the subject" as a product of discourse). For a piece that gets to the heart of what is and is not at stake in the debate over the subject, see John Smith, *The Transcendence of the Individual*, 19 DIACRITICS 80 (1989) (reviewing leading texts on the postmodern constitution of the subject). *See also* DAVID CARROLL, THE SUBJECT IN QUESTION: THE LANGUAGES OF THE-

fact produced by discourse. In applying this concept to feminism, Judith Butler makes the point this way:

> My suggestion is that the presumed universality and unity of the subject of feminism is effectively undermined by the constraints of the representational discourse in which it functions. Indeed, the premature insistence on a stable subject of feminism, understood as a seamless category of women, inevitably generates multiple refusals to accept the category. These domains of exclusion reveal the coercive and regulatory consequences of that construction, even when the construction has been elaborated for emancipatory purposes. Indeed, the fragmentation within feminism and the paradoxical opposition to feminism from "women" whom feminism claims to represent suggest the necessary limits of identity politics.[95]

But if identity, specifically sexual or gender identity, does not exist prior to practice, then from whence does identity issue? The answer, as we have seen, is "the community of discourse."[96] What does this mean? Butler explains:

> The antifoundationalist approach to coalition politics assumes neither that "identity" is a premise nor that the shape of meaning of a coalitional assemblage can be known prior to its achievement. Because the articulation of an identity within available cultural terms instates a definition that forecloses in advance the emergence of new identity concepts in and through politically gauged actions, the foundationalist tactic cannot take the transformation of expansion of existing identity concepts as a normative goal. Moreover, when agreed-upon identities or agreed-upon dialogic structures, through which already established identities are communicated, no longer constitute the theme or subject of politics, then identities can come into being and dissolve depending on the concrete practices that constitute them. Certain political practices institute identities on a contingent basis in order to accomplish whatever aims are new. Coalitional politics requires neither an ex-

---

ORY AND THE STRATEGIES OF FICTION (1982) (essaying the constitution of the subject vis-a-vis critical theory).

95 JUDITH BUTLER, GENDER TROUBLE: FEMINISM AND THE SUBVERSION OF IDENTITY 4 (1990).

96 *See* Murphy, *supra* note 42, at 295.

> In postmodern thought . . . the community plays an indispensable role. It is the community that must decide when to take anomalous facts seriously, and where to make changes in the Quinian network of beliefs. The language games and conventions in which one participates precede individual speech and determine what can and cannot be said. In short, language and the search for knowledge are communal achievements. So escape from either of the modern epistemological or linguistic axes calls for a corresponding detachment from the individualist axis as well.

Id.

panded category of "women" nor an internally multiplicitous self that offers its complexity at once.[97]

The postmodern critique of "the self," here expressed as a critique of gender identity, confirms the claim that ontology—what something is—is not a given but a construct. In the case of "woman," "[o]ne is not born, rather one becomes, a woman."[98] This point does not go far enough, as Butler's analysis of the discourse of "woman" demonstrates; for in every ongoing discursive practice involving the category "woman," that category is open to intervention and resignification.[99] The need to go further, then, leads us at last to consider the roles of sex and gender, and their constitution in law.

> The effort to locate a sexed nature before the law seems to be rooted understandably in the more fundamental project to be able to think that the patriarchal law is not universally true and all-determining. Indeed, if constructed gender is all there is, then there appears to be no "outside," no epistemic anchor in a precultural "before" that might serve as an alternative epistemic point of departure for a critical assessment of existing gender relations. Locating the mechanism whereby sex is transformed into gender is meant to establish not only the constructedness of gender, its unnatural and nonnecessary status, but the cultural universality of oppression in nonbiologic terms.
>
> . . .
>
> Only when the mechanism of gender construction implies the *contingency* of that construction does "constructedness" *per se* prove useful to the political project to enlarge the scope of possible gender configurations. If, however, it is a life of the body beyond the law or a recovery of the body before the law which then emerges as the normative goal of feminist theory, such a norm effectively takes the focus of feminist theory away from the concrete terms of contemporary cultural struggle.[100]

Butler here defines the postmodern project of feminism as nothing less than the subversion, at every turn, of modernist projections of "woman." The target of Butler's postmodern reconstruction of the relationship between gender and sex is the elevation of that relationship into a juridical category that takes the sexed body as gendered prior to its emergence from the order of discourse. Only after a break in this univocal link will the postmodern reconstruction of identity begin to be thought. Only through discourse will we know "woman": the unitary quality and character of

97 BUTLER, *supra* note 95, at 15-16.

98 SIMONE DE BEAUVOIR, THE SECOND SEX 267 (H.M. Parshley trans., 1953).

99 BUTLER, *supra* note 95, at 33.

100 *Id.* at 38.

"woman" will be deconstructed away. As Julia Kristeva puts it, "Strictly speaking 'woman' cannot be said to exist."[101]

II
THE FEMINIST CRITIQUE OF LAW

We began by asking, "What is at stake for feminist jurisprudence in the debate over postmodernism?" That debate implicates one question that stands above all others: the question of critique. If the modernist project of truth, right representation, legitimation, correspondence, and critique is abandoned, will feminist jurisprudence be left with tools adequate for the task of criticism and transformation? As we have seen, the modernist argues that validity and rational critique are not possible without philosophy.[102] On that view, then, feminism is not possible without philosophy. It is precisely this issue that divides contemporary feminist jurisprudence.

This Part considers the work of three contemporary feminist critics of the law.[103] Each scholar maintains a distinct perspective on the question of critique. One embraces the project of modernity. The second criticizes that project, but remains ambivalent about the postmodern option. The third embraces a thoroughly postmodern account of understanding and demonstrates the power of discourse to shape our understanding of the social world. Together, these critics illustrate the need for the current debate over the feminist critique of law to come to terms with the postmodern critique of reason.

---

101 *Id.* at 1 (*quoting* Julia Kristeva). This claim is not as radical as it may first appear.

> Kristeva sees different kinds of feminism as embodying different attitudes to the symbolic. Liberal, equal-rights feminism demands for women an equal rather than a marginal place in the symbolic. Radical feminism extols the distinctively feminine, which means it rejects the value placed on the symbolic altogether. A further stage, which Kristeva speaks of as the "third generation," would reject the very opposition of male and female as metaphysical, and attack the whole notion of sexual, or even general, identity.

DEBORAH CAMERON, FEMINISM & LINGUISTIC THEORY 127 (1985).

102 *See supra* text accompanying notes 38-67.

103 For a number of reasons, I have chosen to focus on individuals rather than themes. While it is true that everyone works within a more or less well-defined tradition or orientation in thought, a position's importance depends on the arguments made in its support. Arguments are developed in specific texts in support of specific points. It is useless to say that a given position makes certain assumptions that turn out to be false and then, on that basis, to impeach the position. Such "criticism" is often dismissed as superficial (I am reminded of the reception given Roberto Unger's critique of liberalism in ROBERTO UNGER, KNOWLEDGE AND POLITICS (1975)).

I also believe that all three of the feminist authors I critique advance arguments found in the work of others. In other words, the positions which I focus on are in no way out of the mainstream. They represent main currents of thought in feminist jurisprudence.

A. Robin West

The feminist struggle with law is a struggle over the categories used to organize legal experience and, thus, legal reality. Robin West extends the critique of legal categories to a critique of the jurisprudence of legal categorization. In *Jurisprudence and Gender*,[104] Professor West advocates a jurisprudence that avoids reduplicating the patriarchal categories of contemporary legalisms. Hers is "a truly feminist jurisprudence, . . . define[d] as a jurisprudence built upon feminist insights into women's true nature, rather than upon masculine insights into 'human' nature."[105] Startling as it may seem, West denies that women are "human beings."[106] This "philosophical fact," as she terms it, is the crux of her dispute with contemporary patriarchal jurisprudence.

We begin by reviewing Professor West's critique of patriarchal jurisprudence, and then turn to her alternative schema. The question to which our attention will ultimately be directed is, "Where does West's position fit on the divide between modern and postmodern?" Is hers a postmodern critique of patriarchal jurisprudence, or does her critique of patriarchy and development of a theoretical alternative simply assume the truth of the modernist conception of reason, thereby substituting one set of problems (modernity) for another (patriarchy)?

Is critical legal theory so different from the liberal legal theory it criticizes? Is the left-wing male "more sensitive to the political underpinnings of purportedly neutral legalistic constructs" than is a liberal legalist?[107] Professor West thinks not. In fact, she sees the struggle between the left and the right as a sort of schoolyard brawl—boys being boys. The differences between radical and mainstream politics are largely illusory, for they both represent "the paradigmatically male experience of the inevitability of separation of the self from the rest of the . . . natural world."[108] Both versions of experience are true, but each presents a different side of *the same experience*. Liberal legalists describe the life of the self as one of freedom and autonomy, a life of choices and assertion of individual personality.[109] The experience of the left is one of alienation and

---

104 Robin West, *Jurisprudence and Gender*, 55 U. CHI. L. REV. 1 (1988).

105 *Id.* at 3-4.

106 *Id.* at 4 ("Women, though, are not human beings.").

107 *Id.*

108 *Id.* at 5.

109 The basic architecture of liberal thought was developed by Kant. *See supra* note 54. For the contemporary expression of this spirit in political theory, see JOHN RAWLS, A THEORY OF JUSTICE (1971). For the legal component of liberal legalism, see Ernest J. Weinrib, *Legal Formality*, 97 YALE L.J. 949 (1988); Ernest J. Weinrib, *Law As a Kantian Idea of Reason*, 87 COLUM. L. REV. 472 (1987).

isolation from the Other.[110] The promise of liberation, so dear to the cheerleaders for democracy, rings hollow for critical theorists. Theirs is a perspective of despair and subjugation; they are crushed under the weight of legal categories.

But why are these two disparate views in fact views of the same thing, the same experience? The answer is that, unlike men, women are connected. Feminists disagree about exactly what this "connectedness" amounts to, or how best to characterize it. There are two principal views on the question. The first is cultural feminism, which emphasizes women's sense of "existential 'connection' to other human life,"[111] a connection not felt by men. This sense of connection is elevated into a *Weltanschauung* described as the "feminine perspective." Suzanna Sherry explains the perspective in the following passage:

> [T]he feminine perspective views individuals primarily as interconnected members of a community. Nancy Chodorow and Carol Gilligan, in groundbreaking studies on the development of self and morality, have concluded that women tend to have a more intersubjective sense of self than men and that the feminine perspective is therefore more other-directed . . . . *The essential difference between the male and female perspectives [is that] . . . "the basic feminine sense of self is connected to the world, the basic masculine sense of self is separate." Women thus tend to see others as extensions of themselves rather than as outsiders or competitors.*[112]

Why, Professor West asks, are men and women different in this essential way?[113] The cultural feminist explanation is that "women are more nurturant, caring, loving and responsible to others than are men."[114] These differences from men are not merely differences (or deficiencies, for that matter) but are strengths to be positively valued. Carol Gilligan has not only valorized these traits, but has also elevated them to the level of an essential social constitution for women—a veritable moral identity. West summarizes this perspective:

> [W]omen's potential for a material connection to life entails (either directly, as I have argued, or indirectly, through the reproduction of mothering) an experiential and psychological sense of connection with other human life, which in turn entails both women's concept of value, and women's concept of harm. Women's concept of value revolves not around the axis of autonomy, indi-

---

110 West, *supra* note 104, at 9-10.

111 *Id.* at 15.

112 *Id.* at 15-16 (quoting Suzanna Sherry, *Civic Virtue and the Feminine Voice in Constitutional Adjudication*, 72 VA. L. REV. 543, 584-85 (1986)).

113 West, *supra* note 104, at 16.

114 *Id.* at 17.

> viduality, justice and rights, as does men's, but instead around the axis of intimacy, nurturance, community, responsibility and care. For women, the creation of value, and the living of a good life, therefore depend upon relational, contextual, nurturant and affective responses to the needs of those who are dependent and weak, while for men the creation of value, and the living of the good life, depend upon the ability to respect the rights of independent co-equals, and the deductive, cognitive ability to infer from those rights rules for safe living. Women's concept of harm revolves not around a fear of annihilation by the other but around a fear of separation and isolation from the human community on which she depends, and which is dependent upon her. If, as I have suggested, cultural feminism is our dominant feminist dogma, then this account of the nature of women's lives constitutes the "official text" of feminism, just as liberal legalism constitutes the official text of legalism.[115]

Alternatively, radical feminism takes a very different stance on the question of difference. Unlike the "official" story of cultural feminism, the radical account describes the essence of "woman" as invasion and torment. Radical feminism views women's connection to others—precisely that which is celebrated by cultural feminists—as "the source of women's debasement, powerlessness, subjugation, and misery."[116] On this view, these debasing connections are the product of women's material constitution (e.g., its aspects of reproduction[117] and intercourse[118]). West glosses these constitutive conditions this way:

> The material, sporadic violation of a woman's body occasioned by pregnancy and intercourse implies an existential and pervasive violation of her privacy, integrity and life projects. According to radical feminists, women's longings for individuation, physical privacy, and independence go well beyond the desire to avoid the dangers of rape or unwanted pregnancy. Women also long for liberation from the oppression of intimacy (and its attendant values) which both cultural feminism and most women officially, and wrongly, overvalue. Intimacy, in short, is *intrusive*, even when it isn't life threatening (perhaps *especially* when it isn't life threatening). An unwanted pregnancy is disastrous, but even a *wanted* pregnancy and motherhood are intrusive. The child *intrudes*, just as the fetus invades.
>
> Similarly, while unwanted heterosexual intercourse is disastrous, even wanted heterosexual intercourse is intrusive. The penis occupies the body and "divides the woman" internally, to use

115 *Id.* at 28.
116 *Id.* at 29.
117 *Id.*
118 *Id.* at 32-35.

> Andrea Dworkin's language, in consensual intercourse no less than in rape. It preempts, challenges, negates, and *renders impossible* the maintenance of physical integrity and the formation of a unified self. The deepest unofficial story of radical feminism may be that intimacy—the official value of cultural feminism—is itself oppressive. Women secretly, unofficially, and surreptitiously long for the very individuation that cultural feminism insists women fear: the freedom, the independence, the individuality, the sense of wholeness, the confidence, the self-esteem, and the security of identity which can only come from a life, a history, a path, a voice, a sexuality, a womb, and a body of one's own.[119]

Just as there is an "official" and an "unofficial" story in legal theory, so too in feminist theory. West captures the contrasts in the following chart:

	THE OFFICIAL STORY (Liberal legalism and cultural feminism)		THE UNOFFICIAL STORY (Critical legalism and radical feminism)	
	Value	**Harm**	**Longing**	**Dread**
LEGAL THEORY (human beings)	**Autonomy**	**Annihilation; Frustration**	**Attachment; Connection**	**Alienation**
FEMINIST THEORY (women)	**Intimacy**	**Separation**	**Individuation**	**Invasion; Intrusion**

FIGURE 2

One might think that the unofficial stories in legal theory and feminism bear some relation to each other, but Professor West dismisses this suggestion as "the widespread and confused claim that critical legal studies already *is* feminist because the critical scholars' description of subjectivity converges with the cultural feminists' description of subjectivity, and the less widespread but equally confused claim that radical feminism is 'just' liberalism, for the parallel reason."[121] The reason such a view of the relationship between feminism and critical theory cannot be anything other than confused is that the very comparison presupposes that women's and men's subjectivities are somehow comparable. Professor West is eager to deny precisely this assumption.

The male Critical Legal theorist values love and intimacy for their liberating effect: they "hel[p us] overcome the distinction be-

---

119 *Id.* at 35.
120 *Id.* at 37.
121 *Id.* at 38-39.

tween self and nature."[122] Women, however, do not want to overcome the distinction between self and nature: "women value love and intimacy because they express the unity of self and nature within [their] own selves."[123] Because "love, for men, is an acquired skill,"[124] men will naturally think that alienation is something to be overcome. For men, "separation (and therefore autonomy) is what comes naturally. The separation that endangers women, by contrast, is what is socially constructed—attachment is natural. Separation, and the dread of it, is the response to the natural (and pleasant) state of connection."[125]

We now see that Professor West grounds her seemingly radical claim that women are not human beings[126] in her belief that, by virtue of their faith in a gender-neutral human subjectivity, male legal theorists have simply elevated their own preconceptions into a notion of subjectivity that fails to capture the true nature of women's subjectivity. As West summarizes the matter:

> These, then, are the differences between the "human beings" assumed by legal theory and women, as their lives are now being articulated by feminist theory. The human being, according to legal theory, values autonomy and fears annihilation, while at the same time he subjectively dreads the alienation that his love of autonomy inevitably entails. Women, according to feminist theory, value intimacy and fear separation, while at the same time longing for the individuation which our fear of separation precludes, and dreading the invasion which our love of intimacy entails. The human being assumed or constituted by legal theory precludes the woman described by feminism.[127]

Women and women's experience are not represented in modern jurisprudence because women are not recognized by the law. Not "until we have a legal doctrine that takes women's lives as seriously as it takes men's"[128] will there be any hope for a "genuinely ungendered jurisprudence (a jurisprudence "unmodified" so to speak)."[129] What must we do to make a place for women in legal discourse? How can women, and women's "distinctive existential and material state of being,"[130] be adequately reflected in and considered by legal discourse? Professor West has a distinctly modernist answer to this question.

122 UNGER, *supra* note 103, at 206.
123 West, *supra* note 104, at 40.
124 *Id.* at 41.
125 *Id.*
126 *Id.* at 4.
127 *Id.* at 42.
128 *Id.* at 60.
129 *Id.*
130 *Id.* at 61.

At no point in Professor West's analysis of the legal subordination of "women" does she view the concept of "woman" as anything other than a single, unitary construct. In the opening paragraphs of her essay, she states that women have a "true nature."[131] Here she makes her key modernist assumption: there *is* a "true nature" to woman, which can then be represented or pictured in language—specifically, in the language of legal discourse. Because their essence is at present not represented in language, women are excluded from this discourse; hence, they cannot be part of the extension of the concept "human being."

Professor West also evinces distinct modernist sensibilities in considering the question of truth. She maintains that to solve the problem of women's exclusion from legal discourse, we must tell "true stories" of women's lives.[132] West suggests a sort of public relations campaign: "We need to flood the market with our own stories until we get one simple point across: men's narrative story and phenomenological description of law is not women's story and phenomenology of law."[133] She believes that turning around legal discourse and forcing it to take account of the perspective of "woman," calls for a rewriting of legal discourse "in direct language that is true to our own [women's] experience and our own [women's] subjective lives."[134] To use the language and expression of modernism, the law must begin to mirror not only the male experience but the female experience as well. Notice, however, the nature of the proposed solution to the problem of exclusion: just widen the scope of the mirror. But what of "woman" or "women"? Where does she (do they) reside? In legal discourse? Not according to West. Yes, contemporary legal discourse includes something called "woman," but that is not "true woman." And this is the point: for West, "woman" exists *as a something* quite apart from what legal discourse makes her. In other words, "woman" exists prior to and apart from her treatment in legal discourse. On West's account, woman, whether gendered or sexed, exists prior to being taken up and constituted by legal discourse. This must be true, for were it not, then the idea of woman as a "unity of self and nature"[135] existing outside legal discourse would be unintelligible.[136]

---

131 *Id.* at 4. *See also* Robin West, *The Difference in Women's Hedonic Lives: A Phenomenological Critique of Feminist Legal Theory*, 3 WIS. WOMEN'S L.J. 81, 140-41 (1987) (strongly emphasizing the need to ground an account of female identity in biology).

132 West, *supra* note 104, at 64.

133 *Id.* at 65.

134 *Id.* at 70.

135 *Id.* at 40.

136 And intelligibility is the name of the game. *See* John H. Schlegel, *The Ten Thousand Dollar Question*, 41 STAN. L. REV. 435, 453 (1989) (reviewing LAURA KALMAN, LEGAL REALISM AT YALE: 1927-1960 (1986)) ("But so long as intelligibility is the name of the

In examining the gendered nature of modern legal discourse, Professor West accepts without reservation the key modernist assumptions that underlie her critique. West claims there is a unitary experience of women which has been systematically excluded from legal discourse. In her view, altering the conditions for the possibility of jurisprudential discourse is not the solution to the problem of jurisprudence and gender—West does not advocate a new approach to jurisprudence. Hers is a much less ambitious project, requiring only that the net be widened to include "women." But can feminist jurisprudence prescind from an uninterrogated modernism?[137] We now turn our attention to a feminist who has specifically addressed this problem.

B. Joan Williams

1. *Epistemology*

In 1987, Joan Williams published *Critical Legal Studies: The Death of Transcendence and the Rise of the New Langdells*.[138] Professor Williams argued that, in attempting to supplant the liberal account of legal rationality, members of the Critical Legal Studies school ("CLS") had duplicated some central conceptual errors of the modernist program they were so eager to displace. What was their mistake? In short, the CLS scholars failed to hear the message of the new epistemology. What role does this failure play in the Critical critique of law, and what is this new epistemology? We turn first to the former question.

The attributes of that all-too-familiar cardboard character, "the liberal legalist," are well-known. She stands for the rule of law, the principles of neutrality and fairness, the even-handed and objective application of rules, and the virtues of consistency and publicity.[139] Critical Legal scholars argue that this liberal message is a lie. In

---

game, epistemology, linguistics, and literary theory suggest that rendering the hermeneutic circle, understanding fully the culture of other thinkers' doing and thinking, is the key to understanding an intellectual text."). For an important discussion of the role of intelligibility in the narrative reconstruction of science, see Joseph Rouse, *The Narrative of Science*, 33 INQUIRY 179 (1990). For a discussion of narrative as a form of explanation, see Paul Roth, *How Narratives Explain*, 56 SOC. RES. 449 (1989).

137 West's unswerving commitment to modernism extends beyond gender to method. In her review of Barbara Herrnstein Smith's book, CONTINGENCIES OF VALUE: ALTERNATIVE PERSPECTIVES FOR CRITICAL THEORY (1988), West rejects what she perceives as Herrnstein Smith's relativism because that relativism contributes to domination and oppression. *See* Robin West, *Relativism, Objectivity, and Law*, 99 YALE L.J. 1473 (1990).

138 Joan Williams, *Critical Legal Studies: The Death of Transcendence & The Rise of the New Langdells*, 62 N.Y.U. L. REV. 429 (1987).

139 For a profound and moving account of liberalism in all its dimensions, see UNGER, *supra* note 103 (particularly chapters two and three).

their view, the law is fraught with contradiction and bias. It cannot, even on its best day, approach anything like "neutral application of rules." Liberal legalism is far from being able to articulate a coherent account of the subject capable of free will and the pursuit of an individual conception of the good, and the liberal individual is at best a fiction.

According to Professor Williams, not only does the CLS critique of liberal legalism fail, but it also fails for the same reason as liberalism. Duncan Kennedy's claim that embedded within liberal legalism is "a fundamental contradiction" between individual and community illustrates this failure.[140] Kennedy's claim implicates the old story of the self and the other: attaining individual freedom simultaneously requires and is threatened by other people. Kennedy makes his point this way:

> [A]t the same time that it forms and protects us, the universe of others . . . threatens us with annihilation and urges upon us forms of fusion that are quite plainly bad rather than good. A friend can reduce me to misery with a single look. Numberless conformities, large and small abandonments of self to others, are the price of what freedom we experience in society.[141]

What could be wrong with this assessment? Professor Williams finds Kennedy's analysis problematic in that it posits an abstract structure underlying the entirety of social experience: a structure which purports to explain the multifarious social and political phenomena that are the everyday fare of life in civil liberal society. Worse yet, Kennedy's analysis of liberal legalism's discourse harbors "claims of privileged access to objective truth."[142] What was originally liberalism's problem—the unjustified claim of access to objective truth—now surfaces in the metaphysics of Critical Legal theory. How did this happen? Professor Williams has a complex but familiar answer.

The members of CLS and their critics have failed to give due attention to what Professor Williams refers to as "the new epistemology."[143] New epistemology replaces the liberal-CLS metaphys-

140 Duncan Kennedy, *The Structure of Blackstone's Commentaries*, 28 Buff. L. Rev. 205 (1979).

141 *Id.* at 211-12.

142 Williams, *supra* note 138, 474-75.

143 In *Deconstructing Gender*, Professor Williams summarizes the new epistemology this way:

> This critique, which I have elsewhere called the new epistemology, consists of a broad and diverse intellectual movement that rejects a range of long-standing Western verities, some dating to the Enlightenment, and others all the way back to Plato. Perhaps the core element of the new epistemology is its rejection of an absolute truth accessible through rigorous, logical manipulation of abstractions.

ics of structure, with its emphasis on the "Either/Or" of subjective-objective, self-other, determinate-indeterminate, with what we have described earlier as the first aspect of postmodernism—that is, linguistic holism. Like the liberal legalist, the Critical Legal critic remains "trapped in dreams of transcendence."[144] Professor Williams, following (early) Wittgenstein, labels the linguistic version of transcendence "the picture theory."[145] We encountered the picture theory in our earlier discussion of language and modernism.[146] Language functions as a medium of representation in which a nonlinguistic edifice that exists outside of language is *re*presented in language.[147] Truth, on this account, is the accurate representation of thing and structure through the medium of language.

By postulating a structure underlying the verbal play of linguistic reality, the CLS critique of liberal legalism evinces "a fundamental failure to abandon the universe shaped by the picture theory."[148] Thus, neither the liberal legal claim that law is determinate nor the CLS claim that law is indeterminate—though both are theoretically appealing—prove workable in practice. The reason is *precisely the same* in *each case*: the picture of "knowledge" each presupposes is essentialist. As mentioned earlier,[149] abandoning the idea of a fixed structure to which law "corresponds" obliges one to avoid "claim[ing] to have discovered *the* canonical, essential structure of thought."[150] But, if we give up essentialism, representationalism, and truth-as-correspondence, what are we left with?

Professor Williams's answer derives from the later work of Wittgenstein. When we give up the language of determinacy and

---

Joan C. Williams, *Deconstructing Gender*, 87 MICH. L. REV. 797, 805 (1989).

144 Williams, *supra* note 138, at 432.

145 *Id.* at 433.

146 *See supra* notes 68-72 and accompanying text.

147 In short, necessity is a function not of the nature of things (Aristotle) nor of mind (Kant) but of language. *See* Gordon E. Michalson, *Theology, Historical Knowledge, and the Contingency-Necessity Distinction*, 14 J. PHIL. OF RELIGION 87, 92 (1983).

> The intelligibility of language does not rely upon its gaining purchase on a realm of static laws and immutable truths waiting to be discovered and articulated, but depends instead on how well language serves us as we go about making our way in the world. The correct response to the relativism that apparently results from this is not to worry about a missing stability anchored "in reality"; the correct response is simply that "there is as much stability as there is." Consequently, as one commentator has recently summarized the matter, "whereas once we thought with Aristotle, that necessity came from things, and later thought with Kant that it came from the structure of our minds, we now know that it comes from language."

Id. (citations omitted).

148 Williams, *supra* note 138, at 489.

149 *See supra* note 74 and accompanying text.

150 James Boyle, *The Politics of Reason: Critical Legal Theory and Local Social Thought*, 133 U. PA. L. REV. 685, 715 (1985).

indeterminacy, we replace truth conditions with assertability conditions. In other words, within a practice, we swap talk of truth for persuasion. When a dispute arises over the judicial application of a rule, for example, the critique will issue not from outside the bounds of language but from within the borders of practice. We make our appeals against the background of "a given cultural context."[151] The question whether there is certainty[152] in our legal practices of justification can only be answered from within particular cultural contexts, for it is only "[t]he context [that] determines what is required."[153] We remain always within our "form of life." We cannot break out of it. This is not a limitation, however, for to see it as a limitation is to play into the very picture of knowledge from which we seek to extricate ourselves.

2. *Feminism*

Where, then, does feminism fit into the picture of knowledge just articulated? To sharpen the question, how can feminism view itself as a liberating discourse if, as Williams urges, it abandons the effort to transcend our current perspective and assume a distanciated position from which to criticize the current configuration of gender relations and the law's constitution of the feminine subject?[154] That is, need the following worry be taken seriously?

> [H]ow are we to draw any principled distinction between the rejection of Enlightenment rationalism and the rejection of legiti-

---

151 Williams, *supra* note 138, at 494.

152 The most far-reaching study of the concept of certainty in the thought of the later Wittgenstein is THOMAS MORAWETZ, WITTGENSTEIN AND KNOWLEDGE (1978).

153 Williams, *supra* note 138, at 493.

154 The tradition of thought invoked by Professor Williams in her critique of CLS suggests the following answer:

> [S]emantic analysis can provide no original information about the world or our knowledge of it. We can expect only an indirect reconstruction or reflection of what our own empirical science and common understanding already tell us, together with information about how this might be expressed within different systems of notation. Semantic analysis discovers notational rather than theoretical options. Given the full corpus of antecedently established truth as parameter, it seeks formal principles for constructing the truth, or for correlating it (or parts of it) with other truth. It seeks truths only about the forms and formal relations of true sentences. It is constrained at its borders not by observation or experience but by antecedently perceived truth. Semantic interpretation is shaped by the truth as seen from the vantage point of some accepted theory of the natural world, rather than by the evidence that shapes such a theory. The interpretational hypotheses of the interpreter or analyst have extralinguistic significance only relative to the already accepted doctrine of a background theory, but they provide *no independent basis* even for understanding that doctrine let alone believing it.

GEORGE D. ROMANOS, QUINE AND ANALYTIC PHILOSOPHY 184-85 (1983) (emphasis added).

> mation as such? The concession is, after all, a very significant one; for having been told that intellectual traditions incorporate a capacity for critical reflection, we might well suppose that the forces of Enlightenment had captured the high ground in the current argument. If discursive communities are capable of self-criticism in principle, we might ask, then who is to dictate how far they shall take it? Won't there always be room for more, so long as any intelligible criticism can be addressed to the moral or cognitive order under which we live? And what is this limitless commitment to the dialectical revision of theory and practice, if not precisely the Enlightenment commitment to haul up everything in life before the tribunal of reason.[155]

We have noted Professor Williams's rejection of this "Either/Or" dichotomy, which suggests that one either accepts that there is a tribunal of Reason in which claims to truth and falsity are interrogated,[156] or gives oneself over to the ill-defined and hopelessly vague contours of discursive practice. Having rejected that dichotomy in *The New Langdells*, however, Professor Williams goes on to consider the implications of this rejection in the specific context of feminism. In *Deconstructing Gender*,[157] she puts the new epistemology[158] to work by attacking the Enlightenment's celebration of "reason over emotion"[159] while simultaneously questioning feminist treatments of gender differences. As this analysis will reveal, Professor Williams is deeply ambivalent about the new epistemology's usefulness as a critical tool for the emancipation of women from the gendered structure of legal relations. Her ambivalence serves to confirm the claim that the modern-postmodern divide is a singularly important point of emphasis for feminist critics of law, for until the question of critique is settled, the status of feminism as a liberatory enterprise will be uncertain. Professor Williams's basic disagreement is with the "difference" feminism advocated by Carol Gilligan and her followers. She maintains that Gilligan's description of gender differences is "inaccurate and potentially destructive."[160] Williams has two specific disagreements with Gilligan. First, she believes that "it is incorrect as a matter of intellectual history to claim, as have Gilligan and others, that the twentieth century's shift to a more contextualizing, antiformalist, and relativizing form of discourse constitutes a rejection of absolutist 'male' epistemology in

155 Lovibond, *supra* note 1, at 11-12.

156 The metaphors of the "Tribunal of Reason" and the "Interrogation of Claims to Truth by Reason" figure prominently and powerfully in the first chapter of GILLIAN ROSE, THE DIALECTIC OF NIHILISM: POST-STRUCTURALISM AND LAW (1984).

157 Williams, *supra* note 143, at 805.

158 *Id.*

159 *Id.* at 804.

160 *Id.* at 801.

favor of 'women's voice.' "[161] Second, Williams contends that Gilligan overlooks what is important in the critique of existing conceptions of gender. In her view, it is not enough to argue, as Gilligan does, that there is "a feminine voice."[162] A feminist critique of "possessive individualism" is necessary;[163] without such a critique, Gilligan's relational discourse may be turned against women. These objections are connected, and may be considered together.

There is a fairly diverse range of opinion among feminists who believe that women have a distinct "voice." Nevertheless, there is basic agreement among them that feminism's contribution to the restructuring of gender relations should take place at the level of what Suzanne Lebsock refers to as "a more humane social order."[164] Williams describes this focus the following way:

> For all these feminists, this "more humane social order" entails a new ethic of care based on a focus on relationships, not competition; on negotiation, not combat; on community, not individual self-interest. "What is needed," concludes the early and influential feminist of difference Elizabeth Wolgast, "is another model. . . . We need a model that acknowledges . . . other kinds of interest than self-interest." A more recent legal feminist echoes this thought, noting his aspiration "to transform our polity and its underlying assumptions from the alienated world of atomistic competition to an interconnected world of mutual cooperation."[165]

There is, however, a downside to this social order. If we view men and women as truly different, then perhaps the two groups ought to receive different treatment.[166] As a strategy, such an approach can backfire, as it did in *EEOC v. Sears, Roebuck & Co.*[167] To

---

161 *Id.* at 800.

162 Professor Williams actually believes that Gilligan is ambivalent on this point. *See* Williams, *supra* note 143, at 813. ("Gilligan's inconsistent signals about whether she is talking about women or 'the feminine' have left relational feminism with the potential to be used as a weapon against women.").

163 Professor Williams describes possessive individualism in this way:

> The term refers to the liberal premises that society consists of market relations, and that freedom means freedom from any relations with others except those relations the individual enters voluntarily with a view to his own self-interest.

Id. at 810 n.40.

164 Suzanne Lebsock, The Free Women of Petersburg: Status and Culture in a Southern Town, 1784-1860 (1984).

165 Williams, *supra* note 143, at 811 (citations omitted).

166 This is Elizabeth Wolgast's position: that equality and equal treatment need to take account of "real differences." *See* Elizabeth H. Wolgast, Equality and the Rights of Women 88 (1980) ("[W]omen should have some rights not applicable to men.").

167 628 F.2d 1264 (N.D. Ill. 1986), *aff'd*, 839 F.2d 302 (7th Cir. 1988). For a discussion of the expert testimony in the case, see Alice Kessler-Harris, *History On Trial*, 35

rebut the charge that the company had discriminated against women in filling its more lucrative commission sales positions, Sears's lawyers successfully argued that the absence of women from those positions was bound up with the nature of women. The lawyers argued that because women focus on family, relationships, care and mothering, they often will forsake high-paying but time-intensive positions in favor of other positions that do not compromise their (family) values.[168] As Professor Williams characterizes the Court's judgment, "Women's 'ethic of care' enables them to rise above the fray, so they are not truly hurt when they are excluded from high-powered, competitive jobs in commission sales."[169] Yes, women *are* different. They require different treatment—but they also make different choices. Women are more "focused on relationships, and averse to capitalist virtues such as competition."[170] Sears did not discriminate; rather, the women freely chose the ethic of care over big bucks.

The relational feminists' critique of gender differences does not take account of the particular economic choices facing both women and men. It is precisely this failure—the failure to offer an *economic* account of gender relations—that renders the relational account of gender differences a feeble approximation of their reality. It is not gender differences but "the gendered structure of American capitalism"[171] that is the source of women's (and men's) oppression. Women do not choose family responsibilities over the fast track. "Women know that if *they* do not sacrifice *no one* will, whereas men assume that if *they* do not, *women* will."[172] Women do not have the same choices as men. Williams goes on to note that

> [t]he underlying point is a deeper one: that society is structured so that everyone, regardless of sex, is limited to two unacceptable choices—men's traditional life patterns or economic marginality. Under the current structure of wage labor, people are limited to being ideal workers, which leaves them with inadequate time to devote to parenting, and being primary parents condemned to relative poverty (if they are single parents) or economic vulnera-

RADICAL HIST. REV. 57 (1986); Thomas Haskell & Sanford Levinson, *Academic Freedom and Expert Witnessing: Historians and the Sears Case*, 66 TEX. L. REV. 1629 (1988); Alice Kessler-Harris, *Academic Freedom and Expert Witnessing: A Response to Haskell and Levinson*, 67 TEX. L. REV. 429 (1988); Thomas Haskell & Sanford Levinson, *On Academic Freedom and Hypothetical Pools: A Reply to Alice Kessler-Harris*, 67 TEX. L. REV. 1591 (1989).

168 *Sears*, 628 F.2d at 320-21.

169 Williams, *supra* note 143, at 814.

170 *Id.* at 815. This short summary of the case fails to do justice to Professor Williams's brilliant demonstration of the manner in which the lawyers for Sears simply turned Gilligan's arguments against women.

171 *Id.* at 822.

172 *Id.* at 831.

bility (if they are currently married to an ideal worker). Wage labor does not have to be structured in this way.[173]

So how did things get to be so bad? How is it that women, and especially feminists like Carol Gilligan,[174] have failed to see that not only are they oppressed by the system of wage labor, but they are, perhaps unwittingly, contributing to their own oppression?[175] Professor Williams's answer comes not from feminist theory but from political theory, and, in particular, from the work of the Italian Marxist philosopher Antonio Gramsci. According to Professor Williams, Gramsci's central notion, that of "cultural hegemony,"[176] demonstrates that although they believe they are making choices, in reality women

> may be unwitting accomplices in the maintenance of existing inequalities. . . . Discovering nearly inexhaustible resources for resistance to domination, many social historians have been reluctant to acknowledge the possibility that their subjects may have been muddled by assimilation to the dominant culture — perhaps even to the point of believing and behaving against their own best interests.[177]

The "language of domesticity"[178]—that is, the notion that women speak "in a different voice" or are possessed of their own "ways of knowing"[179]—has to be, as Professor Williams puts it, de-

---

173 *Id.* at 831-32.

174 I am reluctant to buttress Professor Williams's inevitably logical critique of relational feminism with specific reference to the work of Carol Gilligan. Gilligan's research deals with the psychic development of young children, not the socioeconomic parameters of late capitalist culture. While it is clear that her work is suggestive, there are limits to its extrapolation.

175 *See* Kathryn Abrams, *Ideology and Women's Choice*, 24 GA. L. REV. 761, 767-68 (1990) ("Like the women discussed by MacKinnon, Williams' subjects contribute to their own subordination (this time, economic rather than sexual), with only limited understanding of the constraints on their choices and little sense of these choices as systematically self-destructive.").

176 Professor Williams discusses the notion thus:

> Gramsci painted a complex picture of how the dominant culture rules with the consent of the governed by shaping a "hegemony" of values, norms, perceptions, and beliefs that "helps mark the boundaries of permissible discourse, discourages the clarification of social alternatives, and makes it difficult for the dispossessed to locate the source of their unease, let alone remedy it."

Williams, *supra* note 143, at 828-29.

177 T.J. Jackson Lears, *The Concept of Cultural Hegemony: Problems and Possibilities*, 90 AM. HIST. REV. 567, 573 (1985).

178 Williams, *supra* note 143, at 828.

179 *See* MARY F. BELENKY ET AL., WOMEN'S WAYS OF KNOWING: THE DEVELOPMENT OF SELF, VOICE, AND MIND (1986). An excellent vehicle for raising the question of women's way(s) of knowing is the Marlena Gorris 1984 Dutch film A QUESTION OF SILENCE. For a discussion of the film and its implications for this question, see Linda Williams, *A Jury of Their Peers: Marlene Gorris's* A Question of Silence, *in* POSTMODERNISM AND ITS DISCONTENTS 107-15 (E. Ann Kaplan ed., 1988).

coded.[180] Why is it that women fail to see that they are the victims of the dominant culture? Like Gramsci's proletariat,[181] can it be that women suffer from false consciousness?[182] Women do not make choices, for they are merely cogs in the capitalist wheel of commerce. Their mission is to keep home and hearth intact while the man stakes the family claim in the world of work. Women are not making "choices," for they have no choices to make. They are simply filling a role in the wage labor system.

This analysis is a powerful critique of both the wage labor system and the blindness inherent in relational feminism. But is this a critique Professor Williams, as a proponent of "the new epistemology," gets to make? I propose that, on her own terms, the answer to this question must be negative.[183] The new epistemology rejects the modernist dogma that knowledge can transcend the limits of language, and maintains that claims to truth and "right representation" must be given up in favor of assertion and persuasion within a discursive framework. The first casualty of the move to the new epistemology was the neutral grid of objectivity,[184] which was replaced by "the web of human agreements" as the foundation for cognition.[185] However, by invoking Gramsci's critical posture of cultural hegemony and resorting to words like "decode," "hegemony," and the like, Professor Williams places herself squarely within

---

180 Williams, *supra* note 143, at 828.

181 *See* SELECTIONS FROM THE PRISON NOTEBOOKS OF ANTONIO GRAMSCI (Quintin Hoare & Geoffrey N. Smith eds. & trans., 1971).

182 Professor Williams scrupulously avoids using this phrase; however, her invocation of Gramsci's name, as well as her use of cognate terms, commits her to the view that women, like the proletariat, suffer from this ideological disease.

183 *See* SUSAN J. HEKMAN, HERMENEUTICS AND THE SOCIOLOGY OF KNOWLEDGE 150 (1986).

> [Consider] the Marxist concept of false consciousness. A Marxist social scientist, imposing the Marxist framework of interpretation on a sequence of action might be led to the conclusion that a particular group of social actors [e.g., women] in a particular situation exhibit false consciousness. Again, the Gadamerian would have no difficulty with such a conclusion. The 'text' of the action fused with the interpreter's Marxist horizon yields a particular, yet perfectly legitimate interpretation. It might even be argued that, given the influence of Marxist categories in the social sciences, it is difficult for contemporary interpreters to see past actions in anything *but* Marxist terms. That interpretive social science and especially the Wittgensteinian school has had a great deal of difficulty with the concept of false consciousness is, however, evident in the contemporary literature on this subject.

Id.

184 Professor Williams has elsewhere indicated her reservations about giving up on truth. *See* Joan Williams, *Feminism and Post-Structuralism*, 88 MICH. L. REV. 1776, 1778 (1990) (book review) ("Once we as feminists reject Truth, and are left only with arguments in favor of our interpretations, we are brought face to face with the need to persuade others to see the world as we do.").

185 Williams, *supra* note 138, at 453.

the framework of objectivity, truth, and knowledge which she so successfully deconstructed in *The New Langdells*. Considered together, *The New Langdells* and *Deconstructing Gender* demonstrate the importance of the problem of critique to a postmodernist critic of the law. The contradiction inherent in Williams's work, however, need not be a terminus, for in her critique of the relational feminists, she demonstrates the precise point at which the new epistemology breaks down. Thus, it would be foolish to view her failure to escape the bounds of modernist rhetoric as a sign of an inherent or unavoidable limit to postmodernist criticism. Indeed, a third feminist critic suggests a method for resolving that very contradiction.

C. Zillah Eisenstein

Postmodernism's singular contribution to feminism has been to raise the stakes in the sameness-difference debate. While feminists of the "different voice" stripe were consolidating their position and taking a respite from the arduous task of staking out a defensible theoretical position on the question of gender identity, arguments such as the following were being made:

> There can be no guarantee of the nature of women's experience since, in so far as it is meaningful, this experience is discursively produced by the constitution of women as subjects within historically and socially specific discourses. . . . [W]omen's subjectivity will always be open to the plurality of meaning and the possibilities contained within this plurality will have different political implications.[186]

Zillah Eisenstein introduces *The Female Body and the Law*[187] with this provocative remark: "There is no one body, only bodies, only differences, as well as pluralized conceptions of equality."[188] Eisenstein's target is the familiar reductionism of phallocentric liberal discourse—the notion that women are the same as men (equal) except when the equality of women is being denied. In those instances, the argument goes, the cause of the inequality is women's "differences"—their natural biological constitution. Gender and sex (biology) are simultaneously irrelevant (to equality) and determinative (of inequality). For Eisenstein, the problem is not with the question of the "truth" of biological differences; rather, it lies in how those differences are discursively constructed. Thus, her inquiry is directed to the relationship between gender and power.

Let us begin with method. From the start, Eisenstein rejects the very terms that make traditional epistemology possible. She states

186 CHRIS WEEDON, FEMINIST PRACTICE & POSTSTRUCTURALIST THEORY 167 (1987).
187 ZILLAH R. EISENSTEIN, THE FEMALE BODY AND THE LAW (1988).
188 *Id.* at 5.

that "the dualism of the real and the ideal is overdrawn."[189] The realms of fact and idea, material and immaterial, and idea and essence must be replaced not with new dualisms, but with an entirely different way of thinking about the problems of meaning and understanding. To accomplish this, Eisenstein focuses on the concept of "discourse."[190] In this context, the point of the enterprise is not to look at the object (e.g., woman) and how it is represented in language (e.g., representations of "woman."). Rather, it is to look at how discourse—a "realm of thinking and acting"[191]—produces images of gender and sex.

So what does discourse have to do with the distinction between modernism and postmodernism? As we have seen, the project of right representation is the modernist project of knowledge. We have also seen that it is a belief in the power of truth that underwrites the project of modernist epistemology. Eisenstein's "discourse" approach rejects the project of modernist epistemology as not wrong but impossible. She junks categories like "ideology," which depend for their very existence on the dichotomous verities of truth-ideology, real-unreal, clear-distorted, as worn out and useless. Does not this view, then, lead to relativism?[192] Eisenstein addresses this problem the following way:

---

189 *Id.* at 7. Eisenstein has drawn criticism from proponents of essentialism. *See, e.g.*, Marie Ashe, *Inventing Choreographies: Feminism and Deconstruction*, 90 COLUM. L. REV. 1123, 1138 (1990) (reviewing EISENSTEIN, *supra* note 187).

> [H]ad Eisenstein engaged with comparative anthropological theory in the way that, for example, French feminist Julie Kristeva has done, she would have confronted the deep and apparently universal unconscious operations that may motivate constructions of gender. Kristeva has noted an apparent linkage between the universal tendency toward "abjection"—the naming of particular persons and practices as *absolutely other*—and a designation of certain processes of female bodies, such as birthing and menstruation, as polluted.

Id. (footnote omitted).

190 *See* EISENSTEIN, *supra* note 187, at 10-12.

191 *Id.* at 11.

192 As Alan Hunt formulates the matter, the problem is one of paradox. *See* Alan Hunt, *The Big Fear: Law Confronts Postmodernism*, 35 MCGILL L.J. 507, 538-39 (1990).

> Postmodernism is also characterized by a general espousal of the tradition of discourse analysis and the general emphasis on the role of language in the construction of social reality. This involves adherence to the epistemological view, which is central to Foucault's position, that there are no objects of knowledge constituted outside discourse. This gives rise to a profound paradox in postmodernist thought. If everything is constituted in discourse, how can an alternative politics exist or any criticism take purchase which appeals to other meanings or knowledges?

Id.

> It is only within a standpoint that privileges objectivity and absolutes that relativism and pluralism present a problem. Plurality does not mean that all truths are equal; it merely uncovers the role of power in defining truth. Once truth has been defined, we are free to argue in behalf of our interpretation, but we cannot use the claim to truth itself as our defense. . . . We must leave meanings open at the same time we act on them.[193]
>
> . . . .
>
> If there is no place *outside* discourse, how can one establish its meaning? Is the body completely a construction in discourse, with no *outside*? Is the body sexed? Gendered? A mix?[194]
>
> . . . .
>
> We need to recognize that differences exist within and between the sexes. There are a variety of kinds of female bodies: thin, fat, small-breasted, large-breasted, muscular, flabby, and so forth. These differences exist within other differences as well: sexual preference, economic class, race, age, and so on.[195]

One must appreciate Eisenstein's sensitivity to the charge that, from the postmodernist perspective, all questions of difference are simply a matter of one's own view. It would be unfair to level such a charge at Eisenstein, because as the passages above demonstrate, her concern is not to dispute that "[s]ex and gender differences exist."[196] Instead, she urges the claim that "their significance must remain open-textured."[197] Here we come to the crux of the difference between the modern and postmodern approaches to the question(s) of feminism. If we give up the modernist view—embraced by Robin West—that the significance of gender differences can be settled by appeal to a totalizing structure that transcends discourse, what are our alternatives? Joan Williams sees the new epistemology's answer as critique proceeding from within the bounds of existing culture. *EEOC v. Sears*, however, prompted a re-evaluation of this strategy, and engendered a move back to modernist concepts like "cultural hegemony" and the "decoding" of experience.[198] Is Eisenstein's a truly postmodern approach—one that avoids the traps that caused Williams to fall back into the modernist framework?

---

193 EISENSTEIN, *supra* note 187, at 23-24.

194 *Id.* at 29.

195 *Id.* at 31-32.

196 *Id.* at 35.

197 *Id.*

198 This move is really just a shuffle, since Williams remains within a modernist framework. What happened in *EEOC v. Sears* is a perfect example of what is wrong with modernism; Sears's lawyers successfully sold "woman" as a universal category. Williams simply replicates this form of argument by insisting that another universal category—hegemony—is the true explanatory ground. The proper way to attack the logic of the case is at the level of the *form* of the argument itself.

We can assess the adequacy of Eisenstein's discourse-oriented[199] approach to law by analyzing her treatment of a specific topic: pornography. Among the most bizarre coalitions produced by the politics of the eighties, none could be more curious than that formed by the New Right and certain feminists on the issue of pornography. Seemingly, it was the shared purpose of eliminating pornography's subordination and oppression of women that engendered this unusual coalition. Eisenstein argues, however, that this is an erroneous description of what was at stake in the debate over pornography in the eighties.[200] In fact, her analysis of the pornography debate suggests that by joining in the New Right's wholesale rejection of pornography, some feminists actually contributed to the continuing oppression of women.

Eisenstein notes that "[p]ornography is very much tied to the meaning of engendered sex: in it females are displayed as subjugated, objectified women."[201] But her argument is grounded in her claim that pornography is not just "one thing." Pornography has many meanings, including, but not limited to, "fantasy and rebellion."[202] These multiple meanings "coexist within pornography, and they crisscross the realms of the real and ideal."[203] Further, "some females may feel pleasure in imagining both being subjugated and subjugating others. Because sexual pleasure can be experienced as a liberating feeling (liberation from inhibition), fantasies of subjugation may be emancipatory. Thus, pornography is not a homogenized discourse expressing only women's oppression."[204]

Is this also the New Right's reading of pornography? Hardly. For the New Right, the female is mother, Madonna with child—she needs protection (from pornographers), not emancipation. We must free her from the pornographer's subjugation so that we may enslave her to the role of wife and mother.[205] The New Right chooses to address the evil of pornography on the level of its injurious effects on women. From this picture of pornography's impact on women flows the notion that pornography is something from

199 Professor Eisenstein explicitly invokes Foucault's "discourse" analysis in support of her view of legal knowledge. *See* EISENSTEIN, *supra* note 187, at 10-12. For a discussion of Foucault's thought and postmodernism, see DAVID HARVEY, THE CONDITION OF POSTMODERNITY 45 (1989).

200 Her specific focus is the Attorney General's Commission on Pornography, which issued its final report in 1986. ATTORNEY GENERAL'S COMM'N ON PORNOGRAPHY: FINAL REPORT (1986).

201 EISENSTEIN, *supra* note 187, at 163.

202 *Id.*

203 *Id.*

204 *Id.* at 163-64.

205 *Id.* at 164.

which women need protection. Does this mean that, as Eisenstein asks, to argue against pornography is to "challeng[e] women's status as victims"?[206] The New Right would have us believe that it is.[207] Curiously, some feminists also take it to be the case.

The feminists Eisenstein has most in mind are Andrea Dworkin and Catharine MacKinnon. In their well-publicized promotion of antipornography statutes in Minneapolis and Indianapolis,[208] Dworkin and MacKinnon took the position that pornography is "a practice of sex discrimination, a violation of women's civil rights, the opposite of sexual equality."[209] Nothing could be wrong with opposing sex discrimination. But the problem is not whether one is for or against sex discrimination. Rather, the problem is the link between pornography and sex discrimination; "seeing pornography" from the perspective of (sex) discrimination. The problem concerns the clouding of motives and frames of reference. For the New Right, a desire to protect women fuels the antipornography campaign. Women are different from men, and need protection. Feminists do not share this motivation. Their interest in eliminating pornography is not in protecting women but in empowering them.[210] Again, what could be wrong with this agenda?

First, the New Right and feminists share the view that

> pornography is something men enjoy and women do not, that it is something men do to women, that woman is the victim and man is the aggressor. And both feminists and the right wing assume that pornography is the same as violence, an assumption that makes it difficult to avoid thinking about sex in other than protective terms.[211]

Now comes the rub. By campaigning against pornography across the board, feminists in fact contribute to the subordination of women. They do so because the pornography against which they protest sends *more than one* message. It is true that some pornography contains messages of violence and oppression. However, "[p]ornography carries many messages other than woman-hating: it advocates sexual adventure, sex outside of marriage, sex for no reason other than pleasure, casual sex, anonymous sex, group sex,

206 *Id.* at 165.

207 Eisenstein presents an interesting critique of the New Right's political agenda and its relationship to the social-scientific conclusions of the Presidential Commission. She focuses in particular on the dubious nature of the claimed causal connection(s) between certain forms of pornography and violence against women. *See id.* at 168-70.

208 *See, e.g.*, Indianapolis City-County General Ordinance No. 35, 1984, Proposal No. 298, 1984.

209 MacKinnon, *supra* note 7, at 175.

210 Eisenstein, *supra* note 187, at 171.

211 *Id.*

voyeuristic sex, illegal sex, public sex."[212] If this picture of the relationship between pornography and freedom is persuasive, then Eisenstein's conclusion is inexorable: "If pornography is not universally victimizing, then a sweeping indictment of it can create a new problem—denial of the freedom to engage in multiple sexual practices."[213]

What does this analysis have to do with postmodernism?[214] A great deal. In fact, I believe that Eisenstein's critique of Dworkin and MacKinnon shows how the failure to transcend modernist assumptions (in this instance, modernist assumptions about women, sex, and subordination)[215] contributes to the further denial of wo-

---

212 Lisa Duggan et al., *False Promises: Antipornography Feminist Legislation in the U.S.*, *in* WOMEN AGAINST CENSORSHIP 145 (Varda Burstyn ed., 1985).

213 EISENSTEIN, *supra* note 187, at 171.

214 For one thing, Eisenstein's critique upsets the easy alliance between idea and image. It notes that the idea (of "woman" or "sexuality"), which is a function of image, can be changed at the same moment it is understood. *See* JACQUELINE ROSE, SEXUALITY IN THE FIELD OF VISION 231 (1986).

> Artists engaged in sexual representation (representation *as* sexual) come in at precisely this point, calling up the sexual component of the image, drawing out an emphasis that exists *in potentia* in the various instances they inherit and of which they form a part. Their move is not therefore one of (moral) corrective. They draw on the tendencies they also seek to displace, and clearly belong, for example, within the context of that postmodernism which demands that reference, in its problematised form, re-enter the frame. But the emphasis on sexuality produces specific effects. First, it adds to the concept of cultural artefact or stereotype the political imperative of feminism which holds the image accountable for the reproduction of norms. Secondly, to this feminist demand for scrutiny of the image, it adds the idea of a sexuality which goes beyond the issue of content to take in the parameters of visual form (not just what we see but how we see—visual space as more than the domain of simple recognition). The image therefore submits to the sexual reference, but only in so far as reference itself is questioned by the work of the image.

Id.

215 For a more ideological slant on the question of pornography's relationship to phallic images, which nonetheless affirms that current practices are the best place to begin the rethinking of a gender relations, see JOAN COCKS, THE OPPOSITIONAL IMAGINATION 148 (1989).

> [W]e can remain on ideological territory but take a different flight of the imagination than the one dictated to us. We can conjure up possibilities for eroticism not when the phallus is subject and force, but "merely" when the phallus is assigned by a hegemonic culture to the position of subject and force. Given the veil of secrecy over the actual bedroom, this is surely the more sympathetic course, and it is the one I mean to follow here. It *does* require that we exchange an empirical method for one that is partly literary. We cannot behave as if we were searching for facts when we really are looking for plots that are persuasive and characters that ring true. Yet neither are we free to fix on any erotic possibility that happens to please us. Instead, we must confine our imaginations within narrow, deductive bounds. We must look for plots and characters that are logically possible—given, first of all, the existence of a hegemonic culture of Masculine/feminine; given, second, our rejection of the idea that such a culture is totalitarian in its wielding of control or that it has a one-to-one

men's freedom.[216] I will begin with Dworkin and MacKinnon's position on the relationship between pornography and sexual subordination. Dworkin states that if part of what angers women

> is that we're [Dworkin and MacKinnon] suggesting that there are things that are right and things that are wrong, and one of the things that is wrong is the sexual subordination of women, that's accurate. Politics is about making those kinds of distinctions.[217]

As Eisenstein points out, "this view holds only if pornography treats women exclusively as victims."[218] With this observation, we return to postmodernism. Eisenstein's point is that there is no "truth"[219] to the female sexuality that is subordinated by the pornographer. To reduce "sex to its engendered form,"[220] as MacKinnon does, "is to let the phallus win. It is like saying that the female body is one with the mother's body."[221]

For MacKinnon, women's sexuality is not something that exists apart from its representation in discourse. There is, as MacKinnon puts it, "sexual reality."[222] That "reality" is the product of, and is consistent with, the vision of male sexuality. What is at stake is *not* the question of whether sexuality is real or unreal. Rather, what matters is whether or not one buys into what Eisenstein refers to as the "oppositional mode of thinking."[223] There *is* a physical aspect to sex; call it "the real."[224] There are also ideas about "the real"; call these "the ideal."[225] Dworkin and MacKinnon complain that women are subordinated because men have reduced woman's sexuality to the male ideal. Here Eisenstein makes her postmodernist point: there is no (one) such thing as "female sexuality." On the contrary, there are many ways to think about female sexuality. Like

---

> correspondence to actually lived and felt life; and given, third, our refusal to presume at the start any essential significances to the male and female bodies.

Id.

216 The point is that by thinking about pornography in a totalizing, modernist form, Dworkin and MacKinnon throw out too much. By failing to interrogate specific objects, practices, or forms of depiction, they embrace a conception of pornography that sacrifices freedom on the mantel of totalization.

217 Andrea Dworkin, *quoted in* Mara Math, *Andrea Dworkin Talks About Feminism and Pornography*, GAY COMMUNITY NEWS, Dec. 28, 1985, at 8. MacKinnon echoes this view. *See* MACKINNON, *supra* note 7, at 148 ("[P]ornography institutionalizes the sexuality of male supremacy . . . .").

218 EISENSTEIN, *supra* note 187, at 172.

219 *Id.* at 223 ("Biology—as the body—is always mediated through its discourses.").

220 *Id.* at 172.

221 *Id.*

222 Catharine A. MacKinnon, *Not a Moral Issue*, 2 YALE L. & POL'Y REV. 321, 326-27 (1984).

223 EISENSTEIN, *supra* note 187, at 172.

224 Eisenstein refers to this as "the actual picture." *Id.* at 173.

225 Eisenstein refers to these as "interpretation." *Id.*

pornography, "it has a multiplicity of meanings."[226] "The anti-pornography position does not recognize this and therefore with uncomplicated simplicity can reduce sex to its engendered form: pornography is reduced to violence; sexual equality is reduced to a protectionist stance."[227]

The crux of the matter is that the way to increase the freedom of women is to free both sexes from the oppositional mode of modernist thinking. It is this mode that reduces sexual relations to a series of binary oppositions,[228] enslaving political discourse to the production of unities that have the appearance of being part of the architecture of thought. For Eisenstein, it is a mistake to fight pornography by treating it "as a unity."[229] Like sex, pornography can take a multitude of forms, some of which "have a positive effect in depicting sex as not necessarily tied to pregnancy, marriage, or heterosexuality. Pornography can help to create a multiplicity of sexual imagery that enhances women's equality by differentiating the female body from the mother's body."[230] By reducing pornography's multiplicity of meanings, antipornography feminists risk denying women the very freedom they aspire to secure for them.

III
POSTMODERNISM/FEMINISM/LAW

A. Generalization

Owing to the universalistic nature of the prose, modernist forms of argumentation tend to suffer from the problem of "careless generalization."[231] Postmodernism holds open the possibility of breaking free from careless generalization, of renewing interest in the manifold properties of particular cases.[232] It notes that by eschewing the particular historical circumstances within which our conceptions of self and others are forged, we lose track of the path

---

226 *Id.*

227 *Id.*

228 For an insightful discussion of the entrenchment of oppositional thought, see J.M. Balkin, *Nested Oppositions*, 99 YALE L.J. 1669 (1990) (reviewing JOHN M. ELLIS, AGAINST DECONSTRUCTION (1989)).

229 EISENSTEIN, *supra* note 187, at 173.

230 *Id.*

231 Gary Wickham, *The Political Possibilities of Postmodernism*, 19 ECON. & SOC'Y 121, 122 (1990) (describing the inductive and deductive manifestations of "careless generalization"). Of course, postmodernist modes of expression are themselves hardly free of this problem.

232 For a discussion of the return to particularism in ethics, see ALBERT R. JONSEN & STEPHEN TOULMIN, THE ABUSE OF CASUISTRY (1988). The return to particulars in law began with American Legal Realism. *See* Dennis M. Patterson, *Law's Practice*, 90 COLUM. L. REV. 575 (1990) (book review).

from which we have come to be what we are.[233] We fail to see the extent to which we are as much product as producer. In short, we fail to appreciate culture

> not as some subjective or idealized world view that is to be distinguished from behavior but as a form of behavior itself and as the tangible results of that behavior. . . . The important point is that culture . . . is explicitly produced rather than simply being implicitly embedded in, or constitutive of, social arrangements.[234]

As a postmodernist would frame it, the problem with careless generalization is that it "not only ignores the specific voices of *particular political sites, it effectively works to stop these specific voices being heard*."[235] For example, the most egregious problem with Robin West's critique of gender's place in modern jurisprudence is not the lack of argument in support of the platitude "woman's 'true' nature," but the fact that she does nothing with it. In her critique of the Official and Unofficial versions of legalism, for example, Professor West never questions the empty generalizations ("autonomy," "connection," "alienation") she seeks to criticize. Instead of showing why these context-independent categories have no explanatory value, West substitutes equally empty notions (e.g., "intimacy," "separation," "invasion"). Despite her claim of telling the story of "women's subjectivity,"[236] Professor West never tells any stories. Thus, her call for "direct language"[237] rings hollow—she makes no effort to engage reality, being satisfied instead to dance across a universe of empty abstractions.

In her discussion of wage labor, Joan Williams demonstrates the gains to be reaped from careful attention to context. However, in her critique of the *Sears* decision, she mistakes the political downside of careless generalization for a substantive thesis about "wo-

---

233 A focus on historical circumstances does not foreclose critical analysis of tradition. *See* RICHARD SHUSTERMAN, T.S. ELIOT AND THE PHILOSOPHY OF CRITICISM 161 (1988).

> [T]radition admits of immanent critique. Even the most unified tradition will contain inner tensions or gaps which in the face of new circumstances would yield conflicting responses or troubling indecision as to how to behave. Such situations compel tradition to reflect critically on itself and to adjust or redefine itself to resolve them, where competing reconstructive interpretations of tradition stimulate further critical reflection. To suppose that tradition contains no possibility for internal conflict or different future projections is to conceive of it as a fully programmed and uniformly closed system, rather than the roughly fashioned, open-structured scheme of divergent elements which we know it to be.

Id.

234 ROBERT WUTHNOW, COMMUNITIES OF DISCOURSE 15 (1989).

235 Wickham, *supra* note 231, at 132.

236 West, *supra* note 104, at 37.

237 *Id.* at 70.

men's nature." The reason Sears's attorneys were rhetorically successful is not that they convinced the court of the truth of an essentialist model of women; Sears's lawyers won because they were able to create a reality through the careful use of a generality *coupled with* a finite context. Williams makes this point herself (albeit unknowingly) when she notes that it is only within the framework of the wage labor system that the essentialist argument about women's true nature is successful. The critical counterfactual question is never asked: What if the reality of women's need to work became part of the context within which Sears's conduct was judged? Under the terms of Williams's own argument, by which I am persuaded, the relational feminists' conception of gender differences would not have been outcome-determinative.

This is the point at which Williams's return to modernist forms of explanation undercuts the power of her insight. Williams's argument regarding the structure of wage labor and its relationship to our cultural conceptions of women is in no way undermined if the veiled references to "false consciousness" are dropped. Professor Williams appears unwilling to take the leap into postmodernism and simply make her case on the merits of the facts as she constructs them. But she can, and she should. Her argument trips over the modernist props she would do well to jettison.

Is Professor Williams's worry justified? Does postmodernism in fact leave us without any critical standards? In untangling the pornography debate, Professor Eisenstein explicitly rejects the notion that gender is a product of nature (sex). Yet notice that, despite the seemingly radical nature of that rejection, her claim is not so radical after all.[238] The trick is to see that the argument works backwards: pornography explains sex and, thus, gender. By examining the particulars of pornography, Eisenstein shows that the depiction of women in corporeal form carries no inherent meaning.[239] Pornography is a (cultural-conceptual) manifestation of the physical form. The (cultural) meaning of pornography *can* be singular, but *need not be*. This is Eisenstein's argument against the Dworkin-MacKinnon position on pornography. By reducing "sex to its engendered form,"[240] Dworkin and MacKinnon have foisted upon women an essentialist picture of subordination and, in the process, deprived women of a measure of freedom.

238 In fact, despite its references to postmodern forms of argument, Professor Eisenstein's argument succeeds not because it is "postmodern" but because it is persuasive.

239 Again, Eisenstein does not argue that there are no biological differences between men and women. Rather, her argument is that the *meaning* of those differences is a matter of culture.

240 EISENSTEIN, *supra* note 187, at 172.

B. Understanding and Narrative

If we agree with Judith Butler that "woman" is not a thing represented in language but is "an ongoing discursive practice . . . open to intervention and resignification,"[241] then we are inevitably brought face to face with the question of critique. If the law does not represent—accurately or inaccurately—some conception of "woman," then what is the role of critique?[242] From what perspective does critique issue? What is the *object* of critique? If there is no viable perspective from which to assess the moral and political inadequacies of the law, then how is criticism possible?

Answers to these questions begin to emerge in a reconsideration of Quine's holistic epistemology.[243] If the truth or falsity of a belief is a function of other beliefs, then one intent on changing current understanding is best advised to begin with the network of existing beliefs.[244] On this view, the dubitability or indubitability of a belief is a function neither of the belief itself nor of some transcendent web of understanding. There are infinite measures of a be-

241 BUTLER, *supra* note 95, at 33.

242 Peggy Radin summarizes this worry nicely:

> But how can the pragmatist find a standpoint from which to argue that a system is coherent but bad, if pragmatism defines truth and good as coherence? Inattention to this problem is what makes pragmatism seem complacent, when it does. One answer to the problem of bad coherence, which the pragmatist will reject, is to bring back transcendence, natural law, or abstract idealism. Another answer, which the pragmatist can accept, is to take the commitment to embodied perspective very seriously indeed, and especially the commitment to the perspective of those who directly experience domination and oppression.

Margaret J. Radin, *The Pragmatist and the Feminist*, 63 S. CAL. L. REV. 1699, 1710 (1990).

243 *See supra* notes 72-76 and accompanying text.

244 A "network" is a set of conventions used by participants in a certain activity to coordinate their shared endeavor. The following description of conventionalism in the art world applies equally well to law.

> People who cooperate to produce a work of art usually do not decide things afresh. Instead, they rely on earlier agreements now become customary, agreements that have become part of the conventional way of doing things in that art. Artistic conventions cover all the decisions that must be made with respect to works produced, even though a particular convention may be revised for a given work. Conventions dictate the materials to be used . . . to convey particular ideas or experiences, as when painters use the laws of perspective to convey the illusion of three dimensions or photographers use black, white, and shades of gray to convey the interplay of light and mass. Conventions dictate the form in which materials and abstractions will be combined, as in music's sonata form or poetry's sonnet. Conventions suggest the appropriate dimensions of a work, the proper length of a performance, the proper size and shape of a painting or sculpture. Conventions regulate the relations between artists and audience, specifying the rights and obligations of both.

HOWARD S. BECKER, ART WORLDS 29 (1982). Thus, the way to begin the process of "rethinking" legal concepts is to question our conventions of understanding. For a further discussion of this point in the legal context, see Dennis M. Patterson, *An Introduction to Conventionalism*, 10 W. NEW ENG. L. REV. 43 (1988).

lief.[245] The lesson is this: the question, "Is this belief true?" must be replaced with the question, "How is this belief to be understood (and can it be understood differently) within this story?"[246]

The reason postmodernism ultimately forces feminist jurisprudence to become narrational[247] is tied to the lack of cognitive authority[248] for our practices.[249] In this regard, jurisprudence can take a lesson from contemporary philosophy of science. In *The Structure*

245 This view is expressed by Quine's thesis of "underdetermination": any data can be "explained" by a host of theories. *See* W.V. Quine, *On the Reasons for Indeterminacy of Translation*, 67 J. PHIL. 179-83 (1970). For a discussion of this theory, see ROGER F. GIBSON, JR., THE PHILOSOPHY OF W.V. QUINE 84-90 (1982).

246 On the importance of the storied character of legal understanding, see Robert M. Cover, *The Supreme Court 1982 Term: Foreword:* NOMOS and Narrative, 97 HARV. L. REV. 4, 4-5 (1983).

247 As a reconstructive enterprise, narrative has close affinities to pragmatism. This Article is not the place to detail the differences, but at least one must be mentioned. American pragmatism emphasizes "communities of inquiry," the members of which work toward "convergence" in their beliefs. These beliefs they take to be true. In a narrative account of understanding, on the other hand, "truth" is at best a compliment paid to ways of understanding that are intersubjective—talk of "truth" muddies the water.

Despite these differences, I think it a mistake to say, as Richard Rorty does, that "pragmatism is banal in its application to law." Richard Rorty, *The Banality of Pragmatism and the Poetry of Justice*, 63 S. CAL. L. REV. 1811, 1811 (1990). To take an example from my own field of commercial law, the number of converts to pseudo-scientific methodologies like rational choice theory and game theory is, if anything, on the rise. The dubious philosophical pretensions of these pseudo-scientific methodologies must be shown for what they are, and pragmatism seems well positioned to do that. Additionally, pragmatism is a sound posture for the critique of all forms of judicial pseudo-objectivism. *See, e.g.*, Dennis M. Patterson, *A Fable from the Seventh Circuit: Frank Easterbrook on Good Faith*, 76 IOWA L. REV. 503 (1991) (critiquing judicial lapse into plain meaning, deductivism, and other sins of the nineteenth century).

248 It is the lack of cognitive authority that underwrites the conventionalist belief that understanding is not a matter of theory but is, as Wittgenstein says, "a way of acting." LUDWIG WITTGENSTEIN, ON CERTAINTY § 204 (G.E.M. Anscombe & G.H. Von Wright eds., G.E.M. Anscombe & Denis Paul trans., 1972). It is important to keep in mind that the idea of "knowledge" is not being rejected; rather, it is being reconstructed. The locus of knowledge is being transferred from the individual to the group.

249 *See* Mark Okrent, *The Metaphilosophical Consequences of Pragmatism*, *in* THE INSTITUTION OF PHILOSOPHY: A DISCIPLINE IN CRISIS? 187 (Avner Cohen & Marcelo Dascal eds., 1989).

> Considered on its own grounds, pragmatism is a recommendation in regard to a way of speaking. It suggests that there is no point in searching for the essence of truth, mind, language, etc., and thus no point to the traditional philosophical game. Pragmatism is the application of the philosophical position of anti-essentialism to the objects of philosophical discourse themselves.

It is with respect to this last point—the application of antiessentialist positions to philosophical questions—that I think Richard Posner goes wrong when he describes the view advanced in these pages as "back to basics." *See* RICHARD A. POSNER, THE PROBLEMS OF JURISPRUDENCE 424 (1990). The whole point of the enterprise is not "back" to anything; rather, it is "away" from a set of methods and questions identified with traditional philosophy.

of Scientific Revolutions,[250] Thomas Kuhn demonstrated that, contrary to common philosophical and scientific understanding of the enterprise, "the authority of science has no basis beyond the consensus of its practitioners, specifically, no basis in a privileged, truth-gaining method."[251] One might object that the practice of science is objective because it provides the best explanation of events in the physical world. But what is "best" is simply "the explanation which best suits the purpose of some given explainer."[252] There is no denying that scientific models or "pictures" of reality serve heuristic purposes.[253] Again, however, it is the scientific community that judges the adequacy of these models, according to its own methods and purposes. Nothing validates one picture (or a picture about how to choose a picture) over another. "In the end all you have is what we all agree is self-evident or conceptually necessary or linguistically required."[254]

In this analysis lies a lesson about the relationship between noncognitivism, narrative,[255] and critique. Like all emancipatory

---

250 KUHN, *supra* note 90.

251 Gary Gutting, *Paradigms and Hermeneutics: A Dialogue on Kuhn, Rorty, and the Social Sciences*, 21 AM. PHIL. Q. 1, 4 (1984).

252 Richard Rorty, *Is Natural Science a Natural Kind?*, *in* CONSTRUCTION AND CONSTRAINT 69 (Ernan McMullin ed., 1988).

253 *See* REPRESENTATION IN SCIENTIFIC PRACTICE 5-6 (Michael Lynch & Steve Woolgar eds., 1990) (describing multiple uses of representation). *See also* HILARY PUTNAM, REPRESENTATION AND REALITY 21-22 (1988).

> [N]one of the methods of representation that we know about—speech, writing, painting, carving in stone, etc.—has the magical property that there *cannot be* different representations with the same meaning. None of the methods of representation that we know about has the property that the representations *intrinsically* refer to whatever it is that they are used to refer to. All of the representations we know have an association with their referent which is contingent, and capable of changing as the culture changes or as the world changes.

Id. For recent treatments of representation in the realm of disease, see DOUGLAS CRIMP & ADAM ROLSTON, AIDS/DEMO/GRAPHICS (1990); SANDER L. GILMAN, DISEASE AND REPRESENTATION: IMAGES OF ILLNESS FROM MADNESS TO AIDS (1988); LUDWIK FLECK, GENESIS AND DEVELOPMENT OF A SCIENTIFIC FACT (Thaddeus J. Trenn & Robert K. Merton eds., Fred Bradley & Thaddeus J. Trenn trans., 1979); AIDS: CULTURAL ANALYSIS/CULTURAL ACTIVISM OCTOBER 43 (Douglas Crimp ed., 1987); KENNETH J. CARPENTER, THE HISTORY OF SCURVY & VITAMIN C (1986).

254 Gutting, *supra* note 251, at 6. *See generally* LAUDAN, *supra* note 90 (reviewing contemporary approaches to the relationship between theory, evidence, and judgment).

255 For an argument that objectivity is a condition for the possibility of an objective narrative, see TERRY F. GODLOVE, JR., RELIGION, INTERPRETATION, AND DIVERSITY OF BELIEF: THE FRAMEWORK MODEL FROM KANT TO DURKHEIM TO DAVIDSON 149 (1989).

> [B]y divorcing objectivity and narrative, we mask a deep connection between them. At the empirical level, objectivity is a notion upon which religious (and other) narratives must rely, most obviously when they claim to be true (about the world we have not made). But this same objectivity depends, in turn, upon a narrative function operative at the formal or transcendental level. At stake in the reflexive connection between objectivity and narrative is the integrity of each notion: objectivity, be-

discourses, feminism aspires to alter our current practices of understanding.[256] The inadequacy of modernist programs of reform suggests that the craving for a totalizing critique of gender relations is an illusion from which we have been freed.[257] This freedom comes at a price; more importantly, it reveals certain limitations bounding feminist discourse. The most important of these limitations is the recognition that criticism of existing practices must issue from within those very practices. In other words, "going local" entails holding in place the very practices of understanding being challenged.[258]

This conception of critique forces feminist jurisprudence into a reflexive[259] examination of the very practices of understanding that

---

> cause the activity of relating lies at its base; narrative, because, as [Hilary] Putnam—and, as I read him, Kant before him—points out, unless we narrate about something, we cannot distinguish speech from noise.

Id.

256 The question is where to start—the answer, "From where we are." *See* DAVID KOLB, POSTMODERN SOPHISTICATIONS: PHILOSOPHY, ARCHITECTURE AND TRADITION (1990).

> But where do we start? We start from where we are. We are always moving within and from current conventions, already on the move in projects we did not choose, in languages we did not create. We do not have to choose between architecture and revolution. It is always too late to start from scratch; there is always language and meaning ahead and behind. That is the condition the moderns tried to overcome, but the tabula cannot be razed, and the attempt to do so leaves what was to be denied present as resented.
>
> But if we have no centered overview, if we are extending our languages and forms of life as we build, how do we know which moves to make? Only some new combinations and moves suggest themselves. We work in a disciplined way, judging what is appropriate, and neither the discipline nor the judgment are universally rational.

Id. at 162-63.

257 *But see* Bell Hooks, *Feminism: A Movement to End Sexist Oppression*, *in* FEMINISM AND EQUALITY 62 (Anne Phillips ed., 1987) (arguing that the success of feminism as an emancipatory enterprise is tied to the advancement of a definition of "feminism").

258 This approach is antithetical to and skeptical of the modernist presupposition that the needs of women can be identified apart from some discourse. *See* Bartlett, *supra* note 5, at 887 ("I have argued that feminist methods *are means to feminist ends* . . . .") (emphasis supplied). Such an approach to feminism creates two troublesome assumptions: the idea of "feminist ends" is an intelligible, context-free notion; and that there is a direct connection (in the sense that one leads to the other) between method and insight.

259 Reflexivity—the turning of a critique back onto itself—is a central problem for all forms of postmodern thought. The problem grown directly out of modernist conceptions of intelligibility. *See* HILARY LAWSON, REFLEXIVITY: THE POST-MODERN PREDICAMENT 43 (1985).

> At the end of the turn of a century which has seen language become the central concern of philosophy there is a risk of reading Nietzsche in the light of modern debates. Nevertheless, Nietzsche was writing at a time when the role of the thinking subject was still perhaps the dominant theme of philosophy, he was no longer in a milieu that assumed language to be transparent. (Once Kant had linked concepts with intuitions, experience could no longer be regarded as independent of the concepts by

make gender relations intelligible. Like other practices of critical reflection, feminist jurisprudence will succeed only to the extent that it questions the vocabularies through which gender relations are understood.[260] To force critical reflection on the juridical categories of gender relations, feminist jurisprudence must retell the stories of gender in ways that enable us both to see the old in new ways and to make sense of the new.[261] One myth of modernism is that there is only one method for accomplishing this task.

> which it is described. Kant thus laid the ground for an increasing role for language.) However, in Nietzsche we see the clear expression of an outlook characteristic of our modern stance, namely the virtual elision of thought into language. In a modern form of Occam's razor, Nietzsche almost eliminated thought. Language, instead of representing thought, provided concepts directly. 'Every word immediately becomes a concept, inasmuch as it is not intended to serve as a reminder of the unique and wholly individualized experience to which it owes birth.' This is not to imply that Nietzsche denied the existence of thought . . . but to indicate that the character of language was for him equatable with the character of thought. For Nietzsche, therefore, to speak about language is to speak about thought.

Id. (quoting Nietzsche).

Narrational intelligibility addresses the problem of reflexivity not by *solving* the problem, but by *dissolving* it by showing how the problem lies within modernist forms of thought. *See* C.G. Prado, The Limits of Pragmatism (1987).

> The noumenal must be eradicated as an idea; no philosophical contrast should be tolerated if it allows room for skeptical doubts *within* the linguistic, which exhausts what there is though somehow not in an ontological sense . . . . Philosophical *theory* can only attempt to get beyond the linguistic through transcendental arguments. But if there is *nothing* beyond language—and we cannot even say nothing intelligible—then efforts at such theorizing must be pointless, and truth cannot be any sort of faithful mirroring. The last thing truth can be is correspondence between ideas or sentences and states of affairs as extralinguistic. To the tradition all of this naturally looks like idealism; the Kantian distinction, or something like it, persists.

Id. at 75.

260 *See* Stephen T. Leonard, Critical Theory in Political Practice 247 (1990).

> Against the modernists, feminists show that neither the self, nor knowledge, nor theory, nor emancipation itself can be apprehended *a priori*. To take seriously the fact that we are historical beings, that human life is a continuous process of making and remaking social life, is to recognize that the purported goal of critical theory, "a form of life free of domination in all of its forms," cannot be interpreted as a form of life that is free of all conflicts of interests. To take seriously our historicity is to see that it is neither possible nor desirable for critical theory to treat emancipation in universal terms.

Id.

261 *See* Jeremy Barris, God and Plastic Surgery: Marx, Nietzsche, Freud and the Obvious 45 (1990) ("[Y]ou can only start off changing reality by changing your knowledge, by remembering what you know so that you can change it.").

Another modernist myth is that, with respect to "woman,"[262] there is only one story to tell.[263] To dispel this myth, feminist jurisprudence must shift its focus to different questions—questions that are not "epistemological."[264] Moving beyond the essentialist paradism of looking at "woman" as something represented *in* law, we should produce genealogies of "woman" in all her manifestations.[265] The lesson of postmodernism is that "woman" is not one thing but many; we know "woman" by knowing her multiple (discursive) manifestations. To rethink the idea of "woman" we must rethink the network(s) within which she is constructed.[266] How are we to accomplish that?

With the abandonment of the modernist aspiration toward a master discourse—Habermas's second-order "discourse of discourses"[267]—comes the realization that progressive change in a discipline must be reconceived as coming not from without but from within. That is, change must come from the redesign of our tools.[268] Of course, "tool" is here used metaphorically, for the only actual tools of the law are its concepts and linguistic practices.

---

262 The lesson of hermeneutics is that there is not just "one story to tell." The past is always being understood anew. *See generally* Hans-Georg Gadamer, Truth and Method 306-7 (2d ed. 1989) (introducing the notion of "horizon fusion").

263 For a pioneering study of the importance of narrative in the understanding of cooperative practices, see Bruno Latour & Steve Woolgar, Laboratory Life: The Construction of Scientific Facts (2d ed. 1986) (advocating the abandonment of epistemology as a way of understanding the production of scientific knowledge).

264 Foucault entreats with a similar message.

> [I]t is a question of forming a different grid of historical decipherment by starting from a different theory of power; and, at the same time, of advancing little by little toward a different conception of power through a closer examination of an entire historical material. We must at the same time conceive of sex without the law, and power without the king.

Michel Foucault, 1 The History of Sexuality 90-91 (Robert Hurley trans., 1978). *See also* Charles Taylor, *Overcoming Epistemology*, *in* After Philosophy: End or Transformation, *supra* note 2, at 464-88.

265 For an effective demonstration of the power of the genealogical method in matters of the body, see Anne B. Goldstein, *History, Homosexuality, and Political Values: Searching for the Hidden Determinants of* Bowers v. Hardwick, 97 Yale L.J. 1073 (1988).

266 *See* Weedon, *supra* note 186, at 168.

> The task for feminist criticism is to demonstrate how texts constitute gender for the reader in class- and race-specific ways and how these modes of femininity and masculinity relate to the broader network of discourses on gender both in the past and in the present.

Id.

A fine example of the application of this method in the context of social welfare is found in Nancy Fraser, *Women, Welfare, and the Politics of Need Interpretation*, *in* Unruly Practices: Power, Discourse, and Gender in Contemporary Social Theory 144-60 (1989).

267 For a devastating critique of Habermas's claims for the power of philosophy as a second-order, legitimating enterprise, see James Tully, *Wittgenstein and Political Philosophy: Understanding Practices of Critical Reflection*, 17 Pol. Theory 172 (1989).

268 As Kenneth Gergen puts it:

Thus, to speak of "change," "transformation," or "reform" is to raise what is, at bottom, a pragmatic question: How is "woman" to be understood?[269]

To answer this, we must first note that our understanding of "woman" occurs within a horizon of fixed[270] meaning. For example, the meaning of a sentence within which "woman" appears is a function of that sentence's position within an appropriate horizon. That is, the meaning of the sentence is not some *thing*, or intention or essence but is a function of the horizon within which the sentence is at home. Thus, meaning is a function of a system of interconnected language-games that together constitute a "horizon of understanding."[271] Once the horizon of understanding is delimited, the new and different can be integrated into it.[272] The new becomes

> Any given set of tools both enables and constrains. It facilitates certain lines of action while restricting others. Advancement in understanding largely derives, then, from the development of new forms of discourse. With the emergence of new language frames, the potential for effective human action is augmented. To view social life as an exchange of reinforcements is both fascinating and rich in evocative potential—but ultimately delimited. Greater efficacy can be achieved if one has at one's disposal lenses through which social life may be seen as sets of rituals, theatrical presentations, economically determined patterns, power dynamics, dialectic transformations, and so on. In effect, the socio-behavioral sciences stand in an optimal position to contribute to the symbolic resources of the culture.

Kenneth Gergen, *Correspondence versus Autonomy in the Language of Understanding Human Action*, *in* METATHEORY IN SOCIAL SCIENCE 157 (Donald Fiske & Richard Shweder eds., 1986).

269 *See* Murphy & McClendon, *supra* note 42, at 200 ("Postmodern epistemology moves toward a new form of pragmatism in attempting to answer the question 'Why this network (this rearrangement) rather then another?' ").

270 "Fixed" here means nothing more than "already in place": there is an established network of understanding, a practice.

271 A "one-step hermeneutics," if you will. *See* ROBERT J. ACKERMANN, WITTGENSTEIN'S CITY 19 (1988).

272 No one voices this sentiment better than the late Michael Oakeshott:

> The problem of historical thinking is to detect what modification a new discovery, a new experience produces in the world of history as a whole. And the weakness of many historians is due to their inability to understand, first, that a new discovery, a new experience produces in the world of history as whole. And the weakness of many historians is due to their inability to understand, first that a new discovery cannot be appeased by being fitted into an old world, but only by being allowed to transform the whole of that world; and secondly, that the character of a new discovery is not given and fixed, but is determined by its place in the world of history as a whole. The general scheme, the initial world of ideas, they imagine to have been given and to lie beyond the reach of criticism; and each new discovery is, for them, equally fixed, solid and independent. New knowledge may be used to illustrate or to extend the old world, but never to modify or transform it. But the fact is that this general scheme, with which the historian begins, is a world of ideas given only in order that it may be superseded. And to see the bearing of a new detail upon the world of history as a whole is at once the task and difficulty of historical thought. For each new discovery, whatever it may appear to be, is, in-

manageable, since the horizon of meaning is such that it can be altered to accommodate the novel.

In thinking of understanding this way, we see immediately that the point of interpretation is the reconstitution of understanding within a particular horizon.[273] Owing to its status as a second-order, reflective enterprise, legal interpretation is necessarily reconstructive: it allows us to regain a coherence that has, for one reason or another, been lost.[274] The process of reconstruction is best described as "narrative" because it is through the narrative reconstruction of the point of the practice that the coherence necessary to the intelligibility of law is maintained. Owing to its ongoing, developmental, and transformative character, law is described most perspicuously as a narrative discourse. If we are careful to delimit the proper sphere of its narrational character, we will gain a better understanding of its ways and our role in it.

> deed, not the discovery of a fresh detail, but of a new world. Every experience is, by implication, a complete world of experience. And each new discovery must be seen in its place in that world, its effect must have been felt upon that world, before its meaning can be said to have been apprehended, before it is 'discovered'. The process in historical thinking is never a process of incorporation; it is always a process by which a given world of ideas is transformed into a world that is more of a world.

MICHAEL OAKESHOTT, EXPERIENCE AND ITS MODES 98-99 (1933).

273 This approach is not without its difficulties. For example, the story of women's emancipation from gender oppression is largely entangled with the story of racial oppression. *See* ELIZABETH V. SPELMAN, INESSENTIAL WOMAN (1988); Angela P. Harris, *Race and Essentialism in Feminist Legal Theory*, 42 STAN. L. REV. 581 (1989). For a recent discussion of feminism in light of the relationships and semantic authority, see Richard Rorty, *Feminism and Pragmatism*, 30 MICH. Q. REV. 231 (1991).

274 *See* WILLIAM HUBBARD, COMPLICITY AND CONVICTION: STEPS TOWARD AN ARCHITECTURE OF CONVENTION 128-29 (1980).

> The larger understanding that I speak of is aware not just of the particular case or law at issue but rather sees the whole context in which this particular instance is located. A judge with this understanding would see his task not as one of formulating a single, free-standing decision but rather as forging a new link in a chain—linking his decision to those that came before and making sure that later decisions will be able to link up with his. For this larger understanding would know that a legal decision cannot stand on its own, like a provable scientific statement. There is no real reason why any decision must be the way it is, and any skeptical prying—or conversely, any attempts at verification with data—would only reveal that unprovability. It is the judge's reasoning that serves as a scrim for us, which veils that unverifiability with reasoning that is just convincing enough so that our skepticism doesn't rise up in us. But the reasoning that makes a decision convincing consists almost wholly of a skillful demonstration of how that decision adheres to principles contained in earlier cases. That is why it is so important to keep the chain of cases intact. Unless those cases are there to point to—and unless they are held in esteem so that pointing to them means something—that reasoning will convince no one.

Id.

Narration is the analytical device through which we realize the aspirations of a practice-based, nonpropositional account of legal knowledge. The ability to solve conceptual problems in law means being able to narrate the point of a legal practice in a way that preserves the point for the practice at the same moment it is transformed. This mode of analysis enables a participant in the practice, at any point in its history, to see how the point of that practice got to where it is at present and to imagine possibilities of how it might be different. This process—rethinking the point of the practice—involves reconstructing the point of the practice in such a way that a new point can be seen to emerge from earlier stages of the practice.[275]

Through narrative reconstruction of the point of a practice, one can chart the transformation of that practice as it responds to internal criticism from its participants, unforeseen or anomalous cases, the integration of the practice with other practices, and a host of other aspects. Narrative is successful as an analytical device in capturing these many and varied aspects of legal knowledge because it enables us to see that understanding and interpretation stand in a dynamic relationship. On a narrative account of legal knowledge, understanding emerges not as a conservative notion but as the focus of interpretive activity. Without understanding, interpretation would simply bite on air. Without narration, understanding would be wooden, lifeless, robotic in character. Narration is the dynamic element in the understanding-interpretation dichotomy.

Narrative reconstruction steers a course between the Scylla of essentialism and the Charybdis of free-wheeling Deconstruction.[276]

---

275 *See* Noël Carroll, *Art, Practice and Narrative*, 71 THE MONIST 140, 151 (1988) ("At any point in the history of the practice (or practices) of art, the unity of the later stage of development is rendered intelligible or explained within the practice by filling in the narrative of its emergence from an earlier stage. . . .").

276 Here I would agree, although for different reasons, with Christopher Norris and Andrew Benjamin: Derrida is not postmodern. *See* CHRISTOPHER NORRIS & ANDREW BENJAMIN, WHAT IS DECONSTRUCTION? 30 (1988) ("[P]ost-modernism effectively collapses a whole series of distinctions that still play a vital (though problematic) role in Derrida's thinking."). *See also* CHRISTOPHER NORRIS, *Limited Think: How Not to Read Derrida*, *in* WHAT'S WRONG WITH POSTMODERNISM? 134-64 (1990). Because Deconstruction further atomizes the individual into discursive fragments, it represents the modernist spirit at its most excessive. *See* Murphy & McClendon, *supra* note 42, at 211-12 (critiquing Mark Taylor's Deconstructionist A/Theology).

In the end, Derrida is just a skeptic—Hume in the cafe. Quentin Skinner makes the point nicely:

> Consider [Derrida's] much-discussed analysis in *Spurs* of the fragment, found among Nietzsche's manuscripts, which reads "I have forgotten my umbrella." Derrida concedes that there is no difficulty about understanding the meaning of the sentence. "Everyone knows what 'I have forgotten my umbrella' means. His only objection to the despised figure he labels "the hermeneut" is that such persons fail to recognize that this still

The idea of reforming our habits of understanding presupposes that certain practices of understanding are intelligible, and may therefore be criticized.[277] By postulating that all understanding is interpretation,[278] Deconstruction, and other versions of "hermeneutic holism," give us no place to start.[279] Every place is as good as any other,[280] so no particular set of terms can be taken as the appropriate place to begin.[281] From the perspective of juridical narrative, the world (of law) is neither a representation of essentialist forms nor a deconstructed disunity of discursive fragments. It is a web of linguistic relationships composed of vocabularies wherein and whereby individuals understand themselves and their social reality.[282] We can neither transcend these vocabularies nor remain

---

> leaves us without any "infallible way" of recovering what Nietzsche may have meant. "We will never know *for sure* what Nietzsche wanted to say or do when he uttered these words."
>
> . . .
>
> If we insist, as Derrida does, on . . . an equation between establishing that something in the case and being able to demonstrate it "for sure," then admittedly it follows that we can never hope to establish the intentions with which a text may have been written. But equally it follows that we can never hope to establish that life is not a dream. The moral of this, however, is not that we have no reason to believe that life is not a dream. The moral is rather that the skeptic is insisting on far too stringent an account of what it means to have reasons for our beliefs. Haunted as Derrida seems to be by the ghost of Descartes, he has concentrated on attacking a position which no theorist of intentionality need defend.

Quentin Skinner, *A Reply to My Critics*, *in* MEANING AND CONTEXT: QUENTIN SKINNER AND HIS CRITICS 280-81 (James Tully ed., 1988).

277 Wittgenstein's remarks on rule-following address this presupposition. *See* LUDWIG WITTGENSTEIN, PHILOSOPHICAL INVESTIGATIONS § 201 (G.E.M. Anscombe trans., 2d ed. 1958) (following a rule is a practice).

278 *See* Jacques Derrida, *Differance*, *in* JACQUES DERRIDA, SPEECH AND PHENOMENA AND OTHER ESSAYS ON HUSSERL'S THEORY OF SIGNS 129-60 (David B. Allison trans., 1973).

279 *See* Richard Shusterman, *Beneath Interpretation: Against Hermeneutic Holism*, 73 THE MONIST 181, 196 (1990) (describing variations on the "it's all interpretation" orientation).

280 Thus, to Wittgenstein, "A doubt without an end is not even a doubt." WITTGENSTEIN, *supra* note 248, at § 625.

281 *See* Richard Shusterman, *Organic Unity: Analysis and Deconstruction*, *in* REDRAWING THE LINES: ANALYTIC PHILOSOPHY, DECONSTRUCTION, AND LITERARY THEORY 110 (Reed W. Dasenbrock ed., 1989).

> [Derrida] himself in maintaining that language excludes totalization characterizes its differential field as "a field of infinite substitutions in the closure of a finite ensemble." Moreover, even forgoing the question of totality, the very presumption that *all* the elements or objects in our languaged world are essentially differentially interconnected and reciprocally constitutive of each other (however untotaled or untotalizable they may be) clearly seems in itself to constitute a metaphysical perspective predisposed to cosmic unity and coherence.

Id. (citation omitted).

282 *See* Dennis M. Patterson, *Law's Pragamatism: Law as Practice and Narrative*, 76 VA. L. REV. 937 (1990) (for a full account of this perspective).

their obedient subjects.[283] We must reconstitute them and, in the process, change our self-understanding.[284]

This, then, is the project of a postmodern feminist jurisprudence: to problematize and reconstruct the many vocabularies within which the law creates "woman."[285] The promise of such a project is that "if we change language and practice together, and it [is successful], we have achieved a special kind of explanatory vantage point for the understanding of our past practice."[286] What will the "success" of such a feminist project look like?[287] To answer this question by prescribing a general criterion for success serves only to duplicate the mistakes of previous modes of criticism. Only in specific contexts, with particular problems and vocabularies, can "success" be given content. To acknowledge this fact is not to avoid the question, but to give it the answer it deserves.

And is not this issue of context, after all, the nagging element in everything that is associated with "postmodernism"? The promise of modernism is the forward march from darkness to enlightenment.[288] We know we have made progress because we perceive the distance between where we are and the abyss from which we have escaped. Offering nothing comparable to the promises of Enlight-

---

283 In other words, we must always begin the process of reconstitution from where we are. *See* Taylor, *supra* note 264, at 475-76.

> As those effectively engaged in the activities of getting to perceive and know the world, we are capable of identifying certain conditions without which our activity would fall apart into incoherence. The philosophical achievement is to define the issues properly. Once this is done, as Kant does so brilliantly in relation to Humean empiricism, we find there is only one rational answer. Plainly we couldn't have experience of the world at all if we had to start with a swirl of uninterpreted data. Indeed, these wouldn't even be "data," because even this minimal description depends on our distinguishing what is "given" by some objective source from what we merely supply ourselves.

Id.

284 The mode of reinterpretation is narrative in so far as the methodological inspiration is to render the present intelligible "by filling in the narrative of its emergence from an earlier stage." Carroll, *supra* note 275, at 151. *See also* Dennis M. Patterson, *Law, Practice, Interpretation and Argument: Toward a Narrative Conception of Legal Discourse*, 5 Soc. Epistemology 61 (1991).

285 In much the same way, postmodernism in art problematizes the meaning of "art." *See* Amy M. Adler, Note, *Post-Modern Art and the Death of Obscenity Law*, 99 Yale L.J. 1359, 1378 (1990) ("'Art,' by its nature, will call into question any definition that we ascribe to it. As soon as we put up a boundary, an artist will violate it, because that is what artists do.").

286 Stephen P. Turner, *Social Theory Without Wholes*, 7 Hum. Stud. 259, 265 (1984).

287 I have already provided a specific example in the discussion of Zillah Eisenstein's critique of Dworkin and MacKinnon on pornography. *See supra* notes 199-230 and accompanying text.

288 However, as events in the twentieth century have demonstrated, modernity has its own forms of barbarism. *See* Zygmunt Bauman, Modernity and the Holocaust (1989) (demonstrating how the Holocaust is the outcome of modernity's unique triumvirate of hate, technology, and bureaucracy).

enment rationality, postmodernism seems to merit our skepticism.[289] It is true that postmodernism has no program—it provides no blueprint. So why "go postmodern"?[290] Again, this seems to be the wrong question. If modernism's prospects no longer seem as great as they once did, does it make sense to replace modernism with an approach that only duplicates the problems of the past? A negative answer has been suggested.[291] The lesson of postmodernism is that the answers to our questions are not *already there* waiting to be found; instead they will have to be produced in the ways just described.

Conclusion

We began by asking whether feminism requires the trappings of modernity. This question is problematized by the uncertain status of modernity itself. We have seen that "modernism" takes many forms, and even in the context of the limited definition utilized here, the claim that we are "in postmodernity"[292] is a dubious one. Like the criticism of yesterday, the critical methods of contemporary social and political theory will simultaneously draw their strength from available forms of discourse and seek to break the bounds of existing modes of criticism.[293] When critics assert that theirs is an entirely new vision of the human condition, we must remind ourselves of this humble lesson.[294]

289 In the final analysis, this skepticism seems unwarranted. *See* Zygmunt Bauman, *Is There a Postmodern Sociology?*, 5 THEORY, CULTURE & SOC'Y 217, 233 (1988) ("[T]he faith in a historical agent waiting in the wings to take over and to complete the promise of modernity using the levers of the political state—this faith has all but vanished.").

290 For an ambivalent answer, see Steve Fuller, *Does It Pay to Go Postmodern If Your Neighbors Do Not?*, *in* AFTER THE FUTURE: POSTMODERN TIMES AND PLACES, *supra* note 68, at 273-84. For the midlife crisis version, see Pierre Schlag, *Normative and Nowhere to Go*, 43 STAN. L. REV. 167 (1990) (Due to the influence of postmodernism, law teaching is now just a form of training people to become glorified insurance adjusters.).

291 For a more positive answer, see WILLIAM CORLETT, COMMUNITY WITHOUT UNITY: A POLITICS OF DERRIDIAN EXTRAVAGANCE 201-02 (1989) ("Perhaps more concentration on tactics at the level of the municipality (where common ground is usually taken literally instead of metaphorically) in addition to but alongside strategies on the high frontier of the individual/collective tension is the most radical politics of community available.").

292 *See, e.g.*, Charles Jencks, *Death For Rebirth*, *in* POST-MODERNISM ON TRIAL 6-9 (Andreas C. Papadakis ed., 1990) (trumpeting the triumph of postmodern architectural style).

293 For an application of this process in social theory, see ROBERTO M. UNGER, POLITICS, A WORK IN CONSTRUCTIVE SOCIAL THEORY (1987).

294 I have in mind contemporary intellectuals like Richard Rorty, whose claims for contingency and irony fail to heed the lessons of Wittgenstein, of whose thought Rorty is so enamored. *See* RICHARD RORTY, CONTINGENCY, IRONY, AND SOLIDARITY (1989). There is no reason *in general* why contingency is to be favored over its opposite. There are differences *and* similarities. This mistake is made at a more general level by contemporary social theorists who argue for one or another version of a "philosophy of differ-

At this juncture, feminist jurisprudence is struggling with the implications of the postmodern critique of reason. This state of affairs is both exciting and troubling. The excitement stems from the knowledge that we are in the midst of rethinking ideas that are so firmly embedded in our cultural psyche that we can hardly imagine what it is to be without them. On the other hand, the failures and shortcomings of these notions have become too numerous to overlook.[295] Feminist jurisprudence ignores them at its peril.

---

ence." *See, e.g.*, Alex M. Johnson Jr., *The New Voice of Color*, 100 YALE L.J. 2007 (1991) (advancing the claim that scholarly "voice" is distinct by virtue of one's speaking from one's own experience as a person of color). The irony here is that in their efforts to argue for the priority of "difference," these theorists duplicate the fundamental mistake of past philosophers—the reification of one aspect of a thing or person.

295 *See generally* GIANNI VATTIMO, THE END OF MODERNITY: NIHILISM AND HERMENEUTICS IN POSTMODERN CULTURE (Jon R. Snyder trans., 1988) (surveying the roots of modernism and philosophical efforts to theorize postmodernity).

[9]

ESSAY

WHAT IS A POSTMODERN CONSTITUTIONALISM?

*J.M. Balkin**

I

I begin with a puzzle. It must certainly strike one as odd that the subject of postmodern constitutional law arises at a time when the actual arbiters of the Constitution — the federal judiciary and in particular the Supreme Court of the United States — appear to be more conservative than they have been for many years, and indeed, are likely to remain so for the foreseeable future. Postmodernism is often associated with what is new, innovative, and on the cutting edge of cultural development. Yet if we were to define the elements of a postmodern constitutional culture, it would be clear that one of the most central features of the present period — if the expression "central" still has any remaining currency in an era of postmodernism — is a judiciary which has no intention of being new or innovative in anything. Its intellectual leader, Justice Scalia, has even called for a constitutional jurisprudence of tradition, coupled with a return to an interpretive theory of plain meanings for statutes and original intention with respect to the Constitution.[1]

To be sure, some might be tempted to explain away this phenomenon as an anomaly or an exception. The federal judiciary, they will say, is behind the times, much as the *Lochner*-era justices were. Eventually, when a different administration comes to power, and appoints new judges, the judiciary will catch up with the breathtaking developments we now discuss under the name of "postmodern" jurisprudence. Indeed, all about us we see, in the works of legal commentators and scholars, and even in the speeches of a few enlightened political leaders, the harbingers of a new dawn of constitutional postmodernism.

---

* Charles Tilford McCormick Professor of Law, University of Texas. — Ed. This essay was presented at a conference on postmodern constitutional law at Georgetown University, and I thank the participants for their comments; my special thanks to Pierre Schlag and Steven Winter for their valuable criticisms of an earlier draft.

1. *See, e.g.*, Michael H. v. Gerald D., 491 U.S. 110 (1989); Green v. Bock Laundry Mach. Co., 490 U.S. 504, 527, 528-29 (1989) (Scalia, J., concurring); Blanchard v. Bergeron, 489 U.S. 87, 97-100 (1989) (Scalia, J., concurring); Antonin Scalia, *Originalism, The Lesser Evil*, 57 U. CIN. L. REV. 849 (1989).

The current climate of the federal judiciary is an aberration, a mistake which hinders the progress of a grand new postmodern day.

Nevertheless, I think the attempt to see a postmodern constitutional jurisprudence in opposition to the increasingly conservative practice of constitutional law is mistaken. It is understandable why postmodern theorists might wish to identify postmodernism with the progressive, with the new that will eventually replace the old, and deny that title to the work of the Rehnquist Court and the rest of the Reagan judiciary. Yet to treat constitutional law as it is actually practiced by courts as foreign or exceptional to a postmodern era or as the target of an eventual postmodern revolution fails fully to grasp the meaning of postmodernism as a feature of current culture. Moreover, I think that such an attempted marginalization would be ironic coming from those who claim to adopt a postmodern (and especially poststructuralist) stance. Rather than seeing this political phenomenon as exceptional or aberrational to postmodern constitutional culture, I think we should see it as exemplary of that culture. Postmodern constitutionalism is the constitutionalism of reactionary judges surrounded by a liberal academy that despises or disregards them, and which is despised and disregarded in turn; postmodern constitutional culture is the culture in which the control of constitutional lawmaking apparatus is in the hands of the most conservative forces in mainstream life, while constitutional law as practiced in the legal academy has cast itself adrift, whether out of desperation, disgust, or despair, and engaged itself in spinning gossamer webs of republicanism, deconstruction, dialogism, feminism, or what have you. Postmodern legal culture is the rout of progressive forces, the increasing insularity, self-absorption, and fragmentation of progressive academic writing, and the increasing irrelevence of that writing to the positive law of the U.S. Constitution.

How is this possible? What does postmodernism mean if Chief Justice Rehnquist already presides over the postmodern Supreme Court? What is the promise of postmodernism or of postmodern constitutionalism in such an age? We can resolve this puzzle if we dispel certain notions about what postmodernism is and what is or should be our relationship to it.

II

We must distinguish several different facets of postmodernism. First, postmodernism is the cultural era in which we live — the era of postmodernity.[2] It is in some ways a furtherance of and in other ways an outgrowth of and reaction to an earlier epoch called modernity. Like modernity, it combines changes in politics, art, and philosophy with changes in technology and methods of economic production.[3] In particular, while modernity is often associated with the Industrial Revolution and mass production of material goods, postmodernism is better identified with the rise of mass forms of communication and the commodification of intellectual products and symbolic forms.[4] It is the era of mass culture and mediazation, a term used to describe the ways in which culture and cultural artifacts are adapted to or created for the forms of mass communication.[5] Postmodernism in this sense is neither necessarily a good thing nor a bad thing. It is a cultural moment that needs to be interpreted and understood. In this sense, postmodernism, like modernism, embraces all who live within a culture, comprehending the fact that people will react to changes in society in many different ways.

Furthermore, it is important to recognize that the postmodern epoch as such is already upon us. Postmodernism is a cultural phenomenon that has already happened and that we are only becoming aware of now. Cultural change occurs as we live within a culture, but we only become aware of its full import later. Cultural understanding always works in retrospect.[6] For us to speak of postmodernism as a coherent cultural episode in our lives, it must have already occurred; it must already be a part of our existence, albeit something that we are only now coming to codify, analyze, and understand. By the time that

2. *See* DAVID HARVEY, THE CONDITION OF POSTMODERNITY: AN ENQUIRY INTO THE ORIGINS OF CULTURAL CHANGE (1989); FREDRIC JAMESON, POSTMODERNISM, OR, THE CULTURAL LOGIC OF LATE CAPITALISM (1991); JEAN-FRANÇOIS LYOTARD, THE POSTMODERN CONDITION: A REPORT ON KNOWLEDGE (Geoff Bennington & Brian Massumi trans., 1984).

3. *See* HARVEY, *supra* note 2.

4. Different versions of the "information society" thesis can be found in DANIEL BELL, THE COMING OF POST-INDUSTRIAL SOCIETY (1973); JAMES R. BENIGER, THE CONTROL REVOLUTION: TECHNOLOGICAL AND ECONOMIC ORIGINS OF THE INFORMATION SOCIETY (1986); and WILSON P. DIZARD, JR., THE COMING INFORMATION AGE: AN OVERVIEW OF TECHNOLOGY, ECONOMICS, AND POLITICS (2d ed. 1985). On the concept of "symbolic forms," see JOHN B. THOMPSON, IDEOLOGY AND MODERN CULTURE 136-45 (1990).

5. THOMPSON, *supra* note 4, at 3-4, 11-20. The "photo opportunity," the televised criminal trial, and radio call-in show are all examples of mediazation. The rise of mass forms of electronic communication, including broadcast and cable television, satellite communication and computer networks, is central to understanding the transformation of culture brought about by postmodernity. For a pessimistic view of the consequences of mediazation on politics and culture generally, see JEAN BAUDRILLARD, FOR A CRITIQUE OF THE POLITICAL ECONOMY OF THE SIGN 164-84 (Charles Levin trans., 1981).

6. *See* ARTHUR C. DANTO, ANALYTICAL PHILOSOPHY OF HISTORY 168 (1965); HANS-GEORG GADAMER, TRUTH AND METHOD 179 (1975). The most famous expression of this principle is Hegel's metaphor of the Owl of Minerva, which spreads its wings only after night has fallen. HEGEL'S PHILOSOPHY OF RIGHT 13 (T. M. Knox trans., 1967).

we understand postmodernism, postmodernism itself will already have been transformed into something quite different. We will then be enmeshed in a new cultural ethos of which we will be only dimly aware, not fully conscious of the elements of social life by which we are defined and by which later generations will define us. The best that we can hope to do is to define the present age by extrapolation from what is immediately past, which we can begin to understand and synthesize.

Second, postmodernism is also the set of cultural products created during the era of postmodernity. These cultural products reflect this era in different ways. Some are mimetic. If the postmodern era is an era of fragmentation, diffusion, emphasis on surface (as opposed to substance or as substance itself), then we might expect to see fragmentation, diffusion, and emphasis on surface in cultural artifacts of the postmodern period. And we do find this, for example, in the development of the music video.[7] Some elements of postmodern culture, far from being mimetic of postmodernism, will be reactions to it, just as Romanticism was a reaction to the perceived deadening of modern life brought on by the Industrial Revolution. Often, however, the reaction will include cultural forms that are mimetic of postmodern cultural themes in an unintended and uncanny way. Thus, in the postmodern period we see a renewed interest in "natural" foods and health, and "natural" experiences, which, when viewed more closely, turn out to be high-tech, mediaized, or commodified. The back-to-nature enthusiast who purchases an expensive backpack constructed of artificial fibers, who eats food advertised as containing "all natural ingredients" that is mass produced and preserved in sealed plastic wrappers, and who exercises using the latest electronically monitored cycling machine, reinscribes elements of postmodernism even as she reacts to them. "Health" and "naturalness" become not only focal points of reaction to postmodern life, but also symbols subject to commodification and consumerist manipulation. Nor is this unintentional reinscription of postmodernist culture unique to the food and health industries. The devotee of "authentic performances" in music is able to enjoy them because of recording technology wholly alien to the circumstances in which early music was first performed, a technology that allows her (for example) to experience "authentic" performances

7. Steven Connor, Postmodern Culture 160-61 (1989) (noting that juxtaposition of images within videos as well as juxtaposition of rock images from different decades "flatten[s] rock history into an undifferentiated present"). On MTV's connections to postmodernism generally, see E. Ann Kaplan, Rocking Around the Clock: Music Television, Postmodernism, and Consumer Culture 49-88 (1987).

of church music repeatedly on her car stereo.[8] The politician who aspires to avoid the artificiality of Washington politics and to mount an appeal to "the people" campaigns through a combination of sound bites and photo opportunities. Her private life is carefully reconstructed for public display.

Postmodernism understood as the products of a cultural era is not something uniformly to be prized. Postmodernism as a cultural phenomenon is not necessarily progressive or morally valuable. There is no guarantee that postmodernism will prove to be "politically correct" (this phrase itself, and its use to attack progressivism, are products of the postmodern era). If we recall, modernism itself was not progressive in all of its implications. Modernism brought us industrial methods of mass production and undreamed of technological progress. Modernism also brought us the Holocaust.[9] Like modernism before it, postmodernism is morally ambiguous. MTV is a paradigmatically postmodern phenomenon in its style of pastiche, fragmentation, and mediazation. It is also often violent, mindless, and misogynistic, and many critics fear that it conveys and reinforces these attitudes in the minds of its viewers. The 1988 presidential campaign was the essence of postmodern politics. It featured intensive mediazation of messages and symbols, lack of mass participation except as consumers of these symbols, emphasis on the surface features of political discourse and, indeed, the swallowing of substance by surface, so that surface became the substance of political discourse. The self-referential quality of postmodernist experience was well demonstrated by ubiquitous political polls that came to reflect not only what people thought about events, but what people expected that they and other people would think about events.

The management and manipulation of "photo opportunities" and "media events" had previously been honed throughout the eight years of the Reagan presidency.[10] This presidency, in turn, was led (if that is the proper word) by an actor who played the role of a president, or

8. *See* Sanford Levinson & J.M. Balkin, *Law, Music, and Other Performing Arts*, 139 U. PA. L. REV. 1597, 1622 (1991).

9. The degeneration of modernity into dehumanizing wickedness is the famous argument of MAX HORKHEIMER & THEODOR W. ADORNO, DIALECTIC OF ENLIGHTENMENT (John Cumming trans., Herder and Herder 1972) (1944).

10. On the Reagan administration's development of highly effective methods of media manipulation, see MARK HERTSGAARD, ON BENDED KNEE: THE PRESS AND THE REAGAN PRESIDENCY (1988); DOUGLAS KELLNER, TELEVISION AND THE CRISIS OF DEMOCRACY 134-42 (1990); DONALD T. REGAN, FOR THE RECORD (1988). On the Reagan administration's use of staged media events and political spectacle, see TIMOTHY W. LUKE, SCREENS OF POWER (1989); Jochen Schulte-Sasse, *Electronic Media and Cultural Politics in the Reagan Era*, CULTURAL CRITIQUE, Winter 1987-88, at 123.

rather the role of an actor playing the role of a president, with such bravado that it became difficult to tell the difference between role playing and the real thing. This was a president who so confounded distinctions between surface and substance, between smoke and mirrors and actual events, between real economic development and the creation of fictitious capital financed by a mountain of debt, that it was at last quite impossible to discern what had actually happened during the eight years of his presidency. Thus, for those who desire a postmodern politics, a word of warning: We have already lived through the postmodern presidency; we have already seen the rise of the postmodern presidential campaign. All of this must give anyone who celebrates postmodernism pause. To label something postmodern in this sense, then, is not to hold it up as a model to anyone who wants to be intellectually fashionable, but rather to present it as a cultural event that needs to be studied to understand how culture has changed for better or worse. This done, we must then ask how, given the changes in political culture wrought in the postmodern era, we can make politics better.

This cultural or sociological understanding of the concept of postmodernism is comparatively straightforward, even if the boundaries of the concept are debatable. However, there is a third meaning to postmodernism. Postmodernism is also a set of critical or theoretical claims about how art should be created, or how philosophy should be written (or not written at all!) — a set of general perspectives for interpreting and evaluating culture and the products of culture.[11] The postmodern architect embraces decorative play and decentering; the postmodernist art critic attempts to find postmodern themes in the works of postmodern artists.[12] In this sense, postmodernism is an interpretive practice that is claimed to be artistically or theoretically valuable or beneficial. Postmodernism is something to be celebrated or encouraged rather than simply an epoch to be understood. It is also associated with being on the cutting edge of cultural production or the interpretation or criticism of cultural production. In philosophy, postmodernism is an attack on what are called "totalizing" theories or "master narratives" that seek to explain all or substantially all of soci-

11. *E.g.*, LYOTARD, *supra* note 2; RICHARD RORTY, CONTINGENCY, IRONY, AND SOLIDARITY (1989); UNIVERSAL ABANDON? THE POLITICS OF POSTMODERNISM (Andrew Ross ed., 1989). For jurisprudential applications, see COSTAS DOUZINAS ET AL., POSTMODERN JURISPRUDENCE: THE LAW OF TEXT IN THE TEXTS OF LAW (1991).

12. On the postmodern theory of architecture, see CHARLES JENCKS, THE LANGUAGE OF POST-MODERN ARCHITECTURE (1977). A recurring feature of postmodern art is the "attempt to dissolve the boundaries between 'high' and 'mass' culture." Roy Boyne & Ali Rattansi, *The Theory and Politics of Postmodernism*, *in* POSTMODERNISM AND SOCIETY 1, 9-10 (Roy Boyne & Ali Rattansi eds., 1990).

ety, history, knowledge, the nature of femininity, or virtually anything else within a comprehensive and articulable theory.[13] From the perspective of postmodern philosophy, there is only a set of overlapping and occasionally conflicting "language games" that arise with respect to different spheres of social life, each incomplete and each constantly subject to alteration and development.[14] The analogy to "games" is important because it is also characteristic of postmodern philosophy to view knowledge as an activity infused with social interaction and power rather than merely a set of articulable propositions or truths.[15] Postmodern philosophy contrasts with relativism because conflicting perspectives are embedded in people's lives and activities; it contrasts with objectivism because it eschews the type of totalizing discourse that objectivism involves, as well as the reduction of knowledge to propositions and claims rather than action and power.

III

Thus, postmodernism is both a situation in which we find ourselves and a cultural response to that situation. Because the cultural response becomes part of the cultural situation, the two elements feed upon each other. Similarly, postmodernism is both a cultural situation and a set of claims about how that culture should be interpreted, altered and continued. Because such acts of interpretation, alteration and continuation stem from the culture, they share features in common with that culture.

Nevertheless, the overlapping meanings of postmodernism are liable to produce a number of confusions. The first is what we might call the "bandwagon" phenomenon. This is the attempt to celebrate or applaud certain features of cultural life simply because they are postmodern, or to believe that desirable forms of culture are produced by consciously attempting to incorporate postmodern themes. In short, it is the fallacy that conscious mimesis of postmodernism in the first two senses of that term — the cultural milieu and its products — necessarily achieves postmodernism in the third sense — a set of cultural methods or goals that should be commended and pursued. Obvi-

---

13. *See* LYOTARD, *supra* note 2; Nancy Fraser & Linda J. Nicholson, *Social Criticism without Philosophy: An Encounter between Feminism and Postmodernism*, *in* FEMINISM/POSTMODERNISM 19 (Linda J. Nicholson ed., 1990).

14. *See* LYOTARD, *supra* note 2, at 10.

15. *See* PIERRE BOURDIEU, THE LOGIC OF PRACTICE (Richard Nice trans., 1990); PIERRE BOURDIEU, OUTLINE OF A THEORY OF PRACTICE (Richard Nice trans., 1977); MICHEL FOUCAULT, THE HISTORY OF SEXUALITY — VOLUME 1: AN INTRODUCTION (Robert Hurley trans., 1978); MICHEL FOUCAULT, POWER/KNOWLEDGE: SELECTED INTERVIEWS & OTHER WRITINGS 1972-77 (Colin Gordon ed., 1980).

ously, this can have highly undesirable effects. For example, one might be tempted to create a jurisprudence that is fragmented, celebrates surfaces, irony, and pastiche, and eschews master narratives because those are postmodernist themes and so that is what a postmodern jurisprudence should look like. This confuses postmodernism as a set of cultural phenomena that appear in a particular epoch with a set of criteria for judgment. The jurisprudence produced during the postmodern era will turn out to display elements of postmodernity whether this is consciously desired or not. That does not mean, however, that these are necessarily useful or desirable features of contemporary jurisprudence.

The second problem is the converse of the first. After hearing endless talk of postmodernist manifestos, it is easy to reduce postmodernism to a set of normative claims and thus forget that postmodernism also involves larger cultural forces that occur without any person particularly desiring their ascendancy. In his review of Fredric Jameson's book on postmodernism, Robert Post asserts that it is "obvious[] that postmodernism affects only certain segments of contemporary life."[16] He offers as proof that there is "no postmodern physics, although there are postmodern accounts of physics. There is no postmodern medicine, although there are postmodern histories of medicine. There is no postmodern law, although there are postmodern commentaries on law."[17] A modernist and proud of it, Post finds it impossible to translate the manifestos of postmodernists into actual practices that would make any sense in science, law, or medicine. How, or more significantly why, would anyone set out to eschew master narratives in physics, for example, or produce fragmentation in the practice of law or medicine? Thus, Post argues that although postmodernists can comment on these practices as outsiders, postmodernism can have no effect on the way they are actually performed.[18]

Nevertheless, it is important to distinguish between postmodernism as a set of normative standards and postmodernism as a cultural phenomenon. Even if one believes, as Post does, that postmodern normative claims are unsuited or inapplicable to certain social practices, it does not follow that the cultural forces we collectively label

16. Robert Post, *Postmodern Temptations*, 4 YALE J.L. & HUMAN. (forthcoming 1992) (reviewing JAMESON, *supra* note 2).

17. *Id.*

18. For a contrary view see Stephen Toulmin, *The Construal of Reality: Criticism in Modern and Postmodern Science*, *in* THE POLITICS OF INTERPRETATION 99 (W.J.T. Mitchell ed., 1983) (The standard opposition of norms of scientific theory construction to postmodern critical concepts is based on an idealized and outmoded view of scientific practice that does not adequately take into account what scientists actually do.).

"postmodernity" have not affected these practices. To study these effects is not simply to give a "postmodern" account of them any more than to study the effects of modernity on social practices is to give a "modern" account of them. It is to ask rather how the forces that define any cultural age (whether modernity or postmodernity) affect the practices that take place within that age. In short, I argue that one does not have to be a postmodernist to recognize the pervasive effects of postmodernity in our lives.

The postmodern era is an era of industrial practices and mass organization and production applied not to material objects like automobiles but to the products of the mind — art and music, knowledge and information, accounting and other service industries. In this sense, it is quite clear that we are already witnessing postmodern legal and medical practice. The industrial model of production — where production is reinterpreted according to discrete units of production measurable in temporal or spatial categories — has already arrived in law. We already have the seventy-hour billed week, the canned brief, the 500-person law firm churning out mountains of paper to prove its value to its corporate clientele. We already have mass-produced litigation and mass-produced judicial administration to deal with it. Already most federal judicial opinions are written by twenty-five-year olds, so that the language of opinions does not really mean what it says, because it was not said by the persons whose meaning really counts. In medicine, we already have the industrial model of treatment — the structuring of medical practice around procedures that can be tabulated and described in reports to insurance companies, the physician who is rewarded not for her bedside manner but her ability to perform so many operations in an hour, and who bills accordingly. The age of the independent doctor has been replaced by that of the hospital bureaucrat. Older conceptions of professionalism have already been supplanted by an industrial model where service is defined in terms of discrete units of production that can be duplicated and evaluated on a mass scale. The lawyers let go by large New York law firms after the 1987 stock market crash quickly learned that employment practices in service sectors, and even in professional service sectors, had mutated into a model of employer-employee relations quite like those that Ford or General Motors applied to blue collar workers.[19] Only cognitive resistance to recognizing this transformation led partners at these firms to engage in the disreputable claim that all of these attorneys were let go because they were not good lawyers, thus

19. *See, e.g.*, Michael Orey, *No Longer Risk-Free*, AM. LAW., Dec. 1990, at 5 (noting changes in law firm thinking about hiring and firing of lawyers).

preserving the rhetoric of a preindustrial professionalism to justify what were clearly profit-motivated layoffs.[20] Likewise, the day of the individual scientist boldly grappling with the truths of the universe has given way to a complicated and bureaucratic model of research, where teams of scientists compete for institutional dollars and where scholarly factories are expected to produce a steady stream of papers as justification for their continued existence.

Perhaps the most confusing aspect of postmodernism is the postmodernist insistence on the relation between thought and action. This is a claim of postmodernist philosophy, a feature of postmodernist critical interpretation, and a fact about postmodern culture revealed by postmodern interpretations. The postmodern philosopher asserts that knowledge is always inscribed in a form of life; the historical experience of postmodernity is the unfolding of cultural phenomena that demonstrate the philosopher's claim. Thus, postmodernism is not merely an epistemological stance, nor is it merely a series of claims or statements about knowledge. To be sure, postmodernism is often identified with claims that knowledge is a web of beliefs rather than a Cartesian framework of foundational knowledge, with the idea that instead of a single totalizing discourse, we have a multiplicity of competing and contradictory language games in which we express ourselves and our views about the world.[21] Lyotard even goes so far as to define postmodernism as a hostility to the idea of a master narrative.[22] However, it is this very epistemological interpretation that leads one to think that postmodernism is merely another form of relativism dressed up in fancier clothing and thus leads one to debate postmodernism as a philosophical position like objectivism or relativism.

Yet a purely epistemological reading captures neither the meaning of postmodernist philosophy nor the experience of postmodern culture. Postmodernism is not simply a set of beliefs that persons happen to hold, although those beliefs are surely part of the cultural phenomenon we call postmodernity. Rather, they are those beliefs inscribed in ways of living that characterize the late twentieth century, and especially the life of postindustrial western societies. These features include the growth of mass media and telecommunications and the cultural effects that both mass media and telecommunications have

20. *See, e.g.*, Sheryl Gross-Glaser, *Firing Trends: Laid-off New York Associates Keep Headhunters Busy*, A.B.A. J., Aug. 1990, at 23 (estimating that 750 to 1500 New York associates were fired in cutbacks and that associates are hampered in finding new jobs by their former firms' denial that layoffs were economically motivated).

21. *See* LYOTARD, *supra* note 2, at 10; Dennis Patterson, *Postmodernism/Feminism/Law*, 77 CORNELL L. REV. 254, 256-57 n.9 (1992).

22. LYOTARD, *supra* note 2, at xxiv.

had in society, as well as the rise of computer technologies and the creation of urban and suburban centers quite different from living arrangements found at the turn of the century.[23] Postmodernism concerns the ways in which the material conditions of life have changed, not simply in the Marxist sense of ownership of the means of production, but in the more ordinary sense of how we go about living our daily lives — lives that are imbued with television, telephones, cable TV, international satellite hookups, film, video cassettes, and so on. Surely the epistemological programs of postmodernist philosophers are part of this cultural milieu. But they are only a small part. CNN and the modern enclosed shopping mall have had a much more significant defining influence on the postmodernist age than any of Richard Rorty's writings.

Thus, emphasis on cultural practices and ways of living is a key element of postmodern thought. If to imagine a language is to imagine a form of life, then language, thought, and the material conditions of life are inextricably intertwined. Knowledge is a set of language games, as opposed to a set of true beliefs; games imply activity, lived experience and interaction. Knowledge, then, is not something that we know but something that we do, or that is done to us. The Cartesian *cogito* becomes transformed: Instead of "I think therefore I am," we have "I think as I am."

For the modernist mind, this merging of thought and activity seems unnecessary and perhaps even bizarre. If there is such a thing as postmodernist philosophy, then there must be a set of postmodernist beliefs, and these must be true or false. From the standpoint of modernism, postmodernism is just another ideology — another claim to totalizing discourse.[24] But from its own perspective postmodernism cannot be such a discourse because it is not merely a set of beliefs, but also a cultural environment in which beliefs occur.

IV

What, then, is a postmodern constitutionalism? It should be quite clear from what I have said above that I do not think that the greatest relevance of postmodernism to American constitutional law lies in methods of interpreting the Constitution. Rather, I think constitutional lawyers need to understand postmodernism because they need to understand the cultural changes that have taken place around them

23. *See* HARVEY, *supra* note 2; MARK POSTER, THE MODE OF INFORMATION: POSTSTRUCTURALISM AND SOCIAL CONTEXT (1990).

24. *See* Pierre Schlag, *Missing Pieces: A Cognitive Approach to Law*, 67 TEXAS L. REV. 1195, 1245-46 (1989) (describing how postmodernism is reinterpreted in rationalist accounts).

in art, politics, technology, and economics. Just as one cannot understand modernism without understanding the Industrial Revolution and the spurt of technological and cultural change that accompanied it, one cannot understand postmodernism without understanding the particular technological and cultural changes in society that have accompanied it. Postmodernity is the era in which the industrial model of mass production is applied to the creation and distribution of symbolic forms. Therefore, we might approach the question of postmodern constitutionalism in the following way: How have changes in technology, communication, and the organization of living and working changed the public's understandings and practice of law, the Constitution, human rights, and democracy? How should the various social actors concerned with the Constitution (lawyers, judges, academics, legislators, citizens) understand the forms and practices of democratic self-government in light of the cultural changes occurring during the postmodern period, and what should they do in response to these changes?

In stating the question this way, I wish specifically to contrast my perspective with the view or assumption that constitutional postmodernism primarily involves questions of how to interpret the Constitution using postmodernist theories of interpretation or insights gained from understanding the "postmodern" or the socially constructed self. These projects may be useful ones. Yet they are only part of the story. To focus on postmodern theories of subjectivity without understanding the cultural and technological basis of change risks turning postmodernism into a sterile form of idealism.

Moreover, my analysis seeks to go beyond the concern with the "social construction of the subject" commonly associated with postmodernism in law.[25] Without further development, there is the danger that such analyses will remain rooted in an overly idealist conception of culture. Shared symbols, values, discourses, or ideas are

25. The construction of the individual by culture is a key theme in the emerging category of postmodern jurisprudence. For recent examples of this scholarship, see STANLEY FISH, DOING WHAT COMES NATURALLY: CHANGE, RHETORIC, AND THE PRACTICE OF THEORY IN LITERARY AND LEGAL STUDIES (1989); Guyora Binder, *Beyond Criticism*, 55 U. CHI. L. REV. 888 (1988); James Boyle, *Is Subjectivity Possible? The Postmodern Subject in Legal Theory*, 62 U. COLO. L. REV. 489 (1991); Rosemary J. Coombe, *Room for Manoeuver: Toward a Theory of Practice in Critical Legal Studies*, 14 LAW & SOC. INQUIRY 69 (1989); Drucilla L. Cornell, *Institutionalization of Meaning, Recollective Imagination and the Potential for Transformative Legal Interpretation*, 136 U. PA. L. REV. 1135 (1988); Angela P. Harris, *Race and Essentialism in Feminist Legal Theory*, 42 STAN. L. REV. 581 (1990); Martha Minow, *Identities*, 3 YALE J.L. & HUMAN. 97 (1991); Patterson, *supra* note 21; Jeremy Paul, *The Politics of Legal Semiotics*, 69 TEXAS L. REV. 1779 (1991); Gary Peller, *The Metaphysics of American Law*, 73 CAL. L. REV. 1151 (1985); Pierre Schlag, *The Problem of the Subject*, 69 TEXAS L. REV. 1627 (1991); Steven L. Winter, *Indeterminacy and Incommensurability in Constitutional Law*, 78 CAL. L. REV. 1441 (1990); J.M. Balkin, *Ideology as Constraint*, 43 STAN. L. REV. 1133 (1991) (book review).

implicitly assumed to be the "forces" of social construction. But no account is given of how this force operates in practice. In contrast, the analysis presented here is distinctly material in its concerns. It asks how changes in technology and culture create new opportunities for the exercise of power. It seeks to draw closer connections between the material conditions of life and thought by studying the technological re-creation of forms of life.

A postmodern constitutionalism, in my view, must ask how postmodern culture and technology have affected law as an institution: the way that the courts, Congress, and the executive interact with each other, and the way that law is understood, promulgated, argued about, experienced, and assimilated. How is information about constitutional rights distributed and spread? What changes have occurred in the ways in which politics is organized, and in the ways in which laws are debated publicly or within government institutions? How have advances in technology changed the possible forms of power, control, and surveillance? What effect has mediazation wrought on the practice of American democracy? These are the key questions for a postmodern constitutionalist.

We can divide this general inquiry into several issues.

A. *Technological Changes Affecting Democratic Institutions*

The Constitution regulates democratic self-government. Yet democracy as a set of institutional practices has changed greatly since the Second World War and especially since the 1960s and 1970s. Political action committees have taken advantage of developments in computerization and data processing to manipulate the political process in ways heretofore undreamed of. The past twenty-five years have seen the increasing concentration of media industries into multinational conglomerates.[26] What effects will these changes have on our understanding of free speech and traditional expectations about the press as guardians of democracy? What does the First Amendment mean in an age of increasing economic concentration in media industries, or in an age of organizations specifically devoted to mass distribution of political messages?

Perhaps even more important from the standpoint of postmodernist theory, mediazation has fundamentally changed the terms of public debate.[27] The movement from newspapers to televi-

26. *See* BEN H. BAGDIKIAN, THE MEDIA MONOPOLY (3d ed. 1990); KELLNER, *supra* note 10, at 80-90; LUCAS A. POWE, JR., THE FOURTH ESTATE AND THE CONSTITUTION 201-03 (1991); THOMPSON, *supra* note 4, at 193-205.

27. KELLNER, *supra* note 10, at 111-32; THOMPSON, *supra* note 4, at 218-71. For general

sion broadcasting as the major source of public information has changed the nature of information received by the public. It has changed the public's expectations of political behavior and the content and form of political communication.[28] What constitutional analysis should apply to regulation of public elections in the era of the sound bite, the photo opportunity, and the media event? Technological improvements have also made possible sophisticated polling techniques, whose power has made them indispensable to modern political discourse. What effect have these developments had on the democratic nature of public opinion? Has virtually instantaneous polling created a feedback loop of public expectations about expectations that will lead to volatility in public opinion or put in doubt the meaning or the authority of "majority preferences"? Worse yet, has the very concept of a true "public opinion" that is not manufactured or simulated lost its meaning in the postmodern age?[29]

Mediazation has not only affected the form in which information about public affairs is conveyed to the public; it has also had a profound effect on the presentation of the self in public life. Political fortunes can vanish overnight by the slightest slip of the tongue when it is broadcast nationwide.[30] Mediazation has also permitted revelations about politicians to be broadcast quickly and widely in simplified and highly charged symbolic forms. Similarly, the public's expectations about what will or will not be revealed about political life, and hence what aspects of private life are relevant, have surely been affected by the mediazation of politics.[31]

---

studies, see LUKE, *supra* note 10; DAN NIMMO & JAMES E. COMBS, MEDIATED POLITICAL REALITIES (2d ed. 1990).

28. A classic account of how "pseudo-events" are created for media consumption is DANIEL J. BOORSTIN, THE IMAGE (1962). GUY DEBORD, THE SOCIETY OF THE SPECTACLE (1975), describes how mediazation contributes to the development of spectacles geared for popular consumption. On the transformation of political election campaigning due to mediazation, see KELLNER, *supra* note 10, at 148-58; JOE MCGINNISS, THE SELLING OF THE PRESIDENT (Penguin Books 1988) (1969).

29. Jean Baudrillard's critique of polling and mass media, for example, goes beyond charges of manipulation or distortion of public preferences in modern democracies. Baudrillard argues that the mass media have eliminated the division between political simulation and reality, so that simulation itself has become political reality. It follows that media and polling techniques do not distort the political process — they are constitutive of the political process. It becomes impossible to speak of the distortion of the political process when the thing that is supposed to be distorted is created by the very thing that is supposed to be distorting it. Thus, we no longer even have the comfort of believing that opinion polls manipulate public opinion, because we can no longer isolate political reality, human will, or human nature as something that could be corrupted or distorted by the media reports that create both political reality and our political selves. *See* JEAN BAUDRILLARD: SELECTED WRITINGS 208-10 (Mark Poster ed., 1988). For an introduction to Baudrillard's views, see Christopher Norris, *Lost in the Funhouse: Baudrillard and the Politics of Postmodernism*, *in* POSTMODERNISM AND SOCIETY, *supra* note 12, at 119-53.

30. THOMPSON, *supra* note 4, at 247-48.

31. Thus, it is possible that the "New Puritanism" that has beleaguered political candidates

We must also ask how mediazation has affected methods of interaction among various government officials and branches of government. Does the ability to manipulate symbols in the media alter the ways in which politicians achieve compromises behind closed doors? Does it increase opportunities not only to inform but also to mislead the public about the nature of proposed legislation? Has mediazation increased executive power disproportionately because of the executive's greater opportunities for manipulation of symbolic forms? Finally, has mediazation helped to impose increasingly insuperable barriers to entry for challengers to incumbent politicians or for persons without access to considerable wealth? The study of the Constitution has always had to confront structural effects and limitations on self-government and democratic ideals. A postmodernist constitutionalism, then, simply asks whether the technological and cultural features of the present era have altered these structural effects or limitations or added new ones of supervening importance.

The question of mediazation must also be confronted by anyone who seeks to ground democratic theory on any form of dialogism or informed public discourse. Mediaized communication conveys information on a mass scale, but unidirectionally;[32] it arrives instantaneously, but in the form of highly charged symbols and sound bites. Mediazation of political culture thus jeopardizes the kind of neutral dialogism that many contemporary political theorists view as necessary to the success of their projects.[33] Ironically, these philosophical projects do not always consider the extent to which technology has rendered their dreams impossible of attainment, or even worse, wholly irrelevant. Yet no theory of democracy can succeed unless it takes these technological changes in dissemination of information into account. Dialogism may already have died the death of a thousand

---

in recent years may be a function not only of changing public values but also of the gradual change in public and private conceptions of self traceable to mediazation. *See* THOMPSON, *supra* note 4, at 246-48. On the recently lamented phenomenon of "pack journalism," in which journalists devote inordinate amounts of coverage to sensational allegations about the private lives of public figures, see LARRY J. SABATO, FEEDING FRENZY (1991).

32. MARK POSTER, FOUCAULT, MARXISM, AND HISTORY 115 (1984); THOMPSON, *supra* note 4, at 227-28; L. A. Powe, Jr., *Mass Speech and the Newer First Amendment*, 1982 SUP. CT. REV. 243.

33. Here we should distinguish ideal or "as if" dialogism from actual dialogism. We must distinguish theories that attempt to justify political structures as if they were the result of an ideal dialogue or deliberative process that did not actually occur from theories that insist legitimacy flows from actual deliberation and dialogue, and therefore seek to make the actual political process more deliberative or closer to an ideal dialogic situation. Postmodern culture presents obvious problems for the latter group. However, the postmodern experience also presents problems for ideal dialogic theories, because it reveals the nonnatural, historically contingent, and technologically situated nature of our assumptions about dialogue and deliberation.

sound bites.[34]

B. *Technological Changes Affecting Public Perception and Participation in Law*

What effect have the rise of mass media and the industrialization of symbolic forms had on the way that the public understands their legal rights and their ability to participate in the legal system? One might well invent, by analogy to the phenomenon of "sound bites," the concept of "law bites," or symbols of the legal system that have become the common cultural coin of the general public. A classic example of the law bite in operation are reports of motorists arrested by Canadian police who repeatedly insisted that their *Miranda* rights be read to them.[35] Mass broadcast of American police shows (and later *L.A. Law*) has apparently altered the public's perception of the criminal and civil justice system, and not only in America. These symbolic representations of law become the common forms of discourse and benchmarks of expectation about law among the lay public.[36] The growth of cable networks like C-SPAN, CNN, and Court TV, and extensive coverage of trials on television, has increasingly subjected legal controversies to a process of mediazation that has already infected politics. Judges, prosecutors, and even witnesses become media

34. An innovative attempt to meet the crisis in democratic self-government described here comes from a political philosopher who does believe in the importance of dialogue in refining and reaching a legitimating consensus in liberal democratic societies. Professor James Fishkin has argued that a citizen jury or "deliberative opinion poll" of 600 randomly selected Americans should be allowed to meet with prospective presidential candidates in a weekend retreat. The purpose of the event would be to force face-to-face dialogue and extended discussions of policy issues between candidates and citizens. Although the event would be televised, the personal interactions between candidates and voters would discourage much of the presentation management that modern political campaigning through the mass media encourages. Extended face-to-face interaction with candidates would be designed to give the participants personal knowledge of the characters, strengths, and weaknesses of candidates that is hard to obtain from staged campaign events. After the retreat, the participating citizens would be polled on their views about the candidates as well as on public policy issues, and this information would be made available to the general public. The citizen jury model is described in detail in JAMES S. FISHKIN, DEMOCRACY AND DELIBERATION: NEW DIRECTIONS FOR DEMOCRATIC REFORM (1991). A candidate's retreat along the lines of Fishkin's model was actually planned for the 1992 presidential campaign, and would have taken place in January of 1992, but fell through because funding for the project could not be procured from interested media organizations. A second attempt is currently being planned for 1996. Communication from James S. Fishkin to author.

35. Herbert H. Denton, *Canada Turns to U.S. on Bill of Rights Issues; Meese Joins Debate With Speech*, WASH. POST, Aug. 7, 1986, at A30 (noting that "[m]any Canadians who have spent hours of their childhood watching police on American detective television read suspects their Miranda rights," have mistakenly demanded the same warnings from Canadian police officers).

36. *Cf.* Rosemary J. Coombe, *Objects of Property and Subjects of Politics: Intellectual Property Laws and Democratic Dialogue*, 69 TEXAS L. REV. 1853, 1861-65 (1991) (noting how in postmodernist culture, shared cultural symbols taken from television shows, movies, advertising campaigns, and mass-produced consumer goods become shared resources for construction of social meaning).

stars; Senate confirmation hearings are scheduled to mesh with the demands of prime time viewing.[37] Changes in substance soon follow those of form; indeed, at points the Thomas confirmation hearings were difficult to distinguish from a particularly sordid episode of *Geraldo.*

With the mediazation of law and legal processes, the products of the Supreme Court and lower courts become transformed in the public eye in the same way as the work of politicians. When Supreme Court arguments are finally televised, this mediazation may well be on the way to its culmination. In the interim, the experience of televised confirmation hearings and criminal trials gives us some idea of the brave new world of media-saturated law that awaits us. Ironically, then, the divide between legal and political discourse may eventually be dissolved not by the efforts of critical legal studies, but by those of Ted Turner and the Cable News Network.

As noted above, media communication allows mass participation, but only unidirectional participation, because viewers can watch, distanced in time and/or space, but cannot otherwise interact with the sender. In the same way that mass media create the possibility of unidirectional political participation on a mass scale, so too the mediazation of law will create opportunities for manipulation of symbolic forms, commodification and spectacle. If the Bork hearings symbolized a sea change in the confirmation of Supreme Court nominees and a blurring of lines between judicial and political candidates, as many have argued, this is not simply due to the bad faith of Bork's political opponents. Rather, I suggest that it is at least partly due to the technological and cultural changes of the postmodern era, which made mass political organization and mediazation of the confirmation process possible. Opposition to Bork was raised through forms of mass politics that would have been impossible without contemporary quasi-industrial methods of political organization or the use of mass media for distribution of messages.[38] Hence, the Bork nomination, for all the things that it symbolized, may also have symbolized a breakthrough in the mediazation of law. In this way Bork, the pessimistic modernist, was defeated, for good or ill, by forces unleashed by the postmodern

37. *See* Helen Dewar, *Democrats Criticized for Strategy on Thomas; Approach in Hearings Called Too Cautious,* WASH. POST, Oct. 20, 1991, at A11 (noting Bush administration demands to schedule Clarence Thomas' testimony during prime time, while Professor Hill's testimony was placed during the day when most working people could not watch).

38. *See* ROBERT BORK, THE TEMPTING OF AMERICA: THE POLITICAL SEDUCTION OF THE LAW 267-349 (1989); ETHAN BRONNER, BATTLE FOR JUSTICE: HOW THE BORK NOMINATION SHOOK AMERICA (1989).

era.[39]

C. *The Industrialization of Legal Production*

I have argued above that a key postmodernist phenomenon is the application of methods of industrial production to symbolic forms, intellectual products, and the life of the mind in general. Information and symbol manipulation become important commodities or sources of wealth. We can see these features occurring in the legal profession as it exchanges an earlier professional ethic for an industrial professionalism. Examples of the industrialization of symbolic legal forms include the growth of large law firms which employ large scale discovery practices, computerization of documents, and other quasi-industrial methods of litigation and work production. As noted above, in employer and employee relations, we are seeing the development of a quasi-industrial model whereby lawyers are hired, fired, and laid off like industrial workers.[40]

The judicial chamber and the academy have not escaped the effects of postmodern industrialization of symbolic forms, although these influences are manifested in a somewhat different manner. In the judiciary, we see increasing pressures for application of quasi-industrial methods to the administration of justice. This is evidenced not only in the increasing limitation of time for oral argument, the streamlining of dockets, and administrative regulations designed to minimize caseloads, but also in the increased use of clerks to write opinions and

39. As in the case of the Bork nomination, the success of the Thomas nomination appeared to turn on the views of voters in a handful of southern and midwestern states represented by the few senators who remained publicly undecided. Thus, questions of Thomas' legal qualifications (about which even some of his supporters had doubts) were shelved in favor of the sort of issue that could be packaged for mass consumption and conveniently played out in front of the television cameras — Thomas' sexual behavior. Consequently, the struggle over the nomination inevitably reduced to a struggle over the public's view of the seriousness of the charge of sexual harassment and the comparative credibility of Judge Thomas and Professor Hill. What were by now relatively standard techniques of media manipulation were used to great effect in this cause. Thomas' now-famous "hi-tech lynching" speech, evoking powerful imagery of his destroyed reputation and offering barely concealed accusations of racism against his white opponents, apparently helped to turn the tide in his favor, as did the vigorous attacks on Professor Hill's credibility and emotional stability launched by Senators Hatch, Simpson and Specter. With on-the-spot polling techniques showing a decided swing in voter sympathy towards Thomas after his testimony, the Senate's confirmation was assured. One need not label these events "postmodern" to wonder at what they portend for the future of American constitutionalism. One need merely sit in front of the television and watch.

40. This process of industrializing legal employment and legal production is no doubt related to, but should not be confused with, a perceived decline in professional standards of practice. While the "industrialization" process is a product of the twentieth century, and especially the late twentieth century, laments about the loss of professional values in the practice of law have occurred continuously throughout the history of the American bar.

the lack of time for judicial study and reflection — in short, the creation of an industrial model of adjudication.

In the academy, we can witness the increasing need to evaluate work in terms of discrete units of production. Thus, the equivalent of billable hours in the law firm are articles in the legal academy. Academic organizations are increasingly structured to reward persons who produce measurable units of production. Such a process elevates objective measurements of quantity over subjective measurements of quality, on the grounds that quantity is more easily measurable. This produces increasing pressure for academics to publish, not because it will increase the valuable knowledge of mankind, but as a symbol of scholarly production. The term "productive scholar" thus comes to mean the scholar who produces a continuous stream of units of production, rather than the scholar who produces meaningful work.

D. *The Fragmentation of the "Public Sphere" of Legal Discourse, and the Rise of "Legal Theory"*

One of the most useful of Habermas' conceptions is the idea of a public sphere of discourse arising with the Enlightenment.[41] Through this public sphere the great issues of the day were debated in coffee houses, salons, literature, and eventually through the earliest forms of mass media.[42] An important consequence of the postmodern age is the destruction or at least transformation of this public sphere due to the rise of mass communication, which permits only unidirectional reception as opposed to the participatory dialogue upon which the traditional public sphere depended.[43] We might, by analogy, consider whether there has been a "public sphere" for legal discourse in this country. I would argue that such a public sphere, in which lawyers, judges, and the legal professoriat engaged in a more or less continual discourse on the growth, restatement, and reform of positive law, existed at least from the end of the nineteenth century.[44] This public sphere continues even today, although the growth of mass media as a method for distribution of legal information (Lexis, Westlaw, and computer satellite broadcasts of CLE programs) may also threaten its disintegration. But perhaps an equally important feature of the disin-

41. JÜRGEN HABERMAS, THE STRUCTURAL TRANSFORMATION OF THE PUBLIC SPHERE: AN INQUIRY INTO A CATEGORY OF BOURGEOIS SOCIETY (Thomas Burger & Frederick Lawrence trans., 1989).

42. THOMPSON, *supra* note 4, at 111.

43. *See id.* at 113-20.

44. *See* Edward L. Rubin, *The Practice and Discourse of Legal Scholarship*, 86 MICH. L REV. 1835 (1988).

tegration of this public sphere of legal discourse is the development of the special status of the legal academic. The legal academy has, for the past twenty-five years at least, become increasingly interdisciplinary. At the same time, it has become increasingly distanced from the work of actual lawyers and judges. Pierre Schlag's diatribes against normative legal scholarship[45] attack the retention of the form of the discourse of the public sphere after the sphere itself has dissolved. Schlag's attack is well taken with respect to certain types of law, although a remnant of a public sphere still remains with respect to other types, particularly local and commercial law (with the caveat that this public sphere has also been transformed by mediazation). Nevertheless, constitutional law is perhaps the best example of how a public sphere of legal discourse that once included practitioners, judges, and academics has largely disintegrated. In constitutional law, we clearly see the fragmentation of legal culture into an increasingly conservative body of judges and an academy that is quite liberal and whose work is increasingly irrelevant to the actual practice of constitutional adjudication. In my view, this is the best explanation of the puzzle I began this essay with. Postmodern legal culture is not necessarily a culture of lawyers and judges who embrace postmodern interpretive theories, but rather a legal culture mimetic of postmodernity: fragmented, decentered, diffused.

As the judiciary becomes increasingly conservative, we witness increasing self-absorption within the legal academy and its increasing isolation from legal practice. Once again, these phenomena occur in differing degrees in different areas of the law, but they are especially pronounced with respect to constitutional scholarship. As a result, a new class of academics arises who have little or no interest in practical political activity, practical law reform, or even practical restatement of the law. Thus, the postmodern period is marked by the creation of a species of legal scholarship known as "legal theory." As a result of the rise of interdisciplinary scholarship, genres of scholarship defined by traditional practice areas (e.g., contracts, torts) are replaced by scholarly genres defined by theoretical allegiances (e.g., law and economics, feminist legal theory), which may cut across traditional doctrinal areas or simply be irrelevant to them.[46] As Sanford Levinson and I have described elsewhere, these developments create opportunities for frag-

45. Pierre Schlag, *"Le Hors de Texte, C'est Moi": The Politics of Form and the Domestication of Deconstruction*, 11 CARDOZO L. REV. 1631 (1990); Pierre Schlag, *Normative and Nowhere to Go*, 43 STAN. L. REV. 167 (1990); Pierre Schlag, *Normativity and the Politics of Form*, 139 U. PA. L. REV. 801 (1991); Schlag, *supra* note 25.

46. Levinson & Balkin, *supra* note 8, at 1652-53.

mentation not only between the legal academy and legal practitioners, but within the legal academy itself.[47]

The flip side of academic alienation from practitioners is academics' increasing lack of respect for the products of judges, legislatures, and administrative agencies. Academics increasingly recognize, or rather assume, the product of these bodies is written by clerks, politically biased, incompetently reasoned, or all three at once. At the same time, they attempt to redescribe law in terms of ideas that have no possible chance of being enacted into legal practice, at least absent a miraculous mass indoctrination of the judiciary. We thus witness the creation of a "shadow constitution" by progressive scholars, in which they declaim what the Constitution really means in the face of the increasing likelihood that it will never mean that in practice.

E. *Technological Changes Affecting Privacy and Surveillance Both by the State and by Private Organizations*

Finally, a postmodernist constitutionalism must come to grips with the effects of technology on privacy, and, more generally, on autonomy itself.[48] Each of us, whether we recognize it or not, produces traces of her activities in material form, just as an animal leaves a trail in the dust where it travels. These traces are signs, but, equally important, they are material signs. If one were able to capture and reconstruct increasing numbers of a person's material traces, one would have an increasingly full picture of that person — not only of her locations and activities, but even of her thoughts, beliefs, and desires. With the growth of computers, electronic information collection and retrieval systems, mass media, electronic recording equipment and forensic science, it is now possible to organize an incredible number of facts about individuals from the traces they leave behind them. For example, credit card purchases can be recorded in a data bank that can be used to create a consumer profile of customers and trace their

47. *Id.*

48. There is now an increasingly large and important body of scholarship on technology and privacy, some of which is self-consciously within the body of postmodernist scholarship, but much more which is not. In the latter category, the pathbreaking work is ALAN F. WESTIN, PRIVACY AND FREEDOM (1967). Many philosophical and economic treatments of privacy have emerged recently, although they do not always emphasize technological issues. *E.g.*, KIM L. SCHEPPELE, LEGAL SECRETS (1988); Richard A. Epstein, *Privacy, Property Rights, and Misrepresentations*, 12 GA. L. REV. 455 (1978); Ruth Gavison, *Privacy and the Limits of Law*, 89 YALE L.J. 421 (1980); Richard A. Posner, *Privacy, Secrecy, and Reputation*, 28 BUFF. L. REV. 1 (1979); Richard A. Posner, *The Right to Privacy*, 12 GA. L. REV. 393 (1978). A good introduction to the legal issues of technology and privacy is Spiros Simitis, *Reviewing Privacy in an Information Society*, 135 U. PA. L. REV. 707 (1987). Postmodern treatments have largely been inspired by the work of the historian of ideas Michel Foucault on punishment and surveillance. *See infra* notes 49, 50.

movements. The use of electronic pricing codes by checkout clerks provides a method not only of controlling inventories but also of compiling information about purchasers' tastes and preferences. The growth of computerization has made possible a revolution in the collection and analysis of information whose scope could hardly have been imagined twenty years ago. Matching information from different databases makes increasingly possible the production of new kinds of surveillance and control. This is the nightmare of Bentham's Panopticon — a prison where each individual's mere knowledge that her every movement is known to others is sufficient to effect behavioral control without the use of physical force.[49] A social Panopticism of the kind envisioned by Foucault is now made frighteningly possible by contemporary technological advances.[50] In this way, knowledge, or more correctly information encoded in material form, creates ever new sources of power and ever new possibilities for control in the postmodern age.

These developments pose significant problems for constitutional theory. Both the state and private individuals will have control over the new technologies of information collection and surveillance. What limits should be placed on the ability of public and private organizations to collect, organize, and distribute such information? Traditional First Amendment philosophy has asserted that the best weapon against speech we do not like is still more speech. Does this philosophy continue to make sense in an era of new information and surveillance technologies? Will increased availability of information about the most detailed aspects of our lives lessen the dangers of control through surveillance or data compilation? Or is the problem precisely the opposite — that the availability of the information is itself the problem? Do traditional liberal notions of autonomy continue to make sense in an age where control of information processing increasingly means new forms of control over individuals themselves? Or has the liberal ideal of the free market of ideas now turned in on itself and created a new form of totalitarianism, a prison constructed from access to information rather than from steel bars?

These issues strike at the heart of liberal political philosophy. Pri-

49. MICHEL FOUCAULT, DISCIPLINE AND PUNISH: THE BIRTH OF THE PRISON 200 (Alan Sheridan trans., Vintage Books 1979) (1975). The Panopticon was a prison constructed as a quadrangle with a high tower in the center; the guard in the tower could watch the prisoners, but they could not see the guard. Thus the prisoners knew that they were constantly subject to surveillance, but they could not tell exactly when surveillance was taking place. *Id.* As a result, this technology "induce[s] in the inmate a state of conscious and permanent visibility that assures the automatic functioning of power." *Id.* at 201.

50. *See* POSTER, *supra* note 32, at 102-03, 165-67; POSTER, *supra* note 23, at 69-98.

vacy is deeply related to notions of individualism and individual autonomy. Each of us has both a public and a private self; the public self we reveal to the world, and the private self we retain control over by withholding it from others. Our ability alternatively to provide or withhold aspects of our private selves preserves and constitutes our autonomy. Exchanges of private information signal intimacy and trust, and their disclosure to third parties is usually thought a sign of betrayal. But the ability to withhold information about the private self is not wholly a natural attribute of existence — it is technologically circumscribed and determined. What will happen to the fabric of intimate relations in a world in which technological advancement increasingly shrinks the domain of the private self? Will traditional assumptions about personal privacy (and hence autonomy) still make sense, or will they have to be reimagined in wholly different ways? And if this is so, what will happen to a constitutional jurisprudence based on eighteenth-century notions of privacy and autonomy that assumed a world without our present technological advances? Again, it is important to stress how these issues go beyond standard assertions about the social construction of the subject. We are concerned here with the material linkages of power; we are concerned with how forms of technology create new forms of power that will inevitably shape our own understandings and expectations about ourselves. If changes in material conditions can so alter or undermine our conceptions of privacy, it is neither our shared ideas nor their social construction that become the key issues, but rather technological change and who has control over its shape and direction.

V

Postmodernism is sometimes described as a rejection of the Enlightenment and the values of the Enlightenment.[51] I prefer to see postmodernism as a partial continuation of the Enlightenment, and a reevaluation of what was good and bad about the Enlightenment project. The Enlightenment sought to free humanity from the chains of unthinking tradition and religious bigotry. It sought to master the world through science and remake the world according to the dictates of reason. It sought to understand and to recast society in rational and scientific terms, and it was confident about the ability of the human intellect to do this. Two centuries later, humanity is imprisoned by

51. *See, e.g.*, Alex Callinicos, *Reactionary Postmodernism?*, *in* POSTMODERNISM AND SOCIETY, *supra* note 12, at 97, 97-100; Anthony Carty, *Introduction: Post-Modern Law*, *in* POST-MODERN LAW: ENLIGHTENMENT, REVOLUTION AND THE DEATH OF MAN 1 (Anthony Carty ed., 1990).

new chains that the Enlightenment forged for us. These are the chains created by science, technology, and rationality, which in the course of liberating us subjected us to new forms of control, bureaucracy, mediazation, suburbanization, and surveillance. We still need liberation, we still need emancipation, but now it is from the products of our previous emancipation — from computer data bases, sound bites, political action committees, voodoo economics, electronic surveillance, commodified video images, and the industrialization of professional culture. The emancipation we now require cannot be on the same terms as those proposed by the Enlightenment. It must, at least in part, be a rejection of the terms by which we freed ourselves from pre-Enlightenment thinking.

Moreover, as I have tried to suggest in this essay, viewing postmodernism as a reaction to the Enlightenment neglects a second, equally important issue. The Enlightenment is identified primarily with ideas and with the quest for knowledge. After all, the very motto of the Enlightenment, as announced by Kant, was "Dare to Know."[52] Yet there was much more to modernity than Enlightenment. These ideas did not exist in a vacuum but were rather part of increasingly rapid technological changes that brought on profound changes in the way that individuals led their daily lives.[53] The material conditions in which knowledge and thought were instantiated were just as important to modernity as were Enlightenment ideals themselves. Indeed, these technological changes were in some ways even more important than the liberal humanist ideology of the West. This fact is crucial to understanding the meaning of postmodernity in places outside of North America and Western Europe. The technological progress of modernity reached further throughout the world than its associated Enlightenment ideals ever did. The automobile and the television have traveled to places that never heard of John Stuart Mill. Perhaps the most telling revenge of modernity on itself were scenes broadcast to the United States of the Ayatollah Khomeini's followers carrying handpainted signs (in English) calling for "Death to the United States." Fundamentalist cultures had also learned to manipulate the broadcast media produced by western technology in their war against the Enlightenment values of the West. Our humanist ideals may rise and fall, but our technology goes forward forever, mindlessly and powerfully. If the motto of the Enlightenment was "Dare to Know,"

52. IMMANUEL KANT, *What is Enlightenment?*, *in* FOUNDATIONS OF THE METAPHYSICS OF MORALS & WHAT IS ENLIGHTENMENT? 286 (Lewis W. Beck trans., 2d ed. 1955).

53. *See* MARSHALL BERMAN, ALL THAT IS SOLID MELTS INTO AIR: THE EXPERIENCE OF MODERNITY 18-19 (1982).

the motto of the post-Enlightenment should be that Knowledge is Material. It is with that principle, perhaps, that a postmodern constitutionalism must begin.

[10]

CORRESPONDENCE

Postmodern Constitutionalism as Materialism

Francis J. Mootz III *

Professor J.M. Balkin's recent essay in the *Michigan Law Review*[1] assesses the implications that postmodernism holds for constitutional law. Although I agree with Balkin about many of the specific issues that he believes must be addressed in a postmodern constitutionalism, I find that his manner of talking about postmodernism is unproductive in an important way. Balkin quite correctly argues that a postmodern constitutionalism should not mimic the fragmented and superficial culture of postmodernity, nor should it devolve simply to normative claims that postmodernity is desirable and should be embraced or adopted within the law. However, Balkin's thesis that a postmodern constitutionalism must focus on the material determinants of social life is an ambiguous, if not troubling, alternative. Postmodern thought recognizes that all understanding is context-specific, but this very lesson cautions against attempting to decode the material features of our social context in order to understand ourselves. I shall attempt to explain my reservations about Balkin's postmodern constitutionalism as clearly and concisely as Balkin has written his essay.

Balkin begins by distinguishing different facets of postmodernism. He regards the culture of postmodernity as the primary feature of postmodernism. Postmodernity "is the era of mass culture and mediazation" that has produced cultural artifacts exemplifying "fragmentation, diffusion, and emphasis on surface."[2] Balkin stresses that the culture of postmodernity is not a result of the triumph of progressive politics. Postmodernity is a sociological fact that exhibits both reactionary and progressive elements. Therefore, the fact that the Supreme Court is becoming increasingly reactionary is not inconsistent with the fact that our legal culture is postmodern. Balkin regards

---

* Assistant Professor, Western New England College School of Law. B.A. 1983, Notre Dame; A.M. 1986 (Philosophy), J.D. 1986, Duke University. — Ed. I am grateful to Jim Gardner, Don Korobkin, and Caren Senter for engaging me in many helpful conversations about the ideas in this correspondence. I also would like to thank Jack Balkin for his comments and criticisms of an earlier draft and his willingness to comment on my other works in progress.

1. J.M. Balkin, *What Is a Postmodern Constitutionalism?*, 90 MICH. L. REV. 1966 (1992).

2. *Id.* at 1968, 1969. In this regard Balkin describes MTV as a "paradigmatically postmodern phenomenon." *Id.* at 1970.

postmodern thought as a different facet of postmodernism. Postmodernity is marked by theoretical and critical perspectives that simultaneously grow out of the material conditions of the culture at large and also provide a vocabulary for comprehending them and reflecting on their impact. Postmodern thought challenges prevailing epistemologies and ontologies by rejecting the idea that there is a foundation for knowledge other than the historical flux of existence.

Balkin's central premise is that we can describe the cultural condition of postmodernity without becoming entangled in the difficult problems posed by postmodern thought. He argues that postmodern cultural forces "inscribed in ways of living that characterize the late twentieth century" are more primordial than the "epistemological reading" of postmodernism embodied in postmodern thought, which represents a reflective attitude about knowledge.[3] Balkin believes that his postmodern constitutionalism is immune from the standard critiques leveled at other philosophical orientations "because it is not merely a set of beliefs, but also a cultural environment in which beliefs occur."[4] Postmodernity is a cultural given that exists no matter what we may believe, Balkin asserts, and therefore "one does not have to be a postmodernist to recognize the pervasive effects of postmodernity in our lives."[5] For example, Balkin describes new technologies of information collection, collation, and dissemination, and then asks whether traditional liberal notions of autonomy that subtend American constitutionalism "continue to make sense in an age where control of information processing increasingly means new forms of control over individuals."[6] Balkin's point is that to focus on epistemological theories about the Constitution's indeterminate commitment to privacy rights is less useful than to describe postmodernity and then explore whether privacy is possible given the material features of postindustrial society. Balkin argues that epistemological critiques miss the point that postmodernity shapes our lives and knowledge regardless of whether we adopt a postmodern philosophical position.

Balkin's project holds a certain appeal. We might avoid, or at least put to the side, the messy jurisprudential issues raised by deconstruction and hermeneutics and instead undertake a practical assessment of material social reality and its impact on the legal system. This distinction is suspect from the start, however, and Balkin experiences difficulty maintaining it. On one hand, he argues that rejecting master

3. *Id.* at 1975.

4. *Id.* at 1976.

5. *Id.* at 1974.

6. *Id.* at 1987.

narratives and foundational justifications for knowledge must be subordinated to examining the deeper effects of the changes wrought by material forces. On the other hand, he admits that these forces in turn must retrospectively "be interpreted and understood."[7] Balkin does not explain how we are to investigate (interpret) the material forces that shape our lives, nor does he describe the value that this interpretation holds for us. Balkin's essay might lead the casual reader to believe that empirical sociological inquiry is distinct from and has priority over critical reflection and a questioning engagement in legal dialogue. I do not believe that Balkin intends such a simplistic and misguided approach, but his bifurcation of the "material" and "theoretical" facets of postmodernism tends to confuse this issue.[8] Balkin's emphasis on the material determinants of knowledge does not free us from the epistemological puzzles of postmodern thought. Instead, it elevates the importance of these epistemological concerns.

Balkin's use of the word *material* is misleading. Although his references to the material determinants of knowledge suggest a neo-Marxist approach, Balkin has subsequently explained that his use of *material* is meant to breach the materialist-idealist distinction altogether.[9] Balkin wants his reader to regard our material condition as the forms of life that produce all knowledge. Even granting this qualification, I do not believe that reading such a capacious definition of *material* back into Balkin's essay strengthens his argument.[10] Moreover, Balkin is still drawing a distinction, although the distinction is better termed as an opposition of prereflective and reflective experience. In this correspondence I argue that there are more productive

7. *Id.* at 1968.

8. As a leading deconstructionist legal scholar, Balkin would appear to be the last person one would accuse of having postmodernism all wrong. I have found Balkin's work to be closely related to my jurisprudential writings. *See* Francis J. Mootz III, Hermeneutics and the Rule of Law: Why the Obvious Is Plausible (Oct. 1992) (unpublished manuscript, on file with author). It is this backdrop that makes Balkin's essay all the more puzzling to me.

9. Balkin made this point in a telephone conversation with me in early October 1992.

10. I am reminded of Paul Ricoeur's assessment of neo-Marxist writings that move away from Marx's scientific materialism by greatly expanding the definition of *work*. Ricoeur argues that from this perspective work comes to designate "the entire human condition of man, since there is nothing that man effects but by a toilsome act; there is nothing human which is not *praxis*." Paul Ricoeur, *Work and the Word*, *in* EXISTENTIAL PHENOMENOLOGY AND POLITICAL THEORY: A READER 36, 37 (Hwa Yol Jung ed., 1972) (reprinted from PAUL RICOEUR, HISTORY AND TRUTH 197-219 (Charles A. Kelbley trans., 1965)). As Ricoeur indicates, a "notion which signifies everything no longer signifies anything." *Id.* at 38.

Ricoeur's theme is closely related to my argument. Ricoeur asserts that "there is not a kingdom of work and an empire of the spoken word which would set bounds to each other from without, but there is a power of the spoken word which traverses and penetrates everything human, including the machine, the utensil, and the hand." *Id.* at 39. The word is a "critique of work . . . . It assumes an aloof attitude, it *reflects*." *Id.* at 43.

postmodern readings of the relationship of prereflective life and reflective praxis.

Balkin provocatively characterizes postmodern thought as a "partial continuation of the Enlightenment" that seeks emancipation from "the chains created by science, technology, and rationality, which in the course of liberating us subjected us to new forms of control, bureaucracy, mediazation, suburbanization, and surveillance."[11] The task of a postmodern constitutionalism is to determine how these material "chains" have affected the institution of law. Balkin apparently believes that there has been an epochal transformation from modernity to postmodernity and that this transformation has called forth postmodern thought as an evolutionary revision of the Enlightenment project. He contends that the character of postmodern thought is less important than the new culture of postmodernity, whose material forces transform us regardless of what beliefs we hold. In contrast, I believe that the material forces of contemporary society are a continuing development of the modern era and that postmodern thought is an epochal shift that attempts to deal with modernity on radically different terms than those proposed by Enlightenment thought.[12] Consequently, a postmodern constitutionalism should remain closely allied with the critical perspectives of postmodern thought.

I begin by questioning whether moving beyond epistemological critiques in order to confront the material factors that shape and change social practices makes sense. Balkin presses this agenda by arguing that the material features of industrialization were just as important to the modern era as was the self-understanding embodied in the ideals of Enlightenment. As evidence for this claim, Balkin points to the transformation through technology of fundamentalist cultures that remain steadfastly opposed to the Enlightenment commitment to rational, scientific knowledge. But surely this example cuts the other way: the technological colonization of the rest of the world by European and North American countries has not rendered these foreign cultures *modern* in the way that this term is understood in western cultures. Foreign cultures are not sundered from their traditions by the universalizing imperatives of scientific thought and technology. Rather, technology becomes rooted in the tradition it invades, even as it spurs new developments within that tradition. The material forces of cul-

11. Balkin, *supra* note 1, at 1988-89.

12. *See* MARSHALL BERMAN, ALL THAT IS SOLID MELTS INTO AIR: THE EXPERIENCE OF MODERNITY (1982) (arguing that modernity stretches from the sixteenth century to the present and that epochal shifts mark the manner in which we define and cope with this evolving modern era).

tural life undoubtedly are tremendously important resources in the continual process of defining a society, but they are not brute determinants. We should not relegate critical reflection to the background of inquiry in favor of sociological descriptions of material features of society. Rather, we should demand that critical reflection assume a more practical task.[13]

Recall Balkin's privacy example. The technological threat to privacy only makes sense as a "threat" from some social conception of privacy. The mere presence of new technology does not threaten "privacy" as such. Postmodern constitutionalism need not reassess privacy solely because certain technology has been invented. Instead, technological development holds a certain significance for our society because it fits within our culture in a certain way, revealing stresses within the shared view that our society is an amalgam of rights-bearing individuals and also is a functionally organized and administered community. If postmodern constitutionalism must take account of the

---

13. I do not mean to suggest that reflection is in some way more authentic than life as it is lived, nor that we should regard critical reflection as an external power brought to bear on the mundane realm of experience. Reflection simply is unavoidable once we come to regard life as puzzling. *See infra* note 17. Reflection is an effort to recover, articulate and explore the prereflective significance that lived experience holds for us. *See* MAURICE MERLEAU-PONTY, *The Philosopher and Sociology, in* SIGNS 98 (Richard C. McCleary trans., 1964). Merleau-Ponty rejects the idea that the social sciences will come to replace critical reflection by addressing themselves only to the "facts," and he also rejects the idea that philosophy is unconnected to sociological understanding.

> The sociologist philosophizes every time he is required to not only record but comprehend the facts. At the moment of interpretation, he is already a philosopher. . . .
>
> . . . The philosopher thinks about his experience and his world. Except by decree, how could he be given the right to forget what science says about this same experience and world? Under the collective noun "science" there is nothing other than a systematic handling and a methodical use — narrower and broader, more and less discerning — of this same experience which begins with our first perception. . . .
>
> . . . .
>
> . . . Accordingly, we must not simply say that philosophy is compatible with sociology, but that it is necessary to it as a constant reminder of its tasks; and that each time the sociologist returns to the living sources of his knowledge, to what operates within him as a means of understanding the forms of culture most remote from him, he practices philosophy spontaneously. Philosophy is not a particular body of knowledge; it is the vigilance which does not let us forget the source of all knowledge.

Id. at 101-02, 110.

Merleau-Ponty sees the task of reflection as plunging "into the perceptible, into time and history, toward their articulations. It does not surpass them through forces it has in its own right; it surpasses them only in their meaning." MAURICE MERLEAU-PONTY, *Introduction, in* SIGNS, *supra*, at 3, 21. History is not the progression of material social structures, nor is it the march of a disembodied reason.

> Why ask if history is made by men or by things, since it is obvious that human initiatives do not annul the weight of things, and the 'force of things" always acts through men? It is just this failure of analysis, when it tries to bring everything down to one level, which reveals history's true milieu. There is no "last analysis," because there is a flesh of history in which (as in our own body) everything counts and has a bearing — the infrastructure, our idea of it, and above all the perpetual exchanges between the two in which the weight of things becomes a sign as well, thoughts become forces, and the balance of the two becomes events.

Id. at 20.

material forces that shape our lives in mundane and practical ways, then inevitably it must also take account of both the significance that these forces hold for us and the ways that they are understood. I do not understand Balkin's assertion that "it is neither our shared ideas nor their social construction that become the key issues, but rather technological change and who has control over its shape and direction."[14] If all knowledge is acquired only through our inherence in a historical, material situation, then our efforts to understand this situation cannot help but invoke and critique shared perspectives.[15]

Balkin does acknowledge that material forces need "to be studied to understand how culture has changed for better or worse" under their influences, and that critical theory provides the necessary "general perspectives for interpreting and evaluating culture and the products of culture."[16] But the relationship of social fact and social theory is more immediate than Balkin suggests. We cannot avoid gripping, and being gripped by, a critical theoretical perspective if we pursue the question of postmodernity. Simply by asking how postmodern cultural forces are affecting legal practice, we adopt a critical and interpretive posture toward the social conceptions that define these forces. Otherwise, the question simply would not occur to us, and we would not have "postmodernity": we instead would have diffuse and unthematized social experience.[17] By talking about postmodernism, Balkin has adopted a critical perspective on contemporary American

14. Balkin, *supra* note 1, at 1988.

15. Merleau-Ponty's phenomenology demonstrates how we can accept that knowledge is possible only on account of our situated, material condition as corporeal beings without falling prey to materialism. *See* MAURICE MERLEAU-PONTY, PHENOMENOLOGY OF PERCEPTION 70 (Colin Smith trans., 1962) (arguing that our bodily comportment in the world is the source of all knowledge but that modern thought wrongly regards the "body, which is my point of view upon the world, as one of the objects of that world").

16. Balkin, *supra* note 1, at 1971.

17. Some might argue that abandoning abstract critical perspectives would leave life pretty much as it exists now, but without the useless exercise of philosophical reflection. Talking about the end of philosophy is fashionable, but this is often a rhetorically provocative posture rather than a meaningful commitment. Certainly philosophy as an academic discipline does not create, direct, or justify existence. Such philosophical pretensions are quite ridiculous. However, abandoning philosophy in its truest sense — the questioning and challenging encounter with prereflective meaning relations — is a dangerous, unwarranted, and, I believe, difficult proposition to carry out. Even the ever-playful deconstructionist, Jacques Derrida, brutally criticizes other thinkers in a way that leaves no doubt that he believes doing so is somehow worth his efforts, that he is on to something, and that others should listen.

Devout postmodern legal thinkers inevitably carry forward philosophical reflection. *See, e.g.*, Dennis Patterson, *Postmodernism/Feminism/Law*, 77 CORNELL L. REV. 254 (1992). Patterson's article is appropriately titled because it constitutes a third-order philosophical narrative. The ordinary language game of law is first the subject of a critical perspective loosely organized under the term *feminism*. In turn, Patterson assesses feminism according to the yardstick of postmodernism. The fact that Patterson concludes that a postmodern feminism is one that weaves an emancipatory narrative as part of legal practice does not undo the philosophical structure of his argument. This is not a failing of Patterson's article; things simply cannot be other-

society and therefore must grapple with all of the issues raised by postmodern thought.

Balkin accurately states that postmodernism involves more than merely rejecting philosophical metanarratives by accepting reason and knowledge as the products of localized and overlapping language games.[18] But what does it mean to argue that a postmodern constitutionalism should move beyond epistemological theory and instead should focus on the material determinants of social life by asking "how postmodern culture and technology have affected law as an institution"?[19] We can pursue this question by considering Balkin's essay as an essay. Why was it written? What part does his essay play in a postmodern constitutionalism?

For courts and lawyers to assimilate social changes into constitutional practice (as, for instance, by rearticulating personal privacy within a particular context) is one thing, but for Balkin to write about this potentiality within legal practice is quite another. If the material cultural forces of postmodernity shape legal practice above our wanting and willing, what is the point in telling us this? If postmodernity effects its full influence only after being interpreted or thematized in some manner, what has Balkin told us about how scholars, judges, lawyers, and citizens can influence this thematization? Phrased more concretely, if Balkin intends to tell lawyers and judges that they should read the Constitution in light of evolving cultural practices, has he told them something that they do not already know, or has he suggested a strategy that they do not already employ? If Balkin intends to provide lawyers and judges with a better method for practicing constitutional law, does he claim to have grasped "postmodernity" in such a way as to provide guidance for legal practitioners? Surely, Balkin would concede that the search for a method based on a description of reality is the very target of postmodern thought.[20]

Addressing these questions requires that we return to the age-old dispute in political theory regarding the relationship between emancipatory theory and social practice. Postmodern thought is provocative because it places in question whether theory and practice can be segregated to the extent suggested in the framing of such traditional questions. Postmodern theorists cannot pretend to decipher the mate-

---

wise. In fact, I find many similarities between Patterson's philosophical conclusions and my own.

18. Balkin, *supra* note 1, at 1975.

19. *Id.* at 1978.

20. *See, e.g.*, HANS-GEORG GADAMER, TRUTH AND METHOD (Joel Weinsheimer & Donald G. Marshall trans., 2d rev. ed., Crossroad 1989) (1960).

rial determinants of social life; this dog-chasing-its-tail conception of theory is a primary target of postmodern critiques. Postmodern theory assumes a more humble task: to reveal practice in a way that energizes it.[21] Postmodern thought is significant for law because it opens the possibility that legal practice might embody the critical bite that is always embedded, but often unrecognized, in legal dialogue. Practicing lawyers are no more able than legal theorists to grasp the material forces of social life from a distance; a postmodern legal practice is defined by an open comportment within legal dialogue rather than a conscious, rational seizing of the whole situation. Balkin's essay is not part of everyday legal practice; it is jurisprudential. To assess its value, we must clarify the relationship between postmodern jurisprudence and contemporary legal practice.

Postmodern jurisprudence rejects the idea that the culture in which we live can be separated from the rhetorical means by which we represent that culture to ourselves; it also rejects the idea that our theoretical perspectives stand aloof from the practices under study. In a culture lacking absolute foundations, jurisprudential critique of legal practice occurs when we reinterpret habitual thematizations, not from the privileged perspective of observer, but from the frontline perspective of one who shares in the labor of articulating these thematizations. Postmodern jurisprudence describes the dialogic character of knowledge and encourages a critical engagement that can lead to new understanding of our situation. Critical confrontations are possible only within this dynamic, intersubjective rhetorical space. For example, postmodern jurisprudence discredits the rhetorical power of originalism and attempts to present legal practice in a new light. This effort does not simply propound a new method of legal interpretation. Instead, it embodies a new way of understanding legal practice as a continuing dialogue between the demands of the present and our habituation in a traditional discourse. Postmodern jurisprudence questions the received wisdom about how law is practiced and offers instead a nonfoundational, critical account of all understanding, including legal understanding, that describes practice in an attempt to influence it.[22]

21. My characterization of postmodern jurisprudence and postmodern practice follows the post-Heideggerian hermeneutics of Hans-Georg Gadamer and Paul Ricoeur rather than Jacques Derrida's deconstruction or Ludwig Wittgenstein's ordinary language philosophy. *See* Mootz, *supra* note 8; Francis J. Mootz III, *Is the Rule of Law Possible in a Postmodern World?*, 68 WASH. L. REV. (forthcoming Apr. 1993); Francis J. Mootz III, *The Ontological Basis of Legal Hermeneutics: A Proposed Model of Inquiry Based on the Work of Gadamer, Habermas and Ricoeur*, 68 B.U. L. REV. 523 (1988).

22. Balkin notes the "increasing insularity, self-absorption, and fragmentation of progressive academic writing, and the increasing irrelevance of that writing to the positive law of the U.S.

A postmodern legal practice would embody dialogic openness. The legal practitioner will never be able to define and take account of free-standing technologies that go "forward forever, mindlessly and powerfully" as a means of correcting the practice.[23] Rather, postmodern constitutionalism must work through the tangled connections between legal practice and political power that are revealed in legal discourse. The discourse of legal practice helps to define our world because it is an important venue in which we find our world.[24] Judges cannot help but be aware of increasingly advanced surveillance technologies when they decide cases that they regard as implicating privacy concerns. However, they are able to confront the problem of technological advances only by holding legal dialogue open to the broader dialogues about political and social organization in which the idea of privacy in postindustrial society is molded. The project of postmodern jurisprudence is to cajole decisionmakers to do just that. The attack on originalism presents not only a new description of practice but also a normative injunction that we should free legal practice from artificial and unproductive constraints. Postmodern jurisprudence is grounded in and descriptive of legal practice as an ongoing dialogue. There is no postmodern inquiry outside of or prior to this dialogue.[25]

Constitution." Balkin, *supra* note 1, at 1967. But Balkin's argument contains nothing to convince the reader that his postmodern constitutionalism will be any more successful in shaping legal practice. Balkin's essay is not an argument within legal practice in the same way that a memorandum of law or doctrinal scholarship might be considered legal practice. Instead, his essay is jurisprudential. The task of jurisprudence is to place in question the unexpressed limitations defining practice.

My argument is that Balkin's essay is useful only if it helps us to see that the limits of contemporary legal practice are not limitations inherent in a supposed "nature" of legal practice. Postmodern jurisprudence should not move beyond the epistemological battle; it should win the battle. Just as the legal realists won the battle against doctrinal formalism, postmodern scholars must win the battle against foundationalism, not just on paper but by effecting a change in our very comportment within legal dialogue. Postmodern constitutionalism, as contextual legal practice, will follow in the wake of this reorientation.

23. *But cf.* Balkin, *supra* note 1, at 1989.

24. Of course, legal practice is not the only venue, nor is it necessarily always an important venue. For example, legal dialogue in the area of race relations is now seemingly spent without having achieved reconciliation. Admitting this is nothing more than admitting the limitations of postmodern constitutionalism and acknowledging that we participate in our culture in roles other than lawyer, scholar, or judge.

25. Balkin criticizes dialogic models of democratic legitimation as "impossible of attainment, or even worse, wholly irrelevant" due to "technological changes in dissemination of information." Balkin, *supra* note 1, at 1980. I agree that the ideal of society as a deliberative public body, or polis, appears quite naive to us today, but this is not because material social forces necessarily preclude democratic dialogue. In fact, the opposite seems true. When communism fell in Eastern Europe, observers widely acknowledged that closed societies simply could not operate in a technologically advanced culture. Fax machines, video cameras, and satellite feeds were all used to break the authoritarian grip on society. The failed reform effort in Beijing was put down in large part by removing these technological tools from the hands of the reformers and then brutally stifling dissent by physical coercion. The mediazation of American culture does

Postmodern constitutionalism cannot postpone normative commitments in favor of bare descriptions of the culture of postmodernity. By declaring itself postmodern, legal thought takes a position not only on how we acquire knowledge but also on how we should react to this new description.[26] Justice Scalia's legal opinions should not blithely be accepted as symptoms of a fragmented, incoherent culture; they should be criticized for spinning a fantasy about the character of legal dialogue, a fantasy that ultimately warps the dialogue. Nor should we regard postmodern critiques of Justice Scalia's new textualism as epistemological niceties that overlook the material forces of postmodernity. The postmodern critique of textualism, plain meaning, originalism, and crude Burkean traditionalism ultimately describes legal practice as a situated dialogue with a defining history and an undetermined future. It recognizes that legal practice cannot help but reflect the wider culture, but it also suggests how legal practice can be more responsive. Postmodern constitutionalism is not the study of our material context. It is a recognition that knowledge emerges from situated dialogue and a corresponding effort to hold ourselves open to this meaning-laden situation.

I do not dispute Balkin's insistence that a postmodern constitutionalism must be practiced within the specific contexts of our day and that these contexts include the powerful effect of technology on our lives. Balkin's outline of the effect of postmodern culture is a compelling story. But it is only a story, and a rather simple one at that. We

---

not preclude dialogue; in fact, it feeds on the ideals of democratic dialogue even as it warps them. Political theorists must address what democratic dialogue means in this environment, but they need not abandon the ideal of public debate.

More importantly, discrediting any notion of dialogism runs counter to the central thrust of postmodern thought: all knowledge arises from a situated dialogue. Dialogism is not just a model of political legitimation that may or may not be achieved it is a recognition of certain ways of being and knowing that can either be facilitated or hindered.

26. Balkin does not subscribe to the antinormative, radically deconstructive views of some postmodern legal scholars. *See, e.g.*, Pierre Schlag, *Normative and Nowhere To Go*, 43 STAN. L. REV. 167 (1990); Pierre Schlag, *Normativity and the Politics of Form*, 139 U. PA. L. REV. 801 (1991). I believe that Balkin would align himself with Drucilla Cornell's longstanding efforts to counter these corrosive theoretical programs that destroy the possibility of ethics as part and parcel of their effort to subvert our foundational heritage. *See, e.g.*, Drucilla Cornell, *From the Lighthouse: The Promise of Redemption and the Possibility of Legal Interpretation*, *in* LEGAL HERMENEUTICS: HISTORY, THEORY, AND PRACTICE 147, 156 (Gregory Leyh ed., 1992). Nevertheless, Balkin does separate ethical (normative) prescriptions from a description of the material conditions of postmodernity. Balkin argues that the culture of postmodernity does not compel one vision of how law, medicine, or politics should be practiced. Instead, it serves as the material backdrop against which these normative choices are made. Balkin, *supra* note 1, at 1973. I am arguing against the idea that we can describe contemporary legal culture — as bureaucratized, commodified, and industrialized, for instance — without betraying normative commitments about how law should be practiced. Balkin's postmodern constitutionalism fails because it presumes that we can stand back and describe our condition as a prelude to formulating normative commitments, when in fact our descriptions are always symptomatic of normative commitments.

cannot move from the antifoundationalist epistemology of postmodernism to an investigation that looks behind social conceptions to the material forces shaping social life. We cannot investigate the material features of postmodernity and then set out to change legal dialogue. Rather, the lesson of postmodernism is that we can only push and be pushed by the situated dialogue itself.

[11]

McGILL LAW JOURNAL
REVUE DE DROIT DE McGILL
Montréal
Volume 35 1990 *No 3*

The Big Fear: Law Confronts Postmodernism

Alan Hunt*

Postmodernism has had a marked influence on cultural studies for well over two decades, yet its impact on legal studies has been felt only recently. Despite this, the engagement between law and postmodernism is shown by the author to be profound, and it is argued that the postmodernist perspective now pervades progressive legal thought in general and Critical Legal Studies in particular. The author first explores the impact of postmodernism through its critique of the Enlightenment. While remaining sceptical of the perceived novelty of this critique, he finds much that is valuable in the challenge it poses to the pretensions of rationalism and legal centralism that mark the discourse of the Enlightenment and its legacy in the major variants of liberal legal theory. Attention then shifts to the postmodernist critique of the epistemological presuppositions of both liberal theory and early CLS. This is a more problematic aspect of the postmodernist challenge, and the author shows how it has raised the spectre of nihilism within CLS, resulting in an unmediated opposition between those insisting on claims of certainty and those deriding such absolutist theory. The way out of the "big fear" of nihilism, according to the author, is the realization that both views are trapped in a false dichotomy which is characterized in academic debate by the invocation of the image of the "slippery slope". The effect of this false dichotomy on the politics of CLS is then explored with the author concluding that a pragmatic conception of truth, rooted in social practice, is needed to ground a project of progressive legal thought.

Au cours des deux dernières décennies, le postmodernisme a grandement influencé les sciences humaines. Par contre, son impact dans le domaine juridique est beaucoup plus récent. Néanmoins, l'auteur démontre que le lien entre le droit et le postmodernisme est profond. Il affirme que la perspective postmoderniste soutend la pensée juridique progressive en général, et les *Critical Legal Studies* en particulier. L'analyse de l'auteur commence par une exploration de l'impact de la critique postmoderniste de la pensée du siècle des Lumières. Tout en doutant de la nouveauté de cette critique, l'auteur apprécie le défi qu'elle pose au prétention de rationalisme et au centralisme juridique qui marquent le discours des Lumières ainsi que les principales variantes de la théorie libérale du droit issues de celui-ci. L'auteur examine ensuite la critique postmoderniste des prémisses épistémologiques des théories libérales et, à l'origine, les CLS. Le défi postmoderniste est ici plus problématique. Il soulève le spectre du nihilisme au sein des CLS et donne lieu à une opposition entre les absolutistes et les relativistes. Selon l'auteur, pour échapper à la crainte du nihilisme, il s'agit de reconnaitre que ces deux positions sont issues d'une fausse dichotomie. L'auteur conclut que tout fondement d'une pensée juridique progressive doit reposer sur une conception pragmatique de la vérité, ancrée dans la pratique sociale.

* Professor of Law and Sociology, Carleton University, Ottawa, Canada.

* * *

Synopsis

* * *

> The crisis consists precisely in the fact that the old is dying and the new cannot be born; in this interregnum a great variety of morbid symptoms appear.
>
> — Antonio Gramsci[1]

Introduction

The contemporary situation in legal studies exhibits an unprecedented confusion of intellectual trends and influences. This cacophony is especially pronounced amongst those who explicitly undertake committed and partisan scholarship which may be broadly, if not definitively, labelled 'progressive'. There are marked differences of opinion about what constitutes a progressive approach. The most pronounced differences revolve around the merits of the postmodernist influences which today have a substantial, if not predominant, impact within critical legal studies [hereafter CLS], the most influential progressive movement in legal studies.

---

[1]A. Gramsci, *Selections from the Prison Notebooks*, ed. and trans. by Q. Hoare & G.N. Smith (London: Lawrence & Wishart, 1972) at 276.

What is this thing called postmodernism? Is postmodernism the same as poststructuralism? And what of deconstruction? I will generally employ the label postmodernism and treat it as subsuming poststructuralism and deconstruction: poststructuralism identifies the ground-clearing theoretical critique of both Marxist structuralism and linguistic structuralism while deconstruction names the method employed in opening up 'the text', whether legal judgment, news story or novel, to reveal both what it contains and what it blocks or excludes.[2] But the label postmodernism, even if it does not define the project, at least has the merit of projecting something of its flavour.

For present purposes I take postmodernism to be the embracing of a judgement that we have traversed a significant divide between the modernism of the early twentieth century and the postmodern reality of the late twentieth century. Without attempting to explore the various descriptors employed to map this transition, it is sufficient to stress that we now exist in a new epoch. The most significant step in forming the postmodernist perspective is the inference that if the old world is passing or is already past then its problems and questions have become redundant and so also have the intellectual theories and methods that were fashioned around those old problematics. It is not simply that a new set of questions can and should replace a prior set; the radical self-conception of postmodernism arises from its claim that we must break with the kind of 'big' questions which have traditionally motivated the intellectual projects of the previous epoch. It is not so much that modernism arrived at the wrong answers, but that its questions were unanswerable; they have been too broad, too abstract, riddled with a distinctive mix of naive humanism, an unwarranted faith in science and an over-optimistic view of the capacity of language to capture and share knowledge. Perhaps the most pervasive spirit of postmodernism is that it enjoins us all to the challenges and difficulties of trying to rethink the world and our place in it.[3]

The direct object of this paper is to explore the question which may be baldly stated as: "What is Left in legal studies?" This self-consciously polemical question requires explanation; it arises from a concern to identify which of the array of intellectual and political projects that have emerged from controver-

[2]I am sensitive to the view, strongly pressed by Christopher Norris, that deconstruction should not be conflated with postmodernism; see C. Norris & A. Benjamin, *What Is Deconstruction?* (New York: St. Martin's Press, 1988). My justification for merging them in what follows is that the form in which postmodernism has impacted on legal studies is one in which its exponents and practitioners have themselves conflated these two related, but distinguishable positions.

[3]This sketch of postmodernism is given in lieu of a lengthy bibliographic essay. If the varieties and complexities of postmodernism are ignored my suggestion is that just two texts provide a sufficient introduction: J.-F. Lyotard, *The Postmodern Condition: A Report on Knowledge*, trans. G. Bennington & B. Massumi (Manchester: Manchester U.P., 1984); and Richard Rorty's set of essays in the London Review of Books: "The Contingency of Language" (17 April 1986), and "The Contingency of Selfhood" (8 May 1986).

sies around or touching on law can sustain the progressive claims made by their respective advocates. This situation is not just the oft-repeated sectarianism of progressive opinions preferring to argue with their own kind than to engage with their opponents. What is different are the radically dissimilar images, models and strategies which are on offer today. Confronted with this diversity of views and opinions, I am keen to insist that there is no intention to impose some authoritatively 'correct' or definitive line; rather, my concerns stem from a quest for self-clarification whose pursuit may contribute to the resolution of an important set of disagreements amongst progressives.

This article will argue that neither a simple espousal nor a rejection of postmodernism is adequate; instead it will contend that there are valuable elements of the postmodernist perspective which can contribute to progressive legal studies and which can be separated from its negative dimensions. Lest this sound too even-handed, it is as well to make clear that what is rejected is most of the general perspective that constitutes postmodernism. What is recommended for retention are some useful, yet partial, insights and techniques.

The quote from Gramsci with which I opened catches the flavour of a period of transition in which complex sets of intellectual and cultural manifestations contend. It is probably wise to strike a note of caution about whether the current conjuncture should be identified as a 'crisis', but there is no doubt that the end of the 80s marks a break or transition in both intellectual and political life. Perhaps Gramsci strikes a more negative tone than is necessary in that we are not simply confronted with "morbid symptoms"; rather I will argue that our present difficulties stem from the dilemma which confronts us when we seek to distinguish the morbid from the positive features present in postmodernist thought. What Gramsci succeeded in capturing is the sense of confusion, commotion and instability that permeates current exchanges. He focuses our attention on the distinctive characteristics of the present conjuncture in which many and varied positions contend and in which it is difficult to determine the political implications of the positions deployed. We find a vigorous debate on the Left in which radically incommensurate intellectual positions are offered as 'progressive', whilst the same ideas are denounced by others as 'reactionary'. For example, we find Jurgen Habermas arguing that postmodernism plays into the hands of conservatives, whilst Jean-François Lyotard retorts that it is Habermas who is the conservative.[4]

The closing years of the twentieth century are proving to be an epoch fraught with difficulties for progressive intellectuals. Contemporary Western societies seem further than ever away from the major structural transformations

---

[4]See J. Habermas, "Modernity Versus Postmodernity" (1981) 22 New German Critique 3 and, more generally, *The Philosophical Discourse of Modernity*, trans. F. Lawrence (Cambridge: Polity Press, 1987); for the postmodernist response see Lyotard, *supra*, note 3.

necessary for the dismantling of the hierarchies of class, gender and race and the achievement of social justice. It no longer seems relevant to repeat the old battlecries of the variant forms of the socialist movement. Despite the exciting chinks becoming visible in the monolith of the communist East, orthodox Marxism and the intellectual (if not political) renaissance ushered in by the Western Marxism of the 1960s, Marxist socialism is simply too encrusted with its history to provide contemporary inspiration. But neither has the social democratic tradition been able to transcend its own bureaucratic and paternalistic legacy. The oppositional Leftisms, whether Maoist, Trotskyist or anarchist, that have occasionally surfaced over recent decades, seem ever less relevant to the complexities of sustainable social change in the contemporary world. Despite the commitment of progressive intellectuals to the quest for links between theory and practice, meaningful engagement with 'where people are at' in relatively affluent, consumerist societies is more difficult than ever to achieve. The manifestations of resistance and the glimmers of possible alternatives appear as a bewildering plurality. Few would retain a hope that the working class (or any other unitary subject) has the capacity to bring the fragments together.

If progressive intellectuals confront these big and intractable quandaries a more specific set of dilemmas confront the progressive working in and around the law. The intellectual demography of the 60s and 70s resulted in a significant entry of radical intellectuals into both legal practice and law schools. There had, of course, been progressives working in the legal arena in previous periods. The difference today is that the loose alliance of progressives has achieved a certain critical mass which makes it possible to entertain the aspiration that they might displace the elite servants who have for so long and with such self-satisfaction served the aggrandizement of law's empire.[5]

These dilemmas take the form of a quest for a new intellectual paradigm, one that is demonstrably radical but at the same time avoids the deficiencies of the theories of the 'old Left'. In the field of legal scholarship the alternative which is currently having the greatest impact is the constellation of themes around postmodernism.

The intellectual and political issues associated with postmodernism are having a belated but nevertheless significant impact within legal scholarship. It is belated in the sense that in fields such as literary and cultural studies it was the 1970s which witnessed the impact of postmodernism. In this sense legal studies has, not unusually, lagged behind the main flow of intellectual development. But although the decade of postmodernism and deconstruction may be over in cultural studies, it is certainly not over in legal studies. Indeed it is an important dimension of my argument to insist that law's confrontation with

[5] "We are the subjects of law's empire, liegemen to its methods and ideals" in R. Dworkin, *Law's Empire* (Cambridge: Harvard University Press, 1986) at vii.

postmodernism is both a deep and a profound engagement. It is one that cannot be ignored nor will it go away. The belated encounter between law and postmodernism is serious and presents major challenges to most varieties of existing scholarship. While traditional scholarship has reacted dismissively or has ignored the challenge it is significant that the major location of both the rise of postmodernism and of critical reactions thereto has been within CLS; accordingly it will be this engagement that will provide the major focus of my discussion.

Postmodernism is an extremely variable phenomenon. It significantly changes both its form and its content as it moves between different cultural and intellectual fields. Postmodernism in architecture and in law are very different manifestations. It is not my concern to map the varieties of postmodernism.[6] There is a certain superficial sense in which postmodernism has travelled through the cultural and social studies and is currently visiting law. But to make this analogy more satisfactory it is necessary to insist that postmodernism has not simply been a travelling circus passing from one field to another repeating the same show in different locations. Rather, in the course of its migrations not only the debate itself but the ideas and concepts which it deploys change.

I. Law Encounters Postmodernism

There is now a burgeoning postmodernist literature in and around legal studies. It is diverse in nature and not yet sedimented into schools, groups or factions. I make no attempt to offer a bibliography or even a bibliographical survey; instead some of its more interesting manifestations are noted below.[7] In order to assess the impact of postmodernist thought on legal studies it is desir-

---

[6]On the mapping of postmodernism see A. Huyssen, "Mapping the Postmodern" (1984) 33 New German Critique 5 and F. Jameson, "Postmodernism, or the Cultural Logic of Capitalism" (1984) 146 New Left Rev. 53.

[7]J.M. Balkin, "Deconstructive Practice and Legal Theory" (1987) 96 Yale L.J. 743; D. Cornell, "Toward a Modern/Postmodern Reconstruction of Ethics" (1985) 133 U. Pa. L. Rev. 291; C. Dalton, "An Essay in the Deconstruction of Contract Doctrine" (1985) 94 Yale L.J. 997; C. Douzinas & R. Warrington, "On the Deconstruction of Jurisprudence: Fin(n)is Philosophiae" in P. Fitzpatrick & A. Hunt, eds, *Critical Legal Studies* (Oxford: Basil Blackwell, 1987) 33; G. Frug, "The Ideology of Bureaucracy in American Law" (1984) 97 Harv. L. Rev. 1276; P. Goodrich, *Legal Discourse: Studies in Linguistics, Rhetoric and Legal Analysis* (London: Macmillan, 1987); C.A. Desan Husson, "Expanding the Legal Vocabulary: The Challenge Posed by the Deconstruction and Defense of Law" (1986) 95 Yale L.J. 969; A.C. Hutchinson, *Dwelling on the Threshold: Critical Essays on Modern Legal Thought* (Toronto: Carswell, 1988); C. Norris, "Suspended Sentences: Textual Theory and the Law" in *Contest of Faculties: Philosophy and Theory After Deconstruction* (New York: Methuen, 1985) 167; G. Peller, "The Metaphysics of American Law" (1985) 73 Calif. L. Rev. 1151 and "Reason and the Mob: The Politics of Representation" (1987) 2:3 Tikkun 28; G. Rose, *Dialectic of Nihilism: Post-Structuralism and Law* (Oxford: Basil Blackwell, 1984); and B. de Sousa Santos, "Law: A Map of Misreading. Toward a Postmodern Conception of Law" (1987) 14 J. L. & Soc. 279.

able to identify both what is general about postmodernism and, more importantly, what is specific to the issues and controversies to which it has given rise within legal studies.

Postmodernism has made its presence felt in legal studies at two different but related levels. The more immediate level, which manifests the direct connection with literary theory, is provided by the concern with textuality, whilst the more general level involves the postmodernist challenge to the philosophical and epistemological underpinnings of legal theory [see Part II below]. There is an immediate and common sense plausibility to the idea that what links literary criticism and legal studies is that both are significantly concerned with the interpretation of texts. Legal texts, in particular the privileged form of the appellate judgement, provide the raw material for legal interpretation. This focus on textuality has taken on a special significance in the interpretation debate within legal theory.[8] This is because the abandonment of the quest for authorial intention disrupts the deeply entrenched tradition within common law jurisdictions of grounding the validity of the legal order as a whole on the privileged authorship and authority of constitutional texts and appellate judgements.[9] In an important sense there is a great deal at stake in controversies over the 'correct' interpretation of constitutional or statutory documents. The question of interpretation is not new but rather the awareness of the debates in literary criticism, generating an explicit focus on the textuality of law, has served to sharpen the awareness of the important issues that underlie different interpretive strategies. Yet these debates remain, in Ronald Dworkin's sense "internal", in that they accept the interpretive project whilst arguing about how judges and legal academics should discharge this function.[10]

As deconstruction migrated from literary criticism to legal theory the context changed, as did the issues and their importance. The question is no longer how to interpret the text; rather it is about the legitimacy of legal discourse as a mechanism of power disguised as the pursuit of interpretive truth. Thus the project of deconstructivist critique is to mount a challenge to the legitimacy of

[8]On the interpretation debate see R. Dworkin, "Law as Interpretation" (1982) 9 Critical Inquiry 179; D.C. Hoy, "Interpreting the Law: Hermeneutical and Poststructuralist Perspectives" (1985) 58 S. Cal. L. Rev. 135; S. Fish, "Working on the Chain Gang: Interpretation in Law and Literature" (1982) 60 Tex. L. Rev. 551; O. Fiss, "Objectivity and Interpretation" (1982) 34 Stan. L. Rev. 739; and A. Hutchinson, "Doing Interpretive Numbers: A Jurisprudential Twosome in Three Parts" in *Dwelling on the Threshold*, *supra*, note 7, 125.

[9]The question of authorial intention has taken on special significance in the United States by virtue of the review role of the Supreme Court. This was dramatically underlined in the hearings on the Bork Supreme Court nomination played out before a national TV audience which revolved around the role of the founders' intentions as the source of legitimate constitutional interpretation.

[10]*Supra*, note 5 at 78-86.

the project of law as a means of generating distinctively legal truth.[11] This essay will focus on the wider postmodernist themes because I suggest that with respect to interpretation the postmodernist impulse, while radical in its project, is a variant of a position already well established within the interpretation debate in legal theory.[12] This position, in turn, is a species of social constructionism in which language is not conceived as reflecting some extra-discursive reality; but language, and the understandings and meanings which it generates, are the 'reality' of social being.[13] The radical inflection of the postmodernist intervention lies not, I suggest, in its interpretive strategy or deconstructive methods, but rather in the way in which the tensions, closures and contradictions in judicial texts are linked to the wider dynamics of power and dominant interests.[14]

There is a general sense in which we are all now social constructionists; where postmodernist interpretivism departs is that it denies that there is any possibility of comparing, contrasting, evaluating or interpreting that discourse by reference to some extra-discursive reality.[15] Since this characteristic is a manifestation of postmodernism's general epistemology I turn now to the impact of the wider themes of postmodernism.

To situate the postmodernist challenge it is important to recognize the complex interconnection between the intellectual and political strands which it incorporates, and which make its concrete manifestations so diverse. The suggestion to be explored is that postmodernism involves two distinguishable elements. At its most general level postmodernism is a critique of the rationalism of Enlightenment thought. Postmodernism's more specific features, which may

---

[11]The relationship between the strands of postmodernist thought is complex. For present purposes I treat deconstruction as a specific technique of handling discourses which is commonly, but not necessarily, found in association with postmodernist theoretical themes which, as I suggest in Section III below, primarily involve epistemological (or perhaps anti-epistemological) claims. For an excellent account of the relationship between deconstruction and the interpretation debate in legal theory see Norris, *supra*, note 7 at 168-82.

[12]For overviews of the interpretation debate see D.C. Hoy, *supra*, note 8; D. Kennedy, "The Turn to Interpretation" (1985) 58 S. Calif. L. Rev. 251; and G. Peller, "The Metaphysics of American Law", *supra*, note 7.

[13]P.L. Berger and T. Luckmann provided the classical and elegant account of social constructionism in *The Social Construction of Reality: A Treatise in the Sociology of Knowledge* (Garden City: Doubleday, 1966). Another important strand is provided through the generalization and extension of Thomas Kuhn's study of scientific innovation in *The Structure of Scientific Revolutions*, 2d ed. (Chicago: University of Chicago Press, 1970).

[14]Christopher Norris makes a very similar point about the limitations of the radicalism of deconstruction in *supra*, note 7 at 191.

[15]Note that to posit an extra-discursive reality does not necessarily involve positing a realist ontology; it is sufficient to make use of some distinction between 'discourse' and 'practices' to establish the possibility of some position outside of the discourse under consideration without implying that such an external position is 'objective' or 'neutral'.

be grouped together under the label of poststructuralism, revolve around specific reactions to structuralist thought, Marxism in particular, and more generally to the European socialist tradition. As postmodernism migrated into English-speaking intellectual life the specificity of poststructuralism became latent and was fused with the more generalized anti-Enlightenment mood.

Postmodernism's critique of the Enlightenment is of a failed rationalist project which has run its course but which continues to encumber contemporary thought with illusions of a rational route to knowledge, a faith in science and in progress. The radical core of postmodernism lies in its mission of shedding the illusions of the Enlightenment. The political ambiguity of postmodernism lies in its insistence that our received and familiar dichotomy between Left and Right is itself a product of Enlightenment thought, and that contemporary Left theoretical and political positions, especially Marxism, are deeply inscribed with the illusions of the Enlightenment. This is how postmodernism comes to claim progressive credentials whilst devoting much of its energy to the critique of erstwhile Left positions.

Postmodernism has a pronounced tendency to be absolutist in its judgements. Most noticeably it adopts a decidedly one-dimensional and almost wholly negative view of the Enlightenment and the modern world which is its putative offspring. Postmodernist authors such as Lyotard and Michel Foucault present us with an unhelpful and, I suggest, avoidable dichotomy between the wholesale endorsement of some classical version of the Enlightenment project and its complete abandonment. We are presented with a stark and dramatic choice between the Enlightenment (with the strong implication that to make this choice would reveal one's unreconstructed mind in its most old-fashioned garb) and postmodernism (with the strong inference that this is the up-to-date and radical choice); significantly, no intermediate positions are considered. Any approach which leaves features or elements of the Enlightenment intact is perceived as an attempt to keep that played-out project alive. It is important to note, in passing, that the 'Enlightenment Project' is always presented in the singular and thus assumed to be a unitary and integrated project.

It seems preferable to start out from the contention that modernity and the Enlightenment are much more complex, ambiguous and nuanced than this one-dimensional view permits. Marshall Berman forcefully expresses this by capturing the persistent intellectual and political ambiguity of modernism:

> [F]rom Marx's and Dostoevsky's time to our own, it has been impossible to grasp and embrace the modern world's potentialities without loathing and fighting against some of its most palpable realities.[16]

[16]M. Berman, *All That Is Solid Melts Into Air: The Experience of Modernity* (New York: Simon and Schuster, 1982) at 14.

Berman goes on to make the very important point that whereas the intellectual giants of the nineteenth century were simultaneously enthusiasts for and enemies of modernity having to wrestle with its ambiguities and contradictions, their twentieth century successors have lurched far more toward rigid polarities and flat totalizations. Modernity is either embraced with a blind and uncritical enthusiasm, or else condemned with neo-Olympian remoteness and contempt; in either case it is conceived as a closed monolith.[17]

I want to suggest that we can and should adopt a more dispassionate view of the substance of postmodernism, and in so doing retain many of its insights and techniques, if we first separate its content from its general intellectual outlook or mood. At root postmodernism is grounded in a profound disenchantment with modernity. There is a very specific reason why many progressive intellectuals have come to adopt this disenchantment as their own; as I argued in the opening section none of the available political strategies of the present period seem to offer much hope of foreseeable and radical social transformation. So whether in disillusionment with contemporary socialism since the events of 1968[18] or with the swing to the Right since the late 70s, it is not surprising that postmodernism has had its attractions for progressives.

I am anxious to underline Berman's stress on the ambiguity of modernity. I empathize with postmodernism's critique of instrumental reason, scientism, the cult of progress and much more associated with the Enlightenment; but I also want to affirm that significant projects, in particular, that of human emancipation involving appeal to the discourses of freedom, equality and knowledge remain incomplete. In very different ways both Edward Thompson and Habermas articulate the view that modern liberalism has lost the will and the inclination to pursue these goals and that their realization has fallen to contemporary socialism; this in turn underlines my view that socialism must engage with and draw significantly from liberalism in order to fulfil this objective. It is for these reasons that I am unhappy with the general intellectual and political mood of postmodernism.

In order to explore the impact of postmodernism on legal studies it is important to stress that its inspiration stems from a generalized intellectual empathy with the critique of modernity. There is little sense at all from writers most influenced by postmodernism that the phenomena of law have themselves been subject to any significant transformations or have made any transition from one form to another. In contrast the debates in architecture and in literary criticism have explicitly been concerned to identify historically specific shifts in

[17]*Ibid.* at 24.

[18]I select 1968 as the critical turning point because of the way in which it encapsulates the paradox of the rise and fall of insurrectionary militancy in the West (Paris) and of humanist socialism in the East (Prague).

buildings and books, prior to naming and then theorizing that shift. With respect to law there is no evidence that those most influenced by postmodernism contend that their views are a response to some shift in the phenomena of law which mark a passage or transition from the modern to the postmodern.

It is interesting to note that there exists an almost complete separation between those concerned to track the changes in form and substance of law and those concerned with the postmodernism debate. The debate on the nature and implications of the transformation of law during the twentieth century has been very much the preserve of sociologically oriented scholarship, most noticeably in German sociology, which in turn is part of a wider debate within German social theory, in particular, between Habermas and Niklas Luhmann.[19] Whilst recognizing that my acquiescence adds another brick to the intellectual wall between critical legal studies and theoretical sociology of law, I will not consider any aspects of the empirical transformation of legal systems. My only justification for this major limitation on the scope of this essay is that such issues have played no part in the debates and controversies within legal scholarship over postmodernism.[20] Put at its simplest, the postmodernist offensive has been directed at the theory (or explanation) of law offered by the predominant liberal tradition (and its variants) of a phenomenon which both sides presume to be, in all essentials, immutable.

II. The Double Challenge

The postmodernist challenge within legal studies is two-sided. It is this dual challenge which constitutes the specificity of the postmodernist debate within legal scholarship. The first challenge is to the privileged place that Enlightenment thought and modern liberalism accords to state law. The second challenge is to the organizing protocols of legal scholarship and, in particular, to its epistemological assumptions.

A. *Law in the Discourse of the Enlightenment*

In the discourse of the Enlightenment law is accorded a privileged position as the guardian of the boundary between the state and the citizen and of the boundaries between individuals, both sets of boundaries being marked by legal rights. Law is conceived as a unitary phenomenon, 'the Law', and that law is

---

[19]Gunther Teubner has both been an active participant in these debates and has done the most to make them available to English readers; see G. Teubner, ed., *Dilemmas of Law in the Welfare State* (Berlin: Walter de Gruyter, 1988) and G. Teubner, ed., *Autopoietic Law: A New Approach to Law and Society* (Berlin: Walter de Gruyter, 1988).

[20]One important exception has been the work of Boaventura de Sousa Santos who has explored a much more strongly sociologically oriented conception of postmodernism in exploring the contemporary transformations within legal orders; see Santos, *supra*, note 7 and "The Postmodern Transition: Law and Politics", forthcoming.

state law, the expression of the sovereignty of the nation-state. It is invested with the sanctity of rationality as the most advanced way of social ordering by means of a neutral decision procedure rising above the clash of conflicting interests. At the same time the Law is not only self-validating but validates the constitutional arrangement of the society's political institutions and offices. Law is thus conceived as a teleology endowed with its own purpose of self-referentially policing its boundaries in such a way as to provide an independent guarantee of its capacity to resist the transgressions of both political power (the state) and (potentially) of economic power.[21] Nowhere is this teleological conception of law clearer than in Dworkin's allegorical world of *Law's Empire*. In this scenario law is not only identified with a teleology (law as integrity) but it is a self-activating teleology in which law is personified in terms of'"law's ambition for itself" in which "law works itself pure".[22]

In the discourse of the Enlightenment law plays the role of what Foucault termed a "total history" in that it came to be conceived as constituting the overall form or principle of a civilization; indeed law becomes the very personification of civilization.[23] In this role law is endowed with a teleological self-conception combining four projects: that of totality (the rational organization and ordering of a whole society); unity (the sovereignty of the nation state); civilization (the supercession of a dangerous and unordered past — law versus self-help and feuding); and finally the project of 'the subject' (the constitution of the legal subject as citizen, and citizen as legal subject endowed with self-responsibility and legal liability).

In challenging the Enlightenment's conception of law, postmodernism joins with and supplements other strands of critical theory. Its general thrust is to displace and decentre the privileged position accorded to 'the Law'. In short, its challenge is to legal centralism. Postmodernism challenges the four interconnected projects assigned to law. It denies totality by focusing on the social construction of the plurality and the radical particularity of social life. It denies unity, emphasizing instead the diversity of the micro-constituents of social life and the inability of states to ever fully subordinate such plurality. Postmodernism dismembers civilization by denying the evolutionist illusions on which the conception rests and exposing its suppression and silencing of the expelled and excluded (whether they be the insane, women or colonial peoples).

---

[21]Liberal legalism which has enunciated, worked and reworked these themes has been predominantly concerned, even preoccupied, with the danger of transgression by the state. It has generally been critics from the Left who have pointed to the significance of 'private' economic power. My insertion of 'potentially' indicates that there seems to be no intrinsic barrier to liberalism taking cognisance of this form of power which threatens the boundaries it seeks to police. Concretely it is liberalism's parallel commitment to private property that impedes such a recognition.

[22] Dworkin, *supra*, note 5 and "Law's Ambitions for Itself" (1985) 71 Va. L. Rev. 173.

[23]M. Foucault, *The Archaeology of Knowledge* [1969], trans. A.M. Sheridan Smith (London: Tavistock, 1972) at 9.

Finally, and most famously, postmodernism displaces and decentres the sovereign subject. Thus the postmodernist critique displaces law from its central role as the embodiment of rationality and civilization. The discourses of law are simply a prime example of one of Lyotard's *grands récits* or totalising narratives which tells history as the unified story of one universal subject with a single origin and a unitary telos.[24]

To those who read the postmodern challenge too hurriedly this critique reads as a veritable condemnation of law itself and can, by extrapolation, even be treated as heralding the end of law.[25] But it needs to be stressed that the challenge is capable of quite another and less apocalyptic reading. The alternative version is one which cuts down the aggrandisement of state-law's ambition for itself so that we are better able to address both the limits and the potentialities of law as a form of social ordering. In short, postmodernism can be read as enjoining a more modest framework in which we can debate the real world of law, with its strengths and its limitations. This critique can and should be embraced as a necessary corrective to the over-investment in law characteristic of the discourses of the Enlightenment and of the major variants of liberal legal theory. But while it is true that postmodernism offers a powerfully formulated critique of legal centralism, it cannot be considered to be original. Indeed it is one that is already strongly represented by a range of pre-existing critical traditions, most significantly by American legal realism, by sociological discourses on law, by Marxist theories of law and, perhaps most powerfully, in 'early' critical legal studies.

B. Postmodernism and Legal Scholarship

This second challenge is to the way in which the project of legal scholarship has heretofore been conceived; though linked to the first challenge, the second is distinct and separable. It consists in a wide-ranging challenge to the philosophical and, in particular, the epistemological presuppositions of both liberal legalism and of critical legal studies. In its most general form postmodernism is anti-foundational in the sense that it denies the possibility of philosophy providing any epistemological guarantees for legal discourse, in particular, by undermining claims to tests of legal validity, rules of interpretation and the general positivistic quest for certainty, and if not certainty, then predictability. There is a certain variety within the anti-foundational position. In its most measured form, epitomized by Rorty's pragmatism, the denial is of philosophy as a 'mas-

[24]Lyotard, *supra*, note 3.

[25]It is this apocalyptic fear of a threat to law itself, which in passing it may be noted imports a very distinctive personification of law, that underlies the most outspoken criticisms of the critical legal studies movement; see P.D. Carrington, "Of Law and the River" (1984) 34 J. Legal Ed. 222; O. Fiss, "The Death of the Law?" (1986) 72 Cornell L. Rev. 1; A.B. Rubin, "Does the Law Matter? A Judge's Response to the Critical Legal Studies Movement" (1987) 37 J. Legal Ed. 307.

ter discipline' able to provide external epistemological guarantees for other disciplines.[26] This rejection of the foundational role of philosophy leaves every other discipline free to decide upon its own epistemological conventions. More radical forms of anti-foundationalism, epitomized by Foucault's critique of the human sciences, insist that the epistemological postures of any discipline result from the play of relations of power and are subject to decisive and sometimes abrupt paradigm shifts.[27]

The most important implication of postmodernism's epistemological challenge to legal scholarship is that it confronts the central preoccupation of legal positivism, the dominant strand within liberal legalism, with the search for tests of legal validity.[28] The existence of some governing test of validity is conceived as a precondition for the justification of the imposition of law as a form of state coercion. It proceeds by drawing a distinction between legitimate and illegitimate applications of the coercive capacity of the state. In challenging the very possibility of grounding the validity of law, the epistemological critique mounted by postmodernism thus goes to the very heart of the project of liberal legalism.

Drawing a distinction between these two challenges, the first to legal centralism and the second to legal epistemology, is important to both the argument and the structure of this paper. Most immediately it allows me to approve the first challenge to legal centralism whilst identifying reservations and specific resistances to the epistemological challenge. It is upon this attempt to separate out positive and negative dimensions of the postmodernist challenge that my attention will be focused.

III. Postmodernism and Critical Legal Studies

Within legal scholarship it has been in critical legal studies that the challenges posed by postmodernism have been most influential. My contention is that the trajectory of CLS has involved two different strands, one which has accepted much of the mood and language of postmodernism whilst nevertheless

[26]It is precisely this insistence on the restricted nature of Rorty's critique of foundationalism that Joseph Singer emphasises in "The Player and the Cards: Nihilism and Legal Theory" (1984) 94 Yale L.J. 1 in the course of his criticisms of one of the CLS texts which bears the heaviest stamp of postmodernism, namely, J. Stick, "Can Nihilism be Pragmatic?" (1986) 100 Harvard L. Rev. 332.

[27]M. Foucault, *The Order of Things: An Archaeology of the Human Sciences* [1966] (London: Tavistock, 1970) and *supra*, note 23.

[28]In using the designation 'epistemological challenge' it should be borne in mind that postmodernist positions are generally explicitly anti-epistemological in that they deny the pertinence of epistemological enquiries. For my present purposes it matters little whether this claim to occupy a positon outside epistemology is itself an epistemological position; since little hangs on this matter I persist with the convenient label 'epistemological challenge'. My contention, which I do not seek to develop, is that it is impossible to adopt a position outside epistemology.

maintaining a degree of critical distance and the other which has imported the whole of postmodernist thought.

In its earliest stage of development CLS authors generally saw one of their tasks as being to elaborate an alternative theorization of law; this project was most apparent in the central role played by the concept of 'fundamental contradiction'.[29] This concept is typical of classical theoretical strategy; it deploys a concept which seeks to impose a pattern, and possibly a structure, on wide and diverse elements of social reality. Certainly liberal theory, and possibly the social reality of liberal society, could be modelled on the systematic presence of dichotomies and their accumulation into a general or fundamental contradiction (for example, between self and others).

There was, I suggest, one key text which announced the abandonment of this conventional, albeit radical, theoretical strategy and that was Peter Gabel and Duncan Kennedy's conversational exchange "Roll Over Beethoven".[30] But this piece aside, the transition within CLS work involved an almost imperceptible shift of intellectual reference points; it was imperceptible in the sense that it did not seem to necessitate any explicit acknowledgment that a shift was occurring, nor did it generate any public debate within the CLS community about the merits or problems of the shifts or transitions which were occurring. But it was the Gabel-Kennedy text that marked the moment (if there ever is a single moment) of reception of postmodernism into the emergent tradition of critical legal studies. It was in this text that, Kennedy announced a rejection of the possibility of CLS's theoretical project and indeed about the very "possibility of theory".[31] In adopting this stance he was in step with a generalized reaction against theory which had been particularly sharply debated in the field of literary theory.[32] This rejection of theory has come to have the pervasive influence within CLS and is very close to Rorty's critique of the foundational aspirations of philosophy.[33]

In "Roll Over Beethoven" Kennedy sketched out his preferred project for CLS; his alternative to the project of 'grand theory' included some characteris-

---

[29]The concept 'fundamental contradiction' was the cornerstone of Duncan Kennedy's "The Structure of Blackstone's Commentaries" (1979) 28 Buffalo L. Rev. 205; the concept was taken up with changing emphasis by most other CLS writers in the late 70s and early 80s.

[30](1984) 36 Stan. L. Rev. 1.

[31]*Ibid.* at 47. Throughout the exchange Gabel generally assents to the thrust of Kennedy's argument, but also manifests a lingering predisposition to the general theoretical project that had marked the first stage of the CLS project.

[32]The major contributions to the 'against theory' debate are collected in W.J.T. Mitchell, ed., *Against Theory: Literary Studies and the New Pragmatism* (Chicago: University of Chicago Press, 1985).

[33]See, in particular, R. Rorty, *Philosophy and the Mirror of Nature* (Princeton: Princeton University Press, 1979) and *Consequences of Pragmatism* (Minneapolis: University of Minn. Press, 1982).

tically postmodernist motifs: the rejection of rationalist philosophy, the repudiation of 'privileged' concepts, a reaction against abstraction as being antithetical to 'the real', a valorization of experience, and a focus on the small scale (minimalism or what I prefer to call 'localism').[34]

What is striking about Kennedy's remarks is the assumption that the problems presumed to haunt 'theory' and 'abstraction' can be so readily escaped. He insists that to replace theoretical constructs such as 'fundamental contradiction' by the more homely 'making the kettle boil' abolishes privileged concepts and avoids abstraction. This is part of an unargued assumption that to engage with 'experience', or its close associate 'common sense', provides a direct and unmediated access to 'reality'. Of course, as the more philosophically reflective strands of postmodernism make clear, there can be no such direct connection between reality and knowledge. But of more immediate import is the fact that there is no obvious merit in a move from a theorized privileged concept to an under-theorized privileged concept; 'kettles boiling' is both abstract and privileging, it is simply more fuzzy than 'fundamental contradiction'; its only conceivable merit is that it panders to a populist anti-theoreticism.[35] In a similar vein the appeal to the importance of the small-scale or local reality as a site for political intervention is part of conventional wisdom, but does nothing to address the more complex and intractable problems about the processes of aggregation and over-determination that link the local with the national, the micro with the macro levels.[36]

There is a significant continuity between the more recent postmodernist strand within CLS and its longer lineage which reaches back to the themes of the pre-war Legal Realists. This continuity is provided by the central, even organizing, emphasis upon the indeterminacy of legal doctrine. In the work of the 'new wave' postmodernist CLS this thesis draws less on the pragmatic demonstration of the inconsistency of legal doctrine; instead this argument increasingly relies on the more general themes of postmodernist linguistic and literary theory which, in a more systematic way, have displaced authorial authority, interpretational validity and univocal meaning. In the main the postmodernist shift within CLS has taken place easily without any sign of tension or controversy; it is manifest perhaps most demonstrably in CLS's own distinctive style of authorial privileging in which declarations of intellectual approval and affil-

[34]See further discussion of localism below in Part VI.

[35]The characteristic 'against theory' stance of much postmodernism is taken by some to be a 'rightist' deviation. "The rhetoric of 'against theory' ... cannot help but bring comfort, energy, and ideas to the enemies of change. The rhetoric of 'against theory' is reactionary." F. Lentricchia, "The Return of William James" (1986) 4 Cultural Critique 5 at 29. On the other hand Terry Eagleton characterises the "hair-raising radicalism — the nerve and daring with which it knocks the stuffing out of every smug concept" as 'ultra-leftist'; *Walter Benjamin or Towards a Revolutionary Criticism* (London: Verso, 1981) at 134.

[36]See below in Part VI.

iation are given by means of footnotes referring to the oeuvre of some major thinker. Symbolically Marx, Gramsci, Habermas and Freud have been displaced by Nietzsche, Derrida and Foucault.[37]

Critical legal studies has moved into a second phase in some other senses. Today there is a much more explicit focus on postmodernist themes and issues.[38] This second wave of CLS authors has become increasingly concerned with the reaction of the wider community of legal scholarship to the critical enterprise. There is today a secondary literature of responses to critical legal studies which ranges from intemperate hostility[39] to "friendly critiques" from fellow radicals,[40] as well as critical reactions from major figures of modern legal theory.[41] The focus of current debates about critical legal studies, from friend and foe alike, revolves around the issue of 'nihilism' and its close associate 'relativism'. It is these issues that have become most closely associated with the mark of postmodernist thought. It is the anxieties generated around the issues of nihilism/relativism which is captured in the figure of "The Big Fear" used to title this paper.

IV. The Big Fear and the Slippery Slope

The emergence of postmodernist positions within legal scholarship has raised the temperature of the usually benign style of legal scholarship. One response to critical legal studies and postmodernism has been intemperate. For example, Paul Carrington argues that there is no place for CLS-types within the law school; he hedges the illiberality of his position by not calling for their dismissal but with the ultimately lame gesture of calling for their resig-

---

[37]In the general field of social theory postmodernism has been engaged in a protracted debate with the Marxist tradition, but perhaps most intensively with contemporary critical theory, in particular, as represented by Habermas; see, for example, *The Philosophical Discourse of Modernity*, *supra*, note 4; Lyotard, *supra*, note 3. For a very helpful overview of the debate between postmodernism and critical theory see P. Dews, *Logics of Disintegration: Post-Structuralist Thought and the Claims of Critical Theory* (London: Verso, 1987). Not only does Habermas see modernity as a project as yet uncompleted but he also holds out the possibility for the grounding of truth and validity claims. It is as a result of the shift of CLS towards more explicitly postmodernist positions that Habermas, who had earlier been favourably regarded, has largely been dropped.

[38]For texts drawing on and espousing postmodernist themes see, for example, Balkin, *supra*, note 7; Cornell, *supra*, note 7; Douzinas & Warrington, *supra*, note 7; Hutchinson, *supra*, note 7; and Peller, *supra*, note 7.

[39]See, for example, Carrington, *supra*, note 25 and Rubin, *supra*, note 25.

[40]See, for example, E. Sparer, "Fundamental Human Rights, Legal Entitlements, and the Social Struggle: A Friendly Critique of the Critical Legal Studies Movement" (1984) 36 Stan. L. Rev. 509; F. Munger & C. Seron, "Critical Legal Studies Versus Critical Legal Theory: A Comment on Method" (1984) 6 Law & Policy 257; Symposium, "Minority Critiques of the Critical Legal Studies Movement" (1987) 22 Harv. C.R.-C.L. L. Rev. 297.

[41]See, for example, critical responses to CLS from Dworkin, *supra*, note 5 and J. Finnis, "On 'The Critical Legal Studies Movement'" (1985) 30 Am. J. Juris. 21.

nation.[42] Carrington's response is but the most extreme manifestation of the deep and passionate reactions engendered by the double challenge to law and legal scholarship posed by postmodernism.

What I have termed 'The Big Fear' is a reaction which adopts a catastrophic scenario in which any concession to contingency or any retreat from the objectivity of knowledge-claims necessarily leads, via the associated imagery of the "slippery slope", unwittingly, but unavoidably towards the abyss of relativism and its even more dangerous associate, nihilism. This nihilism is both a generalized loss of belief in the prevailing social order leading to the denials of claims to objectivity and an insistence on the contingency of all values. In respect to law, Peter Goodrich suggests that nihilism

> simply means loss of faith in the community of legal doctrine and refusal to succumb, acquiesce or otherwise believe in the foundational myths of legal doctrine and legal regulation.[43]

Nihilism is conceived as catastrophic because it seems to deny the possibility of cognitive, ethical or moral judgement as anything more than subjective preference or conventional consensus. If "one opinion is as good as another" the project of scholarship itself seems to be doomed if the opinion of the fool is as valuable as that resulting from painstaking study. If "anything goes" it becomes impossible to distinguish between a moral judgement and self-interest. If there is no means to construct an argument which makes it 'better' or 'stronger' than another then all judgements, whether legal, political or moral, are arbitrary, and arbitrariness is a step along the road to either anarchy or tyranny.

Participants on both sides of the debate are propelled towards what Habermas has aptly termed "unmediated confrontations" in which stark and irreconcilable oppositions are forced to do battle. The lines of division are broadly and sharply drawn. The debate gets out of hand. "The Big Fear" pictures people who are presented as claiming that any view is as good as any other; but such a view is a fabrication, there are no witnesses that can be subpoenaed who hold, let alone advocate, such a position. Thus, for example, Allan Hutchinson argues that the charges laid at the door of relativism/nihilism must be false because there simply are no relativists or nihilists to be found on the block:

> Nihilism is only threatening or comprehensible for those who maintain that objective truth and rational knowledge are required for moral action and authority. It is only troublesome to those who continue to believe in the worth of the Enlightenment Project. The nihilistic deep is a construct of that project. If the

[42]Carrington, *supra*, note 25.

[43]P. Goodrich, *Reading the Law: A Critical Introduction to Legal Method and Techniques* (Oxford: Basil Blackwell, 1986) at 217.

> Enlightenment Project is abandoned, the association of nihilism with moral despair will also be rejected.[44]

Yet this defence seems to exhibit the classic weakness of all sceptical epistemological positions, namely, that in denying the possibility of absolute truth they slide into the untenable and unsustainable position that all forms of truth-claims must be absolutist and, as such, are fictions. As Peter Dews observes, the avant-gardism of postmodernism

> has been marked by an astonishingly casual and unquestioning acceptance of certain extremely condensed — not to say sloganistic — characterizations of the history of Western thought, as if this history could be dismissed through its reduction to a set of perfunctory dualisms.[45]

The characteristic response of postmodernist thinkers is to deny the pertinence of 'the big fear' and to insist that they are really the 'good guys' who want to do no more than set aside unjustified illusions about truth, certainty and objectivity. Their claim is one which stresses modesty and humility;[46] if we only abandon grandiose and unsubstantiated faith in reason, they suggest, then we can get along fine, and judges (just like everyone else) must make, and justify, their choices without hiding behind the discourses of truth and objectivity which only serve to obscure our responsibility for the choices that we make. James Boyd White exemplifies this response:

> When we discover that we have in this world no earth or rock to stand or walk upon but only shifting sea and sky and wind, the mature response is not to lament the loss of fixity but to learn to sail.[47]

Appealing though this metaphor is, it tarnishes as soon as we press the question: What must the judge or legal scholar do to learn to sail? Sailing offers a recognizable alternative to standing on the rock; but in letting go of our philosophical aspirations to ground knowledge we are entitled to know what is the functional equivalent to sailing.

One answer which has had considerable appeal to contemporary critical thought in law has been suggested by Richard Rorty, whose philosophy may best be understood as offering a naturalization of the radical relativistic themes of European postmodernism through their articulation within a pragmatism that is much more palatable to the North American intellectual mood. He takes on the role of the modest intellectual, eschewing grandiose claims. The best that we

---

[44] Hutchinson, *supra*, note 7 at 46.

[45] Dews, *supra*, note 37 at xv.

[46] "[T]he purport of post-structuralist texts seems extremely modest ... As to their own text, the post-structuralist is often coy and playful" in David Kennedy, "Critical Theory, Structuralism and Contemporary Legal Scholarship" (1985) 21 New Eng. L. Rev. 209 at 286.

[47] J.B. White, *When Words Lose Their Meaning* (Chicago: University of Chicago Press, 1984) at 278.

can do and all that he enjoins, upon philosopher and citizen alike, is to "keep the conversation going". Once the issue is posed in these terms "The Big Fear" can be safely put aside.[48]

Just as those who raise alarmist fears about nihilism grossly overdramatize the intellectual challenge of postmodernism, so likewise do the postmodernists offer an account of their opponents which is a caricature. Their ruse is to make absolute the ordinary knowledge claims of both traditionalists and unreconstructed modernists by attributing to them unproblematic and unitary conceptions that they do not hold; this ploy is practiced by the heavily used device of the capitalisation of Truth, Knowledge, Morality, etc.; those who have not embraced postmodernism are alleged to believe in absolute 'Truth', 'Objectivity', etc. Another favorite devise is to attribute to all claims of objectivity a commitment to deductive modes of proof and to ignore both the presence of and the claims for other methods of reasoning. Joseph Singer, for example, uses this form of argument against the possibility of objectivity or certainty in legal reasoning.[49]

Both the relativists and their opponents seem trapped in the imagery of the "slippery slope" which operates by extrapolation from the positions actually held to their most extreme *reductio ad absurdum*. The problem is to find a way of posing the important issues at stake in a manner that avoids unmediated confrontations. The issues between the postmodernists and their critics touch upon some of the most important and challenging intellectual and political problems of our times. Rather than attempt to address the full range of issues at stake I will take a more focused approach and explore the important exchange about nihilism between Singer and John Stick.[50]

Critical legal studies has, as Singer observes, raised the spectre of nihilism in the arena of legal studies. It has produced an array of argumentation which, with varying degrees of fervour, insists that law is contingent, indeterminant and non-neutral. This has led to the charge of nihilism being brought against critical scholars because their criticism of law seems to involve the denial of the possibility of law being objective and neutral and thus renders impossible the project of achieving a rational ordering of social relations or of law serving as a means of constraining governmental power.

Singer's strategy is to deny that there is a problem by refusing the relevance of the charge of nihilism. He sets out to show that the absence of determinacy, objectivity and neutrality in law does not condemn us to irrationality, indifference or arbitrariness.[51] The big fear aroused by nihilism rests on the con-

---

[48]Rorty, *supra*, note 33.

[49]Singer, *supra*, note 26.

[50]The principal texts are: Singer, *ibid.*, and Stick, *supra*, note 26.

[51]This stance, it should be noted, is exactly the same as Hutchinson's quoted above.

tention that "if we do not believe in the possibility of using reason to adjudicate value conflicts, we have given up on morality and law entirely."[52] The fear which Singer seeks to allay is the apprehension that uncertainty necessarily leads to arbitrariness, a counterposing of reason to passion:[53]

> [If] we do not believe that reason can adjudicate value conflicts and determine the legitimacy of governmental actions, we are relegated to arbitrariness, insecurity, physical and emotional harm, and tyranny.[54]

Singer is concerned to reassure his readers that this fate is not in store for those who espouse the postmodernist cause. His case invokes a Rortian defence which, in brief, says that the critique of legal rationalism can be sustained without fear of contracting the nihilist disease. Immunization from the nihilist contagion is achieved by way of mild inoculation with a dose of pragmatism; this involves nothing more than eschewing Truth, Proof and Reason in favour of that which we all enjoy so much, conversation.

Stick's reply has two main components. The first is to show, and I think quite correctly, that Singer misappropriates Rorty by forgetting that Rorty's primary critique is directed against the foundationalist pretensions of the discipline of philosophy to ground the knowledge-claims of all other disciples. His critique of logocentrism is more limited than Singer recognizes in that Rorty concedes that each discipline (or as he terms it each "field of natural discourse") has its own canons of rationality. For Stick the difference between philosophy and law is that "law does not seek to impose standards of rationality outside its own sphere."[55]

His second line of criticism is that Singer overstates the case for the contingency and indeterminacy of law because he persistently attributes a deductive account of legal reasoning to liberal legalism. This, Stick insists, is a caricature of modern liberal legal theory; rather it is coherence theories, such as those associated with Dworkin, which are the most influential. Again, I suggest that Stick is correct, for although some traditionalists do seem to assume a deductive model of legal reasoning, nobody who addresses the issue explicitly advances such a position; I will not pursue this issue of the dominant modes of legal reasoning further because it lies outside my present concerns, except to comment that it does provide evidence of a tendency in postmodernist argumentation to throw the charge of logocentrism around in a rather cavalier fashion.

---

[52]Singer, *supra*, note 26 at 48.

[53]On the dichotomy of reason and passion see Peller, *supra*, note 7.

[54]Singer, *supra*, note 26 at 51.

[55]Stick, *supra*, note 26 at 342. Whilst accepting Stick's corrective to Singer's overextension of Rorty's critique of philosophy it may be observed, in passing, that legal discourse is not as benign as Stick presumes. Law has, as I argue below, its own imperialistic attempts to impose its canons of rationality on politics and morality.

In winning the first two rounds against Singer, Stick is confident that he has won the contest.[56] But it is far from clear that he has repulsed the dragon of nihilism which is giving CLS such a bad press. To disallow Singer from invoking Rorty's critique of philosophy as if it were a critique of legal theory, as Stick succeeds in doing, does not dispense with the strength of both the Rortian and the postmodernist (in so far as these are different) critique of philosophy and of all epistemologies. Stick relies on the obvious point that law and philosophy are organizationally distinct disciplines. He fails however to grapple with the problem that legal discourse, and in particular orthodox jurisprudence, is a species of precisely that kind of philosophy which is the main target of Rorty's criticism in that it does seek to provide 'guarantees' (in particular, through the search for validity) for its truths.

Nor are legal discourses content to remain within the framework of law-as-a-discipline. Legal discourses and legal theory do persistently seek to prescribe the proper conduct for other fields of human inquiry. For example, legal discourses seek to convince us that law can provide viable criteria for the limits of state action, and to deny all but constitutionalist legitimations of political action. In so doing law shares with philosophy the same sort of intellectual imperialism against which the Rortian critique of foundationalism complains. So, despite Stick's valiant efforts, he fails to repulse the postmodernist challenge.

Stick's strategy fails to deal directly with the Rortian challenge. Whilst he succeeds in deflecting Singer's attempt to remove the relativist sting from postmodern critical legal thought, there remain in place important issues which need to be addressed. My contention is that the basic objection that has to be levelled against Rortian pragmatism is its denial that critique can call upon cultural and intellectual resources outside the discourse under examination. Not only can we legitimately seek to understand specific cultural or legal forms of life in terms not their own, but they must be so evaluated. Critique strives for transcendence, it refuses the passive acceptance of Rorty's "postmodern bourgeois liberalism",[57] which as Christopher Norris demonstrates amounts to an invitation to accept the "hegemonic values of present-day American society".[58]

[56]I would also have Stick win a third round concerning the merits of their substantive political positions because I am sympathetic to his argument that the Left needs to take liberalism seriously rather than being content to trash it; whereas Singer's edifying legal theory of opposition to cruelty, misery, hierarchy and loneliness is just too mushy and indeterminant for my tastes.

[57]Rorty, "Postmodern Bourgeois Liberalism" (1983) 80 J. of Phil. 583.

[58]Norris, *supra*, note 7.

V. Relativism at the Heart of the Postmodern Challenge: The Search For Theories of the Third Way

The implications of my reservation as to whether Stick has done enough to dispense with the fear of nihilism that surrounds CLS, is that the core anxieties that lie at the heart of and provide a rational core for "The Big Fear" remain intact. This anxiety, which can take many forms, manifests itself in the debates within legal studies under the label of relativism. It generates anxiety because it seems to deny the existence of any firm ground in which knowledge can be rooted and seems to leave us, fully aware of our frailties, in an ever changing and variable existence in which access to reality, truth or objectivity is forever denied. It is, in particular, moral relativism which generates the greatest anxiety since its espousal seems forever to prohibit us from settling any argument about what's right or wrong. We seem incapable of getting beyond personal preference or culturally given consensus.

How did critical legal scholarship get into the problem of relativism?[59] For progressive legal scholars, and critical legal scholars in particular, the problem of relativism arose from the concern to escape the vice of determinism which itself was the central problem generated by the interrogation of the formative influence of Marxist theory on critical legal studies.[60] In short, the reaction against determinism swung the intellectual pendulum full circle and arrived at relativism.

The critique of determinism, however, does not necessarily lead to relativism. The issue of determinism came to be posed in terms of the dominance of external causation in which the problem seemed to be that Marxism, as the most influential version of determinism, posits a causality (whether with regard to law or other 'superstructural' phenomena) located outside the phenomena under consideration, and which is to be found in the causal primacy of 'the economic'. The recognition that an important aspect of the problem of determinism was its apparent dependence on an external account of causality is of special significance because it explains the association between the rejection of determinism and the anti-realist philosophical position associated with relativism. The retreat from a realist epistemology comes about because it is assumed that it posits reality as external in respect to which the knowing subject is conceived as internal. This is seen most vividly in Rorty's rejection of all reflection accounts of

[59]Other strands of legal scholarship have come to face issues revolving around relativism by different routes; for example, liberal legal theorists travelled to the relativist implications of the interpretation debate as a result of the breakdown of traditional legal positivism.

[60]For an account of CLS's engagement with determinism see R. Gordon, "Critical Legal Histories" (1984) 36 Stan. L. Rev. 57. More generally, on alternative responses within the Marxist tradition, see N. Mouzelis, "Marxism or Post-Marxism?" (1988) 167 New Left Rev. 107.

reality as "the mirror of nature" whose imagery invokes the mind as internal and the reality mirrored in it as external.[61]

Once the problem is posed in these terms the rejection of determinism, and of the closely related vices of economism and reductionism, then a radical relativism, which renounces all talk of an external causality or an external reality and also abandons the projects of objectivity and truth, comes to seem the best guarantee against these vices. Of the different varieties of relativism the one which is paramount in recent CLS work is a cultural relativism which emphasizes the social construction of reality without any structures outside of linguistic communities being able to impose limits or constraints. Hence culture, in its infinite diversity and irreducibility, ensures the plasticity and relativity of the social.

We should stop and enquire whether this move to cultural relativism was necessary in the first place. The critique of determinism from which it arose is flawed because it introduces its own reductionism in that it presumes that the root problem of our account of causality is that it involves positing causal factors as external to that which is caused. The effect of this reduction is to set up an opposing dualism between external and internal, with the implication that to reject externality necessarily implies the adoption of an internal or non-objectivist account of causality. The paradox is that a distinctive feature of the CLS critique of liberalism has been to draw attention to liberalism's reliance on precisely such irresolvable dichotomies.[62]

The move to cultural relativism, while apparently intellectually radical and fully 'sociological', gives rise to the unintended consequence of 'social subjectivism', in which the subject conceives sociality as expressing only her own social position and experience.[63] The real difficulty is to find a way of avoiding this false counter-opposition between subjectivity and objectivity. This problem is, of course, a variant of that most pervasive problem of contemporary social

---

[61]See Rorty, *supra*, note 33.

[62]On the critique of the role of dichotomies in liberal legalism see D. Kennedy, "Legal Formality" (1973) 2 J. Legal Stud. 351; F. Olsen, "The Family and the Market: A Study of Ideology and Legal Reform" (1983) 96 Harv. L. Rev. 1497 and M. Tushnet, "Legal Scholarship: Its Causes and Cure" (1981) 90 Yale L.J. 1205.

[63]Karel Kosik describes social subjectivism in the following terms:

> Praxis is not man's being walled in the idol of socialness and of social subjectivity, but his openness toward reality and being. All manner of theories of social subjectivism (sociology of knowledge, anthropologism, [and, we may add, postmodernism]) have walled man in a subjectively conceived socialness and practicality: in their opinion, man expresses only himself and his social position in his creations.

K. Kosik, *The Dialectics of the Concrete: A Study on Problems of Man and World* (Dordrecht: D. Reidel, 1976) at 139.

thought, namely, how to embrace both agency and structure without prioritizing one side or the other.[64]

As legal studies comes to engage the implications of taking its place seriously within the social sciences it has to engage what is one of the most pervasive theoretical questions facing the social sciences. There are many and varied ways in which the problem can be stated: Is it possible to avoid the dualism which haunts the history of social theory? Is there any way to avoid the opposition of structure/agency, objectivism/subjectivism, external/internal, etc.? Is it possible to find a way to articulate the interpenetration of objectivity and subjectivity? Can we find a framework which allows us simultaneously to employ ideas of historical determination and of the relativity and particularity of social life?[65]

The quest is for 'theories of the middle way' which, while avoiding overtly dialectical modes of expression, do seek to offer social and philosophical theory that attempts to overcome or to avoid the counterposing of objectivity and subjectivity, of structure and agency. Although very different in the positions espoused and concepts employed Habermas and Anthony Giddens in social theory and Richard Bernstein in philosophy all seek to steer a path between objectivism and subjectivism.[66] Since so significant a background role in the postmodernist debates has been played by responses to Marxism it is significant to note that Marxism, because of the close proximity of determinist and dialectical traditions within its development, has a long history of attempts to reconcile these strands and has produced a number of significant examples of theories of the middle way.[67]

---

[64]For interesting treatments of the structure/agency problem see A. Giddens, *Central Problems in Social Theory* (Berkeley: University of Calif. Press, 1979) and A. Callinicos, *Making History: Agency, Structure and Change in Social Theory* (Ithaca: Cornell University Press, 1988).

[65]The problem is not so much whether such an account exists, for one significant tradition has a long and distinguished history bearing the name of dialectics, and comes in many varieties of intellectual and political hue, most famously, those associated with the names of Hegel and Marx. The problem about following through with this line of thought is that any mention of dialectics produces an adverse reaction in almost all strands of Anglo-American thought. This suspicion and hostility is one which I share. This is not the occasion to explore the reasons for these resistances. For present purposes it is sufficient to note that dialectical theory offers one possible escape from the mechanical counter-opposition of dichotomies within social theory.

[66]R. Bernstein, *Beyond Objectivism and Relativism: Science, Hermeneutics and Praxis* (Philadelphia: University of Penn. Press, 1983); A. Giddens, *The Constitution of Society* (Berkeley: University of Calif. Press, 1984); J. Habermas, *The Theory of Communicative Action*, trans. T. McCarthy (Boston: Beacon Press, 1984).

[67]Among some of the more important Marxist works which are, to a greater or lesser extent, theories of the middle (or third) way; see L. Colletti, *Marxism and Hegel*, trans. L. Garner (London: NLB, 1973); M. Godelier, *The Mental and the Material: Thought, Economy and Society*, trans. Martin Thom (London: Verso, 1986); P. Bourdieu, *Outline of a Theory of Practice*, trans. R. Nice

For present purposes it is not necessary to adopt or defend any one of these alternative theorizations. It is sufficient to insist that we must reject the false promise of the dichotomized choices within which the debate has been constructed. Relativism can have its necessary place, but it must abandon its paradoxically absolutist pretension that "everything is relative". It can take its useful place as a grounded relativism. By this I mean a position which embraces contingency and social construction, but which insists on limits to the possible variation of social forms. This move is not concerned simply to reintroduce objective structures and conditions of existence, although, of course, it does this; but it seeks to make a more basic point that the varieties of social construction of meaning and signification have their limits in the kind of people who construct their social reality, whose language, ideology and consciousness take particular (not just any) historical forms and thus result in determinant limits to the variability of the social. This attempt to ground relativism is essential in order to recover history in so far as postmodernist thought, whilst appealing to historicism, ends by abolishing history. The postmodernist formula that people cannot step outside of history is taken to establish the impossibility of achieving objective truth. This, however, is an ambiguous formula, since it reduces history to historicity, temporality, transience and irreplicability; historicism breaks up history into transience and a temporality of conditions. Social life is not a pre-historical or a trans-historical and unvarying substance; rather it is formed in the course of history. Reality is more than conditions and historical facticity (although it does not ignore empirical reality). Historical reality exists in this duality of transience and the trans-historical. The only reality of the human world is the unity of empirical conditions, complete with the processes of their formation. Reality is not the chaos of events or of fixed conditions but rather the unity of events and their subjects, a unity of events and the processes of their formation, and thus involves a capacity to transcend conditions. The ability to transcend conditions allows for the possibility of a movement from opinion to knowledge. For it is only if knowledge, not an absolute Knowledge or Truth, is itself a grounded knowledge, that is one which is the best that can be realized under the existing conditions of its production, that history can itself be recovered and in turn made use of in our self-understanding and capacity to transform the social conditions that we encounter. Without some such conception of knowledge the progressive urge behind much postmodernist discourse yields, albeit unintentionally, to a passivity and helplessness which becomes most apparent in the politics of legal postmodernism, the subject of Part VI.

(Cambridge: Cambridge University Press, 1977); Kosik, *supra*, note 63; S. Resnick & R. Wolff, *Knowledge and Class: A Marxist Critique of Political Economy* (Chicago: University of Chicago Press, 1987).

The quest for theory cannot be reduced to attempts to impose rival metanarratives upon the flux of social life. Theory is here to stay, if only in the limited sense that it cannot be evaded or abolished; there can be no discourse outside theory. Theory has the simple but important advantage over common sense in that it specifies its concepts and their connections and thereby brings to the surface the assumptions around which the theory is constructed, and thus it makes their interrogation possible.

VI. The Politics of Postmodernism

Not only are there problems in finding appropriate ways of posing the issues in dispute, but there is just as big a difficulty in deciding what the political implications of these intellectual positions are. One dimension of the dilemma of the progressive intellectual is: How do we decide what is progressive?[68] There is nothing to be gained by bemoaning the loss of the old certainties when relatively simple tests revealed the true political colours of intellectual and political positions. These apparent certainties were themselves the result of an ossification of the political thought of both the Left and the Right. That postmodernism has challenged and disrupted the process of political evaluation is one of its significant contributions, although it should be conceded that this process was already well underway within the fundamental rethinking on the Left of both Marxist and social-democratic politics from the late 70s. Peter Dews expresses the inherent limitation of the politics of postmodernism as exhibiting a

> continuing lack of clarity about the political consequences of its characteristic positions . . . [and] little attempt to think through the ultimate compatibility of progressive political commitments with the dissolution of the subject, or a totalizing suspicion of the concept of the truth.[69]

The most distinctive feature of the politics of postmodernism is the suspicion and renunciation of any strategy of large scale political change since these tend to be premised upon privileged agents (e.g. 'the state', 'the working class') and to be posed in terms of totalities (e.g. capitalism). The alternative to macropolitics is the politics of localism. Localism in a number of different forms is present in much CLS writing; ideas of the fundamental reality of immediate experience, of the self-governing community, that small is beautiful interweave with the CLS tradition.[70]

---

[68] I intentionally invoke the plural that "we" have to make decisions about what is progressive; the choice of intellectual orientation or political strategy needs to be more than a matter of individual preference.

[69] Dews, *supra*, note 37 at xv.

[70] The idea of 'community', standing in contrast to both individual alienation and the totalising state, has long been a motif within CLS and has particular significance in providing one of the linkages between Roberto Unger and the more traditional radicalism of mainstream CLS. The themes

The most extensive and developed argument for localism is advanced by Hutchinson and for this reason discussion will focus on his position which is taken to be representative of much within CLS.[71] Hutchinson derives his political stance directly from postmodernist theoretical premises: "By abandoning the search for foundational truths, we enhance the possibilities for the powerless to engage in the essential dialogue of world re-making."[72] Unfortunately he does not indicate just how the adoption of such an abstract philosophical (or non-philosophical) position helps the powerless. Indeed once it becomes clear that he conceives of politics as Rortian "conversation" it becomes even less clear how this helps the powerless, even though he writes of conversational politics with militant rhetoric: "As conversationalists, we are front-line combatants in the daily struggle to resist, reproduce or change the world."[73]

The hegemony of the discourses of power and knowledge is such that it is far from self-evident that this dialogic conception of politics opens spaces for the subordinated.[74] It is uncertain how the radical subjectivism he espouses can contribute to a change in the pattern of political relations. As Terry Eagleton presses: "the unending 'dialogue' of human history is as often as not a monologue by the powerful to the powerless."[75] But Hutchinson exudes a deep confidence in dialogue and inter-subjective communication: The focus of endeavour must be realigned. Each person must individually and collectively encourage him or herself and others to promote and experience new forms of inter-subjectivity.[76] It is difficult to understand just how such a view of politics can provide any challenge to the institutionalized structures of power and inequality which characterize modern society. Whilst he recognizes that in 'politics as conversation' the powerful have the cards stacked in their favour, he is optimistic that localized politics can provide the enpowerment to activate the pow-

---

of localism and community make contact with a certain mutual attraction between CLS and the revived interest in 'civic republicanism'; this is most apparent in the work of Andrew Fraser and Frank Michelman. See A. Fraser, "Legal Amnesia: Modernism versus the Republican Tradition in Americal Legal Thought" (1984) 60 Telos 15; F. Michelman, "Traces of Self-Government" (1986) 100 Harv. L. Rev. 4.

[71]Hutchinson, *supra*, note 7. Hutchinson offers the most developed account of localism. As already noted it is a theme present in Gabel and Kennedy, *supra*, note 30, and is also a major strand of James Boyle's position in "The Politics of Reason: Critical Legal Theory and Local Social Thought" (1985) 133 U. Pa. L. Rev. 685.

[72]Hutchinson, *ibid.* at 289.

[73]*Ibid.*

[74]Joel Handler offers a significantly more elaborated model of participatory politics in what he calls the "dialogic community", but he recognises that "when power is seriously unequal, something more is required"; "Dependent People, the State, and the Modern/Postmodern Search for the Dialogic Community" (1988) 35 U.C.L.A. L. Rev. 999 at 1076.

[75]T. Eagleton, *Literary Theory: An Introduction* (Oxford: Basil Blackwell, 1983) at 73.

[76]Hutchinson, *supra*, note 7 at 291.

erless. He goes further by insisting that local politics requires the renunciation of politics at the level of the state:

> [W]e must refrain from the familiar attempt to think in total and global terms. The response must be much more local and domestic. By working at ground level, transformative activity becomes a real possibility for disaffected citizens.[77]

It follows directly from this Foucaultian thesis that 'power is everywhere' that politics must also be everywhere. There is an obvious sense in which this is true, but a more important sense in which it is misleading since it fails to take account of the fact that local politics are not autonomous realms, but that states, legal institutions and political parties intervene in and hegemonise local struggles and resistances.

It is important to my case to stress that I do not seek to disapprove of or to denigrate local politics. Indeed the stress on local politics has been an important part of the rethinking of progressive and socialist politics during recent years. But I do challenge the simple substitution of micro- for macro-politics. Postmodernism has a tendency to adopt a wilful self-limitation and thus to disempower itself from undertaking more than the most fragmentary analysis. There are some important questions about the relationship between local and state politics; among the questions that need to be explored are: To what extent can specific politics (including local politics) succeed without at the same time engaging with the multifaceted forms of social oppression? If struggles are not reducible, under what conditions is it possible to go "beyond the fragments" to achieve concerted action, and even alliances, effective at the level of the state? Unless these questions are explored the powerless are doomed forever to engage in an endless series of single-issue struggles. It is not that such struggles are unimportant, indeed they are the starting point of action and enpowerment; but unless they find appropriate forms of articulation at the national or international level they may remain locked into a vicious circle of a reformism that can never achieve its most significant goals.

A second and linked strand within the politics of postmodernism which has had considerable impact on CLS is organized around a strong commitment to a model of an ideal political practice which is participatory, which links the participants in a "dialogic community" and is empowering for those constituencies which are marginalized, silenced or excluded by the dominant discourses.[78] The roots of this configuration involve a sharp reaction against the traditional categories of socialist politics; the working class, political parties and the struggle for state power have no place in postmodernist politics. What is sketched is an admixture of Foucault's conception of a politics which is directed to bringing

[77] *Ibid.*

[78] For an extended commentary on the potentialities and limits of the quest for dialogic community through rights struggles see Handler, *supra*, note 74.

into play "an *insurrection of subjugated knowledges*"[79] and Roberto Unger's concern with the expansion of the capacity to revise the encountered contexts through an "empowered democracy".[80] Such influences do not constitute a political programme nor even an agenda; rather they serve to sketch out the parameters of a potential political space whose major characteristic is precisely its marked departures from traditional progressive politics, whether revolutionary or reformist, which have both been directed to the seizure or acquisition of state power. True to the project of redrawing the map of politics and culture embodied in postmodernism, this 'new politics' defies and seeks to break out of the old categories of Left and Right. It is clear that the present period is one of major transformations whose full characteristics and implications at this early stage we can only partially grasp. I prefer to avoid the label postmodernism and in its place invoke the more neutral designation "New Times".[81] It is unwise, if not impossible, to analyse the new political orientations of the postmodernist trend within CLS as if they formed a stable conception. But we can catch glimpses of the implications for the politics of law.

The politics of postmodernist approaches to law tends to take over from earlier CLS positions a strong reservation about the political role of litigation and of rights.[82] Thus, for example, Hutchinson is suspicious of, if not downright hostile to, institutional politics, and this goes for legal politics as well. His strategic position is: "Resort to the courts can only be a pragmatic and occasional strategy for change."[83] He is trenchant in his critique of the judicialization of politics and of creeping judicial review of legislation.

I started out posing the question: What is Left in legal studies? It is now time to return to this issue.

---

[79]M. Foucault, *Power/Knowledge: Selected Interviews and Other Writings 1972-1977*, ed. by C. Gordon (New York: Pantheon Books. 1980) at 81.

[80]R. Unger, *Politics: A Work in Constructive Theory*, 3 vols (New York: Cambridge University Press, 1987). By far the most interesting discussion of Unger's work is Perry Anderson's essay "Roberto Unger and the Politics of Empowerment" (1989) 173 New Left Rev. 93.

[81]See the October 1988 issue of Marxism Today; in particular, S. Hall, "Brave New World" (1988) 32:10 Marxism Today 24 and C. Leadbeater, "Power to the Person" (1988) 32:10 Marxism Today 14. 'New Times' in this context indicating an attempt at a less absolutist analysis than that provided by 'post-Fordism' and 'post-modernism'. See also D. Hebdige, "After the Masses" (1989) 33:1 Marxism Today 48 for a wide-ranging review of the many faces of postmodernism.

[82]For "early" CLS criticism of rights see, for example, A.D. Freeman, "Legitimizing Racial Discrimination Through Anti-Discrimination Law: A Critical Review of Supreme Court Doctrine" (1978) 62 Minn. L. Rev. 1049; M. Tushnet, "An Essay on Rights" (1984) 62 Texas L. Rev. 1363. This hostility towards rights has already come in for some criticism; see Sparer, *supra*, note 40, and Symposium, "Minority Critiques of the Critical Legal Studies Movement", *supra*, note 40. For fuller discussion of the 'rights debate' within CLS see A. Bartholemew and A. Hunt, "What's Wrong With Rights" in *Law and Inequality* (forthcoming).

[83]Hutchinson, *supra*, note 7 at 291-92.

If there is any common core to progressive thought it is a position which stands astride Enlightenment thinking; it does retain some commitment to the idea of progress, but its sense of modernity is one which focuses on the possibility of change and the role of human agency. The Left's version of modernism is one in which all 'natural' social facts are open to challenge and change, there is no pre-given 'human nature'; rather both history, and most significantly those who make it, remake themselves in the process of making history. The projects, struggles and travails of individual women and men, groups and every kind of collectivity make history and in doing so make themselves, and in this process lift the blanket of superstition, ignorance, fear and oppression. We do not need to be over-optimistic and envisage some brave new world in which fear and ignorance are banished; but there is a positive sense of advance in which whatever reservations we may have about 'Truth' do not inhibit us from saying things are better today than they were yesterday. But, of course, the deep source of the attraction of postmodernism lies in all those aspects of the human condition in which we are no longer as certain as we used to be that things are better today than they were yesterday. The deep significance of the inexorable rise of environmentalism is precisely that what has been the key evidence of the universality of progress, namely, the species' ability to control and subordinate nature, is now the source of the greatest collective danger. There is another, and explicitly political, side to contemporary doubts about progress. The parallel political transformations of the twentieth century, socialism (in both its Communist and Social-Democratic forms) and anti-colonialism have failed to produce societies which offer much encouragement to the progressive commitment to remaking the world. When the cake comes out of the political oven it has persistently failed to live up to its promise.

If the Left is committed to change, but unhappy with its results, and less confident about progress, then it follows that progressives have no alternative but to take the postmodernist challenge seriously. If the engagement with postmodernism is to be fruitful (not simply oppositional) then it is necessary to concede that postmodernism does present a challenge to the normal progressivist embrace of science, rationality and progress. It perhaps reduces the shock of embracing postmodernism to recognize that much recent progressive thought has already taken on board many of the characteristic themes of postmodernism and, most importantly, has done so without embracing its more cataclysmic manifestations. Thus, for example, the commitment to any linear, let alone unilinear, conception of progress has long since been abandoned. But this does not imply that the rejection of progress has been replaced by a radical relativism. The possibility of sustaining the judgement that some situation, circumstance, idea, policy, etc. is an 'advance'/'better' or is a 'retreat'/'worse' can and should be retained. Such judgements are not to be measured against some absolute standard of Truth or Knowledge, but seen as a choice between alternatives in which the options are determinant and in which the ethical or other values employed are made explicit. Similarly the faith in narrowly conceived positivistic methods of 'science' has long been left behind, but again this has not involved the abandonment of the idea that it is possible to compare competing knowledge claims and to make judgements as to which is 'better'. This sense of 'better' is not some covert version of 'the Truth'; absolutism need not creep in. It is sufficient that we specify the context in which the judgement is made and the standpoint which we occupy for our judgements to be grounded and thus avoid the slide to ethical relativism.

Progressive thought has similarly taken important strides towards connecting such grounded conceptions of knowledge with the source and mobilization of power. The most revealing measure of this shift is that it finds expression in the across-the-board influence of Foucault.[84] But, as I have suggested above, it is necessary to redress the over-reaction against orthodox Marxism which led Foucault to simply substitute a prioritization of local politics for state politics; it is important to note that he himself made an effort to distance himself from a simple reversal of priorities.[85] This corrective is not only of general importance but has a special pertinence to the field of legal studies. Much contemporary scholarship quite correctly emphasizes the plurality of legal forms and mechanisms,[86] but this should not lead to a neglect of the central importance of state law, not least because it is engaged in a constant project to bring all the other developing and fluid legal fields under its control. To avoid the lapse into either naive localism or simple legal pluralism a more developed account of the inter-penetration of the macro- and micro-levels is needed.

Postmodernism is also characterized by a general espousal of the tradition of discourse analysis and the general emphasis on the role of language in the construction of social reality. This involves adherence to the epistemological view, which is central to Foucault's position, that there are no objects of knowledge constituted outside discourse. This gives rise to a profound paradox in postmodernist thought. If everything is constituted in discourse, how can an alternative politics exist or any criticism take purchase which appeals to other

[84]One of the reasons for Foucault's current intellectual influence lies in the fact that his work can be seen as a sort of half-way between radical postmodernism and neo-Marxism. If nothing else this gives rise to the great mass of scholarship seeking to push rival interpretations. His key texts in this debate are those brought together in Foucault, *supra*, note 79.

[85]For example, Foucault indicates that

> I do not mean in any way to minimise the importance and effectiveness of State power. I simply feel that excessive insistence on its playing an exclusive role leads to the risk of overlooking all the mechanisms and effects of power which don't pass directly via the State apparatus, yet often sustain the State more effectively than its own institutions, enlarging and maximizing its effectiveness.

Ibid. at 72-73.

[86]For a survey of the debate and literature on legal pluralism see S. Merry, "Legal Pluralism" (1988) 22 Law & Soc. Rev. 869.

meanings or knowledges?[87] The position to be sustained is one which welcomes the advances made possible by discourse analysis as overcoming some of the limitations of ideology theory.[88] But, as Stuart Hall argues, it does not follow that it is either necessary or desirable to treat all social phenomena as only discourses; it is important to retain a concept of 'social practices' which are not reducible to discourses.[89]

This aspiration to grasp both discourse and practice is what I take to underline current concerns from a variety of sources to elaborate a model of 'constitutive theory' whose concern is to hang on to the coexistence and mutual determination of practices and discourses, structure and agency. The quest is for ways of articulating the sense in which law (or better legal relations) are generated within non-legal social relations whose own formation incorporates legal relations; legal relations and social relations interpenetrate.[90] Perhaps this project has not been sufficiently developed to merit the slightly grand designation 'theory'; but it does serve to make a point about the extent to which another element of postmodernist thought has been ingested by wider strands of thought. This sense of 'theory' is not one of a complete or formal model as a condensation or concentration of reality; rather it is a sense of theory as a provisional metaphor, as a potentially useful way of thinking and saying something new. Such a view of theory makes no claims to Truth or truths, but is subject only to a rigorously pragmatic evaluation: does a shift or change in the theoretical metaphor help or hinder articulating something that is otherwise ignored, neglected, or otherwise unsayable? In short it involves a conception of theory without guarantees.

There is then much of value that has emerged during the engagement between law and postmodernism. But the deeper problem remains of the neg-

---

[87]Foucault's own solution to this difficulty was his appeal to the resistances generated by power; "there are no relations of power without resistances". *Supra*, note 79 at 142. Whilst definitionally this strategy solved his immediate problem it lacks credibility since it remains unexplained how alternative discourses are generated or how their challenge could ever be more than oppositional.

[88]For an introduction to the relationship between ideology theory and discourse theory see D. Macdonell, *Theories of Discourse: An Introduction* (Oxford: Basil Blackwell, 1986).

[89]S. Hall, "The Toad in the Garden: Thatcherism Among the Theorists" in C. Nelson & L. Grossberg, eds, *Marxism & the Interpretation of Culture* (Urbana: University of Illinois Press, 1988) 35 at 51.

[90]The quest for constitutive theory has its most general roots in Anthony Giddens' search for integrative theory; see, in particular, Giddens, *supra*, note 64. In social-theoretical studies of law its traces can be found in P. Fitzpatrick, "Law and Societies" (1984) 22 Osgoode Hall L.J. 115; C. Harrington, "Moving From Integrative to Constitutive Theories of Law" (1988) 22 Law & Soc. Rev. 963; S. Henry, "The Construction and Deconstruction of Social Control: Thoughts on the Discurcive Production of State Law and Private Justice" in J. Lowman, R.J. Menzies & T.S. Palys, eds, *Transcarceration: Essays in the Sociology of Social Control* (Aldershot: Gower Press, 1987) 89; and A. Hunt, "The Critique of Law: What Is 'Critical' About Critical Legal Studies" in Fitzpatrick & Hunt, *supra*, note 7, 5.

ative face, and indeed it is the most visible face, of postmodernism. I have been concerned to emphasize the distinctive nature of the engagement between law and postmodernism; this is precisely because the core of the legal project, in Lon Fuller's famous phrase, of "subjecting human conduct to the governance of rules" is itself such a profound manifestation of the commitments and preoccupations of rationalist thought.[91] It is precisely because law seems to carry the whole burden of civilization on its shoulders that legal scholarship has been so deeply, almost passionately, affected by the general mood of self-doubt, failure and hopelessness that has been the most distinctive manifestation of postmodernism.

Yet it is possible to face our age and its problems without relapsing into the pessimism that is the final resting place of relativism and nihilism once their radical guise is stripped away. This future has a place for law, but it will be a place in which law can no longer pretend to guarantee civilization or to provide procedural cures for the real world of conflict. In this more modest role we will have to complete what I have called the 'sociological movement in law'.[92] Intellectually law, or legal studies, will have to be fully part of the social sciences if we are to better understand both its possibilities and its limitations. We will, hopefully, have fewer illusions and there will need to be fewer self-proclaimed spokespersons for the legal project who proselytize for such an inflated project of law that it has always been a myth, but is today a dangerous lie. If the engagement with postmodernism, and the big fear which it has engendered, has brought us nearer to this understanding, then it has played its part.

---

[91] L. Fuller, *The Morality of Law* (New Haven: Yale University Press, 1964) at 96.
[92] A. Hunt, *The Sociological Movement in Law* (Philadelphia: Temple University Press, 1978).

Name Index

www.ingramcontent.com/pod-product-compliance
Lightning Source LLC
LaVergne TN
LVHW102105300926
849161LV00014B/3055